2022 FANTASY FOOTBALL RESOURCE

FANTASY FOOTBALL

- WEEKLY PLAYER SCORE SHEETS
- WAIVER WIRE FORMS
- TRADE FORMS
- DRAFT DAY TABLE
- 2022 NFL SCHEDULE
- OFFENSIVE DEPTH CHARTS
- TABLES FOR EVERYTHING

2022 SEASON ORGANIZER

FOR PRISONERS

Letter from FantasyTakeover

Dear Fellow Fantasy Footballers,

Through the years, those of us at FantasyTakeover have been disappointed with the fantasy magazines and books on the market. Some have crazy made-up systems that make no sense strategically when examined closely. Others have flawed ranking and lack coherent analysis.

We decided to create FantasyTakeover to provide the very best fantasy books to our readers.

Our team is made up of a computer programmer, mathematician, professional oddsmaker, and a former Division 1 football player. We've used all our strengths to work together to create our rankings and analysis.

Our book hopes to consider everything one might need to be the best fantasy football drafter and player.

We've included many things most leave out. Our book includes:

- A proven-successful proprietary ranking system
- Cheat sheets for every major scoring format
- Important draft strategy and tips
- 200+ player profiles
- Team summaries and outlooks
- Stats for every relevant player from the past three seasons
- Stat projections for 2022.
- Game-by-game stats for all fantasy players from 2021

- A mock draft and analysis
- Injury updates
- A list of all off-season moves and the fantasy relevant implications
- Analysis of the rookies that will make a fantasy impact their first year
- A complete list of offensive picks for the 2022 NFL Draft

and much more...

Our goal was to provide a complete resource for everything fantasy football, along with complementary and interesting NFL tidbits, like strength of schedule by position and new contract information.

Our ranking system combines machine learning artificial intelligence that analyzes millions of data points to finds patterns humans are unable to detect, statistical analysis, and a human scouting element.

Over 500,000 people use a machine learning AI in fantasy soccer worldwide (shout-out to all our international buyers), but we are now bringing the technology to the fantasy football community with our rankings. We won't bore you with proprietary names or confusing percentages. We'll just tell you who to draft!

We hope our book fulfills our promise of being the best fantasy football book on the market.

Sincerely,
FANTASYTAKEOVER

CON TENT

TEAM REPORTS

PLAYER PROFILES

FANTASY TAKEOVER

rookie RUNDOWN

It seems like every year multiple rookies are making huge fantasy impacts. Consider some of the names from last season: Ja'marr Chase, Najee Harris, Jaylen Waddle, Amon-Ra St. Brown, and Elijah Moore.

Figuring out which ones to add to your fantasy lineup is the hard part. In this article we hope to provide you with enough insight so that you can emerge from your draft with this year's superstar rookie(s).

QUARTERBACKS

1.20 KENNY PICKETT (STEELERS) - *PITTSBURGH, 6-3, 220*

The only QB taken in the first round, Kenny Pickett emerged as an NFL prospect late into his five seasons at Pittsburgh. But in his final year, the small-handed Pickett threw for 4,319 yards and 42 TDs in 13 games. Pickett creates plays when nothing appears to be available. Now a Steeler, he can walk his equipment across the stadium from one locker room to the other.

The Steelers signed Mitch Trubisky to a two-year, low-money deal this offseason. But Pickett should be Pittsburgh's starter sooner than later. Mike Tomlin has already said that Pickett "came readymade." We'll see how he does with the Steelers quality skill players — Najee Harris, Diontae Johnson, and Chase Claypool, among others.

3.10 DESMOND RIDDER (FALCONS) - *CINCINNATI, 6-4, 215*

The four-year Cincinnati starter is a moderately mobile QB with a big arm. He had some accuracy issues in college but is a sound decision maker. He will benefit from not having to play right away, as Atlanta seems content with Mariota as their Week 1 starter.

KENNY PICKETT SHOULD BE PITTSBURGH'S STARTER SOONER THAN LATER.

3.22 MALIK WILLIS (TITANS) - *LIBERTY, 6-1, 225*

The first-round prospect inexplicably slipped to the third round and may not even see the field as a rookie behind Ryan Tannehill. He has the ability to make big-time throws and abort the pocket when needed to create on the fly. He's raw as a decision maker but has the arm strength, athleticism, and size to develop.

3.30 MATT CORRAL (PANTHERS) - *OLE MISS, 6-2, 205*

Carolina traded up to the third round to draft the Ole Miss product as the hopeful future of the organization. He's a raw talent that needs work in ball placement. He isn't as athletic or flashy as some of the other QBs taken in the draft, but he's more than capable. Matt Corral lands on a team with a glaring need at QB. If we see the same Baker Mayfield and Sam Darnold from years past, Corral could get a chance to start this year.

2.04 BREECE HALL (JETS) - IOWA STATE, 6-1, 220

Breece Hall has the best chance of the RBs drafted to have an immediate impact. The 5-11, 217-pound back has oozes athleticism, with a 40-inch vertical and 4.39 40-yard dash. With over 4,500 scrimmage yards, 82 receptions, and 50 TDs as a Cyclone, the Jets drafted a rugged, potential 3-down back.

His ability as a receiver should bolster what could be a dynamic offense, and help continue the development of second-year QB Zach Wilson. Michael Carter will be forced into a supporting role as Hall takes center stage.

2.09 KEN WALKER III (SEAHAWKS)- MICHIGAN ST., 5-10, 212

After transferring from Wake Forest to Michigan State, Ken Walker III transformed from a negligible player, to a punishing back. Last year as a Spartan, he had 263 carries for 1,636 yards and scored 18 TDs. At 5-10 and 212 pounds, with a thick lower half, Walker has the ability to run through contact and stay upright.

He is also an elusive back who can avoid hits and has the speed to get vertical once in the open field. He needs work as a receiver (only 19 receptions in college) and as a pass blocker, but with Chris Carson retiring after suffering a serious neck injury last season, and Rashaad Penny re-signed for only one year, Walker will have the chance to play a significant role in Seattle's offense early in the year.

2.31 JAMES COOK (BILLS)- GEORGIA, 5-11, 190

James Cook was one of only three backs taken in the first two rounds, but he may be in one of the best situations considering his skill set. He averaged 6.5 yards per carry in the SEC, but his greatest value is as a talented receiver who now joins a powerful, pass-heavy Buffalo offense. It's easy to see Cook in this offense as a third-down pass-catching back, working his way into a bigger role.

Although smaller than his older brother Dalvin Cook, he has similar acceleration and agility. While his size may prevent him from ever becoming a workhorse back, he should have plenty of chances to make an impact, if only because of his receiving ability.

3.27 RACHAAD WHITE (BUCCANEERS) ARIZONA ST., 6-2, 210

Rachaad White, a 6-foot 2, 210-pound back, is coming off a 1,000-yard rushing season with Arizona State. For a back with prototypical ground-and-pound size, White had an impressive 43 receptions for 456 yards last year.

Entering a less-than ideal situation for immediate playing time in a somewhat crowded Tampa Bay backfield, the third-round pick could make himself instantly useful as an effective pass blocker.

White tends to hit the edge too quickly and would be better served with more patience in the middle. He's got the QB and coaching staff to aid him in becoming a more disciplined, nuanced runner. With an injury for Tampa Bay, White could be vaulted into a significant role.

WITH CHRIS CARSON RETIRING AFTER SUFFERING A SERIOUS NECK INJURY LAST SEASON, AND RASHAAD PENNY RE-SIGNED FOR ONLY ONE YEAR, WALKER WILL HAVE THE CHANCE TO PLAY A SIGNIFICANT ROLE IN SEATTLE'S OFFENSE EARLY IN THE YEAR.

WITH ONLY MARLON MACK AND REX BURKHEAD AHEAD OF HIM ON THE DEPTH CHART, AND A HOUSTON OFFENSE THAT'S WILLING TO TRY ANYTHING, PIERCE COULD FIND A SIGNIFICANT ROLE AT SOME POINT THIS SEASON.

3.29 TYRION DAVIS-PRICE (49ERS) LSU, 6-1, 223

Tyrion Davis-Price is a big solid back, who doesn't give the 49ers much in the way of finesse or speed. This pick screams they were unhappy with their 2020 third-round pick, RB Trey Sermon. If last year is any indication, injuries could lead to opportunities for Davis-Price. He could also benefit from a 49ers offensive scheme that makes middle-of-the-pack RBs stars.

3.34 BRIAN ROBINSON JR. (COMMANDERS) - ALABAMA, 6-1, 228

As a bigger back, the Alabama product has the agility of a much smaller runner. Robinson has good field vision and the ability to shred tackles at the point of contact. It's unlikely he gets a lot of touches early, but coach Ron Rivera remembers his Carolina tag team (Jonathan Stewart and DeAngelo Williams), and it's possible he reinstates that scheme with Gibson and Robinson. But not if J.D. McKissic has anything to say about it.

4.02 DAMEON PIERCE (HOUSTON) FLORIDA, 5-10, 215

The thick-framed Pierce is light on his feet and can quickly change directions. He's is a physical runner and incredibly athletic, with plenty of life left in his legs after only 100 carries last season as a Gator. We chalk this up to a mid-season coaching change rather than a reflection of his ability. With only Marlon Mack and Rex Burkhead ahead of him on the depth chart, and a Houston offense that's willing to try anything, Pierce could find a significant role at some point this season.

RUNNING BACKS CONTINUED...

4.17 ZAMIR WHITE (RAIDERS) - *GEORGIA, 6-0, 215*

The former Georgia Bulldog was the No. 1 rated back out of high school. He's built like your average 3-down rusher and has good hands despite not being used much in the passing game in college. His numbers at Georgia are not indicative of his talent or potential, as he shared backfield time with James Cook and Kenny McIntosh. He has incredible ability after contact and can drag defenders with him. After ACL tears in both knees, durability is a concern.

Considering that Josh Jacobs' fifth year option wasn't picked up, and Kenyan Drake is coming off a serious ankle injury and is on a short-term deal, White has a decent chance to get into the rotation at some point in 2022.

4.18 ISAIAH SPILLER (CHARGERS) *TEXAS A&M, 6-1, 215*

Spiller recorded three consecutive seasons of at least 1,100 yards and caught 74 passes over a 35-game span. A poor combine showing, possibly due to an injury, hurt his draft stock. He's an all-around back with good size. Austin Ekeler is the clear No. 1 back in Los Angeles, but with the departure of Justin Jackson, the No. 2 spot seems wide open. Last year in L.A., there were 149 carries by backs not named Austin Ekeler.

CONSIDERING THAT JOSH JACOBS' FIFTH YEAR OPTION WAS NOT PICKED UP AND KENYAN DRAKE IS COMING OFF A SERIOUS ANKLE INJURY, AND IS ON A SHORT-TERM DEAL, WHITE HAS A DECENT CHANCE TO GET INTO THE ROTATION AT SOME POINT IN 2022.

4.22 PIERRE STRONG JR. (PATRIOTS) - *SOUTH DAKOTA ST., 5-11, 205*

Pierre Strong was steadily productive over his career at South Dakota State, albeit at the FCS level. His draft stock was boosted by a great combine (4.37 40-yard dash, 36" vertical). He joins a very crowded New England RB room led by Damien Harris, who will be a free agent next season. But you never know what back will emerge in a Bill Belichick-run offense.

5.08 TYLER ALGEIER (FALCONS) - *BYU, 5-11, 220*

The BYU product had almost 1800 yards from scrimmage and 23 touchdowns last season. He's a runner that can handle both rushing and receiving, but leans more towards a power-back role. Allgeier has the potential to be a lead rusher, even if there are no injuries in front of him. Cordarrelle Patterson, Atlanta's current No. 1 back, is 31 years old and also plays the roles of receiver and kick returner. We wouldn't be shocked to see Algeier emerge as the Falcons RB1 by season's end.

6.23 KEAONTAY INGRAM (CARDINALS) - *USC, 6-1, 228*

Keaontay Ingram showed impressive elusiveness for his size as a Trojan. He struggles finding speed and acceleration at the second level but has a strong ability to stay upright. He'll likely start the year at No. 3 on the depth chart, behind James Conner and newly signed Darrell Williams. Both have injury histories which could lead to game action for Ingram.

WIDE RECEIVERS

1.08 DRAKE LONDON (FALCONS) *USC, 6-5, 210*

Drake London was the first wide receiver taken in this year's draft, and with good reason. He caught 88 passes for 1,084 yards in just eight games before he was sidelined with an ankle injury. At 6-4, 219 pounds, London is a matchup nightmare. He has the ability to go up and get the 50/50 balls. With Calvin Ridley suspended for a year, London immediately assumes the Falcons No. 1 receiving role.

OLAVE MIGHT END UP AS JAMEIS WINSTON'S NEW FAVORITE TARGET.

1.10 GARRETT WILSON (JETS) - *OHIO ST., 6-0, 192*

Wilson was the No. 1 receiver on many draft boards. With great hands and speed, he's a deep-play threat and excellent route runner who can line up anywhere on the field. He posted 27 catches, 371 yards, and 6 TDs in his last three games at Ohio State. This is most impressive because he was sharing the filed with other quality skill players — Chris Olave and Jaxon Smith-Njigba. With excellent body control and elite ball tracking, Wilson should be rewarded with plenty of targets from second-year QB Zach Wilson.

1.11 CHRIS OLAVE (SAINTS) - *OHIO ST., 6-1, 188*

Olave was the second of the two Ohio State WRs drafted back-to-back in Round 1. Olave scored a school career record 35 TDs. A precise route runner, he's smart, fast, and NFL ready. He's already working out with teammate Michael Thomas, who should draw some coverage away from him. Olave might end up as Jameis Winston's new favorite target.

1.12 JAMESON WILLIAMS (LIONS) - *ALABAMA, 6-2, 189*

If not for an ACL tear in the national championship game, Jameson Williams may have been the first WR off the board. After transferring from Ohio State to Alabama in 2021, he immediately made his presence known, recording 79 receptions, 1,500 yards, and 15 TDs. An elite receiver with rare speed, Williams averaged a striking 20 yards per reception last season. Unfortunately, he lands under a QB who ranked last in depth of throw per target. Detroit moved up to take Williams with an outlook to the future. He won't be ready to start the season, and Detroit won't push him until he's ready.

1.16 JAHAN DOTSON (COMMANDERS) - *PENN ST., 5-11, 182*

The Penn state product is smaller than your typical wideout but has good hands and decent speed. He's most dangerous once he gets the ball, and able to turn short plays into house calls. In 2021, he had the eighth most receptions among all WRs drafted. Dotson adds another reliable target to complement Terry McLaurin for newly acquired Commanders QB Carson Wentz.

1.18 TREYLON BURKS (TITANS) - *ARKANSAS, 6-3, 225*

Ironically, prior to the draft, many scouts compared Treylon Burks to A.J. Brown, and then Tennessee traded Brown to draft Burks with the 18th pick. The former Razorback led his team in receiving during his three seasons. His size and speed make it hard to bring him down, as well as a capable blocker. He needs to refine his route-running ability. After laboring in first few days of rookie camp, he also needs to keep an eye on his weight and conditioning. But with Brown and Julio Jones gone, and Robert Woods coming off and ACL tear, Burks is in a position to make an impact from day one.

2.02 CHRISTIAN WATSON (PACKERS)
NORTH DAKOTA ST., 6-5, 208

The Packers finally selected a WR with their third pick. The North Dakota State product may never have caught more than 43 passes in a season during his career, but he's tall and fast, with similar measurables to departed WR Marquez Valdes-Scantling, and should be able to stretch the field in the same way. Of the first 12 WRs drafted, Watson is the only one who landed with a truly elite QB, and Aaron Rodgers has the tendency to turn wide receivers into stars — Watson may be his next product.

> "
> WITH A.J. BROWN AND JULIO JONES GONE, AND ROBERT WOODS COMING OFF AND ACL TEAR, BURKS IS IN A POSITION TO MAKE AN IMPACT FROM DAY ONE.

> "
> AARON RODGERS HAS THE TENDENCY TO TURN WIDE RECEIVERS INTO STARS — WATSON MAY BE HIS NEXT PRODUCT.

2.11 WAN'DALE ROBINSON (GIANTS) - *KENTUCKY, 5-11, 185*

The slightly undersized former Wildcat has the ability to elude defenders with quick cuts and good speed. With a shallow WR room in New York, Robinson should have a chance to prove himself on the field. It helps that Giants head coach Brian Daboll has proven adept at getting the best out of his smaller receivers (e.g. Cole Beasley and Isaiah McKenzie).

2.12 JOHN METCHIE III (TEXANS) - *ALABAMA, 6-0, 195*

Another Alabama receiver, John Metchie III caught 96 passes for over 1,100 yards and 8 TDs. He's a skilled downfield route runner who has the ability and turn and track the ball over his shoulder. He also knows how to use his small frame to gain leverage and create separation. If not for Jameson Williams, his numbers at Alabama would have been much better. Metchie was on pace to be ready at some point this season after tearing his ACL in the SEC Championship, but was recently diagnosed with Leukemia and said he won't play this year.

2.18 TYQUAN THORNTON (PATRIOTS) - *BAYLOR, 6-3, 182*

The former Bear is a solid route-runner and natural hands-catcher. Super-fast (4.28) with good size, he's a tough matchup for defenders who could be a deep-threat option for Mac Jones. Joining DeVante Parker, he should have a chance to prove his value.

2.20 GEORGE PICKENS (STEELERS) - *GEORGIA, 6-3, 190*

The former Bulldog has first-round talent. He's tall and quick with an impressive catch radius, and plays with a chip on his shoulder. An ACL tear and immaturity hurt his draft stock.

2.21 ALEC PIERCE (COLTS) - *CINCINNATI, 6-3, 213*

The Colts have an affinity for big, physical receivers, and Alec Pierce fits the bill. In his three collegiate seasons, he averaged a notable 17 yards per reception. His height gives him the ability to be both a target over the middle and in the end zone. He's a little stiff and needs to work on his route running. Pierce is a little raw but has all the tangibles of a starting NFL receiver. With incredible athleticism (4.33 40 and 40.5" vertical), he'll join Matt Ryan's other tall targets, Michael Pittman Jr. (6-4), Mo Alie-Cox (6-5), and rookie TE Jelani Woods (6-7), in a good offense.

WIDE RECEIVERS CONTINUED...

2.22 SKYY MOORE (CHIEFS)
WESTERN MICHIGAN, 5-10, 195

The 13th WR drafted, Skyy Moore lands in a great spot under one of the best QBs in the league. With a good catch radius for his size, Moore has speed and precise route-running ability. In his junior year at Western Michigan, he caught 95 passes for 1,292 yards and 10 TDs. He's no Tyreek Hill, but should see a share of the vacated targets. On a side note, Moore had the biggest hands (10 1/4") of any WR in the draft — take that, Kenny Pickett!

3.24 JALEN TOLBERT (COWBOYS)
SOUTH ALABAMA, 6-3, 190

The South Alabama product was a dominant force among the smaller colleges. In 2021, he had 1,472 yards and 8 TDs. He's deceptively quick with innate ball-tracking ability. An average route runner with poor yards after the catch, he does know how to get open downfield. With a depleted receiving corps, Tolbert will be given a chance in a pass-heavy Dallas offense.

3.35 DAVID BELL (BROWNS)
PURDUE, 6-2, 210

The former Boilermaker has a powerful frame and decent balance, which make him a problem for opposing defenses after the catch. He recorded seven 100-plus yard games last season. His ball-tracking skills may be enough for him to see some action.

5.5 KHALIL SHAKIR (BILLS)
BOISE ST., 6-0, 190

Khalil Shakir is not the tallest or biggest receiver, but he has good field vision, cuts well, and has good balance on contact. He had some amazing sideline body-contorting catches during his time at Boise State. Sahkir finished his career as the third-highest graded receiver in his class according to Pro Football Focus.

TIGHT ENDS

2.23 TREY MCBRIDE (CARDINALS) - *COLORADO ST., 6-4, 260*

In his last season at Colorado State, Trey McBride had 86 receptions for over 1,000 yards. He is able to create separation underneath and at the intermediate level. McBride has elite route-running ability for a TE, and will get the chance to learn behind veteran Zach Ertz. Like most TEs, his fantasy impact in year 1 will be negligible.

3.09 JELANI WOODS (COLTS) - *VIRGINIA, 6-7, 265*

Though originally recruited as a QB, Jelani Woods finished his college career as a productive TE. After transferring from Oklahoma State to Virginia, Woods had 44 receptions and 8 TDs last season. He is surprisingly fast for his size (4.61). He has the ability to boxout defenders and break tackles. He'll most likely play a blocking role the majority of his rookie NFL campaign.

TOP 25 ROOKIE DYNASTY RANKINGS

	RD	PK		POS	TEAM	COLLEGE
1	2	4	BREECE HALL	RB	NEW YORK JETS	IOWA STATE
2	1	8	DRAKE LONDON	WR	ATLANTA FALCONS	USC
3	1	10	GARRETT WILSON	WR	NEW YORK JETS	OHIO STATE
4	1	12	JAMESON WILLIAMS	WR	DETROIT LIONS	ALABAMA
5	1	18	TREYLON BURKS	WR	TENNESSEE TITANS	ARKANSAS
6	2	9	KEN WALKER III	RB	SEATTLE SEAHAWKS	MICHIGAN STATE
7	1	11	CHRIS OLAVE	WR	NEW ORLEANS SAINTS	OHIO STATE
8	2	22	SKYY MOORE	WR	KANSAS CITY CHIEFS	WESTERN MICHIGAN
9	2	2	CHRISTIAN WATSON	WR	GREEN BAY PACKERS	NORTH DAKOTA ST.
10	1	16	JAHAN DOTSON	WR	WASHINGTON COMMANDERS	PENN STATE
11	2	20	GEORGE PICKENS	WR	PITTSBURGH STEELERS	GEORGIA
12	2	31	JAMES COOK	RB	BUFFALO BILLS	GEORGIA
13	3	27	RACHAAD WHITE	RB	TAMPA BAY BUCCANEERS	ARIZONA STATE
14	3	35	DAVID BELL	WR	CLEVELAND BROWNS	PURDUE
15	4	2	DAMEON PIERCE	RB	HOUSTON TEXANS	FLORIDA
16	4	18	ISAIAH SPILLER	RB	LOS ANGELES CHARGERS	TEXAS A&M
17	2	21	ALEC PIERCE	WR	INDIANAPOLIS COLTS	CINCINNATI
18	2	12	JOHN METCHIE III	WR	HOUSTON TEXANS	ALABAMA
19	2	23	TREY MCBRIDE	TE	ARIZONA CARDINALS	COLORADO STATE
20	3	24	JAYLEN TOLBERT	WR	DALLAS COWBOYS	SOUTH ALABAMA
21	1	20	KENNY PICKETT	QB	PITTSBURGH STEELERS	PITTSBURGH
22	2	11	WAN'DALE ROBINSON	WR	NEW YORK GIANTS	KENTUCKY
23	3	34	BRIAN ROBINSON JR.	RB	WASHINGTON COMMANDERS	ALABAMA
24	4	17	ZAMIR WHITE	RB	LAS VEGAS RAIDERS	GEORGIA
25	5	8	TYLER ALLGEIER	RB	ATLANTA FALCONS	BYU

LESSONS LEARNED

Do you remember the Memorial Day weekend dustup between MLB players Tommy Pham and Joc Pederson? Before a Cincinnati Reds-San Francisco Giants game, Pham came out on the field during warm ups, exchanged a few words with Pederson, then slapped him across the face causing a sports-media firestorm that would culminate in a three-game suspension and eventually implicate All Star Mike Trout before the dust settled.

Why? You ask. Somebody get hit with a pitch? Dirty play on a slide into home plate? Unruly bat flip? No. It was a dispute over something that happened in the fantasy football league they took part in last season. Which brings us to our first point in Lessons Learned: **Know the specific rules of your fantasy football league.**

The Pham-Pederson kerfuffle was about the legality of placing a player from your roster on Injured Reserve. RB Jeff Wilson was placed on IR (fantasy) by Pederson, per the written rules of their league. Pham contends there were additional rules, and that the move was illegal. And now you know the story.

Not knowing the rules of your league can cost you in many ways. Be aware of IR, waiver wire and trade rules. Know your roster and line up deadlines, and the rules on substitutions, in case a player is ruled out last minute (remember covid health and safety protocols?). Knowing the rules will save you heartache, and will help you maximize you fantasy points and minimize your mistakes.

What about Mike Trout? He was the commissioner for the league Pham and Pederson were in. Pham ultimately blamed Trout for not resolving their dispute.

Play in a league with an organized, fair, and firm commissioner. A good commissioner will guide your league's fantasy managers and ensure a smooth season.

yard games? Ja'marr Chase had five last year. Stefon Diggs had just two. Considering the system before you draft will allow you to maximize value with every pick, and target players with the most potential.

Draft preparation is the most important thing you can do to get the most value out of every pick. A mock draft — especially if you know what number you pick — is a great way to get an idea of what players to target in what rounds, based on your needs and draft strategy. When other fantasy managers let high value players slip beyond their ADP, a well prepared drafter will be ready to snatch up the best of the best. Also, a well prepared manager will not let high value players fall easily to other drafters. A well-executed draft is the most important thing you can do to have the best chance of a good season.

Yes, a competitive fantasy season starts with a well prepared draft, but **it's important to remain active throughout the season**, by monitoring the waiver wire for emerging players, to improve your chances of fantasy domination.

boost in production. Consider the NFL teams your starters will face week to week. Look at players in Free Agency who may have high-scoring-probability matchups in the future. We like to look weeks ahead for any possible advantage, and secure those players when there's room on our rosters.

Monitor the Injury Report. When RB1s and WR1s miss time, often their backups reach No. 1 option status. These can be easy pickups on the waiver wire, and big fantasy producers for a given week. Also, a top player returning from injury can often be overlooked, and can be picked up a week or so before they return. We especially like to look ahead a few weeks to consider any matchups for streaming.

Streaming is another way to maximize weekly fantasy point potential for certain positions. So, what does this mean? Streaming is choosing a player or defense/special teams from the waiver wire to start for a limited period of time, usually just one week. For example, if you needed a TE for Week 4 last season, you may have con-

1. Know the specific rules of your league.
2. Play in a league with an organized, fair, and firm commissioner.
3. Know your league's scoring system when preparing for the draft.
4. Draft preparation is the most important thing you can do to get the most value out of every pick.
5. Remain active throughout the season.
6. Actively participate in the Add/Drop process.
7. Monitor the injury Report
8. Streaming is a way to maximize your team's potential.

There will always be disagreements that need to be addressed. An effective commissioner will consult with the affected parties, take input from other fantasy managers, and resolve disputes fair and fast. A league with a bad commissioner can leave you ready to slap someone, or worse yet, getting slapped.

In addition to the rules, you should **know your league's scoring system when preparing for the draft.** Over the years we've seen all kinds of scoring systems. Sure, you know about Standard, PPR, and ½ PPR systems. But what about leagues with crazy bonuses or points for carries? In a system that scores one point for every rushing attempt, I'm targeting Derrick Henry (27.4 carries per game) with my first pick, and then the highest volume RBs with my next two picks. Can you say rushing QB?

How about leagues with bonuses for 100

Every year, players that either went undrafted, or were dropped by another manager, emerge as high value fantasy producers. WR Hunter Renfrow was undrafted in most leagues last season. From Weeks 9-14 he averaged 19.1 fantasy PPG. Closely monitoring available players will allow you to pick up fantasy studs, and drop fantasy liabilities.

How about Amon-Ra St. Brown, also mostly undrafted last season. From Weeks 13-18 he averaged 24.9 PPG, with his best effort in Week 17 (33.4). Even his worst in Week 14 (15.8) was still pretty good.

Cordarrelle Patterson — undrafted — averaged 19.9 PPG in 10 of 11 games from Weeks 2-14.

Actively participating in the Add/Drop process is the path to fantasy championships. At every given opportunity, managers should upgrade their rosters, seeking players who will provide even the slightest

sidered Dawson Knox. He went undrafted in most leagues and was scheduled to play a floundering Texans team that week. He ended up with 20.7 fantasy points.

At FantasyTakeover all of our experts stream positions throughout the season. QBs, TEs, D/STs, and Kickers are all commonly streamed. Houston was so bad last year, you could look ahead to who they would play in upcoming weeks, and stream any available D/ST against them, usually for a fantasy payoff!

Streaming can allow you to draft just only one player at certain positions (e.g. QB), so you can spend you remaining draft picks on potential breakouts and big upside possibilities. Happy streaming!

These bits of advice and lessons we've learned are valuable to both the fantasy rookie and fantasy veteran alike. **Have a great season!** ◆

DOCTOR, DOCTOR, GIVE ME THE NEWS

What's the outlook for players coming off injury?

QUARTER BACKS

LAMAR JACKSON

Lamar Jackson had a grade-two ankle sprain causing him to miss several weeks towards the end of last season. The injury shouldn't affect his 2022 status in any way. He should be just as dynamic as ever. What could make a difference this year is his desire for a contract extension. This situation should be monitored, in case of emotional or financial injury.

JAMEIS WINSTON

Before tearing his ACL in Week 8 last season, Jameis Winston was playing solid, but uninspired football. He had surgery soon after the injury and could be ready to go by the early weeks of this season. It was rumored that his rehab was slowed because he was trying to do too much too fast. He also struggled a bit during OTAs, having trouble getting the ball downfield, and, at one point was limping. Andy Dalton was added in the offseason and will probably play early on if Winston can't, especially considering Ian Book's play last year, and Taysom Hill's new role as a tight end. Winston takes over as soon as he's ready, barring an unlikely Andy Dalton comeback performance.

CAM AKERS

Akers came back from a ruptured Achilles in a little over five months. There hasn't been an athlete in any sport to return that quickly from an Achilles tear. Don't let the lack of production in his brief playoff appearance concern you. He only had 5 carries for 2 yards and 3 catches for 10 yards with no touchdowns, but he is still "that guy" for the Rams. Akers is expected to be 100% by Week 1 of this season and should have no problem reasserting himself as the lead back in a high-powered offense. Achilles injuries can be tough on RBs, but Akers is only 23 years old and should bounce back to fantasy relevance.

SAQUON BARKLEY

After suffering a torn ACL during the 2020 season, the New York Giants wisely chose to be careful with Saquon Barkley going into 2021. Their cautious approach looks to have paid off. He was playing well before a nasty ankle sprain and missed a couple weeks before returning to play the final eight games. Barkley just turned 25, and should be 100% by the start of this season. With new head coach Brian Daboll's pedigree (former Bills offensive coordinator), and a retooled offensive line, a healthy Barkley is poised to have a great year. He remains the featured back for the Giants.

J.K. DOBBINS

Before last season started J.K. Dobbins suffered ACL/LCL injuries and missed the entire year. Baltimore has not had much to say about his recovery and rehab, so we assume he is trending in the right direction. Since the injury occurred before the 2021 season, he'll have almost 12 months to heal before this season starts. Baltimore brought in veteran Mike Davis and drafted rookie Tyler Badie, and still has Gus Edwards on the roster. But as long as Dobbins continues to progress, he should start the season as the lead back. If not, look for a heavy dose of Edwards and Davis.

TRAVIS ETIENNE JR.

In August of 2021 Travis Etienne suffered a Lisfranc injury as well as a possible metatarsal fracture. These injuries can be difficult to return from because of the amount of stress placed on the joint as RBs are constantly pushing off, and, the ligament in this area can have poor blood supply. Etienne has the benefit of youth and nearly a year of recovery time. All reports say rehab is going well and he'll be more than ready by the start of the season. Since James Robinson suffered an Achilles injury in Week 16 last season, he likely won't be ready for a normal workload by the start of this season. Considering Etienne's progress and the lack of additional talent at the running back position, it should be the "Travis Etienne Show" in Jacksonville to start the season, and possibly longer. The Jags have rookie Snoop Conner and Ryquell Armstead, but neither compares to a healthy J-Rob, or can match Etienne's potential.

RUNNING BACKS

LEONARD FOURNETTE

Fournette had a hamstring strain that landed him on IR last season. Tampa Bay didn't rush him back, but, instead, used Ronald Jones II down the stretch. Jones signed a one-year deal in Kansas City this offseason, and Fournette resigned a three-year, $21 million extension with the Bucs, thus solidifying his position as the lead running back in Tampa Bay.

DERRICK HENRY

During the 2021 season Derrick Henry fractured his fifth metatarsal (long bone in foot), but was able to return for the playoffs. Although his play (and that of the Titans as a whole) was underwhelming, there is nothing to indicate he won't be back to his true form for 2022. Broken bones tend to heal well and not cause further complications as ligament and tendon injuries do. Tennessee drafted Hasaan Haskins, brought in Trenton Gannon, and still have Dontrell Hilliard, but none can match Henry's physicality and skill set. There's no chance anyone will replace him as the top back in Tennessee.

CHRISTIAN MCCAFFREY

Christian McCaffrey had a strained hamstring that caused him to miss several games early last season (thus a precautionary stint on IR). Unfortunately, shortly after his return he suffered a lateral ankle sprain that put him on IR for a second time, and caused him to miss the rest of the year per NFL policy. Neither injury should have long term effects. Considering how important McCaffrey is to the Carolina Panthers, and the abysmal play of the offense last year, one could assume that the second stint on IR was just as much about recovery, as it was about maintaining the health of your most talented player. Coming into 2022 CMC should return to his prior elusive and explosive form. The Joe Brady coaching experiment is over and Ben McAdoo is in. McAdoo likes to run the ball and know how to utilize the individual talents of his backs. D'Onta Foreman was brought in on a one-year deal, and Chuba Hubbard will look to improve on his 2021 campaign. But neither is a threat to a healthy CMC.

JAMES ROBINSON

Before injuring his Achilles in Week 16 of 2021, James Robinson had 164 carries, 767 yards, and 8 touchdowns. He also caught the ball 31 times for 222 yards. With an optimal recovery time of nine months (research shows returning prior to nine months increases the risk of reinjury), he won't necessarily be ready by the start of 2022 season. Couple that with Travis Etienne Jr.'s return from a foot injury, and he could easily lose ground in the Jag's run game, depending on how long it takes him to get on the field. When healthy, he has the ability and build of a three-down back.

MILES SANDERS

Miles Sanders suffered a broken hand towards the end of the 2021 season. He should have no lingering issues going into 2022. Sanders is Philadelphia's lead back, with Kenneth Gainwell still the more attractive option in passing situations.

WIDE RECEIVERS

ODELL BECKHAM JR.

Odell Beckham Jr. was a key contributor in the Rams Super Bowl victory last year. Unfortunately, he suffered an ACL tear in the championship game. Because of the recovery timeline he could miss a significant portion of the season, if he plays at all. The Rams brought in veteran WR Allen Robinson II on a three-year $46.5 million deal, with $30.7m in guaranteed money. This could effectively signal the end of Beckham's time with the Rams, as he's yet to be resigned to a new contract. This situation should be monitored. When fully recovered, Beckham could be resigned in L.A., or elsewhere.

DJ CHARK JR.

DJ Chark Jr. broke his ankle in Week 4 of 2021 while still playing for the Jaguars. The Detroit Lions were undeterred by the injury, and Chark was signed to a one-year, fully guaranteed $10 million contract. He joins Amon-Ra St. Brown and rookie Jameson Williams, among others in a crowded wide receiver room. Considering his contract guarantee, other injury concerns for the Lions receivers, and that he'll have 10 months of recovery under his belt by the start of this season, Detroit must be confident in his ability to produce this season.

CHRIS GODWIN

Unfortunately, Chris Godwin suffered both ACL and MCL tears during a contract year. Fortunately for him, Tampa Bay believes he'll make a full recovery, as evidenced by the lucrative contract extension he recently signed. He was surprising left off the PUP list for training camp, which leads us to believe his return may be sooner than later. That said, he still may not be 100% until November, if at all this season, and Mike Evans will have to lead the way. Evans can't do it all, so Russell Gage Jr. and Julio Jones were added in the offseason. Both will probably see more work until Godwin is a full go. Once Godwin is healthy he will resume his role in this high powered offense.

DEANDRE HOPKINS

DeAndre Hopkins suffered a grade 2/3 MCL sprain in 2021. With proper rehab these injuries tend to heal very well. In addition, Hopkins will have an extra six weeks of rest due to a six-game suspension for PEDs. Kyler Murray's college teammate, Marquise Brown was added in the offseason, and their history of positive chemistry has already been noted. Hopkins is by far the most talented receiver in Arizona, and will assume the top spot upon his return.

JUJU SMITH-SCHUSTER

JuJu Smith-Schuster suffered a torn labrum in Week 5 of 2021 while still with the Pittsburgh Steelers, and he has since had surgical repair. These injuries can be troublesome for WRs, affecting range of motion (ROM) in the shoulder which can be important in jump-ball situations. There's been no indication this will be a problem for Smith-Schuster, as ROM can be recovered during rehab, and he'll have several months of rehab prior to the 2022 season. The Kansas City Chiefs have signed him to a one-year contract worth a potential $10.75 million with incentives. He'll be a good sized target who's comfortable working in traffic for QB Patrick Mahomes. Tyreek Hill was traded to Miami this offseason and the Chiefs acquired JuJu in free agency to replace him. In addition, Marquez Valdes-Scantling and Corey Coleman were brought in. Of the three, JuJu has been the most consistent and will have plenty of opportunity along with incumbent Mecole Hardman and rookie Skyy Moore.

MICHAEL THOMAS

Michael Thomas missed most of 2020 and all of last season with a lingering high and medial (inside) ankle sprain. He initially tried to avoid surgery opting for rehab, but to no avail. He had the repair shortly before the 2021 season began, so by the start of this season he'll have had more than a year to recover. In late May, head coach Dennis Allen said Thomas wasn't quite ready to see the field, but rehab is going well. He was a full go for training camp. But the Saints brought in veteran Jarvis Landry and drafted standout rookie Chris Olave, so there's plenty of talent in the receiver room. However, if healthy, Thomas is clearly the No. 1 option.

ADAM THIELEN

Adam Thielen had surgery on what was considered a grade-three lateral ankle sprain during the 2021 season. It's likely he suffered torn ligaments, which, he said, caused his ankle to feel unstable. Thielen will have logged nine-plus months of recovery by the start of the 2022 season, but he'll also be 32 years old. With opposing defenses more concerned with the emergence of teammate Justin Jefferson, an aging but still very talented Thielen should suffer no shortage of opportunity and should continue to make an impact, especially around the goal line where he's been so reliable. There's a long-standing chemistry between him and QB Kirk Cousins.

ROBERT WOODS

Apparently, Robert Woods tore his ACL in Week 10 last year, but wasn't aware of the extent of his injury and continued to practice. During the offseason he was traded to the Titans, and joins a somewhat crowded but inexperienced wide receiver room. Barring major setbacks in recovery, he could be ready to go within the first few weeks of the 2022 season. Until then, with the departures of A.J. Brown and Julio Jones, rookie Treylon Burks will get his shot. Once healthy, the more experienced Woods should play a major role this season as the Titans first or second receiving option.

TIGHT ENDS

T.J. HOCKENSON

T.J. Hockenson broke his hand towards the end of last season and is expected to be ready for 2022, as these injuries can heal in short time. Considering that two of the three best receivers in Detroit are coming off serious injuries, Hockenson has a chance to see a significant increase in production. It doesn't hurt that he is their most experienced and accomplished tight end.

IRV SMITH JR.

After playing well in 2020 it appeared Irv Smith Jr. was poised for a 2021 breakout campaign. Unfortunately, he suffered a torn MCL before the season began. Now, Smith has had close to a year of recovery. He might be a smaller-than-average tight end, but he's a faster and a more-adept pass catcher. Minnesota added Johnny Mundt in the offseason and drafted Nick Muse, but Smith, with his skill set, and experience in Minnesota's offense, will be their top tight end. Barring injury this could finally be Smith's year.

DARREN WALLER

Darren Waller had a tough 2021 season battling both hamstring and ankle injuries. But there's no indication he won't be ready early on in 2022. Normally, the addition of a talented pass catcher like Davante Adams would be cause for concern from a production standpoint. But for Waller it could be the opposite. Adams most likely will become the focal point for opposing defenses, setting Waller up for a possible bounce-back year. Demarcus Robinson and Keelan Cole were added in the offseason, and Hunter Renfrow remains in Vegas, giving Derek Carr a talented receiving corps. However, Waller has the best chance to capitalize on defenses focusing their attention elsewhere.

1

10 Players Primed for a Breakout

Our list of breakout candidates for this season includes five WRs, three RBs, one QB, and one TE. Some of these players have never played a snap in the NFL. Others have shown flashes of greatness, but never put it all together. And a few have already produced a solid fantasy season. But what they all have in common is, we are projecting these players to have their best year yet, to be the players that fantasy managers are talking about by mid-season. It doesn't mean they're great draft picks, because some of them already have an ADP in line with their potential, but it does mean, look out! These players are about to explode onto the scene! Here they are, listed in order of our rankings.

MICHAEL PITTMAN JR. (WR) - INDIANAPOLIS

By all accounts, Michael Pittman Jr. had a successful 2021 campaign. His 88-1,082-6 receiving line with Carson Wentz under center leaves fantasy managers optimistic about what he could be with a better passer like Matt Ryan. All we have to do is look to Julio Jones' time in Atlanta to see what a No. 1 WR under Ryan can be.

Pittman's numbers in 2021 weren't a fluke. He finished in the top-20 among WRs in targets, receptions, yards, TDs, and FPs, lacking only in target depth and red zone production. In run-first Indy, he'll never have a chance to put up Julio Jones' numbers, but a 95-1,250-7 line feels achievable for this third-year break out candidate.

CAM AKERS (RB) - LOS ANGELES RAMS

In early fantasy drafts last season, Akers rarely made it out of the second round. Then he tore his Achilles and missed the entire season, returning for a nominal role in the postseason.

The last time we saw what Akers could do was in 2020, when he had 74% of the Rams' rushing attempts in his final six games. He does have a lower receiving floor than some other RBs in his range, but volume on a high-powered offense will be more than enough to make up for his lack of receiving. Though he missed a season, everything we've seen from Sean McVay says Akers will be their feature back. A 10-TD, 1,400-all-purpose-yard season is not out of the question.

3

TRAVIS ETIENNE JR. (RB) - JACKSONVILLE

Former 2020 undrafted free agent James Robinson, who likely won't be fully healthy by Week 1, is the only thing standing between Etienne and a three-down role. The biggest tell that Etienne is about to take on a huge offensive role is that Jacksonville didn't add another back this offseason when they knew Robinson would be questionable to start the year.

Etienne's ability as a receiver may be his best fantasy attribute. Jacksonville will likely be playing from behind often. The result? Check-downs. And Lawrence ran for his life most of last season. Lawrence gets in trouble? Check-downs. Not even mentioning Lawrence and Etienne's college connection, Etienne could be in for enough volume that regardless of efficiency, he'll be an RB2. He continues to move up our rankings this offseason.

BREECE HALL (RB) - NYJ

Hall was a somewhat surprising second-round pick considering Michael Carter's rookie success. Hall is an athletic phenom who has all the attributes of a workhorse back. He is more than capable in the

4

passing game, recording 93 receptions in his final three FBS seasons.

While we don't expect Hall to approach 300 touches, he should exceed Carter's 2021 output (183), who finished as RB29 even after missing games due to injury. Carter played more than 70% of the snaps on three occasions, which should give us an idea of Hall's potential workload. He's got a good shot to finish as an RB2.

DARNELL MOONEY (WR) - CHICAGO

Last season, Mooney accounted for over a quarter of Chicago's targets. His biggest competition for targets, Allen Robinson II, is now with the Rams. Mooney started off slow but turned it up in the last 10 games, averaging 5.4 receptions per game. Mooney has the speed to turn any catch, or run, into a big play, posting three 50-plus yard plays last season.

His 140 targets from 2021 look to carry over into 2022. With a year under his belt, Justin Fields' accuracy and play should improve enough to help Mooney's numbers. A finish of 1,300 yards and 5 TDs seems well within his range of possible outcomes. Don't shy away from this target glutton.

6

RASHOD BATEMAN (WR) - BALTIMORE

Don't overthink this play. Baltimore lost their No. 1 WR, Marquise brown, to a trade with Arizona. Bateman, after missing the start of 2021, emerged as a consistent option for Lamar Jackson, scoring more than 12 FPs in three of his final five games. The competition for targets is small, with Mark Andrews his only real threat. Brown saw 146 targets last season. With those now up for grabs, Bateman could double his number of targets this season, and post the first 1,000-yard season of his career. He'll also see an uptick in red zone looks and TDs. Bateman has real WR2-appeal and a solid floor.

GABRIEL DAVIS (WR) - BUFFALO

Gabriel Davis is another third-year WR breakout candidate. With the departures of Cole Beasley and Emmanuel Sanders, Davis jumps to No. 2 on the depth chart of this high-powered offense. One only needs to look at last year's instant classic playoff game with Kansas City to see what he's capable of: 8-201-4! Even with Diggs in the fold, volume will not be a problem. Consider that with only a 10% target share last season, he still saw 17 red zone targets. Davis will see the first triple-digit target season of his career and use his impressive 15.7 YPR average from last season to post his first 1,000-yard season. You wouldn't be wrong to draft him in the fringe WR2 range on his potential upside.

PAT FREIRMUTH (TE) - PITTSBURGH

Pat Freiermuth quietly recorded the 10th best fantasy season ever for a rookie TE last season, and he didn't even gain the starting job until a month and a half into the season. Freiermuth finished as TE16, while having the lowest YPR of the top-16 TEs. This is a result of Big Ben's immobility and quick time to throw.

While the QB situation in Pittsburgh is still undecided, Trubisky or Pickett should only improve his numbers. Freiermuth's 7 TDs as a rookie were impressive, but not unexpected considering the was tied for first in red zone targets among TEs, and could even see an uptick this coming year. Lookout for Freiermuth this season as he poised to make a leap in production.

TREY LANCE (QB) - SAN FRANCISCO

Averaging just over 200 passing yards per game last season, Jalen Hurts proved that rushing ability can overcome a lack of passing production to produce a great fantasy QB.

Lance offers a high rushing-based floor for fantasy managers. Though it's unlikely he averages 10 rushing attempts per game, as he did in his three games with extended snaps last season, he'll become a better passer, and still offer plenty of upside with his legs.

Lance has lots of help in the passing game with yards-after-the-catch monsters Deebo Samuel and George Kittle in his arsenal.

When Lance finishes in the top-10 QBs this season and has a ADP of QB5 or better next season, you'll be thinking, "FantasyTakeover was right, and I should have listened."

ALLEN LAZARD (WR) - GREEN BAY

Ironically, Allen Lazard was our place holder name for this article for months, added once we heard of the Davante Adam's trade. As we narrowed down our top-10 candidates, Allen Lazard still stood out.

He has been in the shadows of Davante Adams for too long. QB Aaron Rodgers reminded us of Lazard's capability in his last two games of 2021, when Lazard averaged 21.9 fantasy PPG. It's easy to forget how big (6-foot 5) and quick Lazard is. His size makes him the early favorite for the majority of Adams' vacated red zone targets.

The biggest competition for target share will come from rookie Christian Watson. The best reason to pay attention to Lazard is that you won't find a cheaper WR with legitimate WR2 upside. If a breakout never comes, so what, you now have waiver wire fodder. But if you're right, you may have a weekly starter on your hands. Remember, folks, its A-Rod we're talking about. He's out to prove his success was not a result of Adams.

MOCK DRAFT

STARTING LINEUP
1 QB • 2 RBs • 2 WRs
1 Flex • 1 TE
1 K • 1 D/ST

RD	JOHN	TODD	NICK	MARILYN	COREY OF FANTASYTAKEOVER
1	RB1 JONATHAN TAYLOR (IND)	WR1 COOPER KUPP (LAR)	RB2 DERRICK HENRY (TEN)	RB3 CHRISTIAN MCCAFFREY (CAR)	RB4 AUSTIN EKELER (LAC)
2	WR7 CEEDEE LAMB (DAL)	RB11 LEONARD FOURNETTE (TB)	RB10 EZEKIEL ELLIOT (DAL)	QB1 JOSH ALLEN (BUF)	WR6 DAVANTE ADAMS (LV)
3	RB12 JAVONTE WILLIAMS (DEN)	WR8 DEEBO SAMUEL (SF)	TE2 MARK ANDREWS (BAL)	RB13 SAQUON BARKLEY (NYG)	RB14 AARON JONES (GB)
4	WR15 DJ MOORE (CAR)	RB19 ANTONIO GIBSON (WAS)	WR14 DK METCALF (SEA)	WR13 TERRY MCLAURIN (WAS)	RB18 JAMES CONNER (ARI)
5	RB20 CAM AKERS (LAR)	QB3 JUSTIN HERBERT (LAC)	WR16 JAYLEN WADDLE (MIA)	WR17 AMARI COOPER (CLE)	WR18 MICHAEL PITTMAN JR. (IND)
6	RB24 TRAVIS ETIENNE JR. (JAC)	RB23 J.K. DOBBINS (BAL)	QB6 KYLER MURRAY (ARI)	WR24 ALLEN ROBINSON II (LAR)	WR23 BRANDIN COOKS (HOU)
7	TE6 T.J. HOCKENSON (DET)	RB25 DAMIEN HARRIS (NE)	RB1 CLYDE EDWARDS-HELAIRE (KC)	RB27 KAREEM HUNT (CLE)	WR25 COURTLAND SUTTON (DEN)
8	WR33 JUJU SMITH-SCHUSTER (KC)	QB10 TOM BRADY (TB)	WR32 DRAKE LONDON (ATL)	WR31 HUNTER RENFROW (LV)	QB9 JALEN HURTS (PHI)
9	WR34 ADAM THIELEN (MIN)	RB30 KEN WALKER III (SEA)	RB31 TONY POLLARD (DAL)	RB32 DEVIN SINGLETARY (BUF)	TE8 DALLAS GOEDERT (PHI)
10	QB12 RUSSELL WILSON (DEN)	RB38 CORDARRELLE PATTERSON (ATL)	RB37 NYHEIM HINES (IND)	TE10 PAT FREIERMUTH (PIT)	WR39 ELIJAH MOORE (NYJ)
11	D/ST1 BILLS (BUF)	WR40 CHRISTIAN KIRK (JAC)	WR41 GARRETT WILSON (NYJ)	RB39 JAMES COOK (BUF)	WR42 BRANDON AIYUK (SF)
12	QB16 DEREK CARR (LV)	TE11 MIKE GESICKI (MIA)	WR48 CHASE CLAYPOOL (PIT)	WR47 ROBERT WOODS (TEN)	QB15 TREY LANCE (SF)
13	WR49 CHRIS OLAVE (NO)	RB43 JAMAAL WILLIAMS (DET)	WR50 JAKOBI MEYERS (NE)	RB44 RONALD JONES II (KC)	WR51 ALLEN LAZARD (GB)
14	RB49 JAMES WHITE (NE)	WR58 TYLER BOYD (CIN)	RB48 DAMEON PIERCE (TEN)	D/ST4 49ERS (SF)	D/ST3 SAINTS (NO)
15	WR59 MICHAEL GALLUP (DAL)	D/ST5 STEELERS (PIT)	D/ST6 COWBOYS (DAL)	WR60 JAMISON CROWDER (BUF)	TE13 IRV SMITH JR. (MIN)
16	K10 MASON CROSBY (GB)	K9 BRANDON MCMANUS (DEN)	K8 RYAN SUCCOP (TB)	K7 MATT GAY (LAR)	K6 HARRISON BUTKER (KC)

U sually mock drafts serve as our crew's favorite reading material each offseason. But we've noticed that most outlet's drafts consist of industry experts. These drafts are usually analyzed solely for the merits of the picks rather than addressing any real draft strategy.

After drafting for many years with fantasy football managers of all skill levels, we've found that not everyone is aware of some of the most sound drafting strategies. So in-stead of printing a draft of Fantasy-Takeover experts, we decided to print a typical fantasy draft that one of our experts (Corey) participates in each year.

The participants in this league are of all different skill levels and varying years of fantasy football experience. Rather than only analyze the draft for the best and worst picks, we also want to address some of the most common mistakes for drafters, including many made in this draft. Correcting these mistakes will immensely improve your final team's chance of winning. We hope you find our advice helpful.

PPR SCORING			
OFFENSE	**KICKING**	**DEFENSE / SPECIAL TEAMS**	
10 yards rushing = 1 pt	FG of < 40 yards = 3 pts	Fumble recovery = 2 pts	7-13 points allowed = 3 pts
10 yards receiving = 1 pt	FG of 40-49 yards = 4 pts	Interception = 2 pts	14-20 points allowed = 1 pt
25 yards passing = 1 pt	FG of 50+ yards = 6 pts	Sack = 1 pts	21-28 points allowed = 0 pts
Passing TD = 4 pts	PAT = 1 pt	Defensive/ST TDs = 6 pts	28-35 points allowed = -1 pt
Other TD = 6 pts		0 points allowed = 10 pts	35+ points allowed = -3 pts
Reception = 1 pt		1-6 points allowed = 5 pts	

DYLAN	TONY	GREGORY	EVERETTE	KIM
RB5 JOE MIXON *(CIN)*	RB6 NAJEE HARRIS *(PIT)*	RB7 DALVIN COOK *(MIN)*	RB ALVIN KAMARA *(NO)*	RB9 D'ANDRE SWIFT *(DET)*
WR5 STEFON DIGGS *(BUF)*	WR4 TYREEK HILL *(MIA)*	WR3 JA'MARR CHASE *(CIN)*	TE1 TRAVIS KELCE *(KC)*	WR2 JUSTIN JEFFERSON *(MIN)*
RB15 BREECE HALL *(NYJ)*	RB16 NICK CHUBB *(CLE)*	TE3 KYLE PITTS *(ATL)*	WR9 A.J. BROWN *(PHI)*	WR10 KEENAN ALLEN *(LAC)*
WR12 TEE HIGGINS *(CIN)*	RB17 DAVID MONTGOMERY *(CHI)*	WR11 MIKE EVANS *(TB)*	WR10 DIONTAE JOHNSON *(PIT)*	QB2 PATRICK MAHOMES *(KC)*
TE4 DARREN WALLER *(LV)*	RB21 JOSH JACOBS *(LV)*	QB4 LAMAR JACKSON *(BAL)*	QB5 JOE BURROW *(CIN)*	WR19 MICHAEL THOMAS *(NO)*
WR22 JERRY JEUDY *(DEN)*	WR21 DARNELL MOONEY *(CHI)*	RB22 ELIJAH MITCHELL *(SF)*	WR20 CHRIS GODWIN *(TB)*	TE5 GEORGE KITTLE *(SF)*
WR26 MIKE WILLIAMS *(LAC)*	QB7 AARON RODGERS *(GB)*	RB28 MILES SANDERS *(PHI)*	WR27 AMON-RA ST. BROWN *(DET)*	TE7 DALTON SCHULTZ *(DAL)*
QB8 DAK PRESCOTT *(DAL)*	WR30 RASHOD BATEMAN *(BAL)*	WR29 TYLER LOCKETT *(SEA)*	RB29 A.J. DILLON *(GB)*	WR28 MARQUISE BROWN *(ARI)*
WR35 TRELYON BURKS *(TEN)*	WR36 GABRIEL DAVIS *(BUF)*	RB33 ALEXANDER MATTISON *(MIN)*	WR37 DEANDRE HOPKINS *(ARI)*	RB34 CHASE EDMONDS *(MIA)*
WR38 DEVONTA SMITH *(PHI)*	TE9 ZACH ERTZ *(ARI)*	RB36 RASHAAD PENNY *(SEA)*	RB35 MELVIN GORDON III *(DEN)*	QB11 MATTHEW STAFFORD *(LAR)*
RB40 MICHAEL CARTER *(NYJ)*	D/ST2 BUCCANEERS *(TB)*	RB41 RHAMONDRE STEVENSON *(NE)*	QB13 DESHAUN WATSON *(CLE)*	WR43 KADARIUS TONEY *(NYG)*
QB14 TUA TAGOVAILOA *(MIA)*	WR46 RONDALE MOORE *(ARI)*	WR45 SKYY MOORE *(KC)*	WR44 RUSSELL GAGE *(TB)*	RB42 JAMES ROBINSON *(JAC)*
WR52 KENNY GOLLADAY *(NYG)*	TE12 DAWSON KNOX *(BUF)*	WR53 M. VALDES-SCANTLING *(KC)*	RB45 J.D. MCKISSIC *(WAS)*	WR54 ROBBIE ANDERSON *(CAR)*
WR57 JAHAN DOTSON *(WAS)*	WR56 MARVIN JONES JR. *(JAC)*	WR55 MECOLE HARDMAN *(KC)*	RB47 MARK INGRAM II *(NO)*	RB46 DARRELL HENDERSON *(LAR)*
D/ST7 PACKERS *(GB)*	D/ST8 DOLPHINS *(MIA)*	D/ST9 RAMS *(LAR)*	D/ST10 COLTS *(IND)*	D/ST11 RAVENS *(BAL)*
K5 NICK FOLK *(NE)*	K4 DANIEL CARLSON *(LV)*	K3 TYLER BASS *(BUF)*	K2 EVAN MCPHERSON *(CIN)*	K1 JUSTIN TUCKER *(BAL)*

> **" BUT EVEN IF YOU KNOW NOTHING ABOUT YOUR OPPONENTS, ALWAYS BE AWARE OF THEIR POSITIONAL NEEDS DURING THE DRAFT.**

Draft Strategy

1 ALWAYS BE AWARE OF YOUR OPPONENTS' NEEDS.

Like us, you may have drafted with same group of fantasy managers for years. You know their tendencies, or more specifically, who they are targeting each year. But even if you know nothing about your opponents, always be aware of their positional needs during the draft.

For example, in Round 7, when Tony drafted Aaron Rodgers, the three fantasy managers drafting after him (Gregory, Everette, and Kim) had already drafted QBs, and were unlikely to be drafting a backup that soon, especially in a 1-QB league. So, by taking A-Rod one round too early, Tony gave up the chance to draft the six players who were taken in between his picks. Perhaps he was hoping to take Amon-Ra St. Brown instead of Rashod Bateman, but because he didn't pay attention, he lost out.

More DRAFT STRATEGY

2 ONLY USE YOUR FANDOMHOOD TO BREAK TIES.

We understand. You probably play fantasy football because you love football. And if you love football, you likely have a favorite team. But if your goal is to be a fantasy champion, set your fan bias aside.

Nick is a die-hard Cowboys fan. Corey thought Nick might even jump out the window and take Zeke (or CeeDee Lamb) as early as the first round. Nick ended up taking Zeke with his second pick, probably a round too early this year. While Zeke still has an RB14 ADP and Nick took him at RB10, it wasn't because of a superior valuation on the player.

3 JUST BECAUSE A GUY'S YOUR HIGHEST RANKED PLAYER, DOESN'T MEAN TO DRAFT HIM TOO EARLY.

Corey was really high on Courtland Sutton this year, as many of us are here at Fantasy-Takeover. In fact, Corey had Sutton one spot higher than Brandin Cooks in his ranking. Instead of taking Sutton in Round 6, he drafted Cooks. He knew that Sutton had a pretty good chance of making it back around to him in Round 7, a better chance than Cooks.

If you are pretty certain of the rankings and tendencies of the fantasy managers in your draft, use that to decide when to draft players, rather than going strictly by your rankings. This is why being aware of players' ADPs is important.

4 DON'T DRAFT BACKUPS FOR YOUR TOP-5 QBS AND TES BEFORE THE LAST FEW ROUNDS, IF AT ALL.

If your going to use an early-round pick on a TE or QB, don't draft another one who will likely never play. Those roster spots should be used to find potential upside at other positions. We even support leaving drafts with only one QB and one TE.

Consider last year had you decided to take a chance on Elijah Moore or Amon-Ra St. Brown instead of Kirk Cousins.

Shame on you, Kim. What is Stafford going to do for you when you already have Patrick Mahomes.

5 DON'T DRAFT A QB BEFORE ROUND 3.

The difference, as we've explained elsewhere in this book, between QB1s are minimal and hard to project. While Josh Allen, who Marilyn took in Round 2, has the best chance to finish as the overall QB1, he likely won't finish that far ahead of Jalen Hurts, who was taken in Round 8. Let's look at it another way. If you look at two RBs taken in Rounds 2 and 8, say, Leonard Fournette and AJ Dillon. The difference between the RBs in fantasy PPG is much larger than the difference between the QBs. Your goal is to optimize your team's fantasy-point output, and Leonard Fournette and Jalen Hurts will have a higher output than Josh Allen and AJ Dillon.

Oh, Marilyn. Tsk, tsk.

6 DON'T DRAFT A KICKER OR DEFENSE BEFORE THE LAST FEW ROUNDS.

You may have heard the adage, "Defense wins Super Bowls." Well, not in fantasy football. The difference between the best-ranked defense and the 10th best is 1 fantasy PPG, and that's even hard to project on a game-to-game basis. The same goes for kickers.

Stream your defenses and kickers week-to-week based on matchups and save those all important middle-round picks for bigger upside.

Oh, and definitely don't leave your draft with two defenses or two kickers. Tony. Cough, cough.

Best Pick		Worst Pick

Best Pick

Cam Akers (5.1) Travis Etienne Jr. (6.10)
I love both of his picks in Rounds 5 and 6. Both are potential RB2 Studs with solid floors.

Deebo Samuel (3.2)
With an ADP of 16 and our WR6 ranking, Deebo slipped all the way to Round 3. Kyle Shannahan will continue to get Deebo the ball, no matter who's under center.

Jaylen Waddle (5.3)
Nick's team is one of my least favorites. It felt like he reached on most of his picks. Waddle was a good choice, though. He should be able to reproduce his 2021 numbers, even with the addition of Tyreek Hill.

Christian McCaffrey (1.4)
Quit fading CMC. Yes, he's been injured, but most weren't soft tissue. He's no more likely to get injured than some others being drafted in Round 1. Matt Rhule is going to use CMC to save his job and we don't want to miss out. I only wish Marilyn would have let him slide one more pick to me!

Elijah Moore (10.6)
I love what Moore did in the second half of last year. WR39 is way too low, below even his floor. The team will take a step forward, and Moore will benefit most.

Mike Williams (7.7)
There's no way Williams should have gone after guys like Michael Thomas and Allen Robinson. On the high-octane Chargers offense, he could put up WR10-15 numbers, and at a WR26 price.

Zach Ertz (10.4))
Ertz showed out from the day he arrived in Arizona. Tony didn't panic on getting a TE. The difference in TE5 to TE10 is small, so waiting until the bottom of that tier is good strategy.

Skyy Moore (12.3), Marquez Valdes-Scantling (13.8), Mecole Hardman (14.3)
I think I love this play, but I'm not sure. Gregory took three picks, I assume, to find the one who emerges in the Chiefs potent offense, then feed the rest to waiver sharks. It may just work; I'll be interested to see how this strategy pans out by the end of the season.

J.D. McKissic (13.9)
Everette looked lost most of the draft. He picked four players who might not play Week 1. He started to recover in Rounds 12-14, but it was too late. McKissic was a good pick, because rather than chasing injury-upside in Round 13, he took a player who could fill that flex role until his team is full-strength. But chase upside if your starters are in place.

George Kittle (6.1)
I was hoping Kittle would drop to me in this round. He was that last player in Tier 1 and 2 of the TEs. Kittle has overall TE1 potential, and was a steal in Round 6.

Worst Pick

JOHN

James White (14.10)
I'd much rather have a handcuff or injury-upside back. John already had plenty of starting options — Taylor, Akers, Etienne. I'd have taken Isaiah Spiller or Gus Edwards instead.

TODD

Damien Harris (7.2)
Theres not a lot to pick with here. Overall, Todd had a solid draft, but I'd have taken Miles Sanders over Harris. Sanders should be the Eagles lead back, but Harris, who is TD dependent, will split touches with at least Rhamondre Stevenson and James White.

NICK

DK Metcalf (4.8)
Since I spoke about Elliot earlier in this article, I'll choose another miss. I'd much rather have Michael Pittman Jr. here over Metcalf. There's too much uncertainty in Seattle as they try to rebuild.

MARILYN

Josh Allen (2.7)
I know I mention this pick earlier, but Marilyn's team looks pretty good other than that pick. She should have opted for Fournette in the Round 2 and Allen should have still been there in 3. Fournette has the same upside as Barkley, but with a much safer floor.

COREY

Dallas Goedert (9.5)
I panicked here too much and about lost Elijah Moore. I had Goedert, Zack Ertz, and Pat Freiermuth all ranked about the same. I should have taken Moore in Round 9, and waited for one of the three TEs in 10. Instead, I got lucky it worked out.

DYLAN

Joe Mixon (1.6)
Dylan had Mixon last year, and was proud Mixon justified his Round 2 reach. He'd have been much better off with Najee Harris or Dalvin Cook in this spot.

TONY

Rondale Moore (12.4))
Moore had flashes last season, but taking the third option (or fourth when DeAndre Hopkins returns) on a team feels like a reach. If Tony was looking for a high-floor play, Jakobi Myers would have been a better pick.

GREGORY

Alexander Mattison (9.8)
I like reaching a little for valuable handcuffs, but Mattison's ADP is 116, almost three rounds later. I'd take a chance that he'd still be there in a round or two and grab a flex WR option instead.

EVERETTE

A.J. Brown (3.9)
Many people associate uncertainty with upside. We haven't seen A.J. Brown in Philly yet, competing with DeVonta Smith and Dallas Goedert for targets. But we have seen Keenan Allen, who continues to put up great numbers in a fantasy-friendly Chargers Offense.

KIM

Michael Thomas (5.10)
Besides his unnecessary backup picks of Dalton Schultz and Matthew Stafford, Thomas was his biggest blunder. He hasn't played a game in 18 months. And glancing at his RB deficiency, Elijah Mitchell, J.K. Dobbins, and Travis Etienne Jr. sure do look appealing in that spot.

NEW TEAMS DREAMS

A Look at the Impact of the 10 Biggest Offseason Moves

Every offseason players find themselves on new teams, either by trade or free-agent acquisition. You only need to remember last year to see how impactful some of these moves can be on players' fantasy values. Who would have thought that the addition of Matthew Stafford would turn Cooper Kupp into the best fantasy WR in NFL history? In this section, we look at the fantasy winners and losers the 10 biggest offseason moves.

RUSSELL WILSON

Old Team	Seattle Seahawks
New Team	DeXnver Broncos
The How	Acquired in a trade with the Seattle Seahawks, along with a fourth-round pick, for two first-round picks, two second-rounders, a fifth-rounder, QB Drew Lock, TE Noah Fant and DT Shelby Harris.
Fantasy Winners	Courtland Sutton, Jerry Jeudy, Denver Offense
Fantasy Losers	Tyler Lockett, DK Metcalf, Seattle Offense

Chef Russell Wilson will be cooking for Courtland Sutton and Jerry Jeudy this season. Both will feel the fantasy effects of playing with an elite-level QB for the first time. Wilson and Sutton, who share a love of the deep ball, should have an instant connection, while Jeudy and his precision route running won't be far behind. Even Javonte Williams and Melvin Gordon shouldn't be worried about the inevitable decreased rushing rate, as they will see plenty of additional scoring opportunities.

The losers of this trade are definitely Tyler Lockett and DK Metcalf. Neither Geno Smith nor Drew Lock know as many recipes as Wilson. Lockett will suffer most, as he is on the wrong side of 30, and fighting for targets with the WR Seattle hopes will lead their receiving corps for years to come, Metcalf. Unlike Lockett, Metcalf should see enough volume to remain a WR2.

DESHAUN WATSON

Old Team	Houston Texans
New Team	Cleveland Browns
The How	Acquired in a trade with the Texans, along with a 2024 sixth-round pick, in exchange for three first-round picks (2022-24), a third-rounder ('23) and two fourth-rounders ('22, '24). Watson will receive a fully guaranteed five-year, $230 million contract from Cleveland.
Fantasy Winners	Amari Cooper, Cleveland Offense, Houston Texans
Fantasy Losers	Amari Cooper, Cleveland Offense

The Houston Texans can finally move on and put their chaotic last two years behind them, and have plenty of draft capital to help them heal faster.

Amari Cooper, who was expecting to be catching passes from Baker Mayfield, won the fantasy lottery with the addition of Deshaun Watson. Now that we know Watson is facing a six-game suspension, managers can draft Cooper knowing they'll have an elite QB under center most of the season.

Watson has a chance to be the best QB in fantasy from Week 7 on, and Amari Cooper could be elevated to a WR1 as a result.

In addition, Watson will make all of Cleveland's offensive skill players more valuable, as the offense should put up bigger numbers than in previous years.

BAKER MAYFIELD

Old Team Cleveland Browns

New Team Carolina Panthers

The How Acquired in trade with the Cleveland Browns in exchange for a 2024 fifth-round pick that can convert to a fourth-rounder based on playing time.

Fantasy Winners DJ Moore, Baker Mayfield

Fantasy Losers Sam Darnold

Even before Baker Mayfield arrived in Carolina in a virtually risk-free trade with the Brown, we felt DJ Moore was being undervalued in drafts, mostly because we expected the Panthers to be starting someone other than Sam Darnold the majority of the season.

With the addition of Mayfield, Darnold's days as an NFL QB are numbered. While Christian McCaffrey's fantasy outlook shouldn't change, DJ Moore will be likely be catching passes from the best QB of his career. Moore saw a 28% target share last season and was fifth among all WRs in air yards. He'll will record his first top-20 WR finish under Mayfield. Mark our words.

MATT RYAN

Old Team Atlanta Falcons

New Team Indianapolis Colts

The How Acquired in a trade with the Atlanta Falcons in exchange for a third-round pick.

Fantasy Winners Michael Pittman Jr., Alec Pierce, Nyheim Hines

Fantasy Losers Kyle Pitts, Drake London, Matt Ryan

Matt Ryan had one of the worst fantasy seasons of his career last year in a depleted Falcons offense. Now he's moved to a more run-focused Colts where his numbers are unlikely to improve. Michael Pittman Jr. and rookie Alec Pierce, on the other hand, now have a reliable veteran QB under center, instead of a can't-quite-put-it-all-together Carson Wentz. Pittman is now elevated to a high-end WR2 and Alec Pierce, who would have been forgotten under Wentz, has a shot to be rostered as a potential flex play.

The Atlanta receivers suffered the most in this trade. Kyle Pitts moves out of the top tier for TEs(Travis Kelce and Mark Andrews), having to catch footballs from a less proficient passer, Marcus Mariota. And Drake London, a would-be fringe WR2 with Ryan, is now a fringe WR3.

CARSON WENTZ

Old Team Indianapolis Colts

New Team Washington Commanders

The How Acquired in a trade with the Indianapolis Colts, along with a 2022 seventh-round pick, in exchange for a 2022 third-rounder and a 2023 third-rounder, which can convert to a second-rounder based on Wentz's snap totals. The teams will also swap 2022 second-round picks.

Fantasy Winners Terry McLaurin, Washington Offense, Carson Wentz

Fantasy Losers None

After a year of playing for a team that ran the ball the fifth-most times in the league, Wentz lands in an improved fantasy situation in Washington, as Ron Rivera will at least start the year giving his QB a chance to win games through the air.

If Wentz was able to support a WR3 (Michael Pittman Jr.) in Indy, he definitely should be able to elevate Terry McLaurin to a solid WR2. Wentz, with all his flaws, is the best QB Mclaurin's had during his four years in the league. Wentz may even be able to support another WR, whether it be rookie Jahan Dotson or McLaurin's Ohio State roommate, Curtis Samuel, we don't know. Even Logan Thomas should be in the TE1 mix once he gets fully healthy.

MARCUS MARIOTA

Old Team Tennessee Titans

New Team Atlanta Falcons

The How Signed a two-year deal. Mariota will earn $6.75 million in 2022 ($1.75 million guaranteed base salary, $5 million signing bonus) and has a $12 million option for 2023. He's due a $3 million roster bonus on the fifth day of the league year next March.

Fantasy Winners Marcus Mariota

Fantasy Losers Kyle Pitts, Drake London

Atlanta's offense was, by all accounts, terrible last season. The falcons decided it was time to move on from their franchise QB Matt Ryan. They brought in Marcus Mariota to be a stopgap for the team. Transitioning from backup to starter, Mariota will have some streaming appeal if Atlanta properly utilizes his rushing ability.

As we said under the Matt Ryan section, Kyle Pitts and Drake London got the worst of this deal, but without much competition in the offense, both will have solid fantasy seasons.

TYREEK HILL

Old Team Kansas City Chiefs

New Team Miami Dolphins

The How Acquired in a trade with the Kansas City Chiefs in exchange for 2022 first-, second- and fourth-round picks, and 2023 fourth- and sixth-rounders. Hill has agreed to a four-year, $120 million extension that includes $72.2 million guaranteed.

Fantasy Winners Tua Tagovailoa

Fantasy Losers Patrick Mahomes, Jaylen Waddle, Tyreek Hill

Both Tyreek Hill and Patrick Mahomes' fantasy upside is diminished with the trade of Hill to Miami. Hill will lose many of the deep balls and receptions on unscripted plays he had in Kansas City, now playing with a QB who has one of the lowest average-depth-of-target-per-attempt number in the league, Tua Tagovailoa. More specifically, Mahomes averaged 284 air yards per game over the past two seasons, and Tua, 214. But Hill will help Tua have the best year of his career, and should finally be a solid streaming option throughout the year.

Jaylen Waddle's fantasy value was probably hurt most in the trade, going from a WR1 to WR2. He'll see plenty of good weeks, but his ceiling just got lowered considerably. Don't expect much more than his Year 1 output.

DAVANTE ADAMS

Old Team Green Bay Packers

New Team Las Vegas Raiders

The How Acquired in a trade with the Green Bay Packers in exchange for a 2022 first-round pick and 2022 second-round pick. Adams is expected to sign a new contract with the Raiders worth $141.25 million over five years with an average of $28.25 million per year.

Fantasy Winners Derek Carr, Allen Lazard

Fantasy Losers Aaron Rodgers, Darren Waller, Hunter Renfrow, Davante Adams

The fantasy needle has only slightly moved for Davante Adams after his trade to the Raiders, dropping from the overall WR2 to WR4/5. Derek Carr is the real winner here, with his first chance to be an actual QB1. There is no reason why he shouldn't produce in this three-headed reception eating, pass-oriented offense. Two of the heads, Hunter Renfrow and Darren Waller, have been downgraded with the addition of Adams. There's' simply not enough volume for consistent production among all three. Both should at least benefit from some added scoring opportunities, though.

In Green Bay, Aaron Rodgers who lost 33% of his air yards in the Adams' trade is now only a fringe QB1. But we still can't picture A-rod finishing outside the top-10 QBs. Allen Lazard will finally get his chance to be the No. 1 target for the one of the best QBs in the leagues — WR2/3 is not out of the realm of possibilities for him.

MIAMI RUNNING BACKS

Old Team Chase Edmonds: Arizona Cardinals
Raheem Mostert: San Francisco 49ers
Sony Michel: Los Angeles Rams

New Team Miami Dolphins

The How Chase Edmonds: Signed a two-year, $12.6 million contract that includes $6.1 million guaranteed.
Raheem Mostert: Signed a one-year deal worth $3.125 million.
Sony Michel: Signed a free-agent deal

Fantasy Winners Chase Edmonds, Raheem Mostert, Sony Michel, James Conner

Fantasy Losers Myles Gaskin

Miami revamped their entire skill position group this offseason. The backfield should belong mostly to Chase Edmonds and Raheem Mostert. And if you follow the money, Edmonds should see the majority of the work, especially in the all-important passing-down situations. We expect Mostert, who is already familiar with Mike McDaniel's system, to have first dibs outside of Edmonds for an early-down role. When healthy, he's the best pure runner on the team. But because of his inability to stay on the field, Sony Michel may also have a chance to take some snaps, as he was serviceable in a Rams RB committee last season, especially in goal line situations.

All this action has left Myles Gaskin outside looking in. Gaskin still has a chance to make the roster because of his pass-catching ability, but has little chance of fantasy relevancy this season.

And with Edmonds out of the way in Arizona, James Conner's ranking jumps from a fringe RB2 to a solid RB2 with RB1 upside.

A.J. BROWN

Old Team Tennessee Titans

New Team Philadelphia Eagles

The How Acquired in a trade with the Tennessee Titans, in exchange for a 2022 first-rounder (No. 18 overall) and third-rounder (No. 101).

Fantasy Winners Jalen Hurts

Fantasy Losers Ryan Tannehill, DeVonta Smith

Jalen Hurts finally gets a premier receiving threat in A.J. Brown, who will work opposite DeVonta Smith. Hurts, in an offense that scores a little more often and has a little more passing production, has the potential to be top-three QB. Unfortunately, this increase in passing production comes at the expense of Smith's target share. He's been downgraded from a WR2 to a fringe WR3 in the trade.

While we consider the trade's effect on Brown's fantasy value to be neutral, Ryan Tannehill will suffer the full consequence of losing one of the league's top options. Normally in the QB10-15 range, Tannehill will be lucky to finish in the top 20.

Players Who are Overvalued or Undervalued at Their Current Average Draft Position

For most fantasy outlets, publishing a "Boom or Bust" article is standard operating procedure. Here at FantasyTakeover, we believe that every player could be a boom or bust depending on their average draft position (ADP).

We prefer to call out candidates either overvalued or undervalued. In order to find these players, we examine current ADPs and see how they differ from our rankings.

UNDERVALUED

Leonard Fournette (RB7, RB13 ADP)

Somehow Fournette is currently being drafted in the middle of the third round in most drafts. Did we forget that he was the fourth-best RB in fantasy PPG last season, and sixth overall, after missing three games? Nick Chubb and Javonte Williams are being drafted ahead of him. Come on, folks. Both of those guys are in less-potent offenses and have a smaller share of the backfield snaps than Fournette. Remember, Fournette led all backs in targets last season, and he should be in for a similar workload, especially with Gronk's retirement, and Godwin questionable early on. Fournette won't be making it out of Round 2 in our drafts.

Brandin Cooks (WR19, WR22 ADP)

Though the ranking and ADP don't differ much, Cooks has continued to fall to us in many of our drafts and we thought it important to mention him here. Cooks, with a rotating cast of QBs and teams, has only finished outside the top-20 fantasy WRs twice, his rookie year and a low-volume 2019 with a lost Jared Goff under center. Cooks depends on high volume to excel, and with little competition in Houston for Targets, Cooks will continue to have the ball thrown his way often, as Houston tries to rediscover their identity.

Drake London (WR32, WR38 ADP)

Unless you're a Falcons fan or diehard fantasy footballer, you probably can't name another Atlanta WR. London will essentially be competing with TE Kyle Pitts for the majority of targets this season.

Justin Jefferson and Ja'marr chase have already shown us what first-year receivers with enough targets and ability are capable of. While Atlanta doesn't have the passing volume of Minnesota or Cincinnati, they also don't have an Adam Thielen or Tee Higgins as a No. 2 option competing for targets. Atlanta should struggle on the year as a whole and will at least want to prove to fans that they hit on their first pick. London will see enough action for be a safe WR3/flex.

DJ Moore (WR12, WR18 ADP)

Moore has underperformed his ADP every season, but has had two things to blame: QB play and the offensive line. A bad QB and bad offensive line is a terrible combination for fantasy receivers. Carolina improved their offensive line this offseason in the draft and in free agency. Their QB situation is still up in the air, but our guess is Baker Mayfield starts the majority of the games under center, the best QB Moore has had in his career. The Panthers locked up Moore for a three-year, $61.9 million extension this offseason before WR costs skyrocketed after the Christian Kirk signing. With an improved offensive line, a healthy Christian McCaffrey, and likely a better QB, Carolina's offense has to be much better than their 2021 iteration, and Moore should reap the benefits.

Courtland Sutton (WR25, WR27 ADP)

Here's another instance where our ranking and Sutton's ADP differ only slightly. As the season nears, though, we are getting more and more bullish on Sutton. While we know it's a stretch, Sutton's 2022 looks eerily similar to Copper Kupp's 2021. Both had put up sound numbers in their early years, before declining for a couple of seasons. And then, a great QB comes in, and we saw what happened to Kupp. While we don't expect Sutton to really be this year's Cooper Kupp (we won't see that again for a long time), he certainly a better option than Michael Thomas and Amari Cooper, who are both being drafted ahead of him.

ADP?

OVERVALUED

Nick Chubb (RB16, RB10 ADP)

Early drafts had us penciling in Chubb a possible Sleeper candidate, and then he continued to inexplicably trend upwards. While we're not questioning Chubb's talent, there's a lot about his situation that's worse than some of the backs being drafted behind him. First, we're unsure who will be the QB come Week 1 (or Week 18). Second, Kareem Hunt is back healthy and will not only take most of the passing downs from Chubb, he'll take some of the early-down work, too. Third, as good as Chubb's metrics have been, even D'Ernest Johnson was able to average 6.6 yards per carry against Denver in Week 7 last season, behind the same offensive line that make's Chubb look so talented. And fourth, there's been some offensive line turnover in Cleveland this offseason. Nick Harris is taking over at center and Jack Conklin will likely start the year on the PUP list. We like Chubb, and he's a safe pick, but give us Leonard Fournette, Aaron Jones, Saquon Barkley, or James Conner (all being drafted ahead of Chubb).

A.J. Brown (WR15, WR9 ADP)

Ironically, we were all over A.J. Brown last season at his ADP. What's crazy to us is that Brown's current ADP is higher than we would have projected had he stayed in Tennessee. The blockbuster draft-night trade illuminated his name and talent, and has helped him, puzzlingly, climb the draft board. Jalen Hurts is a worse passer than Ryan Tannehill. If Brown would have received 33% of Hurt's completions, passing yards, and passing TDs last season, a ridiculous offensive share, he would have still only averaged 13.8 fantasy PPG, which would have been 29th-best among WRs. Hurts should improve his passing in 2022, but WR9 is a tall ask. There are plenty of better options going for a cheaper ADP — Keenan Allen, Mike Evans, Tee Higgins, and Jaylen Waddle.

Michael Thomas (WR29, WR24 ADP)

Michael Thomas is a phenomenal player, or was, when he last played 18 months ago. There are still many questions concerning his health, even though he did start training camp "healthy." We're watching him closely before our drafts to see how he's looking in practice, and maybe in limited preseason action. Still, we'd rather have Darnell Mooney, Amon-Ra St. Brown, Jerry Jeudy, or even someone like Elijah Moore who's being drafted almost a round-and-a-half later. All have much less risk and a solid floor.

Adam Thielen (WR38, WR29 ADP)

Adam Thielen is a talented receiver, and one of Cousins' favorite red zone targets. At 32 years old and now an injury risk, Thielen's best days are behind him. He's been extremely lucky in the red zone, with one of the highest TD-per-target rate of any WR over the past three seasons. With Justin Jefferson, a healthy Irv Smith Jr., and an emerging K.J. Osborn, Thielen might just be the one left out, or at least in for a smaller target share than in prior years. Give us Rashod Bateman who's being drafted two rounds later.

Joe Burrow (QB12, QB5 ADP)

We get it. Fantasy football players are football fans, and Joe Burrow was one heck of a football player last season. Most fantasy footballers don't spend hours (or days, or months) studying up for their fantasy draft. If they did, they would know that even in his phenomenal 2021 season, Burrow was a top-five QB only three weeks, and finished as the 10th best QB in fantasy PPG. And if you take away his two monster games, he may have finished outside the top-15. Joe Burrow would have to take a giant step forward to meet his QB5 ADP, and we don't think there's much room in front of him.

POINT PER RECEPTION

We rank the overall top 100. After 100, it is more important to focus on your team's needs.

QUARTERBACKS

	OVERALL	BYE	
1.	37	BUF 7	JOSH ALLEN
2.	46	KC 8	PATRICK MAHOMES
3.	53	LAC 8	JUSTIN HERBERT
4.	58	BAL 10	LAMAR JACKSON
5.	65	PHI 7	JALEN HURTS
6.	74	TB 11	TOM BRADY
7.	75	ARI 13	KYLER MURRAY
8.	85	DAL 9	DAK PRESCOTT
9	92	GB 14	AARON RODGERS
10.	93	DEN 9	RUSSELL WILSON
11.		SF 9	TREY LANCE
12.		CIN 10	JOE BURROW
13.		LAR 7	MATTHEW STAFFORD
14.		MIA 11	TUA TAGOVAILOA
15.		CLE 9	DESHAUN WATSON
16.		LV 6	DEREK CARR
17.		MIN 7	KIRK COUSINS
18.		CHI 14	JUSTIN FIELDS
19.		NO 14	JAMEIS WINSTON
20.		JAC 11	TREVOR LAWRENCE
21.		TEN 6	RYAN TANNEHILL
22.		NYG 9	DANIEL JONES
23.		IND 14	MATT RYAN
24.		NE 10	MAC JONES
25.		NYJ 10	ZACH WILSON
26.		HOU 6	DAVIS MILLS
27.		ATL 14	MARCUS MARIOTA
28.		DET 6	JARED GOFF
29.		CAR 13	BAKER MAYFIELD
30.		WAS 14	CARSON WENTZ
31.		PIT 9	KENNY PICKETT
32.		(SF) 9	JIMMY GAROPPOLO
33.		(CLE) 11	DREW LOCK

TIGHT ENDS

	OVERALL	BYE	
1.	13	KC 8	TRAVIS KELCE
2.	17	BAL 10	MARK ANDREWS
3.	31	ATL 14	KYLE PITTS
4.	45	SF 9	GEORGE KITTLE
5.	54	LV 6	DARREN WALLER
6.	71	DET 6	T.J. HOCKENSON
7.	73	DAL 9	DALTON SCHULTZ
8.	80	PHI 7	DALLAS GOEDERT
9	84	ARI 13	ZACH ERTZ
10.	94	PIT 9	PAT FREIERMUTH
11.		MIA 11	MIKE GESICKI
12.		BUF 7	DAWSON KNOX
13.		MIN 7	IRV SMITH JR.
14.		CHI 14	COLE KMET
15.		SEA 11	NOAH FANT
16.		NE 10	HUNTER HENRY
17.		WAS 14	LOGAN THOMAS
18.		CLE 9	DAVID NJOKU
19.		LAR 7	TYLER HIGBEE
20.		TB 11	ROB GRONKOWSKI
21.		TB 11	CAMERON BRATE
22.		LAC 8	GERALD EVERETT
23.		TEN 6	AUSTIN HOOPER

RUNNING BACKS

	OVERALL	BYE	
1.	1	IND 14	JONATHAN TAYLOR
2.	2	CAR 13	CHRISTIAN MCCAFFREY
3.	3	LAC 8	AUSTIN EKELER
4.	4	TEN 6	DERRICK HENRY
5.	5	PIT 9	NAJEE HARRIS
6.	7	NO 14	ALVIN KAMARA
7.	9	TB 11	LEONARD FOURNETTE
8.	10	MIN 7	DALVIN COOK
9	11	DET 9	D'ANDRE SWIFT
10.	14	CIN 10	JOE MIXON
11.	18	GB 14	AARON JONES
12.	22	ARI 13	JAMES CONNER
13.	23	CHI 14	DAVID MONTGOMERY
14.	27	NYG 9	SAQUON BARKLEY
15.	28	DEN 9	JAVONTE WILLIAMS
16.	29	CLE 9	NICK CHUBB
17.	30	LAR 7	CAM AKERS
18.	35	DAL 9	EZEKIEL ELLIOTT
19.	36	WAS 14	ANTONIO GIBSON
20.	38	LV 6	JOSH JACOBS
21.	39	JAC 11	TRAVIS ETIENNE JR.
22.	43	BAL 10	J.K. DOBBINS
23.	44	NYJ 10	BREECE HALL
24.	51	SF 9	ELIJAH MITCHELL
25.	62	PHI 7	MILES SANDERS
26.	63	KC 8	CLYDE EDWARDS-HELAIRE
27.	64	BUF 7	DEVIN SINGLETARY
28.	66	CLE 9	KAREEM HUNT
29.	67	NE 10	DAMIEN HARRIS
30.	81	DAL 9	TONY POLLARD
31.	82	MIA 11	CHASE EDMONDS
32.	83	DEN 9	MELVIN GORDON III
33.	88	GB 14	AJ DILLON
34.	89	ATL 14	CORDARRELLE PATTERSON
35.	95	SEA 11	KEN WALKER III
36.	96	SEA 11	RASHAAD PENNY
37.	100	NYJ 10	MICHAEL CARTER
38.		NE 10	RHAMONDRE STEVENSON
39.		BUF 7	JAMES COOK
40.		JAC 11	JAMES ROBINSON
41.		MIN 7	ALEXANDER MATTISON
42		KC 8	RONALD JONES II
43.		WAS 14	J.D. MCKISSIC
44.		IND 14	NYHEIM HINES
45.		DET 6	JAMAAL WILLIAMS
46.		MIA 11	RAHEEM MOSTERT
47.		HOU 6	DAMEON PIERCE
48.		ATL 14	TYLER ALLGEIER
49.		BAL 10	GUS EDWARDS
50.		NE 10	JAMES WHITE
51.		PHI 7	KENNETH GAINWELL
52.		LAR 7	DARRELL HENDERSON JR.
53.		HOU 6	MARLON MACK
54.		LAC 8	ISAIAH SPILLER
55.		TB 11	RACHAAD WHITE
56.		MIA 11	SONY MICHEL
57.		CHI 14	KHALIL HERBERT
58.		ARI 13	DARRELL WILLIAMS
59.		CAR 13	D'ONTA FOREMAN
60.		NO 14	MARK INGRAM II
61.		SF 9	JERICK MCKINNON
62.		CAR 13	CHUBA HUBBARD
63.		LV 6	KENYAN DRAKE
64.		MIA 11	MYLES GASKIN
65.		SF 9	TREY SERMON
66.		SF 9	TYRION DAVIS-PRICE
67.		PHI 7	BOSTON SCOTT
68.		WAS 14	BRIAN ROBINSON JR.
69.		CIN 10	SAMAJE PERINE
70.		ATL 14	DAMIEN WILLIAMS
71.		BUF 7	ZACK MOSS
72.		LV 6	ZAMIR WHITE

WIDE RECEIVERS

	OVERALL	BYE	
1.	6	LAR 7	COOPER KUPP
2.	8	MIN 7	JUSTIN JEFFERSON
3.	12	CIN 10	JA'MARR CHASE
4.	15	BUF 7	STEFON DIGGS
5.	16	LV 6	DAVANTE ADAMS
6.	19	SF 9	DEEBO SAMUEL
7.	20	MIA 11	TYREEK HILL
8.	21	DAL 9	CEEDEE LAMB
9.	24	LAC 8	KEENAN ALLEN
10.	25	CIN 10	TEE HIGGINS
11.	26	TB 11	MIKE EVANS
12.	32	CAR 13	DJ MOORE
13.	33	MIA 11	JAYLEN WADDLE
14.	34	IND 14	MICHAEL PITTMAN JR.
15.	40	PHI 7	A.J. BROWN
16.	41	SEA 11	DK METCALF
17.	42	WAS 14	TERRY MCLAURIN
18.	47	PIT 9	DIONTAE JOHNSON
19.	48	HOU 6	BRANDIN COOKS
20.	49	LAC 8	MIKE WILLIAMS
21.	50	CHI 14	DARNELL MOONEY
22.	52	CLE 9	AMARI COOPER
23.	55	ARI 13	MARQUISE BROWN
24.	56	TB 11	CHRIS GODWIN
25.	57	DEN 9	COURTLAND SUTTON
26.	59	DEN 9	JERRY JEUDY
27.	60	NYJ 10	ELIJAH MOORE
28.	61	DET 6	AMON-RA ST. BROWN
29.	68	NO 14	MICHAEL THOMAS
30.	69	SEA 11	TYLER LOCKETT
31.	70	LV 6	HUNTER RENFROW
32.	72	ATL 14	DRAKE LONDON
33.	76	LAR 7	ALLEN ROBINSON II
34.	77	KC 8	JUJU SMITH-SCHUSTER
35.	78	BAL 10	RASHOD BATEMAN
36.	79	BUF 7	GABRIEL DAVIS
37.	86	PHI 7	DEVONTA SMITH
38.	87	MIN 7	ADAM THIELEN
39.	90	ARI 13	DEANDRE HOPKINS
40.	91	TEN 6	TREYLON BURKS
41.	97	SF 9	BRANDON AIYUK
42	98	JAC 11	CHRISTIAN KIRK
43.	99	GB 14	ALLEN LAZARD
44.		TEN 6	ROBERT WOODS
45.		PIT 9	CHASE CLAYPOOL
46.		NYJ 10	GARRETT WILSON
47.		DAL 9	MICHAEL GALLUP
48.		NO 14	CHRIS OLAVE
49.		NYG 9	KADARIUS TONEY
50.		KC 8	M. VALDES-SCANTLING
51.		KC 8	SKYY MOORE
52.		NE 10	DEVANTE PARKER
53.		NYG 9	KENNY GOLLADAY
54.		DET 6	DJ CHARK JR.
55.		CIN 10	TYLER BOYD
56.		TB 11	RUSSELL GAGE
57.		NE 10	JAKOBI MEYERS
58.		NO 14	JARVIS LANDRY
59.		ARI 13	RONDALE MOORE
60.		DET 6	JAMESON WILLIAMS
61.		TB 11	JULIO JONES
62.		NYJ 10	COREY DAVIS
63.		GB 14	CHRISTIAN WATSON
64.		LAR 7	VAN JEFFERSON
65.		KC 8	MECOLE HARDMAN
66.		WAS 14	JAHAN DOTSON
67.		CAR 13	ROBBIE ANDERSON
68.		BUF 7	JAMISON CROWDER
69.		JAC 11	MARVIN JONES JR.
70.		NYG 9	STERLING SHEPARD
71.		NE 6	KENDRICK BOURNE
72.		PIT 9	GEORGE PICKENS

SCORING SYSTEM

PASSING

TD PASS	4 PTS
EVERY 25 PASSING YARDS	1 PT
2-PT PASSING CONVERSION	2 PTS
INTERCEPTIONS THROWN	-2 PTS

RUSHING

TD RUSH	6 PTS
EVERY 10 RUSHING YARDS	1 PT
2-PT RUSHING CONVERSION	2 PTS

RECEIVING

TD RECEPTION	6 PTS
EVERY 10 RECEIVING YARDS	1 PT
2-PT RECEIVING CONVERSION	2 PTS
RECEPTION	1 PT

KICKING

FG MADE (60+ YARDS)	6 PTS
FG MADE (50-59 YARDS)	5 PTS
FG MADE (40-49 YARDS)	4 PTS
FG MADE (0-39 YARDS)	3 PTS
PAT	1 PT
MISSED FG (ANY DISTANCE)	-1 PT

DEFENSE/SPECIAL TEAMS

TD (DEFENSE OR SPECIAL TEAMS)	6 PTS
INTERCEPTION	2 PTS
FUMBLE RECOVERY	2 PTS
BLOCKED PUNT, PAT, OR FG	2 PTS
SAFETY	2 PTS
SACK	1 PT
0 POINTS ALLOWED	5 PTS
1-6 POINTS ALLOWED	4 PTS
7-13 POINTS ALLOWED	3 PTS
14-20 POINTS ALLOWED	1 PT
21-27 POINTS ALLOWED	0 PTS
28-34 POINTS ALLOWED	-1 PT
35-45 POINTS ALLOWED	-3 PTS
46+ POINTS ALLOWED	-5 PTS

KICKERS

		BYE	
1.	BAL	10	JUSTIN TUCKER
2.	KC	8	HARRISON BUTKER
3.	BUF	7	TYLER BASS
4.	CIN	10	EVAN MCPHERSON
5.	LV	6	DANIEL CARLSON
6.	DEN	9	BRANDON MCMANUS
7.	LAR	7	MATT GAY
8.	NE	10	NICK FOLK
9	TB	11	RYAN SUCCOP
10.	DAL	9	JONATHAN GARIBAY
11.	MIN	7	GREG JOSEPH
12.	PHI	7	JAKE ELLIOT
13.	ATL	14	YOUNGHOE KOO
14.	ARI	13	MATT PRATER
15.	PIT	9	CHRIS BOSWELL

DEFENSE/SPECIAL TEAMS

		BYE	
1.	TB	11	BUCCANEERS (@DAL WK. 1)
2.	BUF	7	BILLS (@LAR WK. 1)
3.	NO	14	SAINTS (@ATL WK. 1)
4.	GB	14	PACKERS (@MIN WK. 1)
5.	IND	14	COLTS (@HOU WK. 1)
6.	SF	9	49ERS (@CHI WK. 1)
7.	PIT	9	STEELERS (@CIN WK. 1)
8.	MIA	11	DOLPHINS (NE WK. 1)
9	DAL	9	COWBOYS (TB WK. 1)
10.	LAR	7	RAMS (BUF WK. 1)
11.	CIN	10	BENGALS (PIT WK. 1)
12.	BAL	10	RAVENS (@NYJ WK. 1)
13.	NE	10	PATRIOTS (@MIA WK. 1)
14.	DEN	9	BRONCOS (@SEA WK. 1)
15.	CLE	9	BROWNS (@CAR WK. 1)

1/2 POINT PER RECEPTION

QUARTERBACKS

	OVERALL	BYE	
1.	33	BUF 7	JOSH ALLEN
2.	46	KC 8	PATRICK MAHOMES
3.	54	LAC 8	JUSTIN HERBERT
4.	59	BAL 10	LAMAR JACKSON
5.	61	PHI 7	JALEN HURTS
6.	72	TB 11	TOM BRADY
7.	78	ARI 13	KYLER MURRAY
8.	87	DAL 9	DAK PRESCOTT
9.	91	GB 14	AARON RODGERS
10.	99	DEN 9	RUSSELL WILSON
11.		SF 9	TREY LANCE
12.		CIN 10	JOE BURROW
13.		LAR 7	MATTHEW STAFFORD
14.		MIA 11	TUA TAGOVAILOA
15.		CLE 9	DESHAUN WATSON
16.		LV 6	DEREK CARR
17.		MIN 7	KIRK COUSINS
18.		CHI 14	JUSTIN FIELDS
19.		NO 14	JAMEIS WINSTON
20.		JAC 11	TREVOR LAWRENCE
21.		TEN 6	RYAN TANNEHILL
22.		NYG 9	DANIEL JONES
23.		IND 14	MATT RYAN
24.		NE 10	MAC JONES
25.		NYJ 10	ZACH WILSON
26.		HOU 6	DAVIS MILLS
27.		ATL 14	MARCUS MARIOTA
28.		DET 6	JARED GOFF
29.		CAR 13	BAKER MAYFIELD
30.		WAS 14	CARSON WENTZ
31.		PIT 9	KENNY PICKETT
32.		(SF) 9	JIMMY GARROPPOLO
33.		(CLE) 11	DREW LOCK

TIGHT ENDS

	OVERALL	BYE	
1.	18	KC 8	TRAVIS KELCE
2.	25	BAL 10	MARK ANDREWS
3.	47	SF 9	GEORGE KITTLE
4.	48	ATL 14	KYLE PITTS
5.	62	LV 6	DARREN WALLER
6.	68	DET 6	T.J. HOCKENSON
7.	75	DAL 9	DALTON SCHULTZ
8.	82	PHI 7	DALLAS GOEDERT
9.	90	ARI 13	ZACH ERTZ
10.	100	PIT 9	PAT FREIERMUTH
11.		BUF 7	DAWSON KNOX
12.		MIA 11	MIKE GESICKI
13.		MIN 7	IRV SMITH JR.
14.		CHI 14	COLE KMET
15.		CLE 9	DAVID NJOKU
16.		NE 10	HUNTER HENRY
17.		WAS 14	LOGAN THOMAS
18.		SEA 11	NOAH FANT SEA
19.		TB 11	ROB GRONKOWSKI
20.		LAC 8	GERALD EVERETT
21.		LAR 7	TYLER HIGBEE
22.		TB 11	CAMERON BRATE
23.		TEN 6	AUSTIN HOOPER

RUNNING BACKS

	OVERALL	BYE	
1.	1	IND 14	JONATHAN TAYLOR
2.	2	LAC 8	AUSTIN EKELER
3.	3	CAR 13	CHRISTIAN MCCAFFREY
4.	4	TEN 6	DERRICK HENRY
5.	5	MIN 7	DALVIN COOK
6.	7	TB 11	LEONARD FOURNETTE
7.	8	NO 14	ALVIN KAMARA
8.	9	CIN 10	JOE MIXON
9.	10	PIT 9	NAJEE HARRIS
10.	14	DET 6	D'ANDRE SWIFT
11.	15	ARI 13	JAMES CONNER
12.	19	GB 14	AARON JONES
13.	20	CHI 14	DAVID MONTGOMERY
14.	21	CLE 9	NICK CHUBB
15.	30	NYG 9	SAQUON BARKLEY
16.	31	LAR 7	CAM AKERS
17.	32	DEN 9	JAVONTE WILLIAMS
18.	36	WAS 14	ANTONIO GIBSON
19.	37	LV 6	JOSH JACOBS
20.	38	DAL 9	EZEKIEL ELLIOTT
21.	43	BAL 10	J.K. DOBBINS
22.	44	NYJ 10	BREECE HALL
23.	45	JAC 11	TRAVIS ETIENNE JR.
24.	49	SF 9	ELIJAH MITCHELL
25.	56	PHI 7	MILES SANDERS
26.	57	NE 10	DAMIEN HARRIS
27.	66	BUF 7	DEVIN SINGLETARY
28.	67	KC 8	CLYDE EDWARDS-HELAIRE
29.	69	CLE 9	KAREEM HUNT
30.	71	ATL 14	CORDARRELLE PATTERSON
31.	76	DAL 9	TONY POLLARD
32.	77	DEN 9	MELVIN GORDON III
33.	79	GB 14	AJ DILLON
34.	83	MIA 11	CHASE EDMONDS
35.	84	NE 10	RHAMONDRE STEVENSON
36.	89	JAC 11	JAMES ROBINSON
37.	93	NYJ 10	MICHAEL CARTER
38.	94	WAS 14	J.D. MCKISSIC
39.	98	BUF 7	JAMES COOK
40.		SEA 11	RASHAAD PENNY
41.		SEA 11	KEN WALKER III
42.		MIA 11	RAHEEM MOSTERT
43.		KC 8	RONALD JONES II
44.		MIN 7	ALEXANDER MATTISON
45.		HOU 6	DAMEON PIERCE
46.		IND 14	NYHEIM HINES
47.		BAL 10	GUS EDWARDS
48.		DET 6	JAMAAL WILLIAMS
49.		ATL 14	TYLER ALLGEIER
50.		LAR 7	DARRELL HENDERSON JR.
51.		PHI 7	KENNETH GAINWELL
52.		LAC 8	ISAIAH SPILLER
53.		NE 10	JAMES WHITE
54.		HOU 6	MARLON MACK
55.		TB 11	RACHAAD WHITE
56.		MIA 11	SONY MICHEL
57.		ARI 13	DARREL WILLIAMS
58.		CHI 14	KHALIL HERBERT
59.		CAR 13	D'ONTA FOREMAN
60.		NO 14	MARK INGRAM II
61.		LV 6	KENYAN DRAKE
62.		CAR 13	CHUBA HUBBARD
63.		MIA 11	MYLES GASKIN
64.		PHI 7	BOSTON SCOTT
65.		WAS 14	BRIAN ROBINSON JR.
66.		SF 9	TYRION DAVIS-PRICE
67.		SF 9	TREY SERMON
68.		ATL 14	DAMIEN WILLIAMS
69.		CIN 10	SAMAJE PERINE
70.		LV 6	ZAMIR WHITE
71.		CLE 9	D'ERNEST JOHNSON
72.		BUF 7	ZACK MOSS

WIDE RECEIVERS

	OVERALL	BYE	
1.	6	LAR 7	COOPER KUPP
2.	11	MIN 7	JUSTIN JEFFERSON
3.	12	SF 9	DEEBO SAMUEL
4.	13	CIN 10	JA'MARR CHASE
5.	16	BUF 7	STEFON DIGGS
6.	17	LV 6	DAVANTE ADAMS
7.	22	MIA 11	TYREEK HILL
8.	23	DAL 9	CEEDEE LAMB
9.	24	TB 11	MIKE EVANS
10.	26	CIN 10	TEE HIGGINS
11.	27	CAR 13	DJ MOORE
12.	28	PHI 7	A.J. BROWN
13.	29	LAC 8	KEENAN ALLEN
14.	34	IND 14	MICHAEL PITTMAN JR.
15.	35	MIA 11	JAYLEN WADDLE
16.	39	SEA 11	DK METCALF
17.	40	LAC 8	MIKE WILLIAMS
18.	41	WAS 14	TERRY MCLAURIN
19.	42	PIT 9	DIONTAE JOHNSON
20.	50	HOU 6	BRANDIN COOKS
21.	51	CHI 14	DARNELL MOONEY
22.	52	TB 11	CHRIS GODWIN
23.	53	DEN 9	COURTLAND SUTTON
24.	55	CLE 9	AMARI COOPER
25.	58	ARI 13	MARQUISE BROWN
26.	60	DEN 9	JERRY JEUDY
27.	63	NYJ 10	ELIJAH MOORE
28.	64	BUF 7	GABRIEL DAVIS
29.	65	ATL 14	DRAKE LONDON
30.	70	DET 6	AMON-RA ST. BROWN
31.	73	NO 14	MICHAEL THOMAS
32.	74	LAR 7	ALLEN ROBINSON II
33.	80	SEA 11	TYLER LOCKETT
34.	81	PHI 7	DEVONTA SMITH
35.	85	LV 6	HUNTER RENFROW
36.	86	KC 8	JUJU SMITH-SCHUSTER
37.	88	BAL 10	RASHOD BATEMAN
38.	92	ARI 13	DEANDRE HOPKINS
39.	95	TEN 6	TREYLON BURKS
40.	96	MIN 7	ADAM THIELEN
41.	97	GB 14	ALLEN LAZARD
42.		SF 9	BRANDON AIYUK
43.		JAC 11	CHRISTIAN KIRK
44.		PIT 9	CHASE CLAYPOOL
45.		DAL 9	MICHAEL GALLUP
46.		TEN 6	ROBERT WOODS
47.		NYJ 10	GARRETT WILSON
48.		DET 6	JAMESON WILLIAMS
49.		KC 8	M. VALDES-SCANTLING
50.		NO 14	CHRIS OLAVE
51.		KC 8	SKYY MOORE
52.		DET 6	DJ CHARK JR.
53.		NYG 9	KADARIUS TONEY
54.		NYG 9	KENNY GOLLADAY
55.		NE 10	DEVANTE PARKER
56.		TB 11	RUSSELL GAGE
57.		TB 11	JULIO JONES
58.		CIN 10	TYLER BOYD
59.		GB 14	CHRISTIAN WATSON
60.		NO 14	JARVIS LANDRY
61.		NYJ 10	COREY DAVIS
62.		NE 10	JAKOBI MEYERS
63.		KC 8	MECOLE HARDMAN
64.		LAR 7	VAN JEFFERSON
65.		ARI 13	RONDALE MOORE
66.		WAS 14	JAHAN DOTSON
67.		CAR 13	ROBBIE ANDERSON
68.		NE 10	KENDRICK BOURNE
69.		IND 14	ALEC PIERCE
70.		BUF 7	JAMISON CROWDER
71.		JAC 11	MARVIN JONES JR.
72.		MIN 7	K.J. OSBORN

SCORING SYSTEM

PASSING

TD PASS	4 PTS
EVERY 25 PASSING YARDS	1 PT
2-PT PASSING CONVERSION	2 PTS
INTERCEPTIONS THROWN	-2 PTS

RUSHING

TD RUSH	6 PTS
EVERY 10 RUSHING YARDS	1 PT
2-PT RUSHING CONVERSION	2 PTS

RECEIVING

TD RECEPTION	6 PTS
EVERY 10 RECEIVING YARDS	1 PT
2-PT RECEIVING CONVERSION	2 PTS
RECEPTION	0.5 PTS

KICKING

FG MADE (60+ YARDS)	6 PTS
FG MADE (50-59 YARDS)	5 PTS
FG MADE (40-49 YARDS)	4 PTS
FG MADE (0-39 YARDS)	3 PTS
PAT	1 PT
MISSED FG (ANY DISTANCE)	-1 PT

DEFENSE/SPECIAL TEAMS

TD (DEFENSE OR SPECIAL TEAMS)	6 PTS
INTERCEPTION	2 PTS
FUMBLE RECOVERY	2 PTS
BLOCKED PUNT, PAT, OR FG	2 PTS
SAFETY	2 PTS
SACK	1 PT
0 POINTS ALLOWED	5 PTS
1-6 POINTS ALLOWED	4 PTS
7-13 POINTS ALLOWED	3 PTS
14-20 POINTS ALLOWED	1 PT
21-27 POINTS ALLOWED	0 PTS
28-34 POINTS ALLOWED	-1 PT
35-45 POINTS ALLOWED	-3 PTS
46+ POINTS ALLOWED	-5 PTS

KICKERS

		BYE	
1.	BAL	10	JUSTIN TUCKER
2.	KC	8	HARRISON BUTKER
3.	BUF	7	TYLER BASS
4.	CIN	10	EVAN MCPHERSON
5.	LV	6	DANIEL CARLSON
6.	DEN	9	BRANDON MCMANUS
7.	LAR	7	MATT GAY
8.	NE	10	NICK FOLK
9.	TB	11	RYAN SUCCOP
10.	DAL	9	JONATHAN GARIBAY
11.	MIN	7	GREG JOSEPH
12.	PHI	7	JAKE ELLIOT
13.	ATL	14	YOUNGHOE KOO
14.	ARI	13	MATT PRATER
15.	PIT	9	CHRIS BOSWELL

DEFENSE/SPECIAL TEAMS

		BYE	
1.	TB	11	BUCCANEERS (@DAL WK. 1)
2.	BUF	7	BILLS (@LAR WK. 1)
3.	NO	14	SAINTS (@ATL WK. 1)
4.	GB	14	PACKERS (@MIN WK. 1)
5.	IND	14	COLTS (@HOU WK. 1)
6.	SF	9	49ERS (@CHI WK. 1)
7.	PIT	9	STEELERS (@CIN WK. 1)
8.	MIA	11	DOLPHINS (NE WK. 1)
9.	DAL	9	COWBOYS (TB WK. 1)
10.	LAR	7	RAMS (BUF WK. 1)
11.	CIN	10	BENGALS (PIT WK. 1)
12.	BAL	10	RAVENS (@NYJ WK. 1)
13.	NE	10	PATRIOTS (@MIA WK. 1)
14.	DEN	9	BRONCOS (@SEA WK. 1)
15.	CLE	9	BROWNS (@CAR WK. 1)

SUPER FLEX

QUARTERBACKS

	OVERALL	BYE		
1.	3	BUF	7	JOSH ALLEN
2.	5	KC	8	PATRICK MAHOMES
3.	8	LAC	8	JUSTIN HERBERT
4.	10	BAL	10	LAMAR JACKSON
5.	18	PHI	7	JALEN HURTS
6.	21	TB	11	TOM BRADY
7.	25	ARI	13	KYLER MURRAY
8.	34	DAL	9	DAK PRESCOTT
9.	37	GB	14	AARON RODGERS
10.	38	DEN	9	RUSSELL WILSON
11.	39	SF	9	TREY LANCE
12.	44	CIN	10	JOE BURROW
13.	50	LAR	7	MATTHEW STAFFORD
14.	52	MIA	11	TUA TAGOVAILOA
15.	55	CLE	9	DESHAUN WATSON
16.	66	LV	6	DEREK CARR
17.	67	MIN	7	KIRK COUSINS
18.	72	CHI	14	JUSTIN FIELDS
19.	80	NO	14	JAMEIS WINSTON
20.	81	JAC	11	TREVOR LAWRENCE
21.	86	TEN	6	RYAN TANNEHILL
22.	89	NYG	9	DANIEL JONES
23.	94	IND	14	MATT RYAN
24.	95	NE	10	MAC JONES
25.	99	NYJ	10	ZACH WILSON
26.		HOU	6	DAVIS MILLS
27.		ATL	14	MARCUS MARIOTA
28.		DET	6	JARED GOFF
29.		CAR	13	BAKER MAYFIELD
30.		WAS	14	CARSON WENTZ
31.		PIT	9	KENNY PICKETT
32.		(SF)	9	JIMMY GAROPPOLO
33.		(CLE)	11	DREW LOCK

TIGHT ENDS

	OVERALL	BYE		
1.	16	KC	8	TRAVIS KELCE
2.	22	BAL	10	MARK ANDREWS
3.	41	ATL	14	KYLE PITTS
4.	58	SF	9	GEORGE KITTLE
5.	65	LV	6	DARREN WALLER
6.	85	DET	6	T.J. HOCKENSON
7.	88	DAL	9	DALTON SCHULTZ
8.	36	PHI	7	DALLAS GOEDERT
9.		ARI	13	ZACH ERTZ
10.		PIT	9	PAT FREIERMUTH
11.		MIA	11	MIKE GESICKI
12.		BUF	7	DAWSON KNOX
13.		MIN	7	IRV SMITH JR.
14.		CHI	14	COLE KMET
15.		SEA	11	NOAH FANT
16.		NE	10	HUNTER HENRY
17.		WAS	14	LOGAN THOMAS
18.		CLE	9	DAVID NJOKU
19.		LAR	7	TYLER HIGBEE
20.		TB	11	ROB GRONKOWSKI
21.		TB	11	CAMERON BRATE
22.		LAC	8	GERALD EVERETT
23.		TEN	6	AUSTIN HOOPER

RUNNING BACKS

	OVERALL	BYE		
1.	1	IND	14	JONATHAN TAYLOR
2.	2	CAR	13	CHRISTIAN MCCAFFREY
3.	4	LAC	8	AUSTIN EKELER
4.	6	TEN	6	DERRICK HENRY
5.	7	PIT	9	NAJEE HARRIS
6.	9	NO	14	ALVIN KAMARA
7.	12	TB	11	LEONARD FOURNETTE
8.	13	MIN	7	DALVIN COOK
9.	14	DET	6	D'ANDRE SWIFT
10.	17	CIN	10	JOE MIXON
11.	23	GB	14	AARON JONES
12.	28	ARI	13	JAMES CONNER
13.	29	CHI	14	DAVID MONTGOMERY
14.	33	NYG	9	SAQUON BARKLEY
15.	35	DEN	9	JAVONTE WILLIAMS
16.	36	CLE	9	NICK CHUBB
17.	40	LAR	7	CAM AKERS
18.	46	DAL	9	EZEKIEL ELLIOTT
19.	47	WAS	14	ANTONIO GIBSON
20.	48	LV	6	JOSH JACOBS
21.	49	JAC	11	TRAVIS ETIENNE JR.
22.	56	BAL	10	J.K. DOBBINS
23.	57	NYJ	10	BREECE HALL
24.	63	SF	9	ELIJAH MITCHELL
25.	75	PHI	7	MILES SANDERS
26.	76	KC	8	CLYDE EDWARDS-HELAIRE
27.	77	BUF	7	DEVIN SINGLETARY
28.	78	CLE	9	KAREEM HUNT
29.	79	NE	10	DAMIEN HARRIS
30.	97	DAL	9	TONY POLLARD
31.	98	MIA	11	CHASE EDMONDS
32.	100	DEN	9	MELVIN GORDON III
33.		GB	14	AJ DILLON
34.		ATL	14	CORDARRELLE PATTERSON
35.		SEA	11	KEN WALKER III
36.		SEA	11	RASHAAD PENNY
37.		NYJ	10	MICHAEL CARTER
38.		NE	10	RHAMONDRE STEVENSON
39.		BUF	7	JAMES COOK
40.		JAC	11	JAMES ROBINSON
41.		MIN	7	ALEXANDER MATTISON
42.		KC	8	RONALD JONES II
43.		WAS	14	J.D. MCKISSIC
44.		IND	14	NYHEIM HINES
45.		DET	6	JAMAAL WILLIAMS
46.		MIA	11	RAHEEM MOSTERT
47.		HOU	6	DAMEON PIERCE
48.		ATL	14	TYLER ALLGEIER
49.		BAL	10	GUS EDWARDS
50.		NE	10	JAMES WHITE
51.		PHI	7	KENNETH GAINWELL
52.		LAR	7	DARRELL HENDERSON JR.
53.		HOU	6	MARLON MACK
54.		LAC	8	ISAIAH SPILLER
55.		TB	11	RACHAAD WHITE
56.		MIA	11	SONY MICHEL
57.		CHI	14	KHALIL HERBERT
58.		ARI	13	DARREL WILLIAMS
59.		CAR	13	D'ONTA FOREMAN
60.		NO	14	MARK INGRAM II
61.		SF	9	JERRICK MCKINNON
62.		CAR	13	CHUBA HUBBARD
63.		LV	6	KENYAN DRAKE
64.		MIA	11	MYLES GASKIN
65.		SF	9	TREY SERMON
66.		SF	9	TYRION DAVIS-PRICE
67.		PHI	7	BOSTON SCOTT
68.		WAS	14	BRIAN ROBINSON JR.
69.		CIN	10	SAMAJE PERINE
70.		ATL	14	DAMIEN WILLIAMS
71.		BUF	7	ZACK MOSS
72.		LV	6	ZAMIR WHITE

WIDE RECEIVERS

	OVERALL	BYE		
1.	8	LAR	7	COOPER KUPP
2.	11	MIN	7	JUSTIN JEFFERSON
3.	15	CIN	10	JA'MARR CHASE
4.	19	BUF	7	STEFON DIGGS
5.	20	LV	6	DAVANTE ADAMS
6.	24	SF	9	DEEBO SAMUEL
7.	26	MIA	11	TYREEK HILL
8.	27	DAL	9	CEEDEE LAMB
9.	30	LAC	8	KEENAN ALLEN
10.	31	CIN	10	TEE HIGGINS
11.	32	TB	11	MIKE EVANS
12.	42	CAR	13	DJ MOORE
13.	43	MIA	11	JAYLEN WADDLE
14.	45	IND	14	MICHAEL PITTMAN JR.
15.	51	PHI	7	A.J. BROWN
16.	53	SEA	11	DK METCALF
17.	54	WAS	14	TERRY MCLAURIN
18.	59	PIT	9	DIONTAE JOHNSON
19.	60	HOU	6	BRANDIN COOKS
20.	61	LAC	8	MIKE WILLIAMS
21.	62	CHI	14	DARNELL MOONEY
22.	64	CLE	9	AMARI COOPER
23.	68	ARI	13	MARQUISE BROWN
24.	69	TB	11	CHRIS GODWIN
25.	70	DEN	9	COURTLAND SUTTON
26.	71	DEN	9	JERRY JEUDY
27.	73	NYJ	10	ELIJAH MOORE
28.	74	DET	6	AMON-RA ST. BROWN
29.	82	NO	14	MICHAEL THOMAS
30.	83	SEA	11	TYLER LOCKETT
31.	84	LV	6	HUNTER RENFROW
32.	87	ATL	14	DRAKE LONDON
33.	90	LAR	7	ALLEN ROBINSON II
34.	91	KC	8	JUJU SMITH-SCHUSTER
35.	92	BAL	10	RASHOD BATEMAN
36.	93	BUF	7	GABRIEL DAVIS
37.		PHI	7	DEVONTA SMITH
38.		MIN	7	ADAM THIELEN
39.		ARI	13	DEANDRE HOPKINS
40.		TEN	6	TREYLON BURKS
41.		SF	9	BRANDON AIYUK
42.		JAC	11	CHRISTIAN KIRK
43.		GB	14	ALLEN LAZARD
44.		TEN	6	ROBERT WOODS
45.		PIT	9	CHASE CLAYPOOL
46.		NYJ	10	GARRETT WILSON
47.		DAL	9	MICHAEL GALLUP
48.		NO	14	CHRIS OLAVE
49.		NYG	9	KADARIUS TONEY
50.		KC	8	M. VALDES-SCANTLING
51.		KC	8	SKYY MOORE
52.		NE	10	DEVANTE PARKER
53.		NYG	9	KENNY GOLLADAY
54.		DET	6	DJ CHARK JR.
55.		CIN	10	TYLER BOYD
56.		TB	11	RUSSELL GAGE
57.		NE	10	JAKOBI MEYERS
58.		NO	14	JARVIS LANDRY
59.		ARI	13	RONDALE MOORE
60.		DET	6	JAMESON WILLIAMS
61.		TB	11	JULIO JONES
62.		NYJ	10	COREY DAVIS
63.		GB	14	CHRISTIAN WATSON
64.		LAR	7	VAN JEFFERSON
65.		KC	8	MECOLE HARDMAN
66.		WAS	14	JAHAN DOTSON
67.		CAR	13	ROBBIE ANDERSON
68.		BUF	7	JAMISON CROWDER
69.		JAC	11	MARVIN JONES JR.
70.		NYG	9	STERLING SHEPARD
71.		NE	6	KENDRICK BOURNE
72.		PIT	9	GEORGE PICKENS

SCORING SYSTEM

PASSING

TD PASS	4 PTS
EVERY 25 PASSING YARDS	1 PT
2-PT PASSING CONVERSION	2 PTS
INTERCEPTIONS THROWN	-2 PTS

RUSHING

TD RUSH	6 PTS
EVERY 10 RUSHING YARDS	1 PT
2-PT RUSHING CONVERSION	2 PTS

RECEIVING

TD RECEPTION	6 PTS
EVERY 10 RECEIVING YARDS	1 PT
2-PT RECEIVING CONVERSION	2 PTS
RECEPTION	1 PT

KICKING

FG MADE (60+ YARDS)	6 PTS
FG MADE (50-59 YARDS)	5 PTS
FG MADE (40-49 YARDS)	4 PTS
FG MADE (0-39 YARDS)	3 PTS
PAT	1 PT
MISSED FG (ANY DISTANCE)	-1 PT

DEFENSE/SPECIAL TEAMS

TD (DEFENSE OR SPECIAL TEAMS)	6 PTS
INTERCEPTION	2 PTS
FUMBLE RECOVERED	2 PTS
BLOCKED PUNT, PAT, OR FG	2 PTS
SAFETY	2 PTS
SACK	1 PT
0 POINTS ALLOWED	5 PTS
1-6 POINTS ALLOWED	4 PTS
7-13 POINTS ALLOWED	3 PTS
14-20 POINTS ALLOWED	1 PT
21-27 POINTS ALLOWED	0 PTS
28-34 POINTS ALLOWED	-1 PT
35-45 POINTS ALLOWED	-3 PTS
46+ POINTS ALLOWED	-5 PTS

KICKERS

		BYE	
1.	BAL	10	JUSTIN TUCKER
2.	KC	8	HARRISON BUTKER
3.	BUF	7	TYLER BASS
4.	CIN	10	EVAN MCPHERSON
5.	LV	6	DANIEL CARLSON
6.	DEN	9	BRANDON MCMANUS
7.	LAR	7	MATT GAY
8.	NE	10	NICK FOLK
9.	TB	11	RYAN SUCCOP
10.	DAL	9	JONATHAN GARIBAY
11.	MIN	7	GREG JOSEPH
12.	PHI	7	JAKE ELLIOT
13.	ATL	14	YOUNGHOE KOO
14.	ARI	13	MATT PRATER
15.	PIT	9	CHRIS BOSWELL

DEFENSE/SPECIAL TEAMS

		BYE	
1.	TB	11	BUCCANEERS (@DAL WK. 1)
2.	BUF	7	BILLS (@LAR WK. 1)
3.	NO	14	SAINTS (@ATL WK. 1)
4.	GB	14	PACKERS (@MIN WK. 1)
5.	IND	14	COLTS (@HOU WK. 1)
6.	SF	9	49ERS (@CHI WK. 1)
7.	PIT	9	STEELERS (@CIN WK. 1)
8.	MIA	11	DOLPHINS (NE WK. 1)
9.	DAL	9	COWBOYS (TB WK. 1)
10.	LAR	7	RAMS (BUF WK. 1)
11.	CIN	10	BENGALS (PIT WK. 1)
12.	BAL	10	RAVENS (@NYJ WK. 1)
13.	NE	10	PATRIOTS (@MIA WK. 1)
14.	DEN	9	BRONCOS (@SEA WK. 1)
15.	CLE	9	BROWNS (@CAR WK. 1)

FANTASY TAKEOVER

STANDARD

RUNNING BACKS

	OVERALL		BYE	
1.	1	IND	14	JONATHAN TAYLOR
2.	2	TEN	6	DERRICK HENRY
3.	3	LAC	8	AUSTIN EKELER
4.	4	CAR	13	CHRISTIAN MCCAFFREY
5.	5	MIN	7	DALVIN COOK
6.	6	CIN	10	JOE MIXON
7.	7	NO	14	ALVIN KAMARA
8.	8	TB	11	LEONARD FOURNETTE
9.	9	PIT	9	NAJEE HARRIS
10.	14	ARI	13	JAMES CONNER
11.	16	DET	9	D'ANDRE SWIFT
12.	19	CLE	9	NICK CHUBB
13.	21	CHI	14	DAVID MONTGOMERY
14.	24	GB	14	AARON JONES
15.	25	LAR	7	CAM AKERS
16.	28	WAS	14	ANTONIO GIBSON
17.	29	LV	6	JOSH JACOBS LV
18.	31	DEN	9	JAVONTE WILLIAMS
19.	32	NYG	9	SAQUON BARKLEY
20.	33	DAL	9	EZEKIEL ELLIOTT
21.	40	BAL	10	J.K. DOBBINS
22.	41	SF	9	ELIJAH MITCHELL
23.	43	NYJ	10	BREECE HALL
24.	48	NE	10	DAMIEN HARRIS
25.	50	JAC	11	TRAVIS ETIENNE JR.
26.	53	PHI	7	MILES SANDERS
27.	54	BUF	7	DEVIN SINGLETARY
28.	55	KC	8	CLYDE EDWARDS-HELAIRE
29.	56	DEN	9	MELVIN GORDON III
30.	64	CLE	9	KAREEM HUNT
31.	65	GB	14	AJ DILLON
32.	70	ATL	14	CORDARRELLE PATTERSON
33.	75	DAL	9	TONY POLLARD
34.	76	JAC	11	JAMES ROBINSON
35.	78	NE	10	RHAMONDRE STEVENSON
36.	82	NYJ	10	MICHAEL CARTER
37.	83	SEA	11	RASHAAD PENNY
38.	84	MIA	11	CHASE EDMONDS
39.	92	MIA	11	RAHEEM MOSTERT
40.	93	SEA	11	KEN WALKER III
41.	100	BUF	7	JAMES COOK
42		KC	8	RONALD JONES II
43.		WAS	14	J.D. MCKISSIC
44.		BAL	10	GUS EDWARDS
45.		HOU	6	DAMEON PIERCE
46.		DET	6	JAMAAL WILLIAMS
47.		LAR	7	DARRELL HENDERSON JR.
48.		ATL	14	TYLER ALLGEIER
49.		LAC	8	ISAIAH SPILLER
50.		PHI	7	KENNETH GAINWELL
51.		IND	14	NYHEIM HINES
52.		MIN	7	ALEXANDER MATTISON
53.		HOU	6	MARLON MACK
54.		NE	10	JAMES WHITE
55.		TB	11	RACHAAD WHITE
56.		MIA	11	SONY MICHEL
57.		CHI	14	KHALIL HERBERT
58.		CAR	13	D'ONTA FOREMAN
59.		ARI	13	DARREL WILLIAMS
60.		NO	14	MARK INGRAM II
61.		PHI	7	BOSTON SCOTT
62.		SF	9	TREY SERMON
63.		WAS	14	BRIAN ROBINSON JR.
64.		CAR	13	CHUBA HUBBARD
65.		MIA	11	MYLES GASKIN
66.		SF	9	TYRION DAVIS-PRICE
67.		LV	6	KENYAN DRAKE
68.		LV	6	ZAMIR WHITE
69.		CIN	10	SAMAJE PERINE
70.		CLE	9	D'ERNEST JOHNSON
71.		ATL	14	DAMIEN WILLIAMS
72.		BUF	7	ZACK MOSS

WIDE RECEIVERS

	OVERALL		BYE	
1.	10	LAR	7	COOPER KUPP
2.	11	SF	9	DEEBO SAMUEL
3.	12	MIN	7	JUSTIN JEFFERSON
4.	13	CIN	10	JA'MARR CHASE
5.	17	BUF	7	STEFON DIGGS
6.	18	LV	6	DAVANTE ADAMS
7.	22	TB	11	MIKE EVANS
8.	23	DAL	9	CEEDEE LAMB
9.	26	MIA	11	TYREEK HILL
10.	27	PHI	7	A.J. BROWN
11.	34	CIN	10	TEE HIGGINS
12.	36	CAR	13	DJ MOORE
13.	37	LAC	8	MIKE WILLIAMS
14.	38	SEA	11	DK METCALF
15.	39	IND	14	MICHAEL PITTMAN JR.
16.	44	MIA	11	JAYLEN WADDLE
17.	45	LAC	8	KEENAN ALLEN
18.	46	WAS	14	TERRY MCLAURIN
19.	47	DEN	9	COURTLAND SUTTON
20.	51	CHI	14	DARNELL MOONEY
21.	58	TB	11	CHRIS GODWIN
22.	59	BUF	7	GABRIEL DAVIS
23.	60	NYJ	10	ELIJAH MOORE
24.	61	PIT	9	DIONTAE JOHNSON
25.	62	DEN	9	JERRY JEUDY
26.	63	CLE	9	AMARI COOPER
27.	66	HOU	6	BRANDIN COOKS
28.	67	ARI	13	MARQUISE BROWN
29.	69	PHI	7	DEVONTA SMITH
30.	73	ATL	14	DRAKE LONDON
31.	74	LAR	7	ALLEN ROBINSON II
32.	79	TEN	6	TREYLON BURKS
33.	80	SEA	11	TYLER LOCKETT
34.	81	NO	14	MICHAEL THOMAS
35.	88	DET	6	AMON-RA ST. BROWN
36.	89	BAL	10	RASHOD BATEMAN
37.	97	GB	14	ALLEN LAZARD
38.	94	KC	8	JUJU SMITH-SCHUSTER
39.	95	ARI	13	DEANDRE HOPKINS
40.	99	LV	6	HUNTER RENFROW
41.		MIN	7	ADAM THIELEN
42		SF	9	BRANDON AIYUK
43.		DAL	9	MICHAEL GALLUP
44.		KC	8	M. VALDES-SCANTLING
45.		PIT	9	CHASE CLAYPOOL
46.		NYJ	10	GARRETT WILSON
47.		TEN	6	ROBERT WOODS
48.		NO	14	CHRIS OLAVE
49.		DET	6	JAMESON WILLIAMS
50.		JAC	11	CHRISTIAN KIRK
51.		DET	6	DJ CHARK JR.
52.		KC	8	SKYY MOORE
53.		NYG	9	KENNY GOLLADAY
54.		TB	11	JULIO JONES
55.		GB	14	CHRISTIAN WATSON
56.		NE	10	DEVANTE PARKER
57.		NYJ	10	COREY DAVIS
58.		TB	11	RUSSELL GAGE
59.		KC	8	MECOLE HARDMAN
60.		NYG	9	KADARIUS TONEY
61.		LAR	7	VAN JEFFERSON
62.		NO	14	JARVIS LANDRY
63.		CIN	10	TYLER BOYD
64.		WAS	14	JAHAN DOTSON
65.		CAR	13	ROBBIE ANDERSON
66.		NE	10	JAKOBI MEYERS
67.		ARI	13	RONDALE MOORE
68.		NE	10	KENDRICK BOURNE
69.		MIN	7	K.J. OSBORN
70.		IND	14	ALEC PIERCE
71.		JAC	11	MARVIN JONES JR.
72.		BUF	7	JAMISON CROWDER

SCORING SYSTEM

PASSING

TD PASS	4 PTS
EVERY 25 PASSING YARDS	1 PT
2-PT PASSING CONVERSION	2 PTS
INTERCEPTIONS THROWN	-2 PTS

RUSHING

TD RUSH	6 PTS
EVERY 10 RUSHING YARDS	1 PT
2-PT RUSHING CONVERSION	2 PTS

RECEIVING

TD RECEPTION	6 PTS
EVERY 10 RECEIVING YARDS	1 PT
2-PT RECEIVING CONVERSION	2 PTS

KICKING

FG MADE (60+ YARDS)	6 PTS
FG MADE (50-59 YARDS)	5 PTS
FG MADE (40-49 YARDS)	4 PTS
FG MADE (0-39 YARDS)	3 PTS
PAT	1 PT
MISSED FG (ANY DISTANCE)	-1 PT

DEFENSE/SPECIAL TEAMS

TD (DEFENSE OR SPECIAL TEAMS)	6 PTS
INTERCEPTION	2 PTS
FUMBLE RECOVERY	2 PTS
BLOCKED PUNT, PAT, OR FG	2 PTS
SAFETY	2 PTS
SACK	1 PT
0 POINTS ALLOWED	5 PTS
1-6 POINTS ALLOWED	4 PTS
7-13 POINTS ALLOWED	3 PTS
14-20 POINTS ALLOWED	1 PT
21-27 POINTS ALLOWED	0 PTS
28-34 POINTS ALLOWED	-1 PT
35-45 POINTS ALLOWED	-3 PTS
46+ POINTS ALLOWED	-5 PTS

QUARTERBACKS

	OVERALL		BYE	
1.	35	BUF	7	JOSH ALLEN
2.	49	KC	8	PATRICK MAHOMES
3.	57	LAC	8	JUSTIN HERBERT
4.	68	BAL	10	LAMAR JACKSON
5.	71	PHI	7	JALEN HURTS
6.	86	TB	11	TOM BRADY
7.	87	ARI	13	KYLER MURRAY
8.	90	DAL	9	DAK PRESCOTT
9.	97	GB	14	AARON RODGERS
10.		DEN	9	RUSSELL WILSON
11.		SF	9	TREY LANCE
12.		CIN	10	JOE BURROW
13.		LAR	7	MATTHEW STAFFORD
14.		MIA	11	TUA TAGOVAILOA
15.		CLE	9	DESHAUN WATSON
16.		LV	6	DEREK CARR
17.		MIN	7	KIRK COUSINS
18.		CHI	14	JUSTIN FIELDS
19.		NO	14	JAMEIS WINSTON
20.		JAC	11	TREVOR LAWRENCE
21.		TEN	6	RYAN TANNEHILL
22.		NYG	9	DANIEL JONES
23.		IND	14	MATT RYAN
24.		NE	10	MAC JONES
25.		NYJ	10	ZACH WILSON
26.		HOU	6	DAVIS MILLS
27.		ATL	14	MARCUS MARIOTA
28.		DET	6	JARED GOFF
29.		CAR	13	BAKER MAYFIELD
30.		WAS	14	CARSON WENTZ
31.		PIT	9	KENNY PICKETT
32.		(SF)	9	JIMMY GARROPPOLO
33.		(CLE)	11	DREW LOCK

KICKERS

		BYE	
1.	BAL	10	JUSTIN TUCKER
2.	KC	8	HARRISON BUTKER
3.	BUF	7	TYLER BASS
4.	CIN	10	EVAN MCPHERSON
5.	LV	6	DANIEL CARLSON
6.	DEN	9	BRANDON MCMANUS
7.	LAR	7	MATT GAY
8.	NE	10	NICK FOLK
9	TB	11	RYAN SUCCOP
10.	DAL	9	JONATHAN GARIBAY
11.	MIN	7	GREG JOSEPH
12.	PHI	7	JAKE ELLIOT
13.	ATL	14	YOUNGHOE KOO
14.	ARI	13	MATT PRATER
15.	PIT	9	CHRIS BOSWELL

TIGHT ENDS

	OVERALL		BYE	
1.	15	KC	8	TRAVIS KELCE
2.	20	BAL	10	MARK ANDREWS
3.	30	ATL	14	KYLE PITTS
4.	42	SF	9	GEORGE KITTLE
5.	52	LV	6	DARREN WALLER
6.	72	DET	6	T.J. HOCKENSON
7.	77	DAL	9	DALTON SCHULTZ
8.	85	PHI	7	DALLAS GOEDERT
9.	96	BUF	7	DAWSON KNOX
10.	98	ARI	13	ZACH ERTZ
11.		PIT	9	PAT FREIERMUTH
12.		CLE	9	DAVID NJOKU
13.		MIA	11	MIKE GESICKI
14.		MIN	7	IRV SMITH JR.
15.		NE	10	HUNTER HENRY
16.		WAS	14	LOGAN THOMAS
17.		CHI	14	COLE KMET
18.		SEA	11	NOAH FANT
19.		TB	11	ROB GRONKOWSKI
20.		LAC	8	GERALD EVERETT
21.		TB	11	CAMERON BRATE
22.		LAR	7	TYLER HIGBEE
23.		GB	14	ROBERT TONYAN

DEFENSE/SPECIAL TEAMS

		BYE	
1.	TB	11	BUCCANEERS (@DAL WK. 1)
2.	BUF	7	BILLS (@LAR WK. 1)
3.	NO	14	SAINTS (@ATL WK. 1)
4.	GB	14	PACKERS (@MIN WK. 1)
5.	IND	14	COLTS (@HOU WK. 1)
6.	SF	9	49ERS (@CHI WK. 1)
7.	PIT	9	STEELERS (@CIN WK. 1)
8.	MIA	11	DOLPHINS (NE WK. 1)
9	DAL	9	COWBOYS (TB WK. 1)
10.	LAR	7	RAMS (BUF WK. 1)
11.	CIN	10	BENGALS (PIT WK. 1)
12.	BAL	10	RAVENS (@NYJ WK. 1)
13.	NE	10	PATRIOTS (@MIA WK. 1)
14.	DEN	9	BRONCOS (@SEA WK. 1)
15.	CLE	9	BROWNS (@CAR WK. 1)

STRENGTH OF SCHEDULE ANALYSIS

At FantasyTakeover, we know the slightest advantage can be the difference between a weekly win or loss, or better yet, the key to a fantasy championship. Throughout our publication you'll find in-depth analysis of nearly every possible fantasy metric, all to provide you the best chance of having a successful fantasy football season.

Our Strength of Schedule table shows how easy or difficult a team's entire 2022 schedule is, by position. For example, Chicago's RBs have the easiest overall schedule (1st); their opponents are projected to allow fantasy gold to RBs. Denver, this season, has the best schedule for WRs and the fifth best for QB Russell Wilson. This is part of why we have been so high on the Denver trio – Russell Wilson, Courtland Sutton, and Jerry Jeudy. Sorry, Joe Burrow. Cincinnati has one of the toughest schedules for QBs (29th), and your TE, Hayden Hurst, is in for a rough year (32nd).

Although our rankings take into consideration much more than strength-of-schedule metrics, this chart will prove invaluable information before your draft, and, especially throughout the season, as you choose starters and add new players, to give yourself an advantage over your fantasy opponents.

	QB	RB	WR	TE	K	D/ST
Arizona	31	28	27	17	22	16
Atlanta	14	32	12	30	26	2
Baltimore	30	11	21	25	14	4
Buffalo	16	8	13	15	15	10
Carolina	23	19	22	21	10	11
Chicago	6	1	23	1	20	32
Cincinnati	29	22	18	27	32	6
Cleveland	7	15	4	4	21	3
Dallas	12	6	19	22	4	28
Denver	5	23	1	13	7	17
Detroit	11	7	17	11	17	25
Green Bay	25	13	20	32	9	20
Houston	8	20	16	20	11	9
Indianapolis	19	17	11	29	13	18
Jacksonville	2	12	6	6	12	24
Kansas City	27	21	31	19	2	14
Las Vegas	28	29	29	26	24	13
LA Rams	24	27	26	16	23	22
LA Chargers	20	26	15	8	3	12
Miami	26	3	30	18	28	23
Minnesota	17	10	28	14	29	27
New England	9	2	8	5	6	21
New Orleans	13	16	14	10	5	19
NY Giants	1	18	10	7	27	26
NY Jets	32	5	32	23	31	7
Philadelphia	3	24	7	31	25	29
Pittsburgh	18	14	3	3	19	1
San Francisco	22	30	24	12	16	8
Seattle	15	25	5	28	1	15
Tampa Bay	21	31	2	24	30	5
Tennessee	10	9	25	2	18	28
Washington	4	4	9	9	8	31

2022 NFL SCHEDULE

WEEK 1

THURSDAY, SEPTEMBER 8
BUFFALO AT LA RAMS ... 8:20

SUNDAY, SEPTEMBER 11
NEW ORLEANS AT ATLANTA ... 1:00
CLEVELAND AT CAROLINA ... 1:00
SAN FRANCISCO AT CHICAGO ... 1:00
PITTSBURGH AT CINCINNATI ... 1:00
PHILADELPHIA AT DETROIT ... 1:00
INDIANAPOLIS AT HOUSTON ... 1:00
NEW ENGLAND AT MIAMI ... 1:00
BALTIMORE AT NY JETS ... 1:00
JACKSONVILLE AT WASHINGTON ... 1:00
KANSAS CITY AT ARIZONA ... 4:25
LAS VEGAS AT LA CHARGERS ... 4:25
GREEN BAY AT MINNESOTA ... 4:25
NY GIANTS AT TENNESSEE ... 4:25
TAMPA BAY AT DALLAS ... 8:20

MONDAY, SEPTEMBER 12
DENVER AT SEATTLE ... 8:15

WEEK 2

THURSDAY, SEPTEMBER 15
LA CHARGERS AT KANSAS CITY ... 8:15

SUNDAY, SEPTEMBER 18
MIAMI AT BALTIMORE ... 1:00
NY JETS AT CLEVELAND ... 1:00
WASHINGTON AT DETROIT ... 1:00
INDIANAPOLIS AT JACKSONVILLE ... 1:00
TAMPA BAY AT NEW ORLEANS ... 1:00
CAROLINA AT NY GIANTS ... 1:00
NEW ENGLAND AT PITTSBURGH ... 1:00
ATLANTA AT LA RAMS ... 4:05
SEATTLE AT SAN FRANCISCO ... 4:05
CINCINNATI AT DALLAS ... 4:25
HOUSTON AT DENVER ... 4:25
ARIZONA AT LAS VEGAS ... 4:25
CHICAGO AT GREEN BAY ... 8:20

MONDAY, SEPTEMBER 19
TENNESSEE AT BUFFALO ... 7:15
MINNESOTA AT PHILADELPHIA ... 8:30

WEEK 3

THURSDAY, SEPTEMBER 22
PITTSBURGH AT CLEVELAND ... 8:15

SUNDAY, SEPTEMBER 25
NEW ORLEANS AT CAROLINA ... 1:00
HOUSTON AT CHICAGO ... 1:00
KANSAS CITY AT INDIANAPOLIS ... 1:00
BUFFALO AT MIAMI ... 1:00
DETROIT AT MINNESOTA ... 1:00
BALTIMORE AT NEW ENGLAND ... 1:00
CINCINNATI AT NY JETS ... 1:00
LAS VEGAS AT TENNESSEE ... 1:00
PHILADELPHIA AT WASHINGTON ... 1:00
JACKSONVILLE AT LA CHARGERS ... 4:05
LA RAMS AT ARIZONA ... 4:25
ATLANTA AT SEATTLE ... 4:25
GREEN BAY AT TAMPA BAY ... 4:25
SAN FRANCISCO AT DENVER ... 8:20

MONDAY, SEPTEMBER 26
DALLAS AT NY GIANTS ... 8:15

WEEK 4

THURSDAY, SEPTEMBER 29
MIAMI AT CINCINNATI ... 8:15

SUNDAY, OCTOBER 2
MINNESOTA AT NEW ORLEANS* ... 9:30
CLEVELAND AT ATLANTA ... 1:00
BUFFALO AT BALTIMORE ... 1:00
WASHINGTON AT DALLAS ... 1:00
SEATTLE AT DETROIT ... 1:00
LA CHARGERS AT HOUSTON ... 1:00
TENNESSEE AT INDIANAPOLIS ... 1:00
CHICAGO AT NY GIANTS ... 1:00
JACKSONVILLE AT PHILADELPHIA ... 1:00
NY JETS AT PITTSBURGH ... 1:00
ARIZONA AT CAROLINA ... 4:05
NEW ENGLAND AT GREEN BAY ... 4:25
DENVER AT LAS VEGAS ... 4:25
KANSAS CITY AT TAMPA BAY ... 8:20

MONDAY, OCTOBER 3
LA RAMS AT SAN FRANCISCO ... 8:15

**PLAYED IN LONDON*

WEEK 5

THURSDAY, OCTOBER 6
INDIANAPOLIS AT DENVER ... 8:15

SUNDAY, OCTOBER 9
NY GIANTS AT GREEN BAY* ... 9:30
PITTSBURGH AT BUFFALO ... 1:00
LA CHARGERS AT CLEVELAND ... 1:00
HOUSTON AT JACKSONVILLE ... 1:00
CHICAGO AT MINNESOTA ... 1:00
DETROIT AT NEW ENGLAND ... 1:00
SEATTLE AT NEW ORLEANS ... 1:00
MIAMI AT NY JETS ... 1:00
ATLANTA AT TAMPA BAY ... 1:00
TENNESSEE AT WASHINGTON ... 1:00
SAN FRANCISCO AT CAROLINA ... 4:05
PHILADELPHIA AT ARIZONA ... 4:25
DALLAS AT LA RAMS ... 4:25
CINCINNATI AT BALTIMORE ... 8:20

MONDAY, OCTOBER 10
LAS VEGAS AT KANSAS CITY ... 8:15

**PLAYED IN LONDON*

WEEK 6

THURSDAY, OCTOBER 13
WASHINGTON AT CHICAGO ... 8:15

SUNDAY, OCTOBER 16
SAN FRANCISCO AT ATLANTA ... 1:00
NEW ENGLAND AT CLEVELAND ... 1:00
NY JETS AT GREEN BAY ... 1:00
JACKSONVILLE AT INDIANAPOLIS ... 1:00
MINNESOTA AT MIAMI ... 1:00
CINCINNATI AT NEW ORLEANS ... 1:00
BALTIMORE AT NY GIANTS ... 1:00
TAMPA BAY AT PITTSBURGH ... 1:00
CAROLINA AT LA RAMS ... 4:05
ARIZONA AT SEATTLE ... 4:05
BUFFALO AT KANSAS CITY ... 4:25
DALLAS AT PHILADELPHIA ... 8:20

MONDAY, OCTOBER 17
DENVER AT LA CHARGERS ... 8:15

BYES: DETROIT, HOUSTON, LAS VEGAS, TENNESSEE

WEEK 7

THURSDAY, OCTOBER 20
NEW ORLEANS AT ARIZONA ... 8:15

SUNDAY, OCTOBER 23
CLEVELAND AT BALTIMORE ... 1:00
TAMPA BAY AT CAROLINA ... 1:00
ATLANTA AT CINCINNATI ... 1:00
DETROIT AT DALLAS ... 1:00
NY GIANTS AT JACKSONVILLE ... 1:00
INDIANAPOLIS AT TENNESSEE ... 1:00
GREEN BAY AT WASHINGTON ... 1:00
NY JETS AT DENVER ... 4:05
HOUSTON AT LAS VEGAS ... 4:05
SEATTLE AT LA CHARGERS ... 4:25
KANSAS CITY AT SAN FRAN ... 4:25
PITTSBURGH AT MIAMI ... 8:20

MONDAY, OCTOBER 24
CHICAGO AT NEW ENGLAND ... 8:15

BYES: BUFFALO, LA RAMS, MINNESOTA, PHILADELPHIA

WEEK 8

THURSDAY, OCTOBER 27
BALTIMORE AT TAMPA BAY ... 8:15

SUNDAY, OCTOBER 30
DENVER AT JACKSONVILLE* ... 9:30
CAROLINA AT ATLANTA ... 1:00
CHICAGO AT DALLAS ... 1:00
MIAMI AT DETROIT ... 1:00
ARIZONA AT MINNESOTA ... 1:00
LAS VEGAS AT NEW ORLEANS ... 1:00
NEW ENGLAND AT NY JETS ... 1:00
PITTSBURGH AT PHILADELPHIA ... 1:00
TENNESSEE AT HOUSTON ... 4:05
WASHINGTON AT INDIANAPOLIS ... 4:25
SAN FRANCISCO AT LA RAMS ... 4:25
NY GIANTS AT SEATTLE ... 4:25
GREEN BAY AT BUFFALO ... 8:20

MONDAY, OCTOBER 31
CINCINNATI AT CLEVELAND ... 8:15

**PLAYED IN LONDON*
BYES: KANSAS CITY, LA CHARGERS

WEEK 9

THURSDAY, NOVEMBER 3
PHILADELPHIA AT HOUSTON ... 8:15

SUNDAY, NOVEMBER 6
LA CHARGERS AT ATLANTA ... 1:00
MIAMI AT CHICAGO ... 1:00
CAROLINA AT CINCINNATI ... 1:00
GREEN BAY AT DETROIT ... 1:00
LAS VEGAS AT JACKSONVILLE ... 1:00
INDIANAPOLIS AT NEW ENGLAND ... 1:00
BUFFALO AT NY JETS ... 1:00
MINNESOTA AT WASHINGTON ... 1:00
SEATTLE AT ARIZONA ... 4:05
LA RAMS AT TAMPA BAY ... 4:25
TENNESSEE AT KANSAS CITY ... 8:20

MONDAY, NOVEMBER 7
BALTIMORE AT NEW ORLEANS ... 8:15

BYES: CLEVELAND, DALLAS, DENVER, NY GIANTS, PITTSBURGH, SAN FRANCISCO

WEEK 10

THURSDAY, NOVEMBER 10
ATLANTA AT CAROLINA ... 8:15

SUNDAY, NOVEMBER 13
SEATTLE AT TAMPA BAY* ... 9:30
MINNESOTA AT BUFFALO ... 1:00
DETROIT AT CHICAGO ... 1:00
JACKSONVILLE AT KANSAS CITY ... 1:00
CLEVELAND AT MIAMI ... 1:00
HOUSTON AT NY GIANTS ... 1:00
NEW ORLEANS AT PITTSBURGH ... 1:00
DENVER AT TENNESSEE ... 1:00
INDIANAPOLIS AT LAS VEGAS ... 4:05
DALLAS AT GREEN BAY ... 4:25
ARIZONA AT LA RAMS ... 4:25
LA CHARGERS AT SAN FRAN ... 8:20

MONDAY, NOVEMBER 14
WASHINGTON AT PHILADELPHIA ... 8:15

**PLAYED IN MUNICH*
BYES: BALTIMORE, CINCINNATI, NEW ENGLAND, NY JETS

WEEK 11

THURSDAY, NOVEMBER 17
TENNESSEE AT GREEN BAY ... 8:15

SUNDAY, NOVEMBER 20
CHICAGO AT ATLANTA ... 1:00
CAROLINA AT BALTIMORE ... 1:00
CLEVELAND AT BUFFALO ... 1:00
WASHINGTON AT HOUSTON ... 1:00
PHILADELPHIA AT INDIANAPOLIS ... 1:00
NY JETS AT NEW ENGLAND ... 1:00
LA RAMS AT NEW ORLEANS ... 1:00
DETROIT AT NY GIANTS ... 1:00
LAS VEGAS AT DENVER ... 4:05
KANSAS CITY AT LA CHARGERS ... 4:25
DALLAS AT MINNESOTA ... 4:25
CINCINNATI AT PITTSBURGH ... 8:20

MONDAY, NOVEMBER 21
SAN FRANCISCO AT ARIZONA* ... 8:15

**PLAYED IN MEXICO CITY*
BYES: JACKSONVILLE, MIAMI, SEATTLE, TAMPA BAY

WEEK 12

THURSDAY, NOVEMBER 24 (THANKSGIVING)
BUFFALO AT DETROIT ... 12:30
NY GIANTS AT DALLAS ... 4:30
NEW ENGLAND AT MINNESOTA ... 8:20

SUNDAY, NOVEMBER 27
DENVER AT CAROLINA ... 1:00
TAMPA BAY AT CLEVELAND ... 1:00
BALTIMORE AT JACKSONVILLE ... 1:00
HOUSTON AT MIAMI ... 1:00
CHICAGO AT NY JETS ... 1:00
CINCINNATI AT TENNESSEE ... 1:00
ATLANTA AT WASHINGTON ... 1:00
LA CHARGERS AT ARIZONA ... 4:05
LAS VEGAS AT SEATTLE ... 4:05
LA RAMS AT KANSAS CITY ... 4:25
NEW ORLEANS AT SAN FRAN ... 4:25
GREEN BAY AT PHILADELPHIA ... 8:20

MONDAY, NOVEMBER 28
PITTSBURGH AT INDIANAPOLIS ... 8:15

WEEK 13

THURSDAY, DECEMBER 1
BUFFALO AT NEW ENGLAND ... 8:15

SUNDAY, DECEMBER 4
PITTSBURGH AT ATLANTA ... 1:00
DENVER AT BALTIMORE ... 1:00
GREEN BAY AT CHICAGO ... 1:00
JACKSONVILLE AT DETROIT ... 1:00
CLEVELAND AT HOUSTON ... 1:00
NY JETS AT MINNESOTA ... 1:00
WASHINGTON AT NY GIANTS ... 1:00
TENNESSEE AT PHILADELPHIA ... 1:00
SEATTLE AT LA RAMS ... 4:05
MIAMI AT SAN FRANCISCO ... 4:05
KANSAS CITY AT CINCINNATI ... 4:25
LA CHARGERS AT LAS VEGAS ... 4:25
INDIANAPOLIS AT DALLAS ... 8:20

MONDAY, DECEMBER 5
NEW ORLEANS AT TAMPA BAY ... 8:15

BYES: ARIZONA, CAROLINA

WEEK 14

THURSDAY, DECEMBER 8
LAS VEGAS AT LA RAMS ... 8:15

SUNDAY, DECEMBER 11
NY JETS AT BUFFALO ... 1:00
CLEVELAND AT CINCINNATI ... 1:00
HOUSTON AT DALLAS ... 1:00
MINNESOTA AT DETROIT ... 1:00
PHILADELPHIA AT NY GIANTS ... 1:00
BALTIMORE AT PITTSBURGH ... 1:00
JACKSONVILLE AT TENNESSEE ... 1:00
MIAMI AT LA CHARGERS ... 4:05
TAMPA BAY AT SAN FRANCISCO ... 4:25
CAROLINA AT SEATTLE ... 4:25
KANSAS CITY AT DENVER ... 8:20

MONDAY, DECEMBER 12
NEW ENGLAND AT ARIZONA ... 8:15

BYES: ATLANTA, CHICAGO, GREEN BAY, INDIANAPOLIS, NEW ORLEANS, WASHINGTON

WEEK 15

THURSDAY, DECEMBER 15
SAN FRANCISCO AT SEATTLE ... 8:15

SATURDAY, DECEMBER 17
MIAMI AT BUFFALO ... TBD
BALTIMORE AT CLEVELAND ... TBD
INDIANAPOLIS AT MINNESOTA ... TBD
ATLANTA AT NEW ORLEANS ... TBD
NY GIANTS AT WASHINGTON ... TBD

SUNDAY, DECEMBER 18
PITTSBURGH AT CAROLINA ... 1:00
PHILADELPHIA AT CHICAGO ... 1:00
KANSAS CITY AT HOUSTON ... 1:00
DALLAS AT JACKSONVILLE ... 1:00
DETROIT AT NY JETS ... 1:00
ARIZONA AT DENVER ... 4:05
TENNESSEE AT LA CHARGERS ... 4:25
CINCINNATI AT TAMPA BAY ... 4:25
NEW ENGLAND AT LAS VEGAS ... 8:20

MONDAY, DECEMBER 19
LA RAMS AT GREEN BAY ... 8:15

WEEK 16

THURSDAY, DECEMBER 22
JACKSONVILLE AT NY JETS ... 8:15

SATURDAY, DECEMBER 24
ATLANTA AT BALTIMORE ... 1:00
DETROIT AT CAROLINA ... 1:00
BUFFALO AT CHICAGO ... 1:00
NEW ORLEANS AT CLEVELAND ... 1:00
SEATTLE AT KANSAS CITY ... 1:00
NY GIANTS AT MINNESOTA ... 1:00
CINCINNATI AT NEW ENGLAND ... 1:00
HOUSTON AT TENNESSEE ... 1:00
WASHINGTON AT SAN FRAN ... 4:05
PHILADELPHIA AT DALLAS ... 4:25
LAS VEGAS AT PITTSBURGH ... 8:15

SUNDAY, DECEMBER 25
GREEN BAY AT MIAMI ... 1:00
DENVER AT LA RAMS ... 4:30
TAMPA BAY AT ARIZONA ... 8:20

MONDAY, DECEMBER 26
LA CHARGERS AT INDIANAPOLIS ... 8:15

WEEK 17

THURSDAY, DECEMBER 29
DALLAS AT TENNESSEE ... 8:15

SUNDAY, JANUARY 1
ARIZONA AT ATLANTA ... 1:00
PITTSBURGH AT BALTIMORE ... 1:00
CHICAGO AT DETROIT ... 1:00
JACKSONVILLE AT HOUSTON ... 1:00
DENVER AT KANSAS CITY ... 1:00
MIAMI AT NEW ENGLAND ... 1:00
INDIANAPOLIS AT NY GIANTS ... 1:00
NEW ORLEANS AT PHILADELPHIA ... 1:00
CAROLINA AT TAMPA BAY ... 1:00
CLEVELAND AT WASHINGTON ... 1:00
SAN FRANCISCO AT LAS VEGAS ... 4:05
NY JETS AT SEATTLE ... 4:05
MINNESOTA AT GREEN BAY ... 4:25
LA RAMS AT LA CHARGERS ... 8:20

MONDAY, JANUARY 2
BUFFALO AT CINCINNATI ... 8:30

WEEK 18

SATURDAY, JANUARY 7 (2 GAMES) & SUNDAY, JANUARY 8
TAMPA BAY AT ATLANTA ... TBD
NEW ENGLAND AT BUFFALO ... TBD
MINNESOTA AT CHICAGO ... TBD
BALTIMORE AT CINCINNATI ... TBD
DETROIT AT GREEN BAY ... TBD
HOUSTON AT INDIANAPOLIS ... TBD
TENNESSEE AT JACKSONVILLE ... TBD
NY JETS AT MIAMI ... TBD
CAROLINA AT NEW ORLEANS ... TBD
NY GIANTS AT PHILADELPHIA ... TBD
CLEVELAND AT PITTSBURGH ... TBD
DALLAS AT WASHINGTON ... TBD
LA CHARGERS AT DENVER ... TBD
KANSAS CITY AT LAS VEGAS ... TBD
ARIZONA AT SAN FRANCISCO ... TBD
LA RAMS AT SEATTLE ... TBD

** All Times Eastern Standard*

TIERS

OUR PPR RANKINGS DIVIDED INTO TIERS

Using tiers is an important strategy to apply while drafting. Tiers are made up of players who have similar range of outcomes. While some players in a tier may have a higher floor, others may have better upside.

But, as a drafter, your goal in many situations should be to select players at the bottom of tiers, rather than the top. For example, I'd rather have the sixth overall draft pick than the third because I would be guaranteed a Tier 2 player, whose range of outcomes is very similar. The advantage comes in the next round. If I had the third pick in a 10-team draft, I wouldn't pick again until 18th, and may only have Tier 6 players available. But if I picked sixth overall, then I would pick again at 15, which would guarantee me a player out of Tier 5, before the next dropoff. Selecting the best player available is a good strategy, but you should feel pretty good when selecting a player at the bottom of a tier, knowing you got a good value.

RK		POS	TM	BYE
TIER 1				
1	JONATHAN TAYLOR	RB1	IND	6
2	CHRISTIAN MCCAFFREY	RB2	CAR	13
TIER 2				
3	AUSTIN EKELER	RB3	LAC	8
4	DERRICK HENRY	RB4	TEN	6
5	NAJEE HARRIS	RB5	PIT	9
6	COOPER KUPP	WR1	LAR	7
TIER 3				
7	ALVIN KAMARA	RB6	NO	14
8	JUSTIN JEFFERSON	WR2	MIN	7
9	LEONARD FOURNETTE	RB7	TB	11
TIER 4				
10	DALVIN COOK	RB8	MIN	7
11	D'ANDRE SWIFT	RB9	DET	6
12	JA'MARR CHASE	WR3	CIN	10
TIER 5				
13	TRAVIS KELCE	TE1	KC	8
14	JOE MIXON	RB10	CIN	10
15	STEFON DIGGS	WR4	BUF	7
16	DAVANTE ADAMS	WR5	LV	6
TIER 6				
17	MARK ANDREWS	TE2	BAL	10
18	AARON JONES	RB11	GB	14
19	DEEBO SAMUEL	WR6	SF	9
20	TYREEK HILL	WR7	MIA	11
21	CEEDEE LAMB	WR8	DAL	9
22	JAMES CONNER	RB12	ARI	13
TIER 7				
23	DAVID MONTGOMERY	RB13	CHI	14
24	KEENAN ALLEN	WR9	LAC	8
25	TEE HIGGINS	WR10	CIN	10
26	MIKE EVANS	WR11	TB	11
27	SAQUON BARKLEY	RB14	NYG	9
28	JAVONTE WILLIAMS	RB15	DEN	9
29	NICK CHUBB	RB16	CLE	9
30	CAM AKERS	RB17	LAR	7

TIER 8				
31	KYLE PITTS	TE3	ATL	14
32	DJ MOORE	WR12	CAR	13
33	JAYLEN WADDLE	WR13	MIA	11
34	MICHAEL PITTMAN JR.	WR14	IND	14
35	EZEKIEL ELLIOT	RB18	DAL	9
36	ANTONIO GIBSON	RB19	WAS	14
37	JOSH ALLEN	QB1	BUF	7
38	JOSH JACOBS	RB20	LV	6
39	TRAVIS ETIENNE JR.	RB21	JAC	11
40	A.J. BROWN	WR15	PHI	7
41	DK METCALF	WR16	SEA	11
42	TERRY MCLAURIN	WR17	WAS	14
43	J.K. DOBBINS	RB22	BAL	10
44	BREECE HALL	RB23	NYJ	10
TIER 9				
45	GEORGE KITTLE	TE4	SF	9
46	PATRICK MAHOMES	QB2	KC	8
47	DIONTAE JOHNSON	WR18	PIT	9
48	BRANDIN COOKS	WR19	HOU	6
49	MIKE WILLIAMS	WR20	LAC	8
50	DARNELL MOONEY	WR21	CHI	14
51	ELIJAH MITCHELL	RB24	SF	9
52	AMARI COOPER	WR22	CLE	9
53	JUSTIN HERBERT	QB3	LAC	8
54	DARREN WALLER	TE5	LV	6
55	MARQUISE BROWN	WR23	ARI	13
56	CHRIS GODWIN	WR24	TB	11
57	COURTLAND SUTTON	WR25	DEN	9
58	LAMAR JACKSON	QB4	BAL	10
TIER 10				
59	JERRY JEUDY	WR26	DEN	9
60	ELIJAH MOORE	WR27	NYJ	10
61	AMON-RA ST. BROWN	WR28	DET	6
62	MILES SANDERS	RB25	PHI	7
63	CLYDE EDWARDS-HELAIRE	RB26	KC	8
64	DEVIN SINGLETARY	RB27	BUF	7
65	JALEN HURTS	QB5	PHI	7

66	KAREEM HUNT	RB28	CLE	9
67	DAMIEN HARRIS	RB29	NE	10
68	MICHAEL THOMAS	WR29	NO	14
TIER 11				
69	TYLER LOCKETT	WR30	SEA	11
70	HUNTER RENFROW	WR31	LV	6
71	T.J. HOCKENSON	TE6	DET	6
72	DRAKE LONDON	WR32	ATL	14
73	DALTON SCHULTZ	TE7	DAL	9
74	TOM BRADY	QB6	TB	11
75	KYLER MURRAY	QB7	ARI	13
76	ALLEN ROBINSON II	WR33	LAR	7
77	JUJU SMITH-SCHUSTER	WR34	KC	8
78	RASHOD BATEMAN	WR35	BAL	10
79	GABRIEL DAVIS	WR36	BUF	7
80	DALLAS GOEDERT	TE8	PHI	7
81	TONY POLLARD	RB30	DAL	9
82	CHASE EDMONDS	RB31	MIA	11
83	MELVIN GORDON III	RB32	DEN	9
84	ZACH ERTZ	TE9	ARI	13
85	DAK PRESCOTT	QB8	DAL	9
86	DEVONTA SMITH	WR37	PHI	7
87	ADAM THIELEN	WR38	MIN	7
TIER 12				
88	AJ DILLON	RB33	GB	14
89	CORDARRELLE PATTERSON	RB44	ATL	14
90	DEANDRE HOPKINS	WR39	ARI	13
91	TREYLON BURKS	WR40	TEN	6
92	AARON RODGERS	QB9	GB	14
93	RUSSELL WILSON	QB10	DEN	9
94	PAT FREIERMUTH	TE10	PIT	9
95	KEN WALKER III	RB35	SEA	11
96	RASHAAD PENNY	RB36	SEA	11
97	BRANDON AIYUK	WR41	SF	9
98	CHRISTIAN KIRK	WR42	JAC	11
99	ALLEN LAZARD	WR43	GB	14
100	MICHAEL CARTER	RB37	NYJ	10

2021 ADVANCED QUARTERBACK STATS

		GP	AIR YDS	AIR/A	20+ YDS	50+ YDS	PKT TIME	SK	HRRY	BLITZ	POOR	DROP	RZ ATT
1	JOSH ALLEN (BUF)	17	2,900	4.5	51	3	2.4	26	96	182	108	35	123
2	JUSTIN HERBERT (LAC)	17	2,867	4.3	52	3	2.4	31	50	154	95	38	104
3	TOM BRADY (TB)	17	3,079	4.3	75	4	2.3	22	30	177	135	32	120
4	PATRICK MAHOMES II (KC)	17	2,480	3.8	58	4	2.4	28	76	112	116	31	100
5	JOE BURROW (CIN)	16	2,521	4.8	60	12	2.4	51	46	125	54	23	54
6	MATTHEW STAFFORD (LAR)	17	2,987	5	65	10	2.4	30	32	138	111	31	112
7	AARON RODGERS (GB)	16	2,157	4.1	55	5	2.3	30	59	134	92	14	110
8	JALEN HURTS (PHI)	15	1,912	4.4	44	2	2.6	26	78	125	57	22	54
9	DAK PRESCOTT (DAL)	16	2,638	4.4	55	1	2.4	30	46	188	85	29	97
10	KYLER MURRAY (ARI)	14	2,290	4.7	49	2	2.4	31	68	108	61	16	72
11	KIRK COUSINS (MIN)	16	2,677	4.8	60	4	2.4	28	70	169	92	22	71
12	DEREK CARR (LV)	17	2,806	4.5	67	5	2.5	40	63	166	93	26	76
13	RYAN TANNEHILL (TEN)	17	2,195	4.1	35	3	2.3	47	32	166	83	23	79
14	LAMAR JACKSON (BAL)	12	1,828	4.8	41	0	2.5	38	39	152	72	19	47
15	CARSON WENTZ (IND)	17	2,145	4.2	42	5	2.5	32	46	156	93	25	67
16	TAYLOR HEINICKE (WAS)	16	1,911	3.9	40	2	2.6	38	56	145	80	19	48
17	MAC JONES (NE)	17	2,239	4.3	52	1	2.4	28	29	181	88	16	71
18	JIMMY GAROPPOLO (SF)	15	2,030	4.6	55	5	2.4	29	24	100	56	23	55
19	RUSSELL WILSON (SEA)	14	1,927	4.8	45	7	2.4	33	49	113	72	16	45
20	MATT RYAN (ATL)	17	2,457	4.4	44	2	2.4	40	48	166	79	21	83
21	BEN ROETHLISBERGER (PIT)	16	2,033	3.4	39	4	2.2	38	45	144	109	30	87
22	TEDDY BRIDGEWATER (MIA)	14	1,801	4.2	33	2	2.5	31	65	118	68	13	53
23	TREVOR LAWRENCE (JAC)	17	2,240	3.7	43	2	2.4	32	68	146	118	33	56
24	BAKER MAYFIELD (CLE)	14	1,791	4.3	41	3	2.4	43	52	123	82	20	44
25	JARED GOFF (DET)	14	1,718	3.5	38	1	2.4	35	50	111	77	21	55
26	TUA TAGOVAILOA (MIA)	13	1,589	4.1	30	3	2.2	20	43	101	61	17	52
27	DANIEL JONES (NYG)	11	1,517	4.2	23	2	2.5	22	38	120	63	19	42
28	SAM DARNOLD (CAR)	12	1,322	3.2	30	3	2.5	35	60	130	71	26	41
29	ZACH WILSON (NYJ)	13	1,405	3.7	32	2	2.5	44	71	128	86	26	41
30	DAVIS MILLS (HOU)	13	1,608	4.1	31	1	2.3	31	30	120	64	11	27

2022 PPR RANKINGS

		BYE	
1.	BUF	7	JOSH ALLEN
2.	KC	8	PATRICK MAHOMES
3.	LAC	8	JUSTIN HERBERT
4.	BAL	10	LAMAR JACKSON
5.	PHI	7	JALEN HURTS
6.	TB	11	TOM BRADY
7.	ARI	13	KYLER MURRAY
8.	DAL	9	DAK PRESCOTT
9	GB	14	AARON RODGERS
10.	DEN	9	RUSSELL WILSON
11.	SF	9	TREY LANCE
12.	CIN	10	JOE BURROW
13.	LAR	7	MATTHEW STAFFORD
14.	MIA	11	TUA TAGOVAILOA
15.	CLE	9	DESHAUN WATSON
16.	LV	6	DEREK CARR
17.	MIN	7	KIRK COUSINS
18.	CHI	14	JUSTIN FIELDS
19.	NO	14	JAMEIS WINSTON
20.	JAC	11	TREVOR LAWRENCE
21.	TEN	6	RYAN TANNEHILL
22.	NYG	9	DANIEL JONES
23.	IND	14	MATT RYAN
24.	NE	10	MAC JONES
25.	NYJ	10	ZACH WILSON
26.	HOU	6	DAVIS MILLS
27.	ATL	14	MARCUS MARIOTA
28.	DET	6	JARED GOFF

QUARTERBACKS

RUNNING BACKS

WIDE RECEIVERS

TIGHT ENDS

KICKERS

D/ST

1 JOSH ALLEN

*BUFFALO **BILLS** (7)*

DRAFT: 2018-1(7)   AGE: 26   WT: 237   HT: 6-5   WYOMING

After two consecutive finishes as fantasy's No. 1 QB, Josh Allen lands as our top-ranked passer. What's best for Allen's 2022 fantasy managers is that his numbers from 2021 feel sustainable. Based on his in-game statistics from 2021, Allen finished with the fourth-most fantasy points under expectation. His completion percentage dropped to 63.3%, 25th among QBs with at least six starts. And his QB rating on the year (92) was worse than names like Jared Goff and Teddy Bridgewater.

Allen's ability as both a passer and a rusher make him an elite-level fantasy producer. Among QBs, as a rusher in 2021, Allen was third in every volume-based metric, behind only Lamar Jackson and Jalen Hurts. Allen had 122 rushing attempts, 48 of which were scrambles where he averaged an impressive 9.6 yards each. He also converted 20% of his 30 red zone rushing attempts into TDs. At 6-foot 5, 237 pounds, the 26-year-old has shown no issues staying healthy while taking hits as a rusher.

Where Allen separates himself from other dynamic rushing QBs is his passing ability. Last season, Allen was top-10 in completions per game (24.1), pass yards per game (259), and passing TDs per game (2.1). And when Allen's not the one running in the red zone, he's throwing the ball, finishing second in red zone completions in 2021.

With his top pass catcher Stefon Diggs back, along with breakout candidate, WR Gabriel Davis, Allen's in store for another productive year. He's our definitive No. 1 QB.

YEAR	TEAM	GP	CMP %	PASS YD	PASS TD	INTS	300 YG	RUSH ATT	RUSH YD	RUSH TD	FPPG
2019	BUF	16	58.8	3089	20	9	0	109	510	9	18.2
2020	BUF	16	69.2	4544	37	10	8	102	421	8	25.0
2021	BUF	17	63.3	4407	36	15	6	122	763	8	24.4
PROJ	BUF	17	63.7	4288	35	16	6	118	698	6	22.7

2 PATRICK MAHOMES

*KANSAS CITY **CHIEFS** (8)*

DRAFT: 2017-1(10)   AGE: 26   WT: 227   HT: 6-3   TEXAS TECH

Patrick Mahomes' lackluster 2021 resulted in only a fourth place finish among QBs in fantasy PPG. We're only kind of kidding here. Teams did seem to adjust their defense to prevent the Mahomesesque big plays. As a result, Mahomes had a career low in air yards per catch of 4.9, and led the league in throwaways. These prevent formations did help Mahomes achieve a career high in rushing, though. He had only 2 fewer scrambles than Josh Allen.

With all that said, Mahomes was able to finish 2021 top five among QBs in completions per game (25.6), passing yards per game (285), and passing TDs per game (2.2). He also converted 26% of his red zone pass attempts into TDs.

During the last four seasons, Mahomes has averaged 38 TDs a year and never finished outside the top five in fantasy PPG.

The departure of Tyreek Hill hurts, but Mahomes was QB4 without Hill in the fold through the first five weeks of 2019. Plus, Kansas City added plenty of options in the offseason. Former Packer Marquez Valdes-Scantling will provide a deep threat, while we've already seen the upside of JuJu Smith-Schuster. And second rounder Skyy Moore adds one more option to go with veteran TE Travis Kelce.

With a much-improved offensive line, and an offense that relies on their superstar to be the playmaker, Mahomes' range of outcomes is pretty narrow, and we're positioning him just behind Allen in our rankings.

YEAR	TEAM	GP	CMP %	PASS YD	PASS TD	INTS	300 YG	RUSH ATT	RUSH YD	RUSH TD	FPPG
2019	KC	14	65.9	4031	26	5	7	43	218	2	20.6
2020	KC	15	66.3	4740	38	6	9	62	308	2	24.8
2021	KC	17	66.3	4839	37	13	5	66	381	2	21.5
PROJ	KC	17	65.9	4727	35	12	6	66	374	3	21.2

3 JUSTIN HERBERT

*LOS ANGELES **CHARGERS** (8)*

DRAFT: 2020-1(6)   AGE: 24   WT: 237   HT: 6-6   OREGON

After a sensational first-year campaign where he broke every notable rookie passing record, Justin Herbert avoided the sophomore slump. If you've watched Herbert play, you know he's a generational talent.

Last season, Herbert finished third in fantasy PPG, behind only Josh Allen and Tom Brady. He was second in completions per game (26.1) and passing yards per game (295) and third in TD passes per game (2.2). He had no fewer than 15 fantasy points in any game last year, the highest floor of all QBs last season.

Some of Herbert's success can be attributed to playing on a team whose defense gave up the most points in the league last season. The Chargers defensive improvements this offseason could slightly affect passing volume.

The Chargers, without a real ground-and-pound run game, had the fifth-most red zone passing attempts last season. And while Herbert may not rake in big rushing yards, he's effective at the goal line, and a handful of rushing TDs is well within his reach. He did finish 2021 in the top 10 among QBs in carries and rushing TDs.

The Chargers return their full 2021 receiving corps, led by veterans Keenan Allen and Mike Williams. With pass-catching back Austin Ekeler still in tow, Herbert could be the first QB to produce back-to-back 5,000-yard seasons.

There are few sure things in fantasy football, but Herbert finishing as a top-five QB feels like one of them.

YEAR	TEAM	GP	CMP %	PASS YD	PASS TD	INTS	300 YG	RUSH ATT	RUSH YD	RUSH TD	FPPG
2020	LAC	15	66.6	4336	31	10	8	55	234	5	22.1
2021	LAC	17	65.9	5014	38	15	9	63	302	3	21.8
PROJ	LAC	17	66.3	4671	34	13	8	62	282	3	20.2

4 LAMAR JACKSON

*BALTIMORE **RAVENS** (10)*

DRAFT: 2018-1(32)   AGE: 25   WT: 212   HT: 6-2   LOUISVILLE

In the 11 healthy games Lamar Jackson played last season, he averaged 21.9 FPs, third overall among QBs. The 2019 MVP's fantasy upside comes from his unparalleled rushing ability. For QBs, he finished 2021 first in rushing attempts and rush yards per game. He has the ability to avoid big hits in the run game and slide when needed, as such, durability hasn't been a big concern for fantasy managers. After averaging a rushing touchdown every two games in 2019 and 2020, Jackson had only 2 TDs in 11 games last season. This number is sure to improve in 2022.

Jackson also regressed as a passer in 2021, ranking 28th in clean-pocket passing. Always seeking the big play downfield, he was first in air yards per catch among QBs with at least eight starts. Baltimore's increased number of pass attempts resulted in Jackson's largest expected fantasy PPG output.

Jackson did lose his No. 1 WR this offseason in the unexpected trade of Hollywood Brown to the Cardinals. Fortunately, Rashod Bateman looked like a reliable option as last season progressed, and will step in as Jackson's new top receiver. The Ravens also return Jackson's favorite target, Mark Andrews, who accounted for 23% of Jackson's completions.

Jackson is only 25 years old, and we don't expect his run-first mentality to change this season. He'll likely never return to his 2019, 28 fantasy PPG average, but 22 PPG feels like a reasonable ask. We will be more than happy to walk away from any draft with him as our QB1, a safe pick with big upside.

YEAR	TEAM	GP	CMP %	PASS YD	PASS TD	INTS	300 YG	RUSH ATT	RUSH YD	RUSH TD	FPPG
2019	BAL	15	66.1	3127	36	6	1	176	1206	7	28.0
2020	BAL	15	64.4	2757	26	9	0	159	1005	7	22.6
2021	BAL	12	64.4	2882	16	13	2	133	767	2	20.2
PROJ	BAL	16	65.0	3478	23	13	2	156	886	5	20.0

QUARTERBACKS
RUNNING BACKS
WIDE RECEIVERS
TIGHT ENDS
KICKERS
D/ST

5 JALEN HURTS

PHILADELPHIA EAGLES (7)

DRAFT: 2020-2(21)　AGE: 24　WT: 223　HT: 6-1　　OKLAHOMA

It seems like the fantasy community has more faith in Jalen Hurts than the Eagles do, as they won't commit to Hurts as the future of the organization. But based almost solely on his rushing upside, Hurts rounds out our top-five QBs.

Last season, Hurts finished seventh in fantasy PPG. The QBs who finished nearest him in fantasy points (Jackson, Rodgers, Murray, and Prescott) all lost their top WR. Hurts, on the other hand, added star receiver A.J. Brown to go along with DeVonta Smith and Dallas Goedert. Ranked second in screen plays last season, expect Hurts to find A.J. Brown quickly and let him use his ridiculous yards-after-the-catch ability to get downfield.

Hurts does have some room to grow in the passing game. He ranked in the bottom five of starting QBs for pass attempts and pass yards per game, although his passing numbers are somewhat deceiving. His on-target percentage is higher than QBs like Tom Brady and Patrick Mahomes. And now with a true No. 1 receiver, his passing production will undoubtedly improve.

Hurts ranked No. 1 in our consistency rankings among the top-10 fantasy QBs, mostly due to his high floor, a result of his rushing numbers. Last Season, He finished second in rushing attempts and rush yards per game, and led all QBs with his 10 rushing TDs.

Hurts is likely to be overlooked this year in drafts, as his fantasy numbers are deceptively high for a QB who averaged just over 200 passing yards a game last season. Let him fall, then snag him.

YEAR	TEAM	GP	CMP %	PASS YD	PASS TD	INTS	300 YG	RUSH ATT	RUSH YD	RUSH TD	FPPG
2020	PHI	15	52.0	1061	6	4	2	63	357	3	7.5
2021	PHI	15	61.3	3144	16	9	2	140	782	10	20.7
PROJ	PHI	16	61.4	3285	23	13	2	135	716	8	19.9

7 KYLER MURRAY

ARIZONA CARDINALS (13)

DRAFT: 2019-1(1)　AGE: 25　WT: 207　HT: 5-10　　OKLAHOMA

On paper, there are reasons to be extremely optimistic about Kyler Murray's 2022 fantasy outlook. First, he has never finished outside the top 10 fantasy QBs in his three-year career. Second, his completion rate has improved year-over-year to second in the NFL last year at 69.2%. Third, his receiving corps improved this offseason with the addition of Baltimore's No. 1 wideout, Hollywood Brown.

But there are some concerns. Murray's rushing production fell drastically last season. He had 24% fewer carries and 41% fewer yards per game than in 2020. He still finished fourth in rushing attempts and rush TDs for 2021, but it feels like his rushing upside has now hit a wall.

Also, his No. 1 receiver, DeAndre Hopkins, won't be eligible until Week 8 after serving a suspension for PEDs. Instant chemistry with newcomer Marquise Brown is unlikely.

Because of his size and rushing prowess, Murray's passing ability is often overlooked, but he's more than capable as a passer. Besides an impressive completion rate, Murray was top-10 in completions per game and yards per game last season.

What worries us the most is that in the biggest game of his short career, his first and only playoff game, he threw for only 137 yards and ran for six, with 0 TDs.

We have Murray a little lower than the consensus for his wide range of possible outcomes. Either way, we won't be disappointed walking away from drafts with Murray as our QB1.

YEAR	TEAM	GP	CMP %	PASS YD	PASS TD	INTS	300 YG	RUSH ATT	RUSH YD	RUSH TD	FPPG
2019	ARI	16	64.4	3722	20	12	5	93	544	4	17.7
2020	ARI	16	67.2	3971	26	12	3	133	819	11	24.2
2021	ARI	14	69.2	3787	24	10	3	88	423	5	21.4
PROJ	ARI	17	67.7	4141	26	14	4	101	504	5	18.9

6 TOM BRADY

TAMPA BAY BUCCANEERS (11)

DRAFT: 2000-6(33)　AGE: 45　WT: 225　HT: 6-4　　MICHIGAN

The GOAT continues to defy Father Time. In 2021, only one QB averaged more fantasy PPG than Brady. Moreover, Brady recorded career highs (20-year career!) in pass attempts, completions, completion rate, passing yards, and TDs. He even managed to record 81 rushing yards.

Brady's limited mobility is still not a problem. He compensates by getting the ball out quickly, second fastest in the league last season. Counterintuitively, his in-air yards per target is a solid 8.1, middle of the road among QBs.

But Brady is human. Last season, he lead all QBs in poor throws per game, partly because he was the fourth highest blitzed QB. Because of Brady's field awareness and Tampa Bay's strong offensive line, Brady suffered fewer sacks per game than any other starting QB, despite the high blitz rate.

Because his numbers were elevated in 2021, we are calling for a slight regression in 2022. For example, a remarkable 41% of his red zone completions went for a TD. And though Brady has a large say in the offense, the change of head coach from Bruce Arians to Todd Bowles may equate to a more balanced offensive scheme for the 2021's most pass-heavy offense.

Brady, who is essentially a one-dimensional QB (without rushing upside), could have another standout year but land outside the top-five in fantasy QBs. He's a mid-tier QB1, but with a very high floor. We've given up on calling for his production decline, and will be happy to have Brady on any of our teams.

YEAR	TEAM	GP	CMP %	PASS YD	PASS TD	INTS	300 YG	RUSH ATT	RUSH YD	RUSH TD	FPPG
2019	NE	16	60.8	4057	24	8	5	26	34	3	16.5
2020	TB	16	65.7	4633	40	12	7	30	6	3	21.2
2021	TB	17	67.5	5316	43	12	9	28	81	2	22.4
PROJ	TB	17	66.1	4801	35	12	7	29	50	2	19.1

8 DAK PRESCOTT

DALLAS COWBOYS (9)

DRAFT: 2016-4(37)　AGE: 29　WT: 238　HT: 6-2　　MISSISSIPPI STATE

Dak Prescott was on pace for a record-breaking fantasy year in 2020 before a season-ending broken leg in Week 5. Although 2021 was an impressive comeback, especially in passing production, Prescott's rushing took a hit.

He recorded career lows in rushing attempts per game, rushing yards per game, and rushing TDs. This is likely a combination of coaching strategy to protect their QB and skittishness after his gruesome injury. Either way, we're predicting an increase in rushing yards and rushing TDs in 2022 now that Prescott has had a year to regain his confidence.

His passing in 2021, on the other hand, was arguably the best of his career. He posted career highs in completion rate (67.1%), TDs (37), and attempts (596). He did take fewer deep shots than in years past, but this helped his 3.7-1, TD-to-interception ratio. He also had the fourth most red zone completions (62) and converted 26 of them into TDs.

Dallas finished sixth in total pass attempts last season and return their pass-friendly offensive coordinator, Kellen Moore. The loss of Amari Cooper doesn't concern us too much, as he still has an impressive receiving corps led by CeeDee Lamb. But he did lose two key pieces in his offensive line — La'el Collins and Connor Williams.

Because of his limited rushing upside, his ceiling may not be as high as a player like Kyler Murray. He's a mid-tier QB1 that fantasy managers hope can get his rushing groove back.

YEAR	TEAM	GP	CMP %	PASS YD	PASS TD	INTS	300 YG	RUSH ATT	RUSH YD	RUSH TD	FPPG
2019	DAL	16	65.1	4902	30	11	7	52	277	3	21.2
2020	DAL	5	68.0	1856	9	4	3	18	93	3	25.9
2021	DAL	16	68.8	4449	37	10	5	48	146	1	20.4
PROJ	DAL	17	66.9	4555	33	13	4	54	189	2	18.8

QUARTERBACKS

RUNNING BACKS

WIDE RECEIVERS

TIGHT ENDS

KICKERS

D/ST

9 | AARON RODGERS

GREEN BAY **PACKERS** (14)

DRAFT: 2005-1(24) AGE: 38 WT: 225 HT: 6-2

CALIFORNIA

This QB has finished 13 of the last 14 seasons as a top-10 QB in fantasy PPG. Who is Aaron Rodgers? See what we did there? After a stressful offseason for Packers fans, Rodgers inked a new three-year, $150 million deal.

Last season's MVP produced another top-five fantasy campaign, even after a significant drop from his unsustainable 2020 output. Rodgers continues to be efficient, finishing 2021 as a top-five QB in both TDs and completion rate. He also had a league best 9.25-1 TD-to-interception ratio.

It hurts losing Davante Adams who accounted for 34% of Rodgers' completions last season, but Rodgers has the tendency to turn no-name receivers into stars. Rank him outside your top-10 QBs if you dare.

YEAR	TEAM	GP	CMP %	PASS YD	PASS TD	INTS	300 YG	RUSH ATT	RUSH YD	RUSH TD	FPPG
2019	GB	16	62.0	4002	26	4	4	46	183	1	17.5
2020	GB	16	70.7	4299	48	5	5	38	149	3	24.2
2021	GB	16	68.9	4115	37	4	4	33	101	3	20.8
PROJ	GB	17	67.0	4261	34	8	4	36	121	2	18.5

10 | RUSSELL WILSON

DENVER **BRONCOS** (9)

DRAFT: 2012-3(12) AGE: 33 WT: 215 HT: 5-11

WISCONSIN

Russell Wilson looked unmotivated most of last season after there was speculation he wanted out of Seattle. He got his wish this offseason when he was traded to Denver for extensive draft capital.

Wilson posted eight straight top-10 fantasy finishes before last year's anomaly. The only thing that carried over to last season was Wilson's love of the big play — he had a league-high 9.9 in-air yards per pass attempt. Wilson joins an offense in Denver with plenty of weapons at his disposal: Courtland Sutton, who loves catching the deep ball; Jerry Jeudy, who showed strong ability as a rookie; and Javonte Williams, who should lead the backfield.

The 34-year-old will get back on track in Denver. Draft him, and watch Russ cook. He's a fringe QB1 with a solid floor.

YEAR	TEAM	GP	CMP %	PASS YD	PASS TD	INTS	300 YG	RUSH ATT	RUSH YD	RUSH TD	FPPG
2019	SEA	16	66.1	4110	31	5	3	75	342	3	20.7
2020	SEA	16	68.8	4212	40	13	5	83	513	2	22.9
2021	SEA	14	64.8	3113	25	6	1	43	183	2	17.3
PROJ	DEN	17	64.7	4206	31	11	4	63	284	2	18.3

11 | TREY LANCE

SAN FRANCISCO **49ERS** (9)

DRAFT: 2021-1(3) AGE: 22 WT: 224 HT: 6-4

NORTH DAKOTA STATE

Trey Lance is one of the few who will be drafted outside the top 10 QBs who has the potential to finish inside the top five. The 2020 third overall pick, one-season college starter had only three starts last season. In those games, he averaged 17.3 fantasy PPG, which would have been 13th overall among QBs. While the sample size is small, fantasy manager's caught a glimpse of Lance's potential in those three starts — he averaged 54 rushing yards and 10 rushing attempts per game, which will provide a nice fantasy floor.

At just 22 years old, the 6-foot 4, 224-pound QB has the potential to be the next Josh Allen. With playmakers Deebo Samuel, Brandon Aiyuk, and George Kittle, along with Kyle Shannahan directing traffic, Lance is on our shortlist of QB breakout candidates. We wouldn't be surprised if he ends up being 2021's Jalen Hurts (ADP of QB11, finish of QB7).

YEAR	TEAM	GP	CMP %	PASS YD	PASS TD	INTS	300 YG	RUSH ATT	RUSH YD	RUSH TD	FPPG
2021	SF	6	57.7	603	5	2	0	38	168	1	10.5
PROJ	SF	17	62.8	3811	24	14	2	115	564	5	18.0

12 | JOE BURROW

CINCINNATI **BENGALS** (10)

DRAFT: 2020-1(1) AGE: 25 WT: 221 HT: 6-4

LSU

Joe Burrow, without a doubt, had a sensational 2021 season. He finished 1 TD shy of the Lombardi Trophy while leading all QBs with a 70% completion rate. And he did all this behind an offensive line who gave up the most sacks last season (51), including 11 in a playoff game to Indy, that Cincinnati won.

Burrow is the prime example of a great football player who's only a good fantasy player. Even with such an impressive season, Burrow only finished as the 10th best QB in fantasy PPG. According to Next Gen Stats, his completion rate was a full 6 points higher than expected, one of many metrics we can expect regression in for 2022.

There's no doubt that Burrow will have another impressive season with the best WR duo in the game. But remember to draft the fantasy player, not the football player.

YEAR	TEAM	GP	CMP %	PASS YD	PASS TD	INTS	300 YG	RUSH ATT	RUSH YD	RUSH TD	FPPG
2020	CIN	10	65.3	2688	13	5	5	37	142	3	18.2
2021	CIN	16	70.4	4611	34	14	6	40	118	2	19.8
PROJ	CIN	17	67.0	4451	32	14	5	47	160	2	18.0

13 | MATTHEW STAFFORD

LOS ANGELES **RAMS** (7)

DRAFT: 2009-1(1) AGE: 34 WT: 220 HT: 6-3

GEORGIA

In his first year as a Ram, Matthew Stafford won a Super Bowl and was rewarded with a three-year, $129 million extension. He finished sixth overall in fantasy points among QBs, but only 11th in fantasy PPG. Stafford's value comes from his passing numbers — he finished ninth in passing attempts per game (23.8), fourth in passing yards per game (287), and second in TDs per game (2.4).

Even with the return of his No. 1 partner in crime, Cooper Kupp, and offseason addition Allen Robinson II, Stafford is likely to regress in both yards and TDs. A healthy Cam Akers may also add more balance to an extremely pass-heavy offense.

With zero rushing upside and some passing regression, Stafford's a borderline QB1 or a good matchup play.

YEAR	TEAM	GP	CMP %	PASS YD	PASS TD	INTS	300 YG	RUSH ATT	RUSH YD	RUSH TD	FPPG
2019	DET	8	64.3	2499	19	5	4	20	66	0	21.6
2020	DET	16	64.2	4084	26	10	3	29	112	0	16.2
2021	LAR	17	67.2	4886	41	17	7	32	43	0	19.4
PROJ	LAR	17	67.7	4574	33	17	6	39	81	2	17.7

14 | TUA TAGOVAILOA

MIAMI **DOLPHINS** (11)

DRAFT: 2020-1(5) AGE: 24 WT: 217 HT: 6-1

ALABAMA

Tua Tagovailoa is in for a fantasy boost in 2022, but the question is, how big of boost? Tua has many things going for him this season. First, Miami shored up their offensive line with two key additions, Conner Williams and Terron Armstead. And, of course, they added "peace-out", flyby WR Tyreek Hill to join rookie standout Jaylen Waddle. Also, former 49ers offensive coordinator, Mike McDaniel, Miami's new head coach, has shown he knows how to utilize his playmakers (e.g. Deebo Samuel). Tua might finally be in store for a breakout season.

Tua's past fantasy performances are abysmal, finishing 26th in fantasy points last season, including a bottom-five finish in 20-plus yard plays. Perhaps, with Hill in the fold and with a new coach, Tua will be more apt to take shots downfield. Take a chance on Tua for his upside as your second QB in drafts.

YEAR	TEAM	GP	CMP %	PASS YD	PASS TD	INTS	300 YG	RUSH ATT	RUSH YD	RUSH TD	FPPG
2020	MIA	10	64.1	1814	11	5	2	36	109	3	13.5
2021	MIA	13	67.8	2653	16	10	1	42	128	3	13.9
PROJ	MIA	16	66.3	3885	26	14	3	49	170	3	17.0

15 DESHAUN WATSON

CLEVELAND BROWNS (9)

DRAFT: 2017-1(12) AGE: 26 WT: 215 HT: 6-2
CLEMSON

Deshaun Watson is now a Brown after sitting out all of 2021 and being traded to Cleveland this offseason. The off-field issues that kept Watson off the gridiron last season have now resulted in a six-game suspension for the star QB.

Watson has been a top-six fantasy QB in fantasy PPG all four of his seasons, leading the NFL in passing yards and yards per pass attempt. A true dual-threat QB, Watson has also finished top six among QBs in rushing yards his last three seasons.

Behind an outstanding offensive line and with an average group of pass catchers led by Amari Cooper, Watson will put up top-10 numbers when he gets on the field (likely Week 7 against the Ravens). We'll look to draft Watson once we know we have a guaranteed playoff-ready fantasy team.

YEAR	TEAM	GP	CMP %	PASS YD	PASS TD	INTS	300 YG	RUSH ATT	RUSH YD	RUSH TD	FPPG
2019	HOU	15	67.3	3852	26	12	3	85	413	7	21.2
2020	HOU	16	70.2	4823	33	7	10	90	444	3	23.3
2021	HOU		DID NOT PLAY								
PROJ	CLE	11	65.4	2681	18	9	3	68	341	3	19.4

16 DEREK CARR

LAS VEGAS RAIDERS (6)

DRAFT: 2014-2(4) AGE: 31 WT: 210 HT: 6-3
FRESNO STATE

Derek Carr had his best fantasy season to-date in 2021. He posted career highs in pass attempts and passing yards, and finished top five for QBs in completions per game (25.2) and yards per game (283). Yet, he finished as only the 16th best QB in fantasy PPG.

Carr's fantasy deficiency comes from his lack of rushing production, which is deceptively low for a QB as mobile in the pocket as Carr. Only 4% of his fantasy points last season came from rushing. The addition of Davante Adams to a receiving corps that already boasts Hunter Renfrow and Darren Waller should boost Carr's value and increase his fantasy production, especially his TD numbers. In 2022, he's a solid QB2 and should have multiple top-10 finishes during the season.

YEAR	TEAM	GP	CMP %	PASS YD	PASS TD	INTS	300 YG	RUSH ATT	RUSH YD	RUSH TD	FPPG
2019	LV	16	70.4	4054	21	8	1	27	82	2	15.6
2020	LV	16	67.3	4103	27	9	6	39	140	3	17.9
2021	LV	17	68.4	4804	23	14	6	40	108	0	15.7
PROJ	LV	17	67.6	4754	27	15	7	34	106	1	16.8

17 KIRK COUSINS

MINNESOTA VIKINGS (7)

DRAFT: 2012-4(7) AGE: 34 WT: 205 HT: 6-3
MICHIGAN STATE

No one's going to tell you "good pick" (and mean it) for drafting Kirk Cousins. Though he's never finished as a top-10 QB in fantasy PPG, he's been in the top 12 QBs six of his last seven seasons. Last season he ranked no lower than 12th among QBs in pass attempts per game, passing TDs, and fantasy PPG.

Cousins is extremely efficient in the red zone, converting 50% of his red zone completions into TDs. It helps that he has multiple dynamic weapons at his disposal — Justin Jefferson, Adam Thielen, and Dalvin Cook. Cousins may even see more passing volume in 2022 with new head coach Kevin O'Connell at the helm.

With little rushing upside, Cousins has a narrow range of outcomes, but he feels safe to finish in that 10-15 range again. If you get him as your second QB, good pick!

YEAR	TEAM	GP	CMP %	PASS YD	PASS TD	INTS	300 YG	RUSH ATT	RUSH YD	RUSH TD	FPPG
2019	MIN	15	69.1	3603	26	6	4	31	63	1	16.6
2020	MIN	16	67.6	4265	35	13	5	32	156	1	19.1
2021	MIN	16	66.3	4221	33	7	6	29	115	1	19.0
PROJ	MIN	17	65.5	4259	30	11	5	29	102	1	16.7

18 JUSTIN FIELDS

CHICAGO BEARS (14)

DRAFT: 2021-1(11) AGE: 23 WT: 228 HT: 6-3
OHIO STATE

In Justin Fields' last four full starts in 2021, he averaged over 23 fantasy PPG, just below fantasy's No. 1 QB, Josh Allen. While these numbers aren't yet sustainable for Fields, it provides a glimpse of the upside of the dual-threat QB.

Fields' advantage, like most elite fantasy QBs, comes from his rushing production. He averaged the most scrambles per game of any QB last season, and a remarkable 40% of his total fantasy points on the year came from rushing. He's also a look-deep-first passer, which correlates to big plays, averaging 9.1 in-air yards per attempt (second among QBs).

Without Matt Nagy and his stale play calling to hold him back, Fields will take a step forward in 2022 and have a handful of top-10 weekly finishes. We expect the Bears' new regime to find better ways to utilize the strengths of their QB. He may not be worth drafting, but keep an eye on him early.

YEAR	TEAM	GP	CMP %	PASS YD	PASS TD	INTS	300 YG	RUSH ATT	RUSH YD	RUSH TD	FPPG
2021	CHI	12	58.9	1870	7	10	0	72	420	2	11.4
PROJ	CHI	17	62.6	3621	20	18	2	100	541	4	15.7

19 JAMEIS WINSTON

NEW ORLEANS SAINTS (14)

DRAFT: 2015-1(1) AGE: 28 WT: 231 HT: 6-4
FLORIDA STATE

Jameis Winston, in six healthy games before a Week 7 season-ending ACL tear last year, averaged 18.2 fantasy PPG, 13th best for QBs on the year.

Hoping to prevent the return of 2019, 30-interception Winston, the Saints were careful with play calling, emphasizing ball security. As a result, he finished at the bottom of the league in every passing-per-game metric, except TDs where he was 10th on a per-game basis. But he had top-12 numbers in rushing attempts per game and rush yards per game last season. With a much-improved supporting cast in 2022, that includes Michael Thomas and first round pick, Chris Olave, Winston's totals should improve. Winston has some deceptively solid numbers and may be worth a look on waivers.

YEAR	TEAM	GP	CMP %	PASS YD	PASS TD	INTS	300 YG	RUSH ATT	RUSH YD	RUSH TD	FPPG
2019	TB	16	60.7	5109	33	30	11	59	250	1	19.2
2020	NO	4	63.6	75	0	0	0	8	-6	0	0.6
2021	NO	7	59.0	1170	14	3	0	32	166	1	17.1
PROJ	NO	17	62.7	3645	25	13	2	71	320	2	15.5

20 TREVOR LAWRENCE

JACKSONVILLE JAGUARS (11)

DRAFT: 2021-1(1) AGE: 22 WT: 213 HT: 6-6
CLEMSON

The 2021 No. 1 overall draft pick enters his second season in Jacksonville, after a dreadful 3-14 year was overshadowed by the Urban Meyer circus.

The bad: Among QBs, Lawrence finished an abysmal 34th in fantasy PPG. He also had the third highest bad throw percentage and led the league in interceptions, recording a dreadful 60% completion rate.

The good: He finished with high volumes in both passing and rushing. He was eighth in pass attempts and sixth in rushing attempts among QBs.

A new coaching regime, along with new playmakers (Christian Kirk, Evan Engram, and Travis Etienne Jr.), should provide some breakout potential for Lawrence. Among QBs, expect Lawrence to have the biggest year-to-year jump in fantasy points, but we're not quite ready to draft him yet.

YEAR	TEAM	GP	CMP %	PASS YD	PASS TD	INTS	300 YG	RUSH ATT	RUSH YD	RUSH TD	FPPG
2021	JAC	17	59.6	3641	12	17	2	73	334	2	12.1
PROJ	JAC	17	63.4	3963	22	15	2	72	326	2	15.4

QUARTERBACKS

RUNNING BACKS

WIDE RECEIVERS

TIGHT ENDS

KICKERS

D/ST

21 RYAN TANNEHILL

TENNESSEE TITANS (6)

DRAFT: 2012-1(8) AGE: 34 WT: 217 HT: 6-4 TEXAS A&M

Ryan Tannehill has quietly finished as a top-15 QB in fantasy PPG the last three seasons. He did take a step back in 2021 in passing yards, passing TDs, and interceptions. Tannehill's passing upside is limited, playing on the team that led the NFL in rushing attempts in 2021. But he's is a surprisingly capable rusher, with back-to-back 7 TD seasons. With Malik Willis at his heels and the departure of lead receiver A.J. Brown, Tannehill's outlook is unimproved for 2022.

YEAR	TEAM	GP	CMP %	PASS YD	PASS TD	INTS	300 YG	RUSH ATT	RUSH YD	RUSH TD	FPPG
2019	TEN	12	70.3	2742	22	6	3	43	185	4	19.0
2020	TEN	16	65.5	3819	33	7	2	43	266	7	21.2
2021	TEN	17	67.2	3734	21	14	2	55	270	7	16.1
PROJ	TEN	17	66.3	3548	24	15	1	53	247	4	15.1

22 DANIEL JONES

NEW YORK GIANTS (9)

DRAFT: 2019-1(6) AGE: 25 WT: 230 HT: 6-5 DUKE

New head coach Brian Daboll is hoping Daniel Jones can be his new Josh Allen, saying Jones needs to "turn it loose" more. Jones posted three top-10 finishes in his first four games last season, but was dreadfully inconsistent the rest of the season, finishing as QB20 in fantasy PPG. Durability is a concern, as he has missed multiple games in each of his four seasons. Jones is a very capable rusher, posting top-10 numbers in attempts and YPG. Even so, Jones should only be a streaming option.

YEAR	TEAM	GP	CMP %	PASS YD	PASS TD	INTS	300 YG	RUSH ATT	RUSH YD	RUSH TD	FPPG
2019	NYG	13	61.9	3027	24	12	5	45	279	2	17.9
2020	NYG	14	62.5	2943	11	10	0	65	423	1	13.6
2021	NYG	11	64.3	2428	10	7	1	62	298	2	15.0
PROJ	NYG	17	61.6	3644	21	15	2	85	431	2	15.0

23 MATT RYAN

INDIANAPOLIS COLTS (14)

DRAFT: 2008-1(3) AGE: 37 WT: 217 HT: 6-4 BOSTON COLLEGE

After 14 seasons in Atlanta, Matt Ryan was traded to Indy. Ironically, his fantasy outlook is diminished even though he's on a better team. Ryan's fantasy output is dependent on volume, something a run-heavy Colts team won't provide. Extra scoring opportunities will help to counter the lack of volume. He finished outside the top-10 QBs in FPs five of the last seven seasons. There's a chance that a 30-plus TD season could vault Ryan into the QB2 range, but we're looking for better upside elsewhere.

YEAR	TEAM	GP	CMP %	PASS YD	PASS TD	INTS	300 YG	RUSH ATT	RUSH YD	RUSH TD	FPPG
2019	ATL	15	66.2	4466	26	14	11	34	147	1	18.4
2020	ATL	16	65.0	4581	26	11	5	29	92	2	17.9
2021	ATL	17	67.0	3968	20	12	3	40	82	1	13.5
PROJ	IND	17	64.5	3692	26	12	2	45	137	2	14.9

24 MAC JONES

NEW ENGLAND PATRIOTS (10)

DRAFT: 2021-1(15) AGE: 23 WT: 217 HT: 6-3 ALABAMA

Mac Jones led all rookie QBs in fantasy PPG. But overall, Jones finished in the bottom half in pass attempts, passing yards, YPA, and rushing attempts. He did have an impressive 67.6% completion rate (ninth overall). Like many QBs in the back of our rankings, Jones offers little with his legs. His rushing only accounted for a meager 5% of his total FPs. The Patriots did add WR DeVante Parker to a unimpressive receiving corps, which may help. Jones did have four top-10 finishes in his last eight games. Unfortunately, even with elite efficiency, he won't be able to overcome volume and rushing limitations to make our rosters.

YEAR	TEAM	GP	CMP %	PASS YD	PASS TD	INTS	300 YG	RUSH ATT	RUSH YD	RUSH TD	FPPG
2021	NE	17	67.6	3801	22	13	2	44	129	0	13.3
PROJ	NE	17	65.9	3945	24	14	3	38	140	1	14.5

25 ZACH WILSON

NEW YORK JETS (10)

DRAFT: 2021-1(2) AGE: 23 WT: 214 HT: 6-2 BYU

Among QBs in 2021, Wilson finished almost last in every metric, including FPs, highlighted by a league low 55.6% completion rate. His in-head clock is not fast enough yet, recording the longest time to throw in the league. It's hard to feel excited about Wilson as a fantasy player. But the Jets improved this offseason, including at the skill positions, adding WR Garrett Wilson and RB Breece Hall in the draft. Also, Wilson improved as the 2021 season went on, scoring 9 of his 14 TDs in his last seven games. Even if Wilson makes the typical Year1 to Year 2 jump, he should be available on waivers in most leagues.

YEAR	TEAM	GP	CMP %	PASS YD	PASS TD	INTS	300 YG	RUSH ATT	RUSH YD	RUSH TD	FPPG
2021	NYJ	13	55.6	2334	9	11	0	29	185	4	11.5
PROJ											

26 DAVIS MILLS

HOUSTON TEXANS (6)

DRAFT: 2021-3(3) AGE: 23 WT: 225 HT: 6-4 STANFORD

Davis Mills was fortunate, in a way, to end up in a chaotic Houston, because the 2021 third-round draft pick was able to earn the starting position.

Mills looked serviceable in his rookie year. In his 11 starts, he finished 30th among QBs in fantasy PPG, but he did have four top-10 finishes. His fantasy value comes solely from his passing numbers, as his rushing production was non-existent. With little more than journeyman Brandin Cooks in his supporting cast, and on one of the lowest scoring teams in the NFL, he's a long shot to be fantasy relevant this season.

YEAR	TEAM	GP	CMP %	PASS YD	PASS TD	INTS	300 YG	RUSH ATT	RUSH YD	RUSH TD	FPPG
2021	HOU	13	66.8	2664	16	10	4	18	44	0	11.9
PROJ	HOU	17	64.9	3883	22	16	3	29	92	1	13.3

27 MARCUS MARIOTA

ATLANTA FALCONS (14)

DRAFT: 2015-1(2) AGE: 28 WT: 222 HT: 6-4 OREGON

Even if Mariota can hold off third-round pick Desmond Ridder, he's only had one game with more than 1 pass attempt since 2019. In 2020, in the one game he played extended snaps, he was impressive — 226 passing yards and a TD, and 88 yards on the ground for a TD. He brings a dual-threat element that the Falcons lacked with Ryan under center. But even as a starter, he never recoded a top-13 fantasy campaign. In a tear-down/rebuild Atlanta, Mariota's off our draft board.

YEAR	TEAM	GP	CMP %	PASS YD	PASS TD	INTS	300 YG	RUSH ATT	RUSH YD	RUSH TD	FPPG
2019	TEN	7	59.4	1203	7	2	1	24	129	0	12.1
2020	LV	1	60.7	226	1	1	0	9	88	1	25.8
2021	LV	7	50.0	4	0	0	1	13	87	1	2.1
PROJ	ATL	17	63.8	3425	19	13	1	59	345	2	13.7

28 JARED GOFF

DETROIT LIONS (6)

DRAFT: 2016-1(1) AGE: 27 WT: 217 HT: 6-4 CALIFORNIA

Goff's fantasy value comes exclusively from his passing production. In 2021, he finished in the top half of QBs in pass attempts per game, completion rate, and TDs per game. His decent volume is a result of playing from behind. Conversely, he was bottom five in YPA and aDOT, and had the fewest 40-plus yard plays among all QBs. The offseason addition of DJ Chark Jr., who joins Amon Ra St. Brown and T.J. Hockenson, should give Goff better production, but likely not enough to matter.

YEAR	TEAM	GP	CMP %	PASS YD	PASS TD	INTS	300 YG	RUSH ATT	RUSH YD	RUSH TD	FPPG
2019	LAR	16	62.9	4638	22	16	6	33	40	2	16.1
2020	LAR	15	67	3952	20	13	6	51	99	4	16.4
2021	DET	14	67.2	3245	19	8	1	17	87	0	14.2
PROJ	DET	17	66.0	3541	24	13	2	27	85	1	13.3

2021 ADVANCED RUNNING BACK STATS

		GP	RUSHING							RECEIVING	
			YBC/A	YAC/A	BRKTKL	TK LOSS	20+ YDS	40+ YDS	LONG	RZ TGT	YAC
1	JONATHAN TAYLOR (IND)	17	2.6	2.8	25	32	14	5	83	2	93
2	AUSTIN EKELER (LAC)	16	2.3	2.1	13	16	3	0	28	16	172
3	JOE MIXON (CIN)	16	2.2	1.9	20	24	6	0	32	7	55
4	NAJEE HARRIS (PIT)	17	1.7	2.2	30	26	6	0	37	14	219
5	JAMES CONNER (ARI)	15	1.6	2.1	19	14	3	0	35	1	145
6	EZEKIEL ELLIOTT (DAL)	17	2.5	1.7	9	16	3	1	47	14	66
7	NICK CHUBB (CLE)	14	2.5	3	23	20	12	2	70	1	52
8	LEONARD FOURNETTE (TB)	14	2.2	2.3	11	12	5	1	47	15	163
9	CORDARRELLE PATTERSON (ATL)	16	2.1	1.9	7	10	2	0	39	12	170
10	DAMIEN HARRIS (NE)	15	2.3	2.3	15	19	8	1	64	2	19
11	AARON JONES (GB)	15	2.4	2.3	12	15	5	1	57	15	90
12	DERRICK HENRY (TEN)	8	2.1	2.2	10	21	3	2	76	2	26
13	ALVIN KAMARA (NO)	13	2.3	1.5	22	28	3	0	30	12	87
14	ANTONIO GIBSON (WAS)	16	2.1	1.9	19	21	4	0	27	6	131
15	DALVIN COOK (MIN)	13	2.7	2	16	35	9	1	66	1	53
16	JAVONTE WILLIAMS (DEN)	17	2.2	2.3	31	21	6	1	49	7	91
17	MELVIN GORDON III (DEN)	16	2.3	2.2	20	19	3	2	70	5	36
18	JOSH JACOBS (LV)	15	2	2	20	16	2	0	28	5	93
19	DAVID MONTGOMERY (CHI)	13	1.9	1.9	16	25	5	1	41	7	52
20	AJ DILLON (GB)	17	2.1	2.2	17	8	2	0	36	5	111
21	DARREL WILLIAMS (KC)	17	2.4	1.5	4	12	1	0	21	10	81
22	JAMES ROBINSON (JAC)	14	2.7	1.9	11	12	4	1	58	2	55
23	ELIJAH MITCHELL (SF)	11	2.2	2.5	17	20	6	0	39	1	52
24	D'ANDRE SWIFT (DET)	13	2.5	1.5	9	16	3	1	57	8	122
25	DEVIN SINGLETARY (BUF)	17	2.3	2.3	13	12	6	2	46	6	69
26	DARRELL HENDERSON JR. (LAR)	12	2.7	1.9	3	6	1	0	29	9	42
27	MYLES GASKIN (MIA)	17	2.1	1.4	7	16	2	0	30	9	66
28	TONY POLLARD (DAL)	15	3.1	2.5	7	4	4	1	58	7	101
29	SONY MICHEL (LAR)	17	2.1	1.9	16	13	2	0	39	2	52
30	MICHAEL CARTER (NYJ)	14	2	2.3	13	15	3	1	55	2	103
31	DEVONTA FREEMAN (BAL)	16	2.8	1.5	3	16	4	0	32	8	45
32	SAQUON BARKLEY (NYG)	13	1.9	1.7	4	19	3	1	41	3	54

2022 PPR RANKINGS

		BYE	
1.	IND	14	JONATHAN TAYLOR
2.	CAR	13	CHRISTIAN MCCAFFREY
3.	LAC	8	AUSTIN EKELER
4.	TEN	6	DERRICK HENRY
5.	PIT	9	NAJEE HARRIS
6.	NO	14	ALVIN KAMARA
7.	TB	11	LEONARD FOURNETTE
8.	MIN	7	DALVIN COOK
9.	DET	6	D'ANDRE SWIFT
10.	CIN	10	JOE MIXON
11.	GB	14	AARON JONES
12.	ARI	13	JAMES CONNER
13.	CHI	14	DAVID MONTGOMERY
14.	NYG	9	SAQUON BARKLEY
15.	DEN	9	JAVONTE WILLIAMS
16.	CLE	9	NICK CHUBB
17.	LAR	7	CAM AKERS
18.	DAL	9	EZEKIEL ELLIOTT
19.	WAS	14	ANTONIO GIBSON
20.	LV	6	JOSH JACOBS
21.	JAC	11	TRAVIS ETIENNE JR.
22.	BAL	10	J.K. DOBBINS
23.	NYJ	10	BREECE HALL
24.	SF	9	ELIJAH MITCHELL
25.	PHI	7	MILES SANDERS
26.	KC	8	CLYDE EDWARDS-HELAIRE
27.	BUF	7	DEVIN SINGLETARY
28.	CLE	9	KAREEM HUNT
29.	NE	10	DAMIEN HARRIS
30.	DAL	9	TONY POLLARD
31.	MIA	11	CHASE EDMONDS
32.	DEN	9	MELVIN GORDON III
33.	GB	14	AJ DILLON
34.	ATL	14	CORDARRELLE PATTERSON
35.	SEA	11	KEN WALKER III
36.	SEA	11	RASHAAD PENNY
37.	NYJ	10	MICHAEL CARTER
38.	NE	10	RHAMONDRE STEVENSON
39.	BUF	7	JAMES COOK
40.	JAC	11	JAMES ROBINSON
41.	MIN	7	ALEXANDER MATTISON
42.	KC	8	RONALD JONES II
43.	WAS	14	J.D. MCKISSIC
44.	IND	14	NYHEIM HINES
45.	DET	6	JAMAAL WILLIAMS
46.	MIA	11	RAHEEM MOSTERT
47.	HOU	6	DAMEON PIERCE
48.	ATL	14	TYLER ALLGEIER
49.	BAL	10	GUS EDWARDS
50.	NE	10	JAMES WHITE
51.	PHI	7	KENNETH GAINWELL
52.	LAR	7	DARRELL HENDERSON JR.
53.	HOU	6	MARLON MACK
54.	LAC	8	ISAIAH SPILLER
55.	TB	11	RACHAAD WHITE
56.	MIA	11	SONY MICHEL

QUARTERBACKS

RUNNING BACKS

WIDE RECEIVERS

TIGHT ENDS

KICKERS

D/ST

1 JONATHAN TAYLOR

INDIANAPOLIS COLTS (14)

DRAFT: 2020-2(9)   AGE: 23   WT: 226   HT: 5-10   WISCONSIN

➤ Taylor had more fantasy points than any other player, including QBs, last season, and 30 more fantasy points than the next closest RB. Among RBs, Taylor's touches per game (22) and fantasy PPG (22.18) were second only to Derrick Henry.

While there may be a slight regression this year in Taylor's TD output, Coach Reich has shown he is committed to running Taylor in the red zone, with 39 more attempts (85 total) inside the 20 than the next closest RB in 2021.

We don't expect the addition of Matt Ryan to affect Taylor's role. Ryan's limited mobility may even lead to a few more check-downs. Receptions is one of the few areas where Taylor can improve. Although he averaged almost a target per game more than in his rookie season, he finished 36th among RBs in receptions per game last season. While Ryan, a better passing QB than Wentz, may cause a slight reduction in the red zone run-play rate, he should also provide more scoring opportunities.

Fantasy managers who worried about Nyheim Hines' role eating into Taylor's, especially on third down, worry no more. A healthy Hines averaged fewer than 8 touches per game. Hines' role even decreased as the season went on, with Taylor on the field for 81% of the snaps in the last eight games of the season and Hines' touches at fewer than 4 per game.

At 23 years old, Taylor's consistency and high floor in a run-first offense make him a safe player to take with your first pick, although he probably won't be there unless you pick first overall.

YEAR	TEAM	GP	RUSH ATT	RUSH YD	YD/ATT	RUSH TD	100 YG	TAR	REC	REC YD	REC TD	FPPG
2020	IND	15	232	1169	5	11	3	39	36	299	1	17
2021	IND	17	332	1811	5.5	18	10	53	40	360	2	22.2
PROJ	IND	17	323	1614	5.0	14	9	58	43	365	2	19.8

2 CHRISTIAN MCCAFFREY

CAROLINA PANTHERS (13)

DRAFT: 2017-1(8)   AGE: 26   WT: 205   HT: 5-11   STANFORD

➤ Our team agrees on one thing: a healthy CMC could be the top fantasy-point earner of 2022. With only 10 games played in the last two seasons and an ADP of 1, fantasy managers are becoming weary of drafting McCaffrey. This means he could be there in the middle of Round 1 or later, where you should jump at the chance to roster him.

Even in 2021, in his five healthy games, CMC averaged 23.6 fantasy PPG, second only to Derrick Henry who had 9 more TDs, but played only one more game. CMC did so in an atrocious offense with sub-par offensive-line play. With only 2 TDs in seven games, one can be assured his TDs will improve.

CMC played 80% of the snaps before last year's injury, and Coach Matt Rhule has shown no signs of tapering CMC's role to preserve his star player. In fact, Rhule dismissed talk of moving CMC to the slot to protect him, saying he would remain in the backfield where he's most effective.

CMC finished 2021 as the RB1 in receptions and yards per game. He averaged more YPC than Henry, while facing a stacked box 37% of the time (more than Henry, Taylor, and Cook). CMC even improved Darnold's average QB rating by 40 points when throwing to him, and averaged an impressive seven yards after the catch.

CMC is as bust-proof as they come. The question is, do you believe he is injury prone or just unlucky? We're leaning toward the latter and we'll be taking him early and often in our leagues.

YEAR	TEAM	GP	RUSH ATT	RUSH YD	YD/ATT	RUSH TD	100 YG	TAR	REC	REC YD	REC TD	FPPG
2019	CAR	16	287	1387	4.8	15	6	142	116	1005	4	29.3
2020	CAR	3	59	225	3.8	5	0	19	17	149	1	30.1
2021	CAR	7	99	442	4.5	1	0	41	37	343	1	18.2
PROJ	CAR	15	215	907	4.2	6	4	109	88	696	3	20.1

3 AUSTIN EKELER

LOS ANGELES CHARGERS (8)

DRAFT: 2016-UNDRFT   AGE: 27   WT: 200   HT: 5-10   WESTERN STATE, COLORADO

➤ Austin Ekeler embraces his fantasy managers, advising 2022 drafters to make him their No. 1 overall pick, promising a weekly output of over 20 fantasy points. Ekeler is not too far off with his No. 1 pick advice. He finished 2021 as the second-best fantasy RB, averaging 22.2 fantasy PPG. His upside comes from his pass-catching ability, finishing 2021 top-three among RBs in targets and yards per game.

His ground game saw career highs in both attempts and yards, top-25 among RBs. Many were unsure if Ekeler would be able to handle feature-back duties and remain injury free. While he is not a true three-down workhorse, Ekeler only missed one game to covid and played 64% of his team's snaps.

He also finished second (behind Jonathan Taylor) in red zone carries (46) last season, converting 25% to TDs (12). He saw a total of 63 red zone touches, second among all RBs. You don't score 20 TDs without a little luck, and he'll regress in 2022. But had he scored only 12 TDs (our expected TD total for him last season), he would have still finished as the RB2 overall.

While his weekly numbers do fluctuate, he was the only RB without a finish lower than 9.5 fantasy points and posted only two games with fewer than 3 receptions.

Though he was only 14th in touches per game, his RZ volume and efficiency counter a lower overall volume than the other top-five backs. In a high-powered Chargers offense, and with such a high floor, Ekeler is positioned for another top-three finish.

YEAR	TEAM	GP	RUSH ATT	RUSH YD	YD/ATT	RUSH TD	100 YG	TAR	REC	REC YD	REC TD	FPPG
2019	LAC	16	132	557	4.2	3	1	108	92	993	8	19.6
2020	LAC	10	116	530	4.6	1	0	65	54	403	2	16.5
2021	LAC	16	206	911	4.4	12	1	94	70	647	8	21.6
PROJ	LAC	17	221	949	4.3	10	1	99	74	684	6	19.6

4 DERRICK HENRY

TENNESSEE TITANS (6)

DRAFT: 2016-2(14)   AGE: 28   WT: 247   HT: 6-3   ALABAMA

➤ 2021 fantasy managers who drafted Henry with their first pick were left wondering what might have been after a Week 8 foot injury sidelined him until the playoffs. At 28 years old, Henry should be fully healthy coming into the 2022 season.

Before his injury, Henry averaged 24 fantasy PPG, first for RBs. His 30 touch-per-game average led all RBs, 8 more than superstar Jonathan Taylor. Tennessee showed a commitment to the run game, even after Henry was injured, leading the league in rushing attempts and finishing second in rushing TDs.

The trade of Titans second best player, A.J. Brown, should only slightly affect Henry's fantasy value. Tennessee will be forced to lean more heavily on Henry, but hopefully will not become too one dimensional. The only knock on Henry, if there is any, is his reception numbers, and, that his value is very TD dependent. However, Henry was on pace to double his 2020 reception total, matching that of Jonathan Taylor. Henry handled more than 80% of his team's designed runs in those nine games, and was on pace for 20 rushing TDs, a single season record. He did have three, 3 TD games, which seems unsustainable. Even so, Henry had the highest consistency rating of any RB.

If Henry were to enter 2022 at age 28, a step slower, and not average 1.25 TDs per game, he would still be better than both Hilliard and Foreman, his 2021 replacements, who together averaged top-10 RB numbers in his absence. Be assured, you can feel safe taking him as your RB1.

YEAR	TEAM	GP	RUSH ATT	RUSH YD	YD/ATT	RUSH TD	100 YG	TAR	REC	REC YD	REC TD	FPPG
2019	TEN	15	303	1540	5.1	16	7	24	18	206	2	20
2020	TEN	16	378	2027	5.4	17	10	31	19	114	0	20.9
2021	TEN	8	219	937	4.3	10	5	20	18	154	0	23.4
PROJ	TEN	16	382	1590	4.2	12	7	43	30	227	0	17.7

5 NAJEE **HARRIS**
PITTSBURGH *STEELERS (9)*
DRAFT: 2021-1(24) AGE: 24 WT: 232 HT: 6-1
ALABAMA

Mike Tomlin believes in a three-down, workhorse back — a fantasy manager's dream. Najee Harris took 75% of Pittsburgh's carries and played 84% of snaps last season (first in both categories), finishing second in touches per game for RBs.

Tomlin said, leading into 2021, he wanted to commit more to the run game, and he did, giving Harris 211 carries. While most of Harris' other metrics were average, volume has always had the biggest correlation to fantasy production for RBs.

With these high-volume numbers, Harris finished the 2021 season as the overall RB3, and as RB7 in fantasy PPG. He managed this with a mediocre 3.9 yards per carry, while running behind a terrible offensive line.

Harris may not have the speed of some of the faster backs, but he has skill to elude and break tackles. Last season he broke tackles on 22% of his receptions and 10% of his carries.

The retirement of Big Ben could affect Harris' numbers, both positively and negatively. Kenny Pickett, this years' first-round pick out of Pittsburgh, should start the majority of games at QB. His mobility and creativity may lead to fewer check-downs, as it will allow his receivers more time to develop their routes. On the other hand, we expect the offense to provide more scoring opportunities, so you'll see we bumped Harris' TD numbers and slightly reduced his receptions in our projections.

We would be shocked if a healthy Harris finished outside of the top-10 RBs. You should feel comfortable taking him anywhere beyond the first half of round one in your fantasy draft.

YEAR	TEAM	GP	RUSH ATT	RUSH YD	YD/ATT	RUSH TD	100 YG	TAR	REC	REC YD	REC TD	FPPG
2021	PIT	17	307	1200	3.9	7	3	94	74	467	3	17.7
PROJ	PIT	17	295	1105	3.7	8	3	92	70	431	2	16.7

6 ALVIN **KAMARA**
NEW ORLEANS *SAINTS (14)*
DRAFT: 2017-3(3) AGE: 27 WT: 215 HT: 5-10
TENNESSEE

Kamara's 2021 season was forgettable. He had the lowest average yards per carry of his career at 3.7, averaged under 0.5 TDs per game, and could never get comfortable in the offense, playing with three different QBs.

Despite all obstacles, Kamara still finished the season as the seventh best RB in fantasy PPG, and ninth best on the season. If you look at the games with Jameis Winston under center, Kamara finished with 19.7 fantasy PPG, or fourth best on the season.

While it's unlikely Kamara returns to his 2020 form, we expect his numbers to improve in 2022. He is the biggest offensive weapon for the Saints, and the return of Michael Thomas and the addition of rookie receiver Chris Olave, should open things up for Kamara. Ranked sixth among RBs in targets per game in 2021, we expect an increase in targets for 2022.

Even with his decrease in yards per rushing attempt, he averaged more than 18 carries per game, fifth in the league. And, as a three-down back, Kamara played 75% of the snaps when healthy last year. We think we've had a look at worst case Kamara, and it's not that bad. If the Saints offense can improve a little and provide more scoring opportunities, and if Winston will continue to make the safe throws, Kamara should finish as a top-five back, with a floor of his 2021 numbers.

Kamara was arrested on a battery charge in Las Vegas in February. Keep an eye on a possible suspension.

YEAR	TEAM	GP	RUSH ATT	RUSH YD	YD/ATT	RUSH TD	100 YG	TAR	REC	REC YD	REC TD	FPPG
2019	NO	14	171	797	4.7	5	0	97	81	533	1	17.9
2020	NO	15	187	932	5	16	1	107	83	756	5	25.2
2021	NO	13	240	898	3.7	4	3	67	47	439	5	18.1
PROJ	NO	16	221	863	3.7	7	3	81	58	541	5	16.7

7 LEONARD **FOURNETTE**
TAMPA BAY *BUCCANEERS (11)*
DRAFT: 2017-1(4) AGE: 27 WT: 228 HT: 6-0
LSU

No one's ranking fluctuated more this offseason than Fournette's. In the end, most everything went his way: the return of the ageless Brady and the departure of RB Ronald Jones II. Plus, the Bucs made him the highest paid RB in the NFL this offseason. Fournette is on track for another career year, and not many people are paying attention.

In just 14 games last season, Fournette finished as sixth-best RB on the season and fourth best in fantasy PPG. While averaging only 12.9 carries per game, he led all RBs in targets per game. Yes, Fournette. Not Ekeler, not CMC, Fournette! With the second shortest time to throw, Brady's immobility and refusal to take a sack lends itself to plenty of check-downs, a staple of Brady's career. Brady's quick throws and GOAT status allowed Fournette to face an eight-man front only 13% of the time, less than any other RB last season.

New head coach Byron Leftwich, will defer play calls to the team's real coach, Tom Brady. And Brady has been beating the drum for Fournette. We don't expect the offense to look much different, but there's some concern for Fournette's durability. It wouldn't surprise us if the Bucs try to preserve their star back to ensure he's healthy in the postseason.

Still, a healthy Fournette is a guaranteed top-10 back. With an ADP of 79 last season, we won't be surprised to see Fournette still available in back half of Round 2 in most drafts, where we'll gladly roster him.

YEAR	TEAM	GP	RUSH ATT	RUSH YD	YD/ATT	RUSH TD	100 YG	TAR	REC	REC YD	REC TD	FPPG
2019	JAC	15	265	1152	4.3	3	3	100	76	522	0	17.4
2020	TB	13	97	367	3.8	6	1	47	36	233	0	10.2
2021	TB	14	180	812	4.5	8	2	84	69	454	2	18.3
PROJ	TB	16	205	921	4.5	9	3	85	67	460	2	16.9

8 DALVIN **COOK**
MINNESOTA *VIKINGS (7)*
DRAFT: 2017-2(9) AGE: 27 WT: 210 HT: 5-10
FLORIDA STATE

While Dalvin Cook may not have met the expectations of a player with a No. 2 ADP, he finished last season well within his range of possible outcomes.

He ranked third on the year in rushing attempts per game (19.2) and fourth in rush yards per game (89.2). Among the top-20 RBs last season, Cook was first in yards before contact per rushing attempt (2.7). You can't solely attribute this to good blocking, as backup Alexander Mattison was considerably lower In the same metric. Cook also finished third in red zone carries for the league. He did record a career low in targets per game (3.8) and finished outside the top-10 in both fantasy PPG and total fantasy points.

What gives us the biggest pause is Cook's durability. He has never played more than 14 games in a season. At age 27, he's not quite on the backside of his career, but if you draft him, you may want to reach in the middle rounds for his understudy, Mattison, who averaged 23.7 fantasy PPG in Cook's absences last season.

The coaching changes in Minnesota have only slightly altered our 2022 outlook for Cook. We expect his role to remain the same under new head coach, Kevin O'Connell, who came over from the Rams where he was offensive coordinator.

We're projecting Cook's numbers to look similar to his 2021 season, with a bump in TDs. It's rare to have an elite RB option available at the backend of Round 1, but if Cook makes it that far, snag him.

YEAR	TEAM	GP	RUSH ATT	RUSH YD	YD/ATT	RUSH TD	100 YG	TAR	REC	REC YD	REC TD	FPPG
2019	MIN	14	250	1135	4.5	13	5	63	53	519	0	21.2
2020	MIN	14	312	1557	5	16	8	54	44	361	1	24.1
2021	MIN	13	249	1159	4.7	6	4	49	34	224	0	16
PROJ	MIN	16	275	1204	4.4	10	5	60	46	365	1	16.8

QUARTERBACKS

RUNNING BACKS

WIDE RECEIVERS

TIGHT ENDS

KICKERS

D/ST

9 · D'ANDRE SWIFT

DETROIT **LIONS (6)**

DRAFT: 2020-2(3) AGE: 23 WT: 211 HT: 5-9 GEORGIA

D'Andre Swift is in an ideal situation for fantasy managers. First, he is on a team that's often playing from behind, where dump-offs to the running back are routine. It is no wonder Swift led all RBs last season in targets per game (6). He also, on the season, finished as the fourth best running back in yards per game. And because his team is an afterthought, Swift tends to be forgotten in fantasy drafts.

Before he was injured in Week 8 last year, he was averaging 19.6 fantasy PPG and played 72% of Detroit's snaps. At that pace he would have finished the season as a surefire top-five back.

Detroit, surprisingly, has one of the league's best offensive lines and not much changed in the offseason. If Swift can stay healthy (he's missed seven games in two seasons), you won't find a better value at his ADP.

YEAR	TEAM	GP	RUSH ATT	RUSH YD	YD/ATT	RUSH TD	100 YG	TAR	REC	REC YD	REC TD	FPPG
2020	DET	13	114	521	4.6	8	1	57	46	357	2	14.9
2021	DET	13	151	617	4.1	5	2	78	62	452	2	16.2
PROJ	DET	16	201	827	4.1	7	2	86	66	494	3	16.1

12 · JAMES CONNER

ARIZONA **CARDINALS (13)**

DRAFT: 2017-3(41) AGE: 27 WT: 233 HT: 6-1 PITTSBURGH

James Conner — without a single hundred-yard game and averaging only 2.5 receptions per game — finished as the fifth best RB in fantasy last season. With a TD on almost 5% of his touches, and on a remarkable 63% of his 16 carries inside the 5, Conner's 18 TDs were second only to Jonathan Taylor for RBs.

With Chase Edmonds now in Miami, Conner will see an inevitable increase in touches. When Edmonds was sidelined last season, Conner averaged 2 more receptions per game than when Edmonds was active.

While it's unlikely to see a repeat of his 18-TD season, his extra touches should make up for a TD regression. We're happy drafting him if he can repeat his 2021 performance, but if he's able to get 50% of Edmond's touches, he has top-five RB value.

YEAR	TEAM	GP	RUSH ATT	RUSH YD	YD/ATT	RUSH TD	100 YG	TAR	REC	REC YD	REC TD	FPPG
2019	PIT	10	116	464	4	4	1	38	34	251	3	14.8
2020	PIT	13	169	721	4.3	6	3	43	35	215	0	12.7
2021	ARI	15	202	752	3.7	15	0	39	37	375	3	17.2
PROJ	ARI	16	226	871	3.9	10	1	50	44	362	2	15.0

10 · JOE MIXON

CINCINNATI **BENGALS (10)**

DRAFT: 2017-2(16) AGE: 26 WT: 220 HT: 6-1 OKLAHOMA

Joe Mixon's finish as the fourth best RB in FPs last season can be attributed to three things: volume, health, and Joe Burrow. The loss of third-down back Giovanni Bernard and the vast improvement in the Bengals offense, left Mixon finally living up to his ADP. Even with an impoverished offensive line, defenses were unable to stack the box against a potent passing offense. Mixon posted career bests in TDs and yards last season, playing almost 70% of the snaps in his new three-down role. He did, however, finish outside the top 10 in red zone carries but made the most of his opportunities, finishing fifth in rushing TDs per game. Unfortunately, we think Mixon has reached his fantasy ceiling. He should have a similar role in 2022, so feel confident in drafting him anywhere after the Round 1 turn.

YEAR	TEAM	GP	RUSH ATT	RUSH YD	YD/ATT	RUSH TD	100 YG	TAR	REC	REC YD	REC TD	FPPG
2019	CIN	16	278	1137	4.1	5	4	45	35	287	3	14.1
2020	CIN	6	119	428	3.6	3	1	26	21	138	1	16.9
2021	CIN	16	292	1205	4.1	13	3	48	42	314	3	18.1
PROJ	CIN	16	263	1044	3.8	10	3	50	43	293	3	16.0

13 · DAVID MONTGOMERY

CHICAGO **BEARS (14)**

DRAFT: 2019-3(10) AGE: 25 WT: 224 HT: 5-11 IOWA STATE

We understand, David Montgomery is an unsexy fantasy draft pick. But this is why he often slips in drafts below his actual value. Among RBs in 2021, he finished seventh in red zone carries, eighth in rush yards per game, and fourteenth in receptions per game. Most significantly, he played 75% of the team's snaps — no committee here. He finished the season 15th for RBs in fantasy PPG, and had zero games with fewer than 9 FPs, finishing top-five for RBs in our consistency rating.

While coaching changes in Chicago have us concerned for the offense as a whole, Montgomery's role is cemented. He is a guaranteed top-20 back and we wouldn't be surprised if he finishes top-10. And like the last couple of seasons, he'll likely be drafted outside the top-20.

YEAR	TEAM	GP	RUSH ATT	RUSH YD	YD/ATT	RUSH TD	100 YG	TAR	REC	REC YD	REC TD	FPPG
2019	CHI	16	242	889	3.7	6	2	35	25	185	1	10.9
2020	CHI	15	247	1070	4.3	8	3	68	54	438	2	17.7
2021	CHI	13	225	849	3.8	7	2	51	42	301	0	15.3
PROJ	CHI	16	243	960	3.8	8	3	59	43	334	2	14.3

11 · AARON JONES

GREEN BAY **PACKERS (14)**

DRAFT: 2017-5(39) AGE: 27 WT: 208 HT: 5-9 TEXAS-EL PASO

It looks like Aaron Jones could now face a fantasy manager's worst nightmare — running back by committee. AJ Dillon continues to steal touches from Jones, who is now three years removed from leading the NFL in TDs. When both Dillon and Jones are healthy, they are almost identical in rushing attempts and yards. However, Jones had two times as many targets as Dillon, but Dillon, the bigger back, had almost 25% more red zone carries last year. Having missed multiple games in four out of five seasons, Jones has durability concerns as well. The departure of Davante Adams should help Jones, as Aaron Rodgers will need more targets on the field, and Jones is the superior receiving back. After finishing 2021 as the 14th best back in fantasy, we expect to see similar numbers in 2022.

YEAR	TEAM	GP	RUSH ATT	RUSH YD	YD/ATT	RUSH TD	100 YG	TAR	REC	REC YD	REC TD	FPPG
2019	GB	16	236	1084	4.6	16	5	68	49	474	3	19.9
2020	GB	14	201	1104	5.5	9	3	63	47	355	2	18.5
2021	GB	15	171	799	4.7	4	1	65	52	391	6	15.4
PROJ	GB	16	172	766	4.1	5	1	74	61	513	4	15.0

14 · SAQUON BARKLEY

NEW YORK **GIANTS (9)**

DRAFT: 2018-1(2) AGE: 25 WT: 232 HT: 6-0 PENN STATE

Barkley finished first in FPs among RBs in 2018, but since then he's been more of a fantasy liability than asset.

After missing all but two games in 2020, Barkley was able to stay healthy enough to play 13 games last season. He finished 33rd in fantasy PPG among RBs, 3 PPG away from the top-20, which doesn't quite feel out of reach for someone of his talent. On a Giants offense that's usually playing from behind, he finished 11th among backs in targets per game.

The 25-year-old has two things going for him: (1) a new coaching staff who has no incentive to preserve their feature back, and (2) he has no competition at the position.

We understand drafting Barkley for his RB1 upside, but it's not without risk.

YEAR	TEAM	GP	RUSH ATT	RUSH YD	YD/ATT	RUSH TD	100 YG	TAR	REC	REC YD	REC TD	FPPG
2019	NYG	13	217	1003	4.6	6	4	73	52	438	2	18.8
2020	NYG	2	19	34	1.8	0	0	9	6	60	0	7.7
2021	NYG	13	162	593	3.7	2	1	57	41	263	2	11.6
PROJ	NYG	16	220	829	3.8	5	2	74	55	394	3	14.1

15 JAVONTE WILLIAMS

DRAFT: 2021-2(3) AGE: 22 WT: 220 HT: 5-10

DENVER BRONCOS (9)
NORTH CAROLINA

This offseason, the fantasy pundits were ready to anoint Javonte Williams the next fantasy superstar. Then Melvin Gordon III re-signed with the team, and Denver came out and said their running backs would be splitting touches, again.

Last season, Gordon and Williams were almost identical in every metric, from rushing attempts to snaps played. Williams did outshine Gordon in one area. Williams, the No. 1 back in college for broken tackles, amazingly, led the NFL in the same statistic his rookie year.

The addition of elite QB Russell Wilson will boost numbers for the entire offense. Gordon will be 29 entering this season while Williams will be just 22, so it's possible Williams becomes the dominant back, especially if Wilson wants him on the field. While a top-ten RB finish is well within his range of possible outcomes, we are less bullish on this pick than other rankers.

YEAR	TEAM	GP	RUSH ATT	RUSH YD	YD/ATT	RUSH TD	100 YG	TAR	REC	REC YD	REC TD	FPPG
2021	DEN	17	203	903	4.4	4	2	53	43	316	3	12.2
PROJ	DEN	17	218	966	4.4	6	2	56	44	324	3	13.4

16 NICK CHUBB

DRAFT: 2018-2(3) AGE: 26 WT: 227 HT: 5-11

CLEVELAND BROWNS (9)
GEORGIA

In metrics, Nick Chubb may be the best RB in the league. And if he played a three-down role like Derrick Henry, he would be ranked in our top-three RBs. Chubb has averaged more than 5 yards per carry and 8 TDs in all four of his NFL seasons. Last year, he ranked first among RBs in yards after contact, and first in yards per carry for RBs with at least 200 attempts. We get it: his efficiency seems unsustainable — but he's sustained it!

He finished last season as the 13th best RB in FPs and 12th in fantasy PPG, while only playing just over half the snaps. Chubb won't be a three-down back in 2022, but he's proven he doesn't need to be. Kareem Hunt? Who cares. Only 1.4 receptions per game last year? No problem. Chubb is a solid RB2 that's being drafted a little too high for our liking.

YEAR	TEAM	GP	RUSH ATT	RUSH YD	YD/ATT	RUSH TD	100 YG	TAR	REC	REC YD	REC TD	FPPG
2019	CLE	16	298	1484	5	8	7	49	36	278	0	16.3
2020	CLE	12	190	1067	5.6	12	6	18	16	150	0	13.3
2021	CLE	14	228	1259	5.5	8	5	25	20	174	1	15.5
PROJ	CLE	16	241	1159	4.5	8	5	31	24	220	1	13.3

17 CAM AKERS

DRAFT: 2020-2(20) AGE: 23 WT: 217 HT: 5-10

LOS ANGELES RAMS (7)
FLORIDA STATE

Going into 2021, expectations in the fantasy community for Cam Akers — before his season-ending Achilles tear — were through the roof, including a top-10 overall ranking by many outlets. He took over the lead-back position in Los Angeles in Week 13 of 2020 and averaged 16.6 fantasy PPG, top-10 for RBs, in a Jared Goff-led offense.

Sean McVay is so sold on Akers that he brought him back for the playoffs last season, risking the chemistry of the already established offense, and risking re-injury to his favorite back.

The only concerns we have are that the Rams finished 27th as a team for RB FPs, and Akers' limited role as a pass catcher.

Besides Saquon Barkley, who's a much riskier pick, Akers could be the only RB drafted outside the top-10 backs to have top-five upside.

YEAR	TEAM	GP	RUSH ATT	RUSH YD	YD/ATT	RUSH TD	100 YG	TAR	REC	REC YD	REC TD	FPPG
2020	LAR	13	145	625	4.3	2	1	14	11	123	1	8
2021	LAR	1	5	3	0.6	0	0	3	3	10	0	4.3
PROJ	LAR	16	244	1003	3.9	7	3	43	36	301	1	13.2

18 EZEKIEL ELLIOT

DRAFT: 2016-1(4) AGE: 27 WT: 228 HT: 6-0

DALLAS COWBOYS (9)
OHIO STATE

Ezekiel Elliot's finish as the seventh best fantasy RB last season is deceiving, and more representative of games played rather than productivity. His 17-touches-per-game average resulted in 14.6 fantasy PPG (only 19th best for RBs). Last season, he finished outside the top-20 RBs four times, more than he finished inside the top 10.

While Dallas will never completely turn the keys over to understudy Tony Pollard, he is already getting a third of the touches and averaging over a yard more per carry than Elliot. Elliot should look much the same in 2022. Sadly the 27-year-old is already past his prime. Most drafters will only remember his glory days and draft him too soon. Because of this, the fringe RB2 won't make many of our rosters.

YEAR	TEAM	GP	RUSH ATT	RUSH YD	YD/ATT	RUSH TD	100 YG	TAR	REC	REC YD	REC TD	FPPG
2019	DAL	16	301	1357	4.5	12	7	71	54	420	2	19.7
2020	DAL	15	244	979	4	6	2	71	52	338	2	15.4
2021	DAL	17	237	1002	4.2	10	2	65	47	287	2	14.6
PROJ	DAL	17	224	924	4.1	8	2	60	42	284	2	13.1

19 JOSH JACOBS

DRAFT: 2019-1(24) AGE: 24 WT: 220 HT: 5-10

LAS VEGAS RAIDERS (6)
ALABAMA

On one hand, Josh Jacobs has maintained his lead-back role in Vegas all three of his seasons. Last year he was inside the top 20 in every conceivable rushing and receiving metric for RBs, including a finish as the 12th best fantasy RB on a PPG basis. In addition, his targets have increased year over year, from 0.7 targets per game in 2019, to 2.3 in 2020, to 4.3 in 2021. Believe it or not, Jacobs had the second-most targets of any RB during the second half of last season.

On the other hand, the Raiders haven't shown a great amount of faith in Jacobs this offseason. Not only did they neglect to pick up his fifth-year option, they added RBs Ameer Abdullah and third-round pick Zamir White to the backfield.

He's still a solid RB2 until something changes.

YEAR	TEAM	GP	RUSH ATT	RUSH YD	YD/ATT	RUSH TD	100 YG	TAR	REC	REC YD	REC TD	FPPG
2019	LV	13	242	1150	4.8	7	4	27	20	166	0	14.9
2020	LV	15	273	1065	3.9	12	2	45	33	238	0	15.7
2021	LV	15	217	872	4	9	2	64	54	348	0	15.3
PROJ	LV	16	224	900	3.8	8	2	46	37	268	1	12.9

20 ANTONIO GIBSON

DRAFT: 2020-3(2) AGE: 24 WT: 220 HT: 6-2

WASHINGTON COMMANDERS (14)
MEMPHIS

While Gibson did finish 2021 as the eighth best RB in FPs, he didn't have the breakout year most expected. In fact, he averaged fewer fantasy PPG than in his rookie campaign.

The re-signing of J.D. McKissic and Washington's puzzling Round 3 draft pick of RB Brian Robinson Jr. doesn't bode well for Gibson's outlook. During the 11 games McKissic was healthy last season, Gibson averaged 13.5 fantasy PPG, which would have put him outside the top 20 RBs on the year. Gibson's had 8 fewer touches per game when McKissic was healthy.

It looks like Washington is trying to find their identity, and we have downgraded most of their offensive players accordingly. Nonetheless, Gibson is still their lead back and remains a fringe RB2. You should feel pretty good about your pick if you are able to draft him outside the top-20 backs.

YEAR	TEAM	GP	RUSH ATT	RUSH YD	YD/ATT	RUSH TD	100 YG	TAR	REC	REC YD	REC TD	FPPG
2020	WAS	14	170	795	4.7	11	2	44	36	247	0	14.7
2021	WAS	16	258	1037	4	7	2	52	42	294	3	14.7
PROJ	WAS	16	221	936	4.0	8	0	0	35	246	2	13.1

QUARTERBACKS

RUNNING BACKS

WIDE RECEIVERS

TIGHT ENDS

KICKERS

D/ST

QUARTERBACKS

RUNNING BACKS

WIDE RECEIVERS

TIGHT ENDS

KICKERS

D/ST

21 TRAVIS ETIENNE JR.

JACKSONVILLE JAGUARS (11)

DRAFT: 2021-1(25)   AGE: 23   WT: 215   HT: 5-10
CLEMSON

➤ Travis Etienne Jr. suffered a Lisfranc injury in his rookie preseason last year. Completely recovered and taking full reps at OTAs this spring, he enters the 2022 season in a far better fantasy situation than he would have last year.

Etienne's teammate, and Jag's 2020-21 feature back, James Robinson, is coming off a torn Achilles, leaving his early-season availability in question, though he did remain off the PUP list in training camp, and the field open for Etienne to step into the lead role. New head coach Doug Pederson intends to use Etienne in different spots, and to get him the ball as often as possible.

Etienne has speed (4.40 40-yard dash) and is skilled as both a runner and pass catcher. He draws comparisons to Alvin Kamara, who leads the NFL in receptions and yards since 2017. Etienne's worst case scenario is losing early downs to Robinson upon his return. We're ranking him as an RB2 with upside, and believe he'll secure the No. 1 role before Robinson's return.

YEAR	TEAM	GP	RUSH ATT	RUSH YD	YD/ATT	RUSH TD	100 YG	TAR	REC	REC YD	REC TD	FPPG
PROJ	JAC	17	169	728	4.3	5	1	69	55	452	2	12.6

22 J.K. DOBBINS

BALTIMORE RAVENS (10)

DRAFT: 2020-2(23)   AGE: 23   WT: 209   HT: 5-10
OHIO STATE

➤ J.K. Dobbins led all rushers in yards per carry (6.0) and YAC (2.5) in his 2020 rookie season, but a torn ACL kept him out the entire 2021 season. Dobbins will be fully healthy and just 23 years old coming into this season.

In the last six games of 2020 Dobbins showed fantasy managers his potential, averaging 16.3 fantasy PPG. But in the same span, he only had 3 receptions. Lamar Jackson has ranked last in the league the last four seasons in RB targets, and we don't expect that to change. Even with the return of Gus Edwards, who has never averaged below 5.0 yards per carry in his career, Dobbins should lead the backfield in touches. He's an effective red zone rusher, converting 8 of his 10 carries inside the 5-yard line for TDs in 2020. His role and efficiency is much like Nick Chubb's, a good role to have in one of the leagues highest scoring offenses.

YEAR	TEAM	GP	RUSH ATT	RUSH YD	YD/ATT	RUSH TD	100 YG	TAR	REC	REC YD	REC TD	FPPG
2020	BAL	15	134	805	6	9	2	24	18	120	0	11.0
2021	BAL	DNP	INJURY									
PROJ	BAL	17	189	925	4.9	9	2	45	34	250	1	12.4

23 BREECE HALL

NEW YORK JETS (10)

DRAFT: 2022-2(4)   AGE: 21   WT: 220   HT: 6-1
IOWA STATE

➤ We can't wait to see Breece Hall on an NFL field. He's fast (4.39 40-yard dash) and athletic (40-inch vertical, 126-inch broad jump), and was a bona fide stud at Iowa State. During his three college seasons he accumulated over 4,500 yards from scrimmage, 50 TDs, and 80 receptions. Those 80 catches show he's plenty capable in the passing game, too.

The Jets traded up to get Hall early in the second round, and view him as a three-down back. The pick was surprising considering Michael Carter's solid rookie year with the team. To move up in the draft for a RB, knowing you have already have Michael Carter in the locker room, means they have big expectations for Hall, who will carry much of the workload. We conservatively estimate Hall getting 15 touches per game, which would be enough to land him in the RB15-or-better conversation. Carter averaged 14 touches per game when Tevin Coleman was active last season. Hall is a fringe RB2 with decent upside.

YEAR	TEAM	GP	RUSH ATT	RUSH YD	YD/ATT	RUSH TD	100 YG	TAR	REC	REC YD	REC TD	FPPG
PROJ	NYJ	17	200	904	4.5	6	2	47	38	339	2	12.4

24 ELIJAH MITCHELL

SAN FRANCISCO 49ERS (9)

DRAFT: 2021-6(10)   AGE: 24   WT: 200   HT: 5-10
LOUISIANA

➤ In 2020, the fantasy community sought the wrong guy as the projected breakout RB in San Francisco. Preseason hopes were placed on third-round draft pick, Trey Sermon, but sixth-rounder, Elijah Mitchell, was the 49ers top-back from Week 1.

Even after missing a few games to injury, Mitchell returned to the feature-back position, averaging 21 touches in the 49ers three playoff games. Mitchell is a beast of a runner, averaging 2.5 yards after contact per attempt, third among the top-40 RBs.

New starting QB, Trey Lance, may steal some of Mitchell's rushing attempts, especially around the goal line, but not enough that we're concerned. The addition of RB Tyrion Davis-Price in the draft is an indictment of Sermon rather than a nod of uncertainty concerning Mitchell. Even Though they'll continue to utilize Deebo in the run game, we expect much the same out of Mitchell in 2022. He's a solid backend RB2.

YEAR	TEAM	GP	RUSH ATT	RUSH YD	YD/ATT	RUSH TD	100 YG	TAR	REC	REC YD	REC TD	FPPG
2021	SF	11	207	963	4.7	5	5	20	19	137	1	15.0
PROJ	SF	17	278	1126	4.1	7	6	25	20	140	1	11.4

25 MILES SANDERS

PHILADELPHIA EAGLES (7)

DRAFT: 2019-2(11)   AGE: 25   WT: 211   HT: 5-11
PENN STATE

➤ Miles Sanders' 2021 fantasy point totals are misleading — 163 touches for 912 yards, but *zero* TDs. He did average a significant 5.5 yards per carry in the league's run-heaviest offense.

Sanders has missed nine games over the past two years, so durability is a concern. Also, he is not very active in the passing game; in 2021 he averaged just 2.8 targets per game. Most concerning is that his backup, Boston Scott, had more fantasy PPG than Sanders last season. We expect he'll continue to lose touches to Scott and RB Kenneth Gainwell, again this season.

Nevertheless, Miles is the best back in Philadelphia and his numbers should improve on all fronts in 2022, especially his TD numbers. This is reason enough to select him as a backup/flex option this year.

YEAR	TEAM	GP	RUSH ATT	RUSH YD	YD/ATT	RUSH TD	100 YG	TAR	REC	REC YD	REC TD	FPPG
2019	PHI	16	179	818	4.6	3	1	63	50	509	3	13.7
2020	PHI	12	164	867	5.3	6	2	52	28	197	0	14.2
2021	PHI	12	137	754	5.5	0	2	34	26	158	0	9.8
PROJ	PHI	15	189	926	4.3	4	3	39	29	221	1	11.4

26 CLYDE EDWARDS-HELAIRE

KANSAS CITY CHIEFS (8)

DRAFT: 2020-1(32)   AGE: 23   WT: 205   HT: 5-8
LSU

➤ It's hard to be excited about CEH after two consecutive seasons where he's failed to come close to meeting expectations. The Chiefs coaching staff seems to have lost faith in him too, giving Jerrick McKinnon three times as many snaps as a healthy Edwards-Helaire in the postseason last year.

CEH has yet to produce a top-20 fantasy finish. He especially struggles finding yards in the run game and had an abysmal 1.9 yards after contact per carry and zero broken tackles last year. In addition, he only had 12 red zone rushing attempts, resulting in 4 TDs, 2 of which came from inside the 1-yard line.

We understand drafting the 23-year-old at the right price, and with tempered expectations. But the addition of Ronald Jones II and Jerrick Mckinnon are reasons for concern. If the Chiefs aren't convinced CEH is their future, why should we be?

YEAR	TEAM	GP	RUSH ATT	RUSH YD	YD/ATT	RUSH TD	100 YG	TAR	REC	REC YD	REC TD	FPPG
2020	KC	13	181	803	4.4	4	2	54	36	297	1	13.5
2021	KC	10	119	517	4.3	4	2	23	19	129	2	12
PROJ	KC	16	164	709	4.0	5	2	55	40	279	2	11.1

27 | DEVIN **SINGLETARY**

*BUFFALO **BILLS** (7)*

DRAFT: 2019-3(11) AGE: 24 WT: 203 HT: 5-7 FLORIDA ATLANTIC

Devin Singletary finally emerged as the feature back in Week 15 last season, after sharing duties for most of his three-year career. During the six-game span, stretching into the offseason, Singletary averaged 19.5 touches, and had at least 1 TD in each appearance, resulting in a whopping 20.5 fantasy PPG. A season at that pace would have made him the fourth-best RB on the year. While these numbers are unsustainable, it does provide a glimpse at Singletary's upside in the high-powered Buffalo offense. He's unlikely to be completely dethroned. Unfortunately, it looks like he still won't have the backfield to himself, as rookie RB James Cook will at least take some passing-down situations. With enough upside to produce multiple weekly top-10 finishes, we feel safe drafting him in the 25-30 RB range.

YEAR	TEAM	GP	RUSH ATT	RUSH YD	YD/ATT	RUSH TD	100 YG	TAR	REC	REC YD	REC TD	FPPG
2019	BUF	12	151	775	5.1	2	1	41	29	194	2	12.5
2020	BUF	16	156	687	4.4	2	0	50	38	269	0	9.1
2021	BUF	17	188	870	4.6	7	1	50	40	228	1	11.6
PROJ	BUF	17	195	874	4.5	7	1	40	31	204	1	11.0

28 | KAREEM **HUNT**

*CLEVELAND **BROWNS** (9)*

DRAFT: 2017-3(22) AGE: 27 WT: 216 HT: 5-11 TOLEDO

Kareem Hunt played six fully healthy games in 2021, and split duties with Nick Chubb in all but one. He averaged 17 fantasy PPG, a pace which would have landed him as the 10th best RB on the year. In 2020, he finished as the 14th best fantasy RB with Nick Chubb on the field, and the sixth best in the four games without him. While Chubb gets almost three times as many carries as Hunt per game, Hunt averages twice as many targets.

He ranked sixth last season among RBs in YAC and yards per route, and commanded a 26% target share. He had 11 TDs in 2020 and was on pace for a similar number in 2021 before injury. Hunt's value is twofold: (1) He has RB2 upside if Chubb is healthy and (2) he has RB1 potential if Chubb is sidelined for any reason.

YEAR	TEAM	GP	RUSH ATT	RUSH YD	YD/ATT	RUSH TD	100 YG	TAR	REC	REC YD	REC TD	FPPG
2019	CLE	8	43	179	4.2	2	0	44	37	285	1	12.7
2020	CLE	16	198	841	4.2	6	1	51	38	304	5	13.7
2021	CLE	8	78	386	4.9	5	0	27	22	174	0	13.5
PROJ	CLE	16	125	555	4.1	5	0	55	42	352	2	10.8

29 | DAMIEN **HARRIS**

*NEW ENGLAND **PATRIOTS** (10)*

DRAFT: 2019-3(24) AGE: 25 WT: 213 HT: 5-11 ALABAMA

Damien Harris finished last season as the 20th best RB in fantasy PPG, almost solely as a result of his ground production (top 17 in rushing attempts per game and yards per game). He found the most upside in the red zone where he boasted a TD per game average, only bested by Derrick Henry and Jonathon Taylor, and was fifth among backs in red zone carries.

In 2022, we expect the Patriots to use a three-back rotation, with Harris and Rhamondre Stevenson splitting carries 60-40 and James White, who missed all but three games last season, handling the receiving duties. Everything about 2022 screams regression for Harris — fewer carries; fewer TDs, for sure, and fewer FPs. As the Patriots lean more on their second-year QB, Harris is best viewed as a flex option.

YEAR	TEAM	GP	RUSH ATT	RUSH YD	YD/ATT	RUSH TD	100 YG	TAR	REC	REC YD	REC TD	FPPG
2019	NE	2	4	12	3	0	0	0	0	0	0	0.6
2020	NE	10	137	691	5	2	3	7	5	52	0	9.1
2021	NE	15	202	929	4.6	15	5	20	18	132	0	14.3
PROJ	NE	16	195	847	4.0	9	4	22	17	117	0	10.6

30 | TONY **POLLARD**

*DALLAS **COWBOYS** (9)*

DRAFT: 2019-4(26) AGE: 25 WT: 209 HT: 6-0 MEMPHIS

As Ezekiel Elliot's perennial understudy, Tony Pollard has improved in every fantasy metric over his last three seasons in Dallas. Eating into Elliot's touches last season, Pollard posted his first top-30 campaign. He averaged 70.4 all-purpose yards per game, and his 5.5 yards per carry and 8.6 yards per reception are both better than Zeke's (4.2, 6.1). In fact, he was fourth in yards after contact per attempt among all RBs. Still, Zeke remains the No. 1 back in Dallas, and will continue to see the majority of snaps, in part because of his superior pass-blocking ability. Elliot is also, much to the detriment of Pollard, the main red zone back.

While Pollard has stand-alone value as a potential flex play when Zeke is healthy, his real value arises if Zeke misses time, where he would be a league-winning RB1.

YEAR	TEAM	GP	RUSH ATT	RUSH YD	YD/ATT	RUSH TD	100 YG	TAR	REC	REC YD	REC TD	FPPG
2019	DAL	15	86	455	5.3	2	1	20	15	107	1	5.9
2020	DAL	16	101	435	4.3	4	0	49	28	192	1	7.5
2021	DAL	15	130	719	5.5	2	2	46	39	337	0	10.4
PROJ	DAL	17	156	759	4.9	3	2	54	45	352	1	10.6

31 | CHASE **EDMONDS**

*MIAMI **DOLPHINS** (11)*

DRAFT: 2018-4(34) AGE: 26 WT: 210 HT: 5-9 FORDHAM

Chase Edmonds was never a three-down back during his four seasons in Arizona. Though he's only averaged 6 carries per game in his career, the majority of his fantasy value comes from his receiving production.

Last season among RBs, Edmonds ranked top-13 in targets, receptions, and receiving yards per game. But his very unlucky TD total, along with his limited rushing volume (mostly due to the presence of James Conner) had him finishing outside of the top-40 RBs in fantasy PPG. That Edmonds outshines other Miami backs in overall pass-catching ability (where Myles Gaskin made most of his FPs last year) is why he'll likely emerge as the best fantasy back in the Dolphins new high-powered offense. But since he won't be their bell-cow, he remains only a flex play.

YEAR	TEAM	GP	RUSH ATT	RUSH YD	YD/ATT	RUSH TD	100 YG	TAR	REC	REC YD	REC TD	FPPG
2019	ARI	13	60	303	5	4	1	21	12	105	1	6.4
2020	ARI	16	97	448	4.6	1	0	67	53	402	4	10.5
2021	ARI	12	116	592	5.1	2	1	53	43	311	0	12.1
PROJ	MIA	16	120	558	4.4	3	1	57	50	347	1	10.2

32 | MELVIN **GORDON III**

*DENVER **BRONCOS** (9)*

DRAFT: 2015-1(15) AGE: 29 WT: 215 HT: 6-1 WISCONSIN

Melvin Gordon III would be a surefire top-10 fantasy RB if Javonte Williams were to miss any time. But even with a healthy Williams last season, in a Teddy Bridgewater-run offense, Gordon finished 24th in fantasy PPG and 18th in total FPs for all RBs, and had a career high in yards after contact. The offseason was unkind to dynasty managers who have Williams. Not only did Denver re-sign Gordon, but doubled down by saying the two backs would share touches, again. We think it's fair to assume two things: (1) Russell Wilson will provide an immediate fantasy boost to the entire offense, and (2) a healthy Williams will end the season as the touch leader. Perhaps Wilson will prefer the 29-year-old veteran over Williams. With all that said, we think many popular rankings have Gordon ranked too low.

YEAR	TEAM	GP	RUSH ATT	RUSH YD	YD/ATT	RUSH TD	100 YG	TAR	REC	REC YD	REC TD	FPPG
2019	LAC	12	162	612	3.8	8	1	55	42	296	1	15.6
2020	DEN	15	215	986	4.6	9	2	44	32	158	1	13.8
2021	DEN	16	203	918	4.5	8	3	39	28	213	2	12.6
PROJ	DEN	16	162	698	4.0	7	2	38	27	189	1	10.1

QUARTERBACKS RUNNING BACKS WIDE RECEIVERS TIGHT ENDS KICKERS D/ST

33 | AJ DILLON

GREEN BAY *PACKERS (14)*

DRAFT: 2020-2(30)   AGE: 24   WT: 247   HT: 6-0

BOSTON COLLEGE

AJ Dillon made a big leap in volume in 2021 as he moved up on the Packers depth chart after the departure of Jamaal Williams. He averaged the same number of carries per game as Aaron Jones, but about half as many targets per game, though his receiving did improve (9.2 yards per reception).

His fantasy production is sporadic with a healthy Jones but will have top-15 upside if Jones is ever sidelined. For this reason alone, he's worth a middle round pick.

YEAR	TEAM	GP	RUSH ATT	RUSH YD	YD/ATT	RUSH TD	100 YG	TAR	REC	REC YD	REC TD	FPPG
2020	GB	11	46	242	5.3	2	1	2	2	21	0	3.7
2021	GB	17	187	803	4.3	5	0	37	34	313	2	11
PROJ	GB	17	174	724	4.2	5	0	35	29	239	2	9.8

34 | CORDARRELLE PATTERSON

ATLANTA *FALCONS (14)*

DRAFT: 2013-1(29)   AGE: 31   WT: 220   HT: 6-2

TENNESSEE

After nine seasons, Patterson finally had a breakout season in 2021. From Weeks 2-14, he averaged 11.1 carries, 5.5 targets, 90.8 all-purpose yards, and 18.5 FPs, scoring 10 TDs in the stretch. Patterson will start the season as Atlanta's top back, but the workload will be by committee (Damien Williams and rookie Tyler Allgeier). Our rankings reflect our hesitancy that he'll be the lead back by season's end. As an RB3/flex, keep him on your radar in the middle rounds.

YEAR	TEAM	GP	RUSH ATT	RUSH YD	YD/ATT	RUSH TD	100 YG	TAR	REC	REC YD	REC TD	FPPG
2019	CHI	16	17	103	6.1	0	0	17	11	83	0	1.8
2020	CHI	16	64	232	3.6	1	0	25	21	132	0	4
2021	ATL	16	153	618	4	6	0	68	52	548	5	14.7
PROJ	ATL	17	135	515	3.8	4	0	59	44	431	3	10.6

35 | KEN WALKER III

SEATTLE *SEAHAWKS (11)*

DRAFT: 2022-2(9)   AGE: 21   WT: 212   HT: 5-10

MICHIGAN STATE

Ken Walker III may have been drafted into the perfect storm to see starting reps sooner than later. Chris Carson retired before training camp after suffering a serious neck injury last season, and the likely starter, Rashaad Penny, has only played 57% of possible games since joining the league.

Walker's a talented back who had a 263-1,636-18 rushing line his last year at Michigan State. The injury pandemic might find Walker handling feature-back duties at any moment. We have him ranked just ahead of Penny because we are of the belief that often teams in rebuild-mode will give the nod to the younger guys.

YEAR	TEAM	GP	RUSH ATT	RUSH YD	YD/ATT	RUSH TD	100 YG	TAR	REC	REC YD	REC TD	FPPG
PROJ	SEA	17	152	664	4.4	4	1	33	25	212	1	8.4

36 | RASHAAD PENNY

SEATTLE *SEAHAWKS (11)*

DRAFT: 2018-1(27)   AGE: 26   WT: 220   HT: 5-11

SAN DIEGO STATE

In Weeks 13-18 of the 2021 season, on weeks he recorded at least 10 touches, Rashaad Penny averaged 118 rushing yards, 1.3 TDs, and 19.6 fantasy PPG, best in the NFL during the span among RBs. Penny's talent has been undeniable, especially his running ability (5.6 career average yards per carry), but he struggles to stay healthy, missing 42% of the games in his four-year career. With Chris Carson retiring, Penny may only have to hold off second-round rookie Ken Walker III.

YEAR	TEAM	GP	RUSH ATT	RUSH YD	YD/ATT	RUSH TD	100 YG	TAR	REC	REC YD	REC TD	FPPG
2019	SEA	10	65	370	5.7	3	1	11	8	83	1	7.7
2020	SEA	3	11	34	3.1	0	0	0	0	0	0	1.1
2021	SEA	10	119	749	6.3	6	4	8	6	48	0	12.2
PROJ	SEA	15	139	695	4.4	4	2	20	15	117	0	8.2

37 | MICHAEL CARTER

NEW YORK *JETS (10)*

DRAFT: 2021-4(2)   AGE: 23   WT: 201   HT: 5-8

NORTH CAROLINA

Michael Carter had a good rookie season as the lead RB for the Jets, including a six-game stretch where he averaged 17.1 fantasy PPG. In Week 8, with backup Tevin Coleman sidelined, he had 172 combined yards, 9 receptions, and a TD. With Coleman active, his touch-count reduced from 19 to 14. He finished the season as RB29.

Carter, unfortunately, has been relegated to backup duties with the addition of rookie Breece Hall, a three-down back. He's a good Hall-handcuff or RB injury-roulette play.

YEAR	TEAM	GP	RUSH ATT	RUSH YD	YD/ATT	RUSH TD	100 YG	TAR	REC	REC YD	REC TD	FPPG
2021	NYJ	14	147	639	4.3	4	1	55	36	325	0	11.2
PROJ	NYJ	17	135	608	4.5	4	1	52	37	333	0	9.5

38 | RHAMONDRE STEVENSON

NEW ENGLAND *PATRIOTS (10)*

DRAFT: 2021-4(15)   AGE: 24   WT: 230   HT: 6-0

OKLAHOMA

Rhamondre Stevenson was impressive in his rookie campaign, averaging 4.16 yards per carry and 2.6 yards after contact per carry, second among top-40 RBs. PFF graded Stevenson as the third-best RB last season. Unfortunately, he's got the worst role, fantasy-wise, in a three-man committee. Damien Harris collects the majority of the rushing attempts and red zone work, while James White plays the receiving back. Stevenson has a chance to emerge as a better back than Harris because of his explosive ability, but most likely he'll need an injury to make him fantasy-start worthy.

YEAR	TEAM	GP	RUSH ATT	RUSH YD	YD/ATT	RUSH TD	100 YG	TAR	REC	REC YD	REC TD	FPPG
2021	NE	12	133	606	4.6	5	2	18	14	123	0	9.7
PROJ	NE	17	173	717	4.1	6	2	31	25	197	1	9.3

39 | JAMES COOK

BUFFALO *BILLS (7)*

DRAFT: 2022-2(31)   AGE: 22   WT: 190   HT: 5-11

GEORGIA

The Bills drafted James Cook at the end of the second round in this year. Smaller than his brother, Dalvin Cook, James is an explosive, shifty back. He excels in his pass-catching ability, averaging 9.4 yards per reception with no drops last season.

He'll be the No. 2 back behind Devin Singletary, and should start out taking some passing-down duties. The Bills showed they wanted more backfield options by trying to sign J.D. McKissic this offseason. There's a good chance that Cook, by season's end, could carve out enough production to have more value than just a Singletary-insurance option.

YEAR	TEAM	GP	RUSH ATT	RUSH YD	YD/ATT	RUSH TD	100 YG	TAR	REC	REC YD	REC TD	FPPG
PROJ	BUF	17	110	515	4.7	3	0	53	42	340	2	9.3

40 | JAMES ROBINSON

JACKSONVILLE *JAGUARS (11)*

DRAFT: 2018-UNDRFT   AGE: 24   WT: 219   HT: 5-9

ILLINOIS STATE

The 2020 undrafted free agent has exceeded expectations in his two years as the lead back in Jacksonville. He suffered a late-season Achilles tear last year that puts his early availability and effectiveness into question. When he does return, he'll share backfield duties with Travis Etienne Jr., who missed last season to injury. Robinson was RB23 in fantasy PPG last season, but barring an Etienne injury, his days as a RB3 or better are over. Worst of all Etienne will probably assume pass-catching duties, making Robinson's best value as an insurance option.

YEAR	TEAM	GP	RUSH ATT	RUSH YD	YD/ATT	RUSH TD	100 YG	TAR	REC	REC YD	REC TD	FPPG
2020	JAC	14	240	1070	4.5	7	4	60	49	344	3	17.9
2021	JAC	14	164	767	4.7	8	1	46	31	222	0	12.7
PROJ	JAC	14	140	581	4.2	5	0	28	20	160	1	9.3

41 ALEXANDER **MATTISON**
*MINNESOTA **VIKINGS** (7)*
DRAFT: 2019-3(39) AGE: 26 WT: 221 HT: 5-11
BOISE STATE

Alexander Mattison has spent the last three seasons in Minnesota as Dalvin Cook's backup. Still, he's managed to accrue consistent numbers, averaging 607 all-purpose yards, 110 carries, 18 receptions, and 2.7 TDs per season. Last season he finished as RB37. His real value is when Cook is out — four games last season. During those four games, Mattison was the best fantasy RB in the league. He should be there in the later rounds (10-12), or reach a little bit if you draft Cook early.

YEAR	TEAM	GP	RUSH ATT	RUSH YD	YD/ATT	RUSH TD	100 YG	TAR	REC	REC YD	REC TD	FPPG
2019	MIN	13	100	462	4.6	1	0	12	10	82	0	5.4
2020	MIN	13	96	434	4.5	2	1	15	13	125	1	6.7
2021	MIN	16	134	491	3.7	3	2	39	32	228	1	8
PROJ	MIN	17	128	506	4.0	3	2	37	25	185	1	6.9

42 RONALD **JONES II**
*KANSAS CITY **CHIEFS** (8)*
DRAFT: 2018-2(6) AGE: 25 WT: 208 HT: 5-11
SOUTHERN CALIFORNIA

Ronald Jones II will be the last RB drafted with true top-15 upside that doesn't depend on injury promotion. Kansas City is not convinced Clyde Edwards-Helaire is the answer at the position, evidenced by the fact that Jerrick McKinnon was the postseason lead back in 2021 over a healthy CEH.

Though Jones was overtaken in Tampa Bay by Leonard Fournette last season, he is a solid runner and capable pass catcher, which may be enough to takeover duties in Kansas City.

YEAR	TEAM	GP	RUSH ATT	RUSH YD	YD/ATT	RUSH TD	100 YG	TAR	REC	REC YD	REC TD	FPPG
2019	TB	16	172	724	4.2	6	1	40	31	309	0	10.6
2020	TB	14	192	978	5.1	7	4	42	28	165	1	13.6
2021	TB	15	101	428	4.2	4	0	13	10	164	0	6.2
PROJ	KC	16	134	589	4.1	5	1	27	22	156	1	8.1

43 J.D. **MCKISSIC**
*WASHINGTON **COMMANDERS** (14)*
DRAFT: 2016-UNDRFT AGE: 29 WT: 195 HT: 5-10
ARKANSAS STATE

J.D. McKissic reneged on an agreement with Buffalo this offseason when Washington matched the offer, and chose to stay for a third season. The 29-year-old's fantasy value comes from his ability as a pass catcher. Last season among RBs, he finished eighth in targets and third in receiving yards per game. Antonio Gibson sees most of the red zone action and early-down work, limiting McKissic's upside. Fantasy managers should expect no more than his 2020 per-game output. He's a flex/bench player.

YEAR	TEAM	GP	RUSH ATT	RUSH YD	YD/ATT	RUSH TD	100 YG	TAR	REC	REC YD	REC TD	FPPG
2019	DET	16	38	205	5.4	0	0	42	34	233	1	5.2
2020	WAS	16	85	365	4.3	1	0	110	80	589	2	12.1
2021	WAS	11	48	212	4.4	2	0	53	43	397	2	11.6
PROJ	WAS	17	83	369	4.4	3	0	68	55	447	2	9.8

44 NYHEIM **HINES**
*INDIANAPOLIS **COLTS** (14)*
DRAFT: 2018-4(4) AGE: 25 WT: 196 HT: 5-9
NORTH CAROLINA STATE

Nyheim Hines hasn't missed a game in his four-year career, but the emergence of Jonathan Taylor drastically reduced Hines' fantasy value. Hines only played 32% of the snaps last season and finished the year as the 48th-best RB in fantasy. With Matt Ryan taking over under center, there's potential for more targets, but he will mostly ride the bench while Taylor's healthy. And even if Taylor is sidelined, Hines still won't be in for three-down work, like some better-positioned backups.

YEAR	TEAM	GP	RUSH ATT	RUSH YD	YD/ATT	RUSH TD	100 YG	TAR	REC	REC YD	REC TD	FPPG
2019	IND	16	52	199	3.8	2	0	58	44	320	0	6.7
2020	IND	16	89	380	4.3	3	0	76	63	482	4	12
2021	IND	17	56	276	4.9	2	0	57	40	310	1	6.9
PROJ	IND	17	68	308	4.5	2	0	63	50	391	2	8.5

45 JAMAAL **WILLIAMS**
*DETROIT **LIONS** (6)*
DRAFT: 2017-4(28) AGE: 27 WT: 224 HT: 6-0
BRIGHAM YOUNG

After four years in Green Bay, Jamaal Williams finished his first season in Detroit 30th in carries, 39th in rushing yards, and 43rd in FPs among RBs. He returns to the Lions as the No. 2 behind D'Andre Swift. With Swift on the field, Williams doesn't get enough volume to justify a fantasy start. Last season when Swift was out, Williams averaged 18 rushing attempts and 74 rushing yards. Draft him as Swift insurance, or look for him on waivers if Swift goes down.

YEAR	TEAM	GP	RUSH ATT	RUSH YD	YD/ATT	RUSH TD	100 YG	TAR	REC	REC YD	REC TD	FPPG
2019	GB	14	107	460	4.3	1	1	45	39	253	5	10.5
2020	GB	14	119	505	4.2	2	0	35	31	236	1	8.8
2021	DET	13	153	601	3.9	3	0	28	26	157	0	9.2
PROJ	DET	16	141	561	3.8	4	0	28	24	140	1	7.6

46 RAHEEM **MOSTERT**
*MIAMI **DOLPHINS** (11)*
DRAFT: 2015-UNDRFT AGE: 30 WT: 205 HT: 5-10
PURDUE

Raheem Mostert has a legitimate chance to emerge as the best back in Miami, that is, if he can stay healthy. Plagued by injuries, he has only one season with more than nine games.

The 30-year-old averaged a mammoth 5.4 yards per carry in the both 100-plus carry seasons in San Fran, first in NFL history for RBs with at least 200 carries. A crowded Miami backfield, along with his injury history, has us cautiously drafting him for the right price.

YEAR	TEAM	GP	RUSH ATT	RUSH YD	YD/ATT	RUSH TD	100 YG	TAR	REC	REC YD	REC TD	FPPG
2019	SF	16	137	772	5.6	8	1	22	14	180	2	10.6
2020	SF	8	104	521	5	2	0	19	16	156	1	12.7
2021	SF	1	2	20	10	0	0	0	0	0	0	2
PROJ	MIA	15	122	622	5.1	4	1	19	17	138	1	8.2

47 DAMEON **PIERCE**
*HOUSTON **TEXANS** (6)*
DRAFT: 2022-4(2) AGE: 22 WT: 215 HT: 5-10
FLORIDA

Dameon Pierce, the fourth-round pick in this year's draft, is a freakish athlete, with a 700-pound squat, 37-inch vertical, and 4.59 40-yard dash. He was PFF's highest rated back in this year's draft.

In Houston, he'll compete with Marlon Mack and 32-year-old Rex Burkhead, both of whom are only signed for a combined $3 million. For teams in rebuild mode like Houston, rookies often get the edge. He's familiar playing in a RB committee, as he shared duties during his time as a Gator with Malik Davis. We're giving him the best chance to emerge as the feature back in Houston.

YEAR	TEAM	GP	RUSH ATT	RUSH YD	YD/ATT	RUSH TD	100 YG	TAR	REC	REC YD	REC TD	FPPG
PROJ	HOU	17	157	582	3.7	4	0	36	31	253	1	8.5

48 TYLER **ALLGEIER**
*ATLANTA **FALCONS** (14)*
DRAFT: 2022-5(8) AGE: 21 WT: 220 HT: 5-11
BYU

Fifth-round draft pick Tyler Allgeier joins the Falcons after a sensational season at BYU. Allgeier ran for 1,601 yards (fourth best among college RBs) and 23 TDs (first). He's a monster with the ball in his hands, posting the most rushing yards after contact in college last season.

He's currently behind 31-year-old Cordarrelle Patterson and Damien Williams on the depth chart. Of the three he's the only true workhorse-style back, which could help him emerge as the feature back. Allgeier is worth a late-round flier when the rest of your roster is secure.

YEAR	TEAM	GP	RUSH ATT	RUSH YD	YD/ATT	RUSH TD	100 YG	TAR	REC	REC YD	REC TD	FPPG
PROJ	ATL	17	134	483	3.6	3	1	36	30	248	1	7.5

QUARTERBACKS

RUNNING BACKS

WIDE RECEIVERS

TIGHT ENDS

KICKERS

D/ST

49 | GUS EDWARDS

BALTIMORE **RAVENS (10)**
DRAFT: 2018-UNDRFT   AGE: 27   WT: 238   HT: 6-1
RUTGERS

Gus Edwards missed the entire 2021 season due to a torn ACL. He returns to Baltimore with fantasy managers hoping for a step up from his 2020 season when he finished outside the top-40 RBs. But the return of J.K. Dobbins, who also missed 2021 with an ACL, will leave Edwards' fantasy managers wanting more. Edwards lack of reception volume drastically limits his upside and he has little value with a healthy J.K. Dobbins. Consider Edwards late if you drafted Dobbins; otherwise he's not worth it.

YEAR	TEAM	GP	RUSH ATT	RUSH YD	YD/ATT	RUSH TD	100 YG	TAR	REC	REC YD	REC TD	FPPG
2019	BAL	16	133	711	5.3	2	2	7	7	45	0	5.9
2020	BAL	16	144	723	5	6	1	13	9	129	0	8.1
2021	BAL	DNP	INJURY									
PROJ	BAL	17	152	715	4.7	4	1	20	16	145	0	7.4

50 | JAMES WHITE

NEW ENGLAND **PATRIOTS (10)**
DRAFT: 2014-4(30)   AGE: 30   WT: 204   HT: 5-9
WISCONSIN

White returns to New England after re-signing this offseason. He'll resume pass-catching back duties after missing most of 2021 with a hip injury. In his two healthy games last season, he had 12 receptions for 94 yards. Neither Damien Harris nor Rhamondre Stevenson's receiving ability should threaten White's role in the offense. Consider drafting White for an occasional flex player some weeks. He doesn't have the insurance upside of some other backs in this range, though.

YEAR	TEAM	GP	RUSH ATT	RUSH YD	YD/ATT	RUSH TD	100 YG	TAR	REC	REC YD	REC TD	FPPG
2019	NE	15	67	263	3.9	1	0	95	72	645	5	13.3
2020	NE	14	35	121	3.5	2	0	62	49	375	1	8.3
2021	NE	3	10	38	3.8	1	0	14	12	94	0	10.4
PROJ	NE	17	36	155	4.3	2	0	58	47	391	2	7.4

51 | KENNETH GAINWELL

PHILADELPHIA **EAGLES (7)**
DRAFT: 2021-5(6)   AGE: 23   WT: 200   HT: 5-9
MEMPHIS

Kenneth Gainwell enters his sophomore campaign after a mostly underwhelming rookie season. He'll compete for touches with the Eagles top rusher, Miles Sanders, along with Boston Scott and Kennedy Brooks. Gainwell was surprisingly effective in the red zone, converting 50% of his 10 carries into TDs. His best hope for fantasy relevance is as a pass catcher. A standout receiving back for Memphis, Gainwell showed glimpses of his receiving ability last season, as he finished sixth in yards per route run. He's best seen as a low-end flex option.

YEAR	TEAM	GP	RUSH ATT	RUSH YD	YD/ATT	RUSH TD	100 YG	TAR	REC	REC YD	REC TD	FPPG
2021	PHI	16	68	291	4.3	5	0	50	33	253	1	7.7
PROJ	PHI	17	84	353	4.2	4	0	45	29	228	2	7.2

52 | DARRELL HENDERSON JR.

LOS ANGELES **RAMS (7)**
DRAFT: 2019-3(6)   AGE: 25   WT: 208   HT: 5-8
MEMPHIS

Like many RBs in this range, Darrell Henderson is another back whose fantasy appeal is as insurance if starter Cam Akers misses time. Henderson showed out in 2021 with Akers sidelined all season (Achilles), averaging 17.5 fantasy PPG through Week 8. His output was mostly a result of volume rather than efficiency. He slowed down in the second half of the season and was never fully healthy after Week 12. Akers is the Rams starter; Henderson should be viewed as a high-end handcuff.

YEAR	TEAM	GP	RUSH ATT	RUSH YD	YD/ATT	RUSH TD	100 YG	TAR	REC	REC YD	REC TD	FPPG
2019	LAR	13	39	147	3.8	0	0	6	4	37	0	1.7
2020	LAR	15	138	624	4.5	5	1	24	16	159	1	8.7
2021	LAR	12	149	688	4.6	5	0	40	29	176	3	13.6
PROJ	LAR	16	105	430	3.9	4	0	26	21	157	2	7.1

53 | ISAIAH SPILLER

LOS ANGELES **CHARGERS (8)**
DRAFT: 2022-4(18)   AGE: 20   WT: 215   HT: 6-1
TEXAS A&M

Isaiah Spiller was considered one of the top-three RBs in the draft until a lackluster combine performance. Selected by the Chargers in the fourth round, Spiller is poised to overtake Joshua Kelly for the No. 2 spot behind Austin Ekeler. Spiller is a bigger back and should complement Ekeler's style. Spiller is no threat to Ekeler's status as the Charger's No. 1, but is his likely replacement if he misses any time. For injury roulette players, and especially for Ekeler's managers, in an offense that can turn whoever's starting in the backfield into fantasy relevant, Spiller's worth a late-round pick.

YEAR	TEAM	GP	RUSH ATT	RUSH YD	YD/ATT	RUSH TD	100 YG	TAR	REC	REC YD	REC TD	FPPG
PROJ	LAC	17	124	536	4.3	4	1	22	18	132	1	6.8

54 | MARLON MACK

HOUSTON **TEXANS (6)**
DRAFT: 2017-4(37)   AGE: 26   WT: 213   HT: 5-11
SOUTH FLORIDA

The 26-year-old RB signed with Houston this offseason after spending five years in Indy. He had success as the feature back for the Colts in 2018 and 2019, averaging 4.6 yards per touch. The emergence of Jonathan Taylor along with a torn Achilles in Week 1 of 2020 led to the end of Mack's time in Indy. With only 32-year-old Rex Burkhead and fourth-round rookie Dameon Pierce in his way, Mack may be the favorite for touch-leader in Houston, at least at the start of the season.

YEAR	TEAM	GP	RUSH ATT	RUSH YD	YD/ATT	RUSH TD	100 YG	TAR	REC	REC YD	REC TD	FPPG
2019	IND	14	247	1091	4.4	8	3	17	14	82	0	12.8
2020	IND	1	4	26	6.5	0	0	3	3	30	0	8.6
2021	IND	5	28	101	3.6	0	0	5	2	8	0	2.6
PROJ	HOU	15	139	526	3.4	4	1	13	11	68	0	6.1

55 | RACHAAD WHITE

TAMPA BAY **BUCCANEERS (11)**
DRAFT: 2022-3(27)   AGE: 23   WT: 210   HT: 6-2
ARIZONA STATE

We're projecting rookie Rachaad White to enter the season as Fournette's primary backup over Ke'Shawn Vaughn. White is patient, letting plays develop and exploding through the holes once they do. He led all college RBs in receiving yards and yards per route run, and finished second in receptions. PFF ranked him the best receiving back in the class. His size and athleticism — 38-inch vertical and 125-inch broad jump (both top 15%) — make him a potential bell-cow back. But without an injury to Fournette, or perhaps Giovanni Bernard, White will have little fantasy value. He's another insurance play.

YEAR	TEAM	GP	RUSH ATT	RUSH YD	YD/ATT	RUSH TD	100 YG	TAR	REC	REC YD	REC TD	FPPG
PROJ	TB	17	69	293	4.2	2	0	24	19	145	1	4.8

56 | SONY MICHEL

MIAMI **DOLPHINS (11)**
DRAFT: 2018-1(31)   AGE: 27   WT: 220   HT: 5-11
GEORGIA

Sony Michel joins a crowded Dolphins backfield, after serving backup duties for the Super Bowl winning Rams. The problem for Michel is that there are three RBs ahead of him on the depth chart, all vying for touches. Chase Edmonds is the most probable leader, especially with his reception upside. But with Raheem Mostert, and even Myles Gaskin, looking for carries, Michel's path is obstacle-laden. He'll be lucky to repeat his RB31 finish from last season without some injury help.

YEAR	TEAM	GP	RUSH ATT	RUSH YD	YD/ATT	RUSH TD	100 YG	TAR	REC	REC YD	REC TD	FPPG
2019	NE	16	247	912	3.7	7	0	20	12	94	0	9.7
2020	NE	9	79	449	5.7	1	1	9	7	114	1	8.4
2021	LAR	17	208	845	4.1	4	2	33	21	128	1	8.7
PROJ	MIA	16	60	288	4.8	4	0	16	14	90	0	4.7

2021 ADVANCED WIDE RECEIVER STATS

		GP	YBC/R	AIR/R	YAC/R	YACON/R	BRKTKL	DROP	RZ TGT	20+ YDS	40+ YDS	LONG
1	COOPER KUPP (LAR)	17	7.6	7.6	5.8	1.8	10	8	37	30	9	59
2	DEEBO SAMUEL (SF)	16	8	8	11	3.8	13	10	9	24	10	83
3	JA'MARR CHASE (CIN)	17	9.9	9.9	8	3.1	8	11	12	22	8	82
4	DAVANTE ADAMS (GB)	16	7.8	7.8	4.8	1.2	5	4	27	19	4	59
5	JUSTIN JEFFERSON (MIN)	17	10.5	10.5	4.4	1.4	5	7	20	27	5	56
6	TYREEK HILL (KC)	17	7.2	7.2	4	1	10	7	23	13	3	75
7	STEFON DIGGS (BUF)	17	8.7	8.7	3.2	1.5	7	5	34	12	4	61
8	MIKE EVANS (TB)	16	10.5	10.5	3.5	0.9	2	2	18	20	3	46
9	DK METCALF (SEA)	17	8.5	8.5	4.4	2.1	8	4	19	11	2	84
10	DIONTAE JOHNSON (PIT)	16	5.9	5.9	4.9	0.9	8	5	21	14	4	50
11	MIKE WILLIAMS (LAC)	16	9.6	9.6	5.5	1.8	2	6	19	17	9	72
12	CEEDEE LAMB (DAL)	16	8.4	8.4	5.6	2.5	12	8	10	20	2	49
13	KEENAN ALLEN (LAC)	16	7.6	7.6	3.2	0.8	1	8	23	12	2	42
14	TYLER LOCKETT (SEA)	16	12.3	12.3	3.8	0.9	2	0	7	22	7	69
15	TEE HIGGINS (CIN)	14	10.8	10.8	3.9	1.2	4	5	11	17	2	54
16	CHRIS GODWIN (TB)	14	5.3	5.3	6	1.9	5	5	25	15	1	44
17	HUNTER RENFROW (LV)	17	5.7	5.7	4.4	1.1	2	2	23	10	1	54
18	BRANDIN COOKS (HOU)	16	7.5	7.5	4	0.8	5	5	10	12	5	52
19	MICHAEL PITTMAN JR. (IND)	17	8.3	8.3	4	1.1	2	6	16	12	3	57
20	DJ MOORE (CAR)	17	7.9	7.9	4.6	1.4	4	10	13	16	1	64
21	JAYLEN WADDLE (MIA)	16	5.5	5.5	4.2	1	4	8	15	8	2	57
22	ADAM THIELEN (MIN)	13	7.3	7.3	3.6	0.9	1	1	13	14	0	35
23	MARQUISE BROWN (BAL)	16	6.8	6.8	4.3	1	4	8	16	15	3	49
24	TERRY MCLAURIN (WAS)	17	9.6	9.6	4.1	1.6	4	5	9	15	3	46
25	AMARI COOPER (DAL)	15	9.3	9.3	3.5	1.2	4	4	17	15	1	41
26	CHRISTIAN KIRK (ARI)	17	10	10	3	0.8	1	6	10	16	4	50
27	DARNELL MOONEY (CHI)	17	8.3	8.3	4.7	1.5	5	9	10	14	3	64
28	KENDRICK BOURNE (NE)	17	7.5	7.5	7	1.7	5	2	7	10	5	75
29	AMON-RA ST. BROWN (DET)	16	5.4	5.4	4.7	1.1	2	1	14	11	0	37
30	DEVONTA SMITH (PHI)	17	10.9	10.9	3.4	1	2	2	8	16	1	46
31	TYLER BOYD (CIN)	16	6.6	6.6	5.8	0.9	2	0	7	10	2	68
32	VAN JEFFERSON (LAR)	17	11.7	11.7	4.3	1.6	2	6	15	12	4	79
33	MARQUEZ CALLAWAY (NO)	17	12	12	3.1	1.3	4	4	9	9	3	58
34	DEANDRE HOPKINS (ARI)	10	10.3	10.3	3.3	1.1	0	1	14	7	1	55
35	A.J. BROWN (TEN)	13	9.9	9.9	3.9	1.6	2	8	11	10	3	57
36	BRANDON AIYUK (SF)	17	8.5	8.5	6.2	2.5	3	4	10	16	1	43
37	A.J. GREEN (ARI)	16	12.4	12.4	3.4	1.5	5	5	17	16	3	42
38	K.J. OSBORN (MIN)	17	9.5	9.5	3.6	1.1	2	4	9	10	2	64

2022 PPR RANKINGS

		BYE	
1.	LAR	7	COOPER KUPP
2.	MIN	7	JUSTIN JEFFERSON
3.	CIN	10	JA'MARR CHASE
4.	BUF	7	STEFON DIGGS
5.	LV	6	DAVANTE ADAMS
6.	SF	9	DEEBO SAMUEL
7.	MIA	11	TYREEK HILL
8.	DAL	9	CEEDEE LAMB
9.	LAC	8	KEENAN ALLEN
10.	CIN	10	TEE HIGGINS
11.	TB	11	MIKE EVANS
12.	CAR	13	DJ MOORE
13.	MIA	11	JAYLEN WADDLE
14.	IND	14	MICHAEL PITTMAN JR.
15.	PHI	7	A.J. BROWN
16.	SEA	11	DK METCALF
17.	WAS	14	TERRY MCLAURIN
18.	PIT	9	DIONTAE JOHNSON
19.	HOU	6	BRANDIN COOKS
20.	LAC	8	MIKE WILLIAMS
21.	CHI	14	DARNELL MOONEY
22.	CLE	9	AMARI COOPER
23.	ARI	13	MARQUISE BROWN
24.	TB	11	CHRIS GODWIN
25.	DEN	9	COURTLAND SUTTON
26.	DEN	9	JERRY JEUDY
27.	NYJ	10	ELIJAH MOORE
28.	DET	6	AMON-RA ST. BROWN
29.	NO	14	MICHAEL THOMAS
30.	SEA	11	TYLER LOCKETT
31.	LV	6	HUNTER RENFROW
32.	ATL	14	DRAKE LONDON
33.	LAR	7	ALLEN ROBINSON II
34.	KC	8	JUJU SMITH-SCHUSTER
35.	BAL	10	RASHOD BATEMAN
36.	BUF	7	GABRIEL DAVIS
37.	PHI	7	DEVONTA SMITH
38.	MIN	7	ADAM THIELEN
39.	ARI	13	DEANDRE HOPKINS
40.	TEN	6	TREYLON BURKS
41.	SF	9	BRANDON AIYUK
42.	JAC	11	CHRISTIAN KIRK
43.	GB	14	ALLEN LAZARD
44.	TEN	6	ROBERT WOODS
45.	PIT	9	CHASE CLAYPOOL
46.	NYJ	10	GARRETT WILSON
47.	DAL	9	MICHAEL GALLUP
48.	NO	14	CHRIS OLAVE
49.	NYG	9	KADARIUS TONEY
50.	KC	8	M. VALDES-SCANTLING
51.	KC	8	SKYY MOORE
52.	NE	10	DEVANTE PARKER
53.	NYG	9	KENNY GOLLADAY
54.	DET	6	DJ CHARK JR.
55.	CIN	10	TYLER BOYD
56.	TB	11	RUSSELL GAGE
57.	NE	10	JAKOBI MEYERS
58.	NO	14	JARVIS LANDRY
59.	ARI	13	RONDALE MOORE
60.	DET	6	JAMESON WILLIAMS
61.	TB	11	JULIO JONES
62.	NYJ	10	COREY DAVIS
63.	GB	14	CHRISTIAN WATSON
64.	LAR	7	VAN JEFFERSON
65.	KC	8	MECOLE HARDMAN
66.	WAS	14	JAHAN DOTSON
67.	CAR	13	ROBBIE ANDERSON
68.	BUF	7	JAMISON CROWDER
69.	JAC	11	MARVIN JONES JR.
70.	NYG	9	STERLING SHEPARD
71.	NE	6	KENDRICK BOURNE
72.	PIT	9	GEORGE PICKENS
73.	IND	14	ALEC PIERCE
74.	FA	7	ODELL BECKHAM JR.
75.	LAC	8	JOSHUA PALMER
76.	MIN	7	K.J. OSBORNE

QUARTERBACKS

RUNNING BACKS

WIDE RECEIVERS

TIGHT ENDS

KICKERS

D/ST

1 COOPER **KUPP**

LOS ANGELES ***RAMS (7)***

DRAFT: 2017-3(5)   AGE: 29   WT: 208   HT: 6-2

GEORGIA

▶ Kupp's historic performance last year established him as an elite receiving talent, and landed him 70% of all votes for AP Offensive Player of the Year. He was first in every fantasy metric that matters: targets, receptions, receiving yards, and TDs. His 25-plus fantasy PPG were the most in the league for all players.

Fantasy managers can't deny the bromance between Kupp and Rams QB Matthew Stafford. Kupp's route running ability complements Stafford's experience and ability to read defenses. On the field for 94% of offensive snaps, Kupp accounted for a massive 36% of Stafford's completions. More significantly, Kupp saw a third of all red zone targets, and shouldn't worry about losing targets to new addition Allen Robinson II, a between the 20's receiver. Robinson will fill the role vacated by Robert Woods who departed for the Titans, but Kupp's role is firmly cemented in this offense.

Kupp is clearly Stafford's favorite target, and the pair is efficient. Stafford's QB rating saw a 20-point boost when throwing to his top receiver. And in the infamous playoff game against the Bucs, Stafford looked for Kupp when the game was on the line, as the Bucs knew he would, and they still couldn't stop him.

Kupp will likely see a dip in overall production, as last year's totals will be difficult to repeat He enters the season 29 years old, a drop-off age for most WRs. However, he could have a 20% decline and still finish No. 1. Draft him with any pick, and enjoy having a set-it and forget-it superstar each week.

YEAR	TEAM	GP	TAR	REC	REC YD	YD/REC	REC TDS	100 YG	RUSH ATT	RUSH YD	RUSH TD	FPPG
2019	LAR	16	134	94	1161	12.4	10	5	2	4	0	16.9
2020	LAR	15	124	92	974	10.6	3	3	4	33	0	14
2021	LAR	17	191	145	1947	13.4	16	11	4	18	0	25.7
PROJ	LAR	17	154	124	1570	12.7	12	7	4	21	0	20.9

2 JUSTIN **JEFFERSON**

MINNESOTA ***VIKINGS (7)***

DRAFT: 2020-1(22)   AGE: 23   WT: 195   HT: 6-1

LSU

▶ Justin Jefferson has been a fantasy stud since his debut. He finished his rookie season (2020) as WR5, and his 1,400 receiving yards broke Randy Moss' first-year record.

A 2021 sophomore slump? Not in the slightest. Last season, Jefferson averaged 19.6 fantasy PPG (fourth best) and posted seven 100-plus yard games for the second straight season. He only had four games last year when he scored fewer than 16 FPs.

Jefferson has built a strong rapport with Kirk Cousins, who continues to provide opportunities for his receivers. Cousins' 33 touchdowns in 16 games was tied for seventh best in the league, of which Jefferson reeled in 30%. One reason for the big production is his ability to stretch the field. Jefferson had the most yards before catch in league last season, and a massive 12.4-yard average depth of target.

The Vikings made some key coaching changes in the offseason, hiring Wes Philips, Rams TE coach, as offensive coordinator, and Kevin O'Connell, Rams offensive coordinator, as head coach. This bodes well for Jefferson, as the Rams led the NFL in FPs for receivers in a pass-heavy scheme. Although there are plenty of good pass catchers in Minnesota (Adam Thielen, KJ Osborne, and TE Irv Smith Jr.), Jefferson should still see almost a third of the team's targets in 2022.

If Jefferson can convert more of his red zone targets (20), his TD numbers could see a boost. We feel confident that with such a high floor, Jefferson ranks as our No. 2 receiver, and should have no problems finishing as a top-five receiver.

YEAR	TEAM	GP	TAR	REC	REC YD	YD/REC	REC TDS	100 YG	RUSH ATT	RUSH YD	RUSH TD	FPPG
2020	MIN	16	125	88	1400	15.9	7	7	1	2	0	16.9
2021	MIN	16	167	108	1616	15	10	7	6	14	0	20.7
PROJ	MIN	17	166	102	1517	14.9	9	7	5	17	0	18.2

3 JA'MARR **CHASE**

CINCINNATI ***BENGALS (10)***

DRAFT: 2021-1(5)   AGE: 22   WT: 201   HT: 6-0

LSU

▶ Ja'Marr Chase, much like his LSU teammate Justin Jefferson, had one heck of an NFL debut, tallying 1,455 receiving yards, fourth best in the league. Chase reunited with his college National Championship QB, a now fully healthy Joe Burrow, and they led a high-powered Bengals offense on an unexpected run to the Super Bowl.

Chase has shown more production per opportunity than almost any other WR. His 7.53 targets per game may have ranked 26th among WRs last season, but he finished with 13 TDs (third best) and 18 fantasy PPG (WR5). This can be attributed to what happens before and after Chase gets the ball. He was first in average depth of target, and had more yards after the catch per reception than any other WR with a minimum of 80 catches.

Chase is projected to put up top-five WR numbers this season, but fantasy managers should be aware of some of his production challenges. Fluke or not, his 11 dropped passes were most in the league last season. And he shares the field with Tee Higgins, a likely top-ten receiver who saw an almost identical target share last season. There will be games when Chase's numbers drop (second-lowest consistency rating out of our top-20 WRs) and Higgins' soar. During Weeks 9-17 last season, crucial weeks in any fantasy league, Chase averaged 8.1 fantasy PPG, with Higgins seeing the bulk of the work in that period.

Chase lands at No. 3 in our rankings mostly because last year's top-two ADP WRs are now on new teams, and it's always safer to choose what you know over uncertainty.

YEAR	TEAM	GP	TAR	REC	REC YD	YD/REC	REC TDS	100 YG	RUSH ATT	RUSH YD	RUSH TD	FPPG
2021	CIN	17	128	81	1455	18	13	5	7	21	0	18
PROJ	CIN	17	140	88	1375	15.6	10	6	12	61	0	17.2

4 STEFON **DIGGS**

BUFFALO ***BILLS (7)***

DRAFT: 2015-5(10)   AGE: 28   WT: 191   HT: 6-0

MARYLAND

▶ Entering the 2022 season, there is a good amount of uncertainty surrounding some of the best receivers (Davante Adams and Tyreek Hill to new teams, and Deebo Samuel is playing with a new QB). Stefon Diggs is the exception, as he returns to the same team, same QB, familiar coaches, and a familiar scheme. With this pick, you know what you are going to get.

Diggs had a good, if not great 2021 season, once again finishing as a top-10 fantasy WR, and averaging 16.8 fantasy PPG. He had seven games of at least 18 fantasy points and five games with 20-plus. His 10 TDs — all from plays inside the red zone — was sixth best in the league.

Diggs is hands-down Josh Allen's No. 1 receiving option, accounting for 25.3% of Allen's targets last year. His percentage jumps to 29.7% in the red zone, and his 24 red zone targets were second only to Cooper Kupp. And Diggs saw a league-best 20 end zone targets. red zone targets plus end zone Targets equals TDs, and TDs equal fantasy points.

Diggs signed a four-year $96 million extension with the Bills this offseason, securing his status as their top receiver. The departures of Cole Beasley and Emmanuel Sanders was offset by the addition of Jamison Crowder, who will compete with Gabriel Davis and TE Dawson Knox for the remaining targets.

After four straight 1,000-plus yard seasons, Diggs is a safe pick for your WR1 position.

YEAR	TEAM	GP	TAR	REC	REC YD	YD/REC	REC TDS	100 YG	RUSH ATT	RUSH YD	RUSH TD	FPPG
2019	MIN	15	94	63	1130	17.9	6	5	5	61	0	14.5
2020	BUF	16	166	127	1535	12.1	8	7	1	1	0	20.5
2021	BUF	17	164	103	1225	11.9	10	2	0	0	0	16.8
PROJ	BUF	17	165	103	1316	12.8	9	4	1	5	0	17.0

5 DAVANTE **ADAMS**

LAS VEGAS **RAIDERS (6)**

DRAFT: 2014-2(21) AGE: 29 WT: 215 HT: 6-1   FRESNO STATE

The Raiders and their fans couldn't be happier about the offseason acquisition of proven-bad-ass Davante Adams. And Adams himself is embracing the reunion with his Fresno State teammate, Derek Carr. With a five-year, $141 million contract, the Raiders expect elite production.

Adams' work at Green Bay with Aaron Rodgers was nothing short of elite. Over the last four seasons, he's averaged 10.8 targets per game and 21.8 fantasy PPG.

Last season, for WRs, he finished second in every fantasy-point-generating metric, except total yards, where he finished third, a mere 63 yards behind Justin Jefferson who played one more game. On a per-game basis, Adams averaged more yards and fantasy points than Jefferson. Las Vegas hopes he can produce similar numbers with Carr and the Raiders who played their final ten games last season without a true WR1. While Carr is no Rodgers, he did have more pass attempts, completions, and yards per games last season than Rodgers, and he equaled Rodgers completion percentage.

Carr needs to improve his TD numbers, and perhaps red zone specialist Adams will help. There's no argument that Adams target share will decrease with pass catchers Hunter Renfrow and Darren Waller on the field.

But the money says there should be plenty of work for Adams. With the uncertainty of a new locale, he is no longer a guaranteed top-five receiver, but he could have done a lot worse than LV.

YEAR	TEAM	GP	TAR	REC	REC YD	YD/REC	REC TDS	100 YG	RUSH ATT	RUSH YD	RUSH TD	FPPG
2019	GB	12	127	83	997	12	5	5	0	0	0	17.7
2020	GB	14	148	115	1374	11.9	18	7	0	0	0	25.7
2021	GB	16	169	123	1553	12.6	11	8	0	0	0	21.5
PROJ	LV	17	141	110	1364	12.4	7	4	0	0	0	17.0

7 TYREEK **HILL**

MIAMI **DOLPHINS (11)**

DRAFT: 2016-5(28) AGE: 28 WT: 185 HT: 5-10   WEST ALABAMA

Hill had at least 1,180 yards in four of the last five seasons, and he's averaged more than 10 TDs in each of those campaigns. Last season, he finished third in receptions (career best 111), sixth in total yards and fantasy points, and seventh in targets among WRs. Week to week, Hill had consistency problems: he had five weeks of 10 or fewer fantasy points and five weeks of 27-plus fantasy points. He averaged 17.6 fantasy PPG on the season, but as we know, he is now with a different QB and different team.

This offseason Hill was traded to the Dolphins who gave up first-, second-, and fourth-round picks in 2022 and fourth and sixth rounders in 2023. Then they signed Hill to a $120 million, four-year extension, so Miami is all in. We think it's fair to assume some regression without Mahomes and that high-powered KC offense.

New Miami head coach Mike McDaniel (former 49ers offensive coordinator) promotes getting the ball in the hands of his playmakers, as he did with Swiss army knife Deebo Samuel. And with a deep and talented backfield (Chase Edmonds, Raheem Mostert, and Myles Gaskin), along with pass catchers Jalen Waddle and Mike Gesiscki, defenses will have a hard time double teaming Hill.

We can't be sure of Hill's exact role in Miami this year. What we do know is he'll be used early and often. However, we remain cautiously optimistic about his fantasy season, and we won't look to draft him before Round 3.

YEAR	TEAM	GP	TAR	REC	REC YD	YD/REC	REC TDS	100 YG	RUSH ATT	RUSH YD	RUSH TD	FPPG
2019	KC	12	89	58	860	14.8	7	2	8	23	0	15.7
2020	KC	15	135	87	1276	14.7	15	3	13	123	2	21.9
2021	KC	17	159	111	1239	11.2	9	3	9	96	0	17.6
PROJ	MIA	17	140	98	1156	11.8	8	2	10	69	0	15.8

6 DEEBO **SAMUEL**

SAN FRANCISCO **49ERS (9)**

DRAFT: 2019-2(4) AGE: 26 WT: 215 HT: 6-0   SOUTH CAROLINA

San Francisco's game plan in 2021: Get Deebo Samuel the ball. He finished last season third in fantasy PPG among WRs, putting up 1,770 all-purpose yards. In his first eight regular season games, he amassed elite WR numbers, averaging 21.7 fantasy PPG, and posting three games with more than 150 receiving yards. In that stretch, he had a mere 6 rushing attempts.

Then came the second half of the season. During his last eight regular season games, the 49ers used Samuel as more of a WR/RB hybrid: he carried the ball 53 times for 343 yards and 7 TDs, while averaging 3.5 receptions and 65.3 receiving yards per game (22.68 fantasy PPG). He accounted for 28% of the 49ers total yards from scrimmage!

His ability with the ball in his hands is unmatched. His 10 yards after the catch per reception was easily the most among WRs, and he had 3 more broken tackles than any other WR.

Samuel asked for a trade this offseason, but the 49ers refused. There was speculation that Samuel was concerned with longevity, as playing the "wide-back" role takes a considerable toll on the body. After sitting out to start training camp, the 49ers and Samuel worked out a three-year, $73.5 extension. With his contract now ironed out, expect the 49ers to utilize Deebo in whatever way helps the team most. But, with Trey Lance as the starter, there are some unknowns for this season.

Deebo has proven that no matter his role, he will produce. Expect him to be off the board by the middle of Round 2.

YEAR	TEAM	GP	TAR	REC	REC YD	YD/REC	REC TDS	100 YG	RUSH ATT	RUSH YD	RUSH TD	FPPG
2019	SF	15	81	57	802	14.1	3	3	14	159	3	12.6
2020	SF	7	44	33	391	11.8	1	1	8	26	0	11.5
2021	SF	16	120	77	1405	18.2	6	5	59	365	8	21.1
PROJ	SF	17	105	69	1096	15.9	5	3	75	442	5	16.6

8 CEEDEE **LAMB**

DALLAS **COWBOYS (9)**

DRAFT: 2020-1(17) AGE: 23 WT: 189 HT: 6-2   OKLAHOMA

It seemed as if everyone was calling for 2021 to be a breakout year for CeeDee Lamb after an impressive rookie campaign (74-935-5). To fantasy owner's chagrin, 2021 was much the same as his rookie year. Hunter Renfrow and Mike Williams finished with more fantasy points and fantasy PPG than Lamb.

Lamb's metrics last year were pedestrian for a now top-10-ranked WR. Finishing with a 14.6 fantasy PPG average, Lamb's numbers weren't very consistent, as he had six games with fewer than 10 fantasy points.

We expect 2022 will be better for Lamb. The departure of Amari Cooper and Cedric Wilson leaves 129 targets up for grabs. And the Cowboys WR2, Michael Gallup, is still coming back from an ACL tear. Considering that the current WR3, James Washington, didn't have 300 yards last year and will be out 4-8 weeks this season because of a fractured right foot suffered in training camp, Lamb and TE Dalton Schultz will benefit most.

It helps that Dallas continues a pass-heavy scheme, ranking sixth last year in passes attempted and fourth in fantasy points earned by WRs. The situation for Lamb screams success.

A 10% increase seems like a safe floor for Lamb this season. This would have made him the 12th-best WR on the year last season. In a world where volume is the key, Lamb is in for a strong, much more consistent year. With so much uncertainty surrounding some of the bigger WRs this season, Lamb feels safe and bust-proof.

YEAR	TEAM	GP	TAR	REC	REC YD	YD/REC	REC TDS	100 YG	RUSH ATT	RUSH YD	RUSH TD	FPPG
2020	DAL	16	111	74	935	12.6	5	2	10	82	1	13.2
2021	DAL	16	120	79	1102	13.9	6	3	9	76	0	14.6
PROJ	DAL	17	145	95	1231	13.0	7	4	9	65	0	15.7

QUARTERBACKS

RUNNING BACKS

WIDE RECEIVERS

TIGHT ENDS

KICKERS

D/ST

9 | KEENAN ALLEN

*LOS ANGELES **CHARGERS** (8)*

DRAFT: 2013-3(14) AGE: 30 WT: 211 HT: 6-2 CALIFORNIA

Keenan Allen has been one of the most consistent WRs over the last five seasons, finishing four of those seasons with at least 1,100 yards. For WRs last year, he finished fifth in receptions, sixth in targets per game, 12th in total yards, and 12th in fantasy PPG. He had seven games with 19-plus FPs and only one game with fewer than 10. Allen is the No. 1 option for up-and-coming star QB Justin Herbert, seeing 23% of Herbert's targets. Herbert eclipsed 5,000 yards last season, a mark second only to Tom Brady, so there will be plenty of volume for both Allen and Chargers No. 2 WR, Mike Williams. All 6 of Allen's TDs last season came in the red zone, where Herbert looks for him most often. Last season, he had the fifth most red zone targets and receptions. Even at 30 years old, Allen is a solid WR2 with WR1 potential.

YEAR	TEAM	GP	TAR	REC	REC YD	YD/REC	REC TDS	100 YG	RUSH ATT	RUSH YD	RUSH TD	FPPG
2019	LAC	16	149	104	1199	11.5	6	2	3	16	0	16.3
2020	LAC	14	147	100	992	9.9	8	4	1	-1	0	17.7
2021	LAC	16	157	106	1138	10.7	6	4	0	0	0	16
PROJ	LAC	17	155	105	1129	10.8	7	4	1	1	0	15.3

12 | DJ MOORE

*CAROLINA **PANTHERS** (13)*

DRAFT: 2018-1(24) AGE: 25 WT: 210 HT: 6-0 MARYLAND

DJ Moore had more than 1,050 yards in each of the last three seasons, all with a carousel of subpar QBs. Last season, he finished sixth in targets, 10th in yards, and 11th in receptions as the 26th overall best fantasy WR, averaging 14 PPG.

Like the Panthers, Moore started 2021 on fire, posting 20-plus FPs in three of his first four games, but only averaged 11.3 FPs the rest of the season. His TD numbers need improvement, with just 4 per year in the last three seasons, but that number will rise with improved QB play and a better offense.

The opportunity and talent are there. Moore's ranking upgraded with the addition of Baker Mayfield. Mayfield is the best QB of Moore's career, and we expect Mayfield to win the starting job. Moore should finally exceed his ADP.

YEAR	TEAM	GP	TAR	REC	REC YD	YD/REC	REC TDS	100 YG	RUSH ATT	RUSH YD	RUSH TD	FPPG
2019	CAR	15	135	87	1175	13.5	4	4	6	40	0	15.5
2020	CAR	15	118	66	1193	18.1	4	4	2	22	0	14.1
2021	CAR	17	162	93	1157	12.4	4	3	8	48	0	14
PROJ	CAR	17	148	88	1198	13.6	7	3	7	43	0	14.9

10 | TEE HIGGINS

*CINCINNATI **BENGALS** (10)*

DRAFT: 2020-2(1) AGE: 23 WT: 215 HT: 6-4 CLEMSON

Tee Higgins may be the only fantasy WR1 who's the second-best WR on his team. Sure, he has to compete with Ja'marr Chase, who's exploded out of the starting gates as the Bengals No. 1 receiver, but Higgins was not far behind Chase in production last season. He finished top-15 in total receiving yards and 13th in fantasy PPG. Target volume is not a problem, as Higgins actually averaged more targets per game (7.9) than Chase (7.5). When the Bengals top-three receivers — Chase, Higgins, and Tyler Boyd — are all on the field, Higgins still sees a 23% target share. Chase and Higgins had equal targets in the red zone, but inside the 10, Higgins is the preferred receiver, owing to his size and ability to win 50/50 balls. Drafters may let Higgins fall because they'll be thinking of Chase, and we'll be thinking of drafting Higgins early, somewhere in the third round.

YEAR	TEAM	GP	TAR	REC	REC YD	YD/REC	REC TDS	100 YG	RUSH ATT	RUSH YD	RUSH TD	FPPG
2020	CIN	16	108	67	908	13.6	6	2	5	28	0	12.3
2021	CIN	14	110	74	1091	14.7	6	4	0	0	0	15.6
PROJ	CIN	17	130	88	1188	13.5	8	3	1	2	0	15.0

13 | JAYLEN WADDLE

*MIAMI **DOLPHINS** (11)*

DRAFT: 2021-1(6) AGE: 23 WT: 182 HT: 5-10 ALABAMA

Jaylen Waddle justified his 2021 sixth-overall draft pick with an impressive rookie season. He was one of only 23 WRs to exceed 1,000 receiving yards, and he finished the season 11th in targets, seventh in receptions, and 12th in total fantasy points.

Waddle has great hands, reeling in 80% of his targets inside the red zone last season. Inside the 10 he was even better, catching 88% of targets and scoring 6 TDs, both percentages second only to Adam Thielen.

Waddle has two things working against him this season: (1) the addition of Tyreek Hill, who Miami mortgaged the farm for. And (2) the talent limitations of QB Tua Tagavailoa.

Before the Hill acquisition Waddle was a surefire WR1, but you can still feel good with Waddle as your WR2 entering the 2022 season.

YEAR	TEAM	GP	TAR	REC	REC YD	YD/REC	REC TDS	100 YG	RUSH ATT	RUSH YD	RUSH TD	FPPG
2021	MIA	16	142	104	1015	9.8	6	1	2	3	1	15.5
PROJ	MIA	17	135	96	1045	10.9	7	1	5	26	1	14.8

11 | MIKE EVANS

*TAMPA BAY **BUCCANEERS** (11)*

DRAFT: 2014-1(7) AGE: 29 WT: 231 HT: 6-5 TEXAS A&M

Mike Evans has tallied 1,000-plus yards in each of his eight NFL seasons. Ranked just 25th in targets last season, he finished the year as the ninth-best fantasy receiver. The sure-handed Evans had an average depth of target of 13 yards, first among the top-40 WRs. In 16 games, Evans logged six games of 20-plus and 10 games of 14-plus fantasy points.

Since Tom Brady took over the offense in Tampa, 28-year-old Evans has had his two best seasons for TDs, 13 in 2020 and 14 in 2021. When Brady targets Evans, Brady's QB rating is a whopping 122.6.

With an injury-prone Godwin coming off an ACL tear, Evans should start the season as the featured receiver. A potential WR1, we're inserting him as a solid WR2.

YEAR	TEAM	GP	TAR	REC	REC YD	YD/REC	REC TDS	100 YG	RUSH ATT	RUSH YD	RUSH TD	FPPG
2019	TB	13	118	67	1157	17.3	8	3	0	0	0	17.7
2020	TB	16	109	70	1006	14.4	13	4	0	0	0	15.5
2021	TB	16	113	74	1035	14	14	2	1	10	0	16.4
PROJ	TB	17	128	82	1121	13.7	10	3	1	4	0	15.0

14 | MICHAEL PITTMAN JR.

*INDIANAPOLIS **COLTS** (14)*

DRAFT: 2020-2(2) AGE: 24 WT: 223 HT: 6-4 SOUTHERN CALIFORNIA

Michael Pittman Jr. enters his third season as the Colts No. 1 receiving option, and as a player whose value is on the rise. In Indy's run-heavy offense, Pittman finished last season with top-20 WR numbers in targets, receptions, yards, and TDs.

The Colts acquired Matt Ryan this offseason, a much more fantasy-friendly QB than departing Carson Wentz. Ryan's production in Atlanta with Julio Jones and Calvin Ridley, show the kind of fantasy numbers top receivers in his offense can produce. We wouldn't be surprised if head coach Frank Reich calls fewer run plays with a veteran passer under center.

Pittman should make a jump in production this season, and with such a high floor, he'll provide a solid WR2 option for your fantasy team.

YEAR	TEAM	GP	TAR	REC	REC YD	YD/REC	REC TDS	100 YG	RUSH ATT	RUSH YD	RUSH TD	FPPG
2020	IND	13	61	40	503	12.6	1	1	3	26	0	7.6
2021	IND	17	129	88	1082	12.3	6	2	5	44	0	13.9
PROJ	IND	17	138	93	1114	12.0	7	2	5	45	0	14.8

15 | A.J. BROWN
PHILADELPHIA EAGLES (7)
DRAFT: 2019-2(19) AGE: 25 WT: 226 HT: 6-1 OLE MISS

Of A.J. Browns' three seasons in the NFL, last season was his worst yet. He saw regression in every category that equals fantasy points, finishing as the WR28. For the first time, he posted under 1,000 receiving yards, operating in a run-heavy offense with an average QB. This offseason, Brown was traded to the Eagles, who boast a more run-centric scheme and have a less developed passer in QB Jalen Hurts. Hurts ranked in the bottom 10 for completions, pass attempts, passing TDs, and passing yards per game last year. Almost any other team may have improved Brown's fantasy outlook, except the Eagles. Plus he'll be competing with DeVonta Smith and Dallas Goedert for targets. His wide range of outcomes, from a high-end WR2 to a low-end WR3, has us ranking him lower than most outlets.

YEAR	TEAM	GP	TAR	REC	REC YD	YD/REC	REC TDS	100 YG	RUSH ATT	RUSH YD	RUSH TD	FPPG
2019	TEN	16	84	52	1051	20.2	8	5	3	60	1	13.6
2020	TEN	14	106	70	1075	15.4	11	4	0	0	0	17.4
2021	TEN	13	105	63	869	13.8	5	3	2	10	0	13.9
PROJ	PHI	17	123	78	1205	15.4	8	3	1	11	0	14.6

18 | DIONTAE JOHNSON
PITTSBURGH STEELERS (9)
DRAFT: 2019-3(2) AGE: 26 WT: 183 HT: 5-10 TOLEDO

In his third season, Diontae Johnson put up top WR numbers. He finished third in both targets and receptions, ninth in total yards, and 12th in TDs. He also recorded his first top-10 fantasy campaign, finishing eighth among all WRs.

Johnson was a consistent fantasy point generator, earning 14-plus points in 13 of his 17 games. He was also top-10 in separation at point of catch, and was Ben Roethlisberger's (quickest time to throw among QBs) No. 1 target. With Big Ben retired, the QB position could go to first-rounder Kenny Pickett or to offseason addition, Mitchell Trubisky.

Competition and time will decide who's under center. Johnson will need considerable target volume to finish inside the top 20 this season, no matter who throws him the ball.

YEAR	TEAM	GP	TAR	REC	REC YD	YD/REC	REC TDS	100 YG	RUSH ATT	RUSH YD	RUSH TD	FPPG
2019	PIT	16	92	59	680	11.5	5	0	4	41	0	10.1
2020	PIT	15	144	88	923	10.5	7	2	3	15	0	14.9
2021	PIT	16	169	107	1161	10.9	8	3	5	53	0	17.3
PROJ	PIT	17	148	92	1045	11.4	6	2	5	33	0	13.9

16 | DK METCALF
SEATTLE SEAHAWKS (11)
DRAFT: 2019-2(32) AGE: 24 WT: 235 HT: 6-4 OLE MISS

DK Metcalf's 2021 outing was a tale of two halves. In the first eight games, he averaged 18.1 fantasy PPG, on pace to finish as a top-five WR on the year, and this was under both QBs Geno Smith and Russell Wilson. Starting Week 10, when Russell Wilson played like a shell of himself, Metcalf's production declined considerably. He did, however, maintain a massive target share of 26.5%, but had a huge decline in yards and receptions. He managed to finish the year fourth in TDs (12), but 3 of those came in end-of-season garbage time. With Wilson now in Denver, Metcalf's value has decreased. Drew Lock hasn't yet proven himself a capable starting QB. Metcalf, 24 years old, built like an action figure, and with a massive new contract, should receive enough targets in 2022 to keep him in the WR2 range.

YEAR	TEAM	GP	TAR	REC	REC YD	YD/REC	REC TDS	100 YG	RUSH ATT	RUSH YD	RUSH TD	FPPG
2019	SEA	16	100	58	900	15.5	7	1	2	11	0	11.9
2020	SEA	16	129	83	1303	15.7	10	5	0	0	0	17.1
2021	SEA	17	129	75	967	12.9	12	1	1	6	0	14.4
PROJ	SEA	17	133	82	1105	13.5	8	1	1	3	0	14.2

19 | BRANDIN COOKS
HOUSTON TEXANS (6)
DRAFT: 2014-1(20) AGE: 28 WT: 183 HT: 5-10 OREGON STATE

The Texans have been more of a reality show than football team the last few seasons. Determined to change the culture, the Texans traded Deshaun Watson and hired veteran head coach Lovie Smith. Throughout the drama, Brandin Cooks has been the one fantasy bright spot for Houston. In the last seven seasons, Cooks had six 1,000-plus yard campaigns, and did so with four different teams and seven different QBs. Last season he was 13th in receptions and 20th in yards and fantasy points, despite Houston only winning three games. He posted eight games with 17-plus fantasy points, seven of them with newfound starter, Davis Mills. Plus, Cooks signed a two-year, $36.9 million extension this offseason. He will be overlooked in drafts this year. Scoop him up at the right price and you'll have a great value WR.

YEAR	TEAM	GP	TAR	REC	REC YD	YD/REC	REC TDS	100 YG	RUSH ATT	RUSH YD	RUSH TD	FPPG
2019	LAR	14	72	42	583	13.9	2	1	6	52	0	8.4
2020	HOU	15	119	81	1150	14.2	6	3	0	0	0	15.5
2021	HOU	16	133	90	1037	11.5	6	4	2	21	0	14.5
PROJ	HOU	17	140	93	1101	11.8	5	4	3	25	0	13.9

17 | TERRY MCLAURIN
WASHINGTON COMMANDERS (14)
DRAFT: 2019-3(13) AGE: 26 WT: 210 HT: 6-0 OHIO STATE

Terry McLaurin finished last season 13th in targets and 18th in yards, but failed to crack the top 20 in receptions, TDs, and fantasy points. McLaurin is a long-ball receiver, a fantasy owner's friend — his 13.1 aDOT was No. 1 among WRs with 75-plus receptions, and he finished eighth in yards per reception (13.7). He also posted top-15 numbers in plays of 10 yards or more (45), and 20 yards or more (15). For so many deep plays, McLaurin still lacks in TDs, with only 16 in his first three seasons.

The Commanders spent money this offseason to beef up their offensive line, and added QB Carson Wentz to replace Taylor Heinicke. We're not sold on Washington as a team with fantasy prominence, but McLaurin is the one player we feel comfortable drafting. He's got a safe floor with good upside.

YEAR	TEAM	GP	TAR	REC	REC YD	YD/REC	REC TDS	100 YG	RUSH ATT	RUSH YD	RUSH TD	FPPG
2019	WAS	14	93	58	919	15.8	7	3	0	0	0	13.7
2020	WAS	15	134	87	1118	12.9	4	3	2	30	0	15.1
2021	WAS	17	131	77	1053	13.7	5	4	1	12	0	12.6
PROJ	WAS	17	135	84	1155	13.8	6	4	1	6	0	13.9

20 | MIKE WILLIAMS
LOS ANGELES CHARGERS (8)
DRAFT: 2017-1(7) AGE: 27 WT: 218 HT: 6-4 CLEMSON

Mike Williams was undervalued and underrated last season. He finished 17th in fantasy PPG among WRs, ranking 11th in yards, and 16th in targets. He out-performed Chargers No. 1 passing option, Keenan Allen, in seven games last year. Plus, Williams led the team with 9 TDs.

Newly-minted superstar Justin Herbert's passing volume was second only to Tom Brady, and is easily enough to sustain two top-20 WRs. The Chargers and Herbert believe in Williams, so much so that in what was arguably their most important game last season, Williams was targeted a season high 17 times. Then, this offseason, the team doubled down on Williams with a three-year, $60 million extension. Williams is a solid WR2 for 2022.

YEAR	TEAM	GP	TAR	REC	REC YD	YD/REC	REC TDS	100 YG	RUSH ATT	RUSH YD	RUSH TD	FPPG
2019	LAC	15	90	49	1001	20.4	2	2	1	2	0	10.8
2020	LAC	15	85	48	756	15.8	5	2	1	1	0	10.2
2021	LAC	16	129	76	1146	15.1	9	4	0	0	0	15.3
PROJ	LAC	17	125	71	1097	15.5	9	3	0	0	0	13.8

21 DARNELL **MOONEY**

CHICAGO **BEARS (14)**

DRAFT: 2020-5(28) AGE: 24 WT: 173 HT: 5-11
TULANE

This will be Darnell Mooney's third season with the Bears, where he now has a foothold as their top receiver. Last season, he had four games of 120-plus yards and finished 10th in targets, 17th in yards, and 23rd in fantasy points among WRs.

Mooney has notable skills once he gets the ball in his hands. Last year he was fifth in yards after the catch, among WRs with 80-plus receptions. Playing 88% of Chicago's snaps, fifth most among non-QBs, Mooney gets plenty of opportunities to make big plays.

We expect him to achieve his second 1,000-yard season with the help of starting QB Justin Fields, who looks to improve as the Bears starter. Mooney is a WR3 with plenty of opportunity to land a finish in the WR2 range.

YEAR	TEAM	GP	TAR	REC	REC YD	YD/REC	REC TDS	100 YG	RUSH ATT	RUSH YD	RUSH TD	FPPG
2020	CHI	16	98	61	631	10.3	4	0	4	20	0	9.4
2021	CHI	17	140	81	1055	13	4	4	6	32	1	12.9
PROJ	CHI	17	142	77	1095	14.2	5	3	5	26	1	13.3

22 AMARI **COOPER**

CLEVELAND **BROWNS (9)**

DRAFT: 2015-1(4) AGE: 28 WT: 210 HT: 6-1
ALABAMA

28-year-old Amari Cooper was traded to the Browns this offseason and is slated to be the top target in Cleveland. He spent his first three NFL seasons with the Raiders, the next four with the Cowboys, and put up five 1,000-plus-yard campaigns in seven years. Still, Cooper never ascended to a true fantasy WR1. Last season, he was 27th in total fantasy points and 12th in TDs (8), but was no better than 29th in any other fantasy metric.

There's unlimited possibility in Cleveland, as Cooper looks to create a connection with the Brown's new QB, Deshaun Watson. Watson's likely six-game suspension puts a ceiling on Cooper's early potential, but he should see a considerable fantasy boost when Watson's under center. We like him in the WR3 range, but don't be surprised if he finishes better than that.

YEAR	TEAM	GP	TAR	REC	REC YD	YD/REC	REC TDS	100 YG	RUSH ATT	RUSH YD	RUSH TD	FPPG
2019	DAL	16	119	79	1189	15.1	8	4	1	6	0	15.4
2020	DAL	16	130	92	1114	12.1	5	4	6	14	0	14.7
2021	DAL	15	103	68	865	12.7	8	2	0	0	0	13.5
PROJ	CLE	17	125	82	1008	12.3	7	3	1	2	0	13.2

23 MARQUISE **BROWN**

ARIZONA **CARDINALS (13)**

DRAFT: 2019-1(25) AGE: 25 WT: 180 HT: 5-9
OKLAHOMA

Marquise Brown was traded to the Cardinals this offseason after only three years with Baltimore. His target share and fantasy production saw improvement each year, culminating in his first 1,000-yard effort last season. Among WRs, he was ninth in targets, 12th in receptions, 18th in TDs, and 21st in fantasy points during his last season as a Raven. His 6.8 yards before the catch per reception was 10th best among WRs with 90-plus receptions.

He joins an Arizona team as the No. 2 option behind DeAndre Hopkins, who is suspended for the first six games. This should give Brown some extra value early in the season. Since Kyler Murray has a similar style of play to Lamar Jackson, the adjustment for Brown should be easy. He's a solid WR3 with WR2 upside.

YEAR	TEAM	GP	TAR	REC	REC YD	YD/REC	REC TDS	100 YG	RUSH ATT	RUSH YD	RUSH TD	FPPG
2019	BAL	14	71	46	584	12.7	7	1	0	0	0	10.5
2020	BAL	16	100	58	769	13.3	8	1	1	1	0	11.4
2021	BAL	16	145	91	1008	11.1	6	3	1	5	0	14.3
PROJ	ARI	17	130	80	1005	12.6	7	2	0	0	0	13.1

24 CHRIS **GODWIN**

TAMPA BAY **BUCCANEERS (11)**

DRAFT: 2017-3(20) AGE: 26 WT: 208 HT: 6-1
PENN STATE

Chris Godwin suffered MCL/ACL injuries in Week 15 last season and will be worked back in slowly. He is not on the PUP list for training camp, which is a good sign. In 14 games last year, before the injuries, Godwin finished top-20 in every fantasy point metric except TDs. However, on a per game basis, he was 11th in targets, third in receptions, and sixth in fantasy points.

The question is, where do you consider taking Godwin in your draft, knowing he may not be a full go until later in the season? This depends on how well you've done with your early picks. You should secure your top-four skill position players before considering a post-injury Godwin. If you know you'll have a playoff team anyway, then why not draft a player who could help you win your playoffs at a reduced cost?

YEAR	TEAM	GP	TAR	REC	REC YD	YD/REC	REC TDS	100 YG	RUSH ATT	RUSH YD	RUSH TD	FPPG
2019	TB	14	120	86	1333	15.5	9	6	1	8	0	19.6
2020	TB	12	84	65	840	12.9	7	1	0	0	0	15.9
2021	TB	14	128	98	1103	11.3	5	5	4	21	1	17.6
PROJ	TB	14	110	75	997	13.3	5	2	4	22	1	15.2

25 COURTLAND **SUTTON**

DENVER **BRONCOS (9)**

DRAFT: 2018-2(8) AGE: 26 WT: 216 HT: 6-4
SOUTHERN METHODIST

After missing 15 games in 2020 with ACL/MCL injuries, Courtland Sutton returned to play every game last season. He finished 44th in fantasy points among WRs, but between Weeks 2-7 he had three games of 23-plus fantasy points. Denver never found footing with Drew Lock under center, but he's been traded to Seattle, and star QB Russell Wilson will be taking over for the Broncos. Wilson helped WRs Tyler Lockett and DK Metcalf achieve perennial top-20 WR status, and he'll likely do the same for Sutton and Jerry Jeudy. The question is, who will emerge as Wilson's No. 1 option. We're giving the edge to Sutton. His aDOT was a league-best 15.4 yards last season, just ahead of second-best: Tyler Lockett. And Wilson leads the league in average depth of throw per attempt. Sutton's our WR3 with the biggest upside.

YEAR	TEAM	GP	TAR	REC	REC YD	YD/REC	REC TDS	100 YG	RUSH ATT	RUSH YD	RUSH TD	FPPG
2019	DEN	16	125	72	1112	15.4	6	0	3	17	0	13.8
2020	DEN	1	6	3	66	22	0	0	0	0	0	9.6
2021	DEN	17	98	58	776	13.4	2	0	0	0	0	8.7
PROJ	DEN	17	126	73	1068	14.6	7	2	1	2	0	13.1

36 JERRY **JEUDY**

DENVER **BRONCOS (9)**

DRAFT: 2020-1(15) AGE: 23 WT: 193 HT: 6-1
ALABAMA

Entering his third season in the NFL, Jerry Jeudy has yet to live up to his 2020, 15th overall draft pick. He played just 10 games last season and averaged 8.5 fantasy PPG (WR68).

The good news: Jeudy is an excellent route runner who's only 23 years old. His 7.4 yards before the catch and 4.9 yards after the catch per reception are better than average, and his 10.5-yard average depth of target is respectable when considering the questionable QB play of recent years in Denver.

The great news: Russell Wilson is the new QB in Denver. This is Jeudy's first chance to play under an elite passer. He'll face competition for targets from Courtland Sutton, but there's enough volume for both to put up top-30 numbers. We still give Sutton the edge, but wouldn't be shocked to see Jeudy emerge as Denver's No. 1 option.

YEAR	TEAM	GP	TAR	REC	REC YD	YD/REC	REC TDS	100 YG	RUSH ATT	RUSH YD	RUSH TD	FPPG
2020	DEN	16	113	52	856	16.5	3	2	0	0	0	9.7
2021	DEN	10	56	38	467	12.3	0	0	2	3	0	8.5
PROJ	DEN	17	118	77	1058	13.7	6	2	3	14	0	13.0

27 | ELIJAH **MOORE**

DRAFT: 2021-2(2) AGE: 22 WT: 178 HT: 5-10
OLE MISS

Elijah Moore had a slow start to his rookie season before exploding on the scene to become one of the best WRs in a four-game stretch. Then his year was cut short due to a quad injury. Before the Jets Week 6 bye, Moore's production was limited. But, from Weeks 8-11, he was the third-best WR in fantasy (18.9 fantasy PPG), trailing only Cooper Kupp and Justin Jefferson. He finished the year 32nd in fantasy PPG, scoring 5 TDs in a generally weak offense.

QB Zach Wilson had a disappointing rookie season, and only took the field for 13 games. We expect more from Zach Wilson this year, which should be a boost for Moore.

Before drafting Garrett Wilson, we projected Moore to have a monster year. Now, with a slightly more crowded receiving corps that also includes Corey Davis, we've adjusted our numbers and still have Moore as a strong WR3/flex option.

YEAR	TEAM	GP	TAR	REC	REC YD	YD/REC	REC TDS	100 YG	RUSH ATT	RUSH YD	RUSH TD	FPPG
2021	NYJ	11	77	43	538	12.5	5	1	5	54	1	12.6
PROJ	NYJ	17	112	68	965	14.2	6	2	7	71	1	12.6

28 | AMON-RA **ST. BROWN**

DRAFT: 2021-4(7) AGE: 22 WT: 197 HT: 6-0
SOUTHERN CALIFORNIA

In his rookie outing, Amon-Ra St. Brown had a slow start. In his first 10 NFL games, he averaged 35 yards per game, 7.4 fantasy PPG, and didn't locate the end zone once. Then he found his mojo.

In his next six games, he had 5 TDs and averaged 11.2 targets, 94.8 yards per game, and 24.9 fantasy PPG. Even with his lackluster start, St. Brown finished the season 16th in yards, 14th in receptions, and 22nd in fantasy points.

Having established a connection with QB Jared Goff, St. Brown looks to be the No. 1 receiving option going into 2022, but there will be plenty of competition from a crowded receiver room, including rookie Jameson Williams, newly acquired DJ Chark Jr., and TE T.J. Hockenson. St. Brown is a solid WR3 but in the WR2 conversation.

YEAR	TEAM	GP	TAR	REC	REC YD	YD/REC	REC TDS	100 YG	RUSH ATT	RUSH YD	RUSH TD	FPPG
2021	DET	16	119	90	912	10.1	5	2	7	61	1	14
PROJ	DET	17	114	82	876	10.7	5	2	10	71	1	12.5

29 | MICHAEL **THOMAS**

DRAFT: 2016-2(16) AGE: 29 WT: 212 HT: 6-3
OHIO STATE

Michael Thomas hasn't played an NFL snap since January 2021 due to injury. We have to look back to 2019 to see who Thomas was. That year he set the single-season record for most receptions (149), had 1,725 receiving yards, and scored 9 TDs, averaging 23.4 fantasy PPG! In his last four full seasons, he's finished no worse than the seventh among WRs.

The problem is we don't know who he is now. His four seasons of top-seven production came on the arm QB Drew Brees. Current Saints QB Jameis Winston is not Drew Brees. Thomas enters 2022 as New Orleans No. 1 option, until he's not. He's our riskiest WR3 with a wide range of outcomes. Early reports from training camp, though, are positive. Still he'll likely be drafted too soon based on name recognition and past production.

YEAR	TEAM	GP	TAR	REC	REC YD	YD/REC	REC TDS	100 YG	RUSH ATT	RUSH YD	RUSH TD	FPPG
2019	NO	16	185	149	1725	11.6	9	10	1	-9	0	23.4
2020	NO	7	55	40	438	11	0	2	1	1	0	12.0
2021	NO	DNP		INJURY								
PROJ	NO	17	113	81	949	11.7	6	1	1	2	0	12.5

30 | TYLER **LOCKETT**

DRAFT: 2015-3(5) AGE: 29 WT: 182 HT: 5-10
KANSAS STATE

Besides posting three consecutive 1,000-plus yard seasons, Lockett has been a TD machine, averaging 9 per season over the last four years. Consistency, however, has been an issue. Last season, he had six games of 19 or more fantasy points, and six games of less than eight.

One of the best deep-ball receivers in the game, his 14.6 aDOT was second among WRs, and first among WRs with at least 70 receptions. But much of his long-ball success can be attributed to the look-deep-first play of QB Russell Wilson, who was traded to Denver this offseason. With Drew Lock under center, and Lockett turning 30 years old, he's on the backside of his best fantasy years. DK Metcalf will emerge as Seattle's No. 1 receiver this year and Lockett will be relegated to a fantasy WR3.

YEAR	TEAM	GP	TAR	REC	REC YD	YD/REC	REC TDS	100 YG	RUSH ATT	RUSH YD	RUSH TD	FPPG
2019	SEA	16	110	82	1057	12.9	8	4	4	-5	0	14.7
2020	SEA	16	132	100	1054	10.5	10	2	0	0	0	16.6
2021	SEA	16	107	73	1175	16.1	8	5	2	9	0	15
PROJ	SEA	17	115	79	1007	12.7	5	2	2	8	0	12.4

31 | HUNTER **RENFROW**

DRAFT: 2019-5(11) AGE: 26 WT: 185 HT: 5-10
CLEMSON

Hunter Renfrow became the No. 1 receiving option in Las Vegas last season by default, with the early exit of Henry Ruggs II, and the late-season absence of Darren Waller. Renfrow seized the opportunity and achieved his first 1,000-yard season, finishing ninth in receptions and TDs, 17th in targets, and 10th in total FPs. Inside the red zone is where he did his best work, scoring 9 times and reeling in 78.3% of his 26 targets. Renfrow saw an impressive 31.1% of all Raider's red zone targets last season.

Las Vegas signed Devante Adams in the offseason, and he'll takeover the No. 1 receiving role from day one. And with the return of Waller, Renfrow may assume the role of third-best fantasy receiver on the team, but he should still see enough work to remain in the fantasy WR3 conversation.

YEAR	TEAM	GP	TAR	REC	REC YD	YD/REC	REC TDS	100 YG	RUSH ATT	RUSH YD	RUSH TD	FPPG
2019	LV	13	71	49	605	12.3	4	2	0	0	0	10.3
2020	LV	16	77	56	656	11.7	2	0	0	0	0	8.4
2021	LV	17	128	103	1038	10.1	9	3	3	3	0	15.4
PROJ	LV	17	105	82	848	10.3	7	2	3	11	0	12.3

32 | DRAKE **LONDON**

DRAFT: 2022-1(15) AGE: 21 WT: 219 HT: 6-4
USC

Eighth-overall pick, Drake London had an 88-1084-7 receiving line in only eight games at USC last season, before suffering a season-ending broken ankle. At 6-4, with very skilled hands, he easily outworks and outsizes defenders, catching 19 contested balls, the most among college receivers.

He'll be the top WR in Atlanta from Week 1, and will split target share with TE Kyle Pitts.

With the suspension of Calvin Ridley and the departure of Russell Gage, there's not a lot of competition for targets. London is able to lineup wide or in the slot, and he did both at USC, so Atlanta should find plenty of ways to utilize their new offensive weapon. London is a WR3/Flex with plenty of upside in a depleted offense.

YEAR	TEAM	GP	TAR	REC	REC YD	YD/REC	REC TDS	100 YG	RUSH ATT	RUSH YD	RUSH TD	FPPG
PROJ	ATL	17	116	73	1050	14.4	5	1	1	5	0	12.3

QUARTERBACKS

RUNNING BACKS

WIDE RECEIVERS

TIGHT ENDS

KICKERS

D/ST

33 | ALLEN **ROBINSON II**

*LOS ANGELES **RAMS** (7)*
DRAFT: 2014-2(29)   AGE: 29   WT: 220   HT: 6-2
PENN STATE

➤ After back-to back top-10 fantasy campaigns in 2019 and 2020, Allen Robinson II saw a massive drop-off last season. His 5.5 targets per game, down from 9.5 the year before, was 58th in the league, and he finished as a dreadful WR84 on the season. The 29-year-old inked a three-year, $46.5 million deal with the Rams this offseason. He'll be the No. 2 behind Cooper Kupp in a much more pass-heavy offense than in Chicago. He' should return to a solid WR3/flex this season.

YEAR	TEAM	GP	TAR	REC	REC YD	YD/REC	REC TDS	100 YG	RUSH ATT	RUSH YD	RUSH TD	FPPG
2019	CHI	16	154	98	1147	11.7	7	3	1	2	0	15.9
2020	CHI	16	151	102	1250	12.3	6	4	1	-1	0	16.4
2021	CHI	12	66	38	410	10.8	1	0	0	0	0	7.1
PROJ	LAR	17	110	73	984	13.5	6	0	0	0	0	12.2

34 | JUJU **SMITH-SCHUSTER**

*KANSAS CITY **CHIEFS** (8)*
DRAFT: 2017-2(30)   AGE: 25   WT: 215   HT: 6-1
SOUTHERN CALIFORNIA

➤ JuJu Smith-Schuster signed a one-year, $10.75 million deal with the Chiefs this offseason. Injured in Week 5 last year, Smith-Schuster returned for Big Ben's farewell game, but never amassed significant numbers. We know what JuJu can do: 1,426 yards and 18.5 fantasy PPG in 2018. Now, he has the chance to be the No. 1 WR on one of the most explosive offenses in the league. He's a WR3 with huge upside and unlimited possibilities.

YEAR	TEAM	GP	TAR	REC	REC YD	YD/REC	REC TDS	100 YG	RUSH ATT	RUSH YD	RUSH TD	FPPG
2019	PIT	12	70	42	552	13.1	3	1	0	0	0	9.6
2020	PIT	16	128	97	831	8.6	9	0	0	0	0	14.6
2021	PIT	5	28	15	129	8.6	0	0	3	9	1	7
PROJ	KC	17	108	79	858	10.9	6	1	3	10	1	12.2

35 | RASHOD **BATEMAN**

*BALTIMORE **RAVENS** (10)*
DRAFT: 2021-1(27)   AGE: 22   WT: 210   HT: 6-2
MINNESOTA

➤ 22-year-old Rashod Bateman enters his second NFL season as the top WR in Baltimore. He's a popular breakout candidate among the fantasy community, after the trade of Hollywood Brown this offseason. As a rookie, Bateman missed the first five games but was a steady contributor once healthy. Lamar Jackson missed six of the last eight games, so Bateman had little time to create chemistry with the starting QB. He'll be sharing targets with TE Mark Andrews, but Bateman's easily a WR3 with a massive upside and a possible breakout at hand.

YEAR	TEAM	GP	TAR	REC	REC YD	YD/REC	REC TDS	100 YG	RUSH ATT	RUSH YD	RUSH TD	FPPG
2021	BAL	12	67	46	515	11.2	1	1	0	0	0	0
PROJ	BAL	17	110	76	1002	13.2	5	1	0	0	0	12.1

36 | GABRIEL **DAVIS**

*BUFFALO **BILLS** (7)*
DRAFT: 2020-4(22)   AGE: 23   WT: 210   HT: 6-2
CENTRAL FLORIDA

➤ Gabriel Davis suffered from a lack of opportunity last season, due to the wealth of talent and years of experience in a very crowded receiving corps. WRs Cole Beasley and Emmanuel Sanders have now departed, and Davis appears primed to be the second option in Buffalo behind WR Stefon Diggs. There will still be competition for target share from Jamison Crowder and TE Dawson Knox, but there will be plenty of volume from Josh Allen, in a Bills high-powered offense, to feed multiple fantasy-viable players.

YEAR	TEAM	GP	TAR	REC	REC YD	YD/REC	REC TDS	100 YG	RUSH ATT	RUSH YD	RUSH TD	FPPG
2020	BUF	16	62	35	599	17.1	7	1	1	0	0	8.6
2021	BUF	15	63	35	549	15.7	6	1	0	0	0	8.4
PROJ	BUF	17	98	58	941	16.2	9	1	0	0	0	12.1

37 | DEVONTA **SMITH**

*PHILADELPHIA **EAGLES** (7)*
DRAFT: 2021-1(10)   AGE: 23   WT: 170   HT: 6-0
ALABAMA

➤ 23-year-old Heisman Trophy winner, DeVonta Smith had a good rookie year, finishing as the 29th best WR in fantasy. His 13.9 average depth of target was second best among the top-30 WRs, and he had 39 receptions of 10-plus yards, and 16 of 20-plus.

The Eagles added superstar receiver A.J. Brown this offseason, who should assume the No. 1 receiving role. Smith will still get his share of targets in an offense that's run-heavy. He's a WR3/flex, with a wide range of possible outcomes.

YEAR	TEAM	GP	TAR	REC	REC YD	YD/REC	REC TDS	100 YG	RUSH ATT	RUSH YD	RUSH TD	FPPG
2021	PHI	17	103	64	916	14.3	5	2	0	0	0	10.9
PROJ	PHI	17	110	68	937	13.8	7	2	0	0	0	12.0

38 | ADAM **THIELEN**

*MINNESOTA **VIKINGS** (7)*
DRAFT: 2014-UNDRFT   AGE: 32   WT: 200   HT: 6-2
MINNESOTA STATE (MOREHEAD)

➤ Adam Thielen turned 32 in 2022, but age didn't slow him down last season — until it did. Healthy in the first 11 games, he was a RZ monster, with 10 TDs, averaging 17.4 fantasy PPG.

Durability here is a concern, as he's missed 11 games over the past three seasons. It's highly unlikely Thielen ever returns to his 2018 top-three WR form, especially now that superstar Justin Jefferson has established himself as the Vikings No. 1 receiver. With his best years behind him, Thielen is a flex option.

YEAR	TEAM	GP	TAR	REC	REC YD	YD/REC	REC TDS	100 YG	RUSH ATT	RUSH YD	RUSH TD	FPPG
2019	MIN	10	48	30	418	13.9	6	1	4	6	1	11.4
2020	MIN	15	108	74	925	12.5	14	3	3	15	0	16.8
2021	MIN	13	95	67	726	10.8	10	1	1	2	0	15.4
PROJ	MIN	17	108	73	791	10.8	8	1	1	3	0	11.8

39 | DEANDRE **HOPKINS**

*ARIZONA **CARDINALS** (13)*
DRAFT: 2013-1(27)   AGE: 30   WT: 212   HT: 6-1
CLEMSON

➤ DeAndre Hopkins enters his third season in Arizona with a six-game PED suspension. He's been one of the best WRs in the league, posting top-12 fantasy numbers in six of the last eight seasons. The 30-year-old missed seven games last season to injury, and saw a decline in targets and production. When he returns to the field, he'll still be Kyler Murray's No. 1 option and still could put up WR1 numbers. His fantasy football legacy will probably have him drafted too early for our liking, though.

YEAR	TEAM	GP	TAR	REC	REC YD	YD/REC	REC TDS	100 YG	RUSH ATT	RUSH YD	RUSH TD	FPPG
2019	HOU	15	150	104	1165	11.2	7	5	2	18	0	17.6
2020	ARI	16	160	115	1407	12.2	6	7	1	1	0	18.2
2021	ARI	10	43	42	572	13.6	8	0	0	0	0	14.7
PROJ	ARI	11	88	58	694	12.0	5	2	0	1	0	14.3

40 | TREYLON **BURKS**

*TENNESSEE **TITANS** (6)*
DRAFT: 2022-1(18)   AGE: 22   WT: 225   HT: 6-3
ARKANSAS

➤ Treylon Burks was the 18th overall pick in this year's draft. He'll start the season as the probable No. 1 WR in Tennessee, especially considering the recent departure of A.J. Brown, and with newly acquired Robert Woods coming off a torn ACL.

Burks is big, fast, and athletic, posting a 4.55 40-yard dash and a 33-inch vertical at this year's combine. He boasts an impressive 8.5 yards after catch per reception, ranking 14th among 169 qualifying receivers over the past two seasons. He also finished first in yards per route run, 6.1 when lined up on the outside. He'll be limited in a run-heavy offense, and is a flex with upside.

YEAR	TEAM	GP	TAR	REC	REC YD	YD/REC	REC TDS	100 YG	RUSH ATT	RUSH YD	RUSH TD	FPPG
PROJ	TEN	17	100	65	935	14.4	6	0	5	29	0	11.6

41 BRANDON **AIYUK**
SAN FRANCISCO *49ERS (9)*
DRAFT: 2020-1(25) AGE: 24 WT: 200 HT: 6-0
ARIZONA STATE

Brandon Aiyuk's production last season was directly linked to Deebo Samuel's role. The more Samuel ran the ball, the more targets Aiyuk saw. Through Week 8, when Samuel was used mostly as a receiver, Aiyuk averaged 3.8 touches per game and 5.7 fantasy PPG. When Samuel played the hybrid "wide-back" role, Aiyuk's touches improved to 6.2 per game and his FPs jumped to 13.6 per game. If Shanahan continues a similar offensive scheme to the one he deployed in the second half of last season, Aiyuk could be in store for a breakout year.

YEAR	TEAM	GP	TAR	REC	REC YD	YD/REC	REC TDS	100 YG	RUSH ATT	RUSH YD	RUSH TD	FPPG
2020	SF	12	96	60	748	12.5	5	2	6	77	2	15.4
2021	SF	16	85	56	826	14.8	5	1	5	17	0	10.6
PROJ	SF	17	101	70	868	12.4	6	1	4	25	0	11.5

42 CHRISTIAN **KIRK**
JACKSONVILLE *JAGUARS (11)*
DRAFT: 2018-2(15) AGE: 25 WT: 200 HT: 5-11
TEXAS A&M

Merited or not, Christian Kirk signed a four-year, $72 million contract with the Jaguars this offseason. Last season, with the early exit of DeAndre Hopkins due to a knee injury, Kirk was the best receiver in Arizona posting career highs in receptions and yards in 2021. Kirk, now in his fifth season is the clear front runner among the Jaguars receiving corps for targets in a Trevor Lawrence-led offense.

YEAR	TEAM	GP	TAR	REC	REC YD	YD/REC	REC TDS	100 YG	RUSH ATT	RUSH YD	RUSH TD	FPPG
2019	ARI	13	108	68	709	10.4	3	2	10	93	0	12.8
2020	ARI	14	79	48	621	12.9	6	1	2	3	0	10.5
2021	ARI	17	103	77	982	12.8	5	1	1	11	0	12.1
PROJ	JAC	17	109	79	892	11.3	4	1	1	10	0	11.4

43 ALLEN **LAZARD**
GREEN BAY *PACKERS (14)*
DRAFT: 2018-UNDRFT AGE: 26 WT: 227 HT: 6-5
IOWA STATE

Allen Lazard finished as the No. 48 fantasy WR last season, but things are looking up for him in 2022. (1) Target-hog WR Davante Adams was shipped to the Raiders, and (2) Aaron Rodgers is throwing him the ball. This will be Lazard's fifth season with Rodgers, so they already have a rapport, proved by the 8 TDs (12th best) and 12 end zone targets (eighth best) last season. Pick him up in the late rounds and look for a breakout.

YEAR	TEAM	GP	TAR	REC	REC YD	YD/REC	REC TDS	100 YG	RUSH ATT	RUSH YD	RUSH TD	FPPG
2019	GB	16	52	35	477	13.6	3	1	1	21	0	6.4
2020	GB	10	46	33	451	13.7	3	1	2	17	0	9.8
2021	GB	14	60	40	513	12.8	8	0	3	32	0	10.2
PROJ	GB	17	95	63	790	12.5	8	0	4	29	0	11.3

44 ROBERT **WOODS**
TENNESSEE *TITANS (6)*
DRAFT: 2013-2(10) AGE: 30 WT: 195 HT: 6-0
SOUTHERN CALIFORNIA

Robert Woods was traded to the Titans this offseason where he'll likely be the No. 2 receiving option behind rookie Treylon Burks. When Woods tore his ACL before Week 10 last season, he was on pace to finish as the 18th-best WR in fantasy PPG. Even when healthy, which may be after the start of the season, Woods will not see the target volume he saw in L.A. In an offense featuring Derrick Henry and the run, Woods is a good option with upside to fill your bench.

YEAR	TEAM	GP	TAR	REC	REC YD	YD/REC	REC TDS	100 YG	RUSH ATT	RUSH YD	RUSH TD	FPPG
2019	LAR	15	139	90	1134	12.6	2	3	17	115	1	15.5
2020	LAR	16	129	90	936	10.4	6	2	24	155	2	15.4
2021	LAR	9	69	45	556	12.4	4	1	8	46	1	15
PROJ	TEN	17	103	69	778	11.3	4	0	12	77	1	10.8

45 CHASE **CLAYPOOL**
PITTSBURGH *STEELERS (9)*
DRAFT: 2020-2(17) AGE: 24 WT: 238 HT: 6-4
NOTRE DAME

Twenty-four-year-old Chase Claypool has put up nearly identical numbers in his last two NFL seasons, averaging 107 targets, 61 receptions, and 867 yards. In 2021, he had only 2 TDs, a sharp decline from his 9 in 2020. Mitchell Trubisky or Kenny Pickett look to replace Big Ben, and with less competition after the departures of JuJu and James Washington, Claypool may be in for more targets. Big Ben also had one of the lowest average depth of throw last season. A new QB could change this, which would benefit Claypool most. He is a flex with upside.

YEAR	TEAM	GP	TAR	REC	REC YD	YD/REC	REC TDS	100 YG	RUSH ATT	RUSH YD	RUSH TD	FPPG
2020	PIT	16	109	62	873	14.1	9	2	10	16	2	13.6
2021	PIT	15	105	59	860	14.6	2	1	14	96	0	11.1
PROJ	PIT	17	112	62	890	14.4	4	1	13	74	0	10.7

46 GARRETT **WILSON**
NEW YORK *JETS (10)*
DRAFT: 2022-1(10) AGE: 21 WT: 192 HT: 6-0
OHIO STATE

Tenth overall pick in this year's draft, Garrett Wilson, joins the Jets, to compete for targets with second-year WR Elijah Moore and Corey Davis.

Wilson was outstanding at Ohio State, posting a 70-1,058-12 receiving line last season, all while sharing duties with other top receivers, like Chris Olave. Wilson posted a 4.28 40-yard dash at the combine, so it's no surprise he was open on 84% of targets last year.

He's a WR3/Flex in most leagues, but his value could increase as he develops a rapport with Zach Wilson.

YEAR	TEAM	GP	TAR	REC	REC YD	YD/REC	REC TDS	100 YG	RUSH ATT	RUSH YD	RUSH TD	FPPG
PROJ	NYJ	17	98	58	888	15.3	5	0	2	12	0	10.5

47 MICHAEL **GALLUP**
DALLAS *COWBOYS (9)*
DRAFT: 2018-3(17) AGE: 26 WT: 198 HT: 6-1
COLORADO STATE

In the offseason, Michael Gallup signed a five-year, $57.5 million extension with Dallas. He missed eight games early last season but returned for weeks 10-17, only to suffer a late-season ACL tear. He didn't have surgery and his Week 1 availability is in question. When healthy, he should be the No. 2 option behind CeeDee Lamb, as the Cowboys said farewell to Amari Cooper and Cedrick Wilson. He's a WR3 with WR2 upside when he gets fully healthy.

YEAR	TEAM	GP	TAR	REC	REC YD	YD/REC	REC TDS	100 YG	RUSH ATT	RUSH YD	RUSH TD	FPPG
2019	DAL	14	113	66	1107	16.8	6	4	0	0	0	15.2
2020	DAL	16	105	59	843	14.3	5	2	0	0	0	10.8
2021	DAL	9	62	35	445	12.7	2	1	0	0	0	10.2
PROJ	DAL	17	103	58	853	14.7	6	0	0	0	0	10.6

48 CHRIS **OLAVE**
NEW ORLEANS *SAINTS (14)*
DRAFT: 2022-1(11) AGE: 21 WT: 188 HT: 6-1
OHIO STATE

The Saints traded up to take Chris Olave 11th overall in this year's draft. Olave was the second of back-to-back Ohio State WRs drafted in the first round (Garrett Wilson).

He is a fast (4.39 40-yard dash) and skilled route runner who's hard to cover. Olave is a deep ball threat with an striking 14.1 average depth of target, who caught 7 TDs of 20-plus air yards last season. He's not yet great with the ball in his hands, as his yards after the catch ranked last in his draft class. If Michael Thomas is able to return as some semblance of himself, he'll take some attention away from Olave. He's a flex option with an extremely high ceiling.

YEAR	TEAM	GP	TAR	REC	REC YD	YD/REC	REC TDS	100 YG	RUSH ATT	RUSH YD	RUSH TD	FPPG
PROJ	NO	17	97	60	844	14.1	5	0	2	6	0	10.3

QUARTERBACKS

RUNNING BACKS

WIDE RECEIVERS

TIGHT ENDS

KICKERS

D/ST

QUARTERBACKS
RUNNING BACKS
WIDE RECEIVERS
TIGHT ENDS
KICKERS
D/ST

49 | KADARIUS TONEY

*NEW YORK **GIANTS** (9)*

DRAFT: 2021-1(20) AGE: 23 WT: 193 HT: 6-0
FLORIDA

Before the draft, there were rumors that the Giants were going to trade Kadarius Toney. They didn't, but they did spend a third-round pick on WR Wan'Dale Robinson. But for now he's still in New York. His rookie outing showed flashes of what he could be. In Week 5 he was targeted 13 times for 10 receptions and 189 yards! Inconsistent, he had only two other finishes north of 11 FPs in his nine games. The question is, which WR will be the primary target in 2022. It's possible Toney and Kenny Golladay split the majority of target share among a very crowded receiving corps. Toney's worth a late a pick, if only for his upside.

YEAR	TEAM	GP	TAR	REC	REC YD	YD/REC	REC TDS	100 YG	RUSH ATT	RUSH YD	RUSH TD	FPPG
2021	NYG	9	57	39	420	10.8	0	1	3	6	0	9.1
PROJ	NTG	17	102	71	798	11.2	3	1	10	62	0	10.3

50 | MARQUEZ VALDES-SCANTLING

*KC **CHIEFS** (8)*

DRAFT: 2018-5(37) AGE: 27 WT: 205 HT: 6-5
SOUTH FLORIDA

Marquez Valdes-Scantling signed a three-year, $30 million deal with the Chiefs this offseason, moving from one elite QB to another. He's likely the fourth option in Kansas City behind Travis Kelce, JuJu Smith-Schuster, and Mecole Hardman. With his speed, he has the potential to get open downfield, like Tyreek Hill used to when Mahomes improvised. His 17.9 aDOT in Green Bay was first among qualified WRs last season. He'll be too inconsistent to roster, but keep an eye on him.

YEAR	TEAM	GP	TAR	REC	REC YD	YD/REC	REC TDS	100 YG	RUSH ATT	RUSH YD	RUSH TD	FPPG
2019	GB	16	56	26	452	17.4	2	1	2	9	0	5.3
2020	GB	16	63	33	690	20.9	6	1	4	13	0	8.7
2021	GB	11	55	26	430	16.5	3	1	0	0	0	10.5
PROJ	KC	17	77	50	840	16.8	6	0	1	7	0	10.0

51 | SKYY MOORE

*KANSAS CITY **CHIEFS** (8)*

DRAFT: 2022-2(22) AGE: 21 WT: 195 HT: 5-10
WESTERN MICHIGAN

Skyy Moore arrives in Kansas City by way of the draft and joins a club where the hierarchy of WRs is yet to be established. Of course, Travis Kelce will see a large percentage of target share, but the remaining targets could go anywhere. Moore has the skill set to garner his fair share, as he did in college.

In three seasons at Western Michigan, he saw 32% of all targets, and only had 4 drops in his 256 targets. We've seen what the other receivers for KC can do. With the potential to create instant chemistry with Patrick Mahomes, don't hesitate to use a late-round selection on Moore.

YEAR	TEAM	GP	TAR	REC	REC YD	YD/REC	REC TDS	100 YG	RUSH ATT	RUSH YD	RUSH TD	FPPG
PROJ	KC	17	86	58	745	12.8	6	0	1	6	0	9.9

52 | DEVANTE PARKER

*NEW ENGLAND **PATRIOTS** (10)*

DRAFT: 2015-1(14) AGE: 29 WT: 219 HT: 6-3
LOUISVILLE

DeVante Parker arrives in New England after spending his first seven seasons in Miami. He'll provide another option for three-WR sets, and can lineup as a vertical perimeter target. Parker has had injury issues, only playing an entire season once. Last season, he only managed nine games. Parker will compete with Jakobi Meyers for No. 1 receiving duties. We're giving him the edge because we've seen his ceiling. In 2019, he showed us what he can do, but keep an eye on his progression and durability.

YEAR	TEAM	GP	TAR	REC	REC YD	YD/REC	REC TDS	100 YG	RUSH ATT	RUSH YD	RUSH TD	FPPG
2019	MIA	16	128	72	1202	16.7	9	4	0	0	0	15.4
2020	MIA	14	103	63	793	12.6	4	3	0	0	0	11.9
2021	MIA	9	73	40	515	12.9	2	0	0	0	0	11.5
PROJ	NE	17	110	62	814	13.1	4	0	0	0	0	9.8

53 | KENNY GOLLADAY

*NEW YORK **GIANTS** (9)*

DRAFT: 2017-3(32) AGE: 28 WT: 213 HT: 6-4
NORTHERN ILLINOIS

Kenny Golladay spent the better part of the last two seasons nursing injuries. He played 14 games last year, but was never fully healthy or on the same page as QB Daniel Jones. He only averaged 6.4 fantasy PPG. He's seen a considerable decline in production since he was a top-10 WR in 2019. Golladay, if only because of his contract, will continue to see targets. The 29-year-old is worth a late-round flier and has decent upside if he can turn things around.

YEAR	TEAM	GP	TAR	REC	REC YD	YD/REC	REC TDS	100 YG	RUSH ATT	RUSH YD	RUSH TD	FPPG
2019	DET	16	116	65	1190	18.3	11	5	0	0	0	15.6
2020	DET	5	32	20	338	16.9	2	2	0	0	0	13.2
2021	NYG	14	74	37	521	14.1	0	1	0	0	0	6.4
PROJ	NYG	17	103	59	840	14.2	4	1	0	0	0	9.8

54 | DJ CHARK JR.

*DETROIT **LIONS** (6)*

DRAFT: 2018-2(29) AGE: 25 WT: 198 HT: 6-4
LOUISIANA STATE

DJ Chark Jr. has had one good fantasy season in his four years in Jacksonville. In 2019 he went 73-1,008-8 (WR17), but his trajectory has been downhill since. Last season he broke his ankle in Week 4 ending his 2021 campaign. In Detroit he'll seek targets behind ascending WR Amon-Ra St. Brown, D'Andre Swift, T.J. Hockenson, and rookie Jameson Williams. Chark is a bench-worthy flex who will see early targets as Williams recovers from a torn ACL.

YEAR	TEAM	GP	TAR	REC	REC YD	YD/REC	REC TDS	100 YG	RUSH ATT	RUSH YD	RUSH TD	FPPG
2019	JAC	15	118	73	1008	13.8	8	3	2	20	0	14.9
2020	JAC	13	93	53	706	13.3	5	1	0	0	0	11.8
2021	JAC	3	22	7	154	22	2	0	0	0	0	11.5
PROJ	DET	17	91	56	749	13.4	6	0	1	8	0	9.9

55 | TYLER BOYD

*CINCINNATI **BENGALS** (10)*

DRAFT: 2016-2(24) AGE: 27 WT: 203 HT: 6-2
PITTSBURGH

Tyler Boyd is an excellent slot receiver on a team with an abundance of WR talent. While, he'll post some 4-56-1 receiving lines during the season, he'll likley not have enough volume to be a fantasy starter. From 2018-20, prior to the arrival of Ja'marr Chase and Tee Higgins, Boyd averaged 8.1 targets per game (22% share), but with Chase and Higgins in the fold, it dropped to 5.3 (16% share). While he'll have some WR3 potential, an injury to Chase or Higgins would push him into the fringe WR2 range.

YEAR	TEAM	GP	TAR	REC	REC YD	YD/REC	REC TDS	100 YG	RUSH ATT	RUSH YD	RUSH TD	FPPG
2019	CIN	16	148	90	1046	11.6	5	4	4	23	0	14.2
2020	CIN	15	110	79	841	10.6	4	2	5	49	0	12.8
2021	CIN	16	94	67	828	12.4	5	1	2	22	0	11.4
PROJ	CIN	17	94	68	729	10.7	4	1	3	18	0	9.8

56 | RUSSELL GAGE

*TAMPA BAY **BUCCANEERS** (11)*

DRAFT: 2018-6(20) AGE: 26 WT: 184 HT: 6-0
LSU

Russell Gage joined the Buccaneers this offseason after four seasons in Atlanta, where he finished as the 36th-best WR last season. He's been consistent in production, averaging 102 targets, 59 receptions, 778 yards, and 11.9 fantasy PPG over the last two seasons. With the recent addition of Julio Jones, Gage will have a more difficult road to fantasy relevancy. But, with Godwin on the sideline to start the season, Gage could gain chemistry with Brady that could carry throughout the season.

YEAR	TEAM	GP	TAR	REC	REC YD	YD/REC	REC TDS	100 YG	RUSH ATT	RUSH YD	RUSH TD	FPPG
2019	ATL	16	74	49	446	9.1	1	0	4	12	0	6.3
2020	ATL	16	110	72	786	10.9	4	2	2	9	0	11
2021	ATL	13	93	66	770	11.7	4	2	0	0	0	12.8
PROJ	TB	17	101	70	688	9.8	6	0	1	2	0	10.3

57 JAKOBI MEYERS

NEW ENGLAND PATRIOTS (10)
DRAFT: 2018-UNDRFT AGE: 25 WT: 200 HT: 6-2 NORTH CAROLINA STATE

Jakobi Meyers was incredibly consistent last season, averaging 11.4 fantasy PPG, but lacked in TDs. He has only three end zone targets in the last three seasons. However, his rapport with Mac Jones and target volume should be enough for an uptick in TDs, even with competition for targets.

YEAR	TEAM	GP	TAR	REC	REC YD	YD/REC	REC TDS	100 YG	RUSH ATT	RUSH YD	RUSH TD	FPPG
2019	NE	15	41	26	359	13.8	0	0	0	0	0	4.1
2020	NE	14	81	59	729	12.4	0	2	2	9	0	9.5
2021	NE	16	126	83	866	10.4	2	0	1	9	0	11.4
PROJ	NE	17	105	70	725	10.4	4	0	0	0	0	9.8

58 JARVIS LANDRY

NEW ORLEANS SAINTS (14)
DRAFT: 2014-2(31) AGE: 29 WT: 195 HT: 6-1 LSU

Jarvis Landry's fantasy output has declined year over year since his time in Miami. From 2015-19, he posted five straight top-20 fantasy seasons. He's had at least a 24% target share for seven consecutive seasons. There are likely not enough targets in a Saints offense to make him relevant.

YEAR	TEAM	GP	TAR	REC	REC YD	YD/REC	REC TDS	100 YG	RUSH ATT	RUSH YD	RUSH TD	FPPG
2019	CLE	16	138	83	1174	14.1	6	0	1	10	0	14.8
2020	CLE	15	101	72	840	11.7	3	0	4	10	1	12.1
2021	CLE	12	85	52	570	11	2	0	6	40	2	11.4
PROJ	NO	17	89	58	709	12.2	4	0	4	16	1	9.5

59 RONDALE MOORE

ARIZONA CARDINALS (13)
DRAFT: 2021-2(17) AGE: 22 WT: 180 HT: 5-7 PURDUE

Rondale Moore was a short-game, gadget-style player in his rookie season, and is in for similar role in 2022. Moore, 22, is surrounded by receiving talent, which will make it hard to carve out a bigger role. His average depth of target was a mere 1.3 yards, as the Cardinals were just trying to get him the ball and let him create. He'll have WR3 upside until DeAndre Hopkins returns from suspension, but after that he'll have little weekly value.

YEAR	TEAM	GP	TAR	REC	REC YD	YD/REC	REC TDS	100 YG	RUSH ATT	RUSH YD	RUSH TD	FPPG
2021	ARI	14	65	54	435	8.1	1	1	18	76	0	7.9
PROJ	ARI	17	88	64	615	9.6	4	0	21	99	0	9.4

60 JAMESON WILLIAMS

DETROIT LIONS (6)
DRAFT: 2022-1(12) AGE: 21 WT: 189 HT: 6-2 ALABAMA

Jameson Williams was selected by the Lions 12th overall in the draft, despite an ACL tear in the National Title game. His numbers at Alabama last year were elite (79-1572-15), a result of his size, speed, and athleticism.

It appears Williams won't be ready Week 1, and might not be fantasy relevant until later in the season, if at all. Detroit is in no hurry to put him on the field. He's undraftable in eight-team leagues, and bench-worthy in others.

YEAR	TEAM	GP	TAR	REC	REC YD	YD/REC	REC TDS	100 YG	RUSH ATT	RUSH YD	RUSH TD	FPPG
PROJ	DET	12	75	46	562	12.2	4	0	1	5	0	10.6

61 JULIO JONES

TAMPA BAY BUCCANEERS (11)
DRAFT: 2011-1(6) AGE: 33 WT: 220 HT: 6-1 ALABAMA

Julio Jones likely landed with the only team that would give him a shot at fantasy relevancy. Because Chris Godwin will not be fully healthy Week 1, or later, Jones will have a chance to develop a relationship with the GOAT. He will compete with Russell Gage for Brady's third target, a pretty good spot to be in.

YEAR	TEAM	GP	TAR	REC	REC YD	YD/REC	REC TDS	100 YG	RUSH ATT	RUSH YD	RUSH TD	FPPG
2019	ATL	15	157	99	1394	14.1	6	6	2	-3	0	18.3
2020	ATL	9	68	51	771	15.1	3	3	0	0	0	16.2
2021	TEN	10	48	31	434	14.0	1	1	0	0	0	8.0
PROJ	DEN	17	76	51	719	14.1	6	0	0	0	0	9.3

62 COREY DAVIS

NEW YORK JETS (10)
DRAFT: 2017-1(5) AGE: 27 WT: 209 HT: 6-3 WESTERN MICHIGAN

Corey Davis played only nine games last season and will be the No. 3 option for the Jets. His 11.9 fantasy PPG last season was respectable, but he'll lose targets to Garrett Wilson, who could surpass Elijah Moore by season's end, in 2022. If either Wilson or Moore miss time, Davis will have flex potential.

YEAR	TEAM	GP	TAR	REC	REC YD	YD/REC	REC TDS	100 YG	RUSH ATT	RUSH YD	RUSH TD	FPPG
2019	TEN	15	69	43	601	14	2	0	0	0	0	7.7
2020	TEN	14	92	65	984	15.1	5	5	0	0	0	13.8
2021	NYJ	9	59	34	492	14.5	4	1	0	0	0	11.9
PROJ	NYJ	17	86	53	751	14.2	5	0	0	0	0	9.3

63 CHRISTIAN WATSON

GREEN BAY PACKERS (14)
DRAFT: 2022-2(34) AGE: 23 WT: 208 HT: 6-5 NORTH DAKOTA STATE

Second-round draft pick Christian Watson joins a team looking for a new top receiver. Watson was a gadget-type offensive weapon at North Dakota St. — a vertical threat (104 receptions at 20.5 YPR), a kick returner, and had 49 carries. He shined at the combine (4.36 40-yard dash, 136-inch broad jump), he's got size (6-foot 4), and he could be fantasy relevant immediately with limited competition after the departure of target-hog Davante Adams. He's a mid-to-late round play.

YEAR	TEAM	GP	TAR	REC	REC YD	YD/REC	REC TDS	100 YG	RUSH ATT	RUSH YD	RUSH TD	FPPG
PROJ	GB	17	81	51	748	14.7	5	1	3	18	0	9.3

64 VAN JEFFERSON

LOS ANGELES RAMS (7)
DRAFT: 2020-2(25) AGE: 26 WT: 200 HT: 6-1 FLORIDA

Van Jefferson's fantasy value was largely a result of his massive 16 YPR and his 6 TDs, that tend to come with those deep throws. His 168 FPs were impressive for a team's No. 3 option. He'll play the same role this season when he returns from his broken foot suffered in training camp around Week 4/5.

YEAR	TEAM	GP	TAR	REC	REC YD	YD/REC	REC TDS	100 YG	RUSH ATT	RUSH YD	RUSH TD	FPPG
2020	LAR	16	31	19	220	11.6	1	0	1	-1	0	2.9
2021	LAR	17	89	50	802	16	6	0	2	20	0	9.9
PROJ	LAR	17	90	52	704	13.5	5	0	4	31	0	9.1

65 MECOLE HARDMAN

KANSAS CITY CHIEFS (8)
DRAFT: 2019-2(24) AGE: 24 WT: 187 HT: 5-10 GEORGIA

Mecole Hardman saw a 25% increase in targets last season over 2020, but the fourth-year WR has yet to live up to his second-round-draft-pick expectations. Tyreek Hill's departure leaves plenty of targets up for grab, but still faces a crowded WR room. He'll likely be the third or fourth option for the Chiefs.

YEAR	TEAM	GP	TAR	REC	REC YD	YD/REC	REC TDS	100 YG	RUSH ATT	RUSH YD	RUSH TD	FPPG
2019	KC	16	41	26	538	20.7	6	0	4	17	0	7.3
2020	KC	16	62	41	560	13.7	4	0	4	31	0	7.8
2021	KC	17	83	59	693	11.7	2	1	8	46	0	8.3
PROJ	KC	17	80	52	679	13.1	4	0	10	68	1	9.2

66 JAHAN DOTSON

WASHINGTON COMMANDERS (14)
DRAFT: 2022-1(16) AGE: 22 WT: 182 HT: 5-11 PENN STATE

The Commanders first-round pick will stretch the field for Washington. Dotson will be in the starting lineup from day one. In his final year at Penn State, he saw a massive 31% target share for 91-1,182-12 (eighth most receptions in his draft class). Dotson is likely Washington's No. 2 WR, and could be the perfect complement on the right, to McLaurin on the left. Dotson's a WR3/flex option, whose output is heavily dependent on his chemistry with Wentz.

YEAR	TEAM	GP	TAR	REC	REC YD	YD/REC	REC TDS	100 YG	RUSH ATT	RUSH YD	RUSH TD	FPPG
PROJ	WAS	17	83	53	736	13.9	4	1	1	5	0	8.9

67 | ROBBIE ANDERSON

CAROLINA PANTHERS (13)
DRAFT: 2016-UNDRFT AGE: 29 WT: 190 HT: 6-3
TEMPLE

Despite being targeted 110 times and ranking sixth in snaps last season, Robbie Anderson was hardly fantasy relevant. He finished as the 49th overall WR. His top-20 finish among WRs in 2020 provides some hope. We may take a chance on Anderson with hope he and Baker Mayfield develop a connection.

YEAR	TEAM	GP	TAR	REC	REC YD	YD/REC	REC TDS	100 YG	RUSH ATT	RUSH YD	RUSH TD	FPPG
2019	NYJ	16	96	52	779	15	5	3	1	4	0	10
2020	CAR	16	136	95	1096	11.5	3	3	4	15	0	14
2021	CAR	17	110	53	519	9.8	5	0	3	36	0	8.1
PROJ	CAR	17	101	53	776	14.6	3	0	4	23	0	8.9

68 | JAMISON CROWDER

BUFFALO BILLS (7)
DRAFT: 2015-4(6) AGE: 29 WT: 177 HT: 5-9
DUKE

Jamison Crowder signed a one-year deal with the Bills worth a potential $4 million. He's slated to replace Cole Beasley in the slot. At 29, Crowder has missed 16 games over four seasons, and spent the last three with an ineffective Jets team. In Buffalo's pass-heavy offense, he has WR3/Flex potential.

YEAR	TEAM	GP	TAR	REC	REC YD	YD/REC	REC TDS	100 YG	RUSH ATT	RUSH YD	RUSH TD	FPPG
2019	NYJ	16	122	78	833	10.7	6	0	1	4	0	12.4
2020	NYJ	12	88	59	699	11.8	6	3	1	14	0	13.9
2021	NYJ	12	72	51	447	8.8	2	0	0	0	0	9
PROJ	BUF	17	81	55	577	10.5	5	0	1	3	0	8.4

69 | MARVIN JONES JR.

JACKSONVILLE JAGUARS (11)
DRAFT: 2012-5(31) AGE: 32 WT: 200 HT: 6-2
CALIFORNIA

At 32 and in his 10th year in the league, Marvin Jones Jr. is reliable, playing all 33 games over the last two seasons, while commanding a 21% target share. Last year's performance was TD-deficient even though he saw 34% of Trevor Lawrence's red zone targets. Jones could have a bounce-back season.

YEAR	TEAM	GP	TAR	REC	REC YD	YD/REC	REC TDS	100 YG	RUSH ATT	RUSH YD	RUSH TD	FPPG
2019	DET	13	91	62	779	12.6	9	2	2	0	0	14.9
2020	DET	16	115	76	978	12.9	9	3	0	0	0	14.2
2021	JAC	17	118	73	832	11.4	4	1	0	0	0	10.6
PROJ	JAC	17	85	54	644	11.9	4	1	0	0	0	8.4

70 | STERLING SHEPARD

NEW YORK GIANTS (9)
DRAFT: 2016-2(9) AGE: 29 WT: 196 HT: 5-10
OKLAHOMA

Sterling Shepard suffered a late-season Achilles injury last year that leaves his early availability in question. He's one of many in a crowded receiver room in which the hierarchy is not completely established. Shepard's the third option, behind Golladay and Toney, but could move up, or down in the WR cue.

YEAR	TEAM	GP	TAR	REC	REC YD	YD/REC	REC TDS	100 YG	RUSH ATT	RUSH YD	RUSH TD	FPPG
2019	NYG	10	83	57	576	10.1	3	2	6	72	0	14
2020	NYG	12	90	66	656	9.9	3	1	6	49	1	13.4
2021	NYG	7	53	36	366	10.2	1	1	1	-9	0	11.1
PROJ	NYG	17	88	63	586	9.3	3	0	3	14	0	8.3

71 | KENDRICK BOURNE

NEW ENGLAND PATRIOTS (10)
DRAFT: 2016-UNDRFT AGE: 27 WT: 190 HT: 6-1
EASTERN WASHINGTON

Kendrick Bourne finished 2021 as WR32 overall, but was inconsistent. He recorded three top-eight finishes, but also had eight weeks of WR55 or worse finishes. It looks like he'll be the No. 3 option behind DeVante Parker and Jakobi Meyers, but as injury insurance with TD-upside, he's worth a late-round flier.

YEAR	TEAM	GP	TAR	REC	REC YD	YD/REC	REC TDS	100 YG	RUSH ATT	RUSH YD	RUSH TD	FPPG
2019	SF	16	44	30	358	11.9	5	0	0	0	0	6
2020	SF	15	74	49	667	13.6	2	0	0	0	0	8.5
2021	NE	17	70	55	800	14.5	5	0	12	125	0	10.4
PROJ	NE	17	71	46	548	11.9	5	0	11	91	0	8.2

72 | GEORGE PICKENS

PITTSBURGH STEELERS (9)
DRAFT: 2022-2(20) AGE: 21 WT: 190 HT: 6-3
GEORGIA

George Pickens arrives in Pittsburgh by way of a second-round draft pick from the University of Georgia. He's a tall (6-foot 3) perimeter receiver with great hands (only 2 drops in 142 targets) and average speed (4.5 40-yard dash). Pickens, at 21, has drawn comparisons with A.J. Green. With the departure of JuJu Smith-Schuster, Pittsburgh has some unclaimed targets. Pickens could come in and immediately see action as the Steelers No. 3 option.

YEAR	TEAM	GP	TAR	REC	REC YD	YD/REC	REC TDS	100 YG	RUSH ATT	RUSH YD	RUSH TD	FPPG
PROJ	PIT	17	87	53	678	12.8	3	0	0	0	0	8.1

73 | ALEC PIERCE

INDIANAPOLIS COLTS (14)
DRAFT: 2022-2(21) AGE: 22 WT: 213 HT: 6-3
CINCINNATI

Alec Pierce was the Colt's first pick in this year's draft. He has size (6-foot 3), speed (4.4 40-yard dash), and field awareness. At the combine he posted a WR best 40.5-inch vertical. With T.Y. Hilton gone, Pierce will likely fill the vacated field-stretching role. Unfortunately, Matt Ryan has one of the lowest deep-passing rates in the league. Pierce will be limited by the run-first offense and target vacuum Michael Pittman Jr., but he'll take snaps right away as the likely No. 2 option in the passing game.

YEAR	TEAM	GP	TAR	REC	REC YD	YD/REC	REC TDS	100 YG	RUSH ATT	RUSH YD	RUSH TD	FPPG
PROJ	IND	17	79	49	671	13.7	4	0	0	0	0	8.2

74 | ODELL BECKHAM JR.

LOS ANGELES RAMS (7)
DRAFT: 2014-1(12) AGE: 29 WT: 198 HT: 5-11
LSU

Free agent OBJ has had a press-worthy career with highlights, injuries, and embarrassing sideline incidents. He tore his ACL in the Super Bowl last season, after playing just seven full games. When he finds a home, he'll have flex potential, but he's also a high risk for injury, or something we can't even imagine.

YEAR	TEAM	GP	TAR	REC	REC YD	YD/REC	REC TDS	100 YG	RUSH ATT	RUSH YD	RUSH TD	FPPG
2019	CLE	16	133	74	1035	14	4	2	3	10	0	12.7
2020	CLE	7	43	23	319	13.9	3	0	3	72	1	12.3
2021	LAR	14	82	44	537	12.2	5	0	2	14	0	9.2
PROJ	FA	7	45	28	388	13.9	3	0	2	16	0	12.3

75 | JOSHUA PALMER

LOS ANGELES CHARGERS (8)
DRAFT: 2020-6(8) AGE: 23 WT: 212 HT: 6-2
MICHIGAN

Joshua Palmer will split third-option WR reps with Jalen Guyton this season, but should emerge as the clear No. 3. Palmer is only 23 years old and entering his second season. In his final three games last season he averaged 6.7 targets per game. Though his value is limited due to the presence of Keenan Allen and Mike Williams, an injury makes Palmer immediately relevant in the Chargers high-powered offense.

YEAR	TEAM	GP	TAR	REC	REC YD	YD/REC	REC TDS	100 YG	RUSH ATT	RUSH YD	RUSH TD	FPPG
2021	LAC	15	49	33	353	10.7	4	0	1	6	0	6.2
PROJ	LAC	17	72	49	572	11.7	5	0	0	0	0	8.0

76 | K.J. OSBORNE

MINNESOTA VIKINGS (7)
DRAFT: 2020-5(31) AGE: 25 WT: 203 HT: 5-11
MIAMI

K.J. Osborne is the third-option WR in Minnesota. Osborn played all 17 games last year and finished as WR39 for the league. He had some sneaky-good performances, including finishes of 17.3, 19.8 and 20.1 FPs. He returns to a Vikings team of known quantities and familiar faces, so we expect similar production. His true value though, is as insurance, in case Jefferson or Thielen miss time.

YEAR	TEAM	GP	TAR	REC	REC YD	YD/REC	REC TDS	100 YG	RUSH ATT	RUSH YD	RUSH TD	FPPG
2021	MIN	17	82	50	655	13.1	7	0	1	10	0	9.3
PROJ	MIN	17	73	45	624	13.9	5	0	1	5	0	8.1

2021 ADVANCED TIGHT END STATS

		GP	YBC/R	AIR/R	YAC/R	YACON/R	BRKTKL	DROP	RZ TGT	20+ YDS	40+YDS	LONG
1	MARK ANDREWS (BAL)	17	8.4	8.4	4.3	1.7	4	3	20	20	2	43
2	TRAVIS KELCE (KC)	16	6.1	6.1	6.1	2.7	8	10	16	13	2	69
3	GEORGE KITTLE (SF)	14	6.5	6.5	6.3	2.5	8	2	9	13	1	48
4	DALTON SCHULTZ (DAL)	17	5.9	5.9	4.5	1.4	3	4	14	6	0	32
5	DAWSON KNOX (BUF)	15	6.3	6.3	5.7	1.3	3	4	18	8	2	53
6	DALLAS GOEDERT (PHI)	15	7.9	7.9	6.9	1.8	9	5	6	14	1	45
7	KYLE PITTS (ATL)	17	10.5	10.5	4.6	2	3	6	14	16	2	61
8	HUNTER HENRY (NE)	16	9.2	9.2	2.9	0.8	1	0	17	8	0	35
9	ROB GRONKOWSKI (TB)	12	8.2	8.2	6.4	2.7	9	5	10	16	1	42
10	ZACH ERTZ (PHI & ARI)	17	5.7	5.7	4.6	1	2	6	20	7	1	47
11	MIKE GESICKI (MIA)	17	7.7	7.7	3	0.9	1	3	9	12	1	40
12	NOAH FANT (DEN)	16	5.3	5.3	4.5	0.8	1	2	12	7	0	35
13	PAT FREIERMUTH (PIT)	16	4.2	4.2	4.1	2	8	2	20	2	0	24
14	T.J. HOCKENSON (DET)	12	6.3	6.3	3.3	0.9	4	1	9	8	0	33
15	C.J. UZOMAH (CIN)	16	3.9	3.9	6.1	2.2	5	4	7	7	1	55
16	TYLER CONKLIN (MIN)	17	4.4	4.4	5.4	1	0	3	16	4	1	40
17	JARED COOK (LAC)	16	6.8	6.8	5	1.3	0	6	13	7	1	42
18	DARREN WALLER (LV)	11	7.7	7.7	4.4	1.5	3	5	13	13	0	33
19	DAVID NJOKU (CLE)	15	6.3	6.3	6.9	2.9	2	2	8	8	2	71
20	TYLER HIGBEE (LAR)	15	4.6	4.6	4.6	1.3	1	3	18	3	0	37
21	GERALD EVERETT (SEA)	15	4.8	4.8	5.2	2.3	9	3	8	5	1	41
22	COLE KMET (CHI)	17	6.1	6.1	4.1	1.6	4	5	12	7	0	25
23	EVAN ENGRAM (JAC)	15	4.9	4.9	4	0.7	0	6	4	2	0	30
24	AUSTIN HOOPER (CLE)	15	4.2	4.2	4.9	0.9	1	6	11	4	0	34
25	MO ALIE-COX (IND)	17	6.9	6.9	6.3	2.5	2	2	9	5	0	37
26	FOSTER MOREAU (LV)	15	6.1	6.1	6.3	2.1	2	4	5	6	1	44
27	JACK DOYLE (IND)	15	6.1	6.1	4.3	0.5	0	4	7	3	0	34
28	CAMERON BRATE (TB)	16	5.5	5.5	2.7	0.5	0	3	20	0	0	18
29	ALBERT OKWUEGBUNAM (DEN)	14	2.6	2.6	7.4	2	3	2	5	3	1	64
30	DAN ARNOLD (CAR & JAC)	11	6.3	6.3	5.4	1.9	2	2	4	2	0	28

2022 PPR RANKINGS

		BYE	
1.	KC	8	TRAVIS KELCE
2.	BAL	10	MARK ANDREWS
3.	ATL	14	KYLE PITTS
4.	SF	9	GEORGE KITTLE
5.	LV	6	DARREN WALLER
6.	DET	6	T.J. HOCKENSON
7.	DAL	9	DALTON SCHULTZ
8.	PHI	7	DALLAS GOEDERT
9.	ARI	13	ZACH ERTZ
10.	PIT	9	PAT FREIERMUTH
11.	MIA	11	MIKE GESICKI
12.	BUF	7	DAWSON KNOX
13.	MIN	7	IRV SMITH JR.
14.	CHI	14	COLE KMET
15.	SEA	11	NOAH FANT
16.	NE	10	HUNTER HENRY
17.	WAS	14	LOGAN THOMAS
18.	CLE	9	DAVID NJOKU
19.	LAR	7	TYLER HIGBEE
20.	TB	11	ROB GRONKOWSKI
21.	TB	11	CAMERON BRATE
22.	LAC	8	GERALD EVERETT
23.	TEN	6	AUSTIN HOOPER
24.	DEN	9	ALBERT OKWUEGBUNAM
25.	JAC	11	EVAN ENGRAM
26.	GB	14	ROBERT TONYAN
27.	CIN	10	HAYDEN HURST
28.	NO	14	ADAM TRAUTMAN

1 TRAVIS KELCE

KANSAS CITY CHIEFS (8)
DRAFT: 2013-3(1)   AGE: 32   WT: 256   HT: 6-5
CINCINNATI

After three consecutive seasons as fantasy's No. 1 TE, Kelce fell to No. 2 in 2021. Last season among TEs, he finished second in targets, receptions, and yards, just behind Mark Andrews who had a phenomenal season. More noteworthy is that Kelce would have been the ninth-best WR on the year.

There were almost 100 FPs between Kelce's second place finish and the fifth best finish at the TE position. This is why there is a premium on TE valuations over QBs.

He did post career lows in yards per target, catch rate, yards per route run, and PFF's receiving grade, but he had room to regress and still have elite fantasy output.

With the departure of Tyreek Hill, 159 targets are up for grabs, including a valuable 23 RZ targets, where Kelce had a league best catch rate of 88% last season and the most RZ receptions of any TE. The 32-year-old is still capable of big plays as well, with the second longest play (69 yards) of any TE last season.

In our rankings, Kelce edged out last year's No. 1 TE for multiple reasons: (1) Kelce has been a consistent fantasy producer for six straight seasons. (2) He plays in one of the most pass-heavy offenses with arguably the league's best QB. (3) With the departure of Hill, Kelce is about to see even more targets, especially during the time it takes other WRs to gain a rapport with Mahomes.

While he's no longer in consideration for a top-10 overall pick, he's a difference maker worth drafting at a premium.

YEAR	TEAM	GP	TAR	REC	REC YD	YD/REC	TDS	100 YG	RZ TAR	RZ REC	FPPG
2019	KC	16	136	97	1229	12.7	5	2	19	7	15.6
2020	KC	15	145	105	1416	13.5	11	6	20	13	20.8
2021	KC	16	135	92	1125	12.2	9	4	16	14	16.2
PROJ	KC	17	141	104	1228	11.8	9	5	21	14	16.5

2 MARK ANDREWS

BALTIMORE RAVENS (10)
DRAFT: 2018-3(22)   AGE: 26   WT: 256   HT: 6-5
OKLAHOMA

Besides Cooper Kupp, Mark Andrews was the most common player on fantasy football finalists last season, and for good reason. He finished as the No. 1 TE in all formats, outscoring the 10th best tight end by 7 points per game.

He finished 2021 first in receptions, yards, TDs, red zone targets, and end zone targets, among all TEs. He also led the position in 20-plus-yard plays. He accounted for a massive 25% of Baltimore's targets, which he should be able to sustain with the departure of Hollywood Brown, though he may face more double teams as the Ravens biggest threat. He also led the position in routes run per dropback.

What gives us the most pause is Andrews' production in Lamar Jackson's 11 games last season, versus his production in the other six games. With Jackson, Andrews averaged significantly fewer fantasy PPG than when another QB was under center. Also, Baltimore passed more than ever before out of necessity.

And though Andrews has better hands than Kelce, he has less ability with the ball in his hands, as Kelce's yards after the catch were almost 2 yards more than Andrews'.

We think a complete repeat of 2021's massive numbers is unlikely for Andrews. He hasn't shown consistent improvement over his first four seasons. In fact, his fantasy PPG decreased from 2019 to 2020, before his big leap last season.

Kelce feels just a bit safer to us, but if Andrew's is your top-ranked TE, we won't fault you.

YEAR	TEAM	GP	TAR	REC	REC YD	YD/REC	TDS	100 YG	RZ TAR	RZ REC	FPPG
2019	BAL	15	98	64	852	13.3	10	2	14	7	13.9
2020	BAL	14	88	58	701	12.1	7	0	16	10	12.2
2021	BAL	17	154	107	1361	12.7	9	5	20	12	17.5
PROJ	BAL	17	137	90	1115	12.5	9	5	21	13	15.0

3 KYLE PITTS

ATLANTA FALCONS (14)
DRAFT: 2021-1(4)   AGE: 21   WT: 246   HT: 6-6
FLORIDA

It's rare for a rookie TE to be an effective pass catcher in his first year, but Kyle Pitts lived up to his 2021 number-four overall pick expectations. Finishing in the top four among TEs in targets per game and yards per game, Pitts best asset was his verticality. He posted a ridiculous 15.1 yards per reception, first for TEs by a mile. And his 10.5 air yards per reception helped him finish with the most 20-plus yard plays among all TEs. He also ran routes on 80% of his snaps, third best for the position.

Besides Pitts, the Falcons struggled to find consistency among their pass catchers last season. Pitts held a 20% target share, with a lower than average 61% catch rate among TEs. This was more indicative of his large average depth of target and defenses putting their focus on Pitts rather than on Pitts' catching ability.

His red zone numbers at first glance seem concerning. His 14 targets for 4 receptions and 1 TD are indeed terrible. We consider this an outlier partially caused by playing in an offense that didn't put up great numbers in 2021. If he would have scored 5 more TDs, well within our model's expected prediction, he would have finished the year as the No. 3 TE.

The receiving corps for Atlanta has not improved much this offseason. He'll mostly be competing with rookie Drake London for targets. But by adding another targets, defenses won't be able to focus all their attention on Pitts anymore.

This should give you an idea that it won't take a huge leap for Pitts to put up elite TE numbers. His ceiling has him at our No. 3 ranking, and we are taking as many shares of Pitts as we can get.

YEAR	TEAM	GP	TAR	REC	REC YD	YD/REC	TDS	100 YG	RZ TAR	RZ REC	FPPG
2021	ATL	17	110	68	1026	15.1	1	3	14	4	10.4
PROJ	ATL	17	135	90	1002	12.2	5	4	18	9	13.5

4 GEORGE KITTLE

SAN FRANCISCO 49ERS (9)
DRAFT: 2017-5(2)   AGE: 28   WT: 250   HT: 6-4
IOWA

George Kittle's boom-or-bust weekly fantasy output, along with his inability to stay healthy have left his fantasy managers frustrated the past couple of seasons. He has the ability to be the best TE in fantasy if he can put together a healthy, consistent season.

Kittle finished 2021 top five among TEs in receptions and yards, and finished third in fantasy PPG. He's a big playmaker, with a higher yards per reception than both Travis Kelce and Mark Andrews, and had the best yards after the catch among the top-20 TEs. In addition, Kittle was PFF's highest-graded TE.

His situation for 2022 doesn't scream success. Second-year QB Trey Lance will be under center, and we have little information on his chemistry with Kittle. Also, Kittle is competing with Deebo Samuel and Brandon Aiyuk for touches in an already run-heavy offense that could generate fewer pass attempts with a dual-threat QB under center.

In addition, Kittle's red zone production has been troubling to fantasy managers considering his caliber of talent. He had a career high 6 TDs last seasons and only 9 red zone targets, second fewest among the top-20 TEs.

He's already sat out OTAs with a lower body injury; it's likely not serious, but it's worth monitoring.

He did produce two 34-plus point fantasy weeks last season and has huge upside. And TEs do tend to be the favorite targets of new QBs. Kittle is still a top-five TE with even better upside.

YEAR	TEAM	GP	TAR	REC	REC YD	YD/REC	TDS	100 YG	RZ TAR	RZ REC	FPPG
2019	SF	14	107	85	1053	12.4	5	3	16	10	15.7
2020	SF	8	63	48	634	13.2	2	2	3	2	15.4
2021	SF	14	95	71	910	12.8	6	3	9	8	14.1
PROJ	SF	16	108	79	941	12.7	7	3	17	11	13.4

FANTASY TAKEOVER

5 DARREN **WALLER**

*LAS VEGAS **RAIDERS** (6)*
DRAFT: 2015-6(28)   AGE: 29   WT: 255   HT: 6-6   GEORGIA TECH

After a massive 2020 campaign Darren Waller had little chance of duplicating, his yards per game last season fell by 14, his targets per game by 3, and his TD total fell by 7. This is a significant drop-off considering Derek Carr had a career high 626 pass attempts. We're attributing his decrease in targets to the new coaching staff and the emergence of 2021 breakout WR Hunter Renfrow.

Despite his decreased target share, Waller still finished 2021 second in targets per game and fifth in yards per game among TEs. He only had 2 TDs, hurting his fantasy value, well below his expected 6.4. With 10 end zone targets and terrible luck last season, his TD numbers will definitely improve in 2022, even if Waller is most effective between the 20s. He was also third among TEs in expected fantasy PPG.

Last season among TEs, Waller, a dynamic route runner with good hands, ranked in the top five for yards before the catch but in the bottom five for yards after the catch.

The addition of Adams may hurt Waller's target share, but it may also improve last year's catch rate of 59% by adding a new playmaker that defenses must account for.

At 29 years old, he's still in his prime. A healthy Waller with increased efficiency and an improvement in TD totals has the potential to finish as a top-three TE. Even a below-average Waller, in an offense where target share is harder to come by, is still a solid TE1.

YEAR	TEAM	GP	TAR	REC	REC YD	YD/REC	TDS	100 YG	RZ TAR	RZ REC	FPPG
2019	LV	16	117	90	1145	12.7	3	5	11	7	13.9
2020	LV	16	145	107	1196	11.2	9	5	22	18	17.5
2021	LV	11	93	55	665	12.1	2	2	13	6	12.1
PROJ	LV	17	110	82	998	12.2	5	3	19	14	12.5

7 DALTON **SCHULTZ**

*DALLAS **COWBOYS** (9)*
DRAFT: 2018-4(37)   AGE: 26   WT: 244   HT: 6-5   STANFORD

Dalton Schultz, undrafted in most fantasy leagues last year, was on a remarkable 31% of fantasy teams that made their league's championship.

Schultz's 2020 campaign hinted at what his 2021 turned out to be. He improved in every metric last season, recording career highs in targets, receptions, yards, and TDs. Among TEs, he finished fifth in fantasy PPG, and top-seven in yards per game, receptions per game, and TDs. He was also PFF's sixth highest graded TE, and third among TEs in routes run on the season. The only three TEs who have more fantasy points since 2020 are Darren Waller, Travis Kelce, and Mark Andrews.

Schultz did see the lowest target share among the top-five TEs, but Dallas' pass-heavy offense makes up for it. Schultz should be in for a big workload out of the gate this season, as Dallas Traded Amari Cooper and lost Cedrick Wilson to free agency. Michael Gallup is also coming off injury and won't be ready Week 1. Schultz should have no trouble finding targets this season. One negative is, Schultz doesn't have the big-play potential of some of our top-ranked TEs. He had the fewest plays of 20-plus yards of the top-15 TEs, and his 10.4 yards per reception was in the bottom 10% of TEs.

We think Schultz will sustain most of his numbers from 2021, but may slightly regress in TDs. With our highest consistency rating among all TEs last season, he has less fluctuation from week to week. Schultz should be a safe mid-level TE1.

YEAR	TEAM	GP	TAR	REC	REC YD	YD/REC	TDS	100 YG	RZ TAR	RZ REC	FPPG
2019	DAL	16	2	1	6	6	0	0	0	0	0.1
2020	DAL	16	89	63	615	9.8	4	0	14	9	9.3
2021	DAL	17	104	78	808	10.4	8	0	14	9	12.2
PROJ	DAL	17	101	77	789	10.7	6	0	15	10	11.3

6 T.J. **HOCKENSON**

*DETROIT **LIONS** (6)*
DRAFT: 2019-1(8)   AGE: 25   WT: 248   HT: 6-5   IOWA

T.J. Hockenson has shown growth each of his three NFL seasons. In 2021, he posted career bests in targets, receptions, and FPs.

Though he's missed nine games in his short career, we don't yet consider him an injury risk, as most of his injuries are unrelated and not soft tissue. He missed five games last season to a fluke thumb injury.

As the eighth-best TE in fantasy PPG last season, Hockenson finished top six in both targets per game and yards per game for the position.

In 2022, Hockenson will face more competition for Jared Goff's attention, with emerging WR Amon-Ra St. Brown, newly signed DJ Chark Jr., and rookie Jameson Williams all fighting for targets. Hockenson's impressive 21% target share may see a slight dip, but this may be countered by the additional scoring opportunities on a much-improved Detroit offense.

Most of Hockenson's reception metrics are pedestrian at best. He finished in the middle of the pack for yards after the catch, yards before the catch, and yards after contact. It's his sure-handedness (fewest drops among all TEs in 2021) and volume that make him a solid fantasy producer. He was putting up some good numbers prior to his thumb injury last season.

This season should bring improved totals in the TD department, as he fell multiple scores below his expected output in 2021. We are penciling him in for another TE1 outing.

YEAR	TEAM	GP	TAR	REC	REC YD	YD/REC	TDS	100 YG	RZ TAR	RZ REC	FPPG
2019	DET	12	59	32	367	11.5	2	1	7	3	6.7
2020	DET	16	101	67	723	10.8	6	0	15	8	11
2021	DET	12	83	61	583	9.6	4	0	9	6	11.9
PROJ	DET	16	100	72	697	9.6	7	1	13	8	11.4

8 DALLAS **GOEDERT**

*PHILADELPHIA **EAGLES** (7)*
DRAFT: 2018-2(17)   AGE: 27   WT: 256   HT: 6-5   SOUTH DAKOTA STATE

Dallas Goedert enters 2022 as Philadelphia's clear No. 1 TE for the first time in his career. In the 10 games post Zach Ertz last season, Goedert commanded a stunning 26% target share, but on an offense with the fewest pass attempts in 2021. This equated to 5.8 targets per game, or what would have been 11th best on the year among TEs. During those 10 games, Goedert was the fourth-best fantasy TE, behind only the Big Three: Mark Andrews, Travis Kelce, and George Kittle. He was able to finish the season as the ninth best TE in fantasy PPG, and led all TEs in yards after the catch per reception. He also received PFF's highest receiving grade among all TEs last season.

We are not too concerned with the lack of pass production in Philadelphia's offense. Historically, a negative correlation exists between rushing QBs and the other skill positions, but not TEs. In the last five seasons, QBs with at least 80 rushing attempts have produced the same percentage of top-10 TEs as non-rushing QBs.

Goedert continues to be stymied in the TD department, never scoring more than 5 in a season, including recording the fewest red zone targets of the top-20 TEs last season. He'll need improvement around the goal line if he wants to have a chance at a top-five finish. Goedert will be behind A.J. Brown in target share this season, and will compete with DeVonta Smith as the No. 2 option. He's a good TE to target when most teams in your league have already drafted their TE1.

YEAR	TEAM	GP	TAR	REC	REC YD	YD/REC	TDS	100 YG	RZ TAR	RZ REC	FPPG
2019	PHI	15	87	58	607	10.5	5	0	11	8	9.9
2020	PHI	11	65	46	524	11.4	3	1	6	5	10.6
2021	PHI	15	76	56	830	14.8	4	2	6	5	10.9
PROJ	PHI	16	73	57	765	13.3	5	2	7	6	10.1

QUARTERBACKS

RUNNING BACKS

WIDE RECEIVERS

TIGHT ENDS

KICKERS

D/ST

9 ZACH ERTZ

ARIZONA **CARDINALS (13)**

DRAFT: 2013-2(3)　AGE: 31　WT: 250　HT: 6-5　　　STANFORD

▶ Before the start of 2021, the fantasy community was ready to send Ertz to the TE graveyard, but Ertz had different plans. Last season, after putting up solid number in the first six weeks while sharing duties with Dallas Goedert as an Eagle, Ertz was traded to the Cardinals. He didn't miss a beat, commanding a 24% target share and finishing fourth in fantasy PPG during his 11 games in Arizona.

On the year, Ertz finished third in receptions per game and eighth in yards per game among TEs. He was tied for first among TEs in RZ targets, but had one of the worst RZ catch rates (40%).

He should start 2022 right where he left off. He'll even see a few more targets until D-Hop returns. We'd be surprised to find him outside the top-10 TEs at the end of the season.

YEAR	TEAM	GP	TAR	REC	REC YD	YD/REC	TDS	100 YG	RZ TAR	RZ REC	FPPG
2019	PHI	15	135	88	916	10.4	6	1	16	8	14.4
2020	PHI	11	72	36	335	9.3	1	0	7	4	6.9
2021	ARI	17	112	74	763	10.3	5	0	20	8	10.6
PROJ	ARI	17	110	72	695	9.7	5	0	21	9	10.1

12 DAWSON KNOX

BUFFALO **BILLS (7)**

DRAFT: 2019-3(33)　AGE: 25　WT: 254　HT: 6-4　　　OLE MISS

▶ Dawson Knox made substantial strides in every fantasy metric in 2021, finishing the year as the 10th best TE in both total fantasy points and fantasy PPG. He led all TEs in TDs with 9 total. His value came from efficiency and TDs rather than volume, as he finished only 20th among TEs in targets. Also, he was only targeted on a measly 14% of his routes, which raises some red flags. But he still finished third and fourth, respectively, in red zone and end zone targets among TEs.

We'd like to say that Knox will take another step forward in 2022, but this won't be the case. Even in the high-octane Buffalo offense, we expect a regression in TDs and a slight dip in playing time with the addition of capable TE O.J. Howard. He'll post some top-10 weekly outings but is a TE2 on the year.

YEAR	TEAM	GP	TAR	REC	REC YD	YD/REC	TDS	100 YG	RZ TAR	RZ REC	FPPG
2019	BUF	15	50	28	388	13.9	2	0	6	2	5.3
2020	BUF	12	44	24	288	12	3	0	9	5	5.9
2021	BUF	15	71	49	587	12	9	1	18	11	10.8
PROJ	BUF	16	68	49	549	11.2	7	1	16	9	9

10 PAT FREIERMUTH

PITTSBURGH **STEELERS (9)**

DRAFT: 2021-2(23)　AGE: 23　WT: 258　HT: 6-5　　　PENN STATE

▶ Pat Freiermuth's rookie campaign was impressive, even more so considering first-year TEs are rarely fantasy productive. Once Freiermuth overtook Eric Ebron on the depth chart in Week 7, he averaged 11.1 fantasy PPG, which was seventh best among TEs going forward. Freiermuth ran routes on and above-average 67% of dropbacks. Now, with Ebron gone, that number should improve.

While Freiermuth only averaged 8.3 yards per reception, worst among top-20 TEs, Big Ben's fastest time to throw is to blame rather than Freiermuth's inability to get open downfield. Freiermuth is a monster in the red zone, tied for first among all TEs in targets (20) and converting 7 of them into TDs.

Even with an uncertain QB situation, he'll will see plenty of targets in Pittsburgh's offense. We do approach uncertainty with caution, but Freiermuth has real TE1 upside, and at a good price.

YEAR	TEAM	GP	TAR	REC	REC YD	YD/REC	TDS	100 YG	RZ TAR	RZ REC	FPPG
2021	PIT	16	79	60	497	8.3	7	0	20	13	9.5
PROJ	PIT	17	85	68	623	9.2	6	0	22	16	9.8

13 IRV SMITH JR.

MINNESOTA **VIKINGS (7)**

DRAFT: 2019-2(18)　AGE: 24　WT: 240　HT: 6-2　　　ALABAMA

▶ Irv Smith Jr. missed all of 2021 with a knee injury. We were calling for Smith to have a breakout year after the end of 2019 gave us a glimpse at his potential. When last healthy and Kyle Rudolph sidelined to injury, Smith started the last four games of 2020 and averaged 12.8 fantasy PPG. At 24 years old, Smith should be fully healthy entering 2022.

Last season Minnesota's TEs averaged a combined 9.3 fantasy PPG, sixth worst in the league at the position. But 2021's starter, Tyler Conklin, is nowhere near as capable as Smith. The Minnesota coaching staff has already said they have big plans for Smith this season. Behind Justin Jefferson and Adam Thielen, Smith will be Kirk Cousins No. 3 target. We'll be drafting Smith late in plenty of drafts this season just for his TE1 upside.

YEAR	TEAM	GP	TAR	REC	REC YD	YD/REC	TDS	100 YG	RZ TAR	RZ REC	FPPG
2019	MIN	16	47	36	311	8.6	2	0	10	7	4.9
2020	MIN	13	43	30	365	12.2	5	0	10	7	7.4
2021	MIN	0	0	0	0	0	0	0	0	0	0
PROJ	MIN	16	70	56	592	10.7	5	0	11	5	8.9

11 MIKE GESICKI

MIAMI **DOLPHINS**

DRAFT: 2018-2(10)　AGE: 26　WT: 247　HT: 6-6　　　PENN STATE

▶ Mike Gesicki enters his fifth season in Miami after being franchise tagged this offseason. His 2021 per-game numbers looked similar to his 2020 campaign, except for a noticeable decline in TDs. He was one of only a handful of top-20 TEs to have fewer than 10 red zone targets.

Gesicki finished 15th best among TEs last season in fantasy PPG. He's a better at route running than he is with the ball in his hands. He was the worst among top-20 TEs last season in yards after the catch per reception.

The addition of Tyreek Hill will hurt the 26-year-old's 19% target share, but any loss will be more than offset by a much-improved offense and additional scoring opportunities. He's right there on the edge of our TE1 rankings.

YEAR	TEAM	GP	TAR	REC	REC YD	YD/REC	TDS	100 YG	RZ TAR	RZ REC	FPPG
2019	MIA	16	89	51	570	11.2	5	0	11	5	8.6
2020	MIA	15	85	53	703	13.3	6	1	14	5	10.6
2021	MIA	17	111	73	780	10.7	2	1	9	5	9.6
PROJ	MIA	17	10	62	701	11.3	4	1	8	4	9.2

14 COLE KMET

CHICAGO **BEARS (14)**

DRAFT: 2020-2(11)　AGE: 23　WT: 260　HT: 6-6　　　NOTRE DAME

▶ Cole Kmet was just plain unlucky fantasy-wise last season, as his expected fantasy points were significantly higher than his actual output. Kmet finished the year as the 25th best TE in fantasy PPG. The biggest hit to his fantasy value came from a lack of TDs. He was the only top-30 TE to not have a TD. The goose egg was despite 6 end zone targets and 12 red zone targets, plenty of volume to produce at least a few TDs. He had also been competing with Jimmy Graham for end zone targets, but with Graham gone, he should see a uptick in production. If he had scored with his expected TD total (4), Kmet would have finished 2021 as the 14th best TE.

We expect the 23-year-old's numbers to improve in 2022 and wouldn't be surprised to see a top-15 finish. The uber-athletic TE even has the potential to leapfrog into the top-10,

YEAR	TEAM	GP	TAR	REC	REC YD	YD/REC	TDS	100 YG	RZ TAR	RZ REC	FPPG
2020	CHI	16	44	28	243	8.7	2	0	6	3	4
2021	CHI	17	93	60	612	10.2	0	0	12	5	7.1
PROJ	CHI	17	6	63	648	10.3	4	0	13	6	8.9

15 NOAH FANT

SEATTLE SEAHAWKS (11)
DRAFT: 2019-1(20) AGE: 26 WT: 249 HT: 6-4
IOWA

Noah Fant is the forgotten part of Russell Wilson trade. After a solid rookie campaign in 2019, Fant posted two consecutive top-10 finishes in targets, receptions, and yards among TEs. Unfortunately, this high volume did not carry over to the red zone, with just 12 red zone targets for 7 receptions last season. Fant can attribute some of his goal-line woes to the subpar QB play in Denver — sadly, it may look much the same under his 2020 Broncos QB and Seattle's new projected starter, Drew Lock.

Now as a Seahawk, he'll be third option, behind Tyler Lockett and DK Metcalf. Fant's talent is undeniable and he will have a significant role in the offense, but Seattle is in rebuild mode, and we are expecting Fant to finish outside the top-10 TEs, even if he does already have chemistry with his former QB.

YEAR	TEAM	GP	TAR	REC	REC YD	YD/REC	TDS	100 YG	RZ TAR	RZ REC	FPPG
2019	DEN	16	66	40	562	14	3	2	9	1	7.1
2020	DEN	15	93	62	673	10.9	3	0	10	5	9.8
2021	DEN	16	90	68	670	9.9	4	0	12	7	9.9
PROJ	SEA	17	80	58	631	10.9	4	0	11	6	8.5

18 DAVID NJOKU

CLEVELAND BROWNS (9)
DRAFT: 2017-1(29) AGE: 26 WT: 246 HT: 6-4
MIAMI

David Njoku had an eventful offseason outside of the blockbuster trade of QB Deshaun Watson. First, Njoku was franchise tagged before working out a four-year, $57 million extension with the team. Also, Cleveland released the biggest constraint to his fantasy value, Austin Hooper, who had more targets than Njoku last season. If Njoku had received 80% of the TE FPs for Cleveland last season, he would have finished fifth in fantasy PPG. Instead, he finished 22nd.

Njoku did have a career best yards per reception, and a very impressive 6.9 yards after the catch average (first among the top-25 TEs) in 2021. With improved QB play and an increase in volume as the clear No. 1 TE, Njoku could catapult to high-end TE2 output.

YEAR	TEAM	GP	TAR	REC	REC YD	YD/REC	TDS	100 YG	RZ TAR	RZ REC	FPPG
2019	CLE	4	10	5	41	8.2	1	0	2	1	3.8
2020	CLE	13	29	19	213	11.2	2	0	6	3	4
2021	CLE	15	53	36	475	13.2	4	1	8	4	7.2
PROJ	CLE	15	54	41	536	12.8	5	1	9	5	8.5

16 HUNTER HENRY

NEW ENGLAND PATRIOTS (10)
DRAFT: 2016-2(4) AGE: 27 WT: 250 HT: 6-5
ARKANSAS

Hunter Henry quickly surpassed Jonnu Smith as the best TE in New England last season. His fantasy value and 14th place finish among TEs in fantasy PPG, was heavily dependent on his efficient red zone production. His 9 TDs were tied for most among TEs, converting all 8 of his red zone receptions into scores. It feels a bit lucky, but his TD total wasn't much over our model's expected total, 7.5.

Besides his goal-line work, he was mostly average. He finished just inside the top 20 in receptions per game and yards per game among TEs. He's proven himself to Mac Jones as a QB friendly target, and was the only TE in the top-30 without a drop last season. Because TD production varies so much from year to year and his volume is shaky, Henry is only a TE2.

YEAR	TEAM	GP	TAR	REC	REC YD	YD/REC	TDS	100 YG	RZ TAR	RZ REC	FPPG
2019	LAC	12	76	55	652	11.9	5	1	10	7	12.5
2020	LAC	14	93	60	613	10.2	4	0	14	6	10.4
2021	NE	16	75	50	603	12.1	9	0	17	8	10.3
PROJ	NE	16	72	49	531	11.1	6	0	17	9	8.5

19 TYLER HIGBEE

LOS ANGELES RAMS (7)
DRAFT: 2016-4(12) AGE: 29 WT: 255 HT: 6-6
WESTERN KENTUCKY

Tyler Higbee finished last season as the 13th-best TE in both total FPs and fantasy PPG, which makes his third consecutive finish as a fantasy TE2. His numbers with Matthew Stafford under center resemble his last two seasons with Jared Goff. The differences lie in his yards per reception and goal-line work. Save for his rookie year, Higbee recorded a career low in yards per reception (9.2), which was fourth worst among top-30 TEs. On the other hand, in an offense that provided more scoring opportunities, he posted career highs in end zone targets (9) and TDs (5).

It's hard to imagine a scenario where Higbee finds substantial volume in 2022 with Kupp and Robinson in the fold. He'll post a few top-10 weeks but is a middle-to-low-end TE2.

YEAR	TEAM	GP	TAR	REC	REC YD	YD/REC	TDS	100 YG	RZ TAR	RZ REC	FPPG
2019	LAR	15	89	69	734	10.6	3	4	19	14	10.7
2020	LAR	15	60	44	521	11.8	5	0	6	6	8.4
2021	LAR	15	85	61	560	9.2	5	0	18	12	9.8
PROJ	LAR	16	79	56	547	9.7	4	0	17	12	8.4

17 LOGAN THOMAS

WASHINGTON COMMANDERS (14)
DRAFT: 2014-4(20) AGE: 31 WT: 250 HT: 6-6
VIRGINIA TECH

The third-best fantasy TE in 2020, Logan Thomas, was on pace last season to outperform his 2020 campaign before first suffering a hamstring injury and then a torn ACL. He should be healthy to start the year, but his early-season usage might be diminished.

With the return of Curtis Samuel from injury and the addition of rookie Jahan Dotson, the Washington offense has suddenly become more crowded. Thomas' fantasy production is dependent on high volume — in his breakout 2020 season he was first in routes and snaps and third in receptions among all TEs. But we still feel the 31-year-old, even after an injury as serious as a torn ACL, could return to producing top-10 fantasy numbers at some point in 2022.

YEAR	TEAM	GP	TAR	REC	REC YD	YD/REC	TDS	100 YG	RZ TAR	RZ REC	FPPG
2019	DET	16	28	16	173	10.8	1	0	5	3	2.5
2020	WAS	16	110	72	670	9.3	6	1	17	15	10.9
2021	WAS	5	25	18	196	10.9	3	0	5	4	11.1
PROJ	WAS	17	91	54	542	10.0	6	0	15	14	8.5

20 ROB GRONKOWSKI

TAMPA BAY BUCCANEERS (11)
DRAFT: 2010-2(10) AGE: 33 WT: 265 HT: 6-6
ARIZONA

Rob Gronkowski announced his retirement from the NFL for a second time this offseason. But we wanted to include him in case, like his longtime teammate, he changes his mind.

The 33-year-old finished 2021 fourth in fantasy PPG, and was top four in yards, targets, and TDs per game. Gronk continues to be a big playmaker, leading all TEs in yards per reception (14.1) last season, making it 10 straight top-five seasons. Surprisingly he's not a bigger red zone threat, but he converted an efficient 4 of 5 red zone receptions into TDs.

Most importantly, he's a consistent fantasy producer, finishing eight of his 12 games last season as a top-10 TE on the week. If Gronk returns, he will make an immediate impact. When you start hearing rumors of a return, grab him off waivers.

YEAR	TEAM	GP	TAR	REC	REC YD	YD/REC	TDS	100 YG	RZ TAR	RZ REC	FPPG
2020	TB	16	77	45	623	13.8	7	1	14	6	9.3
2021	TB	12	89	55	802	14.6	6	3	11	5	14.3
PROJ	TB	6	45	26	369	14.2	3	1	7	4	13.5

21 CAMERON **BRATE**

*TAMPA BAY **BUCCANEERS** (11)*
DRAFT: 0-UNDRFT   AGE: 31   WT: 235   HT: 6-5
HARVARD

Cameron Brate has not had a top-10 TE finish since 2017. Last season, he was TE27, 24th in targets, and tied for 11th in TDs. Brate has now been elevated to Tampa's No. 1 TE with the retirement of Rob Gronkowski. Brate enters his ninth season with the Bucs, after working the last two seasons behind Gronk. Even as the No. 2 TE, Brate was Brady's second most-targeted option in the red zone last season. Recently signed veteran Kyle Rudolph should hurt Brate's value, so keep an eye on the Buc's TEs early.

YEAR	TEAM	GP	TAR	REC	REC YD	YD/REC	TDS	100 YG	RZ TAR	RZ REC	FPPG
2019	TB	16	56	36	311	8.6	4	0	6	7	0
2020	TB	16	34	28	282	10.1	2	0	4	3	0
2021	TB	16	57	30	245	8.2	4	0	20	11	0
PROJ	TB	17	82	59	526	8.9	5	0	23	12	8.3

22 GERALD **EVERETT**

*LOS ANGELES **CHARGERS** (8)*
DRAFT: 2017-2(12)   AGE: 28   WT: 240   HT: 6-3
SOUTH ALABAMA

Gerald Everett spent his first four years with the Rams, and last year in Seattle. Now, he moves back to LA to take a turn with the Chargers high-powered, high-volume offense. Everett has improved each season in receptions and yards, posting career highs last season in TDs, targets, receptions, and catch rate. He'll be Justin Herbert's No. 1 pass-catching TE from Game 1. Everett could post another career-best year, but it still may not be enough to put him on your roster.

YEAR	TEAM	GP	TAR	REC	REC YD	YD/REC	TDS	100 YG	RZ TAR	RZ REC	FPPG
2019	LAR	13	60	37	408	11	2	1	8	7	6.9
2020	LAR	16	62	41	417	10.2	1	0	5	2	5.5
2021	SEA	15	63	48	478	10	4	0	8	4	8.0
PROJ	SEA	16	67	54	510	9.5	5	0	8	6	8.3

23 AUSTIN **HOOPER**

*TENNESSEE **TITANS** (6)*
DRAFT: 2016-3(18)   AGE: 27   WT: 254   HT: 6-4
STANFORD

Austin Hooper lands in Tennessee this season, after two years in Cleveland. His productivity declined dramatically in Cleveland, after recording two consecutive TE6 seasons with the Falcons. We don't expect a fantasy revival in 2022. While the Titans have one of the largest TE target shares (24%), the position in Tennessee is usually addressed by committee. Unless Mike Vrabel goes against his track record to make Hooper his No. 1. Hooper's best left on the fantasy sideline.

YEAR	TEAM	GP	TAR	REC	REC YD	YD/REC	TDS	100 YG	RZ TAR	RZ REC	FPPG
2019	ATL	13	97	75	787	10.5	6	2	18	10	14.6
2020	CLE	13	70	46	435	9.5	4	0	9	5	8.7
2021	CLE	14	62	38	345	9.1	3	0	12	9	6.5
PROJ	TEN	15	72	49	445	9.2	4	0	11	9	8.0

24 ALBERT **OKWUEGBUNAM**

*DENVER **BRONCOS** (9)*
DRAFT: 2012-4(12)   AGE: 24   WT: 258   HT: 6-6
MISSOURI

Albert Okwuegbunam won the lottery in an offseason trade that brought Russell Wilson to Denver, and sent TE Noah Fant to Seattle.

Okwuegbunam finished as TE28 for the league last season, but he starts this season as the top TE in Denver. This third-year player has the real chance for a breakout season. His 80% catch rate is third among TEs with at least 50 targets in the past two years. With so many unknowns here — a new QB and his first year as the team's No. 1 TE — he's worth a late-round pick.

YEAR	TEAM	GP	TAR	REC	REC YD	YD/REC	TDS	100 YG	RZ TAR	RZ REC	FPPG
2020	DEN	4	15	11	121	11.0	1	0	4	2	7.3
2021	DEN	13	40	33	330	10.0	2	0	5	4	6.0
PROJ	DEN	17	65	50	511	10.3	5	0	7	5	7.7

25 EVAN **ENGRAM**

*JACKSONVILLE **JAGUARS** (11)*
DRAFT: 2017-1(23)   AGE: 27   WT: 240   HT: 6-3
OLE MISS

Evan Engram spent his first five NFL seasons with the Giants, struggling to produce in a weak offense. He hasn't had a good fantasy year since his 2017 rookie outing. In the offseason, he signed a one-year deal with the Jaguars, another team with offensive woes. New head coach Doug Pederson has a history of passer development and TE heavy schemes (e.g. Zach Ertz). There will be some competition from TE Dan Arnold, but Engram's slated as the No. 1. He has legitimate TE2 potential.

YEAR	TEAM	GP	TAR	REC	REC YD	YD/REC	TDS	100 YG	RZ TAR	RZ REC	FPPG
2019	NYG	8	68	44	467	10.6	3	2	0	0	13.6
2020	NYG	16	109	63	654	10.4	1	1	0	0	8.4
2021	NYG	15	73	46	408	8.9	3	0	0	0	7
PROJ	JAC	15	70	52	504	10.6	3	0	5	3	7.6

26 ROBERT **TONYAN**

*GREEN BAY **PACKERS** (14)*
DRAFT: 2017-UNDRFT   AGE: 28   WT: 240   HT: 6-5
INDIANA STATE

We screamed at anyone who would listen last season, "Robert Tonyan was a one-hit wonder!" His breakout 2020 year, where he finished as the sixth-best TE in fantasy PPG, came from an impractical level of efficiency that was unsustainable.

In 2021, his numbers came crashing back to reality — especially his TD numbers. Davante Adams is gone, but we don't see a significant boost in targets. Coming off an ACL tear that caused him to miss eight games last season, Tonyan's undraftable.

YEAR	TEAM	GP	TAR	REC	REC YD	YD/REC	TDS	100 YG	RZ TAR	RZ REC	FPPG
2019	GB	11	15	10	100	10	1	0	2	2	2.4
2020	GB	16	59	52	586	11.3	11	0	11	10	11.0
2021	GB	8	29	18	204	11.3	2	0	4	3	6.3
PROJ	GB	17	55	47	512	10.9	5	0	10	9	7.5

27 HAYDEN **HURST**

*CINCINNATI **BENGALS** (10)*
DRAFT: 2018-4(25)   AGE: 29   WT: 250   HT: 6-4
SOUTH CAROLINA

Hayden Hurst has yet to live up to his 2018 Round 1 selection, but that's been mainly due to timing and bad luck. He started in Baltimore the same year as Mark Andrews. In 2020 in Atlanta, he posted a 56-571-6 receiving line (TE10), only to have Kyle Pitts added in 2021. Now, on an ascending Bengals team, Hurst gets another shot to prove his top-flight TE status. With only one career drop, the sure-handed Hurst may find his groove with rising-star Joe Burrow throwing him the ball.

YEAR	TEAM	GP	TAR	REC	REC YD	YD/REC	TDS	100 YG	RZ TAR	RZ REC	FPPG
2019	BAL	16	39	30	349	11.6	2	0	7	3	4.8
2020	ATL	16	88	56	571	10.2	6	0	15	6	9.3
2021	ATL	12	31	26	221	8.5	3	0	7	6	5.5
PROJ	CIN	17	55	42	431	10.2	4	0	10	7	6.4

28 ADAM **TRAUTMAN**

*NEW ORLEANS **SAINTS** (14)*
DRAFT: 2020-3(41)   AGE: 25   WT: 255   HT: 6-5
DAYTON

Entering his third NFL season, Adam Trautman has not yet become the receiving behemoth he was in college. Last season, he caught passes from Taysom Hill, Jameis Winston, and Trevor Siemian, on a Saints team that never found its footing with a QB. He fared best with Siemian, while averaging only 2 targets per game with Winston under center. We don't expect much to change for Trautman this season, especially with a much better receiver room. He won't see enough volume with so many options in the lineup. He's best left on waivers.

YEAR	TEAM	GP	TAR	REC	REC YD	YD/REC	TDS	100 YG	RZ TAR	RZ REC	FPPG
2020	NO	15	16	15	171	11.4	1	0	3	3	2.5
2021	NO	11	43	27	263	9.7	2	0	8	4	5.9
PROJ	NO	15	64	40	389	9.8	3	0	8	4	6.3

Kickers

1 | JUSTIN TUCKER
BALTIZMORE RAVENS (10)
AGE: 32 WT: 183 HT: 6-1 TEXAS

Tucker, in his ten seasons, has never finished outside the top 11 fantasy kickers. He converted 95% of his attempts last season, including 19 of 40-plus yards. With the highest floor and most consistency of all kickers, he's our No. 1.

YEAR	TEAM	GP	FGM	FGA	0-39	40-49	50+	PATS	FPPG
2019	BAL	16	28	29	17	10	1	57	9.5
2020	BAL	16	26	29	14	9	3	52	8.9
2021	BAL	17	35	37	16	13	6	39	9.8
PROJ	BAL	17	31	34	18	9	4	39	8.6

2 | HARRISON BUTKER
KANSAS CITY CHIEFS (8)
AGE: 27 WT: 205 HT: 6-4 GEORGIA TECH

Butker has had two down years, including his worst finish as the 12th best kicker last season. Most of his decline came from a dip in FG attempts. With one of the strongest legs in the game, we expect Butker to get back on track in 2022.

YEAR	TEAM	GP	FGM	FGA	0-39	40-49	50+	PATS	FPPG
2019	KC	16	34	38	18	13	3	45	10.1
2020	KC	16	25	27	18	3	4	48	8.2
2021	KC	16	25	28	14	4	7	47	8.6
PROJ	KC	17	28	32	16	8	4	50	8.6

3 | TYLER BASS
BUFFALO BILLS (7)
AGE: 25 WT: 205 HT: 5-10 GEORGIA SOUTHERN

Bass has finished fourth and 11th in FPs for kickers in the past two seasons. He sees a massive amount of extra points in the Bills high-scoring offense. Though his conversion rate is in the bottom half of the league, he'll get enough volume to make up for it. He's a solid option week-in and week-out.

YEAR	TEAM	GP	FGM	FGA	0-39	40-49	50+	PATS	FPPG
2020	BUF	16	28	34	16	8	4	57	9.4
2021	BUF	17	28	32	22	4	2	51	8.1
PROJ	BUF	17	29	34	17	9	3	49	8.6

4 | EVAN MCPHERSON
CINCINNATI BENGALS (10)
AGE: 22 WT: 195 HT: 5-10 FLORIDA

As a rookie fifth-round pick, McPherson was a hero in Cincy his first season. With the fourth highest average kick distance, McPherson has the potential to put up good long-kick numbers, helpful in leagues with favorable distance-kicking bonuses. Cincy will have plenty of red zone trips that will end in FGs or extra points. We're in on McPherson again.

YEAR	TEAM	GP	FGM	FGA	0-39	40-49	50+	PATS	FPPG
2021	CIN	16	28	33	13	6	9	46	9.3
PROJ	CIN	17	30	35	18	8	4	43	8.5

5 | DANIEL CARLSON
LAS VEGAS RAIDERS (6)
AGE: 27 WT: 215 HT: 6-5 AUBURN

Carlson finished last season as the No. 1 fantasy kicker, and was third the prior season. He's an accurate kicker in a pass-heavy offense that finds plenty of red zone trips. The offense should be improved this year. Carlson has a strong outlook for 2022.

YEAR	TEAM	GP	FGM	FGA	0-39	40-49	50+	PATS	FPPG
2019	LV	16	19	26	13	6	0	24	5
2020	LV	16	33	35	26	3	4	34	8.9
2021	LV	17	40	43	22	12	6	30	10.1
PROJ	LV	17	29	33	17	8	4	44	8.4

6 | BRANDON MCMANUS
DENVER BRONCOS (9)
AGE: 31 WT: 201 HT: 6-3 TEMPLE

Yes, we know. Brandon McManus has never had better than a ninth-place fantasy finish in his career. But he's also never had Russell Wilson leading his offense. With highest average depth of kick, McManus could put up some solid numbers in 2022, in a much-improved offense.

YEAR	TEAM	GP	FGM	FGA	0-39	40-49	50+	PATS	FPPG
2019	DEN	16	29	34	15	10	4	25	7.8
2020	DEN	15	28	34	12	13	2	30	8.1
2021	DEN	17	26	31	13	8	5	33	7.3
PROJ	DEN	17	29	32	17	8	4	43	8.4

7 | MATT GAY
LOS ANGELES RAMS (7)
AGE: 28 WT: 232 HT: 6-0 UTAH

Matt Gay has been in the right situations to be a fantasy stud at the kicker position, first in a Brady-led Tampa Bay, and now on the Super Bowl-winning Rams. His accuracy, after a rocky 2019 season has been excellent. He's a definite K1.

YEAR	TEAM	GP	FGM	FGA	0-39	40-49	50+	PATS	FPPG
2019	TB	16	27	35	11	11	5	43	8.6
2020	LAR	7	14	16	7	6	1	16	9.1
2021	LAR	17	32	34	21	7	4	48	9.2
PROJ	LAR	17	29	34	17	8	4	44	8.4

8 | NICK FOLK
NEW ENGLAND PATRIOTS (10)
AGE: 37 WT: 222 HT: 6-1 ARIZONA

Folk's finish as the second-best kicker last season was somewhat of a surprise. He struggled with accuracy on extra points, but New England continues to be stopped on the opposing third of the field, which led Folk to have the third-most FG attempts last season. He's a borderline K1.

YEAR	TEAM	GP	FGM	FGA	0-39	40-49	50+	PATS	FPPG
2019	NE	7	14	17	9	4	1	12	8.1
2020	NE	16	26	28	13	11	2	30	7.6
2021	NE	17	36	39	20	11	5	42	9.9
PROJ	NE	17	29	32	17	8	4	42	8.4

R emember, the difference between kickers on a week-to-week basis is minimal. It is usually good strategy to wait until the final round to draft your kicker. Many times, you'll find streaming different kickers from week-to-week can be as effective as drafting the top-ranked kicker.

If you look at the our top-ranked kicker (Justin Tucker) and our 10th-ranked kicker (Jonathan Garibay), they only differ by 1 fantasy PPG in their projected averages. And kickers can be hard to project. For example, one extra 50-yard field goal could bump a kicker six places or more in the overall rankings for the season.

Be aware of the scoring system for your league. Sometimes leagues offer outrageous bonuses for long kicks. If this is the case, value kickers who are able to kick from distance rather than the kickers who only succeed through volume.

The only time we would draft a kicker before the last round, other than favorable scoring systems, is if we know the player we want will also be available in the last round and the kicker may not.

9 RYAN SUCCOP — TAMPA BAY *BUCCANEERS* (11)
AGE: 36 WT: 218 HT: 6-2 SOUTH CAROLINA

YEAR	TEAM	GP	FGM	FGA	0-39	40-49	50+	PATS	FPPG
2019	TEN	6	1	6	1	0	0	24	3.7
2020	TB	16	28	31	13	6	7	35	8.1
2021	TB	17	25	30	17	7	0	47	7.1
PROJ	TB	17	27	31	16	7	4	47	8.2

10 JONATHAN GARIBAY — DALLAS *COWBOYS* (9)
AGE: 22 WT: 215 HT: 6-1 TEXAS TECH

YEAR	TEAM	GP	FGM	FGA	0-39	40-49	50+	PATS	FPPG
PROJ	DAL	17	28	34	17	7	4	45	8.1

11 GREG JOSEPH — MINNESOTA *VIKINGS* (7)
AGE: 28 WT: 210 HT: 6-0 FLORIDA ATLANTIC

YEAR	TEAM	GP	FGM	FGA	0-39	40-49	50+	PATS	FPPG
2019	TEN	2	0	0	0	0	0	9	4.5
2020	TB	DNP							
2021	MIN	17	33	38	19	7	7	36	8.9
PROJ	MIN	17	27	33	16	8	3	41	7.6

12 JAKE ELLIOT — PHILADELPHIA *EAGLES* (7)
AGE: 27 WT: 167 HT: 5-9 MEMPHIS

YEAR	TEAM	GP	FGM	FGA	0-39	40-49	50+	PATS	FPPG
2019	PHI	16	22	26	15	5	2	35	6.6
2020	PHI	16	14	19	7	5	2	24	4.3
2021	PHI	17	30	33	17	10	3	44	8.6
PROJ	PHI	17	27	32	16	8	3	40	7.6

13 YOUNGHOE KOO — ATLANTA *FALCONS* (14)
AGE: 28 WT: 195 HT: 5-9 GEORGIA SOUTHERN

YEAR	TEAM	GP	FGM	FGA	0-39	40-49	50+	PATS	FPPG
2019	ATL	8	23	26	15	7	1	15	11.25
2020	ATL	15	37	39	21	8	8	33	11.1
2021	ATL	17	27	29	17	6	4	30	7.2
PROJ	ATL	17	29	33	17	8	4	31	7.6

14 MATT PRATER — ARIZONA *CARDINALS* (13)
AGE: 38 WT: 201 HT: 5-10 CENTRAL FLORIDA

YEAR	TEAM	GP	FGM	FGA	0-39	40-49	50+	PATS	FPPG
2019	DET	16	26	31	13	6	7	35	8
2020	DET	16	21	28	11	4	6	38	6.9
2021	ARI	17	30	37	20	3	7	47	5.9
PROJ	ARI	17	26	33	15	8	3	43	7.5

15 CHRIS BOSWELL — PITTSBURGH *STEELERS* (9)
AGE: 31 WT: 185 HT: 6-2 RICE

YEAR	TEAM	GP	FGM	FGA	0-39	40-49	50+	PATS	FPPG
2019	PIT	16	29	31	19	9	1	28	7.8
2020	PIT	13	19	20	11	7	1	34	7.6
2021	PIT	17	36	40	17	8	4	30	7.6
PROJ	PIT	17	29	34	17	8	4	30	7.5

16 RODRIGO BLANKENSHIP — INDIANAPOLIS *COLTS* (14)
AGE: 25 WT: 184 HT: 6-2 GEORGIA

YEAR	TEAM	GP	FGM	FGA	0-39	40-49	50+	PATS	FPPG
2020	IND	16	32	37	22	9	1	43	6.4
2021	IND	5	11	14	6	5	0	7	7
PROJ	IND	17	26	29	16	7	3	39	7.5

17 MASON CROSBY — GREEN BAY *PACKERS* (14)
AGE: 37 WT: 207 HT: 6-1 COLORADO

YEAR	TEAM	GP	FGM	FGA	0-39	40-49	50+	PATS	FPPG
2019	GB	16	22	24	14	7	1	40	7.1
2020	GB	16	16	16	7	5	4	59	7.5
2021	GB	17	25	34	18	4	3	49	7.4
PROJ	GB	17	25	30	15	7	3	44	7.5

18 DUSTIN HOPKINS — LOS ANGELES *CHARGERS* (8)
AGE: 31 WT: 193 HT: 6-2 FLORIDA STATE

YEAR	TEAM	GP	FGM	FGA	0-39	40-49	50+	PATS	FPPG
2019	WAS	16	25	30	15	8	2	21	6.4
2020	WAS	16	27	34	12	13	2	30	7.6
2021	LAC	17	30	34	15	13	2	40	8.4
PROJ	LAC	17	25	31	15	7	3	44	7.4

FANTASY**TAKEOVER**

23 JOEY SLYE

WASHINGTON COMMANDERS (14)

AGE: 26   WT: 213   HT: 5-11

VIRGINIA TECH

YEAR	TEAM	GP	FGM	FGA	0-39	40-49	50+	PATS	FPPG
2019	CAR	16	25	32	9	8	8	31	7.7
2020	CAR	16	29	36	21	7	1	34	7.7
2021	WAS	12	23	25	14	5	4	18	8.2
PROJ	WAS	17	27	33	16	8	3	37	7.4

19 GRAHAM GANO

NEW YORK GIANTS (9)

AGE: 34   WT: 202   HT: 6-2

FLORIDA STATE

YEAR	TEAM	GP	FGM	FGA	0-39	40-49	50+	PATS	FPPG
2019	CAR	DNP	INJURY						
2020	NYG	16	31	32	17	9	5	21	8.25
2021	NYG	17	29	33	17	5	7	17	7
PROJ	NYG	17	28	34	16	8	4	32	7.4

20 ROBBIE GOULD

SAN FRANCISCO 49ERS (9)

AGE: 39   WT: 190   HT: 6-0

PENN STATE

YEAR	TEAM	GP	FGM	FGA	0-39	40-49	50+	PATS	FPPG
2019	SF	13	23	31	17	6	0	41	8.3
2020	SF	15	19	23	8	9	2	36	6.8
2021	SF	13	20	23	10	7	3	39	8.4
PROJ	SF	17	26	32	16	7	3	38	7.2

21 WIL LUTZ

NEW ORLEANS SAINTS (14)

AGE: 28   WT: 184   HT: 5-11

GEORGIA STATE

YEAR	TEAM	GP	FGM	FGA	0-39	40-49	50+	PATS	FPPG
2019	NO	16	28	30	16	13	3	48	10.1
2020	NO	16	32	36	15X	7	1	57	8.2
2021	NO	DNP	INJURY						
PROJ	NO	17	27	34	16	8	3	35	7.2

22 RANDY BULLOCK

TENNESSEE TITANS (6)

AGE: 32   WT: 208   HT: 5-9

TEXAS A&M

YEAR	TEAM	GP	FGM	FGA	0-39	40-49	50+	PATS	FPPG
2019	CIN	16	27	31	16	10	1	24	7
2020	CIN	12	21	26	11	7	3	24	7.9
2021	TEN	16	26	31	17	8	1	42	7.8
PROJ	TEN	17	26	33	15	8	3	37	7.2

13 RILEY PATTERSON

DETROIT LIONS (6)

AGE: 23   WT: 190   HT: 6-0

MEMPHIS

YEAR	TEAM	GP	FGM	FGA	0-39	40-49	50+	PATS	FPPG
2021	DET	7	13	14	9	4	0	16	8.2
PROJ	DET	17	26	32	16	7	3	35	7.1

24 JASON MYERS

SEATTLE SEAHAWKS (11)

AGE: 31   WT: 190   HT: 5-10

YEAR	TEAM	GP	FGM	FGA	0-39	40-49	50+	PATS	FPPG
2019	SEA	16	23	28	17	4	2	40	4.5
2020	SEA	16	24	24	9	13	2	49	5.6
2021	SEA	17	17	23	11	3	3	44	3.2
PROJ	SEA	26	29	16	7	3	30	6.9

25 GREG ZUERLEIN

NEW YORK JETS (10)

AGE: 31   WT: 193   HT: 6-2

MISSOURI WESTERN

YEAR	TEAM	GP	FGM	FGA	0-39	40-49	50+	PATS	FPPG
2019	DAL	16	24	33	14	5	5	42	7.5
2020	DAL	16	34	41	19	12	3	33	9.1
2021	DAL	16	29	35	20	7	2	42	8.4
PROJ	NYJ	17	26	31	16	7	3	31	6.9

25 ZANE GONZALES

CAROLINA PANTHERS (13)

AGE: 27   WT: 193   HT: 6-2

ARIZONA STATE

YEAR	TEAM	GP	FGM	FGA	0-39	40-49	50+	PATS	FPPG
2019	TEN	5	4	9	1	2	1	12	2.2
2020	CHI	16	30	32	19	9	2	36	6.3
2021	CHI	17	26	30	15	11	0	27	5
PROJ	CHI	17	26	30	16	7	3	30	6.9

26 JASON SANDERS

MIAMI DOLPHINS (11)

AGE: 26   WT: 190   HT: 5-11

NEW MEXICO

YEAR	TEAM	GP	FGM	FGA	0-39	40-49	50+	PATS	FPPG
2019	MIA	16	23	30	15	5	3	29	4.6
2020	MIA	16	36	39	16	12	8	36	8.3
2021	MIA	17	23	31	13	6	3	37	4.1
PROJ	MIA	17	22	26	13	6	3	37	6.5

27 CAIRO SANTOS

CHICAGO BEARS (14)

AGE: 30   WT: 160   HT: 58

TULANE

YEAR	TEAM	GP	FGM	FGA	0-39	40-49	50+	PATS	FPPG
2019	TEN	5	4	9	1	2	1	12	2.2
2020	CHI	16	30	32	19	9	2	36	6.3
2021	CHI	17	26	30	15	11	0	27	5
PROJ	CHI	17	23	28	14	6	3	35	6.5

28 CADE YORK

CLEVELAND BROWNS (9)

AGE: 21   WT: 198   HT: 6-1

LSU

YEAR	TEAM	GP	FGM	FGA	0-39	40-49	50+	PATS	FPPG
PROJ	CLE	17	24	33	15	6	3	36	6.5

29 KA'IMI FAIRBAIRN

HOUSTON TEXANS (6)

AGE: 28   WT: 183   HT: 5-11

UCLA

YEAR	TEAM	GP	FGM	FGA	0-39	40-49	50+	PATS	FPPG
2019	HOU	16	20	25	13	4	3	40	4.1
2020	HOU	16	27	31	17	6	4	37	5.7
2021	HOU	13	15	19	9	2	4	13	3.9
PROJ	HOU	17	22	27	13	6	3	36	6.4

30 RYAN SANTOSO

JACKSONVILLE JAGUARS (11)

AGE: 27   WT: 260   HT: 6-5

MINNESOTA

YEAR	TEAM	GP	FGM	FGA	0-39	40-49	50+	PATS	FPPG
2021	NYJ	4	4	4	4	0	0	6	4.5
PROJ	JAC	17	22	27	14	6	2	32	6.1

Defense/Special Teams

1 | TAMPA BAY BUCCANEERS — BYE: 11

'21 PPG: 5TH '21 YPG: 12TH '21 VS RUN: 3RD '21 VS PASS: 22ND

A top-10 defense the past three years, Tampa Bay returns eight starters and adds Logan Hall, Logan Ryan, and Keanu Neal. The Bucs finished 2021 fifth in forced fumbles, sixth in sacks, and fifth in points allowed. Expect good numbers again from a team that plays in an the QB-deficient NFC South.

YEAR	INTS	FUMS	SACKS	YPG	PPG	<14 PTS	>27 PTS	TDS	FPPG
2019	12	16	47	344	28.1	1	9	6	6.7
2020	15	10	48	327	22.2	3	3	1	6.9
2021	17	12	47	331	20.8	4	5	2	6.9
PROJ	15	11	46	334	21.1	3	4	2	7.1

2 | BUFFALO BILLS — BYE: 7

'21 PPG: 1ST '21 YPG: 1ST '21 VS RUN: 13TH '21 VS PASS: 1ST

The Bills finished fifth in fantasy PPG last season with a remarkable 10 top-10 finishes. With nine starters returning, the Bills who were first in PPG, yards per game, and first against the pass are in for another big year. Opponents are destined to continue turning the ball over while playing from behind.

YEAR	INTS	FUMS	SACKS	YPG	PPG	<14 PTS	>27 PTS	TDS	FPPG
2019	14	9	44	298	16.2	5	1	1	7.4
2020	15	11	38	353	23.4	2	5	4	6.7
2021	19	11	42	273	17	6	3	1	7.3
PROJ	15	9	42	302	20.1	4	5	2	7.0

3 | NEW ORLEANS SAINTS — BYE: 14

'21 PPG: 4TH '21 YPG: 6TH '21 VS RUN: 4TH '21 VS PASS: 17TH

Here's another NFC South Team in our top three. The Saints finished fourth in PPG last season, and had five games with fewer than 14 points allowed. With playmakers Malcolm Jenkins, Marshon Lattimore, and new addition, Tyrann Mathieu, the Saints are set for another solid year.

YEAR	INTS	FUMS	SACKS	YPG	PPG	<14 PTS	>27 PTS	TDS	FPPG
2019	13	10	51	33	21.3	5	4	4	7.8
2020	18	8	45	311	21.1	6	5	1	6.2
2021	18	7	46	318	19.7	6	2	2	7.5
PROJ	15	7	44	328	19.9	5	3	2	6.9

4 | GREEN BAY PACKERS — BYE: 14

'21 PPG: 14TH '21 YPG: 11TH '21 VS RUN: 10TH '21 VS PASS: 13TH

The Packers have had respectable but not elite defenses the past few years. With a top secondary, a repeat as the 2021 league-leaders in interceptions is in the realm of possibilities. With some changes to the offense, Green Bay may not be in as many high scoring games, good for points allowed bonuses.

YEAR	INTS	FUMS	SACKS	YPG	PPG	<14 PTS	>27 PTS	TDS	FPPG
2019	17	8	41	353	19.6	4	2	0	6
2020	11	7	41	334	23.1	0	5	2	5
2021	18	8	39	328	21.8	4	7	2	5.5
PROJ	15	8	41	333	20.2	4	6	2	6.8

5 | INDIANAPOLIS COLTS — BYE: 14

'21 PPG: 10TH '21 YPG: 15TH '21 VS RUN: 11TH '21 VS PASS: 18TH

Indy has been top 10 in interceptions and fumbles the last four seasons. The secondary added Stephon Gilmore who will join Kenny Moore. If they can improve their sack numbers (they added two edge rushers in the offseason) and still keep their points allowed low, they are in for a great year.

YEAR	INTS	FUMS	SACKS	YPG	PPG	<14 PTS	>27 PTS	TDS	FPPG
2019	15	8	41	347	23.3	4	6	3	6.3
2020	15	10	40	332	22.6	3	4	6	7.8
2021	19	14	33	343	21.5	2	5	1	6.1
PROJ	15	9	41	341	21.6	2	4	2	6.4

6 | SAN FRANCISCO 49ERS — BYE: 9

'21 PPG: 9TH '21 YPG: 5TH '21 VS RUN: 7TH '21 VS PASS: 7TH

The 49ers finished 2021 top 10 in fumbles, sacks, points allowed, YPG, rush yards allowed, and pass yards allowed. We think the low interception number is just a one-off and numbers should improve in 2021. Nick Bosa, Jimmie Ward, and Arik Armstead will provide a solid D/ST fantasy option for 2022.

YEAR	INTS	FUMS	SACKS	YPG	PPG	<14 PTS	>27 PTS	TDS	FPPG
2019	12	15	48	282	19.4	5	3	5	8.8
2020	12	8	30	314	24.4	4	5	1	4.4
2021	9	11	48	310	21.5	5	6	2	5.6
PROJ	13	9	40	318	21.2	5	5	2	6.2

7 | PITTSBURGH STEELERS — BYE: 9

'21 PPG: 20TH '21 YPG: 26TH '21 VS RUN: 32ND '21 VS PASS: 10TH

After two top-five fantasy campaigns, the Steelers finished 2021 15th overall. They have led the league in sacks the past three seasons, good for sack-favorable scoring systems. The Steelers provide a better streaming option throughout the year rather than a weekly set-it-and-forget it D/ST.

YEAR	INTS	FUMS	SACKS	YPG	PPG	<14 PTS	>27 PTS	TDS	FPPG
2019	20	18	54	304	18.9	4	3	4	10.1
2020	18	9	56	306	19.5	3	2	3	8.6
2021	13	9	55	361	23.4	3	4	1	5.7
PROJ	13	9	47	356	22.7	3	4	2	6.2

8 | MIAMI DOLPHINS — BYE: 11

'21 PPG: 16TH '21 YPG: 16TH '21 VS RUN: 14TH '21 VS PASS: 19TH

Finishing seventh in fantasy PPG in 2021, the Dolphins now have three consecutive top-10 finishes. We did notice some of their numbers last season came from TDs, which tend to fluctuate, but elite corners Xavien Howard and Byron Jones are out to prove it wasn't a fluke.

YEAR	INTS	FUMS	SACKS	YPG	PPG	<14 PTS	>27 PTS	TDS	FPPG
2019	13	3	23	398	30.9	1	10	2	1.9
2020	18	11	41	368	21.1	5	5	3	7.6
2021	14	12	48	338	21.9	5	5	6	7.7
PROJ	14	10	43	345	22.8	3	5	2	6.1

FANTASY TAKEOVER

QUARTERBACKS
RUNNING BACKS
WIDE RECEIVERS
TIGHT ENDS
KICKERS
D/ST

Defense/Special Teams
Continued...

9 DALLAS COWBOYS — BYE: 9
'21 PPG: 7TH | '21 YPG: 21ST | '21 VS RUN: 16TH | '21 VS PASS: 21ST

YEAR	INTS	FUMS	SACKS	YPG	PPG	<14 PTS	>27 PTS	TDS	FPPG
2019	7	10	39	327	20.1	4	3	1	5.4
2020	10	13	31	386	29.6	1	9	3	3.9
2021	26	8	41	351	21.1	2	5	7	9
PROJ	13	10	42	353	23.1	1	5	2	5.8

15 CLEVELAND BROWNS — BYE: 9
'21 PPG: 13TH | '21 YPG: 4TH | '21 VS RUN: 12TH | '21 VS PASS: 5TH

YEAR	INTS	FUMS	SACKS	YPG	PPG	<14 PTS	>27 PTS	TDS	FPPG
2019	14	6	38	362	24.6	2	6	1	4.8
2020	11	10	38	358	26.2	2	8	3	4.7
2021	13	6	43	312	21.8	3	4	2	5.5
PROJ	14	8	42	330	23.1	2	4	2	5.7

10 LOS ANGELES RAMS — BYE: 7
'21 PPG: 15TH | '21 YPG: 17TH | '21 VS RUN: 6TH | '21 VS PASS: 24TH

YEAR	INTS	FUMS	SACKS	YPG	PPG	<14 PTS	>27 PTS	TDS	FPPG
2019	13	11	50	340	22.8	7	5	4	7.8
2020	14	8	53	282	18.5	5	3	4	8.3
2021	19	6	50	345	21.9	3	4	1	6.1
PROJ	14	7	48	341	22.4	3	4	2	6.1

16 WASHINGTON COMMANDERS — BYE: 14
'21 PPG: 25TH | '21 YPG: 22ND | '21 VS RUN: 8TH | '21 VS PASS: 28TH

YEAR	INTS	FUMS	SACKS	YPG	PPG	<14 PTS	>27 PTS	TDS	FPPG
2019	13	9	46	385	27.2	1	8	1	4.7
2020	16	7	47	305	20.6	2	6	3	7.0
2021	11	8	37	359	25.5	1	6	3	4.8
PROJ	12	9	42	351	22.9	1	5	2	5.7

11 CINCINNATI BENGALS — BYE: 10
'21 PPG: 17TH | '21 YPG: 20TH | '21 VS RUN: 5TH | '21 VS PASS: 27TH

YEAR	INTS	FUMS	SACKS	YPG	PPG	<14 PTS	>27 PTS	TDS	FPPG
2019	11	5	31	394	26.3	1	4	1	3.6
2020	11	6	17	389	26.5	0	7	1	2.1
2021	13	8	42	351	21.1	5	4	2	5.7
PROJ	14	8	42	355	22.7	3	4	2	5.9

17 KANSAS CITY CHIEFS — BYE: 8
'21 PPG: 8TH | '21 YPG: 27TH | '21 VS RUN: 21ST | '21 VS PASS: 25TH

YEAR	INTS	FUMS	SACKS	YPG	PPG	<14 PTS	>27 PTS	TDS	FPPG
2019	16	7	45	350	19.3	5	5	4	7.6
2020	16	6	32	358	22.6	2	5	4	6.1
2021	15	14	31	369	21.4	6	7	4	6.2
PROJ	15	9	41	360	24.3	4	6	2	5.6

12 BALTIMORE RAVENS — BYE: 10
'21 PPG: 19TH | '21 YPG: 25TH | '21 VS RUN: 1ST | '21 VS PASS: 32ND

YEAR	INTS	FUMS	SACKS	YPG	PPG	<14 PTS	>27 PTS	TDS	FPPG
2019	13	12	37	301	17.6	5	2	6	8.6
2020	10	12	39	330	18.9	6	5	4	7.2
2021	9	6	34	363	23.1	4	6	1	4.1
PROJ	12	10	40	347	22.4	5	5	2	5.8

18 MINNESOTA VIKINGS — BYE: 7
'21 PPG: 24TH | '21 YPG: 31ST | '21 VS RUN: 26TH | '21 VS PASS: 29TH

YEAR	INTS	FUMS	SACKS	YPG	PPG	<14 PTS	>27 PTS	TDS	FPPG
2019	17	14	48	342	18.9	5	2	2	8.5
2020	15	7	23	393	29.7	1	8	0	2.3
2021	16	8	51	384	25.1	1	9	4	6.2
PROJ	14	8	41	356	23.4	2	6	2	5.6

13 NEW ENGLAND PATRIOTS — BYE: 10
'21 PPG: 2ND | '21 YPG: 3RD | '21 VS RUN: 22ND | '21 VS PASS: 2ND

YEAR	INTS	FUMS	SACKS	YPG	PPG	<14 PTS	>27 PTS	TDS	FPPG
2019	25	11	47	276	14.1	9	2	7	11.3
2020	18	4	24	354	22.1	2	3	4	5.5
2021	23	7	36	311	17.8	8	4	3	7.7
PROJ	14	7	39	326	21.6	4	5	2	5.8

19 TENNESSEE TITANS — BYE: 6
'21 PPG: 6TH | '21 YPG: 13TH | '21 VS RUN: 2ND | '21 VS PASS: 26TH

YEAR	INTS	FUMS	SACKS	YPG	PPG	<14 PTS	>27 PTS	TDS	FPPG
2019	14	9	43	360	20.7	2	3	4	7.1
2020	15	8	19	398	27.4	1	8	2	3.6
2021	16	5	43	330	20.8	3	5	3	6.3
PROJ	14	8	40	350	23.4	2	6	2	5.5

14 DENVER BRONCOS — BYE: 9
'21 PPG: 3RD | '21 YPG: 8TH | '21 VS RUN: 15TH | '21 VS PASS: 8TH

YEAR	INTS	FUMS	SACKS	YPG	PPG	<14 PTS	>27 PTS	TDS	FPPG
2019	10	7	40	337	19.8	2	1	1	5.6
2020	10	5	42	368	27.9	2	9	1	3.3
2021	13	6	36	326	18.9	6	4	1	5.7
PROJ	15	8	42	359	22.6	4	5	2	5.8

20 LOS ANGELES CHARGERS — BYE: 8
'21 PPG: 30TH | '21 YPG: 24TH | '21 VS RUN: 30TH | '21 VS PASS: 11TH

YEAR	INTS	FUMS	SACKS	YPG	PPG	<14 PTS	>27 PTS	TDS	FPPG
2019	11	3	30	313	21.6	4	2	1	4.3
2020	12	7	27	343	26.6	1	8	1	3.3
2021	11	10	35	360	27	1	7	2	3.8
PROJ	12	9	40	356	24.6	2	6	2	5.4

Defense/Special Teams
Continued...

21 NEW YORK GIANTS — BYE: 9
'21 PPG: 23RD | '21 YPG: 18TH | '21 VS RUN: 25TH | '21 VS PASS: 14TH

YEAR	INTS	FUMS	SACKS	YPG	PPG	<14 PTS	>27 PTS	TDS	FPPG
2019	10	6	36	377	28.2	1	11	3	3.1
2020	11	11	40	349	22.3	1	2	2	6
2021	15	7	34	355	24.5	2	7	1	4
PROJ	13	7	39	349	22.6	1	6	2	5.4

27 SEATTLE SEAHAWKS — BYE: 11
'21 PPG: 11TH | '21 YPG: 29TH | '21 VS RUN: 17TH | '21 VS PASS: 31ST

YEAR	INTS	FUMS	SACKS	YPG	PPG	<14 PTS	>27 PTS	TDS	FPPG
2019	16	16	28	382	24.9	2	7	3	6.1
2020	14	8	46	381	23.2	2	5	0	5.5
2021	11	7	34	379	21.5	3	4	1	4.2
PROJ	12	7	39	356	24.6	2	4	2	4.7

22 PHILADELPHIA EAGLES — BYE: 7
'21 PPG: 18TH | '21 YPG: 9TH | '21 VS RUN: 9TH | '21 VS PASS: 9TH

YEAR	INTS	FUMS	SACKS	YPG	PPG	<14 PTS	>27 PTS	TDS	FPPG
2019	11	9	43	332	22.1	3	3	3	6.4
2020	8	11	49	363	26.1	1	6	3	5.8
2021	12	4	29	329	22.7	5	6	5	5.4
PROJ	12	9	42	348	23.7	2	6	2	5.4

28 NEW YORK JETS — BYE: 10
'21 PPG: 32ND | '21 YPG: 32ND | '21 VS RUN: 29TH | '21 VS PASS: 30TH

YEAR	INTS	FUMS	SACKS	YPG	PPG	<14 PTS	>27 PTS	TDS	FPPG
2019	12	9	35	323	22.4	3	5	6	6.6
2020	10	9	31	388	28.6	0	10	1	2.8
2021	7	7	33	398	29.7	0	8	2	2.5
PROJ	12	8	39	360	24.9	1	6	2	4.7

23 ARIZONA CARDINALS — BYE: 13
'21 PPG: 12TH | '21 YPG: 10TH | '21 VS RUN: 20TH | '21 VS PASS: 6TH

YEAR	INTS	FUMS	SACKS	YPG	PPG	<14 PTS	>27 PTS	TDS	FPPG
2019	7	10	40	402	27.6	1	8	0	2.9
2020	11	10	48	352	22.9	3	6	0	5.4
2021	13	14	41	329	21.5	4	5	2	6.2
PROJ	12	10	40	357	24.1	2	6	2	5.2

29 ATLANTA FALCONS — BYE: 14
'21 PPG: 29TH | '21 YPG: 23RD | '21 VS RUN: 27TH | '21 VS PASS: 15TH

YEAR	INTS	FUMS	SACKS	YPG	PPG	<14 PTS	>27 PTS	TDS	FPPG
2019	12	8	28	356	24.9	3	5	3	4.8
2020	12	9	29	398	25.9	1	6	1	3.8
2021	12	8	18	364	27	1	9	2	2.7
PROJ	13	8	36	356	25.1	1	6	2	4.6

24 CAROLINA PANTHERS — BYE: 13
'21 PPG: 21ST | '21 YPG: 2ND | '21 VS RUN: 18TH | '21 VS PASS: 3RD

YEAR	INTS	FUMS	SACKS	YPG	PPG	<14 PTS	>27 PTS	TDS	FPPG
2019	14	7	53	375	29.4	1	9	1	5
2020	7	15	28	360	25.1	2	7	3	4.8
2021	9	7	39	306	23.8	4	7	1	3.4
PROJ	13	8	40	321	24.8	3	6	2	5.0

30 JACKSONVILLE JAGUARS — BYE: 11
'21 PPG: 28TH | '21 YPG: 19TH | '21 VS RUN: 24TH | '21 VS PASS: 16TH

YEAR	INTS	FUMS	SACKS	YPG	PPG	<14 PTS	>27 PTS	TDS	FPPG
2019	10	9	47	375	24.8	3	6	2	5.1
2020	12	5	18	418	30.8	0	10	3	1.9
2021	7	2	32	353	26.9	2	8	1	2.3
PROJ	11	6	39	368	24.8	1	6	2	4.4

25 LAS VEGAS RAIDERS — BYE: 6
'21 PPG: 26TH | '21 YPG: 14TH | '21 VS RUN: 19TH | '21 VS PASS: 12TH

YEAR	INTS	FUMS	SACKS	YPG	PPG	<14 PTS	>27 PTS	TDS	FPPG
2019	9	6	32	455	26.2	1	6	2	4.3
2020	10	5	21	389	29.9	2	11	0	1.1
2021	6	9	35	337	25.8	1	7	0	2.7
PROJ	13	8	39	357	24.6	2	6	2	5.0

31 DETROIT LIONS — BYE: 6
'21 PPG: 31ST | '21 YPG: 28TH | '21 VS RUN: 28TH | '21 VS PASS: 23RD

YEAR	INTS	FUMS	SACKS	YPG	PPG	<14 PTS	>27 PTS	TDS	FPPG
2019	7	11	28	400	26.4	1	5	3	4.2
2020	7	5	24	420	32.4	0	10	1	1.3
2021	11	9	30	380	27.5	2	8	0	2.7
PROJ	12	8	37	363	25.6	1	7	2	4.4

26 CHICAGO BEARS — BYE: 14
'21 PPG: 22ND | '21 YPG: 7TH | '21 VS RUN: 23RD | '21 VS PASS: 4TH

YEAR	INTS	FUMS	SACKS	YPG	PPG	<14 PTS	>27 PTS	TDS	FPPG
2019	10	9	32	324	18.6	3	1	2	5.9
2020	10	8	35	345	23.1	2	3	2	5.2
2021	8	8	49	317	23.9	2	7	3	5.1
PROJ	10	9	41	347	24.5	2	6	2	4.9

32 HOUSTON TEXANS — BYE: 6
'21 PPG: 27TH | '21 YPG: 30TH | '21 VS RUN: 31ST | '21 VS PASS: 20TH

YEAR	INTS	FUMS	SACKS	YPG	PPG	<14 PTS	>27 PTS	TDS	FPPG
2019	12	10	31	388	24.1	2	6	2	4.9
2020	3	6	34	417	29	1	9	1	1.8
2021	17	8	32	384	26.6	1	9	2	4
PROJ	12	8	38	369	25.5	1	7	2	4.4

TEAM SHEETS
A BREAKDOWN OF OUR TEAM SHEETS

1 Commentary and analysis for each team, covering the most important fantasy questions for each franchise in 2022.

2 2021 Individual game stats for key fantasy players.

3 2022/23 Team Schedule. Combined with our team schedule is important matchup analysis. Here's how it works: For each week by position, we tell you what percentage of fantasy points above or below the league average their opponent gave up last year. For example, on Sept. 11, Arizona plays Kansas City this year. Last year, Kansas City allowed 15% more FPs for QBs than the league average. What this means is that if your QB, Kyler Murray, averages 20 fantasy PPG on the season against a neutral schedule, then if your QB played Kansas City every week, he would average 15% more, or 23 fantasy PPG. Negative numbers indicate harder matchups, while positive numbers indicate favorable matchups. We usually this chart to break ties when we are deciding who to start in our lineups. Our rankings already consider similar analysis for each team.

4 2022 NFL Draft picks for each team.

5 Key additions and contract details for new acquisitions and contract extensions.

6 2021 Stats, which includes overall fantasy metrics.

7 Key Losses — who left the team and where they went.

8 Offensive depth chart for key fantasy positions.

ARIZONA CARDINALS

NFC WEST

2021 Stats
Record: 11-6
Rushing Rank: 10th
Passing Rank: 8th
Offensive Fantasy Pts: 9th
Against Run: 20th
Against Pass: 6th
ppg Against: 22.2
ppg: 25.6

Some rankings have Kyler Murray as high as the overall QB2. Is this too high?

We're not yet ready to say that Kyler Murray is injury prone, but injuries have forced him to play hurt or miss games in each of his first three seasons. None of the injuries were related — hamstring, AC joint, ankle sprain — but all limited his fantasy output.

Looking at Murray's numbers, one may think he simply performs better in the first half of seasons. In truth, by the second half of the past two seasons Murray was nursing an ailment, and his fantasy numbers reflect it. In Weeks 1-10 in 2020 prior to his AC joint injury, Murray averaged 29.3 fantasy PPG. Post injury, in Weeks 11-17, his output declined an incredible 12.8 PPG. Similarly, in 2021 after his ankle injury, Murray averaged almost 2.0 fantasy PPG fewer than before the injury. 2021 isn't as concerning because his return also coincided with DeAndre Hopkins' absence, and losing your No. 1 receiver would cause any QB to decline in production.

Murray is an above-average passer, but like most of fantasy's elite QB options, his upside comes from his rushing. The only QBs in NFL history with a higher average rushing yards per game are Lamar Jackson and Michael Vick. Speaking of big names, the only QBs with more top-five weekly finishes among QBs over the past two seasons are Josh Allen, Tom Brady, and Aaron Rodgers.

Murray is surrounded this season by a talented group of pass catchers, which, early on, should be led by newly acquired Marquise Brown until Hopkins returns from his six-game suspension.

We don't think overall QB2 is out of the question for Murray, but if we're chasing rushing upside, give us Lamar Jackson or Jalen Hurts instead.

Is James Conner still a fringe RB1 after the addition of Darrel Williams and Keaontay Ingram?

When Conner shared the backfield with Chase Edmonds last season, he was a backend RB2. When he had the backfield to himself the six weeks Edmonds was sidelined with injury, he was excellent, finishing as the best weekly back twice and outside the top-12 only once.

Conner excelled at all levels for Arizona. He caught 95% of his targets and received PFF's third-highest receiving grade among RBs. He was also the highest-rated back in pass blocking, which should keep him on the field during those all important third downs. Conner's best fantasy attribute volume and efficiency in the RZ. Only Jonathan Taylor had more carries inside the 5-yard line than Conner. If he was able to finish as RB3 last season while sharing touches with Edmonds the majority of games, what could happen if he has the backfield all to himself?

Kliff Kingsbury is not opposed to a three-down back. In his tenure, besides Conner, David Johnson, Kenyan Drake, and Edmonds have all played more than 80% of the snaps at some point.

The signing of Darrel Williams shouldn't deter anyone from drafting Conner. Williams was signed extremely late in the offseason for the veteran minimum. He may see some passing-down usage, but he shouldn't hurt Conner's value. Also, Keaontay Ingram isn't likely to carve much of a role unless Conner gets hurt.

Fantasy managers should be happy with Conner's current ADP. We saw his floor last season, and even if he regresses some in TDs, he has fringe RB1 potential.

Which Arizona receiver offers the best value at their current ADP?

Marquise Brown is projected to be the Cardinals No. 1 option during DeAndre Hopkins' six-game suspension. Brown's numbers in Baltimore as their No. 1 wideout were not spectacular. Among WRs with 100-plus targets since 2019, Brown was 50th in yards per route run, 66th in yards per reception, and 28th in target rate per routes run. Brown's best fantasy finish in Baltimore was last season as WR21. Hopkins, Arizona's No. 1 last season, was only WR17 in fantasy PPG prior to his injury.

Murray has the tendency to spread the ball around the field, and when D-Hop returns for the second half of the season and the fantasy playoffs, Brown will face increased competition for targets. We'd much rather have a player with fantasy playoff upside.

Because of his age, competition for targets, and suspension, it's also hard to get behind drafting Hopkins. It would take a great price for us to draft Hopkins just to sit on our bench for six weeks until he returns.

Rondale Moore and Zach Ertz are the two best-valued receivers at their current ADPs. Arizona made a lot of effort last season to get Moore the ball, using him in all sorts of gadget-type plays. We expect he could see the biggest jump in targets with the departure of Christian Kirk. For a late-round flier, we'll give him a shot.

Ertz was all but left for dead in Philly last season before finding his groove after joining Arizona in Week 7. He had six top-10 finishes during his nine weeks there. Arizona valued him so much that they gave him a three-year, $31 million extension. Ertz will see a high percentage of snaps in Arizona's only real pass-catching TE. Just for his target volume alone, his ADP is too low. If you miss out on the top-five TEs, you could do worse than waiting late for Ertz who should be there in the mid-to-late rounds.

ARIZONA CARDINALS

Some rankings have Kyler Murray as high as the overall QB2. Is this too high?

We're not yet ready to say that Kyler Murray is injury prone, but injuries have forced him to play hurt or miss games in each of his first three seasons. None of the injuries were related — hamstring, AC joint, ankle sprain — but each limited his fantasy output.

Looking at Murray's numbers, one may think he simply performs better in the first half of seasons. In truth, by the second half of the past two seasons Murray was nursing an ailment, and his fantasy numbers reflect it. In Weeks 1-10 in 2020 prior to his AC joint injury, Murray averaged 29.3 fantasy PPG. Post injury, in Weeks 11-17, his output declined an incredible 12.8 PPG. Similarly, in 2021 after his ankle injury, Murray averaged almost 2.0 fantasy PPG fewer than before the injury. 2021 isn't as concerning because his return also coincided with DeAndre Hopkins' absence, and losing your No. 1 receiver would cause any QB to decline in production.

Murray is an above-average passer, but like most of fantasy's elite QB options, his upside comes from his rushing. The only QBs in NFL history with a higher average rushing yards per game are Lamar Jackson and Michael Vick. Speaking of big names, the only QBs with more top-five weekly finishes among QBs over the past two seasons are Josh Allen, Tom Brady, and Aaron Rodgers.

Murray is surrounded this season by a talented group of pass catchers, which, early on, should be led by newly acquired Marquise Brown until Hopkins returns from his six-game suspension.

We don't think overall QB2 is out of the question for Murray, but if we're chasing rushing upside, give us Lamar Jackson or Jalen Hurts instead.

Is James Conner still a fringe RB1 after the addition of Darrel Williams and Keaontay Ingram?

When Conner shared the backfield with Chase Edmonds last season, he was a backend RB2. When he had the backfield to himself the six weeks Edmonds was sidelined with injury, he was excellent, finishing as the best weekly back twice and outside the top-12 only once.

Conner excelled at all levels for Arizona. He caught 95% of his targets and received PFF's third-highest receiving grade among RBs. He was also the highest-rated back in pass blocking, which should keep him on the field during those all important third downs. Conner's best fantasy attribute volume and efficiency in the red zone. Only Jonathan Taylor had more carries inside the 5-yard line than Conner. If he was able to finish as RB3 last season while sharing touches with Edmonds the majority of games, what could happen if he has the backfield all to himself?

2022/23 SCHEDULE — 2021 FANTASY POINTS ALLOWED BY OPPONENT VS LEAGUE AVERAGE

WK	DATE	TIME	OPP	QB	RB	WR	TE
1	9/11	4:25	KC	15%	4%	3%	2%
2	9/18	4:25	@LV	1%	10%	-14%	39%
3	9/25	4:25	LAR	-12%	-8%	7%	-2%
4	10/02	4:05	@CAR	-6%	-12%	-7%	-5%
5	10/09	4:25	PHI	-1%	10%	-17%	46%
6	10/16	4:05	@SEA	2%	-8%	3%	-23%
7	10/20	8:15	NO	-26%	2%	-16%	-45%
8	10/30	1:00	@MIN	6%	2%	23%	-13%
9	11/06	4:05	SEA	2%	-8%	3%	-23%
10	11/13	4:25	@LAR	-12%	-8%	7%	-2%
11	11/21	8:20	SF*	-1%	26%	-3%	20%
12	11/27	4:05	LAC	2%	17%	-11%	23%
13	BYE WEEK						
14	12/12	8:15	NE	-8%	-19%	1%	-20%
15	12/18	4:05	@DEN	-10%	-9%	-6%	-29%
16	12/25	8:20	TB	3%	-4%	3%	4%
17	1/01	1:00	@ATL	13%	8%	7%	-3%
18	1/08	TBD	@SF	-1%	26%	-3%	20%

PLAYED IN MEXICO CITY

2022 NFL DRAFT

RD	PK		POS	COLLEGE	HT	WT
2	23	TREY MCBRIDE	TE	COLORADO STATE	6-4	260
3	23	CAMERON THOMAS	EDGE	SAN DIEGO STATE	6-5	290
3	36	MYJAI SANDERS	EDGE	CINICINNATI	6-5	269
6	22	KEAONTAY INGRAM	RB	NORTHWEST MISSOURI STATE	6-0	215
6	37	LECITUS SMITH	G	VIRGINIA TECH	6-3	320
7	23	CHRISTIAN MATTHEW	DB	VALDOSTA STATE	6-4	200
7	35	JESSE LUKETA	LB	PENN STATE	6-3	247
7	36	MARQUIS HAYES	G	OKLAHOMA	6-5	324

2021 WEEKLY STATS

*RUSH STATS : *REC STATS

	@ TEN (W) 38-13		MIN (W) 34-33		@ JAC (W) 31-19		@ LAR (W) 37-20		SF (W) 17-10		@ CLE (W) 37-14		HOU (W) 31-5		GB (L) 21-24	
QB KYLER MURRAY	21-32 289 (1 INT) (4 TD)	5-20 (1 TD)	29-36 400 (2 INT) (3 TD)	5-31 (1 TD)	28-34 316 (1 INT)	7-19 (1 TD)	24-32 268 (2 TD)	6-39	22-31 239 (1 TD)	7-1	20-30 229 (4 TD)	7-6	20-28 261 (1 INT) (3 TD)	6-10	22-33 274 (2 INT)	6-21
QB COLT MCCOY	DNP		DNP		DNP		0-0	2-[-2]	DNP		0-0	3-1-[-3]	0-0	2-1-[-1]	DNP	
RB JAMES CONNER	16-53	0-0	8-26	0-0	11-43 (2 TD)	1-10	18-50 (2 TD)	2-16	10-29 (1 TD)	1-8	16-71	1-0	10-64 (1 TD)	0-0	5-22 (2 TD)	0-0
RB CHASE EDMONDS	12-63	4-43	8-46	5-29	11-26	7-49	12-120	4-19	6-15	3-19	4-46	3-4	15-81	1-9	7-30 (1 TD)	3-39
WR CHRISTIAN KIRK	0-0	5-70 (2 TD)	0-0	3-65	0-0	7-104	0-0	1-5	1-11	5-39	0-0	5-75 (1 TD)	0-0	4-50 (1 TD)	0-0	4-46
WR A.J. GREEN	0-0	2-25	0-0	3-44 (1 TD)	0-0	5-112	0-0	5-67 (1 TD)	0-0	1-13	0-0	5-79 (1 TD)	0-0	3-66	0-0	5-50
WR DEANDRE HOPKINS	0-0	6-83 (2 TD)	0-0	4-54 (1 TD)	0-0	3-21	0-0	4-67	0-0	6-87 (1 TD)	0-0	3-55 (2 TD)	0-0	7-53 (1 TD)	0-0	2-66
WR RONDALE MOORE	0-0	4-68	0-0	7-114 (1 TD)	1-3	2-1	2-9	3-28	3-38	5-59	3-10	3-16	0-0	2-17	2-1	3-24
TE ZACH ERTZ	DNP		DNP		DNP		DNP		DNP		DNP		1-4	3-66 (1 TD)	0-0	4-42
TE MAXX WILLIAMS	0-0	0-0	0-0	7-94	0-0	3-19	0-0	5-66 (1 TD)	0-0	1-14	DNP		DNP		DNP	

FANTASY TAKEOVER

2021 Stats
Record: 11-6
Rushing Rank: 10th
Passing Rank: 8th
Offensive Fantasy Pts: 9th
Against Run: 20th
Against Pass: 6th
ppg Against: 22.2
ppg: 25.6

Kliff Kingsbury is not opposed to a three-down back. In his tenure, besides Conner, David Johnson, Kenyan Drake, and Edmonds have all played more than 80% of the snaps at some point.

The signing of Darrel Williams shouldn't deter anyone from drafting Conner. Williams was signed extremely late in the offseason for the veteran minimum. He may see some passing-down usage, but he shouldn't hurt Conner's value. Also, Keaontay Ingram isn't likely to carve much of a role unless Conner gets hurt.

Fantasy managers should be happy with Conner's current ADP. We saw his floor last season, and even if he regresses some in TDs, he has fringe RB1 potential.

Which Arizona receiver offers the best value at their current ADP?

Marquise Brown is projected to be the Cardinals No. 1 option during DeAndre Hopkins' six-game suspension. Brown's numbers in Baltimore as their No. 1 wideout were not spectacular. Among WRs with 100-plus targets since 2019, Brown was 50th in yards per route run, 66th in yards per reception, and 28th in target rate per routes run. Brown's best fantasy finish in Baltimore was last season as WR21. Hopkins, Arizona's No. 1 last season, was only WR17 in fantasy PPG prior to his injury.

Murray has the tendency to spread the ball around the field, and when D-Hop returns for the second half of the season and the fantasy playoffs, Brown will face increased competition for targets. We'd much rather have a player with fantasy playoff upside.

Because of his age, competition for targets, and suspension, it's also hard to get behind drafting Hopkins. It would take a great price for us to draft Hopkins just to sit on our bench for six weeks until he returns.

Rondale Moore and Zach Ertz are the two best-valued receivers at their current ADPs. Arizona made a lot of effort last season to get Moore the ball, using him in all sorts of gadget-type plays. We expect he could see the biggest jump in targets with the departure of Christian Kirk. For a late-round flier, we'll give him a shot.

Ertz was all but left for dead in Philly last season before finding his groove after joining Arizona in Week 7. He had six top-10 finishes during his nine weeks there. Arizona valued him so much that they gave him a three-year, $31 million extension. Ertz will see a high percentage of snaps as Arizona's only real pass-catching TE. Just for his target volume alone, his ADP is too low. If you miss out on the top-five TEs, you could do worse than waiting late for Ertz who should be there in the mid-to-late rounds.

KEY ADDITIONS & NEW CONTRACTS

QB **KYLER MURRAY**: SIGNED A FIVE-YEAR, $230.5 MILLION CONTRACT EXTENSION THAT INCLUDES $160 MILLION GUARANTEED

QB **COLT MCCOY**: RE-SIGNED ON A TWO-YEAR CONTRACT.

RB **JAMES CONNER**: SIGNED TO A THREE-YEAR, $21 MILLION EXTENSION THAT INCLUDES $16 MILLION OVER THE FIRST TWO YEARS.

RB **DARREL WILLIAMS**: SIGNED A ONE-YEAR DEAL.

WR **MARQUISE BROWN**: ACQUIRED IN A TRADE WITH THE BALTIMORE RAVENS, ALONG WITH A 2022 THIRD-ROUNDER (NO. 100 OVERALL), FOR THE 18TH OVERALL PICK IN THE 2022 NFL DRAFT.

WR **A.J. GREEN**: RE-SIGNED A ONE-YEAR CONTRACT.

TE **ZACH ERTZ**: RE-SIGNED ON A THREE-YEAR, $31.65 MILLION CONTRACT THAT INCLUDES $17.5 MILLION GUARANTEED.

TE **MAXX WILLIAMS**: RE-SIGNED TO A ONE-YEAR CONTRACT.

OG **WILL HERNANDEZ**: SIGNED A ONE-YEAR DEAL.

DE **MICHAEL DOGBE**: RE-SIGNED ON A ONE-YEAR CONTRACT.

LB **DENNIS GARDECK**: RE-SIGNED ON A THREE-YEAR CONTRACT.

LB **NICK VIGIL**: SIGNED A ONE-YEAR DEAL.

P **ANDY LEE**: SIGNED A ONE-YEAR DEAL.

LS **AARON BREWER**: SIGNED A ONE-YEAR DEAL.

KEY LOSSES

RB **CHASE EDMONDS** (DOLPHINS)

WR **CHRISTIAN KIRK** (JAGUARS)

OL **MAX GARCIA** (GIANTS)

DT **COREY PETERS**

DL **JORDAN PHILLIPS** (BILLS)

LB **JORDAN HICKS** (VIKINGS)

LB **CHANDLER JONES** (RAIDERS)

CB **ROBERT ALFORD**

CB **MALCOLM BUTLER** (PATRIOTS)

S **CHRIS BANJO**

DEPTH CHART

QB1	KYLER MURRAY
QB2	COLT MCCOY
RB1	JAMES CONNER
RB2	DARREL WILLIAMS **N**
RB3	KEAONTAY INGRAM **R**
WR1	DEANDRE HOPKINS
WR2	MARQUISE BROWN **N**
WR3	RONDALE MOORE
WR4	A.J. GREEN
TE1	ZACH ERTZ
TE2	TREY MCBRIDE **R**
K	MATT PRATER

2021 WEEKLY STATS

@ SF (W) 31-17		CAR (L) 10-34		@ SEA (W) 23-13		CHI (W) 33-22		LAR (L) 23-30		@ DET (L) 12-30		IND (L) 16-22		@ DAL (W) 25-22		SEA (L) 30-38	
DNP		DNP		DNP		11-15 123 (2 TD) 10-59 (2 TD)		32-49 383 (2 INT) 7-61		23-41 257 (1 INT) (1 TD) 4-3		27-43 245 (1 TD) 4-74		26-38 263 (2 TD) 9-44		28-39 240 (1 TD) 5-35	
22-26 249 (1 TD) 7-23		11-20 107 (1 INT) 1-[-1]		35-44 328 (2 TD) 6-18		DNP		DNP		6-9 56 1-3		DNP		DNP		0-0 0-0	
21-96 (2 TD)	5-77 (1 TD)	10-39 (1 TD)	3-25	21-62 (1 TD)	5-37	20-75	2-36 (1 TD)	13-31 (2 TD)	9-94	8-39	2-31	DNP		DNP		15-52 (1 TD)	6-41 (1 TD)
1-3	0-0	DNP		DNP		DNP		DNP		6-53	0-0	16-56 (1 TD)	8-71	18-53	5-29	DNP	
0-0	6-91	0-0	7-58	0-0	2-25	0-0	1-4	0-0	3-86	0-0	9-94 (1 TD)	0-0	7-48	0-0	6-79	0-0	2-43
DNP		0-0	1-4	0-0	4-78	0-0	1-14	0-0	7-102	0-0	4-64	0-0	1-33	0-0	3-74	0-0	4-23
DNP		DNP		DNP		0-0	2-32 (1 TD)	0-0	5-54	DNP		DNP		DNP		DNP	
0-0	5-25	1-1	2-10	0-0	11-51	3-2	1-8	2-11	3-5	1-1	3-9	DNP		DNP		DNP	
0-0	3-27	0-0	4-46	0-0	8-88 (2 TD)	0-0	1-10	0-0	5-42	0-0	6-74	0-0	8-54	0-0	7-41	0-0	7-84
DNP		DNP		DNP		DNP		DNP		DNP		DNP		DNP		DNP	

What are the fantasy ceilings of Marcus Mariota and Desmond Ridder?

Marcus Mariota is still the projected Week 1 starter for the Falcons. On the surface, Mariota appears to be the dual-threat option that fantasy rewards. But we're hesitant to expect anything more than his fantasy production as a starter in Tennessee from 2015-19. What's telling is that Ryan Tannehill, who took Mariota's starting job in Tennessee, was a better fantasy QB in the same offense. In his last three seasons as a starter (2017-19), Mariota failed to finish in the top-23 QBs.

Atlanta, under Matt Ryan's tenure, has traditionally been a pass-heavy team, although last year's numbers may have been somewhat skewed, as Atlanta was forced to pass more often while playing from behind. While Mariota may have four-to-five impromptu scrambles per game, we mostly expect Arthur Smith to attempt a more balanced game plan that incorporates a larger rushing attack by his RBs. If this is the case, it's unlikely Mariota's passing efficiency will be enough to make him a realistic fantasy option. He may not even be able to hold off Desmond Ridder who is breathing down his neck.

Ridder is an extremely athletic QB who posted some of the best combine numbers. Among QBs tested at the combine, he finished top four in the 40-yard dash, vertical, broad jump, three-cone drill, and the 20-yard shuttle. But with all this athleticism, Ridder didn't put up big rushing numbers in college. He even relied more on his arm than his legs as his collegiate career progressed.

With one of the worst receiver rooms and offensive lines in the league, any Atlanta QB would need some serious rushing chops to make a splash in fantasy, and neither Mariota or Ridder have it.

Can converted WR Cordarrelle Patterson maintain the feature-back role in Atlanta?

Listed as a WR to start the 2021 season, Cordarrelle Patterson emerged as the lead back after Mike Davis could never quite maintain adequate production.

The Patterson situation is a tough one to figure out. In Weeks 1-9 last season, he was overall RB7. After returning from an ankle injury, in Weeks 9-18, he was RB20 (RB30 in PPG). The differences lie in his receiving numbers. Did he lose targets because he wasn't fully healthy or because of the offensive scheme? We are on the fence here.

The good news for Patterson is that Atlanta didn't add too much competition for him this offseason. They gave Damien Williams what is essentially a league-minimum contract and added RB Tyler Allgeier in the fifth round of the draft.

Patterson, as a result, looks to have the job to himself for now, and at his current

2022/23 SCHEDULE			2021 FANTASY POINTS ALLOWED BY OPPONENT VS LEAGUE AVERAGE			
WK	DATE	TIME	OPP	QB	RB	WR	TE
1	9/11	1:00	NO	-26%	2%	-16%	-45%
2	9/18	4:05	@LAR	-12%	-8%	7%	-2%
3	9/25	4:25	@SEA	2%	-8%	3%	-23%
4	10/02	1:00	CLE	-5%	-5%	-6%	2%
5	10/09	1:00	@TB	3%	-4%	3%	4%
6	10/16	1:00	SF	-1%	26%	-3%	20%
7	10/23	1:00	@CIN	-1%	6%	0%	22%
8	10/30	1:00	CAR	-6%	-12%	-7%	-5%
9	11/06	1:00	LAC	2%	17%	-11%	23%
10	11/10	8:15	@CAR	-6%	-12%	-7%	-5%
11	11/20	1:00	CHI	4%	-7%	0%	-28%
12	11/27	1:00	@WAS	29%	-3%	8%	5%
13	12/04	1:00	PIT	-2%	11%	-3%	-10%
14	BYE WEEK						
15	12/17	TBD	@NO	-26%	2%	-16%	-45%
16	12/24	1:00	@BAL	13%	-12%	12%	29%
17	1/01	1:00	ARI	0%	-11%	10%	-36%
18	1/08	TBD	TB	3%	-4%	3%	4%

2022 NFL DRAFT					
RD	PK		POS	COLLEGE	HT	WT
1	8	DRAKE LONDON	WR	USC	6-5	210
2	6	ARNOLD EBIKETIE	EDGE	PENN STATE	6-3	256
2	26	TROY ANDERSON	LB	MONTANA STATE	6-4	235
3	10	DESMOND RIDDER	QB	CINCINNATI	6-4	215
3	18	DEANGELO MALONE	LB	WESTERN KENTUCKY	6-4	230
5	8	TYLER ALLGEIER	RB	BYU	5-11	220
6	11	JUSTIN SHAFFER	G	GEORGIA	6-4	330
6	35	JOHN FITZPATRICK	TE	GEORGIA	6-7	250

2021 WEEKLY STATS

*RUSH STATS : *REC STATS	PHI (L) 6-32		@ TB (L) 25-48		@ NYG (W) 17-14		WAS (L) 17-34		NYJ (W) 27-20		@ MIA (W) 30-28		CAR (L) 13-19		@ NO (W) 27-25	
QB MATT RYAN	21-35 164 2-8		35-46 300 (3 INT) (2 TD) 2-3		27-36 243 (2 TD) 1-1-(1)		25-42 283 (4 TD) 1-17		33-45 342 (2 TD) 1-1-(1)		25-40 336 (1 INT) (2 TD) 3-0		20-27 146 (2 INT) (1 TD) 2-3		23-30 343 (2 TD) 5-8 (1 TD)	
RB C. PATTERSON	7-54	2-13	7-11 (1 TD)	5-58 (1 TD)	7-20	6-82	6-34	5-82 (3 TD)	14-54	7-60	14-60 (1 TD)	2-1	9-35	5-37 (1 TD)	9-10	6-126
RB MIKE DAVIS	15-49	3-23	9-38	7-25	12-50	4-20	13-14	2-12 (1 TD)	13-53 (1 TD)	2-8	4-10	0-0	9-44	5-22	9-13	1-5
WR RUSSELL GAGE	0-0	0-0	0-0	5-28	DNP		DNP		DNP		0-0	4-67 (1 TD)	0-0	0-0	0-0	7-64
WR OLAMIDE ZACCHEAUS	0-0	0-0	0-0	2-22	0-0	3-32 (1 TD)	0-0	1-15	0-0	2-20	0-0	1-13	0-0	1-12	0-0	3-58 (2 TD)
WR CALVIN RIDLEY	0-0	5-51	0-0	7-63 (1 TD)	0-0	8-61	0-0	7-80	DNP		0-0	4-26 (1 TD)	DNP		DNP	
TE KYLE PITTS	0-0	4-31	0-0	5-73	0-0	2-35	0-0	4-50	0-0	9-119 (1 TD)	0-0	7-163	0-0	2-13	0-0	3-62
TE HAYDEN HURST	0-0	4-28	0-0	1-6	0-0	0-0	0-0	4-29	0-0	4-40 (1 TD)	0-0	3-35	0-0	2-4	0-0	2-16

2021 Stats
Record: 7-10
Rushing Rank: 7th
Passing Rank: 31st
Offensive Fantasy Pts: 16th
Against Run: 26th
Against Pass: 27th
ppg Against: 27.0
ppg: 18.4

KEY ADDITIONS & NEW CONTRACTS

QB **MARCUS MARIOTA**: SIGNED A TWO-YEAR DEAL. MARIOTA WILL EARN $6.75 MILLION IN 2022 ($1.75 MILLION GUARANTEED BASE SALARY, $5 MILLION SIGNING BONUS) AND HAS A $12 MILLION OPTION FOR 2023. HE'S DUE A $3 MILLION ROSTER BONUS ON THE FIFTH DAY OF THE LEAGUE YEAR NEXT MARCH.

RB **CORDARRELLE PATTERSON**: RE-SIGNED TO A TWO-YEAR DEAL.

RB **DAMIEN WILLIAMS**: SIGNED A ONE-YEAR DEAL.

TE **ANTHONY FIRKSER**: SIGNED A ONE-YEAR DEAL.

WR **DAMIERE BYRD**: SIGNED A FREE-AGENT DEAL.

WR **BRYAN EDWARDS**: ACQUIRED IN A TRADE WITH THE RAIDERS, ALONG WITH A 2023 SEVENTH-ROUND PICK, IN EXCHANGE FOR A 2023 FIFTH-ROUND PICK.

WR **KHADAREL HODGE**: SIGNED A ONE-YEAR DEAL.

WR **AUDEN TATE**: SIGNED A ONE-YEAR DEAL.

WR **OLAMIDE ZACCHAEUS**: SIGNED A ONE-YEAR DEAL.

OT **GERMAIN IFEDI**: SIGNED A ONE-YEAR DEAL.

OT **JAKE MATTHEWS**: SIGNED A THREE-YEAR EXTENSION THAT WILL PAY HIM $52.5 MILLION OVER THE FIRST THREE YEARS AND REDUCES HIS 2022 CAP NUMBER.

OL **ELIJAH WILKINSON**: SIGNED A FREE-AGENT DEAL.

DT **GRADY JARRETT**: SIGNED A THREE-YEAR EXTENSION WORTH UP TO $51 MILLION AND REDUCES HIS 2022 CAP NUMBER.

LB **LORENZO CARTER**: SIGNED A ONE-YEAR DEAL.

LB **RASHAAN EVANS**: SIGNED A ONE-YEAR DEAL.

CB **CASEY HAYWARD**: SIGNED A TWO-YEAR, $11 MILLION CONTRACT.

CB **ISAIAH OLIVER**: RE-SIGNED ON A ONE-YEAR DEAL.

S **ERIK HARRIS**: RE-SIGNED ON A ONE-YEAR DEAL.

S **DEAN MARLOWE**: SIGNED A ONE-YEAR DEAL.

K **YOUNGHOE KOO**: RE-SIGNED TO A FIVE-YEAR, $24.25 MILLION CONTRACT EXTENSION THAT INCLUDES $11.5 MILLION GUARANTEED.

LS **BEAU BRINKLEY**: SIGNED A FREE-AGENT DEAL.

RB32 ADP, he's being drafted at his floor, assuming he doesn't lose his starting job.

While fifth-round rookies don't always even make a team's roster, Allgeier has the best chance of supplanting the 31-year-old Patterson. He's three-down capable, and in this shallow backfield, will get a chance to prove himself on the field. He may be worth throwing a dart at in the later rounds in hopes that he can steal the job from Patterson, relegating him to a gadget-type role. Keep an eye on Allgeier this preseason before using a late-round pick on him.

Which pass catcher will you have more shares of, Drake London or Kyle Pitts?

Drake London will be the Falcons No. 1 WR from Day 1. London is not the fastest receiver, but he makes up for it with his size (6-4 and 219 pounds) and physical ability, especially at the point of catch. There are some questions about his ability to create separation, but those indictments have been overblown.

History is also on London's side. Since 2010, seven WRs have been selected with the draft's top-10 overall picks and played at least 13 games their rookie season. Out of the seven, all have exceeded 100 targets and finished inside fantasy's top-30 WRs their rookie years. If London is fully recovered from his broken ankle, which he should be, he's a good value at his current ADP of WR38.

Kyle Pitts will compete with London to be Atlanta's target leader. It was going to be tough for Pitts to meet his outrageous rookie expectations, but he came close. Among TEs, he finished fifth in yards per route run and first in yards per reception on his way to a TE6 finish. Pitts, more of a WR in TE clothing, excels when he's matched up against linebackers and safeties, which occurs at a 50% clip. Pitts will improve in every area in 2022, especially his TD numbers. We prefer Pitts over Kittle and Waller, and will be looking to draft him in the third or fourth round.

KEY LOSSES

QB **AJ MCCARRON**
QB **JOSH ROSEN**
QB **MATT RYAN** (TRADED TO COLTS)
RB **MIKE DAVIS**
WR **RUSSELL GAGE** (BUCCANEERS)
WR **CALVIN RIDLEY** (SUSPENDED)
WR **TAJAE SHARPE** (BEARS)
TE **HAYDEN HURST** (BENGALS)
DE **DANTE FOWLER** (COWBOYS)
DE **STEVEN MEANS**
DT **JONATHAN BULLARD** (VIKINGS)
DT **TYELER DAVISON**
LB **BRANDON COPELAND**
LB **FOYE OLUOKUN** (JAGUARS)
CB **FABIAN MOREAU** (TEXANS)
S **DURON HARMON** (RAIDERS)
LS **JOSH HARRIS** (CHARGERS)
P **THOMAS MORSTEAD** (DOLPHINS)

DEPTH CHART

QB1	MARCUS MARIOTA **N**
QB2	DESMOND RIDDER **R**
RB1	CORDARRELLE PATTERSON
RB2	DAMIEN WILLIAMS **N**
RB3	TYLER ALLGEIER **R**
WR1	DRAKE LONDON **R**
WR2	OLAMIDE ZACCHAEUS
WR3	AUDEN TATE **N**
WR4	BRYAN EDWARDS **N**
TE1	KYLE PITTS
TE2	ANTHONY FIRKSER **N**
K	YOUNGHOE KOO

2021 WEEKLY STATS

@ DAL (L) 3-43		NE (L) 0-25		@ JAC (W) 21-14		TB (L) 17-30		@ CAR (W) 29-21		@ SF (L) 13-31		DET (W) 20-16		@ BUF (L) 15-29		NO (L) 20-30	
9-21 117 (2 INT)		19-28 153 (2 INT)		19-29 190 (1 INT) (1 TD)		30-41 297		19-28 190 (1 TD)		19-32 236 (1 TD)		18-24 215 (1 TD)		13-23 197		20-33 216 (1 INT) (1 TD)	
0-0		0-0		4-6		3-2		4-3		5-20		4-5		2-7		1-2	
4-25	1-14	DNP		16-108 (2TD)	2-27	13-78	3-18	16-58 (1 TD)	2-1	11-18	2-5	7-14 (1 TD)	1-[-1]	9-28	2-24	4-11	1-1
4-18	0-0	3-1	3-20	5-16	3-25	4-32 (1 TD)	4-37	11-44	5-42	6-21	0-0	7-28	1-7	8-42 (1 TD)	1-15	6-30	3-[-2]
0-0	0-0	0-0	5-49	0-0	6-62 (1 TD)	0-0	11-130	0-0	4-64	0-0	8-91 (1 TD)	0-0	4-39	0-0	3-50	0-0	9-126 (1 TD)
0-0	2-22	0-0	3-23	0-0	1-5	1-2	3-44	0-0	0-0	0-0	2-53	0-0	2-32	0-0	2-8	0-0	3-47
DNP		DNP		DNP		DNP		DNP		DNP		DNP		DNP		DNP	
0-0	4-60	0-0	3-29	0-0	2-26	0-0	4-48	0-0	5-61	0-0	4-77	0-0	6-102	0-0	2-69	0-0	2-8
0-0	0-0	DNP		DNP		DNP		0-0	1-3 (1 TD)	0-0	2-6	0-0	2-21 (1 TD)	DNP		0-0	1-33

After an injury-laden 2021, what's the outlook for the 2022 Ravens?

Before last season could get started Baltimore was already missing their top two running backs. Both J.K. Dobbins and Gus Edwards suffered ACL tears, either in preseason action or practice, and just days before Week 1. The parade of third-string and end-of-career backs (emergency acquisitions) commenced in the Baltimore backfield. Ty'Son Williams, Devonta Freeman, Latavius Murray, and Le'Veon Bell all took turns, but achieved no real success for the Ravens.

An ineffective backfield forced QB Lamar Jackson to throw the ball more, and to run less — not the best scheme for a group built to favor the run. From 2019-20 the Ravens ran the ball on 54.5% of snaps, and averaged only 26 passing attempts per game. In 2021 they ran the ball just 44% of plays, while passing attempts had increased to 32 per game.

Jackson himself never returned after a Week 14 ankle injury. He missed five games on the season, and was fully healthy for just 10 of his 12 games.

Of the skill position starters in Baltimore, only TE Mark Andrews managed to play the entire season, and boy did he play, finishing the year as TE1.

This season, both Dobbins and Edwards return to the backfield healthy. Dobbins is projected for top-20 RB fantasy numbers. In his 2020 rookie year he averaged 6.0 yards per carry and 2.5 yards after contact.

Jackson returns to Baltimore in full health in his age-25 season, ready to return to MVP form. Consider this: although Jackson missed five games last season, he still rushed 133 times for 767 yards. His 63.9 rushing yards per game was No. 1 among QBs, and he finished the year QB16 overall in fantasy, even with his missing games. But he was on pace to finish as QB9. We expect Jackson to be a top-five fantasy QB in 2022.

> 'OF THE SKILL POSITION STARTERS IN BALTIMORE, ONLY TE MARK ANDREWS MANAGED TO PLAY THE ENTIRE SEASON, AND BOY DID HE PLAY'

2022/23 SCHEDULE				2021 FANTASY POINTS ALLOWED BY OPPONENT VS LEAGUE AVERAGE			
WK	DATE	TIME	OPP	QB	RB	WR	TE
1	9/11	1:00	@NYJ	-4%	11%	-1%	-1%
2	9/18	1:00	MIA	-6%	-4%	-2%	6%
3	9/25	1:00	@NE	-8%	-19%	1%	-20%
4	10/02	1:00	BUF	-34%	-11%	-27%	-34%
5	10/09	8:20	CIN	-1%	6%	0%	22%
6	10/16	1:00	@NYG	12%	40%	-2%	22%
7	10/23	1:00	CLE	-5%	-5%	-6%	2%
8	10/27	8:15	@TB	3%	-4%	3%	4%
9	11/07	8:20	@NO	-26%	2%	-16%	-45%
10	BYE WEEK						
11	11/20	1:00	CAR	-6%	-12%	-7%	-5%
12	11/27	1:00	@JAC	4%	-1%	5%	-2%
13	12/04	1:00	DEN	-10%	-9%	-6%	-29%
14	12/11	1:00	@PIT	-2%	11%	-3%	-10%
15	12/17	TBD	@CLE	-5%	-5%	-6%	2%
16	12/24	1:00	ATL	13%	8%	7%	-3%
17	1/01	1:00	PIT	-2%	11%	-3%	-10%
18	1/08	TBD	@CIN	-1%	6%	0%	22%

2022 NFL DRAFT					
RD	PK		POS	COLLEGE	HT	WT
1	14	KYLE HAMILTON	S	NOTRE DAME	6-4	219
1	25	TYLER LINDERBAUM	C	IOWA	6-3	290
2	13	DAVID OJABO	EDGE	MICHIGAN	6-5	250
3	12	TRAVIS JONES	DT	CONNECTICUT	6-4	333
4	5	DANIEL FAALELE	OT	MINNESOTA	6-9	380
4	14	JAYLN ARMOUR-DAVIS	CB	ALABAMA	6-1	192
4	23	CHARLIE KOLAR	TE	IOWA STATE	6-6	252
4	25	JORDAN STOUT	P	PENN STATE	6-3	209
4	34	ISAIAH LIKELY	TE	COASTAL CAROLINA	6-4	240
4	36	DAMARION WILLIAMS	CB	HOUSTON	5-10	180
6	17	TYLER BADIE	RB	MISSOURI	5-8	194

2021 WEEKLY STATS

*RUSH STATS :REC STATS	@ LV (L) 27-33		KC (W) 36-35		@ DET (W) 19-17		@ DEN (W) 23-7		IND (W) 31-25		LAC (W) 34-6		CIN (L) 17-41		MIN (W) 34-31	
QB LAMAR JACKSON	19-30 235 (1 TD)	12-86	18-26 239 (2 INT) (1 TD)	16-107 (2 TD)	16-31 287 (1 INT) (1 TD)	7-58	22-37 316 (1 TD)	7-28	37-43 442 (4 TD)	14-62	19-27 167 (2 TD)	8-51	15-31 257 (1 TD)	12-88	27-41 266 (2 INT) (3 TD)	21-120
QB TYLER HUNTLEY	DNP		DNP		DNP		DNP		DNP		0-0 0	3-10	5-11 39	0-0	DNP	
RB DEVONTA FREEMAN	DNP		2-29	0-0	3-8	0-0	1-4	0-0	1-1	3-34	9-53 (1 TD)	0-0	4-14 (1 TD)	3-25	13-79	2-4 (1 TD)
RB LATAVIUS MURRAY	10-28 (1 TD)	0-0	9-36 (1 TD)	0-0	7-28	0-0	18-59 (1 TD)	0-0	6-17	2-13	9-44 (1 TD)	2-12	DNP		DNP	
RB TY'SON WILLIAMS	9-65 (1 TD)	3-29	13-77	2-16	5-22	0-0	DNP		4-6	2-15	DNP		2-10	2-24	0-0	0-0
WR MARQUISE BROWN	1-5	6-69 (1 TD)	0-0	6-113 (1 TD)	0-0	3-53	0-0	4-91 (1 TD)	0-0	9-125 (2 TD)	0-0	4-35	0-0	5-80 (1 TD)	0-0	9-116
WR RASHOD BATEMAN	DNP		DNP		DNP		DNP		DNP		0-0	4-29	0-0	3-80	0-0	5-52
WR DEVIN DUVERNAY	0-0	1-6	0-0	0-0	0-0	2-22 (1 TD)	0-0	3-31	0-0	4-45	1-11	2-15	1-[-2]	1-11	0-0	2-8 (1 TD)
WR SAMMY WATKINS	0-0	4-96	0-0	4-44	0-0	4-68	0-0	4-49	0-0	2-35	DNP		DNP		DNP	
TE MARK ANDREWS	0-0	3-20	0-0	5-57	0-0	5-109	0-0	5-67	0-0	11-147 (2 TD)	0-0	5-68 (1 TD)	0-0	3-48	0-0	5-44

2021 Stats

Record: 8-9
Rushing Rank: 8th
Passing Rank: 3rd
Offensive Fantasy Pts: 13th
Against Run: 1st
Against Pass: 32nd
ppg Against: 23.1
ppg: 22.8

How will the departure of Marquise brown affect the Ravens offense?

Hollywood Brown left for Arizona this offseason and the Ravens didn't add anyone to replace their former No. 1 WR. Moving up in the depth chart to fill the top role is second-year receiver Rashod Bateman, who missed the first five games last season to a core muscle injury. Bateman's numbers last year were ordinary, even on a per-game basis, but this year he's positioned for a breakout if he can seize the moment. Brown had 146 targets last year, ninth among WRs, and that volume has to go somewhere. Bateman is first in line for the work and Baltimore thinks he's ready to be their WR1.

Some of Brown's target share will also surely fall the way of TE Mark Andrews. Last season Andrews finished as the best fantasy tight end in the league, posting top marks in targets, receptions, yards, TDs, and fantasy points, both overall and PPG. He also led the Ravens in targets, yards, receptions, and receiving TDs. Entering his fifth season, Andrews is poised to have a top-three TE performance on a now-healthy Baltimore squad.

Rounding out the list of receivers are Devin Duverrnay, Tylan Wallace, James Proche, and TE Nick Boyle. Duvernay and Wallace may be the only ones who have a real chance at football relevance this year. That said, we don't think any of them have a chance of fantasy relevance.

> **BATEMAN'S NUMBERS LAST SEASON WERE ORDINARY, EVEN ON A PER-GAME BASIS, BUT THIS YEAR HE'S POSITIONED FOR A BREAKOUT IF HE CAN SEIZE THE MOMENT.**

KEY ADDITIONS & NEW CONTRACTS

RB MIKE DAVIS: SIGNED A ONE-YEAR DEAL.

FB PATRICK RICARD: SIGNED A THREE-YEAR DEAL.

OT MORGAN MOSES: SIGNED A THREE-YEAR, $15 MILLION DEAL.

DT MICHAEL PIERCE: SIGNED A THREE-YEAR, $16.5 MILLION CONTRACT.

DL CALAIS CAMPBELL: RE-SIGNED ON A TWO-YEAR, $12.5 MILLION DEAL.

DL BRENT URBAN: SIGNED ON A FREE-AGENT DEAL.

LB JOSH BYNES: RE-SIGNED ON A FREE-AGENT DEAL.

CB KYLE FULLER: SIGNED A ONE-YEAR DEAL.

S MARCUS WILLIAMS: SIGNED A FIVE-YEAR, $70 MILLION CONTRACT THAT INCLUDES $37 MILLION GUARANTEED.

DEPTH CHART

QB1	LAMAR JACKSON
QB2	TYLER HUNTLEY
RB1	J.K. DOBBINS
RB2	MIKE DAVIS N
RB3	GUS EDWARDS
WR1	RASHOD BATEMAN
WR2	DEVIN DUVERNAY
WR3	JAMES PROCHE
WR4	TYLAN WALLACE
TE1	MARK ANDREWS
TE2	NICK BOYLE
K	JUSTIN TUCKER

KEY LOSSES

RB **DEVONTA FREEMAN**

RB **LATAVIUS MURRAY**

WR **MILES BOYKIN** (STEELERS)

WR **MARQUISE BROWN** (TRADED TO CARDINALS)

WR **SAMMY WATKINS** (PACKERS)

OT **ALEJANDRO VILLANUEVA** (RETIRED)

C **BRADLEY BOZEMAN** (PANTHERS)

DE **JUSTIN HOUSTON**

DT **JUSTIN ELLIS** (GIANTS)

DT **BRANDON WILLIAMS**

LB **CHRIS BOARD** (LIONS)

LB **PERNELL MCPHEE**

CB **ANTHONY AVERETT** (RAIDERS)

CB **JIMMY SMITH**

CB **TAVON YOUNG** (BEARS)

S **DESHON ELLIOTT** (LIONS)

DB **ANTHONY LEVINE** (RETIRED)

P **SAM KOCH** (RETIRED)

2021 WEEKLY STATS

@ MIA (L) 10-22		@ CHI (W) 16-13		CLE (W) 16-10		@ PIT (L) 19-20		@ CLE (L) 22-24		GB (L) 30-31		@ CIN (L) 21-41		LAR (L) 19-20		PIT (L) 13-16	
26-43 238 (1 INT) (1 TD) 9-39		DNP		20-32 165 (4 INT) (1 TD) 17-68		23-37 253 (1 INT) (1 TD) 8-55		4-4 17 2-5		DNP		DNP		DNP		DNP	
DNP		26-36 219 (1 INT) 7-40		DNP		DNP		27-38 270 (1 TD) 6-45		28-40 215 (2 TD) 13-73 (2 TD)		DNP		20-32 197 (1 TD) 6-54		16-31 141 (2 INT) 12-72	
10-35	3-23	16-49 (1 TD)	6-31	16-52	1-8	14-52 (1 TD)	5-45	13-64	5-8	6-22	1-2	6-17 (1 TD)	2-3	14-76	1-1	5-21	2-6
DNP		10-32	2-1	8-14	0-0	2-1	2-34	1-1 (1 TD)	0-0	7-48	1-3	5-12	1-12	11-31	0-0	16-150 (1 TD)	0-0
DNP		DNP		1-1	0-0	DNP		DNP		DNP		DNP		DNP		1-4	0-0
0-0	6-37	DNP		0-0	8-51	0-0	5-55	0-0	5-41	0-0	10-43	0-0	5-44	0-0	3-28	0-0	3-27
0-0	6-80	0-0	3-29	0-0	4-31	0-0	0-0	0-0	7-103	0-0	1-5	0-0	4-26 (1 TD)	0-0	7-58	0-0	2-22
1-19	4-28	0-0	4-37	1-13	1-2	0-0	2-21	1-3	2-14	0-0	3-13	DNP		1-4	2-19	1-2	0-0
0-0	1-7	0-0	3-48	0-0	1-8	0-0	4-39 (1 TD)	0-0	0-0	DNP		0-0	0-0	0-0	0-0	0-0	0-0
0-0	6-63 (1 TD)	0-0	8-73	0-0	4-65 (1 TD)	0-0	4-50	0-0	11-115 (1 TD)	0-0	10-136 (2 TD)	0-0	8-125 (1 TD)	0-0	6-89	1-0	8-85

BUFFALO BILLS

Will Josh Allen three-peat as fantasy's No. 1 QB?

With new offensive coordinator Ken Dorsey, Allen's QB coach the past three seasons, expect little to change for Allen and the Buffalo offense.

To fantasy manager's delight, the Bills continue to push the pace of play, finishing top 10 for least amount of time between snaps.

But even before Buffalo became the high-powered, quick-paced offense it is today, Allen was a great fantasy QB. In fact, he was the overall QB1 after returning from injury in 2018. He then finished as the sixth-best QB in 2019, before his two consecutive No. 1 finishes in 2020-21. Moreover, he's the first QB with back-to-back overall No. 1 fantasy finishes since... wait for it... Daunte Culpepper in 2003-04.

Allen regressed in many metrics last season, including QB rating, yards per attempt, and completion percentage, but still managed to top all QBs. He continues to take chances with the ball, sometimes ill-advised, but that's just who he is.

He's also has sneaky-good rushing ability. Since 2018 he's top-10 in rushing TDs among ALL players in the league.

Allen will be the overall QB1 this season, as the most likely candidates to dethrone him, Patrick Mahomes and Lamar Jackson, both lost their top receivers, and Justin Herbert doesn't have enough rushing upside to challenge. But Allen will inevitably be taken too soon in drafts, as QBs usually are, and we won't have too many shares of him on our teams.

Are we buying the Gabriel Davis breakout hype?

First, Diggs is still "That Dude" in Buffalo. Period. He's the fourth-best fantasy WR since joining the Bills two years ago. Now, we must consider if there enough volume and ability for Gabriel Davis to finish as a WR2. Fifteen percent of all teams since 2010 have been able to support two top-24 fantasy receivers, so Buffalo should be plenty capable.

We get it, though. Davis has never commanded even 65 targets in a season, yet Buffalo has shown faith with their 23-year-old receiver by not adding any competition for him this offseason. After the departure of Sanders, while only add-

ing slot receiver Jamison Crowder to the mix, Gabriel should enter 2022 as Buffalo's clear No. 2. This will make it his first year lining up in 2-WR sets.

Would Davis be as big a breakout consensus had he not recorded that monster playoff outing last season? Definitely not. But that doesn't change the legitimacy of this opinion. We expect Davis to finish ahead of some other team's No. 1 receiving options, and have ranked him accordingly. We're in on the hype, and hope his lack of prior production has him being overlooked by drafters.

WK	DATE	TIME	OPP	QB	RB	WR	TE
1	9/08	8:20	@LAR	-12%	-8%	7%	-2%
2	9/19	7:15	TEN	3%	-22%	19%	-29%
3	9/25	1:00	@MIA	-6%	-4%	-2%	6%
4	10/02	1:00	@BAL	13%	-12%	12%	29%
5	10/09	1:00	PIT	-2%	11%	-3%	-10%
6	10/16	4:25	@KC	15%	4%	3%	2%
7	BYE WEEK						
8	10/30	8:20	GB	5%	-13%	3%	0%
9	11/06	1:00	@NYJ	-4%	11%	-1%	-1%
10	11/13	1:00	MIN	6%	2%	23%	-13%
11	11/20	1:00	CLE	-5%	-5%	-6%	2%
12	11/24	12.30	@DET	4%	14%	2%	17%
13	12/01	8:15	@NE	-8%	-19%	1%	-20%
14	12/11	1:00	NYJ	-4%	11%	-1%	-1%
15	12/17	TBD	MIA	-6%	-4%	-2%	6%
16	12/24	1:00	@CHI	4%	-7%	0%	-28%
17	1/02	8:30	@CIN	-1%	6%	0%	22%
18	1/08	TBD	NE	-8%	-19%	1%	-20%

2022/23 SCHEDULE — 2021 FANTASY POINTS ALLOWED BY OPPONENT VS LEAGUE AVERAGE

2022 NFL DRAFT

RD	PK		POS	COLLEGE	HT	WT
1	23	KAIIR ELAM	CB	FLORIDA	6-2	193
2	31	JAMES COOK	RB	GEORGIA	5-11	190
3	25	TERREL BERNARD	LB	BAYLOR	6-1	222
5	5	KHALIL SHAKIR	WR	BOISE STATE	6-0	190
6	1	MATT ARAIZA	P	SAN DIEGO STATE	6-2	200
6	6	CHRISTIAN BENFORD	CB	VILLANOVA	6-1	205
6	31	LUKE TENUTA	OT	VIRGINIA	6-9	322
7	10	BAYLON SPECTOR	LB	CLEMSON	6-2	235

2021 WEEKLY STATS

*RUSH STATS : *REC STATS	PIT (L) 16-23		@ MIA (W) 35-0		WAS (W) 43-21		HOU (W) 40-0		@ KC (W) 38-20		@ TEN (L) 31-34		MIA (W) 26-11		@ JAC (L) 6-9	
QB JOSH ALLEN	30-51 270 (1 TD)	9-44	17-33 179 (1 INT) (2 TD)	5-35	32-43 358 (4 TD)	4-9 (1 TD)	20-30 248 (1 INT) (2 TD)	6-41	15-26 315 (3 TD)	11-59 (1 TD)	35-47 353 (1 INT) (3 TD)	9-26	29-42 249 (2 TD)	8-55 (1 TD)	31-47 264 (2 INT)	5-50
QB MITCHELL TRUBISKY	DNP		0-0 0	2-(-2)	1-11	4-19	1-1 8	4-10 (1 TD)	DNP		DNP		DNP		DNP	
RB DEVIN SINGLETARY	11-72	3-8	13-82 (1 TD)	2-9	11-26	1-0	14-79	1-7	6-25	1-1-2	5-27	5-16	7-28	1-1	6-16	7-43
RB ZACK MOSS	DNP		8-26 (2 TD)	2-8	13-60	3-31 (1 TD)	14-61 (1 TD)	0-0	11-37	3-55	8-24	2-15	8-19	6-39	3-6	2-18
WR STEFON DIGGS	0-0	9-69	0-0	4-60 (1 TD)	0-0	6-62	0-0	7-114	0-0	2-69	0-0	9-89 (1 TD)	0-0	5-40 (1 TD)	0-0	6-85
WR COLE BEASLEY	0-0	8-60	0-0	4-36	0-0	11-98	0-0	2-16	0-0	1-5	0-0	7-88 (1 TD)	0-0	10-110	0-0	8-33
WR EMMANUEL SANDERS	0-0	4-52	0-0	2-48	0-0	5-94 (2 TD)	1-7	5-74	0-0	3-54 (2 TD)	0-0	5-91	0-0	0-0	0-0	4-65
WR GABRIEL DAVIS	0-0	2-40 (1 TD)	0-0	0-0	0-0	1-23	0-0	0-0	0-0	1-16	0-0	2-25	0-0	4-29 (1 TD)	0-0	0-0
TE DAWSON KNOX	0-0	4-41	0-0	2-17 (1 TD)	0-0	4-49 (1 TD)	0-0	5-37 (2 TD)	0-0	3-117 (1 TD)	0-0	3-25	DNP		DNP	

FANTASY TAKEOVER

2021 Stats
Record: 11–6
Rushing Rank: 6th
Passing Rank: 10th
Offensive Fantasy Pts: 5th
Against Run: 13th
Against Pass: 1st
ppg Against: 18.3
ppg: 29.8

KEY ADDITIONS & NEW CONTRACTS

QB **MATT BARKLEY**: SIGNED A ONE-YEAR DEAL.

QB **CASE KEENUM**: ACQUIRED IN A TRADE WITH THE BROWNS FOR A 2022 SEVENTH-ROUND PICK.

WR **TAVON AUSTIN**: SIGNED A ONE-YEAR DEAL.

WR **JAMISON CROWDER**: SIGNED A ONE-YEAR DEAL WORTH UP TO $4 MILLION.

RB **DUKE JOHNSON**: SIGNED A ONE-YEAR CONTRACT.

WR **STEFON DIGGS**: SIGNED TO A FOUR-YEAR, $96 MILLION EXTENSION THAT INCLUDES $70 MILLION IN GUARANTEES AND LOWERS HIS 2022 CAP NUMBER.

WR **JAKE KUMEROW**: RE-SIGNED A ONE-YEAR DEAL.

WR **ISAIAH MCKENZIE**: RE-SIGNED A TWO-YEAR DEAL WORTH $8 MILLION.

TE **O.J. HOWARD**: SIGNED A ONE-YEAR DEAL.

OT **BOBBY HART**: RE-SIGNED ON A ONE-YEAR CONTRACT.

OG **IKE BOETTGER**: RE-SIGNED TO A ONE-YEAR DEAL.

OG **DAVID QUESSENBERRY**: SIGNED A ONE-YEAR DEAL.

OG **RODGER SAFFOLD**: SIGNED A ONE-YEAR DEAL.

OL **GREG VAN ROTEN**: SIGNED TO A ONE-YEAR DEAL.

C **MITCH MORSE**: SIGNED A TWO-YEAR, $19.5 MILLION EXTENSION THAT INCLUDES $12 MILLION GUARANTEED. HIS PAY FOR THE 2022 SEASON INCREASES TO $11.25 MILLION FROM $8.5 MILLION.

DE **SHAQ LAWSON**: SIGNED A TWO-YEAR CONTRACT.

DT **DAQUAN JONES**: SIGNED A TWO-YEAR CONTRACT.

DT **TIM SETTLE**: SIGNED A TWO-YEAR, $9 MILLION DEAL THAT HAS A MAX VALUE OF $10.6 MILLION.

DL **JORDAN PHILLIPS**: SIGNED A ONE-YEAR CONTRACT.

LB **VON MILLER**: SIGNED A SIX-YEAR, $120 MILLION CONTRACT ($51 MILLION IN GUARANTEES) THAT AVERAGES $17.5 MILLION PER YEAR THROUGH THE FIRST FOUR YEARS.

CB **SIRAN NEAL**: RE-SIGNED ON A THREE-YEAR DEAL WITH A MAXIMUM VALUE OF $10.9 MILLION.

What should we make of Devin Singletary after his breakout end-of-season run?

In a wind-heavy game against the Patriots in Week 13 last season, when throwing the ball was impossible at times, the Bills lost because they were unable to run the ball. After the embarrassment, the team made Devin Singletary their feature back going forward. On the field for more than 70% of the snaps in the final seven games, Singletary had only one weekly finish outside of the top-10 RBs.

One would assume the lead back in a top-five offense would be a fantasy stud, but since 2018, no Bills RB has finished inside the top-28 for fantasy. This is partly because Buffalo ranks in the bottom 25% for RB targets and carries inside the 5-yard line, all thanks to Allen's scramble and rushing ability.

We do have some concerns with Singletary's fantasy potential because of moves the Bills made this offseason. First, they tried to sign J.D. McKissic, but when the deal fell through, they drafted James Cook (Round 2, 64th overall), who excels in the pass-catching game. These moves don't scream three-down work for Singletary.

The situation, for now, seems undecided. We're not high on either back, but Singletary should see the majority of the work early on. However, there's a chance by the second half of the season — crucial weeks in fantasy — Cook is the better fantasy player.

Devin Singletary (FPs, Finish)

Week 14	18.9	RB14
Week 15	25.6	RB7
Week 16	18.8	RB10
Week 17	23	RB5
Week 18	19.1	RB3
Wild Card	24.4	
Divisional Round	15.1	

KEY LOSSES

QB **MITCHELL TRUBISKY** (STEELERS)
RB **MATT BREIDA** (GIANTS)
WR **COLE BEASLEY**
WR **EMMANUEL SANDERS**
OT **DARYL WILLIAMS**
OG **JON FELICIANO** (GIANTS)
DE **MARIO ADDISON** (TEXANS)
DE **JERRY HUGHES** (TEXANS)
DE **EFE OBADA** (COMMANDERS)
DL **VERNON BUTLER** (RAIDERS)
DL **HARRISON PHILLIPS** (VIKINGS)
DT **STAR LOTULELEI**
LB **A.J. KLEIN**
CB **LEVI WALLACE** (STEELERS)

DEPTH CHART

QB1	JOSH ALLEN
QB2	CASE KEENUM N
RB1	DEVIN SINGLETARY
RB2	JAMES COOK R
RB3	DUKE JOHNSON N
WR1	STEFON DIGGS
WR2	GABRIEL DAVIS
WR3	JAMISON CROWDER N
WR4	ISAIAH MCKENZIE
TE1	DAWSON KNOX
TE2	O.J. HOWARD N
K	TYLER BASS

2021 WEEKLY STATS

@ NYJ (W) 45-17		IND (L) 15-41		@ NO (W) 31-6		NE 10-14		@ TB (L) 27-33		CAR (W) 31-14		@ NE (W) 33-21		ATL (W) 29-15		NYJ (W) 27-10	
21-28 366 (1 INT) (2 TD)	2-3	21-35 209 (2 INT) (2 TD)	2-18	23-28 260 (2 INT) (4 TD)	8-43	15-30 145 (1 TD)	6-39	36-54 308 (1 INT) (2 TD)	12-109 (1 TD)	19-34 210 (1 INT) (3 TD)	3-24	30-47 314 (3 TD)	12-64	11-26 120 (3 INT)	15-81 (2 TD)	24-45 239 (2 TD)	5-63
DNP		3-5 19 (1 INT) 0-0		DNP		DNP		DNP		DNP		DNP		DNP		1-1 15 3-[-3]	
7-43 (1 TD)	1-6	3-17	3-26	15-44	1-4	10-36	0-0	4-52	6-37	22-86 (1 TD)	1-10	12-39 (1 TD)	5-39	23-110 (2TD)	0-0	19-88 (1 TD)	2-24 (1 TD)
7-27 (1 TD)	0-0	3-5	0-0	DNP		8-21	2-12	DNP		DNP		3-12	1-13	5-39	0-0	5-8	2-6
0-0	8-162 (1 TD)	0-0	4-23 (2 TD)	0-0	7-74 (1 TD)	0-0	4-51	0-0	7-74	0-0	4-35 (1 TD)	0-0	7-85 (1 TD)	0-0	5-52	0-0	9-81 (1 TD)
0-0	2-15	0-0	4-23	0-0	5-46	0-0	1-11	0-0	9-64	0-0	4-35	0-0	0-0	0-0	2-22	0-0	4-31
1-24	2-27	0-0	3-26	0-0	3-28	0-0	3-22	0-0	1-25	DNP		0-0	2-20	DNP		DNP	
0-0	3-105	0-0	2-27	0-0	2-47	0-0	2-30 (1 TD)	0-0	5-43 (1 TD)	0-0	5-85 (2 TD)	DNP		0-0	3-40	0-0	3-39
0-0	1-17	0-0	6-80	0-0	3-32 (2 TD)	0-0	2-14	0-0	7-60 (1 TD)	0-0	4-38	0-0	2-11 (1 TD)	0-0	0-0	0-4	3-49

CAROLINA PANTHERS

Is Christian McCaffrey worthy of the No. 1 overall draft pick?

CMC, who has had the No. 1 overall ADP that last two years, has only played eight full games in those two seasons. Fantasy managers hoped for a repeat of his 2019 season, where he was on another planet in terms of fantasy production. When he did play the last two seasons, he was the CMC of old. In those eight games, he only finished outside the top-five RBs once, and the one exception was because he was being eased back into the lineup after an injury.

Injuries are what concerns fantasy managers. Since September of 2020, CMC has suffered a high ankle sprain, sprained AC joint, strained thigh/glute, sprained hamstring, and most recently, another sprained ankle. Sprained ankles and AC joints are not injuries that become more likely after previous occurrences. The hamstring injury is a little more concerning, but not always indicative of a higher propensity for future injuries.

We could provide all the stats and reasons why, but let's just say that there's very little chance a healthy CMC finishes anywhere other than the overall RB1. Even if he loses some early-down touches to D'Onta Foreman or Chuba Hubbard, his reception potential is enough to keep him at the top. We'll be drafting CMC with almost any pick in the first round.

Are our fantasy expectations too high for DJ Moore, again, considering the QB situation?

Moore has been consistent the last three seasons — 1,200-plus yards and 4 TDs each season. The 25-year-old continues to find ways to make plays, but subpar QB play continues to lower Moore's fantasy ceiling. Last season, Moore led all receivers in incomplete targets deemed to be the fault of the QB. Since 2018, Moore has caught passes from eight different signal callers. As a result of unstable QB play, he's failed to finish inside the top-20 WRs the past two seasons.

Yet, the consensus ranking on Moore is again inside the top 20. We support his current ranking for multiple reasons. First, Moore is PFF's 24th-graded receiver among the 125 receivers with at least 100 targets since 2018. He's also assured more targets than many of our top-10 ranked WRs. Also, Moore's fantasy ranking takes into consideration the possibility of a better QB play. We expect Baker Mayfield to be the Week 1 starter. If he falters, rookie Matt Corral may get a shot. Either way, they both may be the best QB Moore has had during his time in Carolina.

We are happy giving Moore another shot, as the offense has nowhere to go but up.

2022/23 SCHEDULE				2021 FANTASY POINTS ALLOWED BY OPPONENT VS LEAGUE AVERAGE			
WK	DATE	TIME	OPP	QB	RB	WR	TE
1	9/11	1:00	CLE	-5%	-5%	-6%	2%
2	9/18	1:00	@NYG	12%	40%	-2%	22%
3	9/25	1:00	NO	-26%	2%	-16%	-45%
4	10/02	4:05	ARI	0%	-11%	10%	-36%
5	10/09	4:05	SF	-1%	26%	-3%	20%
6	10/16	4:05	@LAR	-12%	-8%	7%	-2%
7	10/23	1:00	TB	3%	-4%	3%	4%
8	10/30	1:00	@ATL	13%	8%	7%	-3%
9	11/06	1:00	@CIN	-1%	6%	0%	22%
10	11/10	8:15	ATL	13%	8%	7%	-3%
11	11/20	1:00	@BAL	13%	-12%	12%	29%
12	11/27	1:00	DEN	-10%	-9%	-6%	-29%
13	BYE WEEK						
14	12/11	4:25	@SEA	2%	-8%	3%	-23%
15	12/18	1:00	PIT	-2%	11%	-3%	-10%
16	12/24	1:00	DET	4%	14%	2%	17%
17	1/01	1:00	@TB	3%	-4%	3%	4%
18	1/08	TBD	@NO	-26%	2%	-16%	-45%

2022 NFL DRAFT					
RD	PK		POS	COLLEGE	HT	WT
1	6	IKEM EKWONU	OT	NORTH CAROLINA STATE	6-4	320
3	30	MATT CORRAL	QB	OLE MISS	6-2	205
4	15	BRANDON SMITH	LB	PENN STATE	6-3	241
6	10	AMARE BARNO	EDGE	VIRGINIA TECH	6-6	245
6	20	CADE MAYES	G	TENNESSEE	6-6	325
7	21	KALON BARNES	CB	BAYLOR	6-0	186

2021 WEEKLY STATS

*RUSH STATS *REC STATS	NYJ (W) 19-14		NO (W) 26-7		@ HOU (W) 24-9		@ DAL (L) 28-36		PHI (L) 18-21		MIN (L) 28-34		@ NYG (L) 3-25		@ ATL (W) 19-13	
QB SAM DARNOLD	24-35 279 (1 TD)	5-[-1] (1 TD)	26-38 305 (1 INT) (2 TD)	1-7	23-34 304	8-11 (2 TD)	26-39 301 (2 INT) (2 TD)	6-35 (2 TD)	21-37 177 (3 INT) (1 TD)	2-10	17-41 207 (1 INT) (1 TD)	4-48	16-25 112 (1 INT)	0-0	13-24 129	8-66
QB CAM NEWTON	DNP		DNP		DNP		DNP		DNP		DNP		DNP		DNP	
RB CHUBA HUBBARD	0-0	2-4	8-10	0-0	11-52	3-27	13-57	2-14	24-101	5-33	16-61 (1 TD)	1-4	12-28	4-28	24-82 (1 TD)	1-9
RB C. MCCAFFREY	21-98	9-89	24-72 (1 TD)	5-65	7-31	2-9	DNP		DNP		DNP		DNP		DNP	
RB AMEER ABDULLAH	DNP		DNP		DNP		DNP		DNP		DNP		DNP		8-31	3-35
WR DJ MOORE	1-14	6-80	0-0	8-79 (1 TD)	1-[-1]	8-126	1-6	8-113 (2 TD)	1-[-4]	5-42	1-6	5-73	0-0	6-73	0-0	4-59
WR ROBBY ANDERSON	0-0	1-57 (1 TD)	0-0	3-38	0-0	1-8	1-3	5-46	0-0	2-30	0-0	3-11 (1 TD)	0-0	3-14	0-0	0-0
WR BRANDON ZYLSTRA	0-0	0-0	0-0	3-44 (1 TD)	0-0	0-0	0-0	2-63	0-0	0-0	0-0	3-32	DNP		DNP	
TE TOMMY TREMBLE	0-0	0-0	0-0	0-0	1-7 (1 TD)	1-30	0-0	0-0	0-0	2-12 (1 TD)	1-0	0-0	0-0	2-12	0-0	3-18

2021 Stats

Record: 5-12
Rushing Rank: 20th
Passing Rank: 30th
Offensive Fantasy Pts: 29th
Against Run: 18th
Against Pass: 3rd
ppg Against: 23.8
ppg: 17.9

KEY ADDITIONS & NEW CONTRACTS

QB BAKER MAYFIELD: ACQUIRED IN TRADE WITH THE CLEVELAND BROWNS IN EXCHANGE FOR A 2024 FIFTH-ROUND PICK THAT CAN CONVERT TO A FOURTH-ROUNDER BASED ON PLAYING TIME.

RB D'ONTA FOREMAN: SIGNED A ONE-YEAR CONTRACT.

WR RASHARD HIGGINS: SIGNED A FREE-AGENT DEAL.

WR DJ MOORE: SIGNED A THREE-YEAR CONTRACT EXTENSION WORTH $61.9 MILLION IN NEW MONEY AND INCLUDES $41.6 MILLION IN GUARANTEES. THE NEW DEAL KEEPS HIM UNDER CONTRACT THROUGH THE 2025 SEASON.

WR/KR/PR ANDRE ROBERTS: SIGNED A ONE-YEAR CONTRACT.

WR BRANDON ZYLSTRA: RE-SIGNED ON A ONE-YEAR CONTRACT.

TE IAN THOMAS: RE-SIGNED WITH CAROLINA.

OG AUSTIN CORBETT: SIGNED A THREE-YEAR DEAL WORTH $29.25 MILLION.

C BRADLEY BOZEMAN: AGREED TO TERMS ON A ONE-YEAR DEAL.

DE MARQUIS HAYNES: SIGNED A TWO-YEAR CONTRACT.

DT MATTHEW IOANNIDIS: SIGNED TO A ONE-YEAR CONTRACT.

LB CORY LITTLETON: SIGNED A ONE-YEAR, $2.6 MILLION DEAL THAT INCLUDES $2 MILLION GUARANTEED.

LB DAMIEN WILSON: SIGNED A TWO-YEAR CONTRACT.

CB DONTE JACKSON: RE-SIGNED ON A THREE-YEAR, $31.5 MILLION CONTRACT.

CB RASHAAN MELVIN: SIGNED A ONE-YEAR DEAL.

S JUSTON BURRIS: RE-SIGNED TO A FREE-AGENT DEAL.

S SEAN CHANDLER: RE-SIGNED ON A ONE-YEAR DEAL.

S XAVIER WOODS: SIGNED A THREE-YEAR, $15.75 MILLION CONTRACT.

P JOHNNY HEKKER: SIGNED A THREE-YEAR DEAL.

K ZANE GONZALEZ: AGREED TO A TWO-YEAR, $4.5 MILLION CONTRACT.

Is there any fantasy value to be had under center for the Panthers this season?

One piece of good news for fantasy managers rostering Carolina players is that their new offensive coordinator, Ben McAdoo, should have a faster pace of play. During his final three years as the Giants head coach, his team finished no worse than fourth in seconds per play.

Now on to the bad news. No one believes Sam Darnold is the future of the organization. Heck, he may never start another game in the NFL again. We won't waste space here explaining how bad his metrics were last season, but they were bad. If we told you Darnold started 2021 as QB16, QB14, QB7, and QB1 in his first four starts, you'd be shocked, but it happened. Besides having the easiest first four games in the leagues last season, Darnold, in Week 4, had more rushing TDs at that point in the season than any other player. His incredibly lucky TD stretch was a big part of his early, deceptively high weekly finishes. Darnold is a bad QB and a worse fantasy QB, and even if he progresses behind and improved offensive line, it won't be enough to make him fantasy relevant.

The Panthers made a no-risk trade for Baker Mayfield right before training camp. We give him a 65% chance to be the starter by Week 1. While its unlikely he'll have any fantasy value in 1-QB leagues, he may be a low-end QB2 for 2-QB leagues.

The Panthers also moved up in the draft to take Ole Miss product Matt Corral in the third round. Matt Corral would likely be a better fantasy option than both Mayfield and Darnold if he starts, if only for his rushing ability. Take Corral's 195 rushing yards against Tennessee last season as proof. Playing behind PFF's 31st ranked offensive line for 2021 with an average group of receivers, except for DJ Moore, is a not a recipe for fantasy success.

We're not excited about any of the Panthers QBs, but Mayfield and Corral may offer the biggest upside to Carolina's other skill players, specifically CMC and DJ Moore.

KEY LOSSES

QB **CAM NEWTON**

RB **AMEER ABDULLAH** (RAIDERS)

OG **JOHN MILLER**

C **MATT PARADIS**

DE **MORGAN FOX** (CHARGERS)

DT **DAQUAN JONES** (BILLS)

LB **JERMAINE CARTER JR.** (CHIEFS)

LB **HAASON REDDICK** (EAGLES)

CB **A.J. BOUYE**

CB **STEPHON GILMORE** (COLTS)

DEPTH CHART

QB1	BAKER MAYFIELD **N**
QB2	SAM DARNOLD
RB1	CHRISTIAN MCCAFFREY
RB2	CHUBA HUBBARD
RB3	D'ONTA FOREMAN **N**
WR1	DJ MOORE
WR2	ROBBY ANDERSON
WR3	TERRACE MARSHALL JR.
WR4	RASHARD HIGGINS **N**
TE1	TOMMY TREMBLE
TE2	IAN THOMAS
K	ZANE GONZALEZ

2021 WEEKLY STATS

NE (L) 6-24		@ ARI (W) 34-10		WAS (L) 21-27		@ MIA (L) 10-33		ATL (L) 21-29		@ BUF (L) 14-31		TB (L) 6-32		@ NO (L) 10-18		@ TB (L) 17-41	
16-33 172 (3 INT) 3-9		DNP		DNP		DNP		DNP		DNP		15-32 190 1-11		17-26 132 (1 INT) 2-7		29-42 219 (1 INT) (2 TD) 8-19	
DNP		3-4 8 (1 TD) 3-14 (1 TD)		21-27 189 (2 TD) 10-46 (1 TD)		5-21 92 (2 TD) 3-5 (2 TD)		15-23 178 (1 INT) 10-47 (1 TD)		18-38 156 (1 INT) (1 TD) 15-71 (1 TD)		7-13 61 (1 INT) 5-42		0-0 1-5		DNP	
3-3	1-33	9-27 (1 TD)	0-0	0-0	0-0	2-6	0-0	10-33 (1 TD)	0-0	8-40	1-1	6-9	0-0	17-55 (1 TD)	3-13	9-48	2-8 (1 TD)
14-52	4-54	13-95	10-66	10-59	7-60 (1 TD)	10-35	0-0	DNP		DNP		DNP		DNP		DNP	
1-0	4-30	9-24	4-27	1-6	0-0	2-4	2-20	4-16	2-17	4-7	4-48 (1 TD)	2-1	3-8	6-21	4-31	7-26	9-56
2-14	3-32	0-0	4-24	0-0	5-50 (1 TD)	0-0	4-103	0-0	6-84	0-0	6-48	0-0	5-55	0-0	3-29	1-13	7-87
0-0	1-2	0-0	4-37 (1 TD)	0-0	5-30	0-0	1-15	0-0	7-84 (1 TD)	2-33	3-29	0-0	5-58	0-0	2-10	0-0	7-50 (1 TD)
DNP		0-0	2-18	0-0	1-7	0-0	1-24	0-0	4-45	0-0	2-17	DNP		0-0	0-0	0-0	0-0
0-0	1-6	0-0	1-3	0-0	2-35	0-0	1-4	0-0	2-23	0-0	1-8	0-0	2-22	DNP		1-4	2-7

CHICAGO BEARS

In Year 2 under a new head coach, what should we expect from Justin Fields?

We're not sure who was worse last season, Justin Fields or Matt Nagy. Matt Nagy took his athletic QB and said, "Be a pocket passer and forget about your athleticism."

A pocket passer Fields is not. He finished 2021 42nd in adjusted completion rate, which, believe it or not, was better than fellow rookies Trevor Lawrence and Zach Wilson. Even if Nagy refused to call RPOs or designed runs for his QB, Fields' instincts led to plenty of scrambles, and he had six games with at least 7 rushing attempts. With play calling that utilizes his best attribute, his athleticism, Fields would have a high rushing floor that would be on par with players like Jalen Hurts.

Last season, Fields had his best numbers on plays with pre-snap motion. Motion often allows a QB to better dissect coverages and can make defenders unorganized. For plays with motion, Fields had a completion rate of 70.5%, 7.8 yards per pass attempt, and a 96.6 passer rating. Without motion, Fields' completion rate fell to 54%, his yards per attempt to 6.5, and his passer rating to 63.7. Week 8 last season demonstrated the best of Fields. Using many of his strengths, he had 10 rushing attempts for 105 yards and a TD.

Fields should improve in Year 2, with Nagy out of the way and Matt Everflus and company designing better plays to utilize the assets of their QB. With enough improvement in passing efficiency, the QB10-15 range feels well within reach.

With Cole Kmet climbing draft rankings all offseason, does he really have TE1 potential?

Kmet has been talking up his QB all offseason. Whether he believes what he says or is just trying to get more balls thrown his way we don't know. We do know Kmet had 86 catches in the last two seasons, and only 2 TDs.

While Kmet is being undervalued, it would take more than a TD bump to move him into TE1 territory. With one of the lower yards-per-reception numbers for TEs in his first two seasons, Kmet would need more targets to go with the TDs in order to cross the TE1 threshold.

We don't believe a triple-digit target season is out the question for Fields' No. 2 option, though. And now that he's no longer losing targets, especially red zone targets, to now-departed Jimmy Graham, he should show improvement all the way around. Luke Getsy, Chicago's new offensive coordinator, was part of the regime that orchestrated Robert Tonyan's 11-TD season in 2019. If you like having a backup TE on your roster, consider Kmet — he may turn into your No. 1 TE by season's end.

2022/23 SCHEDULE				2021 FANTASY POINTS ALLOWED BY OPPONENT VS LEAGUE AVERAGE			
WK	DATE	TIME	OPP	QB	RB	WR	TE
1	9/11	1:00	SF	-1%	26%	-3%	20%
2	9/18	8:20	@GB	5%	-13%	3%	0%
3	9/25	1:00	HOU	1%	13%	5%	13%
4	10/02	1:00	@NYG	12%	40%	-2%	22%
5	10/09	1:00	@MIN	6%	2%	23%	-13%
6	10/13	8:15	WAS	29%	-3%	8%	5%
7	10/24	8:15	@NE	-8%	-19%	1%	-20%
8	10/30	1:00	@DAL	-6%	-14%	2%	5%
9	11/06	1:00	MIA	-6%	-4%	-2%	6%
10	11/13	1:00	DET	4%	14%	2%	17%
11	11/20	1:00	@ATL	13%	8%	7%	-3%
12	11/27	1:00	@NYJ	-4%	11%	-1%	-1%
13	12/04	1:00	GB	5%	-13%	3%	0%
14	BYE WEEK						
15	12/18	1:00	PHI	-1%	10%	-17%	46%
16	12/24	1:00	BUF	-34%	-11%	-27%	-34%
17	1/01	1:00	@DET	4%	14%	2%	17%
18	1/08	TBD	MIN	6%	2%	23%	-13%

2022 NFL DRAFT					
RD	PK		POS	COLLEGE	HT	WT
2	7	KYLER GORDON	CB	WASHINGTON	6-0	200
2	16	JAQUAN BRISKER	S	PENN STATE	6-1	212
3	7	VELUS JONES JR.	WR	TENNESSEE	6-0	200
5	25	BRAXTON JONES	OT	SOUTHERN UTAH	6-7	310
5	31	DOMINIQUE ROBINSON	LB	MIAMI (OHIO)	6-4	256
6	7	ZACHARY THOMAS	G	SAN DIEGO STATE	6-5	300
6	24	TRESTAN EBNER	RB	BAYLOR	5-11	215
6	29	DOUG KRAMER	C	ILLINOIS	6-2	305
7	5	J'ATYRE CARTER	G	SOUTHERN	6-5	275
7	33	ELIJAH HICKS	S	CALIFORNIA	5-11	200
7	34	TRENTON GILL	P	NORTH CAROLINA STATE	6-4	219

2021 WEEKLY STATS

*RUSH STATS : *REC STATS	@ LAR (L) 14-44		CIN (W) 20-17		@ CLE (L) 6-26		DET (W) 24-14		@ LV (W) 20-9		GB (L) 14-24		@ TB (L) 3-38		SF (L) 22-33	
QB JUSTIN FIELDS	2-2 10 1-3 (1 TD)		6-13 60 (1 INT) 10-31		6-20 68 3-12		11-17 209 (1 INT) 3-9		12-20 111 (1 TD) 3-4		16-27 174 (1 INT) (1 TD) 6-43		22-32 184 (3 INT) 8-38		19-27 175 (1 INT) (1 TD) 10-103 (1 TD)	
QB ANDY DALTON	27-38 206 (1 INT) 2-13		9-11 56 (1 TD) 2-25		DNP		DNP		1-1 8 0-0		DNP		DNP		DNP	
RB DAVID MONTGOMERY	16-108 (1 TD)	1-10	20-61	3-18	10-34	2-21	23-106(2 TD)	0-0	DNP		DNP		DNP		DNP	
RB KHALIL HERBERT	0-0	0-0	DNP		0-0	0-0	3-7	0-0	18-75	0-0	19-97 (1 TD)	2-15	18-100	5-33	23-72	2-(-4)
RB DAMIEN WILLIAMS	6-12	4-28	2-6	2-(-2)	0-0	0-0	8-55 (1 TD)	2-15	16-64 (1 TD)	2-20	0-0	0-0	3-5	1-3	2-(-3)	0-0
WR DARNELL MOONEY	0-0	5-26	0-0	6-66	0-0	1-9	1-10	5-125	0-0	3-35	0-0	5-45 (1 TD)	0-0	2-39	0-0	6-64
WR ALLEN ROBINSON II	0-0	6-35	0-0	2-24 (1 TD)	0-0	2-27	0-0	3-63	0-0	4-32	0-0	4-53	0-0	2-16	0-0	3-21
WR DAMIERE BYRD	0-0	3-19	0-0	0-0	0-0	0-0	0-0	0-0	0-0	0-0	0-0	0-0	0-0	1-10	0-0	0-0
WR MARQUISE GOODWIN	1-(-2)	4-45	0-0	1-10	0-0	0-0	1-1	0-0	0-0	1-8	0-0	1-12	0-0	2-16	0-0	2-32
TE COLE KMET	0-0	5-42	0-0	1-0	0-0	1-11	0-0	1-6	0-0	2-22	1-0	4-49	0-0	5-43	0-0	3-24
TE JIMMY GRAHAM	0-0	1-11	0-0	0-0	0-0	0-0	0-0	0-0	0-0	0-0	0-0	0-0	DNP		DNP	

2021 Stats
Record: 6–11
Rushing Rank: 14th
Passing Rank: 25th
Offensive Fantasy Pts: 28th
Against Run: 24th
Against Pass: 4th
ppg Against: 23.9
ppg: 18.3

Is Darnell Mooney in for a monster breakout season?

The fantasy community loves finding third-year WR breakout candidates, and Mooney fits the mold nicely. He has already shown the ability to be Chicago's No. 1 option, and will again be their lead receiver in 2022. Last season, Mooney was targeted on 23% of his routes, 23rd best among WRs.

While the Bears passing offense doesn't likely have enough volume to support another fantasy-relevant WR, I implore you to name one who will be competing with Mooney for Fields' attention. Nothing?

Mooney proved himself last season and established a safe fantasy floor. Chicago's front office was happy enough with his production to let Allen Robinson II go.

He has good WR2 upside going into 2022. He and Rashod Bateman are in similar situations — run-first QB and not too much competition in the WR room. Rashod Bateman's ranking and ADP are lower, though, because, unlike Mooney, he has yet to prove he can be his team's No. 1 option

What are the chances this backfield turns into a committee?

Montgomery started 2021 with a bang but injured his knee in Week 4. Upon his return, Montgomery struggled to regain his rhythm is the Matt Nagy-led offense. His efficiency, by all measures, was terrible.

But we're not giving up on Montgomery yet. He still has one of the easiest paths to a three-down role. Now, out from Matt Nagy's tutelage, Montgomery may be the back he always should have been. New head coach Matt Eberflus has seen what a workhorse back should be, as he had a front row seat to the Jonathan Taylor show last season. The new regime has continued to talk up staying committed to the run this season, and Montgomery should again see the volume to be a top-tier RB2.

We still believe Montgomery's the guy in Chicago, and Khalil Herbert, a more-than-capable backup makes a compelling case for a late-round handcuff for Montgomery's managers.

KEY ADDITIONS & NEW CONTRACTS

QB **TREVOR SIEMIAN**: SIGNED A TWO-YEAR, $4 MILLION DEAL THAT HAS A MAX VALUE OF $5 MILLION.

QB **NATHAN PETERMAN**: SIGNED A ONE-YEAR CONTRACT.

WR **BYRON PRINGLE**: SIGNED A ONE-YEAR, $4 MILLION CONTRACT FULLY GUARANTEED WITH A POTENTIAL OF $2 MILLION MORE IN INCENTIVES.

WR **EQUANIMEOUS ST. BROWN**: SIGNED A ONE-YEAR CONTRACT.

WR **DAVID MOORE**: SIGNED A ONE-YEAR DEAL.

WR **DANTE PETTIS**: SIGNED A ONE-YEAR DEAL.

WR **TAJAE SHARPE**: SIGNED A ONE-YEAR DEAL.

TE **RYAN GRIFFIN**: RE-SIGNED ON A ONE-YEAR, $2.25 MILLION DEAL WITH $750,000 GUARANTEED.

TE **JAMES O'SHAUGHNESSY**: SIGNED A ONE-YEAR DEAL.

OT **JULIE'N DAVENPORT**: SIGNED A FREE-AGENT DEAL.

OG **LUCAS PATRICK**: SIGNED A TWO-YEAR, $8 MILLION CONTRACT WITH $4 MILLION GUARANTEED IN YEAR 1.

OL **DAKOTA DOZIER**: SIGNED A ONE-YEAR CONTRACT.

DE **AL-QUADIN MUHAMMAD**: SIGNED A TWO-YEAR DEAL.

DT **JUSTIN JONES**: SIGNED A TWO-YEAR, $12 MILLION DEAL.

LB **MATT ADAMS**: SIGNED A ONE-YEAR DEAL.

LB **NICHOLAS MORROW**: SIGNED A ONE-YEAR DEAL.

CB **TAVON YOUNG**: SIGNED A ONE-YEAR, $1.365 MILLION DEAL.

DB **DEANDRE HOUSTON-CARSON**: RE-SIGNED ON A ONE-YEAR DEAL.

LS **PATRICK SCALES**: RE-SIGNED ON A ONE-YEAR, $1.27 MILLION VETERAN BENEFIT DEAL WITH THE MAXIMUM $152,500 SIGNING BONUS AND $1,047,500 TOTAL GUARANTEED.

KEY LOSSES

QB **ANDY DALTON** (SAINTS)

QB **NICK FOLES** (COLTS)

RB **TARIK COHEN**

RB **DAMIEN WILLIAMS** (FALCONS)

WR **DAMIERE BYRD** (FALCONS)

WR **JAKEEM GRANT** (BROWNS)

WR **MARQUISE GOODWIN** (SEAHAWKS)

WR **ALLEN ROBINSON II** (RAMS)

TE **JIMMY GRAHAM**

TE **JESSE JAMES**

OT **GERMAIN IFEDI** (FALCONS)

OT **JASON PETERS**

OG **JAMES DANIELS** (STEELERS)

OL **ELIJAH WILKINSON** (FALCONS)

NT **EDDIE GOLDMAN**

DL **AKIEM HICKS** (BUCCANEERS)

DL **BILAL NICHOLS** (RAIDERS)

LB **KHALIL MACK** (TRADED TO CHARGERS)

LB **BRUCE IRVIN**

LB **ALEC OGLETREE**

LB **DANNY TREVATHAN**

CB **ARTIE BURNS** (SEAHAWKS)

S **DEON BUSH** (CHIEFS)

S **TASHAUN GIPSON**

P **PAT O'DONNELL** (PACKERS)

DEPTH CHART

QB1	JUSTIN FIELDS
QB2	TREVOR SIEMIAN N
RB1	DAVID MONTGOMERY
RB2	KHALIL HERBERT
RB3	DARRYNTON EVANS N
WR1	DARNELL MOONEY
WR2	BYRON PRINGLE N
WR3	VELUS JONES R
WR4	E. ST. BROWN N
TE1	COLE KMET
TE2	JAMES O'SHAUGHNESSY N
K	CAIRO SANTOS

2021 WEEKLY STATS

@ PIT (L) 27-29		BAL (L) 13-16		@ DET (W) 16-14		ARI (L) 22-33		@ GB (L) 30-45		MIN (L) 9-17		@ SEA (W) 25-24		NYG (W) 29-3		@ MIN (L) 17-31	
17-29 291 (1 INT) (1 TD) 8-45		4-11 79 4-23		DNP		DNP		18-33 224 (2 INT) (2 TD) 9-74		26-39 285 (1 TD) 7-35		DNP		DNP		DNP	
DNP		11-23 201 (2 TD) 0-0		24-39 317 (1 INT) (1 TD) 6-11		26-41 229 (4 INT) (2 TD) 2-6		DNP		DNP		DNP		18-35 173 (1 INT) (1 TD) 3-14		33-48 325 (2 INT) (1 TD) 1-7	
13-63	2-17	14-58	1-9	17-46	3-28	21-90 (1 TD)	8-51	10-42	6-39	18-60	5-23	21-45 (1 TD)	7-61	22-64 (2 TD)	2-17	20-72	2-7
4-13	0-0	1-0	0-0	4-9	0-0	4-16	1-11	1-3	0-0	0-0	3-34	2-21 (1 TD)	1-7	2-9	0-0	4-11	0-0
0-0	0-0	0-0	0-0	0-0	0-0	0-0	0-0	2-13	1-4	0-0	0-0	1-12	1-2	0-0	0-0	0-0	3-33 (1 TD)
1-15 (1 TD)	3-41 (1 TD)	0-0	5-121 (1 TD)	1-2	5-123	0-0	5-27	0-0	1-19	1-3	5-63	2-2	5-57	0-0	7-69 (1 TD)	0-0	12-126
0-0	4-68	DNP		DNP		DNP		0-0	2-14	DNP		DNP		0-0	4-35	0-0	2-22
0-0	0-0	0-0	1-3	0-0	4-42	0-0	3-36	0-0	2-76 (1 TD)	0-0	5-62	0-0	1-11	0-0	1-23	0-0	5-47
0-0	1-50	0-0	4-104 (1 TD)	DNP		DNP		DNP		0-0	0-0	0-0	2-23	0-0	0-0	0-0	2-13
0-0	6-87	0-0	1-12	0-0	8-65	0-0	3-41	0-0	3-17	0-0	6-71	0-0	4-49	0-0	3-25	DNP	
0-0	1-28	0-0	2-25	0-0	2-34 (1 TD)	0-0	1-1 (1 TD)	0-0	2-9	0-0	1-13	0-0	2-30 (1 TD)	0-0	0-0	0-0	2-16

CINCINNATI BENGALS

Could Joe Burrow really finish outside the top-10 fantasy QBs?

Joe burrow, by any measure, was a rock star last season. He had the second-best QB rating, best yards per attempt, and third-best adjusted completion rate. The last two, yards per attempt and completion rate, usually have a negative correlation — the farther the pass, the less likely it is to get caught. But Joe Cool doesn't care about typical correlations.

Burrow's weekly overall QB1 finishes in Weeks 16 and 17 last season brought home the trophy for many fantasy managers. These two outings, however, were not the best representation of Burrow's season. Prior to Week 16, Burrow had only one top-five finish. With average passing volume and a team with one of the highest times between snaps, Burrow needs extreme efficiency to be a top-10 fantasy QB, especially considering the already low rushing volume he did have in his rookie season decreased by 50% in 2021.

Cincinnati did, however, upgrade their offensive line this offseason, adding Ted Karras, Alex Kappa, and La'el Collins. Perhaps Burrow will be able to stay upright a little more.

Burrow is our second-ranked pure pocket passer, behind Tom Brady. We have Russell Wilson and Dak Prescott ranked ahead of Burrow for their rushing floors. Burrow has yet to prove he can sustain the numbers it takes to be a top-10 QB in a moderate-volume offense.

Will Joe Mixon repeat as a top-five fantasy RB?

Mixon finished as the overall RB4 in FPs and RB6 in fantasy PPG. We were all in on Mixon last season, as Joe Burrow was returning from injury and the Bengals said they would rarely take Mixon off the field. But Mixon was lucky with some of his production last season. In our expected fantasy PPG, he was only RB11, in a very productive Bengals offense. We just don't agree with fantasy managers who are drafting Mixon in the first round this year.

First, Mixon only had 48 targets last season, which means he relies on his groundwork to carry him in fantasy. Even with all of the talk last season about Mixon's greatness, we're not even sure how much the team believes in him. With the Super Bowl on the line, in the final two minutes of the game, Samaje Perine was in the backfield as a healthy Mixon watched from the sideline. If nothing else, it says the team believes Perine is the superior pass-catching back.

Perine might not even be Mixon's biggest competition for third-down touches this season. Rookie Chris Evans showed real flashes in the passing game last season.

Mixon, nonetheless, will still see enough volume to exceed 300 touches. His pedestrian rushing analytics will produce another good year. But as we've said elsewhere in this book, we expect

2022/23 SCHEDULE — 2021 FANTASY POINTS ALLOWED BY OPPONENT VS LEAGUE AVERAGE

WK	DATE	TIME	OPP	QB	RB	WR	TE
1	9/11	1:00	PIT	-2%	11%	-3%	-10%
2	9/18	4:25	@DAL	-6%	-14%	2%	5%
3	9/25	1:00	@NYJ	-4%	11%	-1%	-1%
4	9/29	8:15	MIA	-6%	-4%	-2%	6%
5	10/09	8:20	@BAL	13%	-12%	12%	29%
6	10/16	1:00	@NO	-26%	2%	-16%	-45%
7	10/23	1:00	ATL	13%	8%	7%	-3%
8	10/30	8:15	@CLE	-5%	-5%	-6%	2%
9	11/06	1:00	CAR	-6%	-12%	-7%	-5%
10	BYE WEEK						
11	11/20	8:20	@PIT	-2%	11%	-3%	-10%
12	11/27	1:00	@TEN	3%	-22%	19%	-29%
13	12/04	4:25	KC	15%	4%	3%	2%
14	12/11	1:00	CLE	-5%	-5%	-6%	2%
15	12/18	4:25	@TB	3%	-4%	3%	4%
16	12/24	1:00	@NE	-8%	-19%	1%	-20%
17	1/02	8:30	BUF	-34%	-11%	-27%	-34%
18	1/08	TBD	BAL	13%	-12%	12%	29%

2022 NFL DRAFT

RD	PK		POS	COLLEGE	HT	WT
1	31	DAXTON HILL	S	MICHIGAN	6-0	192
2	28	CAM TAYLOR-BRITT	CB	NEBRASKA	6-0	197
3	31	ZACHARY CARTER	DT	FLORIDA	6-4	285
4	31	CORDELL VOLSON	OT	NORTH DAKOTA STATE	6-7	313
5	23	TYCEN ANDERSON	S	TOLEDO	6-2	210
7	31	JEFFREY GUNTER	EDGE	COASTAL CAROLINA	6-4	260

2021 WEEKLY STATS

'RUSH STATS : 'REC STATS	MIN (W) 27-24	@ CHI (L) 17-20	@ PIT (W) 24-10	JAC (W) 24-21	GB (L) 22-25	@ DET (W) 34-11	@ BAL (W) 41-17	@ NYJ (L) 31-34
QB JOE BURROW	20-27 261 (2 TD) 1-2	19-30 207 (3 INT) (2 TD) 0-0	14-18 172 (1 INT) (3 TD) 5-7	25-32 348 (2 TD) 3-4	26-38 281 (2 INT) (2 TD) 3-11	19-29 271 (1 INT) (3 TD) 5-20	23-38 416 (1 INT) (3 TD) 1-0	21-34 259 (1 TD) (3 TD) 1-(-1)
RB JOE MIXON	29-127 (1 TD) 4-23	20-69 1-2	18-90 1-4	16-67 (1 TD) 1-0	10-33 (1 TD) 1-2	18-94 5-59 (1 TD)	12-59 (1 TD) 0-0	14-33 (1 TD) 4-58 (1 TD)
RB SAMAJE PERINE	5-22 1-7	0-0 0-0	1-1-11 1-8	3-7 1-15	11-59 4-24 (1 TD)	DNP	11-52 (1 TD) 1-23	0-0 2-16
WR JA'MARR CHASE	1-1-21 5-101 (1 TD)	0-0 2-54 (1 TD)	0-0 4-65 (2 TD)	0-0 6-77	0-0 6-159 (1 TD)	0-0 4-97	0-0 8-201 (1 TD)	1-9 3-32 (1 TD)
WR TEE HIGGINS	0-0 4-58 (1 TD)	0-0 6-60 (1 TD)	DNP	DNP	0-0 5-32	0-0 3-44	0-0 7-62	0-0 4-97
WR TYLER BOYD	0-0 3-32	0-0 7-73	0-0 4-36 (1 TD)	0-0 9-118	0-0 4-24	0-0 1-7	0-0 4-39	0-0 5-69 (1 TD)
TE C.J. UZOMAH	0-0 2-35	0-0 2-4	0-0 0-0	0-0 5-95 (2 TD)	0-0 2-16	0-0 3-15 (1 TD)	0-0 3-91 (2 TD)	0-0 4-33

2021 Stats

Record: 10-7
Rushing Rank: 23rd
Passing Rank: 7th
Offensive Fantasy Pts: 8th
Against Run: 5th
Against Pass: 27th
ppg Against: 21.8
ppg: 26.3

the Bengals to regress, and Mixon along with them.

Mixon as a second rounder feels safe, but quit taking him in front of guys like Leonard Fournette and D'Andre Swift, who have bigger receiving upside. We're not completely fading Mixon, but we're much lower on him than the consensus.

Who's the better pick, Ja'marr Chase or Tee Higgins?

After Justin Jefferson showed out in his rookie year, Chase came and one-upped him. The 22-year-old put up ridiculous numbers — 81 receptions, 1,455 yards, and 13 TDs. He also performed in the playoffs, averaging 17.2 fantasy PPG in his four postseason games.

His numbers prove his success wasn't a fluke — tenth in PFF's receiving grade, second in yards per reception, and 35th in targets per route run among WRs with 50-plus targets.

What gives us the slightest pause concerning Chase is that he scored so much higher than his expected fantasy output. With such a deep average depth of target, one would expect his yards after catch to be low, but, instead, he had the fourth-highest yards after the catch per reception number in the league. Some of those monster yards-after-the-catch numbers came from busted coverages and missed tackles. It's possible that some of those plays he took to the house last season are not as frequent in 2022. Either way, Chase will have enough production that we ranked him as our overall WR3; he should be drafted somewhere around the first-round turn.

Call us crazy, but we wouldn't be surprised if Higgins ends the season with more FPs than Chase. Higgins saw similar target numbers as Chase in 2021. Their expected fantasy PPG only differed by 1.2 points.

What makes Higgins' 2021 even more impressive is that he did it with a hurt shoulder the majority of the season. He had surgery in March and should be a full go by training camp.

Since 2021, there have been 14 instances of teams producing two top-12 fantasy WRs. Joe Burrow's ability has us predicting Cincinnati will make it 15 (Miami might be the only other team with a chance this season).

Because of how fantasy drafts are playing out this year, we will end up with more shares of Higgins than Chase, and we are good with that.

Also, don't forget about Tyler Boyd who may have WR3 potential on his own, and WR2 upside with an injury to Chase or Higgins.

KEY ADDITIONS & NEW CONTRACTS

QB **BRANDON ALLEN**: RE-SIGNED ON A ONE-YEAR DEAL.

TE **HAYDEN HURST**: SIGNED A ONE-YEAR CONTRACT.

OL **LA'EL COLLINS**: SIGNED A THREE-YEAR DEAL.

OG **ALEX CAPPA**: SIGNED A FOUR-YEAR, $35 MILLION THAT INCLUDES $20 MILLION OVER THE FIRST TWO YEARS AND $1 MILLION IN PRO BOWL INCENTIVES EACH YEAR.

OL **TED KARRAS**: SIGNED A THREE-YEAR, $18 MILLION CONTRACT.

DT **B.J. HILL**: RE-SIGNED ON A THREE-YEAR, $30 MILLION DEAL THAT INCLUDES $15 MILLION IN YEAR 1.

DL **JOSH TUPOU**: RE-SIGNED TO A ONE-YEAR CONTRACT.

CB **ELI APPLE**: RE-SIGNED TO A ONE-YEAR CONTRACT.

CB **TRE FLOWERS**: RE-SIGNED ON A ONE-YEAR, $1.85 MILLION DEAL WITH $500,000 GUARANTEED.

S **JESSIE BATES**: RECEIVED THE FRANCHISE TAG.

DB **MICHAEL THOMAS**: RE-SIGNED WITH THE BENGALS.

LS **CLARK HARRIS**: RE-SIGNED ON A ONE-YEAR CONTRACT.

P **KEVIN HUBER**: RE-SIGNED ON A ONE-YEAR CONTRACT.

KEY LOSSES

WR **AUDEN TATE** (FALCONS)

TE **C.J. UZOMAH** (JETS)

OT **RILEY REIFF**

OG **QUINTON SPAIN**

C **TREY HOPKINS**

DT **LARRY OGUNJOBI** (STEELERS)

LB **JORDAN EVANS**

CB **VERNON HARGREAVES III**

CB **TRAE WAYNES**

S **RICARDO ALLEN** (RETIRED)

DEPTH CHART

QB1	JOE BURROW
QB2	BRANDON ALLEN
RB1	JOE MIXON
RB2	SAMAJE PERINE
RB3	CHRIS EVANS
WR1	JA'MARR CHASE
WR2	TEE HIGGINS
WR3	TYLER BOYD
WR4	MIKE THOMAS
TE1	HAYDEN HURST **N**
TE2	DREW SAMPLE
K	EVAN MCPHERSON

2021 WEEKLY STATS

CLE (L) 16-41		@ LV (W) 32-13		PIT (W) 41-10		LAC (L) 22-41		SF (L) 23-26		@ DEN (W) 15-10		BAL (W) 41-21		KC (W) 34-31		@ CLE (L) 16-21	
28-40 282 (2 INT) 2-1		20-29 148 (1 TD) 3-11		20-24 190 (1 INT) (1 TD) 1-8 (1 TD)		24-40 300 (2 INT) (1 TD) 1-6 (1 TD)		25-34 348 (2 TD) 2-3		15-22 157 (1 TD) 5-25		37-46 525 (4 TD) 2-11		30-39 446 (4 TD) 5-10		DNP	
13-64 (2 TD)	5-46	30-123(2TD)	0-0	28-165(2TD)	4-1-21	19-54 (1 TD)	0-0	18-58	2-10	17-58	1-2	18-65 (1 TD)	6-70 (1 TD)	12-46	7-40	0-0	0-0
5-20	2-17	2-3	3-18	3-3	1-12	5-36	2-5	4-11	4-22	4-30	2-13	0-0	2-6	1-4	1-10	DNP	
2-0	6-49	2-8	3-32 (1 TD)	0-0	3-39	0-0	5-52	1-6	5-77 (2 TD)	0-0	1-3	0-0	7-125	0-0	11-266 (3TD)	0-0	2-26
0-0	6-78	0-0	2-15	0-0	6-114 (1 TD)	0-0	9-138 (1 TD)	0-0	5-114	0-0	2-23	0-0	12-194 (2 TD)	0-0	3-62	DNP	
0-0	1-11	1-14	6-49	0-0	2-13	0-0	5-85	1-8	4-55	0-0	5-96 (1 TD)	0-0	3-85 (1 TD)	0-0	4-36 (1 TD)	DNP	
0-0	4-24	0-0	2-9	0-0	3-9	0-0	3-20	0-0	4-56	0-0	3-18	0-0	5-36	0-0	4-32	0-0	0-0

CLEVELAND BROWNS

Deshaun Watson or Jacoby Brissett?

Deshaun Watson signed a five-year, $230 million, fully-guaranteed contract this offseason, and the Browns gave up a slew of future draft picks to secure the QB. But, with a recent six-game suspension handed down in the "Massage-gate" scandal, we still don't know who the starting QB will be when the Browns face the Panthers in the season opener.

We know who it won't be, at least not for Cleveland, as the Browns and Baker Mayfield have both moved on, and Mayfield was traded to the Panthers prior to training camp. Baker may get the start against his old team, though.

Watson took all first-team reps at minicamp, ahead of backup Jacoby Brissett. The Browns were planning as if Watson will be available Week 1 and now we should see him Week 7, pending the appeal, against the Ravens. If Watson were to play the entire season, he'd likely be a top-five fantasy producer, especially considering his numbers on a less-than-functional Texans squad. Take a look at his fantasy PPG history over the years: 2017, 24.1 PPG (QB1); 2018, 20.7 (QB4); 2019, 22 (QB3); 2020, 23.8 (QB6). Watson's career average of 22 PPG is third best in NFL history for the position!

However, its looking like Brissett will be the Game 1 starter. His last full campaign was 2019 with the Colts, when he managed 2,942 yards and 18 TDs in 15 games. His fantasy PPG for that year was 16.9 — average at best.

There was some talk about adding Jimmy Garoppolo if Watson had a lengthier-than-expected suspension, but that seems unlikely now that Watson's fate has mostly been decided.

Watson's worth considering after you have drafted your first QB.

Can Amari Cooper achieve WR1 numbers in Cleveland?

Like every fantasy-relevant player in the Browns offense, Cooper's production depends more on who's under center than any other factor. Last season in 15 games with Dallas, he finished as WR27 overall, but had a handful of above average fantasy performances (38.9 vs. Tampa Bay, 26 vs. Minnesota, 16.1 and 21.5 vs. Washington).

In 2020, Deshaun Watson's last season, he was QB1 in passing yards (4,823) and QB9 for passing TDs (33), and he led WR Brandin Cooks to an 81-1,150-6 receiving line. Cooper's a better receiver than Cooks, and Cleveland's a better team than Houston. Cooper, with Watson under center, could return to WR1 status, but is still a WR2 with Jacoby Brissett.

Whether Brissett, Watson, or someone else is under center, Cooper's main competition for targets will come from TE David Njoku, in an otherwise weak receiver room.

Cooper should see plenty of targets, and should only improve with Watson at the helm.

WK	DATE	TIME	OPP	QB	RB	WR	TE
		2022/23 SCHEDULE		2021 FANTASY POINTS ALLOWED BY OPPONENT VS LEAGUE AVERAGE			
1	9/11	1:00	@CAR	-6%	-12%	-7%	-5%
2	9/18	1:00	NYJ	-4%	11%	-1%	-1%
3	9/22	8:15	PIT	-2%	11%	-3%	-10%
4	10/02	1:00	@ATL	13%	8%	7%	-3%
5	10/09	1:00	LAC	2%	17%	-11%	23%
6	10/16	1:00	NE	-8%	-19%	1%	-20%
7	10/23	1:00	@BAL	13%	-12%	12%	29%
8	10/30	8:15	CIN	-1%	6%	0%	22%
9	BYE WEEK						
10	11/13	1:00	@MIA	-6%	-4%	-2%	6%
11	11/20	1:00	@BUF	-34%	-11%	-27%	-34%
12	11/27	1:00	TB	3%	-4%	3%	4%
13	12/04	1:00	@HOU	1%	13%	5%	13%
14	12/11	1:00	@CIN	-1%	6%	0%	22%
15	12/17	TBD	BAL	13%	-12%	12%	29%
16	12/24	1:00	NO	-26%	2%	-16%	-45%
17	1/01	1:00	@WAS	29%	-3%	8%	5%
18	1/08	TBD	@PIT	-2%	11%	-3%	-10%

2022 NFL DRAFT

RD	PK		POS	COLLEGE	HT	WT
3	4	MARTIN EMERSON	CB	MISSISSIPPI STATE	6-2	200
3	14	ALEX WRIGHT	EDGE	UAB	6-7	270
3	35	DAVID BELL	WR	PURDUE	6-2	210
4	3	PERRION WINFREY	DT	OKLAHOMA	6-4	292
4	19	CADE YORK	K	LSU	6-1	198
5	13	JAROME FORD	RB	CINCINNATTI	5-11	220
6	23	MICHAEL WOODS	WR	OKLAHOMA	6-1	198
7	2	ISAIAH THOMAS	EDGE	OKLAHOMA	6-5	266
7	25	DAWSON DEATON	C	TEXAS TECH	6-6	310

2021 WEEKLY STATS

*RUSH STATS : *REC STATS	@ KC (L) 29-33		HOU (W) 31-21		CHI (W) 26-6		@ MIN (W) 14-7		@ LAC (L) 42-47		ARI (L) 14-37		DEN (W) 17-14		PIT (L) 10-15	
QB BAKER MAYFIELD	21-28 321 (1 INT) 1-7		19-21 213 (1 INT) (1 TD) 8-10 (1 TD)		19-31 246 (1 TD) 4-31		15-33 155 2-11		23-32 305 (2 TD) 2-8		19-28 234 (1 INT) (2 TD) 3-8		DNP		20-31 225 1-5	
QB CASE KEENUM	DNP		DNP		0-0 0 3-0		DNP		DNP		1-3 6 0-0		21-33 199 (1 TD) 4-7		DNP	
RB NICK CHUBB	15-83 (2 TD)	2-18	11-95 (1 TD)	1-3	22-84	0-0	21-100	1-5	21-161 (1 TD)	1-9	DNP		DNP		16-61	1-8
RB KAREEM HUNT	6-33 (1 TD)	3-28	13-51	1-2	10-81 (1 TD)	6-74	14-69 (1 TD)	2-17	12-61 (2 TD)	5-28	14-66	3-12	DNP		DNP	
RB D'ERNEST JOHNSON	DNP		0-0	0-0	2-9	0-0	DNP		DNP		1-2	1-7	22-146 (1 TD)	2-22	4-22 (1 TD)	1-7
WR JARVIS LANDRY	2-13 (1 TD)	5-71	0-0	1-9	DNP		DNP		DNP		DNP		0-0	5-37	1-5	5-65
WR D. PEOPLES-JONES	0-0	1-4	0-0	1-14	0-0	2-39	0-0	0-0	0-0	5-70	0-0	4-101 (2 TD)	DNP		DNP	
TE DAVID NJOKU	0-0	3-76	0-0	2-18	0-0	0-0	0-0	2-17	0-0	7-149 (1 TD)	0-0	1-6	0-0	2-18	0-0	3-39
TE AUSTIN HOOPER	0-0	3-27	0-0	5-40	0-0	2-19 (1 TD)	0-0	1-11	0-0	0-0	0-0	1-4	0-0	2-42	0-0	4-26

2021 Stats
Record: 8–9
Rushing Rank: 4th
Passing Rank: 27th
Offensive Fantasy Pts: 21st
Against Run: 12th
Against Pass: 5th
ppg Against: 21.8
ppg: 20.5

KEY ADDITIONS & NEW CONTRACTS

QB DESHAUN WATSON: ACQUIRED IN A TRADE WITH THE TEXANS, ALONG WITH A 2024 SIXTH-ROUND PICK, IN EXCHANGE FOR THREE FIRST-ROUND PICKS (2022-24), A THIRD-ROUNDER ('23) AND TWO FOURTH-ROUNDERS ('22, '24). WATSON WILL RECEIVE A FULLY GUARANTEED FIVE-YEAR, $230 MILLION CONTRACT FROM CLEVELAND.

QB JACOBY BRISSETT: SIGNED A ONE-YEAR, $4.65 MILLION CONTRACT, INCLUDING $4.5 MILLION GUARANTEED.

QB JOSH DOBBS: SIGNED A ONE-YEAR DEAL.

WR AMARI COOPER: ACQUIRED IN A TRADE WITH THE DALLAS COWBOYS IN EXCHANGE FOR A 2022 FIFTH-ROUND DRAFT PICK AND A SWAP OF SIXTH-ROUNDERS.

WR JAKEEM GRANT: SIGNED A THREE-YEAR DEAL WORTH UP TO $13.8 MILLION.

TE DAVID NJOKU: ORIGINALLY RECEIVED THE FRANCHISE TAG, THEN INKED A FOUR-YEAR, $56.75 MILLION EXTENSION, WITH $28 MILLION GUARANTEED AT SIGNING.

OT CHRIS HUBBARD: RE-SIGNED TO A FREE-AGENT DEAL.

OG ETHAN POCIC: SIGNED TO A FREE-AGENT DEAL.

DE JADEVEON CLOWNEY: RE-SIGNED ON A ONE-YEAR, $10 MILLION DEAL WITH AN ADDITIONAL $1MILLION AVAILABLE IN INCENTIVES.

DE STEPHEN WEATHERLY: SIGNED TO A FREE-AGENT DEAL.

DE CHASE WINOVICH: ACQUIRED IN A TRADE WITH THE NEW ENGLAND PATRIOTS IN EXCHANGE FOR LB MACK WILSON.

DT TAVEN BRYAN: SIGNED A ONE-YEAR DEAL WORTH UP TO $5 MILLION.

LB ANTHONY WALKER: RE-SIGNED ON A ONE-YEAR DEAL.

CB DENZEL WARD: SIGNED A FIVE-YEAR, $100.5 MILLION EXTENSION THAT INCLUDES $71.5 MILLION GUARANTEED.

S RONNIE HARRISON: RE-SIGNED TO A FREE-AGENT DEAL.

P COREY BOJORQUEZ: SIGNED A FREE-AGENT DEAL.

K CHASE MCLAUGHLIN: RE-SIGNED ON A FREE-AGENT DEAL.

What's the division of workload between RBs Chubb, Hunt, and Johnson?

If any one of these three RBs had the position to themselves in Cleveland, he would be a top-five fantasy back. Instead, work is divided among the three. While Nick Chubb is clearly the top back, assuming almost double the work as Hunt in the rushing attack, Hunt sees nearly twice the targets in the receiving game. Last season Chubb had 16.3 rushing attempts, 89.9 rushing yards, 1.8 targets, and 12.4 receiving yards per game. Hunt had 9.8 rushing attempts for 48.3 yards, and 3.4 targets for 21.75 yards. In fantasy PPG, Chubb was RB12 on the season, while Hunt was RB22 last year.

Durability has been an issue at the position, but mostly with Hunt. He played only eight games last season, and has missed 17 in three years. Chubb missed three last year, but has only missed seven in a four-year span.

D'Ernest Johnson, the Browns RB3, played 14 games last year, and finished RB52 for the league. Unless Chubb, Hunt, or both are injured, Johnson won't be a fantasy factor. However, he did have three substantial games in Hunt's absence last season (24.8 FPs vs. Denver, 22.7 vs. New England, 20.3 vs. Cincinnati). Johnson's 119 combined touches, 4 TDs, and 671 all-purpose yards last year are at least evidence of his potential to siphon touches from both Chubb and Hunt.

> IF ANY ONE OF THESE THREE RBS HAD THE POSITION TO THEMSELVES IN CLEVELAND, HE WOULD BE A TOP-FIVE FANTASY BACK.

KEY LOSSES

QB BAKER MAYFIELD (TRADED TO PANTHERS)
QB CASE KEENUM (TRADED TO BILLS)
QB NICK MULLENS (RAIDERS)
WR RASHARD HIGGINS (PANTHERS)
WR JARVIS LANDRY (SAINTS)
TE AUSTIN HOOPER (TITANS)
C JC TRETTER
DE TAKKARIST MCKINLEY
DT MALIK JACKSON
LB MALCOLM SMITH
LB MACK WILSON (TRADED TO PATRIOTS)
CB TROY HILL (TRADED TO RAMS)
S M.J. STEWART (TEXANS)
P DUSTIN COLQUITT
K CHRIS BLEWITT
K CHASE MCLAUGHLIN

DEPTH CHART

QB1	DESHAUN WATSON **N**
QB2	JACOBY BRISSETT **N**
RB1	NICK CHUBB
RB2	KAREEM HUNT
RB3	D'ERNEST JOHNSON
WR1	AMARI COOPER **N**
WR2	DONOVAN PEOPLES-JONES
WR3	DAVID BELL **R**
WR4	ANTHONY SCHWARTZ
TE1	DAVID NJOKU
TE2	HARRISON BRYANT
K	CADE YORK **R**

2021 WEEKLY STATS

@ CIN (W) 41-16		@ NE (L) 7-45		DET (W) 13-10		@ BAL (L) 10-16		BAL (W) 24-22		LV (L) 14-16		@ GB (L) 22-24		@ PIT (L) 14-26		CIN (W) 21-16	
14-21 218 (2 TD)	0-0	11-21 73 (1 INT) (1 TD)	0-0	15-29 176 (2 INT) (1 TD)	4-9	18-37 247 (1 TD)	2-4	22-32 190 (1 INT) (2 TD)	6-14	DNP		21-36 222 (4 INT) (2 TD)	2-11	16-38 185 (2 INT) (2 TD)	2-16	DNP	
DNP		8-12 81	0-0	DNP		DNP		DNP		DNP		DNP		DNP		17-24 176 (1 INT) (2 TD)	5-15
14-137 (2 TD)	2-26	DNP		22-130	2-14 (1 TD)	8-16	2-23	17-59	3-6	23-91 (1 TD)	1-2	17-126 (1 TD)	3-58	12-58	0-0	9-58	1-2
DNP		DNP		DNP		7-20	0-0	2-5	2-13	DNP		DNP		DNP		DNP	
8-16	0-0	19-99	7-58	5-26	0-0	0-0	0-0	4-22	1-7	1-[-2]	4-17	4-58	1-8	5-13	1-1	25-123 (1 TD)	1-10
1-0	3-11	0-0	4-26	1-16 (1 TD)	4-26	0-0	6-111	0-0	5-41 (1 TD)	DNP		0-0	4-55	1-6	4-43	0-0	6-75 (1 TD)
0-0	2-86 (1 TD)	0-0	1-16	DNP		0-0	2-10	0-0	5-90	0-0	4-48	0-0	1-5	0-0	3-76	0-0	3-38
0-0	1-18 (1 TD)	0-0	1-11	1-1	2-20	0-0	3-35 (1 TD)	DNP		0-0	3-29	0-0	0-0	0-0	4-28 (1 TD)	0-0	2-11
0-0	2-14	0-0	4-25 (1 TD)	0-0	4-53	0-0	0-0	0-0	5-30 (1 TD)	DNP		0-0	3-26	0-0	2-28	0-0	0-0

DALLAS COWBOYS

With the offseason changes in Dallas, are Dak Prescott's best fantasy days behind him?

In the last three seasons, Dak has been a top-eight QB in fantasy PPG, and finished as the No. 1 QB in PPG in 2020, though only playing five games.

There's a lot to like about Dak's 2022 situation. First, Dallas, the No. 1 pace-of-play offense, finished third last season in overall passing yards. Second, Dak had his worst rushing production ever in 2021, and had below average production out of his top receiver, Amari Cooper, yet still finished as the seventh-best fantasy QB on the year. Also, the defense, which was unsustainably good last season, should regress, which, in turn, will provide even more passing attempts for Prescott.

On the other hand, the loss of Amari Cooper and offensive lineman, La'el Collins hurts. There's also the fear that Dak turns into a one-dimensional QB, evidenced by his continued decline in rushing production. He had a career low 1 TD last season. He did have his best rushing stats in three of his last four games last year, leading us to believe his lack of production may have been a result of post-injury skittishness.

We expect Dak, in an aging offense with fewer playmakers, to step up to the challenge and remain a top-10 QB. We have him ranked as our eighth-best QB, and prefer him over true one-dimensional QBs, Joe Burrow and Aaron Rodgers.

Can CeeDee Lamb, behind Kupp, Jefferson, and Chase, be fantasy's fourth best WR?

CeeDee Lamb, now in his third year in the NFL, continues to improve as a receiver, posting career bests in PFF's receiving grade, yards per reception, yards after the catch, and targets last season. Much of the fantasy community was calling for Lamb to have a breakout year in 2021. While he did finish as WR21, his didn't quite live up to his last year's fantasy ADP. The difference this year, after the departure of Amari Cooper, is that Lamb has the potential to see more targets than any other WR in the league. And at 23 years old, he's still getting better.

'We wouldn't blame you for drafting him at WR4 with all the unknowns surrounding other top receivers'

Lamb is our WR8, but we wouldn't blame you for drafting him at WR4 with all the unknowns surrounding the other top receivers, except for Stefon Diggs whose role in cemented in Buffalo. Deebo Samuel will be playing with a new run-first QB. Davante Adams and Tyreek Hill are both on new teams with QBs who have never supported a top-five fantasy WR.

We just don't see how you can go wrong with Lamb after the top-three WRs; if he's your WR4, we support you.

2022/23 SCHEDULE				2021 FANTASY POINTS ALLOWED BY OPPONENT VS LEAGUE AVERAGE			
WK	DATE	TIME	OPP	QB	RB	WR	TE
1	9/11	8:20	TB	3%	-4%	3%	4%
2	9/18	4:25	CIN	-1%	6%	0%	22%
3	9/26	8:15	@NYG	12%	40%	-2%	22%
4	10/02	1:00	WAS	29%	-3%	8%	5%
5	10/09	4:25	@LAR	-12%	-8%	7%	-2%
6	10/16	8:20	@PHI	-1%	10%	-17%	46%
7	10/23	1:00	DET	4%	14%	2%	17%
8	10/30	1:00	CHI	4%	-7%	0%	-28%
9	BYE WEEK						
10	11/13	4:25	@GB	5%	-13%	3%	0%
11	11/20	4:25	@MIN	6%	2%	23%	-13%
12	11/24	4:30	NYG	12%	40%	-2%	22%
13	12/04	8:20	IND	2%	-12%	4%	23%
14	12/11	1:00	HOU	1%	13%	5%	13%
15	12/18	1:00	@JAC	4%	-1%	5%	-2%
16	12/24	4:25	PHI	-1%	10%	-17%	46%
17	12/29	8:15	@TEN	3%	-22%	19%	-29%
18	1/08	TBD	@WAS	29%	-3%	8%	5%

2022 NFL DRAFT					
RD	PK		POS	COLLEGE	HT WT
1	24	TYLER SMITH	OT	TULSA	6-6 332
2	24	SAM WILLIAMS	EDGE	OLE MISS	6-4 261
3	24	JALEN TOLBERT	WR	SOUTH ALABAMA	6-3 190
4	24	JAKE FERGUSON	TE	WISCONSIN	6-5 244
5	12	MATT WALETZKO	OT	NORTH DAKOTA	6-7 305
5	24	DARON BLAND	CB	FRESNO STATE	6-2 200
5	33	DAMONE CLARK	LB	LSU	6-3 245
5	35	JOHN RIDGEWAY	DT	ARKANSAS	6-6 320
6	14	DEVIN HARPER	LB	OKLAHOMA STATE	6-0 235

2021 WEEKLY STATS

		@ TB (L) 29-31		@ LAC (W) 20-17		PHI (W) 41-21		CAR (W) 36-28		NYG (W) 44-20		@ NE (W) 35-29		@ MIN (W) 20-16		DEN (L) 16-30	
	*RUSH STATS : *REC STATS																
QB DAK PRESCOTT		42-58 403 (1 INT) (3 TD) 4-13		23-27 237 (1 INT) 0-0		21-26 238 (3 TD) 9-6		14-22 188 (4 TD) 4-35		22-32 302 (1 INT) (3 TD) 2-6		36-51 445 (1 INT) (3 TD) 3-10		DNP		19-39 232 (1 INT) (2 TD) 2-16	
RB EZEKIEL ELLIOTT		11-33	2-6	16-71 (1 TD)	2-26	17-95 (2 TD)	3-21	20-143 (1 TD)	0-0	21-110 (1 TD)	2-2 (1 TD)	17-69	7-50	16-50	4-23	10-51	3-25
RB TONY POLLARD		3-14	4-29	13-109 (1 TD)	3-31	11-60	1-5	10-67	0-0	14-75	4-28	10-41	3-22	7-26	1-1	4-11	1-32
WR CEEDEE LAMB		0-0	7-104 (1 TD)	1-13	8-81	1-1-11	3-66	0-0	2-13	1-4	4-84 (1 TD)	1-2	9-149 (2 TD)	0-0	6-112	0-0	2-23
WR AMARI COOPER		0-0	13-139 (2TD)	0-0	3-24	0-0	3-26	0-0	3-69 (1 TD)	0-0	3-60 (1 TD)	0-0	5-55	0-0	8-122 (1 TD)	0-0	2-37
WR CEDRICK WILSON JR.		0-0	3-24	1-5	2-20	0-0	2-17 (1 TD)	0-0	2-30 (1 TD)	1-6	1-35	0-0	4-42	0-0	3-84 (1 TD)	0-0	2-28
WR MICHAEL GALLUP		0-0	4-36	DNP		DNP		DNP		DNP		DNP		DNP		DNP	
TE DALTON SCHULTZ		0-0	6-45	0-0	2-18	0-0	6-80 (2 TD)	0-0	6-58 (1 TD)	0-0	6-79	0-0	5-79	0-0	2-11	0-0	4-54

2021 Stats

Record: 12–5
Rushing Rank: 9th
Passing Rank: 3rd
Offensive Fantasy Pts: 2nd
Against Run: 16th
Against Pass: 21st
ppg Against: 21.2
ppg: 30.4

KEY ADDITIONS & NEW CONTRACTS

WR **MICHAEL GALLUP**: RE-SIGNED A FIVE-YEAR, $57.5 MILLION DEAL THAT INCLUDES $23 MILLION FULLY GUARANTEED AND HAS A MAX VALUE OF $62.5 MILLION. THE DEAL ALSO INCLUDES A $10 MILLION SIGNING BONUS.

WR **JAMES WASHINGTON**: AGREED TO TERMS ON A ONE-YEAR DEAL.

TE **JEREMY SPRINKLE**: RE-SIGNED WITH THE COWBOYS.

TE **DALTON SCHULTZ**: SIGNED THE FRANCHISE TAG.

DE **DEMARCUS LAWRENCE**: AGREED TO A NEW THREE-YEAR, $40 MILLION CONTRACT WITH $30 MILLION GUARANTEED.

DT **CARLOS WATKINS**: SIGNED TO A ONE-YEAR CONTRACT.

LB **DANTE FOWLER**: SIGNED A ONE-YEAR CONTRACT.

LB **LEIGHTON VANDER ESCH**: RE-SIGNED ON A ONE-YEAR DEAL.

S **MALIK HOOKER**: RE-SIGNED ON A TWO-YEAR DEAL WORTH $8 MILLION.

S **JAYRON KEARSE**: RE-SIGNED ON A TWO-YEAR, $10 MILLION DEAL WITH A MAX VALUE OF $11 MILLION.

LS **JAKE MCQUAIDE**: RE-SIGNED ON A ONE-YEAR DEAL WORTH THE VETERAN MINIMUM.

P **BRYAN ANGER**: RE-SIGNED ON A THREE-YEAR, $9 MILLION DEAL.

Is the Ezekiel Elliot RB1 era over?

Post Week 5 last year, Zeke looked like a shell of himself. For fantasy managers, his TDs, for the first time ever, felt like a relief rather than a given. From Week 5 forward, after suffering a torn PCL, Zeke was only the 19th best RB in fantasy PPG. He averaged 1.9 yards per carry and 1.1 yards after contact less than before the injury. We attribute some of this loss directly to the PCL injury and some of it to a normal decline after years of wear and tear on his body.

There's also the fact that Tony Pollard continues to outperform Zeke in every metric, from yards per touch to big-play percentage. So why does Zeke continue to hold the decisive edge in snap count percentage? Perhaps his $90 million contract has something to do with it, but it mostly due to one thing: Zeke is by and large a better pass-protecting back than Pollard. It's true that Pollard would be a better fantasy back if Zeke missed time than Zeke would be if Pollard missed time.

Zeke may enter 2022 injury free, but he has another year of age and wear on his body, having fought through the PCL injury to play all 17 games last season. With his production waning, he had the fewest touches of any season in his career, except his lone 10-game season in 2017.

Gone are the days where Zeke is guaranteed 300 touches and double-digit TDs. Like many of his other seasons, his range of outcomes feels pretty narrow. But this year, it's as a RB2.

EZEKIEL ELLIOT'S 2021 SEASON

Weeks 1-4, 2021

5.3 yards per carry

3.4 YAC per carry

7.1 carries per missed tackle

Weeks 5-18, 2021

3.8 yards per carry

2.5 YAC per carry

16.7 carries per missed tackle

KEY LOSSES

RB **COREY CLEMENT**

WR **AMARI COOPER** (TRADED TO BROWNS)

WR **CEDRICK WILSON** (DOLPHINS)

TE **BLAKE JARWIN**

OT **TY NSEKHE**

OG **CONNOR WILLIAMS** (DOLPHINS)

OL **LA'EL COLLINS** (BENGALS)

DE **RANDY GREGORY** (BRONCOS)

DE **BRENT URBAN** (RAVENS)

S **DAMONTAE KAZEE** (STEELERS)

S **KEANU NEAL** (BUCCANEERS)

K **GREG ZUERLEIN** (JETS)

DEPTH CHART

QB1	DAK PRESCOTT
QB2	COOPER RUSH
RB1	EZEKIEL ELLIOT
RB2	TONY POLLARD
RB3	RYAN NALL **N**
WR1	CEEDEE LAMB
WR2	MICHAEL GALLUP
WR3	JAMES WASHINGTON **N**
WR4	JALEN TOLBERT **R**
TE1	DALTON SCHULTZ
TE2	JAKE FERGUSON **R**
K	JONATHAN GARIBAY **N**

2021 WEEKLY STATS

ATL (W) 43-3		@ KC (L) 9-19		LV (L) 33-36		@ NO (W) 27-17		@ WAS (W) 27-20		@ NYG (W) 21-6		WAS (W) 56-14		ARI (L) 22-25		@ PHI (W) 51-26	
24-31 296 (2 TD)		28-43 216 (2 INT)		32-47 375 (2 TD)		26-40 238 (1 INT) (1 TD)		22-39 211 (2 INT) (1 TD)		28-37 217 (1 TD)		28-39 330 (4 TD)		24-38 226 (3 TD)		21-27 295 (5 TD)	
2-5 (1 TD)		0-0		1-3		3-1-3)		7-15		2-1-1)		4-21		5-20		0-0	
14-41 (2 TD)	3-15	9-32	6-36	9-25 (1 TD)	6-24	13-45	2-2	12-45	1-15	16-52 (1 TD)	3-20	9-37 (1 TD)	1-5 (1 TD)	9-16	1-14	18-87	1-3
11-42	6-56	7-50	2-20	10-36	4-32	7-71 (1 TD)	2-3	DNP		12-74	3-13	8-34	2-16	3-9	3-49	DNP	
1-12	6-94 (2 TD)	0-0	3-14	DNP		1-33	7-89	2-15	7-61	0-0	6-50	1-1-2)	4-66	0-0	3-51	0-0	2-45
0-0	4-51	DNP		DNP		0-0	2-41	0-0	5-51 (1 TD)	0-0	2-8	0-0	7-85 (1 TD)	0-0	3-18 (1 TD)	0-0	5-79
0-0	0-0	0-0	4-36	0-0	7-104	DNP		0-0	2-18	0-0	0-0	0-0	2-10	0-0	6-35 (1 TD)	0-0	5-119 (2 TD)
0-0	3-42	0-0	5-44	0-0	5-106	0-0	5-36 (1 TD)	0-0	5-60	0-0	3-32	0-0	2-53	0-0	3-36 (1 TD)	DNP	
0-0	1-14	0-0	6-53	0-0	3-46 (1 TD)	0-0	5-43	0-0	1-4	0-0	8-67 (1 TD)	0-0	8-82 (1 TD)	0-0	6-54	0-0	3-21 (2 TD)

DENVER BRONCOS

Does Javonte Williams emerge as the clear No. 1 in Denver's backfield?

In 2021, Williams was first among all RBs in broken tackles per carry and seventh in yards after contact per rushing attempt, and he did this as a rookie.

But metrics are just that — numbers. We can distort them to support whatever view we are taking. Williams, with his forced missed tackles and impressive yards after contact, had the same yards per carry as his running mate, Melvin Gordon III. In fact, they were identical in almost every stat, including fantasy PPG.

When Gordon signed a one-year, $2.5 million contract this offseason to return to Denver, the coaching staff said they planned to split work among the backs again. This is more likely a show of support for the signing rather than an actual game plan.

This organization had a complete change in coaches and has a new starting QB. But new head coach Nathanial Hackett has shown a willingness to split carries among his backs (e.g. Aaron Jones and A.J. Dillon). While Williams becoming a three-down back is not out of the question, this seems unlikely. We're predicting, at best, Williams will get around 20% more touches than Gordon. Let's not forget that Williams finished 13th in touches last season. A small increase in touches and an improved offense spells success. Williams has a high floor and an even higher ceiling. If you can get him in the RB2 range, you won't be disappointed, and have a chance to end up with an RB1

Who emerges as Wilson's new favorite target?

In the offseason, Courtland Sutton signed a four-year, $60.8 million extension, and Tim Patrick signed a three-year $34 million extension. General Manager George Paton, who negotiated the deals with the two receivers, was not even with the Broncos when Jerry Jeudy was drafted. Nathaniel Hackett, Denver's new head coach, used two-receiver sets ninth most in the NFL last season with Green Bay. Usually, the slot receiver is the odd man out in these sets. Last season, Sutton played 12% of his snaps from the slot, Patrick 23%, and Jeudy 74%.

Deep-route, big-play Courtland Sutton has suffered the past few seasons, playing under some of the shortest-average-throw QBs in the league. Now he has the longest, the QB with the most air yards per attempt.

Tim Patrick, who had more TDs in the last two seasons than Sutton and Jeudy combined, suffered a season-ending ACL injury in training camp. This should lead to even more targets to Sutton and Jeudy.

Jeudy was dealing with a high ankle sprain the second half of last season, but besides an impressive rookie campaign, he's been average. Sutton will emerge as Wilson's new favorite target, but Jeudy has fringe WR2 potential as well. We'll take whoever slips the farthest in our drafts, which currently seems to be Sutton, according to recent ADPs.

WK	DATE	TIME	OPP	QB	RB	WR	TE
2022/23 SCHEDULE				2021 FANTASY POINTS ALLOWED BY OPPONENT VS LEAGUE AVERAGE			
1	9/12	8:15	@SEA	2%	-8%	3%	-23%
2	9/18	4:25	HOU	1%	13%	5%	13%
3	9/25	8:20	SF	-1%	26%	-3%	20%
4	10/02	4:25	@LV	1%	10%	-14%	39%
5	10/06	8:15	IND	2%	-12%	4%	23%
6	10/17	8:15	@LAC	2%	17%	-11%	23%
7	10/23	4:05	NYJ	-4%	11%	-1%	-1%
8	10/30	9:30AM	@JAC*	4%	-1%	5%	-2%
9	BYE WEEK						
10	11/13	1:00	@TEN	3%	-22%	19%	-29%
11	11/20	4:05	LV	1%	10%	-14%	39%
12	11/27	1:00	@CAR	-6%	-12%	-7%	-5%
13	12/04	1:00	@BAL	13%	-12%	12%	29%
14	12/11	8:20	KC	15%	4%	3%	2%
15	12/18	4:05	ARI	0%	-11%	10%	-36%
16	12/25	4:30	@LAR	-12%	-8%	7%	-2%
17	1/01	1:00	@KC	15%	4%	3%	2%
18	1/08	TBD	LAC	2%	17%	-11%	23%

PLAYED IN LONDON

2022 NFL DRAFT

RD	PK		POS	COLLEGE	HT	WT
2	32	NIK BONITTO	EDGE	OKLAHOMA	6-3	238
3	16	GREG DULCICH	TE	UCLA	6-4	250
4	10	DEMARRI MATHIS	CB	PITTSBURGH	5-11	195
4	11	EYIOMA UWAZURIKE	EDGE	IOWA STATE	6-6	320
5	9	DELARRIN TURNER-YELL	S	OKLAHOMA	5-11	200
5	19	MONTRELL WASHINGTON	WR	SAMFORD	5-10	170
5	28	LUKE WATTENBERG	C	WASHINGTON	6-5	300
6	28	MATT HENNINGSEN	DT	WISCONSIN	6-3	291
7	11	FAION HICKS	CB	WISCONSIN	5-10	192

2021 WEEKLY STATS

*RUSH STATS : *REC STATS	@ NYG (W) 27-13		@ JAC (W) 23-12		NYJ (W) 26-0		BAL (L) 7-23		@ PIT (L) 19-27		LV (L) 24-34		@ CLE (L) 14-17		WAS (W) 17-10	
QB TEDDY BRIDGEWATER	28-36 264 (2 TD) 3-19		26-34 328 (2 TD) 4-1		19-25 235 4-24		7-16 65 (1 TD) 1-2		24-38 288 (1 INT) (2 TD) 1-11		35-49 334 (3 INT) (3 TD) 2-9		23-33 187 (1 INT) (2 TD) 2-3		19-26 213 (1 TD) 1-1	
QB DREW LOCK	DNP		DNP		DNP		12-21 113 (1 INT) 0-0		DNP		DNP		DNP		DNP	
RB JAVONTE WILLIAMS	14-45	1-[-4]	13-64	1-10	12-29 (1 TD)	3-33	7-48	3-11	8-61	3-25	11-53	3-15	4-20	6-32 (1 TD)	9-35	2-13
RB MELVIN GORDON III	11-101 (1 TD)	3-17	13-31	2-38	18-60 (1 TD)	1-21	9-56	2-11	9-34	2-9	10-50	3-23	8-18	2-14 (1 TD)	10-47 (1 TD)	3-15 (1 TD)
WR TIM PATRICK	0-0	4-39 (1 TD)	0-0	3-37 (1 TD)	0-0	5-98	0-0	3-39	0-0	7-89	0-0	3-42 (1 TD)	0-0	2-16	0-0	3-64
WR COURTLAND SUTTON	0-0	1-14	0-0	9-159	0-0	5-37	0-0	3-47	0-0	7-120 (1 TD)	0-0	8-94 (1 TD)	0-0	5-68	0-0	2-40
WR JERRY JEUDY	0-0	6-72	DNP		DNP		DNP		DNP		DNP		1-0	4-39		
TE NOAH FANT	0-0	6-62	0-0	4-33 (1 TD)	0-0	2-15	0-0	6-46 (1 TD)	0-0	3-20	0-0	9-97 (1 TD)	0-0	5-39	0-0	2-8

2021 Stats

Record: 7-10
Rushing Rank: 13th
Passing Rank: 20th
Offensive Fantasy Pts: 22nd
Against Run: 15th
Against Pass: 8th
ppg Against: 18.9
ppg: 19.7

KEY ADDITIONS & NEW CONTRACTS

QB **JOSH JOHNSON**: SIGNED A ONE-YEAR CONTRACT.

QB **RUSSELL WILSON**: ACQUIRED IN A TRADE WITH THE SEATTLE SEAHAWKS, ALONG WITH A FOURTH-ROUND PICK, FOR TWO FIRST-ROUND PICKS, TWO SECOND-ROUNDERS, A FIFTH-ROUNDER, QB DREW LOCK, TE NOAH FANT AND DT SHELBY HARRIS.

RB **MELVIN GORDON III**: RE-SIGNED ON A ONE-YEAR DEAL WORTH UP TO $5 MILLION.

TE **ERIC SAUBERT**: RE-SIGNED ON A ONE-YEAR CONTRACT.

OT **CALVIN ANDERSON**: RE-SIGNED ON A ONE-YEAR CONTRACT.

OL **TOM COMPTON**: SIGNED TO A FREE-AGENT DEAL.

OL **BILLY TURNER**: SIGNED ONE-YEAR DEAL WORTH UP TO $5 MILLION.

DE **RANDY GREGORY**: SIGNED A FIVE-YEAR, $70 MILLION DEAL THAT INCLUDES $28 MILLION GUARANTEED.

DT **D.J. JONES**: SIGNED A THREE-YEAR DEAL WORTH $30 MILLION THAT INCLUDES $20 MILLION GUARANTEED.

DT **DESHAWN WILLIAMS**: RE-SIGNED ON A ONE-YEAR DEAL.

LB **JOSEY JEWELL**: SIGNED A TWO-YEAR DEAL. (JAMES PALMER)

LB **MALIK REED**: SIGNED HIS RIGHT OF FIRST REFUSAL TENDER.

LB **ALEX SINGLETON**: SIGNED A ONE-YEAR, $1.1 MILLION FULLY GUARANTEED CONTRACT.

CB **K'WAUN WILLIAMS**: SIGNED A TWO-YEAR CONTRACT.

S **KAREEM JACKSON**: RE-SIGNED ON A ONE-YEAR DEAL.

How is Russell Wilson's fantasy value affected by his new home?

Wilson's 2021 season was an outlier. It was his first season since 2016 when he didn't throw at least 30 TDs and finish in the top-11 QBs. He also posted a career low PFF passing grade. We'll put some of the blame on his fractured middle finger that kept him out three weeks. He also had a career low in rushing yards per game, which is likely most indicative of an aging QB.

Wilson now joins Denver, who, arguably, has the better group of pass catchers than in Seattle, even with the loss of Tim Patrick to a season-ending ACL tear in training camp. Also, Denver has the more talented backfield with the two-headed monster of Javonte Williams and Melvin Gordon III.

The bad news for Wilson's fantasy managers may be new head coach Nathaniel Hackett's (former Green Bay offensive coordinator) offensive philosophy. His most successful years in Green Bay, 2017 and 2020, were the most run-heavy of his career. And Denver has a solid defense that will allow the offense to lean more on the run.

On the other hand, the AFC West is loaded with powerhouse offenses that will force Hackett to let Russ cook. The better skill players in Denver will counter the slight passing-volume decline he'll likely face. We have him as our QB10, just behind Aaron Rodgers, but ahead of Joe Burrow. He'd likely have the same ranking if were still in Seattle.

WILSON'S FANTASY PPG

2021: 17.3 (QB13)
2020: 22.5 (QB6)
2019: 20.5 (QB5)
2018: 18.7 (QB11)
2017: 21.7 (QB1)
2016: 16.8 (QB15)
2015: 21 (QB3)
2014: 20.6 (QB3)
2013: 16.7 (QB11)
2012: 17.4 (QB9)

KEY LOSSES

QB **TEDDY BRIDGEWATER** (DOLPHINS)
QB **DREW LOCK** (TRADED TO SEAHAWKS)
WR **DAESEAN HAMILTON** (TEXANS)
TE **NOAH FANT** (TRADED TO SEAHAWKS)
OT **CAMERON FLEMING**
OT **BOBBY MASSIE**
DE **STEPHEN WEATHERLY** (BROWNS)
DT **SHELBY HARRIS** (TRADED TO SEAHAWKS)
DL **SHAMAR STEPHEN**
LB **A.J. JOHNSON**
LB **KENNY YOUNG** (RAIDERS)
CB **BRYCE CALLAHAN** (CHARGERS)
CB **KYLE FULLER** (RAVENS)

DEPTH CHART

QB1	RUSSELL WILSON **N**
QB2	JOSH JOHNSON **N**
RB1	JAVONTE WILLIAMS
RB2	MELVIN GORDON III
RB3	MIKE BOONE
WR1	JERRY JEUDY
WR2	COURTLAND SUTTON
WR3	KJ HAMLER
WR4	TYRIE CLEVELAND
TE1	ALBERT OKWUEGBUNAM
TE2	GREG DULCICH **R**
K	BRANDON MCMANUS

2021 WEEKLY STATS

@ DAL (W) 30-16		PHI (L) 13-30		LAC (W) 28-13		@ KC (L) 9-22		DET (W) 38-10		CIN (L) 10-15		@ LV (L) 13-17		@ LAC (L) 13-24		KC (L) 24-28	
19-28 249 (1 TD)		22-36 226		11-18 129 (1 TD)		22-40 257 (2 INT) (1 TD)		18-25 179 (2 TD)		12-22 98		DNP		DNP		DNP	
3-[-1] (1 TD)		0-0		2-10 (1 TD)		4-17		0-0		3-10							
DNP		DNP		4-7 26 (1 INT)		DNP		DNP		6-12 88 (1 TD)		15-22 153		18-25 245 (1 TD)		12-24 162	
				0-0						1-[-2]		2-10		3-10		4-35 (2 TD)	
17-111	0-0	8-48	2-1	14-54 (1 TD)	3-57	23-102	6-76 (1 TD)	15-73 (1 TD)	1-10 (1 TD)	15-72	4-9	7-12 (1 TD)	2-8	14-30	1-2	12-46	2-18
21-80 (1 TD)	2-15	9-45 (1 TD)	1-[-2]	17-83	1-5	DNP		24-111 (2 TD)	0-0	15-53	1-8	7-[-4]	1-4	10-43	3-29	12-110 (1 TD)	1-6
0-0	4-85 (1 TD)	0-0	3-14	0-0	2-26	0-0	1-9	0-0	2-21	0-0	3-42 (1 TD)	0-0	2-18	DNP		0-0	6-95
0-0	1-9	0-0	2-29	0-0	2-17	0-0	2-15	0-0	1-9	0-0	2-12	0-0	4-33	0-0	3-60	0-0	1-13
0-0	6-69	1-3	6-48	0-0	2-25	0-0	4-77	0-0	5-47	0-0	0-0	0-0	3-60	DNP		0-0	2-30
DNP		0-0	5-59	0-0	3-12	0-0	4-33	0-0	4-51	0-0	5-57	0-0	3-30	0-0	6-92 (1 TD)	0-0	1-16

DETROIT LIONS

What is the run game outlook for 2022?

Detroit's top back, D'Andre Swift, ran for a mere 617 yards in 13 games last season, but still finished the year as the overall RB15, and as RB10 in fantasy PPG. What makes Swift so valuable is his pass-catching volume. With 6, he tied Leonard Fournette for most targets per game among RBs last year, and his total of 62 receptions was fourth best on the season. Swift eclipsed 1,000 yards last year, with 452 coming from receiving. For PPR leagues Swift's value is considerable as 42% of his total yards comes from receiving, adding an immediate fantasy boost in PPR leagues.

Jamaal Williams also played only 13 games last year. Williams and Swift totaled almost identical rushing lines last season (Williams 151-617-2, Swift 153-603-3), but the real difference between the backs is receiving. Williams caught just 26 passes for 157 yards and 0 TDs. Williams will still take a cut of the ground work this year, but Swift should see some increase in all areas, while a 27-year-old Williams will see a little decrease. Swift will vie for top-10 fantasy status, while Williams will only be viable if Swift misses time. And there's a slew of backups waiting for their chance.

Is this a breakout year for sophomore Amon-Ra St. Brown?

St. Brown averaged 24.9 fantasy PPG in his last six games last year. Two of those efforts were behind the arm of backup QB Tim Boyle, one of the league's worst. If St. Brown could have put a whole season together maintaining that average, he would have finished as WR2, behind Super Bowl Champion Cooper Kupp.

St. Brown's sudden emergence directly corresponded with Detroit's ability to compete last year, as his first game in the breakout stretch — a 29-27 contest with Minnesota — came with their first win of the season. The Lions would go on to win two of their next five games, and St. Brown would cap his rookie year with 33.4 and 26.1 fantasy point performances against

'St. Brown would cap his rookie year with 33.4 and 26.1 fantasy point performances.'

Seattle and Green Bay respectively.

St. Brown's late season improvement, combined with his ability to sustain that level of performance through the end of the campaign, is the best indicator he may very well continue at this level of performance. Detroit has a relatively soft early schedule and a Week 6 bye, so if St. Brown comes out the gate running, he could carry a high-value confidence deep into 2022.

There will be plenty of competition for targets, especially when rookie Jameson Williams is fully recovered from his ACL tear. And T.J. Hockenson will draw his fair cut of target percentage. But St. Brown is the clear No. 1, and has the chance to finish the year as a top-20 (or better) WR.

2022/23 SCHEDULE				2021 FANTASY POINTS ALLOWED BY OPPONENT VS LEAGUE AVERAGE			
WK	DATE	TIME	OPP	QB	RB	WR	TE
1	9/11	1:00	PHI	-1%	10%	-17%	46%
2	9/18	1:00	WAS	29%	-3%	8%	5%
3	9/25	1:00	@MIN	6%	2%	23%	-13%
4	10/02	1:00	SEA	2%	-8%	3%	-23%
5	10/09	1:00	@NE	-8%	-19%	1%	-20%
6	BYE WEEK						
7	10/23	1:00	@DAL	-6%	-14%	2%	5%
8	10/30	1:00	MIA	-6%	-4%	-2%	6%
9	11/06	1:00	GB	5%	-13%	3%	0%
10	11/13	1:00	@CHI	4%	-7%	0%	-28%
11	11/20	1:00	@NYG	12%	40%	-2%	22%
12	11/24	12.30	BUF	-34%	-11%	-27%	-34%
13	12/04	1:00	JAC	4%	-1%	5%	-2%
14	12/11	1:00	MIN	6%	2%	23%	-13%
15	12/18	1:00	@NYJ	-4%	11%	-1%	-1%
16	12/24	1:00	@CAR	-6%	-12%	-7%	-5%
17	1/01	1:00	CHI	4%	-7%	0%	-28%
18	1/08	TBD	@GB	5%	-13%	3%	0%

2022 NFL DRAFT					
RD	PK		POS	COLLEGE	HT	WT
1	2	AIDAN HUTCHINSON	EDGE	MICHIGAN	6-6	265
1	12	JAMESON WILLIAMS	WR	OHIO STATE	6-2	189
2	14	JOSH PASCHAL	EDGE	KENTUCKY	6-3	278
3	33	KERBY JOSEPH	S	ILLINOIS	6-1	200
5	34	JAMES MITCHELL	TE	VIRGINIA TECH	6-3	255
6	9	MALCOLM RODRIGUEZ	LB	OKLAHOMA STATE	5-11	225
6	39	JAMES HOUSTON	LB	JACKSON STATE	6-1	225
7	16	CHARLES LUCAS	CB	ARIZONA STATE	6-0	185

2021 WEEKLY STATS

*RUSH STATS : *REC STATS	SF (L) 33-41		@ GB (L) 17-35		BAL (L) 17-19		@ CHI (L) 14-24		@ MIN (L) 17-19		CIN (L) 11-34		@ LAR (L) 19-28		PHI (L) 6-44	
QB JARED GOFF	38-57 338 (1 INT) (3 TD) 3-14		26-36 246 (1 INT) (2 TD) 4-46		22-30 217 1-4		24-38 299 (2 TD) 3-8		21-35 203 (1 INT) 0-0		28-42 202 (1 INT) 1-1		22-36 268 (2 INT) (1 TD) 1-3		25-34 222 0-0	
RB D'ANDRE SWIFT	11-39	8-65 (1 TD)	8-37	4-41	14-47 (1 TD)	7-60	8-16	4-33	11-51 (1 TD)	6-53	13-24 (1 TD)	5-43	13-48	8-96 (1 TD)	12-27	5-24
RB JAMAAL WILLIAMS	9-54 (1 TD)	8-56	7-25	3-12	12-42 (1 TD)	2-25	14-66	0-0	13-57	2-8	4-11	1-[-2]	12-57	0-0	DNP	
WR AMON-RA ST. BROWN	0-0	2-23	0-0	3-18	0-0	1-2	0-0	6-70	0-0	7-65	0-0	5-26	0-0	0-0	0-0	3-46
WR KALIF RAYMOND	1-9	3-50	0-0	2-18	0-0	6-68	0-0	3-46 (2 TD)	0-0	0-0	0-0	6-37	1-1	6-115	0-0	0-0
TE T.J. HOCKENSON	0-0	8-97 (1 TD)	0-0	8-66 (1 TD)	0-0	2-10	0-0	4-42	0-0	2-22	0-0	8-74	0-0	6-48	0-0	10-89

2021 Stats

Record: 3-13-1
Rushing Rank: 19th
Passing Rank: 19th
Offensive Fantasy Pts: 20th
Against Run: 28th
Against Pass: 23rd
ppg Against: 27.5
ppg: 19.1

KEY ADDITIONS & NEW CONTRACTS

QB **DAVID BLOUGH**: RE-SIGNED ON A ONE-YEAR, $1.35 MILLION DEAL.

QB **TIM BOYLE**: RE-SIGNED ON A ONE-YEAR, $2 MILLION DEAL THAT INCLUDES $1.75 MILLION GUARANTEED.

WR **DJ CHARK JR.**: SIGNED A ONE-YEAR, $10 MILLION DEAL THAT IS FULLY GUARANTEED.

WR **KALIF RAYMOND**: RE-SIGNED ON A TWO-YEAR DEAL.

WR **JOSH REYNOLDS**: RE-SIGNED ON A TWO-YEAR DEAL WITH A MAX VALUE OF $12 MILLION.

TE **GARRETT GRIFFIN**: SIGNED DEAL.

C/OG **EVAN BROWN**: RE-SIGNED ON A ONE-YEAR, $2.025 MILLION DEAL ($600,000 GUARANTEED) WITH A MAXIMUM VALUE OF $3.025 MILLION INCLUDING INCENTIVES.

DE **CHARLES HARRIS**: RE-SIGNED ON A TWO-YEAR, $14 MILLION DEAL.

LB **ALEX ANZALONE**: RE-SIGNED ON A ONE-YEAR, $2.25 MILLION DEAL ($1.75 MILLION GUARANTEED) WITH A MAXIMUM VALUE OF $4 MILLION INCLUDING INCENTIVES.

LB **CHRIS BOARD**: AGREED TO TERMS ON ONE-YEAR DEAL.

LB **JARRAD DAVIS**: SIGNED A FREE-AGENT CONTRACT.

CB **MIKE HUGHES**: SIGNED A FREE-AGENT CONTRACT.

S **DESHON ELLIOTT**: SIGNING A ONE-YEAR DEAL.

S **TRACY WALKER**: RE-SIGNED ON A THREE-YEAR, $25 MILLION DEAL THAT INCLUDES $17 MILLION GUARANTEED.

DB **C.J. MOORE**: RE-SIGNED ON A ONE-YEAR DEAL WORTH UP TO $2.4 MILLION WITH $800,000 GUARANTEED.

Is this a put up or shut up year for Jared Goff?

Back for his second year as the Lions QB, Goff had a rough go in his first effort in Detroit. After a disappointing 0-9 start, which included two, two-point losses and a 38-point blowout, Goff led his Lions to a 16-16 tie against Pittsburgh last season, and the fans celebrated as if they had won the title. It would be Week 13 before Detroit secured the first of their three wins on the year, with a two-point victory over Minnesota.

Goff finish the year with the 24th best QB rating, 3,245 yards, and 19 TDs — his worst marks in any season — excluding his seven-game effort in 2016.

There was improvement last year in the home stretch, partially attributed to two major factors. First, head coach Dan Campbell assumed play-calling duties halfway through the season, from then offensive coordinator Anthony Lynn. Campbell's slightly-less-conservative approach gave a boost to Goff's league-low average depth of throw (among qualified QBs) of 6.6 yards. Under Campbell's scheme the mark jumped to 7.4, which is still a bottom-half number, but is a considerable upgrade when trying to get the ball downfield.

Also contributing to the late-season improvement was the development of, and chemistry with, emerging WR Amon-Ra St. Brown. When throwing to St. Brown, Goff's QB rating improved to 104.0, top-20 among qualified QB/WR tandems last year. Behind the arm of Goff, St. Brown amassed 401 receiving yards in his final five games, and finished his season 3-2-1.

This is, no doubt, a put-up-or-shut-up year for Goff. With a solid receiving corps, including St. Brown, newly signed DJ Chark, rookie Jameson Williams, TE T.J. Hockenson, and pass-friendly RB D'Andre Swift (not to mention Jamaal Williams and Josh Reynolds), Goff certainly has his choice of quality targets. The offensive line in Detroit is one of the best in the league, so time for excuses is over. Goff either wins enough games this season to prove he's starting QB material or he loses enough so the Lions have a good draft pick to find a replacement. Either way, Goff remains unworthy of a fantasy draft pick.

KEY LOSSES

WR **KHADAREL HODGE** (FALCONS)

DT **NICK WILLIAMS**

LB **TREY FLOWERS**

LB **JALEN REEVES-MAYBIN** (TEXANS)

S **DEAN MARLOWE** (FALCONS)

DEPTH CHART

QB1	JARED GOFF
QB2	TIM BOYLE
RB1	D'ANDRE SWIFT
RB2	JAMAAL WILLIAMS
RB3	CRAIG REYNOLDS
WR1	AMON-RA ST. BROWN
WR2	DJ CHARK JR. **N**
WR3	JAMESON WILLIAMS **R**
WR4	JOSH REYNOLDS
TE1	T.J. HOCKENSON
TE2	GARRETT GRIFFIN **N**
K	AUSTIN SEIBERT

2021 WEEKLY STATS

@ PIT (TIE) 16-16		@ CLE (L) 10-13		CHI (L) 14-16		MIN (W) 29-27		@ DEN (L) 10-38		ARI (W) 30-12		@ ATL (L) 16-20		@ SEA (L) 29-51		GB (W) 37-30	
14-25 114		DNP		21-25 171 (2 TD)		25-41 296 (1 INT) (3 TD)		24-39 215 (1 INT) (1 TD)		21-26 216 (3 TD)		DNP		DNP		21-30 238 (2 TD)	
0-0				0-0		2-1		2-10		0-0						0-0	
33-130	3-5	14-136 (1 TD)	3-0	3-0	3-9	DNP		DNP		DNP		DNP		4-32	2-7	7-30 (1 TD)	4-16
DNP		7-11	0-0	15-65	5-18	17-71	1-9	DNP		DNP		19-77	0-0	11-22 (1 TD)	3-22	13-43	1-9
0-0	4-61	0-0	4-18	0-0	4-23	1-2	10-86 (1 TD)	0-0	8-73	1-5	8-90 (1 TD)	2-19	9-91 (1 TD)	2-23 (1 TD)	8-111 (1 TD)	1-12	8-109 (1 TD)
0-0	4-29	0-0	0-0	0-0	3-16	0-0	2-33	0-0	4-31 (1 TD)	0-0	2-20	1-5	3-12	DNP		1-13	4-101 (1 TD)
0-0	0-0	0-0	6-51	0-0	3-35 (1 TD)	0-0	4-49 (1 TD)	DNP		DNP		DNP		DNP		DNP	

GREEN BAY PACKERS

Has the Green Bay backfield turned into a committee?

We are as bullish as we've been in recent years on Aaron Jones' potential for 2022. If you compare the overall stats for Jones and A.J. Dillon, you would think that their workload is more evenly distributed than it actually is. The truth is that Aaron Jones was clearly the lead back last season before suffering a knee injury in Week 10.

Before his injury, Jones saw one-and-a-half times more carries than Dillon and played exactly twice as many snaps. He also accounted for 64% of the team's premium backfield touches (carries inside the 10 and all receptions).

Green Bay seemed to rush Jones back into action and forced him to take a reduced workload. It's in Weeks 12-17 that Dillon was the lead back. But when it mattered most, in the divisional round of the playoffs against the 49ers, Jones stepped back into his feature-back role. He recorded 64% of the team's carries, and caught 9 passes for 129 yards.

With Adams gone, Jones should see an uptick in targets. During his games without Adams over the past two seasons, Jones has seen an increase of over 2 targets per games.

We're out on believing this is a committee. But we are in on believing Dillon is a great insurance play that has some flex appeal. Unfortunately, Dillon's current ADP is more indicative of hoping Green Bay turns into a two-headed monster, which shouldn't be the case. Dillon is a little to pricey for our liking.

With the stat sheet wide open, what receiver should we target in drafts?

Some combination of Allen Lazard, Sammy Watkins, Randall Cobb, rookie Christian Watson, and Robert Tonyan will fill the role vacated by Adams. Rodgers has already said that Lazard will start the year as his No. 1 receiver. And we are buying plenty of shares of Lazard at his current ADP. It may not work out, but we're willing to risk a late-round pick on his upside.

Christian Watson is another option for Rodgers. Word out of the Green Bay camp is that he is already struggling with drops (but we saw that in Ja'marr Chase last season). Among his draft class, Watson was in the 97th percentile in catch radius, 98th percentile in speed score, and 95th percentile in burst score. We'll see if he can earn the trust of Rodgers as the season progresses.

Finally, the only other possibly relevant fantasy option is TE Robert Tonyan. Tonyan, who tore his ACL in Week 8 last season, may not be ready to play by Week 1, though. His best, and only fantasy attribute is his red zone work. Though his 11 TDs in 2020 were extremely lucky, he did lead all TEs except for Kelce in targets inside the 10 last season. We're not convinced Tonyan is a worthwhile pick, but perhaps you'll be lucky and start him the week he posts 3-27, and 2 TDs.

2022/23 SCHEDULE / 2021 FANTASY POINTS ALLOWED BY OPPONENT VS LEAGUE AVERAGE

WK	DATE	TIME	OPP	QB	RB	WR	TE
1	9/11	4:25	@MIN	6%	2%	23%	-13%
2	9/18	8:20	CHI	4%	-7%	0%	-28%
3	9/25	4:25	@TB	3%	-4%	3%	4%
4	10/02	4:25	NE	-8%	-19%	1%	-20%
5	10/09	9:30AM	NYG*	12%	40%	-2%	22%
6	10/16	1:00	NYJ	-4%	11%	-1%	-1%
7	10/23	1:00	@WAS	29%	-3%	8%	5%
8	10/30	8:20	@BUF	-34%	-11%	-27%	-34%
9	11/06	1:00	@DET	4%	14%	2%	17%
10	11/13	4:25	DAL	-6%	-14%	2%	5%
11	11/17	8:15	TEN	3%	-22%	19%	-29%
12	11/27	8:20	@PHI	-1%	10%	-17%	46%
13	12/04	1:00	@CHI	4%	-7%	0%	-28%
14	BYE WEEK						
15	12/19	8:15	LAR	-12%	-8%	7%	-2%
16	12/25	1:00	@MIA	-6%	-4%	-2%	6%
17	1/01	4:25	MIN	6%	2%	23%	-13%
18	1/08	TBD	DET	4%	14%	2%	17%

*PLAYED IN LONDON

2022 NFL DRAFT

RD	PK		POS	COLLEGE	HT	WT
1	22	QUAY WALKER	LB	GEORGIA	6-4	240
1	28	DEVONTE WYATT	DT	GEORGIA	6-3	315
2	2	CHRISTIAN WATSON	WR	NORTH DAKOTA STATE	6-5	208
3	28	SEAN RHYAN	G	UCLA	6-5	320
4	27	ROMEO DOUBS	WR	NEVADA	6-2	200
4	35	ZACH TOM	C	WAKE FOREST	6-5	295
5	36	KINGSLEY ENAGBARE	LB	SOUTH CAROLINA	6-4	265
7	7	TARIQ CARPENTER	LB	GEORGIA TECH	6-4	225
7	13	JONATHAN FORD	DT	MIAMI	6-5	315
7	28	RASHEED WALKER	OT	PENN STATE	6-6	325
7	37	SAMOURI TOURE	WR	NEBRASKA	6-3	190

2021 WEEKLY STATS

*RUSH STATS : *REC STATS	@ NO (L) 3-38		DET (W) 35-17		@ SF (W) 30-28		PIT (W) 27-17		@ CIN (W) 25-22		@ CHI (W) 24-14		WAS (W) 24-10		@ ARI (W) 24-21	
QB AARON RODGERS	15-28 133 (2 INT) 0-0		22-27 255 (4 TD) 4-6		23-33 261 (2 TD) 0-0		20-36 248 (2 TD) 3-2 (1 TD)		27-39 344 (1 INT) (2 TD) 0-0		17-23 195 (2 TD) 7-19 (1 TD)		27-35 274 (3 TD) 2-17		22-37 184 (2 TD) 2-3	
RB AARON JONES	5-9	2-13	17-67 (1 TD)	6-48 (3 TD)	19-82 (1 TD)	2-14	15-48	3-51	14-103	4-6	13-76	4-34 (1 TD)	6-19	5-20	15-59 (1 TD)	7-51
RB AJ DILLON	4-19	1-7	5-18	1-8	6-18	2-8	15-81	1-16	8-30	4-49 (1 TD)	11-59	0-0	3-6	1-2	16-78	0-0
WR DAVANTE ADAMS	0-0	5-56	0-0	8-121	0-0	12-132 (1 TD)	0-0	6-64	0-0	11-206 (1 TD)	0-0	4-89	0-0	6-76 (1 TD)	DNP	
WR ALLEN LAZARD	0-0	2-16	0-0	0-0	0-0	1-42	0-0	2-33	0-0	2-6	0-0	3-27 (1 TD)	0-0	5-60 (1 TD)	DNP	
WR RANDALL COBB	1-1	1-32	0-0	3-26	0-0	0-0	0-0	5-69 (2 TD)	0-0	2-30	0-0	0-0	0-0	3-22	0-0	3-15 (2 TD)
WR M. VALDES-SCANTLING	0-0	3-17	0-0	0-0	0-0	3-59 (1 TD)	0-0	0-0	DNP		DNP		DNP		DNP	
TE JOSIAH DEGUARA	0-0	0-0	DNP		0-0	1-4	0-0	0-0	0-0	0-0	0-0	1-4	0-0	0-0	0-0	2-20
TE ROBERT TONYAN	0-0	2-8	0-0	3-52 (1 TD)	0-0	1-6	0-0	2-8	0-0	1-8	0-0	2-10	0-0	4-63 (1	0-0	3-49

Fantasy TAKEOVER

2021 Stats
Record: 13–4
Rushing Rank: 18th
Passing Rank: 9th
Offensive Fantasy Pts: 7th
Against Run: 11th
Against Pass: 13th
ppg Against: 21.3
ppg: 25.6

KEY ADDITIONS & NEW CONTRACTS

QB **AARON RODGERS**: SIGNED AN EXTENSION THAT PAYS $150.815 MILLION OVER THE NEXT THREE YEARS, WITH $101.515 MILLION FULLY GUARANTEED. THE NEW DEAL DROPS HIS 2022 SALARY CAP HIT BY ABOUT $18 MILLION.

WR **ALLEN LAZARD**: RECEIVING SECOND-ROUND RESTRICTED FREE AGENT TENDER WORTH $3.986 MILLION.

WR **SAMMY WATKINS**: SIGNED A ONE-YEAR, $4 MILLION DEAL.

TE **ROBERT TONYAN**: RE-SIGNED ON A ONE-YEAR, $3.75 MILLION CONTRACT WITH A MAX VALUE OF $5.5 MILLION.

LB **DE'VONDRE CAMPBELL**: RE-SIGNED ON A FIVE-YEAR DEAL WORTH $50 MILLION.

LB **PRESTON SMITH**: SIGNED A FOUR-YEAR EXTENSION WORTH $52.5 MILLION IN NEW MONEY. IN ALL, SMITH GETS MORE THAN $65 MILLION OVER FIVE YEARS WITH A CHANCE TO MAKE $71 MILLION.

DT **JARRAN REED**: SIGNED A FREE-AGENT CONTRACT.

CB **JAIRE ALEXANDER**: SIGNED A FOUR-YEAR, $84 MILLION EXTENSION THAT WILL PAY HIM $31 MILLION IN YEAR 1.

CB **RASUL DOUGLAS**: SIGNED A THREE-YEAR DEAL WORTH $21 MILLION WITH A MAX VALUE OF $25.5 MILLION.

CB **KEISEAN NIXON**: SIGNED A FREE-AGENT CONTRACT.

P **PAT O'DONNELL**: SIGNED WITH THE PACKERS.

With the departure of Davante Adams, is Aaron Rodgers still a top-10 fantasy QB?

The offense in Green Bay is going to look a lot different without Davante Adams, who accounted for 38% of the team's air yards and 33% of the targets for the last two seasons. Despite the slow-paced, mostly balanced offense in Green Bay, Rodgers has been able to turn in some pretty good fantasy campaigns, including top-five finishes the past two seasons. And he's done this in spite of continuing to record career lows in rushing yards.

Adams' absence isn't the only thing that's different in this offense for 2022. Adam Stanovich, last year's run-game coordinator, will be the team's new offensive coordinator, as Nathaniel Hackett is now the head coach in Denver. Stanovich has hinted at deploying a faster-paced offense, that could lean a little bit more on the run.

While Green Bay's 61.2% pass-play rate in non-garbage time situations is 16th in the league, they hold the third highest pass-play rate (58%) when leading. Green Bay also had the fifth-most pass attempts inside the 10-yard line last season. The departure of Davante Adams and the new offensive scheme could reduce these numbers. Also, Rodgers had the highest completion rate over expected of any QB in the league for the last two seasons, much of which can be attributed to Adams.

Rodgers has played three games without Adams in the past two seasons. Last year in Week 8 without Adams, Rodgers had the fifth-lowest completion rate over expected, throwing for an uninspired 184 yards and 2 TDs. But in the two games in 2020 without Adams, Rodgers threw 7 TDs, which gives us hope for this season.

While, we are no longer expecting MVP numbers, Rodgers should still be a serviceable fantasy QB in 2022. Even if we're unsure who emerges as his new favorite target, He should put up enough points to justify his top-10 QB ADP. We Have Rodgers and Russell Wilson in the same tier this season.

KEY LOSSES

WR **DAVANTE ADAMS** (TRADED TO RAIDERS)

WR **EQUANIMEOUS ST. BROWN** (BEARS)

WR **MARQUEZ VALDES-SCANTLING** (CHIEFS)

OT **DENNIS KELLY** (COLTS)

OG **LUCAS PATRICK** (BEARS)

OL **BILLY TURNER** (BRONCOS)

DE **WHITNEY MERCILUS** (RETIRED)

DL **TYLER LANCASTER**

LB **OREN BURKS** (49ERS)

LB **ZA'DARIUS SMITH** (VIKINGS)

CB **KEVIN KING**

CB **CHANDON SULLIVAN** (VIKINGS)

P **COREY BOJORQUEZ** (BROWNS)

DEPTH CHART

QB1	AARON RODGERS
QB2	JORDAN LOVE
RB1	AARON JONES
RB2	AJ DILLON
RB3	KYLIN HILL
WR1	ALLEN LAZARD
WR2	RANDALL COBB
WR3	SAMMY WATKINS **N**
WR4	CHRISTIAN WATSON **R**
TE1	ROBERT TONYAN
TE2	JOSIAH DEGUARA
K	MASON CROSBY

2021 WEEKLY STATS

KC (L) 7-13		SEA (W) 17-0		@ MIN (L) 31-34		LAR (W) 36-28		CHI (W) 45-30		@ BAL (W) 31-30		CLE (W) 24-33		MIN (W) 37-10		@ DET (L) 30-37	
DNP		23-37 292 (1 INT) 2-8		23-33 385 (4 TD) 2-21		28-45 307 (2 TD) 2-0 (1 TD)		29-37 341 (4 TD) 1-0		23-31 268 (3 TD) 4-11		24-34 202 (3 TD) 1-1-1		29-38 288 (2 TD) 2-8		14-18 138 (2 TD) 1-7	
12-53	0-0	7-25	4-61	DNP		10-23	0-0	5-35 (1 TD)	3-30 (1 TD)	13-58	2-12 (1 TD)	12-66	5-21	8-76	5-30	DNP	
8-46	4-44	21-66 (2 TD)	2-62	11-53	6-44	20-69	5-21 (1 TD)	15-71	0-0	7-22 (1 TD)	1-13	9-41	3-15	14-63 (2 TD)	2-20	14-63	1-4
0-0	6-42	0-0	7-78	0-0	7-115 (2 TD)	0-0	8-104	0-0	10-121 (2 TD)	0-0	6-44 (1 TD)	0-0	10-114 (2 TD)	0-0	11-136 (1 TD)	0-0	6-55
0-0	1-20 (1 TD)	0-0	1-6	DNP		0-0	2-13	1-14	6-75 (1 TD)	1-5	2-23	1-13	2-45 (1 TD)	0-0	6-72 (1 TD)	0-0	5-75 (2 TD)
0-0	3-50	0-0	3-21	0-0	1-15	0-0	4-95 (1 TD)	DNP		DNP		DNP		DNP		DNP	
0-0	2-19	0-0	1-41	0-0	4-123 (1 TD)	0-0	4-50	0-0	3-20	0-0	5-98 (1 TD)	0-0	2-5	0-0	1-3	0-0	0-0
0-0	2-16	0-0	2-9	0-0	2-37 (1 TD)	0-0	2-13	0-0	3-44	0-0	3-16	0-0	2-5	0-0	2-11	0-0	3-66 (1 TD)
0-0	0-0	DNP		DNP		DNP		DNP		DNP		DNP		DNP		DNP	

HOUSTON TEXANS

Besides Brandin Cooks, is there a WR in Houston worth considering?

Rookie John Metchie III (second round, Alabama) has some serious promise and may be another receiver on Houston's roster worth taking a look at in the future. But he may not be fantasy relevant this season. He tore his ACL in the SEC championship game, and then was recently diagnosed with the most treatable form of Leukemia and won't play this season.

The only other receiving option worth considering is Nico Collins. He saw plenty of deep looks and end zone targets, but could never put it all together. He is undraftable for now but is worth keeping and eye on early.

Brandin Cooks, on the other hand, is Houston's one shining star. Underrated on a yearly basis, Cooks has continued to outperform his ADP, regardless of which team he's is playing for or the team's relevance. Last season, he was WR20 on the year, but top 13 in targets and receptions. He averaged 14.5 fantasy PPG, and Cooks could be a middle-to-late round steal again this season. He's a prime example of a good fantasy player who's underrated because he plays on a terrible NFL team.

> *Underrated on a yearly basis, Cooks has continued to outperform his ADP, regardless of which team he's is playing for or the team's relevance.*

What does the run game look like in Houston this year?

Last season the Texans were the league's worst all-around rushing unit. They were last in yards per carry, 24th in yards after contact, and 31st in total rushing yards. This is not for lack of trying. They continued to run the ball despite their inefficiency, posting 377 carries (13th most in the league). The committee approach, with a lack of talent and below-average blocking, was a bad combination for success.

It appears the Texans may try a similar committee approach this season with Marlon Mack, Rex Burkhead, and Dameon Pierce. Because of the low expectations in Houston after the team's terrible outing in 2021, Houston can try to sort out the run game out on their own terms, without pressure.

This provides the rookie Pierce with the biggest upside as Houston tries to figure out the future of the team. Don't draft him with unrealistic expectations, though, because he may never get enough work to make him a fantasy contender, but he's worth a look in later rounds or on waivers as the season progresses.

2022/23 SCHEDULE — 2021 FANTASY POINTS ALLOWED BY OPPONENT VS LEAGUE AVERAGE

WK	DATE	TIME	OPP	QB	RB	WR	TE
1	9/11	1:00	IND	2%	-12%	4%	23%
2	9/18	4:25	@DEN	-10%	-9%	-6%	-29%
3	9/25	1:00	@CHI	4%	-7%	0%	-28%
4	10/02	1:00	LAC	2%	17%	-11%	23%
5	10/09	1:00	@JAC	4%	-1%	5%	-2%
6	BYE WEEK						
7	10/23	4:05	@LV	1%	10%	-14%	39%
8	10/30	4:05	TEN	3%	-22%	19%	-29%
9	11/03	8:15	PHI	-1%	10%	-17%	46%
10	11/13	1:00	@NYG	12%	40%	-2%	22%
11	11/20	1:00	WAS	29%	-3%	8%	5%
12	11/27	1:00	@MIA	-6%	-4%	-2%	6%
13	12/04	1:00	CLE	-5%	-5%	-6%	2%
14	12/11	1:00	@DAL	-6%	-14%	2%	5%
15	12/18	1:00	KC	15%	4%	3%	2%
16	12/24	1:00	@TEN	3%	-22%	19%	-29%
17	1/01	1:00	JAC	4%	-1%	5%	-2%
18	1/08	TBD	@IND	2%	-12%	4%	23%

2022 NFL DRAFT

RD	PK		POS	COLLEGE	HT	WT
1	3	DEREK STINGLEY JR.	CB	LSU	6-1	190
1	15	KENYON GREEN	G	TEXAS A&M	6-4	325
2	5	JALEN PITRE	S	BAYLOR	6-0	197
2	12	JOHN METCHIE III	WR	ALABAMA	6-0	195
3	11	CHRISTIAN HARRIS	LB	ALABAMA	6-2	232
4	2	DAMEON PIERCE	RB	FLORIDA	5-10	215
5	7	THOMAS BOOKER	DT	STANFORD	6-4	309
5	27	TEAGAN QUITORIANO	TE	OREGON STATE	6-6	259
6	27	AUSTIN DECULUS	OT	LSU	6-6	345

2021 WEEKLY STATS

*RUSH STATS : *REC STATS	JAC (W) 37-21		@ CLE (L) 21-31		CAR (L) 9-24		@ BUF (L) 0-40		NE (L) 22-25		@ IND (L) 3-31		@ ARI (L) 5-31		LAR (L) 22-38	
QB DAVIS MILLS	DNP		8-18 102 (1 TD) 2-[-1]		19-28 168 (1 TD) 1-0		11-21 87 (4 INT) 1-2		21-29 312 (3 TD) 1-2		29-43 243 (2 INT) 2-5		23-32 135 0-0		29-38 310 (1 INT) (2 TD) 0-0	
QB TYROD TAYLOR	21-33 291 (2 TD) 4-40		10-11 125 (1 TD) 1-15 (1 TD)		DNP		DNP		DNP		DNP		DNP		DNP	
RB REX BURKHEAD	0-0	1-6	0-0	0-0	0-0	1-5	1-[-1]	0-0	DNP		0-0	0-0	0-0	0-0	4-21 (1 TD)	3-27
RB DAVID JOHNSON	3-10	3-18 (1 TD)	6-25	2-22	2-11	0-0	5-21	3-27	2-5	5-46	2-7	1-14	7-25	5-27	2-4	1-[-1]
RB MARK INGRAM II	26-85 (1 TD)	0-0	14-41	1-[-1]	6-21	1-[-1]	6-24	0-0	16-41	0-0	18-73	2-8	6-9	3-18	DNP	
WR BRANDIN COOKS	0-0	5-132	0-0	9-78 (1 TD)	1-5	9-112	0-0	5-47	0-0	3-23	0-0	9-89	0-0	5-21	0-0	6-83 (1 TD)
WR NICO COLLINS	0-0	1-7	0-0	1-32	DNP		DNP		DNP		0-0	4-44	0-0	2-28	0-0	4-55

2021 Stats

Record: 4–13
Rushing Rank: 32nd
Passing Rank: 26th
Offensive Fantasy Pts: 30th
Against Run: 31st
Against Pass: 20th
ppg Against: 26.6
ppg: 16.5

KEY ADDITIONS & NEW CONTRACTS

QB JEFF DRISKEL: RE-SIGNED ON A ONE-YEAR CONTRACT.

QB KYLE ALLEN: SIGNED A ONE-YEAR CONTRACT.

QB KEVIN HOGAN: SIGNED A FREE-AGENT DEAL WITH HOUSTON.

RB ROYCE FREEMAN: RE-SIGNED TO A ONE-YEAR CONTRACT.

RB MARLON MACK: SIGNED A ONE-YEAR DEAL WORTH $2 MILLION WITH $250,000 GUARANTEED.

RB DARE OGUNBOWALE: SIGNED A TWO-YEAR, $3.3 MILLION DEAL.

FB ANDY JANOVICH: SIGNED A ONE-YEAR CONTRACT.

WR CHAD BEEBE: SIGNED A FREE-AGENT CONTRACT.

WR CHRIS CONLEY: RE-SIGNED ON A ONE-YEAR, $2 MILLION CONTRACT THAT INCLUDES $750,000 GUARANTEED.

WR BRANDIN COOKS: SIGNED A TWO-YEAR, $39.6 MILLION EXTENSION WITH $36 MILLION IN GUARANTEES.

WR DAESEAN HAMILTON: SIGNED A FREE-AGENT CONTRACT.

TE PHARAOH BROWN: SIGNED TO A ONE-YEAR CONTRACT WORTH UP TO $4 MILLION.

OT CEDRIC OGBUEHI: SIGNED A ONE-YEAR DEAL.

OL JUSTIN BRITT: RE-SIGNED ON A CONTRACT.

OL A.J. CANN: AGREED TO A TWO-YEAR, $10.5 MILLION DEAL WITH $4.5 MILLION GUARANTEED.

DE MARIO ADDISON: SIGNED A FREE-AGENT DEAL.

DE RASHEEM GREEN: SIGNED A ONE-YEAR CONTRACT.

DE JERRY HUGHES: SIGNED A FREE-AGENT DEAL.

DT MALIEK COLLINS: RE-SIGNED ON A TWO-YEAR, $17 MILLION DEAL WITH $8.5 MILLION GUARANTEED.

LB BLAKE CASHMAN: ACQUIRED IN A TRADE WITH THE NEW YORK JETS IN EXCHANGE FOR A 2023 SIXTH-ROUND PICK.

LB KAMU GRUGIER-HILL: RE-SIGNED TO A ONE-YEAR, $4 MILLION DEAL.

LB NEVILLE HEWITT: RE-SIGNED TO A ONE-YEAR DEAL.

LB CHRISTIAN KIRKSEY: RE-SIGNED ON A TWO-YEAR, $10 MILLION CONTRACT THAT INCLUDES $4 MILLION GUARANTEED.

LB OGBO OKORONKWO: SIGNED A FREE-AGENT CONTRACT.

LB JALEN REEVES-MAYBIN: SIGNED A TWO-YEAR, $7.5 MILLION DEAL WITH $5 MILLION GUARANTEED AT SIGNING. THE DEAL IS WORTH UP TO $9 MILLION WITH INCENTIVES.

CB FABIAN MOREAU: SIGNED WITH THE TEXANS.

CB STEVEN NELSON: SIGNED A FREE-AGENT DEAL.

S TERRANCE BROOKS: RE-SIGNED ON A ONE-YEAR, $2 MILLION DEAL.

S M.J. STEWART: SIGNED A ONE-YEAR, $3 MILLION CONTRACT.

DB DESMOND KING: RE-SIGNED A TWO-YEAR, $7 MILLION DEAL.

What will new head coach Lovie Smith do this year in Houston?

Promoted from defensive coordinator this offseason, Lovie Smith will assume head coaching duties. The veteran head coach was likely hired to tame the circus that Houston had turned into these past few seasons. This will be a tough assignment on a team in full-rebuild mode for a coach who hasn't had a winning season in years.

His last stint in the NFL was an 8-24 run with the Buccaneers, which resulted in Smith hitting the job market again at the end of 2015. He received the head coaching job at the University of Illinois, where he worked from 2016-20, posting a record of 17-39 with one bowl appearance, a loss.

The Texans also promoted the former QB coach, Pep Hamilton, to offensive coordinator. Both Hamilton and Davis Mills are products of the Stanford football program, so there's a familiarity in terminology and scheme.

The Texans only managed four wins last year, so the bar is set low for Smith and crew. And with Houston's tough schedule this season, he is likely the underdog in Vegas for every game. Their best chances for wins are Week 3 in Chicago and the two meetings with their divisional opponents, the Jaguars. As long as they can finish better than last year, Smith will have succeeded.

KEY LOSSES

QB **TYROD TAYLOR** (GIANTS)

QB **DESHAUN WATSON** (TRADED TO BROWNS)

RB **DAVID JOHNSON**

WR **DANNY AMENDOLA**

WR **DAESEAN HAMILTON**

TE **JORDAN AKINS** (GIANTS)

OT **MARCUS CANNON**

DE **JACOB MARTIN** (JETS)

CB **TERRANCE MITCHELL** (PATRIOTS)

S **JUSTIN REID** (CHIEFS)

DB **LONNIE JOHNSON** (TRADED TO CHIEFS)

DEPTH CHART

QB1	DAVIS MILLS
QB2	KYLE ALLEN **N**
RB1	MARLON MACK **N**
RB2	REX BURKHEAD
RB3	DAMEON PIERCE **R**
WR1	BRANDIN COOKS
WR2	NICO COLLINS
WR3	CHRIS CONLEY
WR4	PHILLIP DORSETT
TE1	BREVIN JORDAN
TE2	PHARAOH BROWN
K	KA'IMI FAIRBAIRN

2021 WEEKLY STATS

@ MIA (L) 9-17		@ TEN (W) 22-13		NYJ (L) 14-21		IND (L) 0-31		SEA (L) 13-33		@ JAC (W) 30-16		LAC (W) 41-29		@ SF (L) 7-23		TEN (L) 25-28	
DNP		DNP		DNP		6-14 49 2-11		33-49 331 (1 TD) 2-8		19-30 209 (1 INT) (2 TD) 1-2		21-27 254 (2 TD) 1-(-1)		21-32 163 (1 INT) (1 TD) 1-4		23-33 301 (3 TD) 4-12	
24-43 240 (3 INT) 3-23		14-24 107 6-28 (2 TD)		17-26 158 (1 INT) (2 TD) 2-30		5-13 45 (1 INT) 3-15		DNP		DNP		DNP		DNP		DNP	
2-9	0-0	18-40	0-0	12-27	3-27	8-30	1-15	11-40	4-26	16-41	1-6	22-149 (2TD)	2-0	16-47	6-32	12-24	3-42
4-11	3-29	13-18	3-16	10-39	2-16	DNP		DNP		6-24	1-3	DNP		DNP		5-28	3-8
DNP		DNP		DNP		DNP		DNP		DNP		DNP		DNP		DNP	
0-0	6-56	0-0	2-18	0-0	3-45 (1 TD)	1-16	3-38	0-0	8-101	0-0	7-102 (2 TD)	DNP		0-0	7-66 (1 TD)	0-0	3-26
0-0	3-25	0-0	1-9	0-0	2-28	0-0	0-0	0-0	5-69	0-0	2-14	0-0	3-33 (1 TD)	0-0	2-35	0-0	3-67

INDIANAPOLIS COLTS

Will the move to Indy revitalize Matt Ryan's career?

Matt Ryan was better last year at nearly every metric than Carson Wentz, except total TDs, rushing, and yards per game. These few measures were enough for Wentz to finish as QB14, while Ryan was QB18. Some of the differences can be attributed to the teams, rather than the QBs themselves. Indy, undoubtedly, had a better offense than Atlanta, and arguably better receiving options. For decision making, based on past stats and the eye-test, Ryan is a better QB, but he's also at the backend of his career.

Ryan has had some monster fantasy seasons, earned primarily with his passing yardage, which makes it all the more impressive. He finished as QB7 in 2014, and had QB2 finishes in 2016 and 2018. Since 2018, though, he has declined in production every year. Add in the fact that he's a pure pocket passer with few rushing attempts (40 for 82 yards and 1 TD in 2021), and you'll understand how he can throw for almost 4,000 yards and still finish as QB18.

Ryan won't have the overall passing volume in Indy as he had in Atlanta, so his ceiling will be lower. He'll now be playing on a run-heavy offense that boasted the overall RB1 last season. Ryan will be a solid QB for Indy, but a less solid QB for fantasy managers.

What will Michael Pittman Jr. do with Matt Ryan at the helm, and are there other fantasy-viable receivers in Indy?

Michael Pittman Jr. is established as the Colts' first option for the pass this season, and likely for several years to come. QB Matt Ryan should throw for more yards and do so more accurately than Carson Wentz did last year. Pittman shares elite company on a list of WRs with at least 25% of their team's targets and 30% of their team's air yards. Last season, only eight WRs were better in these two metrics: Cooper Kupp, Davante Adams, Justin Jefferson, and Stefon Diggs are four.

In his third year, Pittman is primed for a breakout — the talent and development

'Pittman is with elite company in a list of WRs with at least 25% of their team's targets and 30% of their team's air yards.'

is there, no doubt — but the one obstacle that may continue to hinder him is the run-first, give-the-ball-to-Jonathan-Taylor offensive mentality. Pittman is secure in the WR2 range, but without a flashy name he could slip below his actual value.

Other than Pittman, the other WRs in Indy are mere afterthoughts. Rookie Alec Pierce was selected in the second round and should see some on-field work right away. But unless Pittman misses time, Pierce is only viable in the deepest leagues for fantasy bench consideration.

2022/23 SCHEDULE				2021 FANTASY POINTS ALLOWED BY OPPONENT VS LEAGUE AVERAGE			
WK	DATE	TIME	OPP	QB	RB	WR	TE
1	9/11	1:00	@HOU	1%	13%	5%	13%
2	9/18	1:00	@JAC	4%	-1%	5%	-2%
3	9/25	1:00	KC	15%	4%	3%	2%
4	10/02	1:00	TEN	3%	-22%	19%	-29%
5	10/06	8:15	@DEN	-10%	-9%	-6%	-29%
6	10/16	1:00	JAC	4%	-1%	5%	-2%
7	10/23	1:00	@TEN	3%	-22%	19%	-29%
8	10/30	4:25	WAS	29%	-3%	8%	5%
9	11/06	1:00	@NE	-8%	-19%	1%	-20%
10	11/13	4:05	@LV	1%	10%	-14%	39%
11	11/20	1:00	PHI	-1%	10%	-17%	46%
12	11/28	8:15	PIT	-2%	11%	-3%	-10%
13	12/04	8:20	@DAL	-6%	-14%	2%	5%
14	BYE WEEK						
15	12/17	TBD	@MIN	6%	2%	23%	-13%
16	12/26	8:15	LAC	2%	17%	-11%	23%
17	1/01	1:00	@NYG	12%	40%	-2%	22%
18	1/08	TBD	HOU	1%	13%	5%	13%

2022 NFL DRAFT						
RD	PK		POS	COLLEGE	HT	WT
2	21	ALEC PIERCE	WR	CINCINNATI	6-3	213
3	9	JELANI WOODS	TE	VIRGINIA	6-7	265
3	13	BERNHARD RAIMANN	OT	CENTRAL MICHIGAN	6-7	305
3	32	NICK CROSS	S	MARYLAND	6-1	215
5	16	ERIC JOHNSON	DT	MISSOURI STATE	6-5	298
6	13	ANDREW OGLETREE	TE	YOUNGSTOWN STATE	6-7	250
6	38	CURTIS BROOKS	DT	CINCINNATI	6-2	285
7	18	RODNEY THOMAS II	S	YALE	6-1	200

2021 WEEKLY STATS

*RUSH STATS *REC STATS	SEA (L) 16-28		LAR (L) 24-27		@ TEN (L) 16-25		@ MIA (W) 27-17		@ BAL (L) 25-31		HOU (W) 31-3		@ SF (W) 30-18		TEN (L) 31-34	
QB CARSON WENTZ	25-38 251 (2 TD) 4-23		20-31 247 (1 INT) (1 TD) 5-37		19-37 194 0-0		24-32 228 (2 TD) 5-8		25-35 402 (2 TD) 2-5		11-20 223 (2 TD) 2-1		17-26 150 (2 TD) 4-23 (1 TD)		27-51 231 (2 INT) (3 TD) 3-11	
RB JONATHAN TAYLOR	17-56	6-60	15-51	1-2	10-64	1-8	16-103 (1 TD)	3-11	15-53 (1 TD)	3-116 (1 TD)	14-145 (2 TD)	1-13	18-107 (1 TD)	3-3	16-70 (1 TD)	3-52
RB NYHEIM HINES	9-34	6-48	1-5	1-17	6-25 (1 TD)	5-54	2-6	2-5	4-18	0-0	4-13	1-9	8-14	1-(-2)	1-2	4-22
WR MICHAEL PITTMAN JR.	0-0	3-29	0-0	8-123	1-5	6-68	0-0	6-59	0-0	6-89 (1 TD)	1-3	2-35	0-0	4-105 (1 TD)	0-0	10-86 (2 TD)
WR ZACH PASCAL	0-0	4-43 (2 TD)	0-0	5-38 (1 TD)	0-0	2-31	0-0	4-44	0-0	3-48	0-0	0-0	0-0	3-14	0-0	5-43
WR T.Y. HILTON	DNP		DNP		DNP		DNP		DNP		0-0	4-80	DNP		0-0	2-16
TE MO ALIE-COX	0-0	0-0	0-0	1-18	0-0	2-14	0-0	3-42 (2 TD)	0-0	3-50	0-0	1-28 (1 TD)	0-0	3-25 (1 TD)	0-0	0-0
TE JACK DOYLE	0-0	3-21	0-0	5-64	0-0	1-10	0-0	1-24	0-0	1-4	0-0	0-0	0-0	0-0	0-0	2-12 (1 TD)

2021 Stats
Record: 9–8
Rushing Rank: 2nd
Passing Rank: 28th
Offensive Fantasy Pts: 15th
Against Run: 10th
Against Pass: 18th
ppg Against: 21.5
ppg: 26.5

Is Jonathan Taylor a lock to repeat as fantasy's RB1 this season?

Taylor blew the socks (and shoes) off every other RB in the league last year with his 2,171 all-purpose yards. On the ground, his 1,272 yards after contact was more than any other back had for their entire rushing total. Taylor tied Austin Ekeler (RB2) for rushing TD leader with 20 scores. This comes as a result of his groundwork in the red zone, where he had almost twice as many carries as any other back (85 carries, 251 yards, 12 TDs). Ekeler's 46 touches were second best. There's more. Taylor had the most forced missed tackles (66) and the most first downs (106, 41 more than any other rusher).

That said, Taylor will have competition for the RB1 spot this season. Starting with Derrick Henry, who actually averaged more fantasy PPG last season (24.0), but played only eight games. Christian McCaffrey is another high-production back who could challenge for top billing if he could put together a healthy campaign. His numbers per game during his career are also better than Taylor's. Alvin Kamara, Najee Harris, Leonard Fournette, and, of course, Ekeler, could all attain that No. 1 position, but they would need plenty of things to go right for them. So, Taylor could be the best again this season, as could another rusher. But if I have the first pick in my league's draft, after a brief pause to heighten the drama... "Jonathan Taylor."

'TAYLOR BLEW THE SOCKS (AND SHOES) OFF EVERY OTHER RB IN THE LEAGUE LAST YEAR WITH HIS 2,171 ALL-PURPOSE YARDS.'

KEY ADDITIONS & NEW CONTRACTS

QB NICK FOLES: SIGNED A TWO-YEAR DEAL.

QB MATT RYAN: ACQUIRED IN A TRADE WITH THE ATLANTA FALCONS IN EXCHANGE FOR A THIRD-ROUND PICK.

RB PHILLIP LINDSAY: SIGNED A ONE-YEAR DEAL WITH THE COLTS.

TE MO ALIE-COX: RE-SIGNED ON A THREE-YEAR, $18 MILLION CONTRACT.

OT DENNIS KELLY: SIGNED WITH THE COLTS.

OT MATT PRYOR: RE-SIGNED ON A ONE-YEAR, $5.5 MILLION DEAL WITH A MAX VALUE OF $6 MILLION WITH INCENTIVES.

DE TYQUAN LEWIS: RE-SIGNED ON A ONE-YEAR, $3 MILLION CONTRACT.

DE YANNICK NGAKOUE: ACQUIRED IN A TRADE WITH THE LAS VEGAS RAIDERS IN EXCHANGE FOR CB ROCK YA-SIN.

LB ZAIRE FRANKLIN: RE-SIGNED WITH THE COLTS.

CB BRANDON FACYSON: SIGNED A ONE-YEAR, $3.84 MILLION DEAL.

CB STEPHON GILMORE: SIGNED A TWO-YEAR, $20 MILLION DEAL WITH A MAX VALUE OF $23 MILLION. THE DEAL INCLUDES $10.51 FULLY GUARANTEED AND $14 MILLION IN TOTAL GUARANTEES.

S RODNEY MCLEOD: SIGNED WITH THE COLTS.

DEPTH CHART

QB1	MATT RYAN **N**
QB2	SAM EHLINGER
RB1	JONATHAN TAYLOR
RB2	NYHEIM HINES
RB3	PHILLIP LINDSAY **N**
WR1	MICHAEL PITTMAN JR.
WR2	PARRIS CAMPBELL
WR3	ALEC PIERCE **R**
WR4	ASHTON DULIN
TE1	MO ALIE-COX
TE2	JELANI WOODS **R**
K	RODRIGO BLANKENSHIP

KEY LOSSES

QB **CARSON WENTZ** (TRADED TO COMMANDERS)

RB **MARLON MACK** (TEXANS)

WR **T.Y. HILTON**

WR **ZACH PASCAL** (EAGLES)

TE **JACK DOYLE** (RETIRED)

OT **JULIE'N DAVENPORT** (BEARS)

OT **ERIC FISHER**

OT **SAM TEVI**

OG **MARK GLOWINSKI** (GIANTS)

OG **CHRIS REED** (VIKINGS)

DE **AL-QUADIN MUHAMMAD** (BEARS)

DE **KEMOKO TURAY** (49ERS)

DT **ANTWAUN WOODS**

LB **MATT ADAMS** (BEARS)

CB **T.J. CARRIE**

CB **XAVIER RHODES**

CB **ROCK YA-SIN** (TRADED TO RAIDERS)

S **JAHLEEL ADDAE**

S **GEORGE ODUM** (49ERS)

S **ANDREW SENDEJO**

S **KHARI WILLIS** (RETIRED)

K **MICHAEL BADGLEY**

2021 WEEKLY STATS

NYJ (W) 45-30	JAC (W) 23-17	@ BUF (W) 41-15	TB (L) 31-38	@ HOU (W) 31-0	NE (W) 27-17	@ ARI (W) 22-16	LV (L) 20-23	@ JAC (L) 11-26
22-30 272 (3 TD) 4-13	22-34 180 4-(-11)	11-20 106 (1 TD) 2-18	27-44 306 (2 INT) (3 TD) 3-21	16-22 158 (1 TD) 3-8	5-12 57 (1 INT) (1 TD) 8-17	18-28 225 (2 TD) 2-4	16-27 148 (1 TD) 3-10	17-29 185 (1 INT) (1 TD) 3-17
19-172 (2TD)	2-28	21-116 (1 TD)	6-10	32-185(4TD)	3-19 (1 TD)	16-83 (1 TD)	4-14	32-143 (2TD)	0-0	29-170 (1 TD)	0-0	27-108	0-0	20-108(1 TD)	1-6	15-77	3-18
6-74 (1 TD)	4-34	2-12	2-17	4-31	0-0	1-3	3-26	3-24	3-32	0-0	1-8 (1 TD)	3-11	1-7	2-4	4-14	0-0	2-19
0-0	5-64 (1 TD)	0-0	5-71	0-0	2-23	0-0	4-53	2-33	6-77	0-0	1-7	1-3	8-82	0-0	6-47	0-0	6-64 (1 TD)
0-0	4-58	0-0	2-9	1-9	0-0	0-0	2-12	1-12	1-6	0-0	1-23	DNP		0-0	1-8	0-0	1-7
DNP		0-0	1-5	0-0	2-26	0-0	4-28 (1 TD)	0-0	2-22	0-0	1-19	0-0	4-51 (1 TD)	0-0	1-45 (1 TD)	0-0	2-39
0-0	1-28	0-0	1-6	0-0	0-0	0-0	1-8	0-0	1-0	0-0	0-0	0-0	2-42	0-0	3-28	0-0	2-27
0-0	1-1 (1 TD)	0-0	3-31	0-0	3-30	0-0	6-81 (1 TD)	0-0	1-13	0-0	1-0	0-0	0-0	0-0	0-0	0-0	1-11

JACKSONVILLE JAGUARS

Will James Robinson be relegated to backup RB with the return of Travis Etienne Jr.?

Etienne was slated to be the top back for the Jaguars in 2021 until he suffered a season-ending foot injury weeks before Week 1. James Robinson stepped in and played the role of lead back for a second straight season. The former undrafted free agent was on pace for his second consecutive 1,000-yard season before tearing his Achilles in Week 16. In 2022, both backs are ready to prove themselves fully recovered from their injuries. Robinson may have to wait a little longer than Etienne to get back on the field, as his early season availability is in question. There's even a chance Robinson does not see the field until late in the season.

Etienne, on the other hand, should start the season as the undisputed three-down back. His last snap under the whis-

'The real question is what happens when Robinson is ready to reintegrate into the Jaguars offense.'

tle came in his final year at Clemson, playing with QB Trevor Lawrence. Etienne's lost year won't slow down his development, he's already established years of chemistry with Lawrence.

The real question is what happens when Robinson is ready to reintegrate into the Jaguars offense. There's a chance that Etienne earns the No. 1 job outright, and Robinson only plays a limited role. There's also the possibility that Robinson returns to top-back status, with Etienne as the change-of-pace backup. However, the most likely scenario is somewhere in between. We wouldn't be surprised to see the backs split touches on early downs and Etienne take the majority of passing-down situations, which gives Etienne the big advantage in fantasy.

Who emerges as the No. 1 pass catcher inside a crowded receiver room?

The $72 million deal Christian Kirk signed this offseason suggests the Jaguars plan to make him their top man. He had a good 2021 in Arizona, and we project similar numbers for him in Jacksonville this season. Kirk's production, or the output of any player from this crowded receiving corps, is dependent on the improvement of QB Trevor Lawrence. If Lawrence can emerge as a real passing

threat, there are plenty of hungry route runners looking for their target share.

Among Jacksonville's current receivers, only Marvin Jones Jr. has eclipsed 1,000 yards in a season (Detroit, 2017). The only other to come close was Kirk last season (982 yards).

Kirk's route-running ability is his biggest strength. He has embarrassed defenders, specifically when matched up

2022/23 SCHEDULE				2021 FANTASY POINTS ALLOWED BY OPPONENT VS LEAGUE AVERAGE			
WK	DATE	TIME	OPP	QB	RB	WR	TE
1	9/11	1:00	@WAS	29%	-3%	8%	5%
2	9/18	1:00	IND	2%	-12%	4%	23%
3	9/25	4:05	@LAC	2%	17%	-11%	23%
4	10/02	1:00	@PHI	-1%	10%	-17%	46%
5	10/09	1:00	HOU	1%	13%	5%	13%
6	10/16	1:00	@IND	2%	-12%	4%	23%
7	10/23	1:00	NYG	12%	40%	-2%	22%
8	10/30	9:30AM	DEN*	-10%	-9%	-6%	-29%
9	11/06	1:00	LV	1%	10%	-14%	39%
10	11/13	1:00	@KC	15%	4%	3%	2%
11	BYE WEEK						
12	11/27	1:00	BAL	13%	-12%	12%	29%
13	12/04	1:00	@DET	4%	14%	2%	17%
14	12/11	1:00	@TEN	3%	-22%	19%	-29%
15	12/18	1:00	DAL	-6%	-14%	2%	5%
16	12/22	8:15	@NYJ	-4%	11%	-1%	-1%
17	1/01	1:00	@HOU	1%	13%	5%	13%
18	1/08	TBD	TEN	3%	-22%	19%	-29%
*PLAYED IN LONDON							

2022 NFL DRAFT					
RD	PK		POS	COLLEGE	HT WT
1	1	TRAVON WALKER	EDGE	GEORGIA	6-5 275
1	27	DEVIN LLOYD	LB	UTAH	6-3 232
3	1	LUKE FORTNER	C	KENTUCKY	6-6 300
3	6	CHAD MUMA	LB	WYOMING	6-3 242
6	18	GREGORY JUNIOR	CB	MISSOURI	6-0 190
7	1	MONTARIC BROWN	CB	ARKANSAS	6-0 190

2021 WEEKLY STATS

*RUSH STATS *REC STATS			@ HOU (L) 21-37		DEN (L) 13-23		ARI (L) 19-31		@ CIN (L) 21-24		TEN (L) 19-37		MIA (W) 23-30		@ SEA (L) 7-31		BUF (W) 9-6	
QB TREVOR LAWRENCE			28-51 332 (3 INT) (3 TD) 1-[-2]		14-33 118 (2 INT) (1 TD) 2-21		22-34 219 (2 INT) (1 TD) 6-27		17-24 204 8-36 (1 TD)		23-33 273 (1 INT) (1 TD) 7-28 (1 TD)		25-41 319 (1 TD) 2-11		32-54 238 (1 INT) (1 TD) 3-11		15-26 118 3-4	
RB JAMES ROBINSON	5-25	3-29	11-47	3-17	15-88 (1 TD)	6-46	18-78 (2 TD)	1-1-2]	18-149 (1 TD)	1-1-21	17-73 (1 TD)	3-28	4-22	1-17	DNP	
RB DARE OGUNBOWALE	DNP		DNP		0-0	0-0	2-3	0-0	0-0	1-19	DNP		2-9	1-9	1-1	1-4
RB CARLOS HYDE	9-44	2-14	2-7	0-0	8-44	0-0	0-0	0-0	5-13	0-0	0-0	0-0	9-32	6-40	21-67	1-6
WR MARVIN JONES JR.	0-0	5-77 (1 TD)	0-0	6-55 (1 TD)	0-0	6-62	0-0	3-24	0-0	1-25	0-0	7-100 (1 TD)	0-0	5-35	0-0	3-21
WR LAVISKA SHENAULT JR.	1-9	7-50	1-0	2-1-3]	0-0	4-48	1-11	6-99	0-0	1-58	0-0	6-54	1-8	2-13	1-1-4]	4-24
TE DAN ARNOLD	0-0	0-0	0-0	0-0	0-0	0-0	0-0	2-29	0-0	6-64	0-0	2-27	0-0	8-68	0-0	4-60

FANTASY TAKEOVER

2021 Stats

Record: 3-14
Rushing Rank: 22nd
Passing Rank: 24th
Offensive Fantasy Pts: 31st
Against Run: 23rd
Against Pass: 16th
ppg Against: 26.9
ppg: 14.9

KEY ADDITIONS & NEW CONTRACTS

WR **ZAY JONES**: SIGNED A THREE-YEAR, $24 MILLION CONTRACT THAT HAS A MAX VALUE OF $30 MILLION.

WR **CHRISTIAN KIRK**: SIGNED A FOUR-YEAR, $72 MILLION CONTRACT THAT INCLUDES $37 MILLION FULLY GUARANTEED AND HAS A MAX VALUE OF $84 MILLION.

WR **LAQUON TREADWELL**: RE-SIGNED A FREE-AGENT CONTRACT.

TE **EVAN ENGRAM**: SIGNED A ONE-YEAR DEAL.

OT **CAM ROBINSON**: SIGNED THE FRANCHISE TAG. ROBINSON LATER AGREED TO A THREE-YEAR, $54 MILLION DEAL.

OG **BRANDON SCHERFF**: SIGNED A THREE-YEAR, $49.5 MILLION DEAL THAT INCLUDES $30 MILLION FULLY GUARANTEED AND $33 MILLION IN THE FIRST TWO YEARS.

OL **TYLER SHATLEY**: RE-SIGNED ON A TWO-YEAR DEAL WORTH UP TO $6.8 MILLION WITH $2.35 MILLION GUARANTEED.

DE **ADAM GOTSIS**: RE-SIGNED WITH THE JAGUARS.

DE **ARDEN KEY**: SIGNED A ONE-YEAR DEAL WORTH UP TO $7 MILLION.

DT **FOLEY FATUKASI**: SIGNED A THREE-YEAR, $30 MILLION DEAL THAT INCLUDES $20 MILLION FULLY GUARANTEED.

LB **FOYE OLUOKUN**: SIGNED A THREE-YEAR, $45 MILLION DEAL THAT INCLUDES $28 MILLION FULLY GUARANTEED AND HAS A MAX VALUE OF $46.5 MILLION.

CB **TRE HERNDON**: RE-SIGNED ON A FREE-AGENT CONTRACT.

CB **DARIOUS WILLIAMS**: SIGNED A THREE-YEAR, $30 MILLION DEAL THAT INCLUDES $18 MILLION FULLY GUARANTEED AND HAS A MAX VALUE OF $39 MILLION.

against linebackers and safeties (16th best). But when lined up against corners, his ranking dropped to 49th. As the No. 1 receiver, he likely won't have too many linebackers across the line of scrimmage this season.

Besides Kirk, and possibly Zay Jones, no one else should see enough target volume to be a viable fantasy option. We'll give Kirk a chance, though, because the Jaguars have to give him the ball enough to justify his high-dollar contract.

What can we expect from Trevor Lawrence in year two?

Trevor Lawrence was terrible in his rookie outing, but its hard to determine how much of the failure to attribute directly to him. The Urban Meyer experiment is over, and so is the team dysfunction that lasted until Meyer's firing after 13 games. In addition, there were offensive line issues, and a lack of talent available at the offensive skill positions. The Jaguars, last year, could never find their rhythm. For every two TDs Lawrence threw, he threw three interceptions. While he had over 600 pass attempts, he completed a mere 59.6% and finished as QB34 in fantasy PPG. He also had plenty of rushing volume (5th most among QBs), but was incredibly inefficient, finishing only 15th in rushing yards per game. But, again, many of those rushing attempts were out of necessity caused by offensive line breakdown.

The setup is much better for Lawrence this year. New head coach Doug Pederson is known as a quarterback whisperer, getting Alex Smith, Michael Vick, Carson Wentz, and Nick Foles to perform at their full potential. Pederson is a Super Bowl-winning coach with a proven track record, and he's brought in QB-minded Press Taylor as his offensive coordinator.

Lawrence will play behind a rebuilt offensive line, which includes Probowl guard Brandon Scherff. The Jaguars have more offensive weapons, too, with the offseason additions of Christian Kirk, Zay Jones, and Evan Engram.

Still, while Lawrence is in store for a better year, there are plenty of QBs who have a better outlook for your fantasy needs.

KEY LOSSES

RB **CARLOS HYDE**
RB **DARE OGUNBOWALE** (TEXANS)
WR **TAVON AUSTIN** (BILLS)
WR **DJ CHARK JR.** (LIONS)
TE **JACOB HOLLISTER** (RAIDERS)
TE **JAMES O'SHAUGHNESSY** (BEARS)
OG **A.J. CANN** (TEXANS)
OG **ANDREW NORWELL** (COMMANDERS)
C **BRANDON LINDER** (RETIRED)
DE **JIHAD WARD** (GIANTS)
DT **TAVEN BRYAN** (BROWNS)
LB **MYLES JACK** (STEELERS)
LB **DAMIEN WILSON** (PANTHERS)
CB **NEVIN LAWSON**

DEPTH CHART

QB1	TREVOR LAWRENCE
QB2	C.J. BEATHARD
RB1	JAMES ROBINSON
RB2	TRAVIS ETIENNE JR.
RB3	SNOOP CONNER **R**
WR1	CHRISTIAN KIRK **N**
WR2	MARVIN JONES JR.
WR3	ZAY JONES **N**
WR4	LAVISKA SHENAULT JR.
TE1	EVAN ENGRAM **N**
TE2	DAN ARNOLD
K	RYAN SANTOSO

2021 WEEKLY STATS

@ IND (L) 17-23		SF (L) 10-30		ATL (L) 14-21		@ LAR (L) 7-37		@ TEN (L) 0-20		HOU (L) 16-30		@ NYJ (L) 21-26		@ NE (L) 10-50		IND (W) 26-11	
16-35 162		16-25 158		23-42 228 (1 INT) (1 TD)		16-28 145		24-40 221 (4 INT)		22-38 210		26-39 280		17-27 193 (3 INT) (1 TD)		23-32 223 (2 TD)	
5-33		3-23		5-39		4-10		1-2		5-21		6-37		2-16		10-17	
12-57 (1 TD)	4-27	12-29 (1 TD)	2-9	17-86	3-29	8-24	1-11	6-4	0-0	18-75 (1 TD)	3-13	3-10	0-0	DNP		DNP	
0-0	0-0	DNP		0-0	0-0	DNP		0-0	2-5	1-1	1-5	17-57 (1 TD)	2-15	9-36	2-32 (1 TD)	11-30	3-25
2-4	1-0	0-0	0-0	6-16	0-0	9-24 (1 TD)	1-1-1	1-2	1-6	DNP		DNP		DNP		DNP	
0-0	2-35	0-0	4-52	0-0	4-43	0-0	2-11	0-0	6-70	0-0	2-14	0-0	8-74	0-0	2-46	0-0	7-88 (1 TD)
2-6	3-15	0-0	5-50	0-0	5-33	3-1	3-30	0-0	4-34	1-10	4-39	DNP		0-0	2-13	0-0	5-62
0-0	5-67	DNP		DNP		DNP		DNP		DNP		DNP		DNP		DNP	

Will Patrick Mahomes have another "down" year?

Patrick Mahomes looked almost human at times last season. He had the lowest QB rating and average depth of throw of his career. While always fun to watch, he wasn't as efficient as years past. Even during this "down" season, Mahomes finished as QB5 in fantasy PPG, better than his 2019 campaign.

Undoubtedly, losing Tyreek Hill hurts, but Mahomes' average in the four games he played without Hill were not statistically different than from his average with him. We are certain that Mahomes will have no issues getting his new WRs on the same page, and he's likely to turn one of them into a fantasy stud. And he still has Ole Faithful, TE Travis Kelce.

In the past two seasons, Mahomes has finished in the top-12 QBs almost 70% of the time on a weekly basis. He has enough of a rushing floor (career high last season) to give him a legitimate chance to be the overall QB1.

At FantasyTakeover we likely won't have many shares of Mahomes on our fantasy teams, and there are multiple reasons why. His name as a football player has someone reaching as high as the second round to draft him, ignoring solid fantasy strategy. And the range of outcomes in our first tier of QBs (Allen, Mahomes, Herbert, Jackson, and Hurts) are all close enough together that we'll settle for who's left out of the five rather than taking the top names.

Who's going to emerge as the No. 1 WR?

After Kelce, there are three WRs who could become the Chiefs No. 1 receiving option — JuJu Smith-Schuster, Marquez Valdes-Scantling, and Skyy Moore.

JuJu is our favorite of the three. His recent injury history and receiving metrics aren't great, but he has proven he can produce WR1 numbers, unlike Moore and MVS. He's also been stuck playing with Big Ben the past few years who has been immobile and unable to get the ball down the field.

MVS is our second choice. He never quite panned out in Green Bay, but he was competing with target monster Davante Adams. His $30 million-contract is evidence that Kansas City sees something in him. His ability to get to the second level and how he uses speed to create space will help him find targets when Mahomes goes into scramble mode. He'll post a couple 5-125-2 lines this season, but predicting when is the tricky part.

Skyy Moore, the second-round rookie, is the wild card. He excels lining up in the slot and winning in the underneath routes. He has a knack for evading defenders and improvising when plays break down. He may end up being Mahome's new guy.

While JuJu is our top choice, Mahomes will have the final say. Keep an eye out during preseason to see who Mahomes is targeting.

WK	DATE	TIME	OPP	QB	RB	WR	TE
	2022/23 SCHEDULE			2021 FANTASY POINTS ALLOWED BY OPPONENT VS LEAGUE AVERAGE			
1	9/11	4:25	@ARI	0%	-11%	10%	-36%
2	9/15	8:15	LAC	2%	17%	-11%	23%
3	9/25	1:00	@IND	2%	-12%	4%	23%
4	10/02	8:20	@TB	3%	-4%	3%	4%
5	10/10	8:15	LV	1%	10%	-14%	39%
6	10/16	4:25	BUF	-34%	-11%	-27%	-34%
7	10/23	4:25	@SF	-1%	26%	-3%	20%
8	BYE WEEK						
9	11/06	8:20	TEN	3%	-22%	19%	-29%
10	11/13	1:00	JAC	4%	-1%	5%	-2%
11	11/20	4:25	@LAC	2%	17%	-11%	23%
12	11/27	4:25	LAR	-12%	-8%	7%	-2%
13	12/04	4:25	@CIN	-1%	6%	0%	22%
14	12/11	8:20	@DEN	-10%	-9%	-6%	-29%
15	12/18	1:00	@HOU	1%	13%	5%	13%
16	12/24	1:00	SEA	2%	-8%	3%	-23%
17	1/01	1:00	DEN	-10%	-9%	-6%	-29%
18	1/08	TBD	@LV	1%	10%	-14%	39%

2022 NFL DRAFT

RD	PK		POS	COLLEGE	HT	WT
1	21	TRENT MCDUFFIE	CB	WASHINGTON	5-11	195
1	30	GEORGE KARLAFTIS	EDGE	PURDUE	6-4	275
2	22	SKYY MOORE	WR	WESTERN MICHIGAN	5-10	195
2	30	BRYAN COOK	S	CINCINNATI	6-1	210
3	39	LEO CHENAL	LB	WISCONSIN	6-2	261
4	30	JOSHUA WILLIAMS	CB	FAYETTEVILLE STATE	6-3	195
5	2	DARIAN KINNARD	G	KENTUCKY	6-5	345
7	22	JAYLEN WATSON	CB	WASHINGTON STATE	6-3	204
7	30	ISAIH PACHECO	RB	RUTGERS	5-11	215
7	38	NAZEEH JOHNSON	S	MARSHALL	6-2	189

2021 WEEKLY STATS

*RUSH STATS : *REC STATS	CLE (W) 33-29		@ BAL (L) 35-36		LAC (L) 24-30		@ PHI (W) 42-30		BUF (L) 20-38		@ WAS (W) 31-13		@ TEN (L) 3-27		NYG (W) 20-17	
QB PATRICK MAHOMES	27-36 337 (3 TD) 5-18 (1 TD)		24-31 343 (1 INT) (3 TD) 1-3		27-44 260 (2 INT) (3 TD) 4-45		24-30 278 (1 INT) (5 TD) 5-26		33-54 272 (2 INT) (2 TD) 8-61		32-47 397 (2 INT) (2 TD) 3-31		20-35 206 (1 INT) 6-35		29-48 275 (1 INT) (1 TD) 3-10	
RB DARREL WILLIAMS	1-4	0-0	3-1-2 (1 TD)	0-0	7-28	2-11	10-42 (1 TD)	2-16	5-27	3-18	21-62 (2 TD)	3-27	5-20	3-30	13-49	6-61
RB C. EDWARDS-HELAIRE	14-43	3-29	13-46	0-0	17-100	2-9 (1 TD)	14-102	2-12 (1 TD)	7-13	1-11	DNP		DNP		DNP	
RB DERRICK GORE	DNP		DNP		DNP		DNP		DNP		DNP		0-0	1-7	11-48 (1 TD)	0-0
WR TYREEK HILL	1-4	11-197 (1 TD)	1-15	3-14	1-11	5-56	0-0	11-186 (3 TD)	1-15	7-63	0-0	9-76 (1 TD)	1-18	6-49	0-0	12-94 (1 TD)
WR MECOLE HARDMAN	0-0	3-19	0-0	5-55	1-2	3-33 (1 TD)	2-25	2-16	0-0	9-76	1-6	4-62	0-0	4-28	0-0	5-63
WR BYRON PRINGLE	0-0	1-6	0-0	2-63 (1 TD)	0-0	2-12	0-0	2-23	0-0	2-11 (1 TD)	0-0	3-55	0-0	5-73	0-0	1-12
TE TRAVIS KELCE	0-0	6-76 (2 TD)	0-0	7-109 (1 TD)	0-0	7-104	0-0	4-23	0-0	6-57 (1 TD)	0-0	8-99	0-0	7-65	0-0	4-27

2021 Stats

Record: 12–5
Rushing Rank: 16th
Passing Rank: 4th
Offensive Fantasy Pts: 4th
Against Run: 21st
Against Pass: 25th
ppg Against: 22.4
ppg: 29.4

KEY ADDITIONS & NEW CONTRACTS (KC)

QB **CHAD HENNE**: RE-SIGNED ON A ONE-YEAR DEAL WORTH $2 MILLION.

RB **RONALD JONES II**: SIGNED A ONE-YEAR DEAL WORTH UP TO $5 MILLION.

RB **JERICK MCKINNON**: SIGNED A FREE-AGENT DEAL.

WR **COREY COLEMAN**: SIGNED WITH KANSAS CITY; COLEMAN LAST APPEARED IN AN NFL GAME WITH THE GIANTS IN 2018.

WR **JUJU SMITH-SCHUSTER**: SIGNED A ONE-YEAR DEAL WITH A MAX VALUE OF $10.75 MILLION WITH INCENTIVES.

WR **MARQUEZ VALDES-SCANTLING**: SIGNED A THREE-YEAR, $30 MILLION DEAL THAT HAS A MAX VALUE OF $36 MILLION.

TE **BLAKE BELL**: RE-SIGNED ON A FREE-AGENT DEAL.

OT **ORLANDO BROWN**: RECEIVED THE FRANCHISE TAG.

C **AUSTIN REITER**: RE-SIGNED ON A FREE-AGENT DEAL.

DE **FRANK CLARK**: SIGNED A NEW TWO-YEAR, $29 MILLION DEAL THAT HAS A MAX VALUE OF $36 MILLION WITH INCENTIVES. THE NEW DEAL SCRAPS THE FINAL YEAR OF THE ORIGINAL FIVE-YEAR CONTRACT HE SIGNED IN 2019, SIGNIFICANTLY LOWERING HIS CAP NUMBER FOR 2022.

DT **DERRICK NNADI**: SIGNED A FREE-AGENT DEAL.

LB **JERMAINE CARTER JR.**: SIGNED A FREE-AGENT DEAL.

S **DEON BUSH**: SIGNED A FREE-AGENT DEAL.

S **JUSTIN REID**: SIGNED A THREE-YEAR, $31.5 MILLION DEAL THAT INCLUDES $20 MILLION GUARANTEED.

DB **LONNIE JOHNSON**: ACQUIRED IN A TRADE WITH THE HOUSTON TEXANS IN EXCHANGE FOR A 2024 CONDITIONAL SEVENTH-ROUND PICK.

Is this a make-it-or-break-it year for Clyde Edwards-Helaire?

You could try to justify CEH's lack of production as a result of a series of unfortunate injuries. Since arriving in Kansas City, he has suffered two ankle sprains, a hip strain, a knee sprain, and a bruised shoulder. Maybe we haven't seen CEH at his best, but we're no longer confident that his best is enough, and we think the Chiefs agree with us.

Since 2020, among backs with at least 100 carries, CEH ranks 34th in yards per carry, 49th in yards after contact per carry, and 36th in forced missed tackles.

One would assume CEH would make his money in the passing game after all his success at LSU, but so far this hasn't been the case. In his 27 NFL games, he's only had three games with more than three receptions.

The fact that Jerrick McKinnon was the featured back in the 2021 postseason over a healthy CEH, speaks volumes. While the Chiefs may not be ready to give up on CEH yet, the signing of Ronald Jones II and the re-signing of McKinnon indicates they want to make sure they have a backup plan.

Jones figures to have the best opportunity to takeover early-down backfield duties from CEH. His yards per carry and yards after contact are remarkably better than CEH's. Receiving limitations will prevent Jones from having the backfield to himself, but he could have big TD upside in a top-five offense.

While McKinnon will compete with CEH for passing-down duties, CEH will have first dibs. But if he falters, expect McKinnon to step in.

We're not buying CEH at his current ADP, but we will have some shares of Ronald Jones II.

'THE FACT THAT JERRICK MCKINNON WAS THE FEATURED BACK LAST POSTSEASON OVER A HEALTHY CEH SPEAKS VOLUMES.'

KEY LOSSES

RB **DARREL WILLIAMS** (CARDINALS)
WR **TYREEK HILL** (TRADED TO DOLPHINS)
WR **BYRON PRINGLE** (BEARS)
WR **DEMARCUS ROBINSON** (RAIDERS)
OT **MIKE REMMERS**
OG **KYLE LONG**
C **AUSTIN BLYTHE** (SEAHAWKS)
DE **ALEX OKAFOR**
DT **JARRAN REED** (PACKERS)
LB **ANTHONY HITCHENS**
LB **MELVIN INGRAM** (DOLPHINS)
CB **MIKE HUGHES** (LIONS)
CB **CHARVARIUS WARD** (49ERS)
S **TYRANN MATHIEU** (SAINTS)
S **DANIEL SORENSON** (SAINTS)

DEPTH CHART

QB1	PATRICK MAHOMES
QB2	CHAD HENNE
RB1	CLYDE EDWARDS-HELAIRE
RB2	RONALD JONES II **N**
RB3	JERRICK MCKINNON
WR1	JUJU SMITH-SCHUSTER **N**
WR2	MECOLE HARDMAN
WR3	M. VALDES-SCANTLING **N**
WR4	SKYY MOORE **R**
TE1	TRAVIS KELCE
TE2	BLAKE BELL
K	HARRISON BUTKER

2021 WEEKLY STATS

GB (W) 13-7		@ LV (W) 41-14		DAL (W) 19-9		DEN (W) 22-9		LV (W) 48-9		@ LAC (W) 34-28		PIT (W) 36-10		@ CIN (L) 31-34		@ DEN (W) 28-24	
20-37 166 (1 TD) 2-[-2]		35-50 406 (5 TD) 0-0		23-37 260 (1 INT) 7-11		15-29 184 (1 INT) 4-12 (1 TD)		20-24 258 (2 TD) 4-20		31-47 410 (1 INT) (3 TD) 3-32		23-30 258 (3 TD) 0-0		26-35 259 (2 TD) 2-25		27-44 270 (2 TD) 9-54	
19-70	3-7	11-43	9-101 (1 TD)	5-15	1-11	5-20	3-60	2-8	3-31 (1 TD)	5-12	0-0	11-55	3-30	14-88 (2 TD)	3-19	7-17	3-30
0-0	0-0	0-0	0-0	12-63 (1 TD)	2-13	14-54	3-28	10-37 (2 TD)	3-5	9-32	2-18	9-27 (1 TD)	1-4	DNP		DNP	
3-13	1-6	6-19	0-0	DNP		DNP		9-66 (1 TD)	2-23	DNP		12-43	3-61	3-37	1-8	7-30	0-0
1-[-4]	4-37	1-2	7-83 (2 TD)	1-33	9-77	0-0	2-22	0-0	4-76	0-0	12-148 (1 TD)	0-0	2-19	1-2	6-40	0-0	1-2
0-0	3-20	1-3	2-27	0-0	2-25	0-0	1-12	1-0	2-59	1-0	2-11	0-0	3-31 (1 TD)	0-0	1-53	1-10	8-103
0-0	0-0	0-0	4-46 (1 TD)	0-0	1-37	0-0	1-14	0-0	1-28	0-0	3-22	0-0	6-75 (2 TD)	0-0	3-35	0-0	5-56
0-0	5-68 (1 TD)	0-0	8-119	1-4 (1 TD)	5-74	0-0	3-27	0-0	3-27	0-0	10-191 (2 TD)	DNP		1-[-1]	5-25 (1 TD)	0-0	4-34 (1 TD)

Will Derek Carr finally finish as a top-15 fantasy QB?

Carr's best fantasy years, 2015 and 2016, were when he had two dynamic weapons at his disposal — Amari Cooper and Michael Crabtree. But even then Carr wasn't a top-15 fantasy QB. He's improved drastically as a passer since then, but his receivers have not, until now. Carr's three-headed receiving monster — Davante Adams, Hunter Renfrow, and Darren Waller — says it's now or never.

Carr had elite-speed option in Henry Ruggs II for the first seven games last season, and was off to the best start of his career. Unfortunately, he was only the 11th-best QB in this span, and

'The problem is he's never averaged more than 10 rushing yards per game in a season'

then fell to 30th after Rugg's early-season departure.

The problem with Carr is he's never averaged more than 10 rushing yards per game in a season, and his passing numbers are not enough on their own to sustain a QB1 ranking. It won't help that new head coach Josh McDaniels has been outside the top-20 teams in pass-play rate for last four seasons in New England.

Top 15 for Carr? We'll flip a coin. Top 10? Unlikely, as he'd have to have his first 30-plus TD year, and surpass 5,000 yards. We'll be chasing more dual-threat options with higher upsides as our backups.

Is Darren Waller still a top-five fantasy TE?

Unlike wide receivers and running backs, tight ends don't tend to regress as quickly with age because they don't rely as much on their athleticism as much as they do their size. If Darren Waller, who enters the 2022 season at age 30, can avoid the injury bug, he can definitely be a top-five TE.

Waller played most of last season on a sprained ankle before hurting his knee in Week 13. He still had flashes of greatness, though, with three games of at least 7 receptions and 60 yards. Considering his target count (90 in 11 games), Waller's fantasy output was almost 30 points less than projected, and he finished on the opposite side of the expected FPs last

season. We'll chalk up some of his inefficiency in 2021 to injury and not as a sign of decline in ability.

With the addition of WR Davante Adams, we're projecting Waller to see plenty of targets while defenses are having to focus on the additional offensive threat. Of the four TEs ranked ahead of Waller, George Kittle is the only one who might not be their team's No. 1 receiver going into the season, and there's a possibility that Waller, is now the No. 3 option on his team.

Either way, he is still top-five material and, unfortunately, the fantasy community agrees and has pushed his ADP a little too high.

2022/23 SCHEDULE			2021 FANTASY POINTS ALLOWED BY OPPONENT VS LEAGUE AVERAGE			
WK	DATE	TIME	OPP	QB	RB	WR	TE
1	9/11	4:25	@LAC	2%	17%	-11%	23%
2	9/18	4:25	ARI	0%	-11%	10%	-36%
3	9/25	1:00	@TEN	3%	-22%	19%	-29%
4	10/02	4:25	DEN	-10%	-9%	-6%	-29%
5	10/10	8:15	@KC	15%	4%	3%	2%
6	BYE WEEK						
7	10/23	4:05	HOU	1%	13%	5%	13%
8	10/30	1:00	@NO	-26%	2%	-16%	-45%
9	11/06	1:00	@JAC	4%	-1%	5%	-2%
10	11/13	4:05	IND	2%	-12%	4%	23%
11	11/20	4:05	@DEN	-10%	-9%	-6%	-29%
12	11/27	4:05	@SEA	2%	-8%	3%	-23%
13	12/04	4:25	LAC	2%	17%	-11%	23%
14	12/08	8:15	@LAR	-12%	-8%	7%	-2%
15	12/18	8:20	NE	-8%	-19%	1%	-20%
16	12/24	8:15	@PIT	-2%	11%	-3%	-10%
17	1/01	4:05	SF	-1%	26%	-3%	20%
18	1/08	TBD	KC	15%	4%	3%	2%

2022 NFL DRAFT					
RD	PK		POS	COLLEGE	HT	WT
3	26	DYLAN PARHAM	G	MEMPHIS	6-3	285
4	17	ZAMIR WHITE	RB	GEORGIA	6-0	215
4	21	NEIL FARRELL JR.	DT	LSU	6-4	325
5	32	MATTHEW BUTLER	DT	TENNESSEE	6-4	295
7	17	THAYER MUNFORD	OT	OHIO STATE	6-6	321
7	29	BRITTAIN BROWN	RB	UCLA	6-1	205

2021 WEEKLY STATS

*RUSH STATS : *REC STATS		BAL (W) 33-27		@ PIT (W) 26-17		MIA (W) 31-28		@ LAC (L) 14-28		CHI (L) 9-20		@ DEN (W) 34-24		PHI (W) 33-22		@ NYG (L) 16-23	
QB DEREK CARR		34-56 435 (1 INT) (2 TD) 4-6		28-37 382 (2 TD) 4-9		26-43 386 (1 INT) (2 TD) 2-[-2]		21-34 196 (1 INT) (2 TD) 3-6		22-35 206 (1 INT) 3-10		18-27 341 (2 TD) 2-1-1)		31-34 323 (1 INT) (2 TD) 2-1		30-46 296 (2 INT) (1 TD) 2-5	
RB JOSH JACOBS	10-34 (2 TD)	1-6	DNP		DNP		13-40	5-17	15-48 (1 TD)	4-19	16-53 (1 TD)	1-29	6-29 (1 TD)	3-39	13-76	4-19
RB KENYAN DRAKE	6-11	5-59	7-9	5-46	8-24	3-33	1-2	0-0	2-11	0-0	4-34 (1 TD)	2-39 (1 TD)	14-69 (1 TD)	3-10	4-30	6-70
WR HUNTER RENFROW	0-0	6-70	0-0	5-57	0-0	5-77 (1 TD)	0-0	6-45 (1 TD)	0-0	6-56	0-0	3-36	0-0	7-58	0-0	7-49 (1 TD)
WR BRYAN EDWARDS	0-0	4-81	0-0	3-40	0-0	3-89	0-0	1-4	0-0	2-22	0-0	2-67	0-0	3-43 (1 TD)	0-0	0-0
WR ZAY JONES	0-0	2-46 (1 TD)	0-0	0-0	0-0	1-15	0-0	1-5	0-0	1-6	0-0	0-0	0-0	1-43	0-0	1-20
WR HENRY RUGGS III	0-0	2-46	1-2	5-113 (1 TD)	1-7	4-78	0-0	3-60	0-0	3-51	0-0	3-97 (1 TD)	1-7	4-24	DNP	
TE DARREN WALLER	0-0	10-105 (1 TD)	0-0	5-65	0-0	5-54	0-0	4-50 (1 TD)	0-0	4-45	0-0	5-59	DNP		0-0	7-92
TE FOSTER MOREAU	0-0	0-0	0-0	2-34 (1 TD)	0-0	1-8	0-0	0-0	0-0	0-0	0-0	1-11	0-0	6-60 (1	0-0	0-0

2021 Stats
Record: 10-7
Rushing Rank: 28th
Passing Rank: 6th
Offensive Fantasy Pts: 11th
Against Run: 19th
Against Pass: 12th
ppg Against: 25.8
ppg: 21.8

KEY ADDITIONS & NEW CONTRACTS

QB **DEREK CARR**: SIGNED A THREE-YEAR EXTENSION WORTH $121.5 MILLION. THE DEAL INCLUDES A NO-TRADE CLAUSE.

QB **GARRETT GILBERT**: SIGNED A FREE-AGENT DEAL.

QB **NICK MULLENS**: SIGNED A FREE-AGENT DEAL.

QB **JARRETT STIDHAM**: ACQUIRED IN A TRADE WITH THE NEW ENGLAND PATRIOTS, ALONG WITH A SEVENTH-ROUND PICK, IN EXCHANGE FOR A SIXTH-ROUNDER.

RB **AMEER ABDULLAH**: SIGNED WITH THE RAIDERS.

RB **BRANDON BOLDEN**: SIGNED A FREE-AGENT CONTRACT WITH THE RAIDERS.

FB **JAKOB JOHNSON**: SIGNED DEAL.

WR **DAVANTE ADAMS**: ACQUIRED IN A TRADE WITH THE GREEN BAY PACKERS IN EXCHANGE FOR A 2022 FIRST-ROUND PICK AND 2022 SECOND-ROUND PICK. ADAMS IS EXPECTED TO SIGN A NEW CONTRACT WITH THE RAIDERS WORTH $141.25 MILLION OVER FIVE YEARS WITH AN AVERAGE OF $28.25 MILLION PER YEAR.

WR **KEELAN COLE**: SIGNED WITH THE RAIDERS.

WR **HUNTER RENFROW**: SIGNED A TWO-YEAR EXTENSION WORTH $32 MILLION, INCLUDING $21 MILLION GUARANTEED.

WR **DEMARCUS ROBINSON**: SIGNED A FREE-AGENT CONTRACT.

TE **JACOB HOLLISTER**: SIGNED A ONE-YEAR DEAL.

OT BRANDON PARKER: SIGNED A FREE-AGENT CONTRACT.

DE **MAXX CROSBY**: SIGNED A FOUR-YEAR, $98.98 MILLION CONTRACT EXTENSION WITH $95 MILLION IN NEW MONEY AND $53 MILLION GUARANTEED.

DE **CHANDLER JONES**: SIGNED A DEAL THAT WILL PAY HIM ROUGHLY $52.5 MILLION OVER THREE YEARS, INCLUDING $34 MILLION GUARANTEED.

DT **VERNON BUTLER**: SIGNED A ONE-YEAR CONTRACT.

DT **JOHNATHAN HANKINS**: RE-SIGNED WITH THE RAIDERS.

DT **BILAL NICHOLS**: SIGNED A TWO-YEAR, $11 MILLION DEAL WITH $9 MILLION GUARANTEED.

LB **JAYON BROWN**: SIGNED WITH THE RAIDERS.

LB **KYLER FACKRELL**: SIGNED A ONE-YEAR CONTRACT.

LB **KENNY YOUNG**: SIGNED WITH THE RAIDERS.

CB **ANTHONY AVERETT**: SIGNED A FREE-AGENT CONTRACT.

CB **ROCK YA-SIN**: ACQUIRED IN A TRADE WITH THE INDIANAPOLIS COLTS IN EXCHANGE FOR DE YANNICK NGAKOUE.

S **DURON HARMON**: SIGNED WITH THE RAIDERS.

What's Davante Adams' ceiling?

One must travel all the way back to 2017 to see examples of Adams without Aaron Rodgers. In eight games with Brett Hundley under center, Davante Adams averaged a WR12 finish. Volume has been more indicative of Adams' success than anything else, and he should receive plenty of targets in Las Vegas, as the Raiders made him one of the highest paid WRs in the league.

There are examples of star receivers being traded, and both succeeding and busting. We argue Adams is more like the booms (Stefon Diggs and DeAndre Hopkins) than the busts (Odell Beckham Jr. and Jarvis Landry).

Adams isn't totally in a new situation. He is joining his college teammate Derek Carr. Together at Fresno State, the two shined, and though it was nine years ago, athletes say that once chemistry is formed it's never lost. Adams has top-three potential and a higher floor than most WRs would have in a new home.

How did the offseason affect Josh Jacob's fantasy value?

We don't believe Josh McDaniels when he says Josh Jacobs could work across all three downs. McDaniels' track record says otherwise. Over the past five seasons in New England, McDaniels has rushed by committee, with his No. 1 back finishing top-18 only once (James White, 2019, RB9). McDaniels' top back last season, Damien Harris, scored a remarkable 16 TDs, yet finished RB20. The pass-catching back has the most value in a McDaniels-run offense, and though Jacobs posted career highs in targets, receptions, and receiving yards last season, he's limited in his pass-catching upside.

The consensus ranking of Jacobs at RB15 is too high for our liking.

KEY LOSSES

QB **MARCUS MARIOTA** (FALCONS)

RB **PEYTON BARBER**

RB **JALEN RICHARD**

FB **ALEC INGOLD** (DOLPHINS)

WR **BRYAN EDWARDS** (TRADED TO FALCONS)

WR **DESEAN JACKSON**

WR **ZAY JONES** (JAGUARS)

TE **DEREK CARRIER**

OG **RICHIE INCOGNITO**

C **NICK MARTIN**

DE **CARL NASSIB**

DE **YANNICK NGAKOUE** (TRADED TO COLTS)

DT **QUINTON JEFFERSON** (SEAHAWKS)

DT **GERALD MCCOY**

DL **SOLOMON THOMAS** (JETS)

LB **NICK KWIATKOSKI** (FALCONS)

LB **CORY LITTLETON** (PANTHERS)

LB **NICHOLAS MORROW** (BEARS)

LB **K.J. WRIGHT**

CB **BRANDON FACYSON** (COLTS)

CB **CASEY HAYWARD** (FALCONS)

CB **KEISEAN NIXON** (PACKERS)

CB **DESMOND TRUNDRFTNT**

DEPTH CHART

QB1	DEREK CARR
QB2	JARRETT STIDHAM **N**
RB1	JOSH JACOBS
RB2	KENYAN DRAKE
RB3	ZAMIR WHITE **R**
WR1	DAVANTE ADAMS **N**
WR2	HUNTER RENFROW
WR3	DEMARCUS ROBINSON **N**
WR4	MACK HOLLINS
TE1	DARREN WALLER
TE2	FOSTER MOREAU
K	DANIEL CARLSON

2021 WEEKLY STATS

KC (L) 14-41		CIN (L) 13-32		@ DAL (W) 36-33		WAS (L) 15-17		@ KC (L) 9-48		@ CLE (W) 16-14		DEN (W) 17-13		@ IND (W) 23-30		LAC (W) 35-32	
25-35 261 (1 INT) (2 TD)	3-18	19-27 215 (1 INT) (1 TD)	0-0	24-39 373 (1 TD)	2-21	28-38 249	2-24	33-45 263 (1 INT) (1 TD)	0-0	25-38 236 (1 INT) (1 TD)	3-7	20-25 201 (1 INT) (1 TD)	7-5	24-31 255 (2 INT) (1 TD)	0-0	20-36 186 (2 TD)	1-1(-1)
7-16	5-20	9-37	5-24	22-87 (1 TD)	2-25	13-52 (1 TD)	9-38	9-24	5-46	15-52	3-42	27-129	1-1(-5)	16-63 (1 TD)	4-17	26-132 (1 TD)	2-12
4-16	2-15	5-23	1-6	7-25	2-5	1-0	1-8	DNP		DNP		DNP		DNP		DNP	
0-0	7-46 (1 TD)	1-5	4-30	1-2	8-134	0-0	9-102	0-0	13-117 (1 TD)	0-0	3-32	0-0	3-40 (1 TD)	0-0	7-76 (1 TD)	1-1(-4)	4-13 (2 TD)
0-0	3-88 (1 TD)	1-0	0-0	0-0	1-12	0-0	3-30	0-0	2-24	0-0	3-8 (1 TD)	DNP		0-0	0-0	0-0	4-63
0-0	1-22	0-0	1-20	1-4	5-59	0-0	3-21	0-0	5-25	0-0	6-67	0-0	6-50	1-1(-1)	8-120	0-0	5-27
DNP		DNP		DNP		DNP		DNP		DNP		DNP		DNP		DNP	
0-0	4-24	0-0	7-116	0-0	2-33	DNP		DNP		DNP		DNP		DNP		0-0	2-22
0-0	0-0	0-0	1-19 (1 TD)	0-0	1-3	0-0	1-34	0-0	3-13	0-0	7-65	0-0	4-67	0-0	1-9	0-0	2-50

LOS ANGELES CHARGERS

Can Justin Herbert finish as Fantasy's No. 1 QB?

We don't understand why the Chargers are so conservative with Herbert in the deep-ball game. Herbert's deep-ball pass rate (pass attempts of 20-plus yards) is an abysmal 9.5%, or about the same as Jared Goff. Herbert is an excellent long-ball passer, with PFF's sixth-best passing grade on 20-plus-yard throws. His only chance of finishing as QB1 is if head coach Brandon Staley opens up his playbook a little more.

Herbert set an NFL record for most TDs (77) in the first two season of a QB's career. During those first two seasons, he had the fifth highest percentage of top-12 weekly finishes, and sixth highest for top-five finishes.

Herbert, however, has outplayed his expected fantasy PPG the last two seasons, a measure hard to sustain in the long run. Unlike four of our top-six-ranked QBs, Herbert's upside comes from his massive passing numbers and not his rushing ability. We doubt he can finish ahead of a healthy Josh Allen, but with the reins loosened just a little, Herbert is easily capable of finishing as the overall QB2.

> *'Herbert, however, has outplayed his expected fantasy PPG the last two seasons, a measure hard to sustain in the long run.'*

Is Ekeler a lock to repeat as a top-three fantasy RB?

In his first four seasons, Ekeler averaged a TD every 24.5 touches. Last season, he averaged a TD every 13.8 touches. Historically, for RBs who have scored at least 20 TDs in a season, the following year they averaged a 33% drop-off, with only 60% scoring at least 10 TDs.

The primary concern for Ekeler doubters last season was his red zone volume. He quieted skeptics, finishing second in red zone carries and sixth in carries inside the 5.

Ekeler will never see the touch count of a Najee Harris or Derek Henry, both behind Ekeler in our rankings, but a reception is more valuable than a carry, and Ekeler's receiving workload is enormous. In fact, he would have been RB24 without a single carry.

While we rank Ekeler as our third-best back, we wouldn't fault you for drafting Harris or Henry ahead of him. Henry's injury last season and Harris' new QB situation leaves more unknowns than in Ekeler's situation.

A top-three lock? No. But being the top back with massive receiving upside in the league's fifth-best offense is enough to make him a top-seven RB lock.

2022/23 Schedule — 2021 Fantasy Points Allowed by Opponent vs League Average

WK	DATE	TIME	OPP	QB	RB	WR	TE
1	9/11	4:25	LV	1%	10%	-14%	39%
2	9/15	8:15	@KC	15%	4%	3%	2%
3	9/25	4:05	JAC	4%	-1%	5%	-2%
4	10/02	1:00	@HOU	1%	13%	5%	13%
5	10/09	1:00	@CLE	-5%	-5%	-6%	2%
6	10/17	8:15	DEN	-10%	-9%	-6%	-29%
7	10/23	4:25	SEA	2%	-8%	3%	-23%
8	BYE WEEK						
9	11/06	1:00	@ATL	13%	8%	7%	-3%
10	11/13	8:20	@SF	-1%	26%	-3%	20%
11	11/20	4:25	KC	15%	4%	3%	2%
12	11/27	4:05	@ARI	0%	-11%	10%	-36%
13	12/04	4:25	@LV	1%	10%	-14%	39%
14	12/11	4:05	MIA	-6%	-4%	-2%	6%
15	12/18	4:25	TEN	3%	-22%	19%	-29%
16	12/26	8:15	@IND	2%	-12%	4%	23%
17	1/01	8:20	LAR	-12%	-8%	7%	-2%
18	1/08	TBD	@DEN	-10%	-9%	-6%	-29%

2022 NFL Draft

RD	PK		POS	COLLEGE	HT	WT
1	17	ZION JOHNSON	G	BOSTON COLLEGE	6-3	316
3	15	JT WOODS	S	BAYLOR	6-2	195
4	18	ISAIAH SPILLER	RB	TEXAS A&M	6-1	215
5	17	OTITO OGBONNIA	DT	UCLA	6-4	320
6	16	JAMAREE SALYRE	G	GEORGIA	6-4	325
6	36	JA'SIR TAYLOR	CB	WAKE FOREST	5-10	185
7	15	DEANE LEONARD	CB	OLE MISS	6-0	195
7	39	ZANDER HORVATH	FB	PURDUE	6-3	230

2021 Weekly Stats

	*RUSH STATS / *REC STATS		@ WAS (W) 20-16		DAL (L) 17-20		@ KC (W) 30-24		LV (W) 28-14		CLE (W) 47-42		@ BAL (L) 6-34		NE (L) 24-27		@ PHI (W) 27-24	
QB JUSTIN HERBERT			31-47 337 (1 INT) (1 TD) 4-[-1]		31-41 338 (2 INT) (1 TD) 4-12		26-38 281 (4 TD) 4-16		25-38 222 (3 TD) 3-4		26-43 398 (4 TD) 4-29 (1 TD)		22-39 195 (1 INT) (1 TD) 2-12		18-35 223 (2 INT) (2 TD) 2-9		32-38 356 (2 TD) 5-14 (1 TD)	
RB AUSTIN EKELER	15-57 (1 TD)	0-0	9-54	9-61	11-55	6-52 (1 TD)	15-117 (1 TD)	3-28 (1 TD)	17-66 (2 TD)	5-53 (1 TD)	6-7	4-48	11-64 (1 TD)	6-60	17-59	3-23
RB JUSTIN JACKSON	1-5	1-2	4-21	1-8	2-0	0-0	3-[-4]	4-17	DNP		0-0	1-7	3-79	0-0	DNP	
WR KEENAN ALLEN	0-0	9-100	0-0	4-108	0-0	8-50 (1 TD)	0-0	7-36	0-0	6-75	0-0	5-50	0-0	6-77 (1 TD)	0-0	12-104
WR MIKE WILLIAMS	0-0	8-82 (1 TD)	0-0	7-91 (1 TD)	0-0	7-122 (2 TD)	0-0	1-11	0-0	8-165 (2 TD)	0-0	2-27	0-0	2-19	0-0	2-58
WR JALEN GUYTON	0-0	3-49	1-9	2-13	1-3	0-0	2-20	1-9	0-0	2-35	0-0	1-15	0-0	1-18	0-0	1-19
TE JARED COOK	0-0	5-56	0-0	3-28	0-0	2-27	0-0	6-70 (1 TD)	0-0	1-29	0-0	4-25 (1 TD)	0-0	2-25	0-0	4-48
TE DONALD PARHAM	0-0	0-0	0-0	0-0	0-0	1-19	0-0	2-17 (1 TD)	0-0	2-29 (1 TD)	0-0	2-10	0-0	0-0	0-0	3-39 (1 TD)

2021 Stats
Record: 9–8
Rushing Rank: 21st
Passing Rank: 2nd
Offensive Fantasy Pts: 3rd
Against Run: 30th
Against Pass: 11th
ppg Against: 27th
ppg: 27.9

KEY ADDITIONS & NEW CONTRACTS

QB **CHASE DANIEL**: RE-SIGNED ON A FREE-AGENT CONTRACT.

WR/KR **DEANDRE CARTER**: SIGNED A ONE-YEAR, $1.135 MILLION DEAL WITH $100,000 GUARANTEED.

WR **MIKE WILLIAMS**: RE-SIGNED ON A THREE-YEAR, $60 MILLION DEAL THAT INCLUDES $40 MILLION FULLY GUARANTEED OVER THE FIRST TWO YEARS.

TE **GERALD EVERETT**: SIGNED A TWO-YEAR, $12 MILLION DEAL WITH A MAX VALUE OF $13.5 MILLION.

DE **MORGAN FOX**: SIGNED A FREE-AGENT DEAL.

DT **CHRISTIAN COVINGTON**: RE-SIGNED ON A FREE-AGENT CONTRACT.

DT **AUSTIN JOHNSON**: SIGNED WITH THE CHARGERS.

DL **SEBASTIAN JOSEPH-DAY**: SIGNED A THREE-YEAR, $24 MILLION DEAL WITH $15 MILLION FULLY GUARANTEED.

LB **KHALIL MACK**: ACQUIRED IN A TRADE WITH THE LOS ANGELES CHARGERS IN EXCHANGE FOR A 2022 SECOND-ROUND DRAFT PICK AND A SIXTH-ROUNDER IN 2023.

LB **KYLE VAN NOY**: SIGNED A FREE-AGENT DEAL WITH THE CHARGERS.

CB **BRYCE CALLAHAN**: SIGNED A FREE-AGENT DEAL WITH THE CHARGERS.

CB **J.C. JACKSON**: SIGNED A FIVE-YEAR, $82.5 MILLION DEAL WITH $40 MILLION GUARANTEED.

LS **JOSH HARRIS**: SIGNED A FOUR-YEAR, $5.6 MILLION DEAL WITH $1.92 MILLION GUARANTEED.

K **DUSTIN HOPKINS**: RE-SIGNED ON A MULTI-YEAR CONTRACT.

What are the chances of Mike Williams having a better year than Keenan Allen?

After Week 5 last season, the fantasy community was sure that Mike Williams had supplanted Allen as the Charger's No. 1 WR. During that span, Williams averaged 7.4 more fantasy PPG than Allen. What people didn't notice was that Allen still had more targets than Williams in that stretch.

Williams came back to earth in Week 6, finishing 2021 with about the same number of yards as Allen, but with 3 more TDs and 40 fewer receptions.

The receivers had almost identical PFF receiving grades. But in fantasy football where volume is the key, it's hard to find a scenario where one could reasonably rank Williams higher than Allen. It would take a large TD discrepancy along with a play-calling change that promotes more deep-balls, to put Williams ahead of Allen.

We are concerned, however, with Allen's age (30), an age often associated with WR performance decline. While his upside may not be as high as years' past, he still has a solid floor.

Here's some history. Over the past 10 years, looking at top-five QBs with fewer than 75 rushing attempts (like Herbert), the teams' top receiving option has an average finish of WR9, while the teams' second option has an average finish of WR33. History doesn't bode well for Williams' outlook.

'It's hard to find a scenario where one could reasonably rank Williams higher than Allen.'

The two receivers, each now making $10 million a year, are both slated for big years. In PPR leagues we expect Allen to outscore Williams, but in less reception-friendly leagues, we wouldn't be shocked to see Williams finish as the team's leading fantasy WR.

KEY LOSSES

RB **JUSTIN JACKSON**

WR **ANDRE ROBERTS** (PANTHERS)

TE **JARED COOK**

OG **ODAY ABOUSHI**

OG **MICHAEL SCHOFIELD**

OT **BRYAN BULAGA**

DT **LINVAL JOSEPH**

DL **JUSTIN JONES** (BEARS)

LB **KYLER FACKRELL** (RAIDERS)

LB **UCHENNA NWOSU** (SEAHAWKS)

LB **KYZIR WHITE** (EAGLES)

CB **CHRIS HARRIS**

CB **RYAN SMITH**

LS **MATT OVERTON**

DEPTH CHART

QB1	JUSTIN HERBERT
QB2	CHASE DANIEL
RB1	AUSTIN EKELER
RB2	ISAIAH SPILLER **R**
RB3	JOSHUA KELLEY
WR1	KEENAN ALLEN
WR2	MIKE WILLIAMS
WR3	JOSH PALMER
WR4	JALEN GUYTON
TE1	GERALD EVERETT **N**
TE2	DONALD PARHAM
K	DUSTIN HOPKINS

2021 WEEKLY STATS

MIN (L) 20-27		PIT (W) 41-37		@ DEN (L) 13-28		@ CIN (W) 41-22		NYG (W) 37-21		KC (L) 28-34		@ HOU (W) 29-41		DEN (W) 34-13		@ LV (L) 32-35	
20-34 195 (1 INT) (1 TD) 2-22		30-41 382 (1 INT) (3 TD) 9-90		28-44 303 (2 INT) (2 TD) 4-36		26-35 317 (1 INT) (3 TD) 1-6		23-31 275 (3 TD) 4-19		22-38 236 (1 INT) (2 TD) 5-16 (1 TD)		27-35 336 (2 INT) (1 TD) 4-15		22-31 237 (2 TD) 4-2		34-64 383 (1 INT) (3 TD) 2-1	
11-44	3-15 (1 TD)	11-50 (2 TD)	6-65 (2 TD)	12-31	6-68 (1 TD)	14-59 (1 TD)	5-45	12-67 (1 TD)	2-17	12-59 (1 TD)	4-23	DNP		17-54 (1 TD)	3-54	16-64 (1 TD)	5-35 (1 TD)
DNP		1-2	0-0	DNP		6-15	2-6	9-35	1-7	13-86	1-13	11-64 (2 TD)	8-98	12-41	3-20	3-20	0-0
0-0	8-98	0-0	9-112	0-0	7-85	0-0	5-34 (2 TD)	DNP		0-0	6-78 (1 TD)	0-0	4-35	0-0	4-44 (1 TD)	0-0	6-52
0-0	4-33	0-0	5-97 (1 TD)	0-0	4-39	0-0	5-110	0-0	6-61	0-0	3-49	DNP		0-0	3-63 (1 TD)	0-0	9-119 (1 TD)
0-0	0-0	1-2	1-18	0-0	2-23	1-1-1	4-90 (1 TD)	0-0	3-87 (1 TD)	0-0	2-10 (1 TD)	DNP		1-1	2-10	0-0	6-52
0-0	1-10	0-0	3-28	0-0	2-25 (1 TD)	0-0	3-29	0-0	2-8 (1 TD)	0-0	3-32	0-0	3-44	DNP		0-0	4-80
0-0	1-17	0-0	4-38	0-0	1-5	0-0	2-3	0-0	2-13	0-0	0-0	DNP		DNP		DNP	

Is Matthew Stafford a top-10 fantasy QB in 2022?

Stafford finally got out of Detroit, landing on a Rams team full of talent. All he did in his first year in his new locale was win the Lombardi Trophy.

Stafford was terrific last season: He threw for 4,886 yards and 41 TDs (second best among QBs), had a QB rating of 102.9 (seventh), and had 8.1 yards per attempt (third). He was the 11th-best QB in fantasy PPG. Josh Allen, last season's QB1, averaged 4.3 more fantasy PPG last season than Stafford, but the QB3 had only 2 more PPG, and the QB6 1 more. The difference in QBs in a certain range is nominal, and it's not worth overvaluing them in drafts.

Stafford's 2022 fantasy managers should be more than happy to see a repeat of his 2021 performance. He retains the best part of his receiving corps in Cooper Kupp and will still have Sean McVay directing traffic. In a competitive division that should generate plenty of shootouts, Stafford should see ample opportunity to throw the ball down the field.

Without any rushing stats to speak of, He and Joe Burrow have similar outlooks as they are both pure pocket passers. We'll take either one for our fantasy team, but we give the slight edge to Burrow. Stafford may not finish in the top-10 QBs, but he shouldn't finish outside the top 15 either.

Is Cam Akers finally the Rams three-down back this season?

We've seen a small sample size of what Cam Akers could be. In his rookie year (2020), he was used sparingly as part of a committee approach, while he nursed various injuries. Then, in the last six games that year he was charged with the workload, averaging almost 24 touches per game.

In July 2021, Akers tore his Achilles, and it appeared his season was over. In Aker's absence, Darrell Henderson took the lead in Weeks 1-12, averaging 15.7 fantasy PPG. Then from Weeks 13-18, Sony Michel took over the backfield, averaging 14.8 fantasy PPG. Akers, amazingly, returned in Week 18 to play throughout the playoff run to the Super Bowl. While mostly ineffective during this stretch, he did average 19.3 touches per game.

What may be the most telling is the division of work between RBs in the championship game. While Akers saw the bulk of the workload, he still only played 57% of the snaps, after playing 81% of the snaps in the divisional round against the Bucs, two games prior. Henderson played 33% of the snaps, and Michel, 11%. We consider 60% the threshold for lead-back or committee, and Akers was

2022/23 SCHEDULE			2021 FANTASY POINTS ALLOWED BY OPPONENT VS LEAGUE AVERAGE			
WK	DATE	TIME	OPP	QB	RB	WR	TE
1	9/08	8:20	BUF	-34%	-11%	-27%	-34%
2	9/18	4:05	ATL	13%	8%	7%	-3%
3	9/25	4:25	@ARI	0%	-11%	10%	-36%
4	10/03	8:15	@SF	-1%	26%	-3%	20%
5	10/09	4:25	DAL	-6%	-14%	2%	5%
6	10/16	4:05	CAR	-6%	-12%	-7%	-5%
7	BYE WEEK						
8	10/30	4:25	SF	-1%	26%	-3%	20%
9	11/06	4:25	@TB	3%	-4%	3%	4%
10	11/13	4:25	ARI	0%	-11%	10%	-36%
11	11/20	1:00	@NO	-26%	2%	-16%	-45%
12	11/27	4:25	@KC	15%	4%	3%	2%
13	12/04	4:05	SEA	2%	-8%	3%	-23%
14	12/08	8:15	LV	1%	10%	-14%	39%
15	12/19	8:15	@GB	5%	-13%	3%	0%
16	12/25	4:30	DEN	-10%	-9%	-6%	-29%
17	1/01	8:20	@LAC	2%	17%	-11%	23%
18	1/08	TBD	@SEA	2%	-8%	3%	-23%

2022 NFL DRAFT					
RD	PK		POS	COLLEGE	HT	WT
3	40	LOGAN BRUSS	G	WISCONSIN	6-5	316
4	37	DECOBIE DURANT	CB	SOUTH CAROLINA STATE	6-2	165
5	21	KYREN WILLIAMS	RB	NOTRE DAME	5-9	195
6	33	QUENTIN LAKE	S	UCLA	6-1	205
6	34	DERION KENDRICK	CB	GEORGIA	6-0	190
7	14	DANIEL HARDY	EDGE	MONTANA STATE	6-3	223
7	32	RUSS YEAST	S	KANSAS STATE	5-10	195
7	40	AJ ARCURI	OT	MICHIGAN STATE	6-7	320

2021 WEEKLY STATS

*RUSH STATS : REC STATS		CHI (W) 34-14		@ IND (W) 27-24		TB (W) 34-24		ARI (L) 20-37		@ SEA (W) 26-17		@ NYG (W) 38-11		DET (W) 28-19		@ HOU (W) 38-22	
QB MATTHEW STAFFORD		20-26 321 (3 TD) 5-[-5]		19-30 278 (1 INT) (2 TD) 2-1		27-38 343 (4 TD) 2-[-2]		26-41 280 (1 INT) (2 TD) 6-21		25-37 365 (1 INT) (1 TD) 1-[-1]		22-28 251 (1 INT) (4 TD) 2-12		28-41 334 (3 TD) 2-[-2]		21-32 305 (3 TD) 0-0	
RB DARRELL HENDERSON	16-70 (1 TD)	1-17	13-53 (1 TD)	3-29	DNP		14-89	5-27	17-82 (1 TD)	1-17	21-78 (1 TD)	2-29 (1 TD)	15-45	3-19	14-90 (1 TD)	1-3 (1 TD)
RB SONY MICHEL	1-2	0-0	10-46	0-0	20-67	3-12	3-11	0-0	11-37 (1 TD)	1-8	9-42	0-0	2-4	0-0	9-42	2-14
WR COOPER KUPP	0-0	7-108 (1 TD)	1-[-5]	9-163 (2 TD)	0-0	9-96 (2 TD)	0-0	5-64	0-0	7-92	0-0	9-130 (2 TD)	0-0	10-156 (2TD)	0-0	7-115 (1 TD)
WR VAN JEFFERSON	0-0	2-80 (1 TD)	0-0	1-14	0-0	4-42	0-0	6-90 (1 TD)	0-0	1-16	0-0	3-19	0-0	4-43 (1 TD)	0-0	3-88
WR ROBERT WOODS	1-7	3-27 (1 TD)	2-6	5-64	1-5	3-33	0-0	4-48 (1 TD)	0-0	12-150	0-0	2-31 (1 TD)	0-0	6-70	3-22 (1 TD)	3-35 (1 TD)
WR ODELL BECKHAM JR.	DNP		DNP		DNP		DNP		DNP		DNP		DNP		DNP	
TE TYLER HIGBEE	0-0	5-68	0-0	1-8	0-0	5-40 (1 TD)	0-0	4-36	0-0	2-14 (1 TD)	0-0	5-36	0-0	5-46	0-0	3-25

2021 Stats

Record: 12–5
Rushing Rank: 25th
Passing Rank: 5th
Offensive Fantasy Pts: 6th
Against Run: 6th
Against Pass: 24th
ppg Against: 21.3
ppg: 27.0

in a committee in the Super Bowl. His lack of snaps could have been because he was still not in playing shape after his injury or even fully healthy. While most in FantasyTakeover believe Akers will play more than 65% of the snaps as the clear lead back for the Rams this season, not everyone agrees.

With that said, Henderson is his only real competition for touches, as Michel is now in Miami. Nonetheless, Akers will have a large role for the Rams this season, but how large has yet to be seen.

KEY ADDITIONS & NEW CONTRACTS

QB **MATTHEW STAFFORD**: SIGNED WHAT IS EFFECTIVELY A THREE-YEAR, $129 MILLION EXTENSION THAT INCLUDES A $60 MILLION SIGNING BONUS. THE EXTENSION SHOULD CLEAR CLOSE TO $10 MILLION OFF OF THE RAMS' 2022 SALARY CAP.

WR **COOPER KUPP**: AGREED TO A THREE-YEAR EXTENSION WORTH UP TO $80 MILLION. KUPP IS NOW UNDER CONTRACT WITH THE RAMS THROUGH 2026.

WR **ALLEN ROBINSON II**: SIGNED A THREE-YEAR, $46.5 MILLION DEAL THAT INCLUDES $30.7 MILLION FULLY GUARANTEED.

OT **JOE NOTEBOOM**: RE-SIGNED ON A THREE-YEAR, $40 MILLION DEAL THAT INCLUDES $25 MILLION GUARANTEED AND HAS A MAX VALUE OF $47.5 MILLION.

C **BRIAN ALLEN**: RE-SIGNED TO A THREE-YEAR DEAL.

DT **AARON DONALD**: SIGNED A RESTRUCTURED CONTRACT THAT WILL PAY HIM $65 MILLION GUARANTEED OVER THE NEXT TWO SEASONS. THE DEAL IS DESIGNED TO ALLOW DONALD TO RETIRE IN YEAR 3 OR RETURN IN 2024 FOR AN ADDITIONAL $30 MILLION GUARANTEED. DONALD IS NOW THE HIGHEST-PAID NON-QB IN NFL HISTORY.

LB **BOBBY WAGNER**: SIGNED WHAT IS FUNCTIONALLY A TWO-YEAR DEAL WORTH $17.5 MILLION IN BASE SALARY WITH ANOTHER $23.5 MILLION POSSIBLE IN INCENTIVES. IF WAGNER HITS HIS INCENTIVES, HE CAN OPT-OUT OF THE DEAL AND BECOME A FREE AGENT AGAIN.

CB **TROY HILL**: ACQUIRED IN A TRADE WITH THE CLEVELAND BROWNS FOR A 2023 FIFTH-ROUND PICK.

P **RILEY DIXON**: SIGNED A FREE-AGENT DEAL.

Can Cooper Kupp repeat last season's performance, and can Allen Robinson II be viable in his wake?

Cooper Kupp had one of the best fantasy seasons in the history of football. Last season, he scored more fantasy points than any other WR in the NFL, ever. Over the past 50 years, only three other receivers have led the league in each: receptions, receiving yards, and receiving TDs (Jerry Rice, 1990; Sterling Sharpe, 1992; and Steve Smith, 1995).

Kupp rightfully enters this season as the projected WR1 for the league. Of 21 games played last season, in only four did he see fewer than 10 targets. In eight games, he had 9 or more receptions, with a notable 13.4 yards per reception in the regular season. With such a massive target volume in 2021, it will be difficult for Kupp to repeat last year's numbers, but even with a semi-significant drop he still could finish as the overall WR1.

Allen Robinson II signed with the Rams this offseason and looks to fill the void left by Robert Woods (Tennessee) and then Odell Beckham (free agent). Before Woods' season-ending ACL tear last year, Woods was on pace for 130 targets, 85 receptions, and 1,050 yards. With Robinson filling that void, he should see similar numbers in targets, yards, and receptions.

Robinson had a poor outing in 12 games with a terrible Matt Nagy-led Bears last season. He was also dealing with injuries most of the season. This was his first season in three without at least 1,100 yards. Both the previous seasons he was a top-20 WR. He'll finally have the first good passing QB of his career, and we expect an A-Rob comeback.

KEY LOSSES

RB **SONY MICHEL** (DOLPHINS)

WR **ODELL BECKHAM JR.**

WR **ROBERT WOODS** (TRADED TO TITANS)

OT **ANDREW WHITWORTH** (RETIRED)

OG **AUSTIN CORBETT** (PANTHERS)

DL **SEBASTIAN JOSEPH-DAY** (CHARGERS)

LB **VON MILLER** (BILLS)

LB **OGBO OKORONKWO** (TEXANS)

CB **DONTE DEAYON**

CB **DARIOUS WILLIAMS** (JAGUARS)

P **JOHNNY HEKKER** (PANTHERS)

DEPTH CHART

QB1	MATTHEW STAFFORD
QB2	JOHN WOLFORD
RB1	CAM AKERS
RB2	DARRELL HENDERSON JR.
RB3	JAKE FUNK
WR1	COOPER KUPP
WR2	ALLEN ROBINSON II **N**
WR3	VAN JEFFERSON
WR4	BEN SKOWRONEK
TE1	TYLER HIGBEE
TE2	KENDALL BLANTON
K	MATT GAY

2021 WEEKLY STATS

	TEN (L) 16-28	@ SF (L) 10-31	@ GB (L) 28-36	JAC (W) 37-7	@ ARI (W) 30-23	SEA (W) 20-10	@ MIN (W) 30-23	@ BAL (W) 20-19	SF (L) 24-27
	31-48 294 (2 INT) (1 TD); 2-13	26-41 243 (2 INT) (1 TD); 1-1	21-38 302 (1 INT) (3 TD); 1-[-1]	26-38 295 (3 TD); 1-2	23-30 287 (3 TD); 0-0	21-29 244 (1 INT) (2 TD); 3-[-3]	21-37 197 (3 INT) (1 TD); 3-8	26-35 309 (2 INT) (2 TD); 1-[-1]	21-32 238 (2 INT) (3 TD); 0-0
	11-55; 3-3	5-31; 4-10	16-55; 4-18 (1 TD)	DNP	DNP	6-23; 2-4	1-17; 0-0	DNP	DNP
	7-20; 2-6 (1 TD)	4-20; 2-11	3-14; 1-11	24-121 (1 TD); 3-8	20-79; 0-0	18-92; 2-23	27-131 (1 TD); 1-4	19-74 (1 TD); 3-25	21-43; 1-6
	0-0; 11-95	0-0; 11-122	0-0; 7-96	0-0; 8-129 (1 TD)	0-0; 13-123 (1 TD)	1-1; 9-136 (2 TD)	1-4; 10-109	0-0; 6-95 (1 TD)	1-18; 7-118 (1 TD)
	0-0; 3-41	0-0; 3-54	0-0; 3-93 (1 TD)	0-0; 6-41 (1 TD)	1-10; 2-58 (1 TD)	1-10; 2-23	0-0; 1-6	0-0; 4-63	0-0; 2-31
	1-6; 7-98	TBD	TBD	TBD	TBD	TBD	TBD	TBD	TBD
	DNP	0-0; 2-18	0-0; 5-81 (1 TD)	0-0; 2-28 (1 TD)	0-0; 6-77 (1 TD)	0-0; 1-7	0-0; 4-37 (1 TD)	0-0; 5-39 (1 TD)	0-0; 2-18
	0-0; 5-51	0-0; 3-20 (1 TD)	0-0; 1-3	0-0; 5-48	DNP	DNP	0-0; 5-41	0-0; 6-69	0-0; 6-55 (2 TD)

MIAMI DOLPHINS

What's Tua's fantasy outlook for 2022?

By all measures, Tua Tagovailoa should improve his fantasy output this season. He's been a non-factor thus far, with only two career top-10 weekly finishes. He's a conservative passer, which is directly reflected by his numbers: 7.0 air yards per attempt (last among QBs with at least 12 starts), and a 68% completion rate (tied for second best). So, what does Tua need to do to reach the next level?

His best chance of raising his fantasy stock comes at the hands of newly-acquired WR Tyreek Hill. He's been a top-six receiver three of the last four seasons in Kansas City, and could produce similar numbers with Tua. Hill's been Tua's most vocal supporter this offseason, controversially stating that Tua was even more accurate than his former QB, Patrick Mahomes (not sure we agree).

Where Tua needs work is in the deep game. He's got the arm strength, and despite his low average depth of throw, when he does throw the ball for at least 20-plus air yards, he's second best in the league on yards per attempt. With Hill and second-year stud, Jaylen Waddle, as primary targets, Tua should improve in yards, completions, and passing TDs, and should see an increase in production of the all-important big plays.

The fantasy reality is that without any significant rushing production, entering 2022 as our 14th-ranked QB, Tua will be limited to a streaming option outside of 2-QB leagues.

Can Miami's offense support two top-15 WRs?

The short answer is, yes. This offseason, Miami made Tyreek Hill one of the highest paid WRs in the NFL. His worst fantasy finish over the last five seasons was as the WR12 in 2019, when he only played 12 games.

But to understand Hill's potential in Miami, one must look at his games where Patrick Mahomes wasn't under center. Way back in 2017, with Alex Smith at QB in Kansas City, Hill finished the season as WR5. Yes, he's older now, but hasn't yet been limited by his age.

The harder situation to assess is that of Jaylen Waddle, now the No. 2 receiving option. Is it still possible for him to finish in the top-15 WRs?

In the past ten years, on average only 4.3 teams per season have supported two top-24 WRs. No more than six teams have done so in a given season. But, other than Cincinnati, Miami has the best chance of posting two top-15 WRs this year. Waddle would have been a definite top-10 pick had Miami not added Hill. While Waddle's 2021 season now may be more of a ceiling (WR12) than a floor, he will still see enough targets to be a top-15 WR.

2022/23 SCHEDULE				2021 FANTASY POINTS ALLOWED BY OPPONENT VS LEAGUE AVERAGE			
WK	DATE	TIME	OPP	QB	RB	WR	TE
1	9/11	1:00	NE	-8%	-19%	1%	-20%
2	9/18	1:00	@BAL	13%	-12%	12%	29%
3	9/25	1:00	BUF	-34%	-11%	-27%	-34%
4	9/29	8:15	@CIN	-1%	6%	0%	22%
5	10/09	1:00	@NYJ	-4%	11%	-1%	-1%
6	10/16	1:00	MIN	6%	2%	23%	-13%
7	10/23	8:20	PIT	-2%	11%	-3%	-10%
8	10/30	1:00	@DET	4%	14%	2%	17%
9	11/06	1:00	@CHI	4%	-7%	0%	-28%
10	11/13	1:00	CLE	-5%	-5%	-6%	2%
11	BYE WEEK						
12	11/27	1:00	HOU	1%	13%	5%	13%
13	12/04	4:05	@SF	-1%	26%	-3%	20%
14	12/11	4:05	@LAC	2%	17%	-11%	23%
15	12/17	TBD	@BUF	-34%	-11%	-27%	-34%
16	12/25	1:00	GB	5%	-13%	3%	0%
17	1/01	1:00	@NE	-8%	-19%	1%	-20%
18	1/08	TBD	NYJ	-4%	11%	-1%	-1%

2022 NFL DRAFT					
RD	PK		POS	COLLEGE	HT WT
3	38	CHANNING TINDALL	LB	GEORGIA	6-2 230
4	20	ERIK EZUKANMA	WR	TEXAS TECH	6-3 220
7	3	CAMERON GOODE	EDGE	CALIFORNIA	6-4 240
7	26	SKYLAR THOMPSON	QB	KANSAS STATE	6-2 223

2021 WEEKLY STATS

*RUSH STATS : *REC STATS	@ NE (W) 17-16		BUF (L) 0-35		@ LV (L) 28-31		IND (L) 17-27		@ TB (L) 17-45		@ JAC (L) 20-23		ATL (L) 28-30		@ BUF (L) 11-26	
QB TUA TAGOVAILOA	16-27 202 (1 INT) (1 TD) 4-1 (1 TD)		1-4 13 0-0		DNP		DNP		DNP		33-47 329 (1 INT) (2 TD) 3-22		32-40 291 (2 INT) (4 TD) 4-29		21-39 205 (1 INT) 4-10 (1 TD)	
QB JACOBY BRISSETT	0-0 0 2-4		24-40 169 (1 INT) 4-8		32-49 215 7-37 (1 TD)		20-30 199 (2 TD) 3-8		27-39 275 (1 INT) (2 INT) 0-0		1-1 25 0-0		DNP		DNP	
RB MYLES GASKIN	9-49	5-27	5-25	4-21	13-65	3-9	2-3	0-0	5-25	10-74 (2 TD)	5-9	2-5	15-67	4-10 (1 TD)	12-36	3-19
RB DUKE JOHNSON	DNP		DNP		DNP		DNP		DNP		DNP		DNP		DNP	
WR JAYLEN WADDLE	0-0	4-61 (1 TD)	0-0	6-48	0-0	12-58	0-0	3-33	1-2	2-31	0-0	10-70 (2 TD)	0-0	7-83	0-0	4-29
WR DEVANTE PARKER	0-0	4-81	0-0	5-42	0-0	4-42	0-0	4-77 (1 TD)	DNP		DNP		DNP		0-0	8-85
WR MACK HOLLINS	0-0	0-0	0-0	0-0	0-0	0-0	0-0	0-0	0-0	1-10	0-0	4-61	0-0	2-13 (1 TD)	0-0	0-0
TE MIKE GESICKI	0-0	0-0	0-0	3-41	0-0	10-86	0-0	5-57 (1 TD)	0-0	4-43	0-0	8-115	0-0	7-85 (1 TD)	0-0	3-48
TE DURHAM SMYTHE	0-0	1-9	0-0	0-0	0-0	0-0	0-0	2-6	0-0	2-23	0-0	5-59	0-0	3-37	0-0	0-0

2021 Stats

Record: 9-8
Rushing Rank: 30th
Passing Rank: 18th
Offensive Fantasy Pts: 23rd
Against Run: 14th
Against Pass: 19th
ppg Against: 21.9
ppg: 20.1

KEY ADDITIONS & NEW CONTRACTS

QB **TEDDY BRIDGEWATER**: SIGNED A ONE-YEAR, $6.5 MILLION FULLY GUARANTEED DEAL THAT'S WORTH UP TO $10 MILLION WITH INCENTIVES.

RB **CHASE EDMONDS**: SIGNED A TWO-YEAR, $12.6 MILLION CONTRACT THAT INCLUDES $6.1 MILLION GUARANTEED.

RB **SONY MICHEL**: SIGNED A FREE-AGENT DEAL

RB **RAHEEM MOSTERT**: SIGNED A ONE-YEAR DEAL WORTH $3.125 MILLION.

FB **ALEC INGOLD**: SIGNED A TWO-YEAR DEAL WORTH UP TO $7.5 MILLION.

WR **TYREEK HILL**: ACQUIRED IN A TRADE WITH THE KANSAS CITY CHIEFS IN EXCHANGE FOR 2022 FIRST-, SECOND- AND FOURTH-ROUND PICKS, AND 2023 FOURTH- AND SIXTH-ROUNDERS. HILL HAS AGREED TO A FOUR-YEAR, $120 MILLION EXTENSION THAT INCLUDES $72.2 MILLION GUARANTEED.

WR **TRENT SHERFIELD**: SIGNED A ONE-YEAR DEAL.

WR **PRESTON WILLIAMS**: RE-SIGNED ON A ONE-YEAR DEAL WORTH UP TO $1.99 MILLION.

WR **CEDRICK WILSON**: SIGNED A THREE-YEAR, $22.8 MILLION DEAL THAT INCLUDES $12.75 MILLION FULLY GUARANTEED.

TE **MIKE GESICKI**: SIGNED THE FRANCHISE TAG.

TE **DURHAM SMYTHE**: RE-SIGNED WITH MIAMI.

LT **TERRON ARMSTEAD**: SIGNED A FIVE-YEAR, $75 MILLION DEAL THAT HAS A MAX VALUE OF $87.5 MILLION.

OG **CONNOR WILLIAMS**: SIGNED A TWO-YEAR, $14 MILLION DEAL THAT INCLUDES $7.5 MILLION FULLY GUARANTEED.

DE **EMMANUEL OGBAH**: RE-SIGNED ON A FOUR-YEAR, $65.4 MILLION DEAL THAT WILL PAY HIM $32.7 MILLION OVER THE FIRST TWO YEARS.

DT **JOHN JENKINS**: RE-SIGNED WITH MIAMI.

LB **MELVIN INGRAM**: SIGNED A ONE-YEAR, $5 MILLION DEAL.

LB **DUKE RILEY**: RE-SIGNED A ONE-YEAR, $3 MILLION DEAL.

LB **ELANDON ROBERTS**: RE-SIGNED ON A ONE-YEAR, $3.25 MILLION DEAL.

LB **BRENNAN SCARLETT**: RE-SIGNED TO A ONE-YEAR DEAL.

CB **XAVIEN HOWARD**: AGREED TO A NEW FIVE-YEAR CONTRACT WORTH $90 MILLION. HOWARD HAD THREE YEARS AND ROUGHLY $39.3 MILLION REMAINING ON HIS OLD DEAL.

P **THOMAS MORSTEAD**: SIGNED A FREE-AGENT DEAL.

Who emerges from Miami's RB room?

The Dolphins signed several backs this offseason setting up a competition to determine the RB hierarchy. Although talented, some backs vying for position may not even make the roster. Salary could give a hint as to who will take the lead in Miami's backfield.

At $5.5 million, Chase Edmonds stands to make the most this season. However, salary aside, there are arguments that suggest, the lead back position is anybody's job to win.

Edmonds has the best preseason outlook. Beyond salary, his receiving potential makes him the most fantasy viable RB in the Miami offense. In just 12 games last season he had 53 targets and 43 receptions, 10th best among RBs on a per-game basis. He finished the season as RB28 in fantasy PPG.

Raheem Mostert signed a $1.9 million contract this offseason. The 30-year-old missed almost the entire 2021 season due to injury, but returns ready to go. Among active backs with 200-plus carries, he has the most yards per carry. Mostert also has a history of with new head coach Mike McDaniel, his offensive coordinator in San Francisco. Mostert may be the most talented pure rusher of the bunch, but durability and age are now an issue.

Myles Gaskin will enter his fourth season in Miami and stands to make $2.5 million this season. In 2021, he played his first full season finishing as the No. 25 RB overall and as RB16 in receptions per game. However, it's unlikely he has much of a role this season with all the new additions.

Then, there's Sony Michel, who split RB duties for the Super Bowl Champion Rams last season. In five games, when Michel was asked to assume the lead role, he averaged 111.4 yards per game and 16.5 fantasy PPG.

Chase Edmonds is the frontrunner to end the year with the highest fantasy value, but Mostert and Michel have the best chance for the early-down RB role. Edmonds is worth a pick, and should be drafted in the middle rounds. Mostert and Michel are also worth late-round consideration.

KEY LOSSES

QB **JACOBY BRISSETT** (BROWNS)

RB **MALCOLM BROWN**

RB **DUKE JOHNSON** (BILLS)

RB **PHILLIP LINDSAY** (COLTS)

WR **WILL FULLER**

WR **ALLEN HURNS**

WR **ALBERT WILSON** (VIKINGS)

OL **JESSE DAVIS** (VIKINGS)

CB **JUSTIN COLEMAN** (SEAHAWKS)

CB **JASON MCCOURTY**

P **MICHAEL PALARDY**

DEPTH CHART

QB1	TUA TAGOVAILOA
QB2	TEDDY BRIDGEWATER **N**
RB1	CHASE EDMONDS **N**
RB2	SONY MICHEL **N**
RB3	RAHEEM MOSTERT **N**
WR1	TYREEK HILL **N**
WR2	JAYLEN WADDLE
WR3	CEDRICK WILSON **N**
WR4	PRESTON WILLIAMS
TE1	MIKE GESICKI
TE2	DURHAM SMYTHE
K	JASON SANDERS

2021 WEEKLY STATS

HOU (W) 17-9		BAL (W) 22-10		@ NYJ (W) 24-17		CAR (W) 33-10		NYG (W) 20-9		NYJ (W) 31-24		@ NO (W) 20-3		@ TEN (L) 3-34		NE (W) 33-24	
DNP		8-13 158 3-0 (1 TD)		27-33 273 (1 INT) (2 TD) 3-6		27-31 230 (1 TD) 4-0		30-41 244 (2 TD) 2-1		16-27 196 (2 INT) (2 TD) 7-19		19-26 198 (1 INT) (1 TD) 1-1		18-38 205 (1 INT) 2-1		15-22 109 (1 TD) 5-38	
26-43 244 (2 INT) (1 TD) 1-7		11-23 156 1-4		DNP		DNP		DNP		0-0 0 1-2		DNP		DNP		DNP	
20-34 (1 TD)	6-23	14-31	1-14	23-89	3-7 (1 TD)	16-49 (2 TD)	2-3	15-44	2-5	10-54	0-0	3-10	1-6	5-23	0-0	1-[-1]	3-11
DNP		DNP		4-18	0-0	DNP		DNP		22-107 (2TD)	1-20	13-39	0-0	7-49	2-16	25-117 (1 TD)	1-5
0-0	8-83	0-0	4-61	1-1 (1 TD)	8-65	0-0	9-137 (1 TD)	0-0	9-90	DNP		0-0	10-92 (1 TD)	0-0	3-47	0-0	5-27 (1 TD)
DNP		DNP		DNP		DNP		0-0	5-62	0-0	4-68 (1 TD)	0-0	0-0	0-0	4-46	0-0	2-12
0-0	3-22 (1 TD)	0-0	0-0	0-0	2-72 (1 TD)	0-0	0-0	0-0	1-5 (1 TD)	0-0	0-0	0-0	1-40	0-0	0-0	0-0	0-0
0-0	4-54	0-0	0-0	0-0	5-50	0-0	3-17	0-0	7-46	0-0	5-43	0-0	3-22	0-0	4-51	0-0	2-22
0-0	2-27	0-0	1-23	0-0	4-37	2-3	5-32	0-0	0-0	0-0	1-4	0-0	3-31	0-0	3-37	0-0	2-32

MINNESOTA VIKINGS

Can new head coach Kevin O'Connell take QB Kirk Cousins to the next level?

Kirk Cousins hasn't been a bad quarterback, or a bad fantasy quarterback, for that matter, but he hasn't been a good one either. In three of four years in Minnesota, Cousins has consistently finished just inside the top half of fantasy QBs in PPG average (2018: 17.6 fantasy PPG [QB16], 2019: 16.3 [QB18], 2020: 19.1 [QB12], 2021: 18.8 [QB12]), but who wants a 12th-ranked QB, unless you're in a Superflex or 2-QB league? Nobody.

Cousins, however, is a better QB than he seems, and numbers can be deceiving. For example: Since 2018, according to PFF, Cousins has had the No. 6 passing grade (90.7) and QB rating (103.5), and the No. 3 adjusted completion rate (78.9%). Last season, he had eight games of 21.9 fantasy points or more, totaling more than 25 PPG in four of those contests. He also threw 33 TDs, but only 7

'The Vikings front office hopes the answer is new head coach Kevin O'Connell, and it's possible they may be right.'

interceptions. So with a four-year record of 33-29-1 with the Vikings, what will it take to get Cousins over the just-better-than-average hump?

The Vikings front office hopes the answer is new head coach Kevin O'Connell, and it's possible they may be right. O'Connell comes from the Super Bowl-winning Rams, where he was offensive coordinator. Under O'Connell the Rams were pass heavy, with the seventh-highest usage of shift/motion plays, and led the league in play-action rate since 2018. If O'Connell can bring some of that aggressive and deceptive play calling to Minnesota, Cousins, and the Vikings as a whole, have a chance to improve, and the Ceiling is high. And the Vikings have the highly skilled playmakers to do it.

Is Dalvin Cook still a top-10 RB?

Cook has certainly has some durability issues, missing 13 games over the last four years, but when he's on the field he's produced (2018: 13.8 Fantasy PPG [RB19], 2019: 20.9 [RB2], 2020: 24.1 [RB2], 2021: 15.9 [RB11]).

Last year he saw some regression, tallying only five games of 21.5 fantasy points or more, while battling an ongoing shoulder problem. He saw his lowest career total of targets per game (3.8), and we expect that to increase with the play

calling of Kevin O'Connell. If Cooks can match last year's rushing numbers — which we expect he will — and can see a slight boost in the receiving game, he should re-enter the top 10 among backs, and regain his reputation as a RB1 in fantasy. But consider RB Alexander Mattison as a handcuff. Mattison has always produced in Cooks' absence, and history tells us Cook's likely to miss a couple of games.

2022/23 SCHEDULE			2021 FANTASY POINTS ALLOWED BY OPPONENT VS LEAGUE AVERAGE			
WK	DATE	TIME	OPP	QB	RB	WR	TE
1	9/11	4:25	GB	5%	-13%	3%	0%
2	9/19	8:30	@PHI	-1%	10%	-17%	46%
3	9/25	1:00	DET	4%	14%	2%	17%
4	10/02	9:30AM	@NO*	-26%	2%	-16%	-45%
5	10/09	1:00	CHI	4%	-7%	0%	-28%
6	10/16	1:00	@MIA	-6%	-4%	-2%	6%
7	BYE WEEK						
8	10/30	1:00	ARI	0%	-11%	10%	-36%
9	11/06	1:00	@WAS	29%	-3%	8%	5%
10	11/13	1:00	@BUF	-34%	-11%	-27%	-34%
11	11/20	4:25	DAL	-6%	-14%	2%	5%
12	11/24	8:20	NE	-8%	-19%	1%	-20%
13	12/04	1:00	NYJ	-4%	11%	-1%	-1%
14	12/11	1:00	@DET	4%	14%	2%	17%
15	12/17	TBD	IND	2%	-12%	4%	23%
16	12/24	1:00	NYG	12%	40%	-2%	22%
17	1/01	4:25	@GB	5%	-13%	3%	0%
18	1/08	TBD	@CHI	4%	-7%	0%	-28%
* PLAYED IN LONDON							

2022 NFL DRAFT					
RD	PK		POS	COLLEGE	HT	WT
1	32	LEWIS CINE	S	GEORGIA	6-1	200
2	10	ANDREW BOOTH	CB	CLEMSON	6-0	200
2	27	ED INGRAM	G	LSU	6-4	320
3	2	BRIAN ASAMOAH	LB	OKLAHOMA	6-1	228
4	13	AKAYLEB EVANS	CB	MISSOURI	6-2	198
5	22	ESEZI OTOMEWO	EDGE	MINNESOTA	6-6	285
5	26	TY CHANDLER	RB	NORTH CAROLINA	6-0	210
6	5	VEDERIAN LOWE	OT	ILLINOIS	6-6	320
6	12	JALEN NAILOR	WR	MICHIGAN STATE	6-0	190
7	6	NICK MUSE	TE	SOUTH CAROLINA	6-5	249

2021 WEEKLY STATS

*RUSH STATS :*REC STATS	@ CIN (L) 24-27		@ ARI (L) 33-34		SEA (W) 30-17		CLE (L) 7-14		DET (W) 19-17		@ CAR (W) 34-28		DAL (L) 16-20		@ BAL (L) 31-34	
QB KIRK COUSINS	36-49 351 (2 TD)	0-0	22-32 244 (3 TD)	2-35	30-38 323 (3 TD)	1-2	20-38 203 (1 INT) (1 TD)	2-0	25-34 275 (1 INT) (1 TD)	1-4	33-48 373 (3 TD)	2-16	23-35 184 (1 TD)	3-18	17-28 187 (2 TD)	1-1 (1 TD)
RB DALVIN COOK	20-61 (1 TD)	6-43	22-131	2-17	DNP		9-34	2-10	DNP		29-140 (1 TD)	2-3	18-78	0-0	17-110	3-12
RB ALEXANDER MATTISON	1-2	1-4	3-11	1-17	26-112	6-59	10-20	0-0	25-113	7-40 (1 TD)	3-10	0-0	2-5	2-(-5)	4-0	1-3
WR JUSTIN JEFFERSON	0-0	5-71	0-0	6-65 (1 TD)	0-0	9-118 (1 TD)	0-0	6-84 (1 TD)	0-0	7-124	0-0	8-80	0-0	2-21	1-11	3-69 (1 TD)
WR ADAM THIELEN	0-0	9-92 (2 TD)	0-0	6-39 (1 TD)	0-0	6-50 (1 TD)	0-0	3-46	0-0	2-40	1-2	11-126 (1 TD)	0-0	6-78 (1 TD)	0-0	2-6 (1 TD)
WR K.J. OSBORN	0-0	7-76	0-0	5-91 (1 TD)	0-0	2-26	1-10	3-26	0-0	3-14	0-0	6-78 (1 TD)	0-0	2-10	0-0	1-20
TE TYLER CONKLIN	0-0	4-41	0-0	2-15	0-0	7-70 (1 TD)	0-0	4-18	0-0	2-25	0-0	3-71	0-0	5-57	0-0	5-45

FANTASY TAKEOVER

2021 Stats
Record: 8–9
Rushing Rank: 17th
Passing Rank: 11th
Offensive Fantasy Pts: 10th
Against Run: 26th
Against Pass: 19th
ppg Against: 25.1
ppg: 25.0

KEY ADDITIONS & NEW CONTRACTS

QB **KIRK COUSINS**: SIGNED A ONE-YEAR, $35 MILLION FULLY GUARANTEED EXTENSION THAT PUTS HIM UNDER CONTRACT THROUGH 2023 AND REDUCES HIS 2022 CAP NUMBER BY ALMOST $14 MILLION.

QB **SEAN MANNION**: RE-SIGNED ON A ONE-YEAR DEAL.

WR **ALBERT WILSON**: SIGNED A ONE-YEAR DEAL.

OG **CHRIS REED**: SIGNED A TWO-YEAR DEAL WORTH $4.5 MILLION WITH A MAX VALUE OF $6.5 MILLION.

OL **JESSE DAVIS**: SIGNED WITH MINNESOTA.

DT **JONATHAN BULLARD**: SIGNED WITH MINNESOTA.

DL **HARRISON PHILLIPS**: SIGNED A THREE-YEAR, $19.5 MILLION DEAL, INCLUDING $8.5 MILLION IN YEAR 1 WITH $13 MILLION GUARANTEED OVERALL.

LB **JORDAN HICKS**: AGREED TO A TWO-YEAR, $10 MILLION CONTRACT WITH A MAX VALUE OF $12 MILLION, INCLUDING $6.5 MILLION GUARANTEED.

LB **ZA'DARIUS SMITH**: SIGNED A THREE-YEAR, $42 MILLION DEAL THAT HAS A MAX VALUE OF $47 MILLION.

CB **PATRICK PETERSON**: RE-SIGNED WITH THE VIKINGS ON A ONE-YEAR DEAL. THE CONTRACT HAS A BASE OF $4 MILLION DEAL WITH $3.5 MILLION GUARANTEED AND $1 MILLION MORE AVAILABLE IN INCENTIVES.

K **GREG JOSEPH**: RE-SIGNED.

P **JORDAN BERRY**: RE-SIGNED ON A ONE-YEAR DEAL.

What's the outlook for the Vikings receiving corps?

Justin Jefferson has exploded to relevance in his two short NFL seasons, putting up 3,016 yards and 17 TDs, on 199 total receptions. In that span, Jefferson has earned a PFF receiving grade of 91.7 (No. 2 among 78 WRs with 100 or more targets), and averaged 15.4 yards per reception, sixth best in the league. Only four WRs have more fantasy PPG over the last two years: Davante Adams (23.4), Cooper Kupp (20.3), Tyreek Hill (19.5), and Stefon Diggs (18.6). That's pretty good company.

With Kevin O'Connell assuming head coach duties, it's entirely possible that Jefferson could see a boost in targets, more work from the slot, and a few more touches out of the backfield. But no matter where he lines up, he's already one of the best, and his volume should be similar to last year's.

Adam Thielen has been one of the best WRs over the last six seasons in Minnesota. Yes, he'll be 32 years old by the start of this season, but over the last two years, even with Jefferson in the mix, Thielen's been a scoring machine, with 10 TDs last year, and 14 in 2020. Thielen has seen 203 targets, 4 more than Jefferson, but has played five less games over the span. Sure, there are some wear-and-tear concerns here, and Jefferson is clearly the star receiver, but Cousins threw 561 pass attempts last year, and will likely exceed that number this year. With this many targets to go around, Thielen should be fantasy relevant at least one more year. With O'Connell calling the show, it's likely the Vikings will see more three-WR sets this season. This should help developing receiver K.J. Osborne see the field for more snaps with more opportunity.

And, don't forget about TE Irv Smith Jr. There's little competition at the position for the third-year starter, with both Kyle Rudolph and Tyler Conklin gone. Smith looks to be the only full-time receiving TE, with both Johnny Mundt and Nick Muse perpetual block-first options.

KEY LOSSES

RB **WAYNE GALLMAN**

WR **DEDE WESTBROOK**

TE **TYLER CONKLIN** (JETS)

OL **MASON COLE** (STEELERS)

OL **RASHOD HILL**

DE **EVERSON GRIFFEN**

DT **MICHAEL PIERCE** (RAVENS)

DT **SHELDON RICHARDSON**

LB **ANTHONY BARR**

LB **NICK VIGIL** (CARDINALS)

CB **MACKENSIE ALEXANDER**

S **XAVIER WOODS** (PANTHERS)

DEPTH CHART

QB1	KIRK COUSINS
QB2	KELLEN MOND
RB1	DALVIN COOK
RB2	ALEXANDER MATTISON
RB3	C.J. HAM
WR1	JUSTIN JEFFERSON
WR2	ADAM THIELEN
WR3	K.J. OSBORN
WR4	OLABISI JOHNSON
TE1	IRV SMITH JR.
TE2	JOHNNY MUNDT **N**
K	GREG JOSEPH

2021 WEEKLY STATS

@ LAC (W) 27-20		GB (W) 34-31		@ SF (L) 26-34		@ DET (L) 27-29		PIT (W) 36-28		@ CHI (W) 17-9		LAR (L) 23-30		@ GB (L) 10-37		CHI (W) 31-17	
25-37 294 (2 TD) 4-[-3]		24-35 341 (3 TD) 2-[-4]		20-32 238 (1 INT) (2 TD) 0-0		30-40 340 (2 TD) 2-6		14-31 216 (2 INT) (2 TD) 2-14		12-24 87 (1 INT) (2 TD) 2-10		27-38 315 (1 INT) (1 TD) 4-17		DNP		14-22 250 (3 TD) 1-[-1]	
24-94 (1 TD)	3-24	22-86 (1 TD)	3-29	10-39	6-64	DNP		27-205 (2TD)	1-17	28-89	2-2	DNP		9-13	3-0	14-79	1-3
4-16	1-24	3-5	0-0	7-21 (1 TD)	2-7	22-90 (1 TD)	3-34	6-27	0-0	DNP		13-41 (1 TD)	3-29	0-0	4-13	5-18	1-3
1-[-4]	9-143	1-3	8-169 (2 TD)	0-0	4-83	1-4	11-182 (1 TD)	1-[-4]	7-79 (1 TD)	0-0	4-47 (1 TD)	0-0	8-116	0-0	6-58	1-4	5-107 (1 TD)
0-0	5-65	0-0	8-82 (1 TD)	0-0	5-62 (2 TD)	0-0	1-0	DNP		DNP		0-0	3-40	DNP		DNP	
0-0	0-0	0-0	1-19	0-0	1-5	0-0	4-47 (1 TD)	0-0	3-83 (1 TD)	0-0	3-21	0-0	5-68 (1 TD)	0-0	3-50 (1 TD)	0-0	1-21 (1 TD)
0-0	3-11 (2 TD)	0-0	3-35	0-0	2-25	0-0	7-56	0-0	2-20	0-0	1-7	0-0	4-44	0-0	5-47	0-0	2-6

NEW ENGLAND PATRIOTS

How much improvement can we expect from Mac Jones in year two?

Mac Jones' fantasy history is a tale of two sides. The first side had four top-10 finishes in his final eight games last season. The other side? He's one of only five QBs who had 10 or more weekly finishes outside the top-20 fantasy passers. As QB24 on the year, Jones posted mostly middle-of-the-road metrics. He was efficient enough, and capable of running Bill Belichick's offense but, as we like to say, being a good NFL QB and being a good fantasy QB are two different things. Jones has neither the passing volume or rushing ability to raise his fantasy ceiling to draft-worthy status. The combination of averaging fewer than 3 rushing attempts per game, and New England's bottom-five pass-play rate, is too big of obstacle to overcome in fantasy. There's just better upside QBs with a similar ADP.

Should fantasy managers avoid New England RBs altogether?

The New England backfield is a messy situation for fantasy managers. It appears as if Damien Harris and Rhamondre Stevenson will share first- and second-down duties, with Harris getting the edge in touch-count, while James White will handle most of the passing-down work.

Before drafting any player, you should always consider their best-case scenario. With New England's backfield, there's hardly a scenario, even with injuries, where anyone transitions into a three-down role.

Harris, the Patriots top fantasy back in 2021, may have reached his ceiling in this offense already. Sadly, his 15 TDs last year only resulted in a RB20 finish. Only two New England RBs in the last 10 years (eight-game minimum) have finished inside the top-15 for fantasy PPG.

Belichick has already shown he has no plans to use Stevenson or Harris as a passing-down back. When White was out with injury last season, nothing-special Brandon Bolden took on that role.

When considering one of New England's top-three backs — Harris, Stevenson, and White — consider your team's needs. If you're weak at the RB position and need a potential starter for a particular week, then a New England RB may be a good option. But if your RB starting spots are secure, opt to take a back with more injury-insurance upside, like Alexander Mattison or AJ Dillon.

While Harris is our highest-ranked, because of his TD upside, White could very well be the most productive fantasy back this year in New England. But we won't be drafting them to find out.

2022/23 SCHEDULE · 2021 FANTASY POINTS ALLOWED BY OPPONENT VS LEAGUE AVERAGE

WK	DATE	TIME	OPP	QB	RB	WR	TE
1	9/11	1:00	@MIA	-6%	-4%	-2%	6%
2	9/18	1:00	@PIT	-2%	11%	-3%	-10%
3	9/25	1:00	BAL	13%	-12%	12%	29%
4	10/02	4:25	@GB	5%	-13%	3%	0%
5	10/09	1:00	DET	4%	14%	2%	17%
6	10/16	1:00	@CLE	-5%	-5%	-6%	2%
7	10/24	8:15	CHI	4%	-7%	0%	-28%
8	10/30	1:00	@NYJ	-4%	11%	-1%	-1%
9	11/06	1:00	IND	2%	-12%	4%	23%
10	BYE WEEK						
11	11/20	1:00	NYJ	-4%	11%	-1%	-1%
12	11/24	8:20	@MIN	6%	2%	23%	-13%
13	12/01	8:15	BUF	-34%	-11%	-27%	-34%
14	12/12	8:15	@ARI	0%	-11%	10%	-36%
15	12/18	8:20	@LV	1%	10%	-14%	39%
16	12/24	1:00	CIN	-1%	6%	0%	22%
17	1/01	1:00	MIA	-6%	-4%	-2%	6%
18	1/08	TBD	@BUF	-34%	-11%	-27%	-34%

2022 NFL DRAFT

RD	PK		POS	COLLEGE	HT	WT
1	29	COLE STRANGE	G	UT-CHATTANOOGA	6-6	301
2	18	TYQUAN THORNTON	WR	BAYLOR	6-3	182
3	21	MARCUS JONES	CB	HOUSTON	5-8	185
4	16	JACK JONES	CB	ARIZONA STATE	5-10	175
4	22	PIERRE STRONG JR.	RB	SOUTH DAKOTA STATE	5-11	205
4	32	BAILEY ZAPPE	QB	WESTERN KENTUCKY	6-1	220
6	4	KEVIN HARRIS	RB	SOUTH CAROLINA	5-10	220
6	21	SAM ROBERTS	DT	NORTHWEST MISSOURI STATE	6-5	292
6	32	CHASEN HINES	C	LSU	6-3	350
7	24	ANDREW STUEBER	G	MICHIGAN	6-7	338

2021 WEEKLY STATS

	*RUSH STATS · *REC STATS	MIA (L) 16-17		@ NYJ (W) 25-6		NO (L) 13-28		TB (L) 17-19		@ HOU (W) 25-22		DAL (L) 29-35		NYJ (W) 54-13		@ LAC (W) 27-24	
QB MAC JONES		29-39 281 (1 TD) 0-0		22-30 186 0-0		30-51 270 (3 INT) (1 TD) 6-28		31-40 275 (1 INT) (2 TD) 1-[-1]		23-30 231 (1 INT) (1 TD) 1-3		15-21 229 (1 INT) (2 TD) 2-[-4]		24-36 307 (2 TD) 3-19		18-35 217 4-10	
RB DAMIEN HARRIS		23-100	2-17	16-62 (1 TD)	1-2	6-14	2-[-3]	4-[-4]	2-30	14-58 (1 TD)	0-0	18-101 (1 TD)	1-7	14-106 (2 TD)	2-7	23-80 (1 TD)	0-0
RB BRANDON BOLDEN		1-5	0-0	DNP		3-[-1]	3-23	1-0	6-51	2-25	4-6	1-[-1]	1-3	2-0	6-79 (1 TD)	4-26	0-0
RB R. STEVENSON		1-2	1-9	DNP		DNP		DNP		11-23	0-0	5-23 (1 TD)	3-39	DNP		8-26	1-5
WR JAKOBI MEYERS		0-0	6-44	0-0	4-38	0-0	9-94	0-0	8-70	0-0	4-56	0-0	5-44	0-0	5-44	0-0	4-36
WR KENDRICK BOURNE		0-0	1-17	1-16	2-10	0-0	6-96 (1 TD)	0-0	5-58	1-12	3-26	0-0	1-75 (1 TD)	0-0	4-68	0-0	4-38
WR NELSON AGHOLOR		0-0	5-72 (1 TD)	0-0	3-21	0-0	2-17	1-4	3-55	0-0	3-32	1-1	1-27	0-0	2-51 (1 TD)	0-0	3-60
TE HUNTER HENRY		0-0	3-31	0-0	2-42	0-0	5-36	0-0	4-32 (1 TD)	0-0	6-75 (1 TD)	0-0	2-25 (1 TD)	0-0	2-23 (1 TD)	0-0	1-33
TE JONNU SMITH		1-6	5-42	0-0	4-28	0-0	1-4	0-0	3-14 (1 TD)	1-5	2-27	0-0	1-9	1-5	2-52	0-0	2-13

FANTASY TAKEOVER

2021 Stats

Record: 10-7
Rushing Rank: 8th
Passing Rank: 14th
Offensive Fantasy Pts: 14th
Against Run: 22nd
Against Pass: 2nd
ppg Against: 19.4
ppg: 26.6

KEY ADDITIONS & NEW CONTRACTS

QB **BRIAN HOYER**: RE-SIGNED A TWO-YEAR CONTRACT.

RB **TY MONTGOMERY**: SIGNED A FREE-AGENT DEAL.

RB **JAMES WHITE**: RE-SIGNED ON A TWO-YEAR, $5 MILLION DEAL THAT INCLUDES $500,000 GUARANTEED.

WR **LIL'JORDAN HUMPHREY**: SIGNING A ONE-YEAR DEAL.

WR **DEVANTE PARKER**: ACQUIRED IN A TRADE WITH THE MIAMI DOLPHINS, ALONG WITH A 2022 FIFTH-ROUND PICK, IN EXCHANGE FOR A 2023 THIRD-ROUNDER.

OT **TRENT BROWN**: RE-SIGNED ON A TWO-YEAR, $22 MILLION DEAL THAT INCLUDES $4 MILLION GUARANTEED.

C/OG **JAMES FERENTZ**: RE-SIGNED WITH NEW ENGLAND.

OL **DARRYL WILLIAMS**: SIGNED WITH NEW ENGLAND.

LB **JA'WHAUN BENTLEY**: RE-SIGNED ON A TWO-YEAR DEAL WORTH A MAXIMUM OF $9 MILLION.

LB **MACK WILSON**: ACQUIRED IN A TRADE WITH THE CLEVELAND BROWNS IN EXCHANGE FOR DE CHASE WINOVICH.

CB **MALCOLM BUTLER**: SIGNED A TWO-YEAR CONTRACT.

CB **TERRANCE MITCHELL**: SIGNED A FREE-AGENT CONTRACT.

S **DEVIN MCCOURTY**: RE-SIGNED TO A ONE-YEAR CONTRACT WORTH $9 MILLION.

S **JABRILL PEPPERS**: SIGNED A ONE-YEAR, $2 MILLION DEAL THAT HAS A MAX VALUE OF $5 MILLION.

K **NICK FOLK**: RE-SIGNED ON A TWO-YEAR, $5 MILLION EXTENSION THAT INCLUDES $2.19 MILLION GUARANTEED AND HAS A MAX VALUE OF $5.6 MILLION WITH INCENTIVES.

ST **MATTHEW SLATER**: RE-SIGNED ON A ONE-YEAR, $2.6 MILLION DEAL THAT IS FULLY GUARANTEED.

Should fantasy managers avoid New England's WRs altogether?

New England has had only one WR finish in the top 29 in the past seven years, Brandin Cooks, WR15, in 2017. Some blame can be put on an offense that distributed a large portion of targets to TEs (Gronk), and RBs (White).

New England's WRs face two hurdles to fantasy success: (1) Volume — New England had the third fewest pass attempts in the league last season. (2) Target distribution — the Pats had six players with at least 45 targets last season.

Jakobi Meyers was the Pats' clear No. 1 last season with at least 51 more targets than any other receiver. He should enter 2022 as the first option, even with addition of DeVante Parker. The former undrafted free agent has improved each year in volume but struggles to find the end zone. In fact, he's one of only 11 players in NFL history with at least 1,500 yards, but fewer than 6 TDs in their first three seasons.

Kendrick Bourne flashed a few games last season, but mostly fizzled on the rest. While he did have three top-eight finishes, he finished outside the top 50 in twice as many games. He wasn't on the field enough to put up consistent numbers, only playing a more than 60% of the snaps in four games. We don't expect his target share to increase enough this season to make him draftable.

Parker is the most interesting of New England's WRs. He's just three years removed from his WR9 finish (72-1,202-9). Belichick is keenly aware of Parker's capabilities, as he's posted three 100-plus-yard games against the Patriots. Parker hasn't been able to put together another complete campaign since 2018, but we'll keep an eye on his preseason chemistry with Mac Jones.

We're going to give the edge to Meyer, but because of Parker's proven pedigree, he may still have the higher ceiling. If you're throwing darts in a late round, you might decide that ceiling is more important to you.

KEY LOSSES

QB **JARRETT STIDHAM** (TRADED TO RAIDERS)

RB **BRANDON BOLDEN** (RAIDERS)

FB **JAKOB JOHNSON** (RAIDERS)

OG **SHAQ MASON** (TRADED TO BUCS)

C **TED KARRAS** (BENGALS)

DE **CHASE WINOVICH** (TRADED TO BROWNS)

LB **JAMIE COLLINS**

LB **DONT'A HIGHTOWER**

LB **KYLE VAN NOY** (CHARGERS)

CB **J.C. JACKSON** (CHARGERS)

DEPTH CHART

QB1	MAC JONES
QB2	BAILEY ZAPPE **R**
RB1	DAMIEN HARRIS
RB2	RHAMONDRE STEVENSON
RB3	JAMES WHITE
WR1	JAKOBI MEYERS
WR2	DEVANTE PARKER **N**
WR3	KENDRICK BOURNE
WR4	NELSON AGHOLOR
TE1	HUNTER HENRY
TE2	JONNU SMITH
K	NICK FOLK

2021 WEEKLY STATS

@ CAR (W) 24-6	CLE (W) 45-7	@ ATL (W) 25-0	TEN (W) 36-13	@ BUF (W) 14-10	@ IND (L) 17-27	BUF (L) 21-33	JAC (W) 50-10	@ MIA (L) 24-33
12-18 139 (1 INT) (1 TD) 2-4	19-23 198 (3 TD) 0-0	22-26 207 (1 INT) (1 TD) 6-1	23-32 310 (2 TD) 2-11	2-3 19 5-(-3)	26-45 299 (2 TD) 1-12	14-32 145 (2 INT) 6-33	22-30 227 (3 TD) 2-12	20-30 261 (1 INT) (1 TD) 3-4
15-30 (1 TD) 1-3	DNP	10-56 1-9	11-40 (1 TD) 1-12	10-111 (1 TD) 0-0	DNP	18-103 (3TD) 0-0	9-35 (2 TD) 1-12	11-37 (1 TD) 4-36
8-54 2-27	3-32 3-38	1-1 2-15	0-0 4-54	4-28 1-7	4-3 3-41	2-4 2-20	1-4 2-21	7-46 (1 TD) 2-20 (1 TD)
10-62 2-44	20-100(2TD) 4-14	12-69 1-6	9-46 0-0	24-78 0-0	10-36 1-4	DNP	19-107 (2 TD) 0-0	4-34 1-2
0-0 1-8	0-0 4-49 (1 TD)	0-0 4-39	0-0 5-98	0-0 1-9	0-0 6-44	0-0 6-59	0-0 8-73 (1 TD)	0-0 4-70
0-0 3-34	3-43 4-98 (1 TD)	1-7 4-42	0-0 5-61 (2 TD)	1-3 0-0	2-19 3-44	0-0 2-33	2-17 5-76	1-8 3-24
0-0 0-0	0-0 2-21	0-0 5-40 (1 TD)	0-0 3-20	1-6 0-0	0-0 4-34	DNP	DNP	0-0 1-23
0-0 2-19 (1 TD)	0-0 4-37 (2 TD)	0-0 2-25	0-0 2-16	0-0 0-0	0-0 6-77 (2 TD)	0-0 1-9	0-0 3-37	0-0 5-86
1-4 1-4	DNP	0-0 1-17	1-9 3-49	1-[-1] 1-12	1-2 1-3	0-0 0-0	1-5 1-20	1-5 0-0

With an entirely new set of pass catchers, what's Jameis Winston's ceiling?

Keeping things in house, New Orleans promoted former defensive coordinator Dennis Allen to head coach when Sean Payton stepped away after 15 years with the organization. We expect Allen to follow suit with what we've seen from New Orleans in recent years. Long gone are the days of the fast-paced, pass-heavy offense of the Drew Brees era. Last season, New Orleans was middle-of-the-pack in time between plays, but dead last in the league is pass-play rate.

If Winston had the rushing ability of a Jalen Hurts, then he could overcome these passing-volume deficiencies, but he doesn't. He was a capable enough rusher last season, finishing 11th among QBs with 4.6 rushing attempts per game. That was enough to elevate him to two top-five weekly finishes in his seven starts last season, but he also finished outside the top 25 in four of those starts. Still, he did enough to finish as QB14 in fantasy PPG. Winston, however, looked like a different QB than the guy who had a 30-TD, 30-interception performance in 2019, where volume alone vaulted him to a QB8 finish in fantasy PPG.

Winston has a much-improved receiver room this season, featuring three talented options: Michael Thomas, Chris Olave, and Jarvis Landry. We've seen Thomas and Landry at their best, and if New Orleans sees a semblance of that production, they'll be much better than last season. Winston should also see an uptick in passing volume simply because he'll have better options on the field.

Still, the Saints' offensive scheme just doesn't lend itself to fantasy success. There are more consistent options at QB (Kirk Cousins) in Winston's range. He may have QB1 upside some weeks, but predicting when would be impossible.

What concerns are there with the Saints' impressive trio of receivers?

Thomas is supposedly a full go for training camp, and reports are in that his movements are fluid, and that he looks healthy. However, he hasn't played football in 18 months and there are a lot of unknowns about what percentage of the old Thomas is left.

There's no doubt, a healthy Thomas is one of the best WRs in the league. He makes most of his money on slants and comeback routes, where he's ranked in the top six among qualified receivers. But Thomas is now older, his health is in question, and he's facing competition from two good pass catchers. Draft Thomas with all that in mind rather than with visions of his 2019 glory days. The WR3 range feels pretty safe.

Where Thomas struggles on go-routes, rookie Chris Olave excels. Olave is able to create space in one-on-ones downfield, and defenses will be unable to dou-

2022/23 SCHEDULE				2021 FANTASY POINTS ALLOWED BY OPPONENT VS LEAGUE AVERAGE			
WK	DATE	TIME	OPP	QB	RB	WR	TE
1	9/11	1:00	@ATL	13%	8%	7%	-3%
2	9/18	1:00	TB	3%	-4%	3%	4%
3	9/25	1:00	@CAR	-6%	-12%	-7%	-5%
4	10/02	9:30AM	MIN*	6%	2%	23%	-13%
5	10/09	1:00	SEA	2%	-8%	3%	-23%
6	10/16	1:00	CIN	-1%	6%	0%	22%
7	10/20	8:15	@ARI	0%	-11%	10%	-36%
8	10/30	1:00	LV	1%	10%	-14%	39%
9	11/07	8:20	BAL	13%	-12%	12%	29%
10	11/13	1:00	@PIT	-2%	11%	-3%	-10%
11	11/20	1:00	LAR	-12%	-8%	7%	-2%
12	11/27	4:25	@SF	-1%	26%	-3%	20%
13	12/05	8:15	@TB	3%	-4%	3%	4%
14	BYE WEEK						
15	12/17	TBD	ATL	13%	8%	7%	-3%
16	12/24	1:00	@CLE	-5%	-5%	-6%	2%
17	1/01	1:00	@PHI	-1%	10%	-17%	46%
18	1/08	TBD	CAR	-6%	-12%	-7%	-5%

PLAYED IN LONDON

2022 NFL DRAFT					
RD	PK		POS	COLLEGE	HT	WT
1	11	CHRIS OLAVE	WR	OHIO STATE	6-1	188
1	19	TREVOR PENNING	OT	NORTHERN IOWA	6-7	329
2	17	ALONTAE TAYLOR	CB	TENNESSEE	6-0	195
5	18	D'MARCO JACKSON	LB	APPALACHIAN STATE	6-1	230
6	15	JORDAN JACKSON	DT	AIR FORCE	6-5	290

2021 WEEKLY STATS

*RUSH STATS :*REC STATS	GB (W) 38-3		@ CAR (L) 7-26		@ NE (W) 28-13		NYG (L) 21-27		@ WAS (W) 33-22		@ SEA (W) 13-10		TB (W) 36-27		ATL (L) 25-27	
QB TAYSOM HILL	1-13	2-1	0-0-0	2-16	0-0-0	6-32 (1 TD)	2-3 9 (1 INT)	6-28 (2 TD)	0-0-0	0-0	DNP		DNP		2-2 33	1-4
QB JAMEIS WINSTON	14-20 148 (5 TD)	6-37	11-22 111 (2 INT)	3-19 (1 TD)	13-21 128 (2 TD)	5-4	17-23 226 (1 TD)	0-0	15-30 279 (1 INT) (4 INT)	6-26	19-35 222 (1 TD)	8-40	6-10 56 (1 TD)	4-40	DNP	
RB ALVIN KAMARA	20-82	3-8 (1 TD)	8-5	4-25	24-89	3-29 (1 TD)	26-120	0-0	16-71 (1 TD)	5-51 (1 TD)	20-51	10-128 (1 TD)	19-61 (1 TD)	3-15	13-50 (1 TD)	4-54
RB MARK INGRAM II	DNP		DNP		DNP		DNP		DNP		DNP		6-27	2-25	9-43	5-21
WR MARQUEZ CALLAWAY	0-0	1-14	0-0	2-8	0-0	4-41 (1 TD)	0-0	2-74	0-0	4-85 (2 TD)	0-0	3-32	0-0	3-30	0-0	3-25 (1 TD)
WR DEONTE HARRIS	0-0	2-72 (1 TD)	1-1	1-9	0-0	3-31	0-0	5-52	0-0	1-72 (1 TD)	DNP		1-22	3-35	0-0	6-52
WR TRE'QUAN SMITH	DNP		DNP		DNP		DNP		DNP		0-0	1-11	0-0	3-33 (1 TD)	0-0	3-53
TE ADAM TRAUTMAN	0-0	3-18	0-0	0-0	0-0	0-0	0-0	1-3	0-0	2-43	0-0	3-36	0-0	2-4	0-0	4-47

ble team both Olave and Thomas.

When considering Olave, consider this: out of the past 10 seasons, the top three WRs drafted had a median finish of WR51 in their rookie year. Names like Courtland Sutton, DJ Moore, and Marquise brown all finished outside the top-50 receivers in their rookie year. There's simply too much competition to draft Olave as anything more than a flex option.

While we are not totally fading Landry, he has the widest range of outcomes on the team. He could finish as high as No. 2 in targets, or may not even make a splash in the bucket. We may look his way late in certain drafts in hopes of finding the Landry of old, or just in case the Thomas situation isn't what it appears.

KEY ADDITIONS & NEW CONTRACTS

QB JAMEIS WINSTON: RE-SIGNED ON A TWO-YEAR, $28 MILLION DEAL THAT INCLUDES $15.2 MILLION FULLY GUARANTEED.

QB ANDY DALTON: SIGNED A ONE-YEAR, $3 MILLION GUARANTEED DEAL THAT HAS A MAX VALUE OF $6 MILLION.

WR JARVIS LANDRY: SIGNED A ONE-YEAR, $3 MILLION DEAL WITH A MAX VALUE OF $6 MILLION.

WR TRE'QUAN SMITH: RE-SIGNED A TWO-YEAR, $6 MILLION THAT INCLUDES $2 MILLION GUARANTEED AND HAS A MAX VALUE OF $10 MILLION.

DE TACO CHARLTON: SIGNED A FREE-AGENT CONTRACT.

DE KENTAVIUS STREET: SIGNED A FREE-AGENT CONTRACT.

CB P.J. WILLIAMS: RE-SIGNED ON A ONE-YEAR, FULLY GUARANTEED DEAL WORTH $2.537 MILLION.

S TYRANN MATHIEU: SIGNED A THREE-YEAR, $33 MILLION DEAL.

S MARCUS MAYE: SIGNED A THREE-YEAR DEAL WORTH $28.5 MILLION, WITH $15 MILLION GUARANTEED.

S DANIEL SORENSON: SIGNED A FREE-AGENT DEAL.

With Alvin Kamara's 2020 efficiency issues and a potential suspension, what should be considered before drafting a Saints' back?

It feels pretty certain Kamara will face a suspension for a charge of battery and project he misses four-to-six games. According to sources, there's film of the Las Vegas incident, which will make the situation worse, considering how the NFL has handled past domestic violence cases caught on video (think Ray Rice). His next scheduled hearing is in August, which could be continued until after the 2022 season. We're guessing there's about a 25% chance he'll serve some of the suspension this year.

Kamara's subpar 2021 season, in terms of per-attempt metrics, still resulted in a respectable RB6 finish in fantasy PPG. Among backs with at least 100 carries last season, he was 42nd in yards per carry, 30th in yards after contact per carry, and 15th in forced missed tackles per carry. When a player finishes this far below his expected fantasy output, it's usually due to a combination of inefficiency and bad luck. Kamara should see more than enough volume in 2022 to achieve another top-five RB finish. And if a suspension is definitely off the table, he should be drafted as such. But until his case is decided, I would elevate some other backs ahead of him.

Mark Ingram II is currently Kamara's backup. Though inefficient last season, he was given enough volume to produce some solid fantasy finishes. But the 32-year-old is, well, 32. There's a chance that the Saints add another back if Kamara is guaranteed to miss time, and with that said, Ingram is worth a late-round pick, and is a good Kamara handcuff.

KEY LOSSES

QB BLAKE BORTLES

QB TREVOR SIEMIAN (BEARS)

RB TY MONTGOMERY (PATRIOTS)

WR LIL'JORDAN HUMPHREY (PATRIOTS)

WR KENNY STILLS

TE GARRETT GRIFFIN (LIONS)

LT TERRON ARMSTEAD (DOLPHINS)

LB KWON ALEXANDER

S JEFF HEATH

S MALCOLM JENKINS (RETIRED)

S MARCUS WILLIAMS (RAVENS)

DEPTH CHART

QB1	JAMEIS WINSTON
QB2	IAN BOOK
RB1	ALVIN KAMARA
RB2	MARK INGRAM II
RB3	TONY JONES JR.
WR1	MICHAEL THOMAS
WR2	JARVIS LANDRY **N**
WR3	CHRIS OLAVE **R**
WR4	MARQUEZ CALLAWAY
TE1	TAYSOM HILL
TE2	NICK VANETT
K	WILL LUTZ

2021 WEEKLY STATS

@ TEN (L) 21-23		@ PHI (L) 29-40		BUF (L) 6-31		DAL (L) 17-27		@ NYJ (W) 30-9		@ TB (W) 9-0		MIA (L) 3-20		CAR (W) 18-10		@ ATL (W) 30-20	
2-2 11 3-23		DNP		DNP		19-41 264 (4 INT) (2 TD) 11-101		15-21 175 11-73 (2 TD)		13-27 154 11-33		DNP		17-28 222 (1 TD) 12-45		7-9 107 (1 TD) 5-18	
DNP		DNP		DNP		DNP		DNP		DNP		DNP		DNP		DNP	
DNP		DNP		DNP		DNP		27-120 (1 TD)	4-25	11-18	2-13	13-52	2-7	13-32	5-68 (1 TD)	30-146	2-16
14-47 (1 TD)	4-61	16-88	6-25	DNP		10-28	1-(-2)	DNP		9-10	2-8	4-17	0-0	DNP		DNP	
0-0	2-37 (1 TD)	0-0	1-26 (1 TD)	0-0	2-24	0-0	1-13	0-0	2-34	0-0	6-112	0-0	4-46	0-0	6-97	0-0	0-0
1-6	3-84	0-0	2-11	0-0	1-9	1-3	4-96 (1 TD)	DNP		DNP		DNP		0-0	2-23	1-9	3-24
0-0	4-44 (1 TD)	0-0	5-64	0-0	4-31	0-0	2-15	0-0	3-33	0-0	2-17	0-0	0-0	DNP		0-0	5-76 (1 TD)
0-0	5-32	0-0	5-58 (1 TD)	DNP		DNP		DNP		0-0	1-4	DNP		0-0	0-0	0-0	1-18 (1 TD)

NEW YORK GIANTS

Should we avoid Saquon Barkley in our drafts?

Just when it looked like the old Barkley might be returning in Weeks 3 and 4 last season (RB9, RB2), he suffered a high ankle sprain in Week 5. When he came back he showed flashes of the 2019 Barkley, but he was never fully healthy. His statistical efficiency numbers were downright terrible last season. Among the 50 RBs with at least 100 carries, he ranked in the bottom 10 in yards per carry, yards after contact per attempt, and broken tackles. But we could take these same stats and others, like yards per route run, and show how Barkley outshined backs like Alvine Kamara, D'Andre Swift, and Najee Harris.

In an offense with little competition for RB touches, Barkley will have plenty of volume in a better Brian Daboll-led scheme. Daboll showed his willingness to use Devin Singletary in a tremendously fantasy productive three-down role in the final six games in Buffalo last season.

A healthy Barkley is a lock for 250-plus touches, and we're no more concerned with his injury outlook than some other top RBs, like CMC. Since 2010, only 8% of the 173 RBs who had 250-plus touches landed outside the top-20 fantasy RBs at the end of the season.

While Barkley 1.0 is over, Barkely 2.0 still has RB1 potential and a pretty high floor. We'll invest at his middle RB2 ADP.

Is Daniel Jones worth a roster spot in one-QB leagues?

This offseason the Giants hired former Bills offensive coordinator Brian Daboll as their new head coach. He is joined by new offensive coordinator Mike Kafka from the Chiefs. As the Bills offensive coordinator, Daboll increased their pass-play percentage each of the last three years. But rather than a pass-happy coach, Daboll is a more of a find-what-works-and-go-with-it kind of guy.

Daniel Jones is a dynamic rusher. It was the rushing production that led Jones to three top-12 QB finishes in the first four games last season. That same production also resulted in the second most 30-plus fantasy point finishes in 2019.

To say that Jones has been an unreliable fantasy producer would be an understatement. Some of his inconsistency can be attributed to a 30th-ranked offensive line and poor coaching. Either way, most of his metrics — QB rating, yards per attempt, completion rate — ranked in the bottom quarter for starting QBs.

Then there's the fact that Jones' group of skill players are either past their prime or simply unproven. Perhaps the receiving corps shows out in 2022, with Toney, Golladay, and Shepard leading the way. And maybe Barkley returns to 2019 form.

Daboll helped make Josh Allen the fantasy superstar he is today, but Jones is no Allen. For fantasy teams there are better backup options, and Jones is best served as a bye-week streaming option rather than a dead spot on your roster.

	2022/23 SCHEDULE			2021 FANTASY POINTS ALLOWED BY OPPONENT VS LEAGUE AVERAGE			
WK	DATE	TIME	OPP	QB	RB	WR	TE
1	9/11	4:25	@TEN	3%	-22%	19%	-29%
2	9/18	1:00	CAR	-6%	-12%	-7%	-5%
3	9/26	8:15	DAL	-6%	-14%	2%	5%
4	10/02	1:00	CHI	4%	-7%	0%	-28%
5	10/09	9:30AM	@GB*	5%	-13%	3%	0%
6	10/16	1:00	BAL	13%	-12%	12%	29%
7	10/23	1:00	@JAC	4%	-1%	5%	-2%
8	10/30	4:25	@SEA	2%	-8%	3%	-23%
9	BYE WEEK						
10	11/13	1:00	HOU	1%	13%	5%	13%
11	11/20	1:00	DET	4%	14%	2%	17%
12	11/24	4:30	@DAL	-6%	-14%	2%	5%
13	12/04	1:00	WAS	29%	-3%	8%	5%
14	12/11	1:00	PHI	-1%	10%	-17%	46%
15	12/17	TBD	@WAS	29%	-3%	8%	5%
16	12/24	1:00	@MIN	6%	2%	23%	-13%
17	1/01	1:00	IND	2%	-12%	4%	23%
18	1/08	TBD	@PHI	-1%	10%	-17%	46%

PLAYED IN LONDON

	2022 NFL DRAFT				
RD	PK		POS	COLLEGE	HT WT
1	5	KAYVON THIBODEAUX	EDGE	OREGON	6-5 258
1	7	EVAN NEAL	OT	ALABAMA	6-7 350
2	11	WAN'DALE ROBINSON	WR	KENTUCKY	5-11 185
3	3	JOSHUA EZEUDU	G	NORTH CAROLINA	6-4 325
3	17	CORDALE FLOTT	CB	LSU	6-2 170
4	7	DANIEL BELLINGER	TE	SAN DIEGO STATE	6-6 255
4	9	DANE BELTON	S	IOWA	6-1 205
5	3	MICAH MCFADDEN	LB	INDIANA	6-2 232
5	4	D.J. DAVIDSON	DT	ARIZONA STATE	6-5 325
5	30	MARCUS MCKETHAN	G	NORTH CAROLINA	6-7 335
6	3	DARRIAN BEAVERS	LB	CINCINNATI	6-4 255

2021 WEEKLY STATS

*RUSH STATS / *REC STATS	DEN (L) 13-27		@ WAS (L) 29-30		ATL (L) 14-17		@ NO (W) 27-21		@ DAL (L) 20-44		LAR (L) 11-38		CAR (W) 25-3		@ KC (L) 17-20	
QB DANIEL JONES	22-37 267 (1 TD)	6-27 (1 TD)	22-32 249 (1 TD)	9-95 (1 TD)	24-35 266	8-39	28-40 402 (1 INT) (2 TD)	4-27	5-13 98	3-9	29-51 242 (3 INT)	3-4	23-33 203 (1 TD)	8-28	22-32 222 (1 INT) (2 TD)	5-12
QB MIKE GLENNON	DNP		DNP		DNP		DNP		16-25 196 (2 INT) (1 INT)	2-2	DNP		DNP		DNP	
RB SAQUON BARKLEY	10-26	1-1	13-57	2-12	16-51 (1 TD)	6-43	13-52 (1 TD)	5-74 (1 TD)	2-9	0-0	DNP		DNP		DNP	
RB DEVONTAE BOOKER	4-7	1-6	2-9	1-2	DNP		1-6	1-6	16-42 (1 TD)	3-16 (1 TD)	12-41	4-28	14-51 (1 TD)	2-15	15-60	5-65
WR KENNY GOLLADAY	0-0	4-64	0-0	3-38	0-0	4-64	0-0	6-116	0-0	0-0	DNP		DNP		DNP	
WR KADARIUS TONEY	0-0	2-[-2]	0-0	0-0	0-0	2-16	1-1	6-78	1-7	10-189	0-0	3-36	DNP		0-0	4-26
WR STERLING SHEPARD	0-0	7-113 (1 TD)	1-[-9]	9-94	0-0	2-16	DNP		DNP		0-0	10-76	DNP		0-0	4-25
WR DARIUS SLAYTON	0-0	3-65	0-0	3-54 (1 TD)	0-0	1-8	DNP		DNP		DNP		0-0	5-63	0-0	0-0
TE EVAN ENGRAM	DNP		DNP		0-0	2-21	1-[-3]	5-27	0-0	4-55	0-0	3-24	0-0	6-44	0-0	3-15 (1 TD)
TE KYLE RUDOLPH	0-0	2-8	0-0	2-25	0-0	0-0	0-0	2-24	0-0	1-14	0-0	1-8	0-0	2-8	0-0	2-12 (1 TD)

2021 Stats

Record: 4–13
Rushing Rank: 24th
Passing Rank: 31st
Offensive Fantasy Pts: 32th
Against Run: 25th
Against Pass: 14th
ppg Against: 24.5
ppg: 15.2

What do you make of the Giants receiving corps, and are there any WRs worth targeting in the draft?

Golladay has the best chance to emerge as the Giants No. 1 fantasy WR. We'd like to credit his lack of production the past two seasons to his inability to stay healthy. Last season alone, he suffered from a hamstring injury, strained hip, hyperextended knee, and rib injury. And when he did return in Week 13, he was forced to play with backup QBs.

Golladay's outlook is better for 2022. He should at least be healthy to start the season and will have less competition for targets, as Shepard is rehabbing a late-season Achilles injury and Evan Engram is now a Jaguar. With a current 50-plus ADP for WRs, we'll be happy to take a late-round shot at Golladay and hope he can turn things around (remember he was the overall WR9 just two years ago).

The only other potentially draft-worthy candidate is Kadarius Toney. Toney flashed as a rookie, providing glimpses of his potential. Over the previous five seasons, the only rookies with a higher average yards per route run are A.J. Brown, Justin Jefferson, Ja'marr Chase, and JuJu Smith-Schuster (see chart) — pretty good company. While Golladay is our first choice in this offense, both have the potential to see triple-digit target numbers.

We firmly believe in using late-round picks to draft season-winning potential players that offer true starting potential if things go right. Golladay and Toney are both examples of this type of player.

KEY ADDITIONS & NEW CONTRACTS

QB **TYROD TAYLOR**: SIGNED A TWO-YEAR, $11 MILLION DEAL WITH A MAX VALUE OF $17 MILLION WITH INCENTIVES.

RB **MATT BREIDA**: SIGNED A ONE-YEAR DEAL.

WR **RICHIE JAMES**: SIGNED A ONE-YEAR DEAL.

TE **JORDAN AKINS**: SIGNED A FREE-AGENT CONTRACT.

TE **RICKY SEALS-JONES**: SIGNED A FREE-AGENT CONTRACT.

OL **JON FELICIANO**: SIGNED A FREE-AGENT CONTRACT.

OL **MARK GLOWINSKI**: SIGNED A THREE-YEAR, $20 MILLION CONTRACT WITH $11.4 MILLION GUARANTEED.

DE **JIHAD WARD**: SIGNED A FREE-AGENT DEAL.

DT **JUSTIN ELLIS**: SIGNED A ONE-YEAR DEAL.

LS **CASEY KREITER**: SIGNED A FREE-AGENT DEAL.

Rookie WRs Who Averaged More Than 2 Yards Per Route Run in The Last Five Seasons

A.J. Brown (2.67)
Justin Jefferson (2.66)
Ja'Marr Chase (2.51)
JuJu Smith-Schuster (2.17)
Kadarius Toney (2.14)
Hunter Renfrow (2.09)
Terrry McLaurin (2.05)
Cooper Kupp (2.04)
Deebo Samuel (2.04)
Chris Godwin (2.03)
Chase Claypool (2)

DEPTH CHART

QB1	DANIEL JONES
QB2	TYROD TAYLOR **N**
RB1	SAQUON BARKLEY
RB2	MATT BREIDA
RB3	GARY BRIGHTWELL
WR1	KENNY GOLLADAY
WR2	KADARIUS TONEY
WR3	STERLING SHEPARD
WR4	DARIUS SLAYTON
TE1	RICKY SEALS-JONES **N**
TE2	DANIEL BELLINGER **R**
K	GRAHAM GANO

KEY LOSSES

QB **MIKE GLENNON**

RB **DEVONTAE BOOKER**

RB **ELIJHAA PENNY**

WR **JOHN ROSS**

TE **EVAN ENGRAM** (JAGUARS)

TE **KYLE RUDOLPH**

OT **NATE SOLDER**

OG **WILL HERNANDEZ** (CARDINALS)

OL **BILLY PRICE**

OL **MATT SKURA**

DT **DANNY SHELTON**

DT **AUSTIN JOHNSON** (CHARGERS)

OLB **LORENZO CARTER** (FALCONS)

LB **BENARDRICK MCKINNEY**

LB **REGGIE RAGLAND**

LB **JAYLON SMITH**

CB **JAMES BRADBERRY** (EAGLES)

S **JABRILL PEPPERS** (PATRIOTS)

DB **LOGAN RYAN** (BUCCANEERS)

P **RILEY DIXON** (RAMS)

2021 WEEKLY STATS

LV (W) 23-16		@ TB (L) 10-30		PHI (W) 13-7		@ MIA (L) 9-20		@ LAC (L) 21-37		DAL (L) 6-21		@ PHI (L) 10-34		@ CHI (L) 3-29		WAS (L) 7-22	
15-20 110 (1 TD) 4-17		23-38 167 (2 INT) (1 TD) 3-10		19-30 202 (1 TD) 9-30		DNP		DNP		DNP		DNP		DNP		DNP	
DNP		DNP		DNP		23-44 187 (1 INT) 0-0		17-36 191 (1 INT) (2 TD) 1-7 (1 TD)		13-24 99 (3 INT) 1-0		17-27 93 (1 INT) (1 TD) 2-11		4-11 24 (2 INT) 1-13		DNP	
DNP		6-25	6-31	13-40	4-13	11-55	6-19	16-64	3-31 (1 TD)	15-50	4-24	15-32	1-[-4]	21-102	0-0	11-30	3-19
21-99	3-23	3-15	1-5	3-10	1-17	6-36	4-18	8-56	4-28	8-74	2-8	6-27	4-19	18-46	2-0	8-14	2-12
0-0	2-28	0-0	1-12	0-0	3-50	0-0	3-37	0-0	2-15	0-0	3-53	0-0	3-22	0-0	0-0		3-22
1-[-2]	1-9	0-0	7-40	DNP		DNP		DNP		DNP		0-0	4-28	DNP		DNP	
DNP		DNP		DNP		DNP		0-0	2-27	0-0	2-15	DNP		DNP		DNP	
0-0	0-0	0-0	4-37	1-[-1-13	3-40	0-0	2-13	0-0	0-0	0-0	2-23	0-0	1-7	0-0	0-0	0-0	2-29 (1 TD)
0-0	3-38 (1 TD)	0-0	2-12	0-0	3-37	0-0	4-61	0-0	1-8	0-0	4-33	0-0	4-17 (1 TD)	0-0	1-12		1-4
0-0	4-20	0-0	1-28	DNP		0-0	2-18	0-0	2-66	0-0	1-9	0-0	0-0	0-0	0-0		4-17

NEW YORK JETS

Elijah Moore or Garrett Wilson? Who's the Jets No. 1 WR?

Expect healthy competition for targets between second-year WR Elijah Moore and rookie Garrett Wilson. Moore had flashes of brilliance last season (Weeks 7-13, WR3 overall), but also a few lackluster performances, and he missed six games to injury.

Wilson, this year's tenth overall pick, crushed the competition at Ohio State last season. Opposing defenses will now have to decide where to put their best corners — Wilson or Moore — while the other benefits from weaker coverage. Wilson's sure-handedness and ability to get open underneath, may make him the more favorable receiver when playing from behind, which the Jets should be doing more often than not. It's possible that Wilson could be Zach Wilson's new favorite target from Week 1, but we think that their chemistry will take some time to develop.

While Wilson may have the higher ceiling, we already know what Moore is capable of, and the higher floor and less uncertainty wins in our ranking. Had Garrett Wilson not showed up this season, we had Moore penciled in as a top-15 option.

> While Wilson may have the higher ceiling, we already know what Moore is capable of, and the higher floor and less uncertainty wins in our ranking.

What's the division of workload between Breece Hall and Michael Carter?

Second-round draft pick Breece Hall comes to the Jets as this season's assumed three-down back. But you can't discount Michael carter as he's sure to be involved, possibly on the ground and definitely in the passing game.

Carter had a good rookie outing last season, especially in the passing game, where he finished 15th in targets and 27th in receptions per game. When the Jets used Carter in a heavier workload, he produced. He also lost time to injury last season.

Enter Hall, who is the more talented, fantasy-ready back, with the ability to take on a workhorse-like load. He's young, fast, athletic, and slated to be the clear-cut No. 1.

While there will be some competition for touches, Hall could takeover the backfield duties all together, with Carter coming in for some third-down passing duties. Carter has good insurance upside if Hall were to miss time.

2022/23 SCHEDULE — 2021 FANTASY POINTS ALLOWED BY OPPONENT VS LEAGUE AVERAGE

WK	DATE	TIME	OPP	QB	RB	WR	TE
1	9/11	1:00	BAL	13%	-12%	12%	29%
2	9/18	1:00	@CLE	-5%	-5%	-6%	2%
3	9/25	1:00	CIN	-1%	6%	0%	22%
4	10/02	1:00	@PIT	-2%	11%	-3%	-10%
5	10/09	1:00	MIA	-6%	-4%	-2%	6%
6	10/16	1:00	@GB	5%	-13%	3%	0%
7	10/23	4:05	@DEN	-10%	-9%	-6%	-29%
8	10/30	1:00	NE	-8%	-19%	1%	-20%
9	11/06	1:00	BUF	-34%	-11%	-27%	-34%
10	BYE WEEK						
11	11/20	1:00	@NE	-8%	-19%	1%	-20%
12	11/27	1:00	CHI	4%	-7%	0%	-28%
13	12/04	1:00	@MIN	6%	2%	23%	-13%
14	12/11	1:00	@BUF	-34%	-11%	-27%	-34%
15	12/18	1:00	DET	4%	14%	2%	17%
16	12/22	8:15	JAC	4%	-1%	5%	-2%
17	1/01	4:05	@SEA	2%	-8%	3%	-23%
18	1/08	TBD	@MIA	-6%	-4%	-2%	6%

2022 NFL DRAFT

RD	PK		POS	COLLEGE	HT	WT
1	4	AHMAD GARDNER	CB	CINCINNATI	6-3	200
1	10	GARRETT WILSON	WR	OHIO STATE	6-0	192
1	26	JERMAINE JOHNSON	EDGE	FLORIDA STATE	6-5	262
2	4	BREECE HALL	RB	IOWA STATE	6-1	220
3	37	JEREMY RUCKERT	TE	OHIO STATE	6-5	250
4	6	MAX MITCHELL	OT	LOUSIANA	6-6	299
4	12	MICHAEL CLEMONS	EDGE	TEXAS A&M	6-5	270

2021 WEEKLY STATS

*RUSH STATS : *REC STATS		@ CAR (L) 14-19		NE (L) 6-25		@ DEN (L) 0-26		TEN (W) 27-24		@ ATL (L) 20-27		NE (L) 13-54		CIN (W) 34-31		@ IND (L) 30-45	
QB ZACH WILSON		20-37 258 (1 INT) (2 TD) 0-0		19-33 210 (4 INT) 3-19		19-35 160 (2 INT) 1-2		21-34 297 (1 INT) (2 TD) 3-[-2]		19-32 192 (1 INT) 1-3		6-10 51 0-0		DNP		DNP	
QB MIKE WHITE		DNP		DNP		DNP		DNP		DNP		20-32 202 (2 INT) (1 TD) 0-0		37-45 405 (2 INT) (3 TD) 5-[-1]		7-11 95 (1 TD) 0-0	
RB MICHAEL CARTER		4-6	1-14	11-59	2-29	9-24	2-5	13-38 (1 TD)	1-[-4]	10-38 (1 TD)	3-20	11-37	8-67	15-77 (1 TD)	9-95	13-49	1-37
RB TY JOHNSON		4-15	1-11	12-50	0-0	3-17	1-6	3-1	2-12	4-12 (1 TD)	2-22	5-6	6-65	4-15	5-71 (1 TD)	4-21	2-40 (1 TD)
WR ELIJAH MOORE		0-0	1-[-3]	0-0	4-47	0-0	3-22	DNP		0-0	0-0	1-19 (1 TD)	1-13	1-4	6-67	0-0	7-84 (2 TD)
WR BRAXTON BERRIOS		0-0	5-51	0-0	7-73	0-0	2-26	2-15	1-0	0-0	1-6	0-0	0-0	0-0	2-13 (1 TD)	0-0	2-5
WR JAMISON CROWDER		DNP		DNP		DNP		0-0	7-61 (1 TD)	0-0	4-24	0-0	4-34	0-0	8-84	0-0	5-38
WR COREY DAVIS		0-0	5-97 (2 TD)	0-0	2-8	0-0	5-41	0-0	4-111 (1 TD)	0-0	4-45	0-0	4-47 (1 TD)	DNP		DNP	

2021 Stats
Record: 4–13
Rushing Rank: 27th
Passing Rank: 17th
Offensive Fantasy Pts: 25th
Against Run: 29th
Against Pass: 30th
ppg Against: 29.6
ppg: 18.2

KEY ADDITIONS & NEW CONTRACTS

QB **JOE FLACCO**: RE-SIGNED ON A ONE-YEAR DEAL.

QB **MIKE WHITE**: SIGNED HIS ORIGINAL-ROUND TENDER, A ONE-YEAR CONTRACT WORTH $2.54 MILLION.

RB **TEVIN COLEMAN**: RE-SIGNED ON A ONE-YEAR, $1.5 MILLION DEAL ($650,000 GUARANTEED) THAT HAS A MAX VALUE OF $2.3 MILLION.

WR **BRAXTON BERRIOS**: RE-SIGNED ON A TWO-YEAR, $12 MILLION CONTRACT.

TE **TYLER CONKLIN**: SIGNED A FREE-AGENT DEAL.

TE **C.J. UZOMAH**: SIGNED A THREE-YEAR DEAL WORTH $24 MILLION.

OT **CONOR MCDERMOTT**: RE-SIGNED TO A ONE-YEAR CONTRACT.

OG/OL **DAN FEENEY**: RE-SIGNED TO A FREE-AGENT DEAL.

OG **LAKEN TOMLINSON**: SIGNED A THREE-YEAR, $40 MILLION DEAL THAT INCLUDES $27 MILLION GUARANTEED AND HAS A MAX VALUE OF $41.2 MILLION.

DT **NATHAN SHEPHERD**: RE-SIGNED ON A FREE-AGENT CONTRACT.

DL **SOLOMON THOMAS**: SIGNED A ONE-YEAR, $2.25 MILLION DEAL THAT INCLUDES $1.91 MILLION GUARANTEED AND HAS A MAX VALUE OF $3.75 MILLION.

LB **JACOB MARTIN**: SIGNED A THREE-YEAR, $13.5 MILLION CONTRACT THAT INCLUDES $6 MILLION GUARANTEED.

CB **D.J. REED**: SIGNED A THREE-YEAR, $33 MILLION CONTRACT.

S **JORDAN WHITEHEAD**: SIGNED A TWO-YEAR CONTRACT WORTH $14.5 MILLION.

DB **LAMARCUS JOYNER**: RE-SIGNED ON A ONE-YEAR CONTRACT.

K **GREG ZUERLEIN**: SIGNED A FREE-AGENT CONTRACT.

Is Zach Wilson fantasy viable this season?

By all measures, Zach Wilson had a terrible rookie season. His 11.5 fantasy PPG ranked 32nd in the league among QBs with at least 12 games played. His completion rate of 55.6% was 47th of 51 qualified passers. But a poor start for a rookie QB on a bad team is not unusual.

Wilson spent the offseason in the weight room, adding 13 pounds of muscle to his 6-foot 2 frame. At 221 pounds, with a stronger lower half, he should be ready to endure a 17-game schedule, after missing four-and-a-half weeks to a sprained knee in Year 1.

So, will Wilson be worth a shot in fantasy leagues this season? Since 2012, of 14 QBs who averaged less than 15 fantasy PPG (minimum eight games) in their first year, only four improved in Year 2.

Wilson is surrounded by talent, much of it added in the offseason, and that should help him. With skill players Breece Hall, Elijah Moore, and Garrett Wilson, the Jets have a excess of young talent. The group should grow together and gain a chemistry that could make them very competitive in the near future.

For now, he's likely not even a streaming option in 1-QB leagues, and in 2-QB leagues he'll be a starter most weeks.

'Since 2012, of 14 QBs who averaged less than 15 fantasy PPG (minimum eight games) in their first year, only four improved in Year 2.'

KEY LOSSES

WR **KEELAN COLE** (RAIDERS)	
WR **JAMISON CROWDER** (BILLS)	
TE **RYAN GRIFFIN** (BEARS)	
TE **TYLER KROFT** (49ERS)	
OG **LAURENT DUVERNAY-TARDIF**	
OG **ALEX LEWIS**	
OT **MORGAN MOSES** (RAVENS)	
OL **GREG VAN ROTEN** (BILLS)	
DE **SHAQ LAWSON** (BILLS)	
DT **FOLEY FATUKASI** (JAGUARS)	
LB **BLAKE CASHMAN** (TRADED TO TEXANS)	
LB **JARRAD DAVIS** (LIONS)	
S **MARCUS MAYE** (SAINTS)	
K **MATT AMMENDOLA**	

DEPTH CHART

QB1	MAC JONES
QB2	BAILEY ZAPPE **R**
RB1	DAMIEN HARRIS
RB2	RHAMONDRE STEVENSON
RB3	JAMES WHITE
WR1	JAKOBI MEYERS
WR2	DEVANTE PARKER **N**
WR3	KENDRICK BOURNE
WR4	NELSON AGHOLOR
TE1	HUNTER HENRY
TE2	JONNU SMITH
K	NICK FOLK

2021 WEEKLY STATS

BUF (L) 17-45		MIA (L) 17-24		@ HOU (W) 21-14		PHI (L) 18-33		NO (L) 9-30		@ MIA (L) 24-31		JAC (W) 26-21		TB (L) 24-28		@ BUF (L) 10-27	
DNP		DNP		14-24 145 (1 INT) 2-3 (1 TD)		23-38 226 (1 INT) (2 TD) 3-0 (1 TD)		19-42 202 4-33		13-23 170 4-12 (1 TD)		14-22 102 (1 TD) 4-91 (1 TD)		19-33 234 (1 TD) 2-0		7-20 87 (1 TD) 2-24	
24-44 251 (4 INT) 0-0		DNP		DNP		DNP		DNP		DNP		DNP		DNP		DNP	
16-39 (1 TD)	4-43	9-63	1-2	DNP		DNP		DNP		8-18	1-2	16-118	2-6	3-54	1-9	9-19	0-0
2-2	5-36	1-5	1-8	6-42	0-0	1-1	2-14	6-17	4-40	DNP		0-0	0-0	5-35 (1 TD)	3-47	1-[-1]	0-0
0-0	3-44 (1 TD)	1-15	8-141 (1 TD)	1-7	4-46	1-9	6-77 (1 TD)	DNP		DNP		DNP		DNP		DNP	
0-0	3-19	0-0	0-0	0-0	2-47	0-0	1-11	0-0	6-52	2-10 (1 TD)	1-26	1-3	5-37	2-12 (1 TD)	8-65 (1 TD)	DNP	
0-0	3-20	0-0	6-44 (1 TD)	0-0	1-5	0-0	4-62	0-0	3-19	0-0	5-40	DNP		DNP		0-0	1-16
0-0	5-93	0-0	3-35	DNP		0-0	2-15	DNP		DNP		DNP		DNP		DNP	

How will the backfield touches be distributed this season?

Fantasy managers who rostered Eagles RBs last season were likely left frustrated at the uncertainty in the division of touches within the position. Presumed 2022 lead back, Miles Sanders, had an unusual 2021 season. In his 12 games, he was 15th in yards per game (62.8), but 43rd in fantasy PPG. With a total of 754 rushing yards on the season, Sanders did not find the end zone once! The next highest RB without a TD was Tevin Coleman who had 354 yards.

Boston Scott was 47th in yards per game, but finished as RB55, just behind Sanders' RB46. All of Scott's TDs came in the red zone, 7 TDs on 19 red zone carries. Sanders had more red zone carries (20) with no TDs. Scott is not a better rusher, just the more fortunate one last season.

Then, there's also second-year back, Kenneth Gainwell, who saw the most targets out of all the backs. Like in most cases with RB committees, the back with the most receiving upside is the best fantasy option. In this case, Gainwell's RB40 finish was highest on the team.

Sanders is the only draftable option in the backfield for Philly in 2022. While Sanders in projected to be a top-30 back this season (our RB25), he'll need to stay healthy in order to live up to his ranking. We're more likely this season to roster Philly's actual leading rusher, Jalen Hurts rather than Sanders.

How does the addition of A.J. Brown affect DeVonta Smith's upside?

DeVonta Smith was the Eagles leading pass catcher last season, but in 17 games he saw only 104 targets (33rd among WRs). Of course, his 6.1 targets per game, fewest among team's No. 1 WRs, makes sense when you consider he was a rookie. It didn't help that he played on the team that finished first in rushing yards, second in rushing attempts, and dead last in passing attempts. Unfortunately, the addition of A.J. Brown could hinder his potential Year 2 improvement.

Brown is no stranger to run-heavy offenses. The Titans, last season, were No. 1 in rushing attempts, with just one more carry than the Eagles. Brown still had 105 targets on only 13 games, 2 more targets per game than Smith.

Brown is the better receiver of the two, and will assume top-receiver duties for the Eagles this season. While Brown will take a larger target share, we expect Hurts to have more passing attempts and more scoring opportunities, which, along with focused coverage on Brown, may make up for the target share decline for Smith.

Both Brown and Smith are worth drafting, Brown as WR2 and Smith as a flex option.

2022/23 SCHEDULE				2021 FANTASY POINTS ALLOWED BY OPPONENT VS LEAGUE AVERAGE			
WK	DATE	TIME	OPP	QB	RB	WR	TE
1	9/11	1:00	@DET	4%	14%	2%	17%
2	9/19	8:30	MIN	6%	2%	23%	-13%
3	9/25	1:00	@WAS	29%	-3%	8%	5%
4	10/02	1:00	JAC	4%	-1%	5%	-2%
5	10/09	4:25	@ARI	0%	-11%	10%	-36%
6	10/16	8:20	DAL	-6%	-14%	2%	5%
7	BYE WEEK						
8	10/30	1:00	PIT	-2%	11%	-3%	-10%
9	11/03	8:15	@HOU	1%	13%	5%	13%
10	11/14	8:15	WAS	29%	-3%	8%	5%
11	11/20	1:00	@IND	2%	-12%	4%	23%
12	11/27	8:20	GB	5%	-13%	3%	0%
13	12/04	1:00	TEN	3%	-22%	19%	-29%
14	12/11	1:00	@NYG	12%	40%	-2%	22%
15	12/18	1:00	@CHI	4%	-7%	0%	-28%
16	12/24	4:25	@DAL	-6%	-14%	2%	5%
17	1/01	1:00	NO	-26%	2%	-16%	-45%
18	1/08	TBD	NYG	12%	40%	-2%	22%

2022 NFL DRAFT					
RD	PK		POS	COLLEGE	HT	WT
1	13	JORDAN DAVIS	DT	GEORGIA	6-6	340
2	19	CAM JURGENS	C	NEBRASKA	6-3	290
3	19	NAKOBE DEAN	LB	GEORGIA	6-0	225
5	11	SNOOP CONNER	RB	OLE MISS	5-10	220
6	2	KYRON JOHNSON	LB	KANSAS	6-1	235
6	19	GRANT CALCATERRA	TE	SMU	6-5	247

2021 WEEKLY STATS

*RUSH STATS / *REC STATS	@ ATL (W) 32-6		SF (L) 11-17		@ DAL (L) 21-41		KC (L) 30-42		@ CAR (W) 21-18		TB (L) 22-28		@ LV (L) 22-33		@ DET (W) 44-6	
QB JALEN HURTS	27-35 264 (3 TD)	7-62	12-23 190	10-82 (1 TD)	25-39 326 (2 INT) (2 TD)	9-35	32-48 387 (2 TD)	8-47	22-37 198 (1 INT)	9-30 (2 TD)	12-26 115 (1 INT) (1 TD)	10-44 (2 TD)	18-34 236 (2 TD)	13-61	9-14 103	7-71
QB GARDNER MINSHEW II	DNP		DNP		DNP		DNP		DNP		DNP		DNP		2-2 11	0-0
RB KENNETH GAINWELL	9-37 (1 TD)	2-6	6-14	2-18	1-2	3-32	3-31 (1 TD)	6-58	2-16	1-8	0-0	1-1	5-20	4-41 (1 TD)	13-27	0-0
RB MILES SANDERS	15-74	4-39	13-55	1-4	2-27	3-28	7-13	3-34	11-45	5-6	9-56	2-10	6-30	1-1 (-3)	DNP	
RB BOSTON SCOTT	DNP		DNP		0-0	2-5	DNP		DNP		DNP		7-24 (1 TD)	1-5	12-60 (2 TD)	0-0
WR DEVONTA SMITH	0-0	6-71 (1 TD)	0-0	2-16	0-0	3-28	0-0	7-122	0-0	7-77	0-0	2-31	0-0	5-61	0-0	1-15
WR QUEZ WATKINS	0-0	3-23	0-0	2-117	0-0	2-46	0-0	3-33	0-0	3-48	0-0	3-44	0-0	2-37	0-0	2-18
WR JALEN REAGOR	0-0	6-49 (1 TD)	0-0	2-5	0-0	5-53	1-12	1-9	0-0	3-24	0-0	1-0	1-0	2-25 (1 TD)	2-21	1-0
TE DALLAS GOEDERT	0-0	4-42 (1 TD)	0-0	2-24	0-0	2-66	0-0	5-56 (1 TD)	0-0	2-28	DNP		0-0	3-70	0-0	6-72
TE ZACH ERTZ	0-0	2-34	0-0	1-6	0-0	4-53 (1 TD)	0-0	6-60	0-0	1-7	0-0	4-29 (1 TD)	0-0	0-0	DNP	

2021 Stats

Record: 9-8
Rushing Rank: 1st
Passing Rank: 29th
Offensive Fantasy Pts: 19th
Against Run: 9th
Against Pass: 9th
ppg Against: 23.1
ppg: 25.5

KEY ADDITIONS & NEW CONTRACTS

RB **BOSTON SCOTT**: RE-SIGNED A ONE-YEAR, $1.75 MILLION DEAL WORTH UP TO $2.25 MILLION WITH INCENTIVES, INCLUDING $1.1 MILLION GUARANTEED.

WR **A.J. BROWN**: ACQUIRED IN A TRADE WITH THE TENNESSEE TITANS, IN EXCHANGE FOR A 2022 FIRST-ROUNDER (NO. 18 OVERALL) AND THIRD-ROUNDER (NO. 101).

WR **ZACH PASCAL**: SIGNED A ONE-YEAR DEAL.

WR **GREG WARD**: SIGNED A ONE-YEAR CONTRACT.

C **JASON KELCE**: SIGNED A NEW ONE-YEAR CONTRACT WORTH $14 MILLION.

DE **DEREK BARNETT**: RE-SIGNED TO A TWO-YEAR CONTRACT.

DT **FLETCHER COX**: SIGNED A ONE-YEAR CONTRACT WORTH $14 MILLION.

LB **HAASON REDDICK**: SIGNED A THREE-YEAR, $45 MILLION DEAL THAT INCLUDES $30 MILLION FULLY GUARANTEED AND HAS A MAX VALUE OF $49.5 MILLION.

LB **KYZIR WHITE**: SIGNED A ONE-YEAR DEAL WORTH UP TO $5 MILLION.

CB **JAMES BRADBERRY**: SIGNED A ONE-YEAR, $10 MILLION DEAL.

S **ANTHONY HARRIS**: RE-SIGNED ON A ONE-YEAR, $2.5 MILLION DEAL.

S **JAQUISKI TARTT**: SIGNED A ONE-YEAR CONTRACT

Is Jalen Hurts a top-five fantasy QB?

Jalen Hurts' passing efficiency ranked towards the bottom of the league last season. So, how is it that a QB who ranked 32nd in completions and attempts per game, and 35th in completion rate (61.3%) finished the year as the QB7 in fantasy PPG? Simply put, the man's got wheels.

He made up for the lack of passing with his feet, rushing for 784 yards (second among QBs) and scoring 10 rushing TDs (first). Last season, he finished just inside the top-10 for fantasy QBs on the year, but can he crack the top-five like our rankings predict?

First, consider that last year's passing woes were not entirely Hurts' fault. He was working with limited receiving talent. Outside of DeVonta Smith, Dallas Goedert, and Zach Ertz (traded after seven games), Hurts was limited to Quez Watkins and Jalen Reagor as his third and fourth options.

Another factor was the offensive scheme. Weeks 1-7, Hurts passed for 245 yards per game with 10 TDs and only 4 interceptions. He had another 5 TDs on the ground. But the Eagles changed their approach and it was reflected in his numbers. For the rest of the season, Hurts averaged 178 yards per game, threw 6 TDS, had 5 interceptions, and rushed for 5 more TDs. The volume decrease in the passing game affected his fantasy output.

'So, how is it that a QB who ranked 32nd in completions and attempts per game, and 35th in completion rate finished the year as the QB7 in fantasy PPG?'

With the addition of A.J. Brown to the WR room, pass-catching talent will no longer be an issue. Smith should also show overall improvement in Year 2, as some outlets are naming him a sleeper this season. Hurts, without a doubt, has the tools and ability to be a top-five QB, and we'd be shocked if he ended the year outside of the RB1 range.

KEY LOSSES

RB **JORDAN HOWARD**

OG **BRANDON BROOKS** (RETIRED)

DE **RYAN KERRIGAN**

DT **HASSAN RIDGEWAY** (49ERS)

LB **GENARD AVERY** (STEELERS)

LB **ALEX SINGLETON** (BRONCOS)

CB **STEVEN NELSON** (TEXANS)

S **RODNEY MCLEOD** (COLTS)

DEPTH CHART

QB1	JALEN HURTS
QB2	GARDNER MINSHEW II
RB1	MILES SANDERS
RB2	KENNETH GAINWELL
RB3	BOSTON SCOTT
WR1	A.J. BROWN **N**
WR2	DEVONTA SMITH
WR3	JALEN REAGOR
WR4	QUEZ WATKINS
TE1	DALLAS GOEDERT
TE2	TYREE JACKSON
K	JAKE ELLIOT

2021 WEEKLY STATS

	LAC (L) 24-27	@ DEN (W) 30-13	NO (W) 40-29	@ NYG (L) 7-13	@ NYJ (W) 33-18	WAS (W) 27-17	NYG (W) 34-10	@ WAS (W) 20-16	DAL (L) 26-51
	11-17 162 (1 TD) / 10-62	16-23 178 (1 INT) (2 TD) / 13-55	13-24 147 / 18-69 (3 TD)	14-31 129 (3 INT) / 8-77	DNP	20-26 296 (1 INT) (1 TD) / 8-38 (2 TD)	17-29 199 (2 TD) / 2-7	17-26 214 / 7-44	DNP
	DNP	DNP	DNP	DNP	20-25 242 (2 TD) / 4-11	DNP	DNP	DNP	19-33 186 (1 INT) (2 TD) / 5-10
	2-3 (1 TD) | 0-0	2-5 | 1-9	DNP	0-0 | 3-32	12-54 (1 TD) | 5-33	0-0 | 0-0	0-0 | 1-6	1-4 | 0-0	12-78 (1 TD) | 4-9
	DNP	DNP	16-94 | 0-0	9-64 | 1-0	24-120 | 3-22	18-131 | 2-15	7-45 | 1-3	DNP	DNP
	10-40 | 0-0	11-81 | 2-24	6-16 | 2-2	15-64 (1 TD) | 2-8	0-0 | 0-0	DNP	12-41 (1 TD) | 0-0	14-47 (2 TD) | 4-39	DNP
	0-0 | 5-116 (1 TD)	0-0 | 4-66 (2 TD)	0-0 | 4-61	0-0 | 2-22	0-0 | 2-15	0-0 | 3-40	0-0 | 5-80 (1 TD)	0-0 | 3-54	0-0 | 3-41
	0-0 | 2-9	0-0 | 4-33	0-0 | 0-0	1-3 | 2-23	0-0 | 3-60	0-0 | 2-14	0-0 | 3-43	0-0 | 2-15	0-0 | 5-84 (1 TD)
	0-0 | 1-1-6]	1-1-81 | 1-12	0-0 | 1-1-1]	0-0 | 2-31	1-0 | 1-7	0-0 | 3-57	0-0 | 2-15	1-1-3] | 0-0	3-10 | 2-19
	0-0 | 3-43	0-0 | 2-28	0-0 | 5-62	0-0 | 1-0	0-0 | 6-105 (2 TD)	0-0 | 7-135	0-0 | 2-28	0-0 | 6-71	DNP
	DNP	DNP	DNP	DNP	DNP	DNP	DNP	DNP	DNP

Can Najee Harris repeat as a top-five RB this season?

Najee Harris is difficult to get to the ground. Nobody in the NFL had more broken tackles than Harris last season. But that's not all. He led the league in snaps, touches, targets, and receptions, totaling 1,667 yards on 381 combined touches, with 10 TDs. Indeed, it's true — volume is king.

Volume is the reason Harris had so much value, as his efficiency wasn't pretty at 3.9 yards per carry and 5.0 yards per touch. The good news is we expect his efficiency to improve this year, while his usage should remain the same.

Sure, Big Ben won't be available for the check-down; Harris led the league with 34 check-down targets last year. Comparatively, from 2017-19 Tarik Cohen had

'This season Canada will be more involved, so we should expect plenty of check-down action to go along with an increase of Najee's use on screens'

just 24 check-down targets from Mitchell Trubisky, Pittsburgh's presumed Week 1 starter. But offensive coordinator Matt Canada deferred to Big Ben on his farewell tour last season, allowing Ben to call his own shots. This season Canada will be more involved, so we should expect plenty of check-down action to go along with an increase of Najee's use on screens (last year only 14% of Harris' targets came on screens, sixth-lowest among qualified backs).

Pittsburgh did nothing to improve the running back position this offseason, signaling their commitment to Harris. Harris will indeed repeat this year, he's a solid RB1 who will be drafted in the first round.

Can the Steelers support multiple fantasy-worthy receivers this year?

Like Najee Harris, WR Diontae Johnson has made his fantasy money in Pittsburgh by way of volume. In his last 31 regular-season games, he was targeted 313 times. Only Stefon Diggs, Davante Adams, and Cooper Kupp had more targets in the past two seasons.

It's good that Johnson gets the heavy volume, because his efficiency has been less than stellar. Last season he only reeled in 63% of passes thrown his way, and his 10.7 yards per touch and 11.4 yards per reception ranked 59th in the league. Still, thanks to volume, Johnson finished eighth overall in FPs for wide receivers.

The second WR option in Pittsburgh is Chase Claypool. While he has flashed over the last two seasons, he's still second to Johnson, and will have to compete for target share with up-and-coming TE Pat Freiemuth.

Considering all factors, including the unknowns at the QB position in Pittsburgh, it's unlikely that the Steelers produce any fantasy-viable WRs other than Johnson this season. Claypool's only worth of a look as injury insurance or as a WR4/5 in deep leagues.

2022/23 SCHEDULE			2021 FANTASY POINTS ALLOWED BY OPPONENT VS LEAGUE AVERAGE			
WK	DATE	TIME	OPP	QB	RB	WR	TE
1	9/11	1:00	@CIN	-1%	6%	0%	22%
2	9/18	1:00	NE	-8%	-19%	1%	-20%
3	9/22	8:15	@CLE	-5%	-5%	-6%	2%
4	10/02	1:00	NYJ	-4%	11%	-1%	-1%
5	10/09	1:00	@BUF	-34%	-11%	-27%	-34%
6	10/16	1:00	TB	3%	-4%	3%	4%
7	10/23	8:20	@MIA	-6%	-4%	-2%	6%
8	10/30	1:00	@PHI	-1%	10%	-17%	46%
9	BYE WEEK						
10	11/13	1:00	NO	-26%	2%	-16%	-45%
11	11/20	8:20	CIN	-1%	6%	0%	22%
12	11/28	8:15	@IND	2%	-12%	4%	23%
13	12/04	1:00	@ATL	13%	8%	7%	-3%
14	12/11	1:00	BAL	13%	-12%	12%	29%
15	12/18	1:00	@CAR	-6%	-12%	-7%	-5%
16	12/24	8:15	LV	1%	10%	-14%	39%
17	1/01	1:00	@BAL	13%	-12%	12%	29%
18	1/08	TBD	CLE	-5%	-5%	-6%	2%

2022 NFL DRAFT					
RD	PK		POS	COLLEGE	HT	WT
1	20	KENNY PICKETT	QB	PITT	6-3	220
2	20	GEORGE PICKENS	WR	GEORGIA	6-3	190
3	20	DEMARVIN LEAL	DT	TEXAS A&M	6-4	290
4	33	CALVIN AUSTIN III	WR	MEMPHIS	5-9	162
6	30	CONNOR HEYWARD	FB	MICHIGAN STATE	6-0	230
7	4	MARK ROBINSON	LB	OLE MISS	5-11	235
7	20	CHRIS OLADOKUN	QB	SOUTH DAKOTA STATE	6-2	195

2021 WEEKLY STATS

*RUSH STATS / *REC STATS	@ BUF (W) 23-16		LV (L) 17-26		CIN (L) 10-24		@ GB (L) 17-27		DEN (W) 27-19		SEA (W) 23-20		@ CLE (W) 15-10		CHI (W) 29-27	
QB BEN ROETHLISBERGER	18-32 188 (1 TD) 4-5		27-40 295 (1 INT) (1 TD) 0-0		38-58 318 (2 INT) (1 TD) 1-5		26-40 232 (1 INT) (1 TD) 0-0		15-25 253 (2 TD) 1-1-1		29-40 229 (1 TD) 2-[-3]		22-34 266 (1 TD) 1-0		21-30 205 (2 TD) 2-0	
RB NAJEE HARRIS	16-45	1-4	10-38	5-43 (1 TD)	14-40	14-102	15-62 (1 TD)	6-29	23-122 (1 TD)	2-20	24-81	6-46 (1 TD)	26-91 (1 TD)	3-29	22-62 (1 TD)	3-16
WR DIONTAE JOHNSON	0-0	5-36 (1 TD)	0-0	9-105	DNP		0-0	9-92 (1 TD)	0-0	2-72 (1 TD)	1-25	9-71	0-0	6-98	2-11	5-56
WR CHASE CLAYPOOL	1-25	3-45	1-[-3]	3-70	0-0	9-96	DNP		0-0	5-130 (1 TD)	0-0	2-17	2-16	4-45	2-13	3-30
WR RAY-RAY MCCLOUD	0-0	0-0	0-0	0-0	0-0	3-33	0-0	1-2	0-0	1-1	0-0	2-18	1-10	0-0	0-0	1-12
WR JAMES WASHINGTON	0-0	2-10	0-0	0-0	0-0	3-20	0-0	4-69	DNP		0-0	1-9	0-0	1-4	2-13	1-42
TE PAT FREIERMUTH	0-0	1-24	0-0	4-36	0-0	3-22 (1 TD)	0-0	1-11	0-0	2-7	0-0	7-58	0-0	4-44 (1 TD)	0-0	5-43 (2 TD)

2021 Stats
Record: 9-7-1
Rushing Rank: 29th
Passing Rank: 15th
Offensive Fantasy Pts: 18th
Against Run: 32nd
Against Pass: 10th
ppg Against: 24.4
ppg: 20.2

KEY ADDITIONS & NEW CONTRACTS

QB **MITCHELL TRUBISKY**: SIGNED A TWO-YEAR, $14.25 MILLION DEAL THAT'S WORTH UP TO $27 MILLION WITH INCENTIVES.

WR **MILES BOYKIN**: CLAIMED OFF WAIVERS BY THE STEELERS.

OT **CHUKWUMA OKORAFOR**: RE-SIGNED ON A THREE-YEAR, $29.25 MILLION DEAL WITH $20 MILLION GUARANTEED.

OG **JAMES DANIELS**: SIGNED A THREE-YEAR, $26.5 MILLION DEAL.

OL **MASON COLE**: SIGNED A THREE-YEAR CONTRACT.

DT **LARRY OGUNJOBI**: SIGNED A ONE-YEAR DEAL WORTH UP TO $8 MILLION WITH INCENTIVES.

LB **GENARD AVERY**: SIGNED A FREE-AGENT DEAL.

LB **MYLES JACK**: SIGNED A TWO-YEAR DEAL.

LB **ROBERT SPILLANE**: RE-SIGNED ON A ONE-YEAR RE-STRICTED FREE AGENT TENDER WORTH $2.433 MILLION.

CB **ARTHUR MAULET**: RE-SIGNED A TWO-YEAR DEAL.

CB **LEVI WALLACE**: SIGNED A TWO-YEAR CONTRACT.

CB **AHKELLO WITHERSPOON**: RE-SIGNED TO A TWO-YEAR CONTRACT.

S **TERRELL EDMUNDS**: RE-SIGNED ON A ONE-YEAR, $2.5 MILLION DEAL.

S **MINKAH FITZPATRICK**: AGREED TO A FOUR-YEAR EXTEN-SION WORTH MORE THAN $73.6 MILLION. FITZPATRICK IS NOW UNDER CONTRACT WITH THE STEELERS THROUGH 2026

S **DAMONTAE KAZEE**: SIGNED A ONE-YEAR DEAL.

S **MILES KILLEBREW**: RE-SIGNED ON A TWO-YEAR, $4 MILLION DEAL.

DB **KARL JOSEPH**: SIGNED TO A FREE-AGENT DEAL.

KR **GUNNER OLSZEWSKI**: SIGNED A TWO-YEAR, $4.2 MILLION CONTRACT.

Who wins the starting QB job in Pittsburgh?

The Big Ben era has finally ended in Pittsburgh, and the QB job is anyone's to win. Although there's been an offseason competition for the starting position, it seems clear that Mitchell Trubisky will begin this season under center. However, the Steelers didn't spend their first-round pick on Kenny Pickett (20th overall), just so he could watch from the bench all season. The real question is how long before Pittsburgh transitions to the guy they hope is their future?

Trubisky was acquired from the Bills this offseason. He watched QB Josh Allen from the bench in Buffalo last season, after spending his first four years in Chicago. You have to go all the way back to 2018 to see quality fantasy production from Trubisky. That year, between Weeks 1-11, he had finishes of QB1, QB1, QB2, QB5 and QB9. In the eleven-week span he was QB7 overall. The problem is, there's been nothing but negative regression since. Pittsburgh signed him to a two-year, $24.3 million contract, with just $5.25m guaranteed. When they're ready, it'll be easy to move on from Trubisky.

Kenny Pickett comes in as the hometown favorite after four years as the starting QB for the Pitt Panthers. 2021 was his breakout campaign, where he posted 4,319 yards, threw for 47 TDs, and scrambled for over 400 yards. It's only a matter of time before Pickett takes the helm to lead the offense. We expect the change by mid-season.

The problem with QBs in Pittsburgh is this — none of them are fantasy viable, including perennial backup Mason Rudolph, the only returning Steelers QB. That is, unless you're drafting for Superflex or Dynasty leagues, then consider Pickett.

> 'The real question is how long before Pittsburgh transitions to the guy they hope is their future?'

KEY LOSSES

QB **JOSH DOBBS** (BROWNS)
QB **BEN ROETHLISBERGER** (RETIRED)
RB **KALEN BALLAGE**
WR **RAY-RAY MCCLOUD** (49ERS)
WR **JUJU SMITH-SCHUSTER** (CHIEFS)
WR **JAMES WASHINGTON** (COWBOYS)
TE **ERIC EBRON**
OT **ZACH BANNER**
OG **TRAI TURNER** (COMMANDERS)
DE **TACO CHARLTON** (SAINTS)
DE **STEPHON TUITT** (RETIRED)
LB **JOE SCHOBERT**
CB **JOE HADEN**

DEPTH CHART

QB1	MITCHELL TRUBISKY **N**
QB2	KENNY PICKETT **R**
RB1	NAJEE HARRIS
RB2	BENNY SNELL JR.
RB3	ANTHONY MCFARLAND JR.
WR1	DIONTAE JOHNSON
WR2	CHASE CLAYPOOL
WR3	GEORGE PICKENS **R**
WR4	ANTHONY MILLER
TE1	PAT FREIERMUTH
TE2	ZACH GENTRY
K	CHRIS BOSWELL

2021 WEEKLY STATS

DET (TIE) 16-16		@LAC (L) 37-41		@CIN (L) 10-41		BAL (W) 20-19		@MIN (L) 28-36		TEN (W) 19-13		@KC (L) 10-36		CLE (W) 26-14		@BAL (W) 16-13	
DNP		28-44 273 (3 TD)	0-0	24-41 263 (2 INT) (1 TD)	0-0	21-31 236 (2 TD)	1-[-1]	28-40 308 (1 INT) (3 TD)	1-5	16-25 148	3-0 (1 TD)	23-35 159 (1 INT)	0-0	24-46 123 (1 INT) (1 TD)	1-[-1]	30-44 244 (1 INT) (1 TD)	3-[-4]
26-105	4-28	12-39 (1 TD)	5-20	8-23	3-14	21-71	5-36	20-94 (1 TD)	3-10 (1 TD)	12-18	2-8	19-93	5-17	28-188 (1TD)	3-18	11-28	4-27
0-0	7-83	0-0	7-101 (1 TD)	0-0	9-95	0-0	8-105 (2 TD)	1-7	5-76	1-10	5-38	0-0	6-51 (1 TD)	0-0	8-31 (1 TD)	0-0	7-51
DNP		2-1	5-93	0-0	3-82	1-2	2-52	1-2	8-93	1-7	0-12	0-0	4-41	0-0	3-17	3-33	5-37 (1 TD)
0-0	9-63	1-5	2-12	DNP		0-0	1-7	0-0	6-32	0-0	1-0	0-0	4-25	0-0	4-35	0-0	4-37
0-0	2-15 (1 TD)	0-0	2-12	0-0	1-3	0-0	0-0	0-0	4-65 (1 TD)	0-0	3-36	0-0	0-0	0-0	0-0	DNP	
0-0	5-31	0-0	4-11 (1 TD)	0-0	4-40 (1 TD)	0-0	3-26	0-0	2-32 (1 TD)	0-0	4-37	DNP		0-0	5-22	0-0	6-53

SAN FRANCISCO 49ERS

Does Trey Lance have top-five QB potential?

After Kyle Shannahan said Jimmy Garoppolo would be traded before the season, we are certain that Trey Lance will be the starter come Week 1. Lance is one our breakout candidates for 2022. His rushing floor, almost on its own, is enough to push him into the QB1 range.

Lance averaged 10 rushing attempts per game in his three games as the No. 1 QB last season. At that rate, he would finish with well over 150 attempts on the year. Of the 12 QBs with at least 125 carries in the last five seasons, only one has finished outside the top-12 QBs in fantasy PPG, and seven finished in the top five!

Lance does need improvement as a passer. While he had an impressive 8.5 yards per attempt, it was only because he was throwing to yards-after-the-catch monsters Deebo Samuel and George Kittle.

We don't want to be overly optimistic about his potential, as he finished as QB20, QB18, and QB10 in his three games with extended snaps last season. But don't be surprised when our ranking of Lance above Burrow comes to fruition.

Does the backfield still belong to Elijah Mitchell?

Mostly due to injuries, the 49ers have had five different No. 1 backs in five seasons, and in most cases, it was not the back with the highest ADP.

With almost 300 touches and no fumbles, Elijah Mitchell in on track to repeat as the 49ers touch leader. While Mitchell largely played a three-down role last season, he still had fewer targets than his backup, Jamycal Hasty. The reception deficiency leaves the door cracked enough for rookie Tyrion Davis-Price, who features the skillset needed to be a true three-down back, to possibly squeeze his way in to a role.

With a dual-threat QB now under center, whoever carries the ball could see a volume decrease, which traditionally occurs with highly mobile QBs. Mitchell won't have the receiving production to counter any potential loss in volume.

Both Mitchell and TDP have fair ADPs. Mitchell, nonetheless, should maintain his No. 1 back role unless he misses time or TDP shows out. With Kyle Shannahan's tendency to go with whoever's working, TDP is worth throwing a dart at in a later round.

Is it possible that Deebo is a one-hit wonder?

No matter what the stats showed last season, Deebo the receiver is a better fantasy player than Deebo the hyrbid (RB/WR). In weeks 1-9 last season, when Deebo was primarily used as a receiver, he averaged 21.2 fantasy PPG. Post Week 9, when used as both a rusher and receiver, he averaged 20 fantasy PPG.

WK	DATE	TIME	OPP	QB	RB	WR	TE
			2022/23 SCHEDULE	2021 FANTASY POINTS ALLOWED BY OPPONENT VS LEAGUE AVERAGE			
1	9/11	1:00	@CHI	4%	-7%	0%	-28%
2	9/18	4:05	SEA	2%	-8%	3%	-23%
3	9/25	8:20	@DEN	-10%	-9%	-6%	-29%
4	10/03	8:15	LAR	-12%	-8%	7%	-2%
5	10/09	4:05	@CAR	-6%	-12%	-7%	-5%
6	10/16	1:00	@ATL	13%	8%	7%	-3%
7	10/23	4:25	KC	15%	4%	3%	2%
8	10/30	4:25	@LAR	-12%	-8%	7%	-2%
9	BYE WEEK						
10	11/13	8:20	LAC	2%	17%	-11%	23%
11	11/21	8:20	@ARI*	0%	-11%	10%	-36%
12	11/27	4:25	NO	-26%	2%	-16%	-45%
13	12/04	4:05	MIA	-6%	-4%	-2%	6%
14	12/11	4:25	TB	3%	-4%	3%	4%
15	12/15	8:15	@SEA	2%	-8%	3%	-23%
16	12/24	4:05	WAS	29%	-3%	8%	5%
17	1/01	4:05	@LV	1%	10%	-14%	39%
18	1/08	TBD	ARI	0%	-11%	10%	-36%

PLAYED IN MEXICO CITY

2022 NFL DRAFT

RD	PK		POS	COLLEGE	HT	WT
2	29	DRAKE JACKSON	LB	USC	6-4	250
3	29	TYRION DAVIS-PRICE	RB	LSU	6-1	223
3	41	DANNY GRAY	WR	SMU	6-2	199
4	29	SPENCER BURFORD	G	UTSA	6-5	295
5	29	SAMUEL WOMACK	CB	TOLEDO	5-10	187
6	8	NICK ZAKELJ	DT	FORDHAM	6-5	325
6	42	KALIA DAVIS	DT	UCF	6-2	310
6	43	TARIQ CASTRO-FIELDS	CB	PENN STATE	6-0	194
7	41	BROCK PURDY	QB	IOWA STATE	6-1	220

2021 WEEKLY STATS

*RUSH STATS *REC STATS		@ DET (W) 41-33		@ PHI (W) 17-11		GB (L) 28-30		SEA (L) 21-28		@ ARI (L) 10-17		IND (L) 18-30		@ CHI (W) 33-22		ARI (L) 17-31	
QB JIMMY GAROPPOLO		17-25 314 (1 TD) 3-2		22-30 189 (1 TD) 11-20 (1 TD)		25-40 257 (1 TD) (2 TD) 1-4		14-23 165 (1 INT) (1 TD) 0-0		DNP		16-27 181 (2 INT) (1 TD) 2-0		17-28 322 5-4 (2 TD)		28-40 326 (1 INT) (2 TD) 1-3	
QB TREY LANCE		1-15 (1 TD) 3-2		DNP		0-0 0 1-1 (1 TD)		9-18 157 (2 TD) 7-41		15-29 192 (1 INT) 16-89		DNP		DNP		DNP	
RB ELIJAH MITCHELL		19-104 (1 TD)	0-0	17-42	2-11	DNP		DNP		9-43	2-19	18-107 (1 TD)	0-0	18-137 (1 TD)	0-0	8-36	5-43
RB JAMYCAL HASTY		1-3 (1 TD)	1-15	5-38	4-21	DNP		DNP		DNP		3-1	3-15	3-4	2-29	1-2	3-11
RB JEFF WILSON		DNP		DNP		DNP		DNP		DNP		DNP		DNP		DNP	
WR DEEBO SAMUEL		0-0	9-189 (1 TD)	2-8	6-93	2-0	5-52	1-1	8-156 (2 TD)	1-13 (1 TD)	3-58	0-0	7-100 (1 TD)	0-0	6-171	0-0	5-63
WR BRANDON AIYUK		0-0	0-0	0-0	1-6	1-8	4-37 (1 TD)	0-0	1-15	0-0	2-32	1-3	1-6	0-0	4-45	1-[-2]	6-89 (1 TD)
TE GEORGE KITTLE		0-0	4-78	0-0	4-17	1-9	7-92	0-0	4-40	DNP		DNP		DNP		0-0	6-101 (1 TD)

2021 Stats

Record: 10-7
Rushing Rank: 7th
Passing Rank: 12th
Offensive Fantasy Pts: 12th
Against Run: 7th
Against Pass: 7th
ppg Against: 20.6
ppg: 24.0

KEY ADDITIONS & NEW CONTRACTS

RB JAMYCAL HASTY: SIGNED TO A ONE-YEAR EXTENSION.

RB JEFF WILSON: RE-SIGNED ON A ONE-YEAR, $1.085 MILLION CONTRACT WITH $530,000 GUARANTEED.

WR DEEBO SAMUEL: SIGNED A THREE-YEAR, $73.5 MILLION EXTENSION WITH $58.1 MILLION GUARANTEED.

WR MARCUS JOHNSON: SIGNED A ONE-YEAR DEAL.

WR RAY-RAY MCCLOUD: SIGNED A TWO-YEAR CONTRACT WORTH UP TO $10.4 MILLION.

WR MALIK TURNER: SIGNED A ONE-YEAR DEAL.

TE ROSS DWELLEY: SIGNED A ONE-YEAR CONTRACT.

DE KERRY HYDER JR.: SIGNED A FREE-AGENT CONTRACT.

DE KEMOKO TURAY: SIGNED A ONE-YEAR CONTRACT.

DT MAURICE HURST: RE-SIGNED ON FREE-AGENT DEAL.

DT HASSAN RIDGEWAY: SIGNED A ONE-YEAR CONTRACT.

LB OREN BURKS: SIGNED A TWO-YEAR CONTRACT.

CB DARQUEZE DENNARD: RE-SIGNED TO A ONE-YEAR DEAL.

CB DONTAE JOHNSON: RE-SIGNED ON A ONE-YEAR DEAL.

CB JASON VERRETT: RE-SIGNED ON A FREE-AGENT DEAL.

CB CHARVARIUS WARD: SIGNED A THREE-YEAR, $40.5 MILLION DEAL.

S GEORGE ODUM: SIGNED A THREE-YEAR, $10.95 MILLION CONTRACT.

While not a significant difference on the surface, his expected fantasy output decreased by 4 PPG when being used as a combination rusher and receiver.

San Francisco's offense was already one of the slowest-paced, run-heaviest offenses in the NFL. Starting a QB who will lean more on the run and is a less proficient passer will hurt Deebo's fantasy value.

With some uncertainty of his offensive role and the new QB situation, we can see how one would be a little hesitant on making Deebo a top-five WR. We figure Deebo is the 49ers biggest playmaker, and he now has a contract that agrees. The 49ers will continue to find ways to get the ball in his hands, where he's the best in the league.

Behind Deebo, is their enough volume in the run-heavy 49ers offense to support George Kittle and Brandon Aiyuk?

Kittle is a top-five TE. Period. If he played on any of the three teams the TEs ranked ahead of him played on (Kansas City, Baltimore, Atlanta), he'd probably be the No. 1-ranked TE. To add perspective, among TEs with at least 100 targets last season, Kittle ranked first in yards per route run and yards after the catch per reception, fifth in PFF's run-blocking grade, and fifth in yards per reception.

In his tiny two-game sample size with Lance under center last season, Kittle's numbers were unimpressive, but we're not concerned. And, shockingly, he's failed to score more than 6 TDs in a single season, which may no longer be true after 2022. We expect a good year from Kittle and will be looking to draft him in the early-middle rounds.

Brandon Aiyuk probably won't have enough volume to be relevant week-in and week-out, unless Kittle or Deebo misses time, which is very possible. Since 2017, the No. 2 WR for teams whose QB had at least 80 carries has a median finish of WR51. We're more bullish than that for Aiyuk, but we don't expect consistent numbers unless something changes.

KEY LOSSES

RB **RAHEEM MOSTERT** (DOLPHINS)
WR **TRAVIS BENJAMIN**
WR **RICHIE JAMES JR.** (GIANTS)
WR **MOHAMED SANU**
WR **TRENT SHERFIELD** (DOLPHINS)
OG **LAKEN TOMLINSON** (JETS)
C **ALEX MACK** (RETIRED)
OL **TOM COMPTON** (BRONCOS)
DE **ARDEN KEY** (JAGUARS)
DT **D.J. JONES** (BRONCOS)
DT **KENTAVIUS STREET** (SAINTS)
CB **JOSH NORMAN**
CB **K'WAUN WILLIAMS** (BRONCOS)
S **JAQUISKI TARTT** (EAGLES)
S **TAVON WILSON**

DEPTH CHART

QB1	TREY LANCE
QB2	JIMMY GAROPPOLO
RB1	ELIJAH MITCHELL
RB2	JEFF WILSON JR.
RB3	TYRION DAVIS-PRICE **R**
WR1	DEEBO SAMUEL
WR2	BRANDON AIYUK
WR3	JAUAN JENNINGS
WR4	DANNY GRAY **R**
TE1	GEORGE KITTLE
TE2	ROSS DWELLEY
K	ROBBIE GOULD

2021 WEEKLY STATS

LAR (W) 31-10		@ JAC (W) 30-10		MIN (W) 34-26		@ SEA (L) 23-30		@ CIN (W) 26-23		ATL (W) 31-13		@ TEN (L) 17-20		HOU (W) 23-7		@ LAR (W) 27-24	
15-19 182 (2 TD) 2-1		16-22 176 (2 TD) 2-6		17-26 230 (1 INT) (1 TD) 3-0		20-30 299 (2 INT) (2 TD) 2-0		27-41 296 (2 TD) 1-3		18-23 235 (2 TD) 3-4		26-35 322 (2 INT) (1 TD) 1-3		DNP		23-32 316 (2 INT) (1 TD) 1-1	
DNP		0-0 0 3-4		DNP		DNP		DNP		DNP		DNP		16-23 249 (1 INT) (2 TD) 8-31		DNP	
27-91	0-0	DNP		27-133 (1 TD)	5-35	22-66 (1 TD)	3-18	DNP		DNP		DNP		21-119	2-11 (1 TD)	21-85	0-0
DNP		DNP		DNP		0-0	0-0	0-0	3-10	1-13	1-3	1-3	3-26	0-0	1-6	1-4	2-21
10-28	0-0	19-50	1-8	2-5	1-2	0-0	0-0	13-56	0-0	21-110 (1 TD)	2-9	14-45 (1 TD)	3-12	0-0	0-0	0-0	0-0
5-36 (1 TD)	5-97 (1 TD)	8-79 (1 TD)	1-15	6-66 (2 TD)	1-12	DNP		8-37 (1 TD)	1-22	6-29 (1 TD)	4-60	5-32	9-159	7-19	3-63 (1 TD)	8-45 (1 TD)	4-95
0-0	3-26	0-0	7-85 (1 TD)	1-4	3-91	0-0	3-55	1-4	6-62 (1 TD)	0-0	1-36	0-0	4-40 (1 TD)	0-0	4-94	0-0	6-107
0-0	5-50 (1 TD)	0-0	4-34 (1 TD)	0-0	1-13	1-5	9-181 (2 TD)	0-0	13-151 (1 TD)	0-0	6-93	0-0	2-21	1-6	1-29	0-0	5-10

SEATTLE SEAHAWKS

Is their any way a Seattle QB should end up on your fantasy team?

Seattle ran the fewest offensive plays in the league last season, which isn't the foundation for fantasy success.

Even though Geno Smith appears to be a better QB in terms of recent metrics, Drew Lock is currently the presumed started. Let's recall that this is the same QB who was unable to beat out current Jaguars backup QB, Teddy Bridgewater, for the starting job in Denver last season. Among the 51 QBs with at least 300 dropbacks since 2019, Lock is 44th in QB rating, 37th in yards per attempt, and 48th in adjusted completion rate. Lock has finished outside the top-20 QBs in fantasy PPG the two seasons he started in Denver. He's simply given us no indication he can put up and sustain decent fantasy production.

Geno Smith is much the same. His metrics in a small three-and-a-half game sample size last season do outshine lock. Among the 44 QBs with at least 100 drop backs in 2021, Smith was an impressive sixth in QB rating, 13th in yards per attempt, and second in adjusted completion rate. Even with those measurements, he finished inside the top-20 weekly QBs just once, mostly due to a 9-42-1 rushing line.

There's still a chance that Seattle ends up with Baker Mayfield or Jimmy Garoppolo as their starter. If so, a QB2 may in the realm of possibility. But don't draft Lock or Geno unless you're in a 4-QB league.

With the loss of Russ, what's the outlook for Tyler Lockett and DK Metcalf?

Seattle finished 16th in PPG last season. Among teams who have finished in the bottom half of the league in scoring in the past five years, the team's top WR has averaged a WR26 finish and the No. 2 option a WR51 finish.

We expected Metcalf to emerge as Seattle's No. 1 option during Wilson's tenure, but Lockett kept hanging around. Even with Geno Smith under center last season, Lockett saw more targets than Metcalf, but Metcalf did have more fantasy points.

'This is the season Metcalf will ascend to the clear No. 1 option in Seattle.'

This is the season Metcalf will ascend to the clear No. 1 option in Seattle. Lockett will still have some good weekly finishes, but will not be as consistent as Metcalf, or as productive. There's simply no longer enough volume to support both on a weekly basis. Seattle inked a massive new deal with Metcalf at the beginning of training camp, and we expect them to demonstrate the merits of the deal by providing him with a bombardment of targets this year.

	2022/23 SCHEDULE			2021 FANTASY POINTS ALLOWED BY OPPONENT VS LEAGUE AVERAGE			
WK	DATE	TIME	OPP	QB	RB	WR	TE
1	9/12	8:15	DEN	-10%	-9%	-6%	-29%
2	9/18	4:05	@SF	-1%	26%	-3%	20%
3	9/25	4:25	ATL	13%	8%	7%	-3%
4	10/02	1:00	@DET	4%	14%	2%	17%
5	10/09	1:00	@NO	-26%	2%	-16%	-45%
6	10/16	4:05	ARI	0%	-11%	10%	-36%
7	10/23	4:25	@LAC	2%	17%	-11%	23%
8	10/30	4:25	NYG	12%	40%	-2%	22%
9	11/06	4:05	@ARI	0%	-11%	10%	-36%
10	11/13	9:30AM	@TB*	3%	-4%	3%	4%
11	BYE WEEK						
12	11/27	4:05	LV	1%	10%	-14%	39%
13	12/04	4:05	@LAR	-12%	-8%	7%	-2%
14	12/11	4:25	CAR	-6%	-12%	-7%	-5%
15	12/15	8:15	SF	-1%	26%	-3%	20%
16	12/24	1:00	@KC	15%	4%	3%	2%
17	1/01	4:05	NYJ	-4%	11%	-1%	-1%
18	1/08	TBD	LAR	-12%	-8%	7%	-2%

* PLAYED IN MUNICH

2022 NFL DRAFT

RD	PK		POS	COLLEGE	HT	WT
1	9	CHARLES CROSS	OT	MISSISSIPPI STATE	6-5	310
2	8	BOYE MAFE	LB	MINNESOTA	6-4	265
2	9	KEN WALKER III	RB	MICHIGAN STATE	5-10	212
3	8	ABRAHAM LUCAS	OT	WASHINGTON STATE	6-7	319
4	4	COBY BRYANT	CB	CINCINNATI	6-1	198
5	10	TARIQ WOOLEN	CB	UTSA	6-4	205
5	15	TYREKE SMITH	EDGE	OHIO STATE	6-3	265
7	8	BO MELTON	WR	RUTGERS	5-11	195
7	12	DAREKE YOUNG	WR	LENOIR RHYNE	6-3	220

2021 WEEKLY STATS

*RUSH STATS *REC STATS	@ IND (W) 28-16		TEN (L) 30-33		@ MIN (L) 17-30		@ SF (W) 28-21		LAR (L) 17-26		@ PIT (L) 20-23		NO (L) 10-13		JAC (W) 31-7	
QB RUSSELL WILSON	18-23 254 (4 TD) 5-9		22-31 343 (2 TD) 3-16		23-32 298 (1 TD) 3-7		16-23 149 (2 TD) 4-26 (1 TD)		11-16 152 (1 INT) (1 TD) 2-10		DNP		DNP		DNP	
QB GENO SMITH	DNP		DNP		DNP		DNP		10-17 131 (1 INT) (1 INT) 3-23		23-32 209 (1 TD) 1-1-11		12-22 167 (1 TD) 3-12		20-24 195 (2 TD) 2-8 (1 TD)	
RB RASHAAD PENNY	2-8	0-0	DNP		DNP		DNP		DNP		DNP		6-9	0-0	7-7	0-0
RB ALEX COLLINS	DNP		1-25	0-0	2-8	0-0	10-44 (1 TD)	2-34	15-47	2-25	20-101 (1 TD)	1-[-3]	16-35	1-9	10-44	0-0
WR DK METCALF	0-0	4-60 (1 TD)	0-0	6-53	0-0	6-107 (1 TD)	0-0	4-65 (1 TD)	0-0	5-98 (2 TD)	0-0	6-58	0-0	2-96 (1 TD)	0-0	6-43 (2 TD)
WR TYLER LOCKETT	0-0	4-100 (2 TD)	0-0	8-178 (1 TD)	0-0	4-31	0-0	4-24	0-0	5-57	0-0	2-35	0-0	2-12	0-0	12-142
WR FREDDIE SWAIN	1-5	0-0	1-5	5-95 (1 TD)	1-11	1-10	0-0	3-20 (1 TD)	0-0	1-9	0-0	2-[-4]	1-8	4-39	0-0	0-0
TE GERALD EVERETT	0-0	2-20 (1 TD)	0-0	1-3	0-0	5-54	DNP		DNP		0-0	2-40	1-12	3-11	1-[-5]	1-7

2021 Stats
Record: 7-10
Rushing Rank: 11th
Passing Rank: 21st
Offensive Fantasy Pts: 16th
Against Run: 17th
Against Pass: 31st
ppg Against: 21.5
ppg: 23.2

KEY ADDITIONS & NEW CONTRACTS (SEA)

QB DREW LOCK: ACQUIRED IN A TRADE WITH THE DENVER BRONCOS, ALONG WITH DT SHELBY HARRIS, TE NOAH FANT, TWO FIRST-ROUNDERS, TWO SECOND-ROUNDERS AND A FIFTH-ROUNDER, FOR QB RUSSELL WILSON AND A FOURTH-ROUND PICK.

QB GENO SMITH: SIGNED A ONE-YEAR, $3.5 MILLION DEAL THAT INCLUDES ANOTHER $3.5 MILLION IN INCENTIVES.

RB RASHAAD PENNY: RE-SIGNED ON A ONE-YEAR, $5.75 MILLION DEAL THAT HAS A MAX VALUE OF $6.5 MILLION.

WR DK MECALF: SIGNED A THREE-YEAR, $72 MILLION EXTENSION WITH $58.2 MILLION GUARANTEED, AND A $30 MILLION SIGNING BONUS (HIGHEST SIGNING BONUS FOR A WR EVER).

WR MARQUISE GOODWIN: SIGNED A FREE-AGENT DEAL.

TE WILL DISSLY: RE-SIGNED ON A THREE-YEAR, $24 MILLION CONTRACT.

TE NOAH FANT: ACQUIRED IN A TRADE WITH THE DENVER BRONCOS, ALONG WITH QB DREW LOCK, DT SHELBY HARRIS, TWO FIRST-ROUNDERS, TWO SECOND-ROUNDERS AND A FIFTH-ROUNDER, FOR QB RUSSELL WILSON AND A FOURTH-ROUND PICK.

C AUSTIN BLYTHE: SIGNED A ONE-YEAR, $4 MILLION DEAL.

C/OG KYLE FULLER: RE-SIGNED.

DT SHELBY HARRIS: ACQUIRED IN A TRADE WITH THE DENVER BRONCOS, ALONG WITH QB DREW LOCK, TE NOAH FANT, TWO FIRST-ROUNDERS, TWO SECOND-ROUNDERS AND A FIFTH-ROUNDER, FOR QB RUSSELL WILSON AND A FOURTH-ROUND PICK.

DT QUINTON JEFFERSON: SIGNED A FREE-AGENT CONTRACT.

DT AL WOODS: RE-SIGNED ON A TWO-YEAR, $9 MILLION DEAL THAT INCLUDES $4.75 MILLION FULLY GUARANTEED.

LB UCHENNA NWOSU: SIGNED A TWO-YEAR, 20-MILLION DEAL THAT INCLUDES $10.5 MILLION FULLY GUARANTEED.

CB ARTIE BURNS: SIGNED A ONE-YEAR, $2 MILLION DEAL.

CB JUSTIN COLEMAN: SIGNED A ONE-YEAR DEAL.

CB SIDNEY JONES: RE-SIGNED ON A ONE-YEAR, $3.6 MILLION CONTRACT THAT HAS A MAX VALUE OF $4.4 MILLION.

S QUANDRE DIGGS: RE-SIGNED ON A THREE-YEAR, $40 MILLION DEAL.

What's the backfield situation look like?

Chris Carson has taken his last snap in an NFL uniform. Recovering from neck surgery, Carson wasn't cleared to participate in OTAs. Coach Pete Carroll alluded to the idea that it was time for Carson to hang it up, even though it is a tough thing to admit to oneself. And, just recently, Carson made his retirement official.

This leaves the backfield duties to either rookie Ken Walker III or incumbent Rashaad Penny. Penny was one of the most rostered players on fantasy championship teams last season, which makes sense considering his RB1 finish in Week 17, when the majority of leagues hold their championship. Including Week 17, Penny was sensational during his 10 games last season. He ranked first in yards per carry and yards after contact, and ranked seventh in forced missed tackles.

Just when it felt like Penny would have at least the early-down role to himself in 2022, the Seahawks drafted Walker in the second round. We just can't see Walker in a backup role considering the draft capital used. If we were to compare Walker to another NFL RB, we'd choose the only other RB in FBS history to average more than 4.0 yards after contact per rushing attempt besides Walker — Rashaad Penny. Walker and Penny share many attributes. If you saw a Michigan State game last season, you know who Walker is, and the ability he has with the ball in his hands.

Where Walker struggles, like Penny, is in the passing game. He is not an effective pass-blocker or receiver, which means he won't slide into a three-down role immediately.

With both Penny and Walker healthy, neither holds elite value on their own. It doesn't help that both will be playing behind last year's 32nd-ranked offensive line. We're going to give Walker a slight edge in our rankings, but it may take an injury, which seems to happen quite often to the Seattle backfield, to make either a viable starter.

KEY LOSSES

QB RUSSELL WILSON (TRADED TO BRONCOS)
RB CHRIS CARSON (RETIRED)
RB ALEX COLLINS
RB ADRIAN PETERSON
TE GERALD EVERETT (CHARGERS)
OL JAMARCO JONES (TITANS)
OT DUANE BROWN
OT BRANDON SHELL
OG ETHAN POCIC (BROWNS)
DE CARLOS DUNLAP
DE RASHEEM GREEN (TEXANS)
DE KERRY HYDER JR. (49ERS)
DE BENSON MAYOWA
DT ROBERT NKEMDICHE
LB BOBBY WAGNER (RAMS)
CB D.J. REED (JETS)

DEPTH CHART

QB1	DREW LOCK **N**
QB2	GENO SMITH
RB1	KEN WALKER III **R**
RB2	RASHAAD PENNY
RB3	DEEJAY DALLAS
WR1	DK METCALF
WR2	TYLER LOCKETT
WR3	D'WAYNE ESKRIDGE
WR4	FREDDIE SWAIN
TE1	NOAH FANT **N**
TE2	WILL DISSLY
K	JASON MYERS

2021 WEEKLY STATS

@ GB (L) 0-17		ARI (L) 13-23		@ WAS (L) 15-17		SF (W) 30-23		@ HOU (W) 33-13		@ LAR (L) 10-20		CHI (L) 24-25		DET (W) 51-29		@ ARI (W) 38-30	
20-40 161 (2 INT)		14-26 207		20-31 247 (2 TD)		30-37 231 (1 INT) (2 TD)		17-28 260 (2 TD)		17-31 156 (1 INT)		16-27 181 (2 TD)		20-29 236 (4 TD)		15-26 238 (1 INT) (3 TD)	
5-32		2-2		2-16		3-15		2-8		0-0		2-13		6-24		4-5 (1 TD)	
DNP		DNP		DNP		DNP		DNP		DNP		DNP		DNP		DNP	
0-0	0-0	2-19	0-0	0-0	0-0	10-35	1-27	16-137 (2 TD)	1-1	11-39	2-5	17-135 (1 TD)	0-0	25-170 (2TD)	2-15	23-190 (1TD)	0-0
10-41	1-8	10-36	0-0	7-14	1-13	DNP		7-16	1-1	DNP		DNP		DNP		DNP	
0-0	3-26	0-0	4-31	0-0	1-13	0-0	5-60	0-0	4-43	0-0	6-52	0-0	2-41 (1 TD)	1-6	6-63 (3 TD)	0-0	5-58
0-0	2-23	0-0	4-115	0-0	3-96	0-0	7-68 (1 TD)	0-0	5-142 (1 TD)	DNP		0-0	3-30	1-7	3-24 (1 TD)	1-2	5-98 (2 TD)
0-0	0-0	0-0	0-0	0-0	1-32 (1 TD)	0-0	3-18	1-3	0-0	0-0	1-25	0-0	1-9	0-0	2-65	0-0	1-25 (1 TD)
0-0	8-63	0-0	3-37	0-0	5-37 (1 TD)	0-0	4-7	1-13	2-15 (1 TD)	0-0	4-60	0-0	4-68 (1 TD)	0-0	3-36	0-0	1-20

Can an aging Tom Brady put up top-five QB numbers again this season?

Tom Brady's GOAT status is no longer a contended opinion anymore. The stats and rings speak for themselves. So, what would make anyone think that Brady could not have another elite NFL season? Of course there are reasons he shouldn't, the first being his age. Brady will be 45 by the start of the year. Then there's the loss of his favorite career target, Gronk. But anyone who's bet against Brady before (for me it was five years ago, when he was 40 and threw for over 500 yards in the Super Bowl), generally learns their lesson and won't do it again.

In two years and 33 games since he moved to Tampa Bay, Tampa Tom has thrown for 9,949 yards, 83 TDs, and won a Super Bowl. He also got inebriated after the Super Bowl win and threw the Lombardi Trophy over the water, from one boat to another — another completion.

Last season, Brady was first in completions, attempts, yards, and passing TDs. And he also supported four top-11 receivers in fantasy PPG: Chris Godwin (WR6), Antonio Brown (WR8), Mike Evans (WR11), and Rob Gronkowski (TE4). After a six-week retirement, Brady has returned to the field rejuvenated.

Even after his overall QB3 finish last season, we still think Allen, Herbert, Mahomes, Jackson, and Hurts are all better options, mostly because of their rushing upside. Either way, you should feel really good about ending your draft with the old man as your QB1.

Can the Bucs produce two top-20 receivers again?

Mike Evans finished as the overall WR9 last season and should put up similar numbers this season as long as he stays healthy, which hasn't been a problem in the past (only missed seven games in eight years). Evans should have an early-season boost in production as Chris Godwin will still be sidelined while recovering from his ACL tear from Week 15 last season.

While it's not out of the question that Godwin is ready by Week 1, the Bucs have no reason to rush last year's WR13 onto the field before he's completely ready. The Bucs believe Godwin to be a valuable asset to the team, evidenced by his three-year, $60 million extension signed in the offseason, after his injury. Godwin's ADP is in the mid-twenties among WRs, a little too high for our liking.

Russell Gage — fresh from Atlanta — looks to benefit most from Godwin's paced recovery. Gage was good for the Falcons, but never reached his full potential. He'll be the No. 2 option until Godwin returns to full reps, giving Gage a chance to build a rapport with Brady. Gage has the chance to finish the year as the best No. 3 WR on any team.

There are plenty of vacated targets from both Gronk and Antonio Brown to support two top-20 WRs, and maybe a third flex option.

2022/23 SCHEDULE				2021 FANTASY POINTS ALLOWED BY OPPONENT VS LEAGUE AVERAGE			
WK	DATE	TIME	OPP	QB	RB	WR	TE
1	9/11	8:20	@DAL	-6%	-14%	2%	5%
2	9/18	1:00	@NO	-26%	2%	-16%	-45%
3	9/25	4:25	GB	5%	-13%	3%	0%
4	10/02	8:20	KC	15%	4%	3%	2%
5	10/09	1:00	ATL	13%	8%	7%	-3%
6	10/16	1:00	@PIT	-2%	11%	-3%	-10%
7	10/23	1:00	@CAR	-6%	-12%	-7%	-5%
8	10/27	8:15	BAL	13%	-12%	12%	29%
9	11/06	4:25	LAR	-12%	-8%	7%	-2%
10	11/13	9:30AM	SEA*	2%	-8%	3%	-23%
11	BYE WEEK						
12	11/27	1:00	@CLE	-5%	-5%	-6%	2%
13	12/05	8:15	NO	-26%	2%	-16%	-45%
14	12/11	4:25	@SF	-1%	26%	-3%	20%
15	12/18	4:25	CIN	-1%	6%	0%	22%
16	12/25	8:20	@ARI	0%	-11%	10%	-36%
17	1/01	1:00	CAR	-6%	-12%	-7%	-5%
18	1/08	TBD	@ATL	13%	8%	7%	-3%

PLAYED IN MUNICH

2022 NFL DRAFT						
RD	PK		POS	COLLEGE	HT	WT
2	1	LOGAN HALL	EDGE	HOUSTON	6-6	275
2	25	LUKE GOEDEKE	OT	CENTRAL MICHIGAN	6-5	310
3	27	RACHAAD WHITE	RB	ARIZONA STATE	6-2	210
4	1	CADE OTTON	TE	WASHINGTON	6-5	250
4	28	JAKE CAMARDA	P	GEORGIA	6-2	180
5	14	ZYON MCCOLLUM	CB	SAM HOUSTON STATE	6-4	200
6	40	KO KIEFT	TE	MINNESOTA	6-5	265
7	27	ANDRE ANTHONY	EDGE	LSU	6-4	251

2021 WEEKLY STATS

*RUSH STATS : *REC STATS	DAL (W) 31-29		ATL (W) 48-25		@ LAR (L) 24-34		@ NE (W) 19-17		MIA (W) 45-17		@ PHI (W) 28-22		CHI (W) 38-3		@ NO (L) 27-36	
QB TOM BRADY	32-50 379 (2 INT) (4 TD) 0-0		24-36 276 (5 TD) 1-6		41-55 432 (1 TD) 3-14 (1 TD)		22-43 269 4-3		30-41 411 (5 TD) 1-13		34-42 297 (1 INT) (2 TD) 4-1		20-36 211 (4 TD) 0-0		28-40 375 (2 INT) (4 TD) 1-2	
RB LEONARD FOURNETTE	9-32	5-27	11-52	4-24	4-8	3-26	20-92	3-47	12-67 (1 TD)	4-43	22-81 (2 TD)	6-46	15-81 (1 TD)	2-9	8-26	3-17
RB RONALD JONES II	4-14	0-0	6-27	1-9	5-11	0-0	6-25 (1 TD)	0-0	5-21	1-15	5-20	1-9	10-63	0-0	3-13	1-6
RB GIOVANI BERNARD	0-0	2-12	0-0	2-16	0-0	9-51 (1 TD)	DNP		4-21	2-14 (1 TD)	0-0	2-4	0-0	2-5	2-30	1-7 (1 TD)
WR MIKE EVANS	0-0	3-24	0-0	5-75 (2 TD)	0-0	8-106	0-0	7-75	0-0	6-113 (2 TD)	0-0	2-27	0-0	6-76 (3 TD)	0-0	2-48 (1 TD)
WR CHRIS GODWIN	0-0	9-105 (1 TD)	0-0	4-62 (1 TD)	1-2 (1 TD)	6-74	0-0	3-55	0-0	7-70	0-0	5-43	0-0	8-111 (1 TD)	0-0	8-140 (1 TD)
WR ANTONIO BROWN	1-6	5-121 (1 TD)	0-0	1-17	DNP		0-0	7-63	0-0	7-124 (2 TD)	0-0	9-93 (1 TD)	DNP		DNP	
TE ROB GRONKOWSKI	0-0	8-90 (2 TD)	0-0	4-39 (2 TD)	0-0	4-55	DNP		DNP		DNP		DNP		0-0	0-0
TE CAMERON BRATE	0-0	0-0	0-0	1-8	0-0	4-35	0-0	2-29	0-0	1-12	0-0	3-26	0-0	0-0	2-15	

2021 Stats
Record: 13-4
Rushing Rank: 26th
Passing Rank: 1st
Offensive Fantasy Pts: 1st
Against Run: 3rd
Against Pass: 22nd
ppg Against: 20.9
ppg: 29.9

KEY ADDITIONS & NEW CONTRACTS

QB **TOM BRADY**: ANNOUNCED HE WILL COME OUT OF RETIREMENT AND RETURN TO THE TAMPA BAY BUCCANEERS FOR THE 2022 NFL SEASON.

QB **BLAINE GABBERT**: RE-SIGNED ON A ONE-YEAR DEAL WORTH $2.25 MILLION WITH $1.75 MILLION GUARANTEED.

RB **GIOVANI BERNARD**: RE-SIGNED ON A ONE-YEAR DEAL.

RB **LEONARD FOURNETTE**: RE-SIGNED ON A THREE-YEAR, $21 MILLION CONTRACT WITH A MAX VALUE OF $24 MILLION.

OG **SHAQ MASON**: ACQUIRED IN A TRADE WITH THE NEW ENGLAND PATRIOTS IN EXCHANGE FOR A 2022 FIFTH-ROUND PICK.

WR **RUSSELL GAGE**: SIGNED WITH THE BUCCANEERS.

WR **CHRIS GODWIN**: RECEIVED THE FRANCHISE TAG. GODWIN LATER SIGNED A THREE-YEAR, $60 MILLION CONTRACT WITH $40 MILLION GUARANTEED AT SIGNING.

WR **BRESHAD PERRIMAN**: RE-SIGNED ON A ONE-YEAR DEAL.

TE **KYLE RUDOLPH**: SIGNED A ONE-YEAR DEAL.

OT **JOSH WELLS**: RE-SIGNED TO A FREE-AGENT DEAL.

OG **AARON STINNIE**: RE-SIGNED WITH TAMPA BAY.

C **RYAN JENSEN**: RE-SIGNED TO A THREE-YEAR, $39 MILLION DEAL THAT INCLUDES $23 MILLION GUARANTEED.

DE **WILLIAM GHOLSTON**: RE-SIGNED WITH TAMPA BAY.

DT **AKIEM HICKS**: SIGNED A ONE-YEAR CONTRACT WORTH UP TO $10 MILLION.

CB **CARLTON DAVIS**: RE-SIGNED ON A THREE-YEAR, $45 MILLION DEAL THAT INCLUDES $30 MILLION GUARANTEED.

S **KEANU NEAL**: SIGNED A FREE-AGENT CONTRACT.

DB **LOGAN RYAN**: SIGNED WITH THE BUCCANEERS.

LS **ZACH TRINER**: RE-SIGNED.

Are Leonard Fournette and the other Tampa Bay RBs being overvalued in this pass-first offense?

Leonard Fournette established himself as the preferred back last season, after Ronald Jones II got the bulk of the workload in 2020. Jones had a front row seat as Fournette took over the backfield last season, and then Jones departed for Kansas City.

Fournette has been both effective as a rusher and pass catcher. He had more targets per game last season than any other RB. He'll have plenty of scoring chances in the Bucs offense and should produce back-to-back double-digit TD years. The Bucs signed Fournette to a three-year, $21 million extension this offseason, and we're projecting the highest paid RB this offseason will produce a top-10 season.

In Round 3 of the draft, Tampa Bay selected Rachaad White, who averaged 6.3 yards per carry at Arizona State. White has the tools to be a three-down back, but while Fournette's healthy, he'll likely be used as a gadget player or when Fournette takes a breather. There are plenty of touches vacated by Jones, which will provide an opportunity for White to display his ability. He could see some of the third-down work with backup Giovanni Bernard. White has the biggest insurance play upside if Fournette were to be sidelined for any reason, as Bernard is not a three-down back.

All in all, the Bucs high-powered, high-scoring offense offers plenty of opportunity for whoever is in the backfield with Brady.

> **White has the tools to be a three-down back, but while Fournette's healthy, he'll likely be used as a gadget player or when Fournette needs a breather.**

KEY LOSSES

RB **RONALD JONES II** (CHIEFS)
TE **ROB GRONKOWSKI** (RETIRED)
TE **O.J. HOWARD** (BILLS)
OG **ALEX CAPPA** (BENGALS)
OG **ALI MARPET** (RETIRED)
DE **JASON PIERRE-PAUL**
DT **NDAMUKONG SUH**
LB **KEVIN MINTER**
CB **RICHARD SHERMAN**
S **JORDAN WHITEHEAD** (JETS)
P **BRADLEY PINION**

DEPTH CHART

QB1	TOM BRADY
QB2	KYLE TRASK
RB1	LEONARD FOURNETTE
RB2	GIOVANI BERNARD
RB3	RACHAAD WHITE **R**
WR1	MIKE EVANS
WR2	CHRIS GODWIN
WR3	JULIO JONES **N**
WR4	RUSSELL GAGE JR. **N**
TE1	KYLE RUDOLPH **N**
TE2	CAMERON BRATE
K	RYAN SUCCOP

2021 WEEKLY STATS

@ WAS (L) 19-29		NYG (W) 30-10		@ IND (W) 38-31		@ ATL (W) 30-17		BUF (W) 33-27		NO (L) 0-9		@ CAR (W) 32-6		@ NYJ (W) 28-24		CAR (W) 41-17	
23-34 220 (2 INT) (2 TD) 1-2		30-46 307 (1 INT) (2 TD) 1-10		25-34 226 (1 INT) (1 TD) 2-2		38-51 368 (1 INT) (4 TD) 1-[-1]		31-46 363 (2 TD) 7-16 (1 TD)		26-48 214 (1 INT) 1-2		18-30 232 (1 TD) 1-11		34-50 410 (1 INT) (3 TD) 0-0		29-37 326 (3 TD) 0-0	
11-47	8-45	10-35	6-39	17-100 (3 TD)	7-31 (1 TD)	13-44	7-48 (1 TD)	19-113 (1 TD)	4-19	9-34	7-33	DNP		DNP		DNP	
0-0	0-0	8-33 (1 TD)	0-0	7-37 (1 TD)	0-0	1-2	1-0	3-8	0-0	8-63	2-8	20-65 (1 TD)	2-16	10-26	1-1	DNP	
1-4	1-4	0-0	1-3	0-0	0-0	1-3	1-7	0-0	0-0	DNP		DNP		DNP		DNP	
0-0	2-62 (1 TD)	1-10	6-73 (1 TD)	0-0	3-16	0-0	7-99	0-0	6-91 (1 TD)	0-0	1-14	DNP		0-0	4-47 (1 TD)	0-0	6-89 (2 TD)
0-0	7-57	1-7	6-65 (1 TD)	1-3	4-24	1-9	15-143	0-0	10-105	0-0	6-49	DNP		DNP		DNP	
DNP		DNP		DNP		DNP		DNP		DNP		0-0	10-101	0-0	3-26	DNP	
DNP		0-0	6-71	0-0	7-123	0-0	4-58 (2 TD)	0-0	5-62	0-0	2-29	0-0	1-23	0-0	7-115	0-0	7-137
0-0	1-6 (1 TD)	0-0	2-27	0-0	3-23	0-0	1-3 (1 TD)	0-0	2-11	0-0	2-22	0-0	2-11 (1 TD)	0-0	2-5 (1 TD)	0-0	2-12

TENNESSEE TITANS

Should fantasy mangers think twice about drafting Tannehill after Tennessee drafted Malik Willis?

The Titans selected Liberty product Malik Willis in the third round, but heading into Week 1, Ryan Tannehill remains the starter. Tannehill may not have been flashy, but he's been good in Tennessee. Since 2019, he's posted a PFF passing grade of 91 (third), a QB rating of 102, and 7.9 yards per reception (tied for sixth). Last season, he rushed for 15.9 yards per game (19th), but it's not his yardage that's impressive, it's his back-to-back seasons with 7 rushing TDs that's most remarkable. In fact, over the past three seasons, Tannehill had more end zone visits than Lamar Jackson!

With a 12-5 record, Tannehill led the Titans to the playoffs last season, only to throw three embarrassing interceptions in a loss to the Bengals. Tannehill needed therapy to get over his division-round loss, and is using it for motivation this season.

At 34, the veteran QB may have reached his full potential, and the Titans will look to see what the future might hold with Willis. But Willis will spend most, if not all, of 2022 watching from the sideline, with the exception of a few designed snaps or if Tannehill misses time with injury.

But if Willis were to get the start for any reason, he'll have immediate top-ten upside. Drawing comparisons to Lamar Jackson, Willis' fantasy upside comes from his rushing ability. Since 2015, among all college QBs with at least 100 rushing attempts, Willis' 8.4 yards per carry is second only to Lamar Jackson.

While we won't be drafting either QB in traditional leagues (Tannehill's a QB2 in 2-QB leagues), we will always consider Tannehill as a streaming option as in years past. He's usually sitting there on waivers waiting for us.

With the departure or A.J. Brown, who becomes the No. 1 receiving option?

A.J. Brown's absence won't be felt too strongly in this run-first offense. Still, his workload must go somewhere. The Titans acquired Robert Woods from the Rams, but Woods tore his ACL in Week 10 last season, and the timeline for his availability remains unknown. He could be ready sometime in the first half of the season, and should make an impact upon return. You should wait until your starters are secure before selecting woods for your bench.

The Titans picked Treylon Burks in Round 1 of the draft. Burks is a big-body receiver who will have a chance to establish himself as Woods reintegrates. He's currently being drafted in Rounds 9-11, and has also drawn comparisons to Deebo Samuel. He could end up as the No. 1 option for the Titans, and that's enough upside to make him draftable at his current range.

2022/23 SCHEDULE			2021 FANTASY POINTS ALLOWED BY OPPONENT VS LEAGUE AVERAGE			
WK	DATE	TIME	OPP	QB	RB	WR	TE
1	9/11	4:25	NYG	12%	40%	-2%	22%
2	9/19	7:15	@BUF	-34%	-11%	-27%	-34%
3	9/25	1:00	LV	1%	10%	-14%	39%
4	10/02	1:00	@IND	2%	-12%	4%	23%
5	10/09	1:00	@WAS	29%	-3%	8%	5%
6	BYE WEEK						
7	10/23	1:00	IND	2%	-12%	4%	23%
8	10/30	4:05	@HOU	1%	13%	5%	13%
9	11/06	8:20	@KC	15%	4%	3%	2%
10	11/13	1:00	DEN	-10%	-9%	-6%	-29%
11	11/17	8:15	@GB	5%	-13%	3%	0%
12	11/27	1:00	CIN	-1%	6%	0%	22%
13	12/04	1:00	@PHI	-1%	10%	-17%	46%
14	12/11	1:00	JAC	4%	-1%	5%	-2%
15	12/18	4:25	@LAC	2%	17%	-11%	23%
16	12/24	1:00	HOU	1%	13%	5%	13%
17	12/29	8:15	DAL	-6%	-14%	2%	5%
18	1/08	TBD	@JAC	4%	-1%	5%	-2%

2022 NFL DRAFT					
RD	PK		POS	COLLEGE	HT	WT
1	18	TREYLON BURKS	WR	ARKANSAS	6-3	225
2	3	ROGER MCCREARY	CB	AUBURN	6-0	190
3	5	NICHOLAS PETIT-FRERE	OT	OHIO STATE	6-5	315
3	22	MALIK WILLIS	QB	LIBERTY	6-1	225
4	26	HASSAN HASKINS	RB	MICHIGAN	6-1	220
4	38	CHIGOZIE OKONKWO	TE	MARYLAND	6-3	250
5	20	KYLE PHILIPS	WR	UCLA	5-11	191
6	26	THEO JACKSON	S	TENNESSEE	6-2	203
6	41	CHANCE CAMPBELL	LB	OLE MISS	6-2	240

2021 WEEKLY STATS

*RUSH STATS	*REC STATS	ARI (L) 13-38		@ SEA (W) 33-30		IND (W) 25-16		@ NYJ (L) 24-27		@ JAC (W) 37-19		BUF (W) 34-31		KC (W) 27-3		@ IND (W) 34-31	
QB RYAN TANNEHILL		21-35 212 (1 INT) (1 TD) 2-17 (1 TD)		27-40 347 4-27		18-27 197 (2 INT) (3 TD) 5-56		30-49 298 (1 INT) 3-9		14-22 197 (1 INT) 3-21		18-29 216 (1 INT) 2-3 (1 TD)		21-27 270 (1 INT) (1 TD) 2-6 (1 TD)		23-33 265 (2 INT) (3 TD) 2-26	
RB DERRICK HENRY		17-61	3-19	35-182(3TD)	6-55	28-113	3-31	33-157 (1 TD)	2-20	29-130(3TD)	0-0	20-143 (3TD)	2-13	29-86	2-16	28-68	0-0
RB D'ONTA FOREMAN		DNP		DNP		DNP		DNP		DNP		DNP		DNP		DNP	
RB DONTRELL HILLIARD		DNP		DNP		DNP		DNP		DNP		DNP		DNP		DNP	
WR A.J. BROWN		0-0	4-49 (1 TD)	0-0	3-43	1-3	0-0	DNP		0-0	3-38	0-0	7-91	0-0	8-133 (1 TD)	0-0	10-155 (1 TD)
WR WESTBROOK-IKHINE		0-0	1-10	0-0	1-6	0-0	4-53 (1 TD)	0-0	3-29	DNP		0-0	3-27	0-0	0-0	0-0	2-16 (1 TD)
WR JULIO JONES		0-0	3-29	0-0	6-128	0-0	3-47	DNP		DNP		0-0	3-59	0-0	2-38	DNP	
TE ANTHONY FIRKSER		0-0	3-19	DNP		DNP		0-0	3-23	0-0	3-33	0-0	1-11	0-0	1-9	0-0	1-8

FANTASY TAKEOVER

2021 Stats
Record: 12–5
Rushing Rank: 5th
Passing Rank: 23rd
Offensive Fantasy Pts: 17th
Against Run: 2nd
Against Pass: 26th
ppg Against: 20.7
ppg: 24.2

A year older and coming off injury, will Derrick Henry still be a top-three RB this season?

Henry broke his foot in Week 8 last season and missed the rest of the regular season. He returned in the playoffs, rushing 20 times for 62 yards and a TD, in a divisional loss to the Bengals. Henry says his foot is healed, but the playoff loss still stings.

In 2020, Henry became one of only seven NFL RBs to rush for 2,000 yards in a season, ever. Over the last three seasons, his worst fantasy PPG average is 19.6 (RB4, 2019). Last season, in his eight games, he was first in fantasy PPG (24.1).

When healthy, we know what to expect from Henry. He's missed very little time in his NFL career, only two games prior to last season. The real question becomes, where do you consider drafting Henry with his current history? The answer for us is that he's still a first-round pick. Henry may not be the No. 1 overall guy, but he's still top five.

Fantasy drafts are about risk minimization, and there is still very little risk here for three reasons: (1) The playoff loss. Henry is motivated not to have that feeling again. (2) Henry is only guaranteed $3 million this season and is out to prove he deserves to earn a nice contract extension. (3) He'll still be giving plenty of volume, especially with the departure of A.J. Brown.

With a healthy Henry, there's not much fantasy value in the other Titan's RBs, other than as insurance. Both D'onta Foreman and Dontrell Hilliard did well last season in Henry's absence. If Henry were to miss time this year, Hassaan Haskins and Hilliard would carry the load, with Haskins as the primary backup.

> IN 2020, HENRY BECAME ONE OF ONLY SEVEN NFL RBs TO RUSH FOR 2,000 YARDS IN A SEASON, EVER.'

KEY ADDITIONS & NEW CONTRACTS

RB **DONTRELL HILLIARD**: RE-SIGNED WITH THE TITANS.

WR **ROBERT WOODS**: ACQUIRED IN A TRADE WITH THE RAMS FOR A 2023 SIXTH-ROUND PICK.

TE **AUSTIN HOOPER**: SIGNED A ONE-YEAR, $6 MILLION DEAL.

TE **GEOFF SWAIM**: SIGNED TO A ONE-YEAR, $3.5 MILLION EXTENSION WITH ALL BUT A $100,000 WORKOUT BONUS FULLY GUARANTEED.

C **BEN JONES**: RE-SIGNED A TWO-YEAR, $14 MILLION DEAL.

OL **JAMARCO JONES**: SIGNED A MULTI-YEAR CONTRACT.

LB **HAROLD LANDRY**: RE-SIGNED TO A FIVE-YEAR, $87.5 MILLION EXTENSION WITH $52.5 MILLION GUARANTEED.

CB **BUSTER SKRINE**: RE-SIGNED WITH THE TITANS.

LS **MORGAN COX**: SIGNED TO A ONE-YEAR EXTENSION.

K **RANDY BULLOCK**: RE-SIGNED A TWO-YEAR, $4.68 MILLION DEAL.

KEY LOSSES

RB **DARRYNTON EVANS** (BEARS)

RB **D'ONTA FOREMAN** (PANTHERS)

WR **A.J. BROWN** (TRADED TO EAGLES)

WR **JULIO JONES**

WR **CHESTER ROGERS**

TE **ANTHONY FIRKSER** (FALCONS)

TE **MYCOLE PRUITT**

OG **DAVID QUESSENBERRY** (BILLS)

OG **RODGER SAFFOLD** (BILLS)

LB **JAYON BROWN** (RAIDERS)

LB **RASHAAN EVANS** (FALCONS)

CB **JACKRABBIT JENKINS**

DEPTH CHART

QB1	RYAN TANNEHILL
QB2	MALIK WILLIS **R**
RB1	DERRICK HENRY
RB2	HASSAN HASKINS **R**
RB3	DONTRELL HILLIARD
WR1	ROBERT WOODS **N**
WR2	TREYLON BURKS **R**
WR3	NICK WESTBOOK-IKHINE
WR4	RACEY MCMATH
TE1	AUSTIN HOOPER **N**
TE2	GEOFF SWAIM
K	RANDY BULLOCK

2021 WEEKLY STATS

@LAR (W) 28-16		NO (W) 23-21		HOU (L) 13-22		@NE (L) 13-36		JAC (W) 20-0		@PIT (L) 13-19		SF (W) 20-17		MIA (W) 34-3		@HOU (W) 28-25	
19-27 143 (1 INT) (1 TD)		19-27 213 (1 TD)		35-52 323 (4 INT) (1 TD)		11-21 93 (1 INT) (1 TD)		20-31 191		23-32 153 (1 INT)		22-29 209 (1 TD)		13-18 120 (2 TD)		23-32 287 (4 TD)	
2-3 (1 TD)		5-1 (1 TD)		2-3		5-24		4-29 (1 TD)		5-18 (1 TD)		3-22		4-7		2-[-2]	
DNP		DNP		DNP		DNP		DNP		DNP		DNP		DNP		DNP	
5-29	0-0	11-30	2-48	7-25	1-15	19-109	1-3	13-47 (1 TD)	2-15	22-108	2-27	9-17 (1 TD)	0-0	26-132 (1TD)	0-0	21-69	1-15
DNP		DNP		7-35	8-47	12-131 (1 TD)	1-2	6-13	0-0	9-49	4-10	5-20	2-[-6]	8-45 (1 TD)	3-33	9-57	1-1
0-0	5-42	1-7	1-16	0-0	5-48	DNP		DNP		DNP		0-0	11-145 (1 TD)	0-0	2-41	0-0	4-68 (1 TD)
0-0	1-14	0-0	1-10	0-0	7-107	0-0	2-25 (1 TD)	0-0	3-31	0-0	4-32	0-0	2-38	0-0	0-0	0-0	4-78 (1 TD)
0-0	4-35	DNP		DNP		DNP		0-0	4-33	0-0	0-0	0-0	1-7	DNP		0-0	5-58 (1 TD)
0-0	1-7	0-0	1-2	0-0	5-26	0-0	1-7	0-0	4-34	0-0	2-19	0-0	1-13	0-0	3-24 (1 TD)	0-0	4-56 (1 TD)

How does a healthy J.D. McKissic affect Antonio Gibson's production?

Antonio Gibson is the top back in Washington, no questions asked, but early last season it was apparent that there would be a division of touches: Gibson on the ground, McKissic on passing downs.

In the first 12 weeks, Gibson's numbers were average (RB17). Recording fewer touches but with pass-catching upside, McKissic wasn't far behind (RB22). In Week 12 the two backs both put up monster performances against a depleted Seattle, with Gibson recording 21.6 fantasy points and McKissic 22.6. Unfortunately, McKissic was injured that game, not to return for the remainder of the season.

With the entire workload falling to Gibson, he posted three top-10 performances in the final six games, boosted by an increase in passing-down production.

This season, with both backs healthy, the division of touches should resemble the first 12 weeks of last season. McKissic is the second-most targeted back in the last two seasons, behind only Alvin Kamara.

We are content with drafting Gibson at that fringe RB2 range. If McKissic were to miss time again, we know his upside. While an injury to Gibson would not affect McKissic as much because he would never be a three-down back, he still has good flex potential in most leagues. We value him over some other pass-catching backs in the league like James White and Nyheim Hines.

Does rookie Jahan Dotson have a chance to pass Terry McLaurin as Washington's top receiver?

Terry McLaurin's potential ascension to full-fledged star has been hindered by the Washington QB carousel. McLaurin will be catching balls from the best passer of his career this season with Carson Wentz under center. Despite a handful of terrible games last season, Wentz had some success, elevating Michael Pittman Jr. to WR24 on a run-heavy offense.

McLaurin sat out OTAs in hopes of negotiating a new contract. Without much delay, the Commanders worked out a three-year, $70 million extension with McLaurin, cementing him as Washington's No. 1 target for the next few years.

Jahan Dotson will provide some competition for targets with McLaurin, though. The first-round pick was active at all preseason team activities, and with his sure hands and the ability to haul in everything thrown his way, there's no doubt he's the type of receiver a QB could quickly learn to trust.

Still, its highly unlikely Dotson will out-pace McLaurin in fantasy production this year. Even with the missed OTAs, McLaurin is still better equipped and more experienced. We expect the Wentz-McLaurin connection to produce plenty of big plays this season.

2022/23 SCHEDULE				2021 FANTASY POINTS ALLOWED BY OPPONENT VS LEAGUE AVERAGE			
WK	DATE	TIME	OPP	QB	RB	WR	TE
1	9/11	1:00	JAC	4%	-1%	5%	-2%
2	9/18	1:00	@DET	4%	14%	2%	17%
3	9/25	1:00	PHI	-1%	10%	-17%	46%
4	10/02	1:00	@DAL	-6%	-14%	2%	5%
5	10/09	1:00	TEN	3%	-22%	19%	-29%
6	10/13	8:15	@CHI	4%	-7%	0%	-28%
7	10/23	1:00	GB	5%	-13%	3%	0%
8	10/30	4:25	@IND	2%	-12%	4%	23%
9	11/06	1:00	MIN	6%	2%	23%	-13%
10	11/14	8:15	@PHI	-1%	10%	-17%	46%
11	11/20	1:00	@HOU	1%	13%	5%	13%
12	11/27	1:00	ATL	13%	8%	7%	-3%
13	12/04	1:00	@NYG	12%	40%	-2%	22%
14	BYE WEEK						
15	12/17	TBD	NYG	12%	40%	-2%	22%
16	12/24	4:05	@SF	-1%	26%	-3%	20%
17	1/01	1:00	CLE	-5%	-5%	-6%	2%
18	1/08	TBD	DAL	-6%	-14%	2%	5%

2022 NFL DRAFT					
RD	PK		POS	COLLEGE	HT	WT
1	16	JAHAN DOTSON	WR	PENN STATE	5-11	182
2	15	PHIDARIAN MATHIS	DT	ALABAMA	6-4	312
3	34	BRIAN ROBINSON JR.	RB	ALABAMA	6-1	228
4	8	PERCY BUTLER	S	LOUISIANA	6-0	191
5	1	SAM HOWELL	QB	NORTH CAROLINA	6-1	220
5	6	COLE TURNER	TE	NEVADA	6-6	240
7	9	CHRIS PAUL	G	TULSA	6-4	324
7	18	CHRISTIAN HOLMES	CB	OKLAHOMA STATE	6-1	205

2021 WEEKLY STATS

*RUSH STATS : *REC STATS	LAC (L) 16-20		NYG (W) 30-29		@ BUF (L) 21-43		@ ATL (W) 34-30		NO (L) 22-33		KC (L) 13-31		@ GB (L) 10-24		@ DEN (L) 10-17	
QB TAYLOR HEINICKE	11-15 122 (1 TD) 3-17		34-46 336 (1 INT) (2 TD) 4-6		14-24 212 (2 INT) (2 TD) 8-21 (1 TD)		23-33 290 (3 TD) 5-43		20-41 248 (2 INT) 5-40		24-39 182 (1 INT) (1 TD) 0-0		25-37 268 (1 INT) (1 TD) 10-95		24-39 270 (2 INT) (1 TD) 1-10	
RB ANTONIO GIBSON	20-90	3-18	13-69	2-4	12-31	1-73 (1 TD)	14-63 (1 TD)	2-12	20-60 (2 TD)	2-12	10-44	2-0	14-51	2-5	8-34	3-20
RB J.D. MCKISSIC	1-8	0-0	4-10 (1 TD)	5-83	3-23	2-15	7-15	5-44 (1 TD)	2-[-1]	1-8	8-45	8-65	4-22	4-34	3-10	8-83
WR TERRY MCLAURIN	0-0	4-62	0-0	11-107 (1 TD)	0-0	4-62	0-0	6-123 (2 TD)	0-0	4-46	0-0	4-28	0-0	7-122 (1 TD)	1-12	3-23
WR DEANDRE CARTER	0-0	0-0	1-2	0-0	0-0	0-0	0-0	1-24	1-11	4-62	0-0	0-0	1-27	1-4	0-0	3-51 (1 TD)
TE LOGAN THOMAS	0-0	3-30 (1 TD)	0-0	5-45	0-0	4-42 (1 TD)	0-0	0-0	DNP		DNP		DNP		DNP	

2021 Stats
Record: 7–10
Rushing Rank: 12th
Passing Rank: 22nd
Offensive Fantasy Pts: 24th
Against Run: 8th
Against Pass: 28th
ppg Against: 25.5
ppg: 19.7

KEY ADDITIONS & NEW CONTRACTS

QB **CARSON WENTZ**: ACQUIRED IN A TRADE WITH THE INDIANAPOLIS COLTS, ALONG WITH A 2022 SEVENTH-ROUND PICK, IN EXCHANGE FOR A 2022 THIRD-ROUNDER AND A 2023 THIRD-ROUNDER, WHICH CAN CONVERT TO A SECOND-ROUNDER BASED ON WENTZ'S SNAP TOTALS. THE TEAMS WILL ALSO SWAP 2022 SECOND-ROUND PICKS.

RB **J.D. MCKISSIC**: RE-SIGNED ON A TWO-YEAR, $7 MILLION DEAL.

WR **TERRY MCLAURIN**: AGREED TO TERMS ON A THREE-YEAR EXTENSION WORTH UP TO $70 MILLION.

WR **CAM SIMS**: RE-SIGNED ON A FREE-AGENT CONTRACT.

OT **CORNELIUS LUCAS**: RE-SIGNED A TWO-YEAR, $8.2 MILLION DEAL.

OG **ANDREW NORWELL**: SIGNED WITH THE COMMANDERS.

OG **TRAI TURNER**: SIGNED A ONE-YEAR, $3 MILLION CONTRACT.

C **TYLER LARSEN**: RE-SIGNED WITH THE COMMANDERS.

DE **EFE OBADA**: SIGNED TO A FREE-AGENT DEAL.

DB **BOBBY MCCAIN**: RE-SIGNED ON A TWO-YEAR, $11 MILLION CONTRACT.

K **JOEY SLYE**: SIGNED A TWO-YEAR DEAL WORTH UP TO NEARLY $5 MILLION WITH $2 MILLION IN GUARANTEES.

Will QB woes continue for Carson Wentz and the Commanders?

Carson Wentz hasn't had a good fantasy season since 2017. He was above average in 2019 but only played 12 games, leaving fantasy managers hanging. His 2021 campaign, ordinary at best, had some notable lows. In Week 8 he found a way to lose a game that was all but in the bag against the Titans. In Week 15, Wentz managed only 57 yards and 1 TD, along with an interception, against the Patriots (somehow a win). And his final game under center for Indy, a must-win Week 18, he looked lifeless as he was defeated by a hopeless Jaguars team, dashing the Colts playoff hopes. In Washington, Wentz will be surrounded by talent as well as a solid offensive line, but is it enough to make him a viable fantasy option?

Washington has been through a basket full of starting QBs since 2017, but has not yet found their man. For Wentz, this may be a make-or-break season for his future as a starter in the NFL. He has a big-play arm and a triple-digit QB rating on passes of 20-plus yards, so with a receiving corps that includes Terry McLaurin, rookie Jahan Dotson, and TE Logan Thomas, along with pass-catching backs J.D. McKissic and Antonio Gibson, Wentz is set up for a bounce-back year. However, unless you're in a 2-QB league, or looking for a streaming option, Wentz is best left undrafted.

IN WASHINGTON, WENTZ WILL BE SURROUNDED BY TALENT AS WELL AS A SOLID OFFENSIVE LINE, BUT IS IT ENOUGH TO MAKE HIM A VIABLE FANTASY OPTION?

KEY LOSSES

QB **RYAN FITZPATRICK**

WR/KR **DEANDRE CARTER** (CHARGERS)

WR **ADAM HUMPHRIES**

TE **RICKY SEALS-JONES** (GIANTS)

OG **BRANDON SCHERFF** (JAGUARS)

OL **ERECK FLOWERS**

DT **MATTHEW IOANNIDIS** (PANTHERS)

DT **TIM SETTLE** (BILLS)

LB **JON BOSTIC**

CB **D.J. HAYDEN**

CB **DARRYL ROBERTS**

S **LANDON COLLINS**

S **DESHAZOR EVERETT**

DEPTH CHART

QB1	CARSON WENTZ **N**
QB2	TAYLOR HEINICKE
RB1	ANTONIO GIBSON
RB2	J.D. MCKISSIC
RB3	BRIAN ROBINSON JR. **R**
WR1	TERRY MCLAURIN
WR2	JAHAN DOTSON **R**
WR3	CURTIS SAMUEL
WR4	CAM SIMS
TE1	LOGAN THOMAS
TE2	JOHN BATES
K	JOEY SLYE

2021 WEEKLY STATS

TB (W) 29-19		@ CAR (W) 27-21		SEA (W) 17-15		@ LV (W) 17-15		DAL (L) 20-27		@ PHI (L) 17-27		@ DAL (L) 14-56		PHI (L) 16-20		@ NYG (W) 22-7	
26-32 256 (1 TD) 3-15		16-22 206 (3 TD) 6-29		27-35 223 (1 INT) (1 TD) 4-3		23-30 196 (1 INT) (2 TD) 3-10		11-25 122 (1 INT) (1 TD) 3-8		DNP		7-22 121 (2 INT) (1 TD) 1-(-1)		27-36 247 (1 INT) 2-14		9-18 120 2-3	
24-64 (2 TD)	2-14	19-95	0-0	29-111	7-35	23-88	5-23 (1 TD)	10-36	2-5	15-26 (1 TD)	6-39	6-29	2-29 (1 TD)	DNP		21-146 (1 TD)	1-5
2-4	4-35	7-46	1-4	7-30 (1 TD)	5-26 (1 TD)	DNP		DNP		DNP		DNP		DNP		DNP	
0-0	6-59	0-0	5-103 (1 TD)	0-0	4-51	0-0	3-22	0-0	0-0	0-0	2-51	0-0	3-40	0-0	7-61	0-0	4-93
1-4	3-56 (1 TD)	1-(-3)	2-22 (1 TD)	1-4	4-42	0-0	1-6	0-0	2-12	1-12	2-12	1-15	1-5	1-6	0-0	1-11	0-0
DNP		DNP		0-0	3-31	DNP		DNP		DNP		DNP		DNP		DNP	

STATS 2021
Sorted by Average Fantasy Points per Game

QUARTERBACKS

			GP	COMS	ATTS	YARDS	TDS	INTS	ATTS	YARDS	TDS	TOTAL	AVG
				PASSING					**RUSHING**			**PPR**	
1	JOSH ALLEN	BUF	17	409	646	4407	36	15	122	763	6	408.6	24.0
2	JUSTIN HERBERT	LAC	17	443	672	5014	38	15	63	302	3	382.8	22.5
3	TOM BRADY	TB	17	485	719	5316	43	12	28	81	2	380.7	22.4
4	PATRICK MAHOMES	KC	17	436	658	4839	37	13	66	381	2	369.7	21.7
5	KYLER MURRAY	ARI	14	333	481	3787	24	10	88	423	5	300.5	21.5
6	JALEN HURTS	PHI	15	265	432	3144	16	9	139	784	10	316.2	21.1
7	AARON RODGERS	GB	16	366	531	4115	37	4	33	101	3	333.3	20.8
8	DAK PRESCOTT	DAL	16	410	596	4449	37	10	48	146	1	332.6	20.8
9	LAMAR JACKSON	BAL	12	246	382	2882	16	13	133	767	2	246.0	20.5
10	JOE BURROW	CIN	16	366	520	4611	34	14	40	118	2	318.2	19.9
11	MATTHEW STAFFORD	LAR	17	404	601	4886	41	17	32	43	0	333.7	19.6
12	KIRK COUSINS	MIN	16	372	561	4221	33	7	29	115	1	304.3	19.0
13	RUSSELL WILSON	SEA	14	259	400	3113	25	6	43	183	2	244.8	17.5
14	JAMEIS WINSTON	NO	7	95	161	1170	14	3	32	166	1	119.4	17.1
15	RYAN TANNEHILL	TEN	17	357	531	3734	21	14	55	270	7	276.4	16.3
16	DANIEL JONES	NYG	11	232	361	2428	10	7	62	298	2	173.5	15.8
17	CARSON WENTZ	IND	17	322	516	3563	27	7	57	215	1	268.0	15.8
18	DEREK CARR	LV	17	428	626	4804	23	14	40	108	0	267.0	15.7
19	JIMMY GAROPPOLO	SF	15	301	441	3810	20	12	38	51	3	233.5	15.6
20	TREVOR SIEMIAN	NO	6	108	188	1154	11	3	9	20	1	92.2	15.4
21	JARED GOFF	DET	14	332	494	3245	19	8	17	87	0	206.5	14.8
22	TEDDY BRIDGEWATER	DEN	14	285	426	3052	18	7	30	106	2	204.7	14.6
23	BEN ROETHLISBERGER	PIT	16	390	605	3740	22	10	20	5	0	228.1	14.3
24	TAYLOR HEINICKE	WAS	16	321	494	3419	20	15	60	313	1	226.9	14.2
25	TUA TAGOVAILOA	MIA	13	263	388	2653	16	10	42	128	3	182.9	14.1
26	GENO SMITH	SEA	4	65	95	702	5	1	9	42	1	56.3	14.1
27	SAM DARNOLD	CAR	12	243	406	2527	9	13	48	222	5	165.3	13.8
28	TYROD TAYLOR	HOU	6	91	150	966	5	5	19	151	3	81.7	13.6
29	MAC JONES	NE	17	352	521	3801	22	13	44	129	0	230.9	13.6
30	MATT RYAN	ATL	17	375	560	3968	20	12	40	82	1	230.9	13.6
31	BAKER MAYFIELD	CLE	14	253	418	3010	17	13	37	134	0	186.9	13.4
32	TYLER HUNTLEY	BAL	7	122	188	1081	3	4	47	294	2	88.6	12.7
33	CAM NEWTON	CAR	7	69	126	684	4	5	47	230	5	88.4	12.6
34	TREVOR LAWRENCE	JAX	17	359	602	3641	12	17	73	334	2	209.0	12.3
35	DAVIS MILLS	HOU	13	263	394	2664	16	10	18	44	0	159.0	12.2
36	ZACH WILSON	NYJ	13	213	383	2334	9	11	29	185	4	153.9	11.8
37	JUSTIN FIELDS	CHI	12	159	270	1870	7	10	72	420	2	136.8	11.4
38	GARDNER MINSHEW II	PHI	3	41	60	439	4	1	9	21	0	33.7	11.2
39	MIKE WHITE	NYJ	4	88	132	953	5	8	5	-1	0	44.0	11.0
40	TREY LANCE	SF	6	41	71	603	5	2	38	168	1	64.9	10.8

TIGHT ENDS

			GP	TARS	RECS	YARDS	TDS	TOTAL	AVG
				RECEIVING				**PPR**	
1	MARK ANDREWS	BAL	17	153	107	1361	9	301.1	17.7
2	TRAVIS KELCE	KC	16	134	92	1125	9	264.8	16.6
3	GEORGE KITTLE	SF	14	94	71	910	6	200.0	14.3
4	ROB GRONKOWSKI	TB	12	89	55	802	6	171.2	14.3
5	DALTON SCHULTZ	DAL	17	104	78	808	8	208.8	12.3
6	DARREN WALLER	LV	11	93	55	665	2	133.5	12.1
7	T.J. HOCKENSON	DET	12	84	61	583	4	145.3	12.1
8	ZACH ERTZ	ARI	11	81	56	574	3	131.8	12.0
9	DALLAS GOEDERT	PHI	15	76	56	830	4	165.0	11.0
10	DAWSON KNOX	BUF	15	71	49	587	9	164.1	10.9
11	KYLE PITTS	ATL	17	110	68	1026	1	176.6	10.4
12	NOAH FANT	DEN	16	90	68	670	4	159.0	9.9
13	TYLER HIGBEE	LAR	15	85	61	560	5	147.0	9.8
14	MIKE GESICKI	MIA	17	112	73	780	2	165.0	9.7
15	HUNTER HENRY	NE	17	75	50	603	9	164.3	9.7
16	PAT FREIERMUTH	PIT	16	79	60	497	7	153.7	9.6
17	LOGAN THOMAS	WAS	6	25	18	196	3	55.6	9.3
18	JARED COOK	LAC	16	83	48	564	4	132.4	8.3
19	MAXX WILLIAMS	ARI	5	17	16	193	1	41.3	8.3
20	ZACH ERTZ	PHI	6	31	18	189	2	48.9	8.2
21	TYLER CONKLIN	MIN	17	87	61	593	3	138.3	8.1
22	GERALD EVERETT	SEA	15	63	48	478	4	121.8	8.1
23	C.J. UZOMAH	CIN	16	63	49	493	5	128.3	8.0
24	DAN ARNOLD	JAC	8	41	28	324	0	62.4	7.8
25	J. O'SHAUGHNESSY	JAC	7	34	24	244	0	50.4	7.2
26	COLE KMET	CHI	17	93	60	612	0	121.2	7.1
27	EVAN ENGRAM	NYG	15	73	46	408	3	104.5	7.0
28	DAVID NJOKU	CLE	16	53	36	475	4	107.6	6.7
29	ROBERT TONYAN	GB	8	29	18	204	2	50.4	6.3
30	BREVIN JORDAN	HOU	9	28	20	178	3	55.8	6.2
31	AUSTIN HOOPER	CLE	16	61	38	345	3	90.5	5.7
32	A. OKWUEGBUNAM	DEN	14	40	33	330	2	78.0	5.6
33	RICKY SEALS-JONES	WAS	13	49	30	271	2	69.1	5.3
34	DAN ARNOLD	CAR	3	11	7	84	0	15.4	5.1
35	HAYDEN HURST	ATL	13	31	26	221	1	66.1	5.1
36	ADAM TRAUTMAN	NO	13	43	27	263	2	65.3	5.0
37	FOSTER MOREAU	LV	17	44	30	373	3	85.3	5.0
38	ANTHONY FIRKSER	TEN	15	43	34	291	2	75.1	5.0
39	MO ALIE-COX	IND	17	45	24	316	4	79.6	4.7
40	JACK DOYLE	IND	17	43	29	302	3	79.2	4.7

FANTASY**TAKEOVER**

RUNNING BACKS

			GP	RUSHING			RECEIVING				PPR	
				ATTS	YARDS	TDS	TARS	RECS	YARDS	TDS	TOTAL	AVG
1	DERRICK HENRY	TEN	8	219	940	10	20	18	154	0	191.6	24.0
2	JONATHAN TAYLOR	IND	17	332	1811	18	51	40	360	2	377.1	22.2
3	AUSTIN EKELER	LAC	16	206	907	12	94	70	647	8	349.4	21.8
4	LEONARD FOURNETTE	TB	14	180	812	8	84	69	454	2	255.6	18.3
5	CHRISTIAN MCCAFFREY	CAR	7	99	442	1	41	37	343	1	127.5	18.2
6	JOE MIXON	CIN	16	292	1205	13	48	42	314	3	289.9	18.1
7	ALVIN KAMARA	NO	13	240	897	4	67	47	439	5	234.6	18.0
8	NAJEE HARRIS	PIT	17	307	1200	7	94	74	467	3	300.7	17.7
9	JAMES CONNER	ARI	15	202	752	15	39	37	375	3	257.7	17.2
10	D'ANDRE SWIFT	DET	13	151	617	5	78	62	452	2	210.9	16.2
11	DALVIN COOK	MIN	13	249	1159	6	49	34	224	0	210.3	16.2
12	NICK CHUBB	CLE	14	228	1259	8	25	20	174	1	217.3	15.5
13	AARON JONES	GB	15	171	799	4	65	52	391	6	231.0	15.4
14	JOSH JACOBS	LV	15	217	872	9	64	54	348	0	230.0	15.3
15	DAVID MONTGOMERY	CHI	13	225	849	7	51	42	301	0	197.0	15.2
16	ELIJAH MITCHELL	SF	11	207	963	5	20	19	137	1	165.0	15.0
17	EZEKIEL ELLIOTT	DAL	17	237	1002	10	65	47	287	2	254.1	14.9
18	ANTONIO GIBSON	WAS	16	258	1037	7	52	42	294	3	235.1	14.7
19	C. PATTERSON	ATL	16	153	618	6	69	52	548	5	234.6	14.7
20	DAMIEN HARRIS	NE	15	202	929	15	21	18	132	0	214.1	14.3
21	KAREEM HUNT	CLE	8	78	386	5	27	22	174	0	110.0	13.8
22	DARRELL HENDERSON	LAR	12	149	688	5	40	29	176	3	163.4	13.6
23	JAMES ROBINSON	JAC	14	164	767	8	46	31	222	0	177.9	12.7
24	MELVIN GORDON III	DEN	16	203	918	8	38	28	213	2	201.1	12.6
25	CHRIS CARSON	SEA	4	54	232	3	6	6	29	0	50.1	12.5
26	JAVONTE WILLIAMS	DEN	17	203	903	4	53	43	316	3	206.9	12.2
27	RASHAAD PENNY	SEA	10	119	749	6	8	6	48	0	121.7	12.2
28	C. EDWARDS-HELAIRE	KC	10	119	517	4	23	19	129	2	121.6	12.2
29	CHASE EDMONDS	ARI	12	116	592	2	53	43	311	0	145.3	12.1
30	DUKE JOHNSON	MIA	5	71	330	3	5	4	41	0	59.1	11.8
31	DEVIN SINGLETARY	BUF	17	188	870	7	50	40	228	1	197.8	11.6
32	J.D. MCKISSIC	WAS	11	48	212	2	53	43	397	2	127.9	11.6
33	SAQUON BARKLEY	NYG	13	162	593	2	57	41	263	2	150.6	11.6
34	DARREL WILLIAMS	KC	17	144	558	6	57	47	452	2	196.0	11.5
35	MICHAEL CARTER	NYJ	14	147	639	4	55	36	325	0	156.4	11.2
36	AJ DILLON	GB	17	187	803	5	37	34	313	2	187.6	11.0
37	DONTRELL HILLIARD	TEN	7	56	350	2	26	19	87	0	74.7	10.7
38	D'ONTA FOREMAN	TEN	9	133	566	3	11	9	123	0	95.9	10.7
39	TONY POLLARD	DAL	15	130	719	2	46	39	337	0	156.6	10.4
40	JAMES WHITE	NE	3	10	38	1	14	12	94	0	31.2	10.4
41	MYLES GASKIN	MIA	17	173	612	3	63	49	234	4	175.6	10.3
42	BOSTON SCOTT	PHI	10	87	373	7	16	13	83	0	100.6	10.1
43	MILES SANDERS	PHI	12	137	754	0	34	26	158	0	119.2	9.9
44	R. STEVENSON	NE	12	133	606	5	18	14	123	0	116.9	9.7
45	MARK INGRAM II	NO	7	68	260	1	26	20	138	0	65.8	9.4
46	JAMAAL WILLIAMS	DET	13	153	601	3	28	26	157	0	119.8	9.2
47	DEVONTA FREEMAN	BAL	16	133	576	5	42	34	190	1	146.6	9.2
48	DEVONTAE BOOKER	NYG	16	145	593	2	45	40	268	1	144.1	9.0
49	JORDAN HOWARD	PHI	7	86	406	3	5	2	19	0	62.5	8.9
50	SONY MICHEL	LAR	17	208	845	4	33	21	128	1	148.3	8.7

WIDE RECEIVERS

			GP	RECEIVING				RUSHING			PPR	
				TARS	RECS	YARDS	TDS	ATTS	YARDS	TDS	TOTAL	AVG
1	COOPER KUPP	LAR	17	191	145	1947	16	4	18	0	439.5	25.9
2	DAVANTE ADAMS	GB	16	169	123	1553	11	0	0	0	344.3	21.5
3	DEEBO SAMUEL	SF	16	121	77	1405	6	59	365	8	343.0	21.4
4	JUSTIN JEFFERSON	MIN	17	167	108	1616	10	6	14	0	332.4	19.6
5	JA'MARR CHASE	CIN	17	128	81	1455	13	7	21	0	306.6	18.0
6	CHRIS GODWIN	TB	14	127	98	1103	5	4	21	1	246.4	17.6
7	TYREEK HILL	KC	17	159	111	1239	9	9	96	0	298.5	17.6
8	DIONTAE JOHNSON	PIT	16	169	107	1161	8	5	53	0	278.4	17.4
9	ANTONIO BROWN	TB	7	62	42	545	4	1	6	0	121.1	17.3
10	STEFON DIGGS	BUF	17	164	103	1225	10	0	0	0	285.5	16.8
11	MIKE EVANS	TB	16	114	74	1035	14	1	10	0	262.5	16.4
12	KEENAN ALLEN	LAC	16	157	106	1138	6	0	0	0	257.8	16.1
13	TEE HIGGINS	CIN	14	110	74	1091	6	0	0	0	221.1	15.8
14	JAYLEN WADDLE	MIA	16	140	104	1015	6	2	3	1	247.8	15.5
15	MIKE WILLIAMS	LAC	16	129	76	1146	9	0	0	0	246.6	15.4
16	ADAM THIELEN	MIN	13	95	67	726	10	1	2	0	199.8	15.4
17	HUNTER RENFROW	LV	17	128	103	1038	9	3	3	0	261.1	15.4
18	ROBERT WOODS	LAR	9	69	45	556	4	8	46	1	137.2	15.2
19	TYLER LOCKETT	SEA	16	107	73	1175	8	2	9	0	241.4	15.1
20	DEANDRE HOPKINS	ARI	10	64	42	572	8	0	0	0	147.2	14.7
21	CEEDEE LAMB	DAL	16	120	79	1102	6	9	76	0	232.8	14.6
22	BRANDIN COOKS	HOU	16	134	90	1037	6	2	21	0	231.8	14.5
23	DK METCALF	SEA	17	129	75	967	12	1	6	0	244.3	14.4
24	MARQUISE BROWN	BAL	16	146	91	1008	6	1	5	0	228.3	14.3
25	CALVIN RIDLEY	ATL	5	52	31	281	2	0	0	0	71.1	14.2
26	DJ MOORE	CAR	17	163	93	1157	4	8	48	0	239.5	14.1
27	MICHAEL PITTMAN JR.	IND	17	129	88	1082	6	5	44	0	236.6	13.9
28	A.J. BROWN	TEN	13	105	63	869	5	2	10	0	180.9	13.9
29	AMARI COOPER	DAL	15	104	68	865	8	0	0	0	202.5	13.5
30	AMON-RA ST. BROWN	DET	17	119	90	912	5	7	61	1	227.3	13.4
31	DARNELL MOONEY	CHI	17	140	81	1055	4	6	32	1	219.7	12.9
32	ELIJAH MOORE	NYJ	11	77	43	538	5	5	54	1	138.2	12.6
33	TERRY MCLAURIN	WAS	17	130	77	1053	5	1	12	0	213.5	12.6
34	CHRISTIAN KIRK	ARI	17	103	77	982	5	1	11	0	207.6	12.2
35	HENRY RUGGS III	LV	7	36	24	469	2	3	16	0	84.5	12.1
36	RUSSELL GAGE	ATL	14	94	66	770	4	0	0	0	167.0	11.9
37	COREY DAVIS	NYJ	9	59	34	492	4	0	0	0	107.2	11.9
38	TYLER BOYD	CIN	16	94	67	828	5	3	22	0	183.8	11.5
39	JARVIS LANDRY	CLE	12	87	52	570	2	6	40	2	137.0	11.4
40	CHASE CLAYPOOL	PIT	15	105	59	860	2	14	96	0	166.6	11.1
41	STERLING SHEPARD	NYG	7	53	36	366	1	1	-9	0	77.7	11.1
42	JAKOBI MEYERS	NE	17	126	83	866	2	1	9	0	188.3	11.1
43	DEVONTA SMITH	PHI	17	104	64	916	5	0	0	0	187.6	11.0
44	ODELL BECKHAM JR.	LAR	8	48	27	305	5	0	0	0	87.5	10.9
45	KENDRICK BOURNE	NE	17	70	55	800	5	12	125	0	182.5	10.7
46	MARVIN JONES JR.	JAC	17	120	73	832	4	0	0	0	180.2	10.6
47	DEVANTE PARKER	MIA	10	73	40	515	2	0	0	0	103.5	10.4
48	MICHAEL GALLUP	DAL	9	62	35	445	2	0	0	0	91.5	10.2
49	BRANDON AIYUK	SF	17	84	56	826	5	1	17	0	172.3	10.1
50	COLE BEASLEY	BUF	16	112	82	693	1	0	0	0	159.3	10.0

GLOSSARY

100 YG, 300 YG	100-yard games, 300-yard games
/A	Per attempt
/R	Per reception
aDOT	Average depth of target
ADP	Average Draft Position — Where fantasy players are being drafted on average.
AIR/R	Air yards per reception
BRKTKL	Broken tackle
Ceiling	The upper limit of a player's fantasy potential.
Commissioner	The person responsible for maintaining all aspects of a fantasy league.
D/ST	Defense/special teams
FGA	Field goals attempted
FGM	Field goals made
Flex	A spot in some fantasy starting lineups that allows you to start a player from multiple positions, usually a RB, WR, or TE.
Flier	To take a chance on a player in hopes that he exceeds expectations, usually a late-round draft pick or waiver wire addition.
Floor	The lower limit of a player's fantasy potential.
FP(s)	Fantasy point(s)
FPPG	Fantasy points per game
FUM	Fumble
GP	Games Played
Handcuff	Drafting your top RB's backup to mitigate injury risk.
INT	Interception
K	Kicker
Manager	The person who makes decisions for his or her fantasy team (sometimes referred to as "owner").
PAT	Point after touchdown (extra point)
PFF	Pro Football Focus
PPG	Points per game
PPR	Point per reception — A scoring system that rewards one point for each reception.
PROJ	Projected stats
QB	Quarterback
QB1, QB2...	In a 10-team league, a QB1 is a quarterback who ranks as a top-10 option, while a QB2 is ranked from 11-20 at the position.
RB	Running Back
RB1, RB2...	In a 10-team league, a RB1 is a running back who ranks as a top-10 option, while a RB2 is ranked from 11-20 at the position.
REC	Reception
RZ	Red zone
Streaming	Using the waiver wire/free agency to fill a roster spot each week, rather than locking one player into that spot for the long term. This approach is most commonly used for the D/ST roster spot.
Superflex	A flex position that also allows a manager to start a QB, in addition to the usual RB, WR, or TE.
TD	Touchdown
TE	Tight end
TE1, TE2...	In a 10-team league, a TE1 is a tight end who ranks as a top-10 option, while a TE2 is ranked from 11-20 at the position.
TGT	Target
TK	Tackle
Waivers	A player is on waivers after being dropped by another team. When on waivers, the waiver order of the interested teams determines which roster he joins. Should the player clear waivers (that is, no manager labels him as worth their spot in the waiver line), he is added to the free-agency pool and, thus, available for the first team that wants his services.
WR	Wide receiver
WR1, WR2...	In a 10-team league, a WR1 is a wide receiver who ranks as a top-10 option, while a WR2 is ranked from 11-20 at the position.
YAC	Yards after contact (carries), Yards after catch (receptions)
YACON	Yards after contact
YBC	Yards before contact (carries), Yards before catch (receptions)
YDS	Yards
YPA	Yards per attempt
YPC	Yards per carry

FANTASY**TAKEOVER**

Printed in Great Britain
by Amazon

84129469R00086